MIGRANTS, REFUGEES, ... and .... SOCIETIES

WORLD BANK GROUP

The priestly leaders of the Parsis were brought before the local ruler, Jadhav Rana, who presented them with a vessel full of milk to signify that the surrounding lands could not possibly accommodate any more people. The Parsi head priest responded by slipping some sugar into the milk to signify how the strangers would enrich the local community without displacing them. They would dissolve into life like sugar dissolves in the milk, sweetening the society but not unsettling it. The ruler responded to the eloquent image and granted the exiles land and permission to practice their religion unhindered if they would respect local customs, and learn the local language, Gujarati.

—Parsi legend

As a global community, we face a choice. Do we want migration to be a source of prosperity and international solidarity, or a byword for inhumanity and social friction?

—António Guterres, Secretary-General of the United Nations, 2018

Contents

Boxes

Figures

Maps

Tables

Foreword

The World Bank's annual *World Development Reports*, or *WDRs*, are staples of the global community's reservoir of knowledge and data about key development issues. This year's Report discusses migration, one of the world's most important and pressing challenges. There are 184 million migrants worldwide. Of them, 43 percent live in low- and middle-income countries. Migration issues are becoming even more widespread and urgent due to severe divergences between and within countries—in terms of real wages, labor market opportunities, demographic patterns, and climate costs.

Migration makes substantial contributions to economic development and poverty reduction but also involves difficulties and risks. Migrants often bring skills, dynamism, and resources that strengthen destination economies. In many cases, they also strengthen the country of origin, providing a vital support mechanism for communities by sending remittances as a lifeline for their families, especially during times of turmoil. This *World Development Report 2023* proposes policies to better manage migration in destination, transit, and origin countries. These policies can help harness economic opportunities and mitigate the difficulties and risks that migrants face.

The *WDR* discusses the migration trade-offs using a "Match-Motive Framework." The "match" aspect is grounded in labor economics and focuses on how well migrants' skills and related attributes match the needs of the destination countries. This determines the extent to which migrants, countries of origin, and countries of destination gain from migration: the stronger the match, the larger the gains. The "motive" refers to the circumstances under which a person moves in search of opportunity or due to fear of persecution, armed conflict, or violence. The latter may create international law obligations for the destination country: people who move because of a "well-founded fear" of harm at home are entitled to international protection. By combining "match" and "motive," the framework identifies policy priorities for countries of origin, transit, and destination, and the international community. It also discusses how the policy response can be improved through bilateral, plurilateral, or multilateral initiatives and instruments. The way that policies are designed and implemented can help migrants move toward better opportunities and improved matches so that the benefits of migration for all are increased.

Origin countries can maximize the development impacts of labor migration on their own societies by providing ways to facilitate remittance inflows, for example, by lowering the costs of sending and receiving transfers. Origin countries can also improve educational opportunities often in collaboration with destination countries, including language skills. They can also incentivize investment by diasporas, and support returning migrants as they reenter the labor market.

Destination countries can harness the potential of migration to meet their long-term labor market needs, especially to meet labor shortages triggered by aging or a lack of particular skills. They can improve efforts to treat migrants humanely and address social and economic impacts on their own citizens. Transit countries need to coordinate with countries of destination to address distressed migration. International cooperation is critical in sharing the costs for hosting refugees.

Recognizing the challenges and complexities of migration, this *WDR* provides data-driven and evidence-based examples and assessment of trade-offs, showing how migration can work for development. The Report will contribute to a better understanding of migration and should provide a useful reference for policy makers and other stakeholders as they make informed choices and formulate effective strategies that contribute to better outcomes for communities and individuals.

David Malpass
President
The World Bank Group

Acknowledgments

World Development Report 2023 was prepared by a World Bank team led by Xavier Devictor, Quy-Toan Do, and Çağlar Özden. Joyce Antone Ibrahim served as Task Team Leader. Overall guidance was provided by Carmen Reinhart (through June 2022), former Senior Vice President and Chief Economist; Indermit Gill (as of September 2022), Senior Vice President and Chief Economist; and Aart Kraay, Director of Development Policy, Development Economics, and Deputy Chief Economist. The Report was sponsored by the Development Economics Vice Presidency.

The core author team comprised Paige Casaly, Viviane Clement, Vikram Raghavan, Kanta Rigaud, Sandra Rozo Villarraga, Zara Sarzin, Kirsten Schuettler, Ganesh Seshan, Maheshwor Shrestha, Mauro Testaverde, Solomon Walelign, Christina Wieser, and Soonhwa Yi, together with research analysts Laura Caron, Narcisse Cha'ngom, Jessica Dodo Buchler, Sameeksha Khare, Matthew Martin, Elham Shabahat, Samikshya Siwakoti, and Adesola Sunmoni. Selome Missael Paulos provided the team with administrative support, assisted by Aidara Janulaityte. Barthelemy Bonadio, April Frake, Janis Kreuder, and Tony Zurui Su assisted chapter authors at various stages. Bruce Ross-Larson provided developmental guidance in drafting the Report.

Members of the extended team were Caroline Sergeant and Thamesha Tennakoon. Erhan Artuc developed the methodology used to construct the Report's bilateral migration matrix. Gero Carletto contributed to spotlight 2 on data, and Lucia Hanmer, Laura Montes, and Laura Rawlings contributed to spotlight 4 on gender. Anne Koch, Nadine Biehler, Nadine Knapp, and David Kipp authored box 6.3 on lessons from Germany. Irene Bloemraad, Victoria Esses, Connie Eysenck, William Kymlicka, Rachel McColgan, and Yang-Yang Zhou contributed to sections of chapter 6 on destination countries. Paulo Bastos, Irina Galimova, Rebeca Gravatá, Alreem Kamal, and He Wang assisted with reviewing translations.

The communications and engagement strategy was led by a team comprising Chisako Fukuda, Karolina Ordon, Anugraha Palan, Elizabeth Price, Joe Rebello, Shane Romig, and Mariana Teixeira. Paul Blake led and coordinated the video production. Kristen Milhollin, Mikael Reventar, and Roula Yazigi provided web and online services and related guidance.

Special thanks are extended to Stephen D. Pazdan, who coordinated and oversaw formal production of the Report, and to the World Bank's Formal Publishing Program, including Cindy Fisher and Patricia Katayama. Mary C. Fisk facilitated the multiple translations of the overview and main messages by the Translations and Interpretation team, coordinated by Bouchra Belfqih. Deb Barker and Yaneisy Martinez managed the printing and electronic conversions of the Report and its many ancillary products.

The concept note was edited by Anne Koch. The Report was edited by Sabra Ledent and Nancy Morrison and proofread by Gwenda Larsen and Catherine Farley. Robert Zimmermann verified the Report's extensive citations. Reyes Work designed some of the Report's figures and infographics, as did Bill Pragluski at Critical Stages. Puntoaparte Editores was the principal graphic designer, and BMWW and Datapage supplied typesetting services.

Van Thi Hong Do, Dayana Leguizamon, Monique Pelloux Patron, and Ghulam Ahmad Yahyaie provided the team with resource management support. Rolf Parta facilitated the team retreats and other team sessions. The team would also like to thank colleagues from various World Bank country offices who assisted with the logistics and stakeholder engagement of team members' missions. Special thanks to Maria Alyanak, Gabriela Calderon Motta, Maria del Camino Hurtado, Grace Soko, and Sebastian Stolorz for their help with coordination and high-level engagement strategies.

The team relied on the guidance and inputs of an Internal Advisory Committee: Dina Abu-Ghaida, Loli Arribas-Banos, Caroline Bahnson, Michel Botzung, Gero Carletto, Ximena del Carpio, Stephane Hallegatte, David McKenzie, Pia Peeters, and Dilip Ratha. The team is also grateful for the guidance, comments, and inputs provided by other World Bank Group colleagues, particularly from the Development Economics Vice Presidency; Economics and Private Sector Development Vice Presidency (International Finance Corporation); Legal Vice Presidency; Environment, Natural Resources, and Blue Economy Global Practice; Finance, Competitiveness, and Innovation Global Practice; Poverty and Equity Global Practice; Social Protection and Jobs Global Practice; Social Sustainability and Inclusion Global Practice; Climate Change Group; Fragility, Conflict, and Violence Group; as well as the Multilateral Investment Guarantee Agency and the Balance of Payments Division at the International Monetary Fund. The team would also like to thank the many World Bank colleagues who provided written comments during the formal Bank-wide review process. Those comments provided invaluable guidance at a crucial stage in the Report's production.

The team also gratefully received suggestions and guidance from a High-Level Advisory Panel: Nasser Alkahtani, Executive Director, Arab Gulf Programme for Development, Saudi Arabia; Davinia Esther Anyakun, Minister of State for Relief, Disaster Preparedness and Refugees, Uganda; Alejandra Botero Barco, former Director-General, National Planning Department, Colombia; Karl Chua, former Secretary of Socioeconomic Planning, National Economic and Development Authority, the Philippines; Reha Denemeç, former Deputy Minister of National Education, Turkey; Tiébilé Dramé, former Minister of Foreign Affairs and former Member of Parliament, Mali; Filippo Grandi, High Commissioner, United Nations High Commissioner for Refugees (UNHCR); Carlos Gutierrez, former Secretary of Commerce, United States; Gilbert F. Houngbo, Director-General, International Labour Organization (ILO) (as of October 2022); Mary Kawar, former Minister of Planning and International Cooperation, Jordan; Yuba Raj Khatiwada, former Minister of Finance, former Minister of Planning, and former Central Bank Governor, Nepal; Janez Lenarčič, Commissioner for Crisis Management, European Commission; David Miliband, President and CEO, International Rescue Committee; Guy Ryder, former Director-General, ILO (through September 2022); Asif Saleh, Executive Director, BRAC Bangladesh; and António Vitorino, Director-General, International Organization for Migration. Volker Türk also served as a member of the panel in his personal capacity through September 2022.

The team also received suggestions and inputs from an Academic Advisory Committee: Ran Abramitzky (Stanford University), Emmanuelle Auriol (Toulouse School of Economics), Alexander Betts (University of Oxford), Michael Clemens (Center for Global Development), Alexander de Sherbinin (Columbia University Climate School), Frédéric Docquier (Catholic University of Louvain/Luxembourg Institute of Socio-Economic Research), Esther Duflo (Massachusetts Institute of Technology), Filiz Garip (Princeton University), Guy Goodwin-Gill (University of Oxford), Jennifer Hunt (Rutgers University), Ana María Ibáñez (Inter-American Development Bank/Universidad de los Andes), Susan Martin (Georgetown University), Anna Maria Mayda (Georgetown University), Edward Miguel (University of California, Berkeley), Mushfiq Mobarak (Yale University), Giovanni Peri (University of California, Davis), Lant Pritchett (University of Oxford), Jaya Ramji-Nogales (Beasley School of Law, Temple University), Hillel Rapoport (University of Paris 1 Pantheon-Sorbonne/Paris School of Economics), and Jackie Wahba (University of Southampton).

The team conducted a series of bilateral consultations and field visits with several governments and development partners, including Armenia, Azerbaijan, Bangladesh, Cameroon, the Central African Republic, Colombia, Côte d'Ivoire, Denmark, Estonia, Ethiopia, Finland, France, Georgia, Germany, Guatemala, Indonesia, Italy, Japan, Jordan, Kuwait, Latvia, Lithuania, Mexico, Morocco, the Netherlands, Peru, the Philippines, Portugal, Saudi Arabia, Sweden, Switzerland, Tunisia, the United Kingdom, and the United States; as well as the European Commission's Directorate-Generals for Climate Action, International Partnerships, Migration and Home Affairs, and Neighborhood and Enlargement Negotiations; the European External Action Service; the Expert Council on Integration and Migration (Germany); and the Vatican.

The team also consulted several international and regional organizations, including the Asian Development Bank, Caribbean Community (CARICOM), ILO, Inter-American Development Bank (Migration Unit), Intergovernmental Authority on Development, International Committee of the Red Cross, International Organization for Migration (IOM), Organisation for Economic Co-operation and Development (OECD), United Nations Department of Economic and Social Affairs (UN DESA, Population Division), United Nations Economic Commission for Africa, United Nations High Commissioner for Refugees, and the UN Secretary-General's High-Level Panel on Internal Displacement.

The team thanks Columbia University, Cornell University, InterAction, International Council of Voluntary Agencies, Japan International Cooperation Agency (JICA), Overseas Development Institute, Peterson Institute for International Economics, and Refugees International for organizing and hosting a series of roundtable discussions and seminars with academics and nongovernmental organizations.

The team benefited from the inputs of several think tanks and research institutes, including the Center for Global Development, Chatham House, Freedom House, German Institute for International and Security Affairs, Institute of International and European Affairs, Japan External Trade Organization (JETRO) Institute of Developing Economies, JICA Ogata Research Institute, Migration Policy Institute, and National Council of Research of Italy.

The team also benefited from inputs from a number of civil society organizations, including ActionAid Bangladesh; Adventist Development and Relief Agency; Agency for Migration and Adaptation; Ain O Salish Kendra; Aligarh Muslim University; All for Integral

Development; Alliance for Peacebuilding; American University of Beirut; AMIGA z.s.; Angels Refugee Support Foundation; Arab Renaissance for Democracy and Development; Asia Displacement Solutions Platform; Association of Rehabilitation Nurses; Bangladesh Nari Sramik Kendra; Bangladeshi Ovhibashi Mohila Sramik Association; Basmeh and Zeitooneh; Bill & Melinda Gates Foundation; Bond; Bordeaux-Montaigne University; BRAC; British International Investments; Business Fights Poverty; CARE International; CARE International Jordan; CARE International UK; Catholic Agency for Overseas Development; Catholic Relief Services; Center for Disaster Philanthropy; Center for Global Development; Center for Intercultural Dialogue; Center for Peace and Advocacy; Centre for Policy Development; Centre for Policy Dialogue; Church World Service; CLEAR Global; Columbia Global Centers; Congolese Banyamulenge community; Cordaid International; Cultuur in Harmonie; Danish Refugee Council; Delegation of the European Union to Bangladesh; Dilla University; Durrat AlManal for Development and Training; Economic, Social and Environmental Council; Embassy of Denmark; Encuentros SJM; European External Action Service; Films 4 Peace Foundation; Fondazione Compagnia di San Paolo; Food for the Hungry; Foreign, Commonwealth and Development Office, UK; German Centre for Integration and Migration Research; Global Campaign for Equal Nationality Rights; Global Recordings Network USA; Global Research Forum on Diaspora and Transnationalism; Good Neighbors; GRACE; Grassroot Leadership Organizations; Grupo Equilibrium; Guilford College; HasNa; Hebrew Immigrant Aid Society; Helvetas International; Hope of Children and Women Victims of Violence; Hungarian Migrant Women's Association (she4she); IHH Humanitarian Relief Foundation; ILO; Independent Living Institute; Institute for Government; Institute of International and European Affairs; InterAction; Internal Displacement Monitoring Centre; International Centre for Migration Policy Development; International Committee of the Red Cross; International Council of Voluntary Agencies; International Independent Hockey League; International Institute for Strategic Studies; INTERSOS; IOM; Islamic Relief USA; Islamic Relief Worldwide; ITASTRA; Jeronimo Martins; Jesuit Refugee Service; Jordanian Hashemite Fund for Human Development; Justus Liebig University Giessen; Kakuma Vocational Center; Kids in Need of Defense; Kivu Kwetu Développement; Living Water Community; Lutheran World Federation; Manusher Jonno Foundation; McGill University; Medecins du Monde Japon; MedGlobal; Me For You Organization; Mercy Corps; Mercy Corps Jordan; Middle East and North Africa Civil Society Network for Displacement; MiGreat; MISEREOR; Moltivolti; National Agency for the Promotion of Employment and Competencies; National Human Rights Council of Morocco; Netherlands Refugee Foundation; Newcomers with Disabilities in Sweden; New School for Social Research; New Sorbonne University; New York University; Norwegian Refugee Council; Norwegian Refugee Council Jordan; Norwegian Refugee Council USA; Norwegian University of Science and Technology; Ocasiven; OECD; Osun Rise Regenerative Experiences; Overseas Development Institute; Ovibashi Karmi Unnayan Program; Oxfam IBIS; Oxfam International; Oxfam Jordan; Oxfam Novib; Oxfam UK; Pan American Development Foundation; Pasos Firmes; Permanent Mission of the Republic of Kenya to the United Nations; Permanent Representation of the Kingdom of the Netherlands to the European Union; Plan International; Plan International Jordan; Policy Center for the New South; RA Studio; Refugee and Migratory Movements Research Unit; Refugee Company; Refugee Consortium of Kenya; Refugee Council; Refugee Integration via Internet-Based Revitalization of Rural Europe; Refugee

Investment Fund; Refugee Investment Network; Refugee Self-Reliance Initiative; Refugees International; Regional Durable Solutions Secretariat; Relief International; RW Welfare Society; Samuel Hall; Save the Children; Sawiyan; SEEK Feminist Research Network; SEP Jordan; 17 Ventures; Soccer Without Borders Uganda; Society for Human Rights and Prisoners' Aid-Pakistan; Solidarity Center; Souq Fann; Stand for the Refugee Africa SRA; Swiss Agency for Development and Cooperation; Syria Justice and Accountability Centre; Tamkeen; Tent Partnership for Refugees; UMI; UNHCR; UNHCR Global Youth Advisory Council; UNHCR Representation in the Netherlands; United Nations Office on Drugs and Crime; United Nations Resident Coordinator Office; United Nations Women; United States Refugee Advisory Board; University of Oxford; University of Virginia; WARBE Development Foundation; War Child Canada; Wilton Park; Winrock International; Women's Refugee Commission; World Bank Group Geneva; World Refugee and Migration Council; World Vision; World Vision International; Youth Cooperation for Ideas; and Youth Up Foundation.

The team extends special thanks to the many migrant- and refugee-led organizations it consulted, allowing the team to ensure that the voices of migrants and refugees were heard. They included the Afghan Refugees Solidarity Association, Africa Refugee-Led Network RELON, ARCI Porco Rosso, Asylum Access, ChangeMakers Resettlement Forum, Darfur Refugees Association in Uganda, European Coalition of Migrants and Refugees, Global Refugee-Led Network, Hope for Refugees in Action, International Rescue Committee, Irish Refugee Advisory Board, Mediterranean Hope, Migrants' Rights Network, Mosaico, New Women Connectors, Organization for Children's Harmony, People for Peace and Defense of Rights, PLACE Network, Plethora Social Initiative, PPDR Uganda, Refugee Advisory Group, Refugee Advisory Network of Canada, Refugee-Led Organization Network (RELON) Uganda, SITTI Soap, Umoja Refugee, and Youth Social Advocacy Team.

In addition, the team consulted academics, including Tendayi Achiume (University of California, Los Angeles), T. Alexander Aleinikoff (The New School), Mustapha Azaitraoui (University of Sultan Moulay Slimane, Beni Mellal, Faculty of Khouribga), Massimo Livi Bacci (University of Florence), Kaushik Basu (Cornell University), Bernd Beber (WZB), Irene Bloemraad (University of California, Berkeley), Chad Bown (Peterson Institute for International Economics), Nancy Chau (Cornell University), Huiyi Chen (Cornell University), Vincent Chetail (Geneva Graduate Institute), Cathryn Costello (Hertie School), Jishnu Das (Georgetown University), Glen Denning (Columbia University), Shanta Devarajan (Georgetown University), Jasmin Diab (Lebanese American University), Mamadou Diouf (Columbia University), Ángel A. Escamilla García (Cornell University), Victoria Esses (University of Western Ontario), Ama R. Francis (Columbia University), Feline Freier (Universidad del Pacífico, Peru), Filiz Garip (Princeton University), Shannon Gleeson (Cornell University), Guy Grossman (University of Pennsylvania), Yuki Higuchi (Sophia University), Walter Kälin (member, Expert Advisory Group for the United Nations Secretary-General's High-Level Panel on Internal Displacement and University of Bern), Ravi Kanbur (Cornell University), Neeraj Kaushal (Columbia University), Will Kymlicka (Queen's University), Jane McAdam (University of New South Wales, Sydney), Gustavo Meireles (Kanda University of International Studies), Pierluigi Montalbano (La Sapienza University), Yuko Nakano (University of Tsukuba), Daniel Naujoks (Columbia University), Izumi Ohno (National Graduate Institute for Policy Studies), Obiora Chinedu Okafor (Johns Hopkins University School of Advanced International Studies), Brian Park (Cornell University), Eleanor Paynter

(Cornell University), Paolo Pinotti (Bocconi University), Adam Posen (Peterson Institute for International Economics), Furio Rosati (University of Tor Vergata), Yasuyuki Sawada (University of Tokyo), Alexandra Scacco (WZB), Mai Seki (Ritsumeikan University), Akira Shibanuma (University of Tokyo), Dana Smith (Cornell University), Aya Suzuki (University of Tokyo), Jan Svejnar (Columbia University), Saburo Takizawa (Touyo Eiwa University), Joel Trachtman (Tufts University, Fletcher School of Law and Diplomacy), Carlos Vargas-Silva (University of Oxford), Nicolas Veron (Peterson Institute for International Economics), Tatsufumi Yamagata (Ritsumeikan Asia Pacific University), Keiichi Yamazaki (Yokohama National University), and Yang-Yang Zhou (University of British Columbia).

The background papers, along with stakeholder engagement and dissemination activities, were generously supported by the Multi-Donor Trust Fund for Forced Displacement.

Finally, the team apologizes to any individuals or organizations inadvertently omitted from this list. It is grateful for the help received from all who contributed to this Report, including those whose names may not appear here. Team members would also like to thank their families for their support throughout the preparation of this Report.

Key takeaways

This Report provides a comprehensive analysis of international migration and its potential to serve as a force for growth and shared prosperity in *all* countries.

○ **It focuses on people who lack citizenship in the country in which they live: about 184 million people across the world, including 37 million refugees.** About 43 percent of them live in low- and middle-income countries. Migrants are sometimes defined as "foreign-born." This Report takes a different view because people who have been naturalized enjoy the same rights as all other citizens.

○ **Rapid demographic change is making migration increasingly necessary for countries at all income levels.** High-income countries are aging fast. So are middle-income countries, which are growing older before they become rich. The population of low-income countries is booming, but young people are entering the workforce without the skills needed in the global labor market. These trends will spark a global competition for workers.

○ **This Report presents a powerful framework to guide policy making based on how well migrants' skills and related attributes *match* the needs of destination countries and on the *motive* for their movement.** The match determines the extent to which migrants, countries of origin, and countries of destination gain from migration. The motive may create international law obligations for the destination country: people who move because of a "well-founded fear" of harm or persecution at home—refugees, by definition—are entitled to international protection.

○ **The match and motive framework enables policy makers to respond appropriately, and the Report identifies the policies needed.**

  • *When the match of migrants is strong, the gains are large for themselves and for countries of origin and destination.* This is the case for the vast majority of migrants, whether high- or low-skilled, regular or irregular. The policy objective should be to maximize gains for all.

  • *For refugees, when the match is weak, the costs need to be shared—and reduced—multilaterally.* Refugee situations can last for years. The policy objective should be to lower the hosting costs while maintaining adequate standards of international protection.

  • *When the match is weak and people are not refugees, difficult policy challenges arise,* especially when migrants are in irregular and distressed circumstances. It is the prerogative of destination countries to regulate entry of these migrants, but deportation and refusal of entry can lead to inhumane treatment. The restrictive policies adopted by destination countries can also impose costs on some transit countries. The policy goal should be to reduce the need for distressed migration—and development can play a critical role.

- **Origin countries should actively manage migration for development.** They should make labor migration an explicit part of their development strategy. They should lower remittance costs, facilitate knowledge transfers from their diaspora, build skills in high demand globally, mitigate the adverse effects of "brain drain," protect their nationals while abroad, and support them upon return.
- **Destination countries can also manage migration more strategically.** They should use "strong match" migration to meet their labor needs, facilitating migrants' inclusion while addressing social impacts that raise concerns among their citizens. They should let refugees move, get jobs, and access national services wherever they are available. And they should also reduce distressed, high-risk movements in a humane manner.
- **International cooperation is essential to turn migration into a strong force for development.** Bilateral cooperation can strengthen migrants' match with destination countries' needs. Multilateral efforts are needed to share the costs of refugee-hosting and to address distressed migration. New financing instruments should be developed to help countries care for noncitizens in a predictable manner. Voices that are underrepresented in the migration debate must be heard, including developing countries, the private sector and other stakeholders, and migrants and refugees themselves.

Glossary

This list provides general descriptions, not precise legal definitions, of the terms commonly used in this Report. However, the descriptions include legal and policy elements relevant to how these terms are understood and applied in practice.

asylum or refugee status   A legal status arising from judicial or administrative proceedings that a country grants to a refugee in its territory. This status confers on refugees international refugee protection by preventing their return (in line with the principle of *non-refoulement*), regularizing their stay in the territory, and providing them with certain rights while there.

asylum-seeker   A person outside of their home country who is seeking asylum. For statistical purposes, it is a person who has submitted their application for asylum but has not yet received a final decision.

complementary (international) protection   Forms of international protection provided by countries or regions to people who are not refugees, but who still may need international protection. Countries use various legal and policy mechanisms to regularize the entry or stay of such individuals or prevent their return (in line with the principle of *non-refoulement*).

co-national   A person who holds the same citizenship as another person.

destination country/society   The country or society to which a migrant moves.

diaspora   The population of a given country that is scattered across countries or regions that are separate from its geographic place of origin.

distressed migrant   A migrant who moves to another country under distressed circumstances but who does not meet the applicable criteria for refugee status. Their movements are often irregular and unsafe.

economic migrant   A migrant who crosses an international border motivated not by persecution or possible serious harm or death, but for other reasons, such as to improve living conditions by working or reuniting with family abroad. This term encompasses labor migrants or migrant workers, who move primarily to work in another country.

emigrant   A person who leaves their country of habitual residence to reside in another country. This term is used from the perspective of the person's country of origin.

host country/society   The country or society to which a refugee moves, either temporarily or permanently.

immigrant   A person who moves to a country to establish habitual residence. This term is used from the perspective of the person's destination country.

internally displaced persons (IDPs)   People who have been displaced within a state's borders to avoid persecution, serious harm, or death, including through armed conflict, situations of generalized violence, violations of human rights, or natural or humanmade disasters.

international protection   Legal protection granted by countries to refugees or other displaced people in their territory who cannot return to their home countries because they would be at risk there and because their home countries are unable or unwilling to protect them. International protection takes the form of a legal status that, at a minimum, prevents their return (in line with the principle of *non-refoulement*) and regularizes their stay in the territory.

irregular migrant   A migrant who is not legally authorized to enter or stay in a given country (also called an *undocumented migrant*).

migrant   In this Report, those who change their country of habitual residence and who are not citizens of their country of residence. Such changes of country exclude short-term movement for purposes such as recreation, business, medical treatment, or religious pilgrimage.

naturalized citizen   A migrant who has obtained citizenship in their country of destination.

nonnational   A person who does not hold the citizenship of the country in which that person resides.

non-refoulement   The legal principle prohibiting countries from returning people to places where they may be at risk of persecution, torture, or other serious harm.

origin country/society   The country or society from which a migrant or refugee moves.

refugee   A person who has been granted international protection by a country of asylum because of feared persecution, armed conflict, violence, or serious public disorder in their origin country. The international protection granted by countries to refugees takes the form of a distinct legal status (see **asylum or refugee status**) preventing their return (in line with the principle of *non-refoulement*), regularizing their stay in the territory, and providing them with certain rights while there, under the 1951 Convention Relating to the Status of Refugees and its 1967 Protocol or other international, regional, or national legal instruments.

regular migrant   A migrant who is legally authorized to enter or stay in a given country.

stateless person   A person who is not a citizen of any country.

transit country   A country that a migrant transits through to reach their destination country.

Abbreviations

APTC	Australia Pacific Training Coalition
ASEAN	Association of Southeast Asian Nations
BAMF	Bundesamt für Migration und Flüchtlinge (Federal Office for Migration and Refugees, Germany)
BLA	bilateral labor agreement
BoP	balance of payments
CARICOM	Caribbean Community
COVID-19	coronavirus disease 2019
CSME	Caribbean Community (CARICOM) Single Market and Economy
DAC	Development Assistance Committee (OECD)
ECOWAS	Economic Community of West African States
EGRISS	Expert Group on Refugee, IDP and Statelessness Statistics (formerly EGRIS, Expert Group on Refugee and Internally Displaced Persons Statistics)
ETPV	Estatuto Temporal de Protección para Migrantes Venezolanos (Temporary Protection Status for Venezuelan Migrants, Colombia)
EU	European Union
FDI	foreign direct investment
GBV	gender-based violence
GCC	Gulf Cooperation Council
GCR	Global Compact on Refugees
GDP	gross domestic product
GSP	Global Skills Partnership
G20	Group of Twenty
IASC	Inter-Agency Standing Committee
IDA	International Development Association
IDMC	Internal Displacement Monitoring Centre
IDP	internally displaced person
IGAD	Intergovernmental Authority on Development
ILO	International Labour Organization
IMF	International Monetary Fund
JDC	Joint Data Center on Forced Displacement
KNOMAD	Global Knowledge Partnership on Migration and Development

LGBTQ+	lesbian, gay, bisexual, transgender, queer/questioning, plus (others)
MTO	money transfer operator
NGO	nongovernmental organization
ODA	official development assistance
OECD	Organisation for Economic Co-operation and Development
PPP	purchasing power parity
RPRF	Refugee Policy Review Framework
RPW	Remittance Prices Worldwide
SAR	special administrative region
SDG	Sustainable Development Goal
STEM	science, technology, engineering, and mathematics
TMF	Tarjeta de Movilidad Fronteriza (Border Mobility Card, Colombia)
UN	United Nations
UN DESA	United Nations Department of Economic and Social Affairs
UNHCR	United Nations High Commissioner for Refugees
UNRWA	United Nations Relief and Works Agency for Palestine Refugees in the Near East
WAEMU	West African Economic and Monetary Union
WDI	World Development Indicators
WDR	*World Development Report*
WHR	Window for Host Communities and Refugees (IDA)

Overview

Migration has been part of the human experience since the earliest days of civilization. *Homo sapiens* left Africa's Omo Valley some 200,000 years ago, and since then humans have never ceased to move, producing distinct cultures, languages, and ethnicities.[1] Migration has proved to be a powerful force for development, improving the lives of hundreds of millions of migrants, their families, and the societies in which they live across the world. But there are challenges as well—for migrants, their countries of origin, and their countries of destination.

This Report defines migrants as people who live outside their country of nationality (box O.1)—whether they moved in search of better economic opportunities or were displaced by conflict or persecution (refugees). It does not consider as migrants people who have been naturalized in their country of residence. It is the lack of citizenship—and of the associated civil, political, and economic rights—that creates distinct challenges for migrants and policy makers, not the fact that people moved at some point in their life.

The Report proposes a framework to best manage the economic, societal, and human impacts of migration. Combining insights from labor economics and international law, it looks at the degree to which migrants' skills and attributes are in demand at their destination (match) and whether they seek opportunities or fear for their lives in their country of origin (motive). It distinguishes between four different types of movements and identifies priority policies and interventions to fully realize the development benefits in all situations. To make change happen, international cooperation is critical—and so is empowering new voices that can change the nature and tone of the current debates.

Box O.1 How many migrants are there, and where do they live?

Today's cross-border movements are characterized by their diversity: there is no typical migrant or typical origin or destination country. Migrants differ by their reasons to move, their skills and demographic characteristics, their legal statuses, and their circumstances and prospects. There are countries of origin and countries of destination at all levels of income, and, in fact, many countries are simultaneously both origin and destination, such as Mexico, Nigeria, and the United Kingdom.

As defined in this Report, there are globally about 184 million migrants (about 2.3 percent of the world's population)—37 million of them refugees:

- About 40 percent (64 million economic migrants and 10 million refugees) live in high-income countries that belong to the Organisation for Economic Co-operation and Development (OECD).[a] These are high- and low-skilled workers and their families, people with an intent to settle, temporary migrants, students, as well as undocumented migrants and people seeking international protection. This number includes 11 million European Union (EU) citizens living in other EU countries with extensive residency rights.

(Box continues next page)

- About 17 percent (31 million economic migrants) live in Gulf Cooperation Council (GCC) countries. Nearly all of them are temporary workers with renewable work visas. They represent, on average, about half of the population across GCC countries.
- About 43 percent (52 million economic migrants and 27 million refugees) live in low- and middle-income countries.[b] They moved primarily for jobs or family reunification or to seek international protection.

The share of migrants in the global population has remained relatively stable since 1960. However, this apparent stability is misleading because demographic growth has been uneven across the world. Global migration increased more than three times faster than population growth in high-income countries and only half as fast as population growth in low-income countries.

Source: WDR2023 Migration Database, World Bank, Washington, DC, https://www.worldbank.org/wdr2023/data.
a. This estimate does not include approximately 61 million foreign-born naturalized citizens.
b. This estimate does not include approximately 31 million foreign-born naturalized citizens.

Migration is necessary for all countries

Migration is a response to shocks and global imbalances, such as the massive gaps in income and well-being across countries. Economic migration is driven by prospects of higher wages and access to better services.[2] In 2020, about 84 percent of migrants lived in a country that was wealthier than their own. Yet moving has costs that most poor people cannot afford. Largely from middle-income countries, most migrants are not among the poorest or the wealthiest in their country of origin.

Demographic changes have sparked an intensifying global competition for workers and talent. Consider three countries. Italy, with a population of 59 million, is projected to shrink by almost half, to 32 million, by 2100, with those above age 65 increasing from 24 to 38 percent of the population. Mexico, traditionally an emigration country, has seen its fertility rate drop to barely replacement level. Nigeria, by contrast, is expected to expand its population from 213 million to 791 million, becoming the second-most populous country in the world, after India, by the end of the century (figure O.1).

Such trends are already having profound impacts, changing where workers are needed and where they can be found.[3] Regardless of politics, wealthy countries will need foreign workers to sustain their economies and honor their social commitments to older citizens. Many middle-income countries, traditionally the main sources of migration, will soon need to compete for foreign workers—and many are not ready to do so. Low-income countries have large numbers of unemployed and underemployed young people, but many of them do not yet have skills in demand in the global labor market.[4]

Climate change is compounding the economic drivers of migration.[5] About 40 percent of the world's population—3.5 billion people—live in places highly exposed to the impacts of climate change: water shortages, drought, heat stresses, sea level rise, and extreme events such as floods and tropical cyclones.[6] Economic opportunities are dwindling in affected regions, amplifying vulnerabilities and fueling pressures for migration.[7] Climate impacts are threatening the habitability of entire regions in places as diverse as the Sahel, low-lying Bangladesh, and the Mekong Delta.[8] In some Small Island Developing States, these impacts are forcing leaders to contemplate planned relocations.[9] Most of the movements attributed to climate change have so far been over short distances, mainly within a

Figure O.1 Widely different demographic forces are at play in Italy, Mexico, and Nigeria

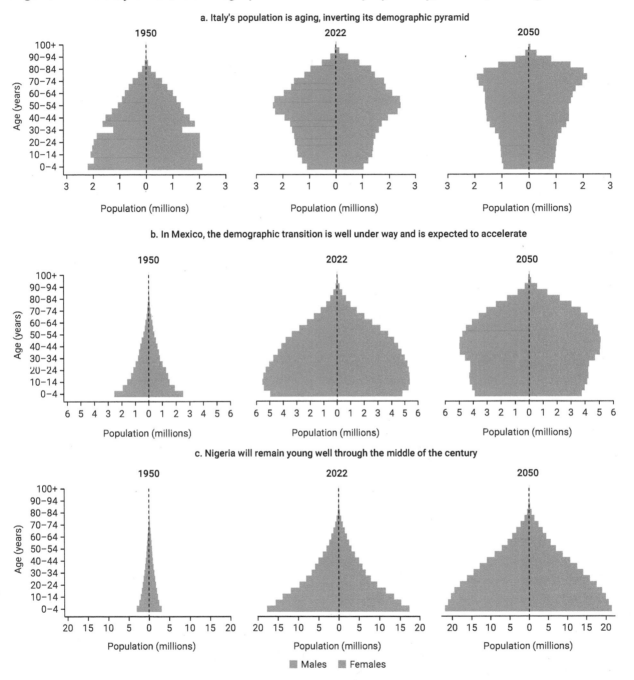

a. Italy's population is aging, inverting its demographic pyramid

b. In Mexico, the demographic transition is well under way and is expected to accelerate

c. Nigeria will remain young well through the middle of the century

■ Males ■ Females

Source: 2022 data (medium scenario): World Population Prospects (dashboard), Population Division, Department of Economic and Social Affairs, United Nations, New York, https://population.un.org/wpp/.

country.[10] But this may change. Whether and how much climate change will amplify international movements in the coming decades depend on the global and national policies for mitigation and adaptation adopted and implemented now.

Meanwhile, conflict, violence, and persecution continue to drive large numbers of people out of their home countries. The number of refugees has more than doubled over the last decade.[11]

Forced displacement and economic migration patterns are largely distinct. Refugee movements are often sudden and rapid.[12] Because refugees aim for the closest safe destination, they are concentrated in a small number of neighboring host countries. Refugees also include large numbers of vulnerable people—children account for 41 percent of the total.[13]

In the face of such forces, migration needs to be managed so that its development benefits can fully materialize. Current approaches often fail both migrants and nationals. They create large inefficiencies and missed opportunities in both destination and origin countries.[14] At times, they lead to human suffering. In many countries at all income levels, broad segments of society are challenging migration as part of a broader discourse against globalization.[15]

A practical framework for policy makers: The Match and Motive Matrix

Migration entails both benefits and costs—for the migrants, the origin countries, and the destination countries. For all, favorable outcomes depend on migrants' individual characteristics, the circumstances of their move, and the policies they face. Yet countries have unequal roles in setting such policies. Most origin countries have little sway in regulating movements. By contrast, destination countries define and regulate who crosses their borders, who is legally allowed to stay, and with what rights. They encourage some movements and discourage others. Their policies largely shape the impacts of cross-border movements.[16]

Labor economics and international law provide the two main lenses to understand migration patterns and to design the appropriate migration policies. These two perspectives arise from distinct intellectual and scholarly traditions, and they focus on different aspects of cross-border movements. As a result, each provides important insights, and yet until now there has been no simple framework to integrate them into a coherent whole.

Labor economics focuses on the "match" between migrants' skills and related attributes and destination countries' needs (figure O.2, panel a). The starting point for migration policies in many destination countries is a simple question: Does migration yield benefits that exceed the costs? Migrants bring skills for which there are different levels of demand. The more migrants' skills match the needs of the destination labor market, the larger are the gains for the destination economies and the migrants themselves—and often for the origin countries as well (through remittances and knowledge transfers).[17] This applies regardless of skills level and legal status. But migrants also use public services, and they must be integrated into a society that can be unfamiliar. Both involve costs, at least in the short term. The net gains can thus be either positive or negative.

Under international law, migrants' motives determine destination countries' obligations. Countries decide which migrants to let in and under what status as a matter of state sovereignty (figure O.2, panel b). Yet when people flee their country because of a "well-founded fear" of persecution, conflict, or violence—and when they cannot return without risking harm—they are entitled to international protection under the 1951 Refugee Convention, and the cost-benefit calculations by destination countries no longer apply. Under international law, these people are refugees, and they are not to be returned to their country of origin regardless of the cost of hosting them.[18] There are other migrants who require special support because they face daunting challenges, such as some women and children (especially girls), LGBTQ+ people, and victims of racism, xenophobia, and other forms of discrimination. In fact, some people move for a combination of reasons, blurring the strict distinction between refugees and economic migrants. The need for international protection provides a second lens through which migration policies should be viewed as they are designed.

Figure O.2 Two perspectives on cross-border migration

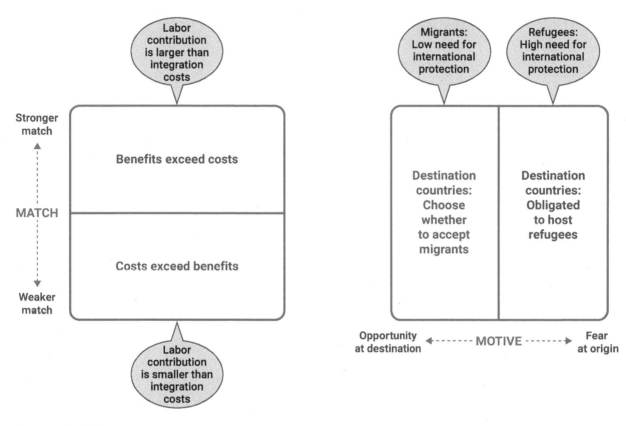

a. Labor economics: When migrants' skills and attributes are a strong match, labor contributions exceed integration costs

b. International law: If migrants fear harm in their country of origin, destination countries are obligated to host them

Source: WDR 2023 team.

Note: Panel a: *Match* refers to the degree to which a migrant's skills and related attributes meet the demand in the destination country. *Benefits* include greater economic output, a larger tax base, and a greater availability and affordability of some goods and services. *Costs* include greater demand for public services, effects on competing workers, as well as the costs of economic and social integration. Panel b: *Motive* refers to the circumstances under which a person moves—whether in search of opportunity or because of a "well-founded fear" of persecution, armed conflict, or violence in their origin country. Under the 1951 Refugee Convention, those who have such fear are entitled to a refugee status and shall be provided with international protection. They cannot be returned to their country of origin or to a country where they would face inhuman or degrading treatment or other irreparable harm (*non-refoulement* principle).

This Report offers an analytical framework that incorporates both dimensions—match as well as motive. It distinguishes between four types of movements, and it identifies policy priorities for each situation (figure O.3):[19]

- *Economic migrants with a strong match* (upper-left quadrant). Most migrants move in search of better opportunities and choose destinations where they are likely to be a strong match.[20] Their movement generates substantial development benefits for the migrants, the destination country, as well as the country of origin, regardless of their legal status. There are costs as well, but they are typically smaller. For such movements, the interests of all parties are generally aligned. The policy goal should be to further increase the benefits and to reduce the costs.

Figure O.3 "Match" determines the net gains of receiving migrants; "motive" determines their international protection needs

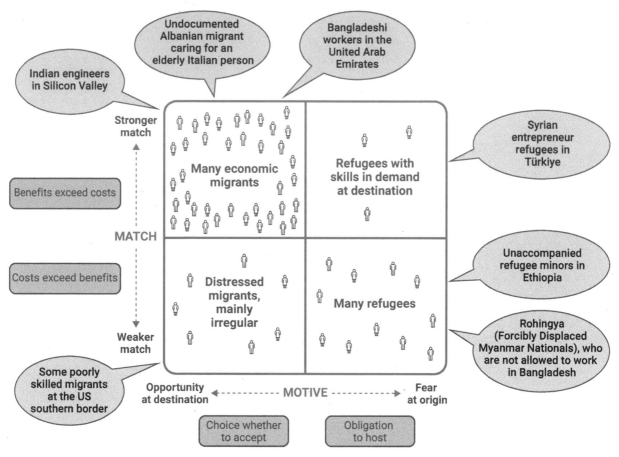

Source: WDR 2023 team.

Note: Match refers to the degree to which a migrant's skills and related attributes meet the demand in the destination country. *Motive* refers to the circumstances under which a person moves—whether in search of opportunity or because of a "well-founded fear" of persecution, armed conflict, or violence in their origin country.

- *Refugees with a strong match* (upper-right quadrant). Some refugees have skills and attributes that match the destination country's needs, even though they are moving out of fear and not to seek opportunities. Their movement brings to the destination society the same development benefits as those brought by voluntary migrants. The policy goal should be to further increase net gains.
- *Refugees with a weak match* (lower-right quadrant). Many refugees bring skills and attributes that are a weak match with the needs of the destination society. They choose their destination based on their immediate need for safety, not labor market considerations. Yet under international law they must be accommodated, regardless of the costs. The policy goal for the destination country should be to reduce these costs and to share them internationally.
- *Distressed migrants* (lower-left quadrant). Other migrants neither qualify as refugees nor are a strong match at their destination. Their aggregate numbers are not large, but their movements are often irregular and unsafe, raising significant challenges for destination countries. The term *distressed migrants*, as they are called in this Report, is an acknowledgment of the circumstances

under which they move, not a normative category. Some of these distressed migrants, while not refugees, may still have protection needs on humanitarian grounds or otherwise. Others may be returned to the country of origin—but they must be treated humanely.

Where migrants stand in the Match and Motive Matrix is determined in part by destination countries' policies. For example, the match of a migrant's skills and attributes with the needs of the destination country depends on whether that migrant has the right to work at the level of his or her qualifications. The match can evolve over time, based on changing labor needs, economic regulations, and social norms in the destination country. Similarly, the determination of who should receive international protection varies significantly across countries within the broader parameters of international law.

Ultimately, government policies should aim to both maximize the development gains of migration—for the migrants, origin societies, and destination societies—and provide refugees with adequate international protection. Over time, policies should aim to strengthen the match of all migrants' skills and attributes with the needs of the destination societies so that the benefits can be further increased. They should also aim to reduce the need for distressed movements, which often entail considerable suffering.

When the match is strong, the gains are large

When migrants bring skills and attributes in demand in the destination country, the benefits typically outweigh the costs, regardless of motives, skill levels, or legal status. These migrants fill gaps in the destination labor market, with benefits for the destination economy, as well as for themselves and their origin country. There are costs as well, both social and economic, but they typically are much smaller than the benefits. Both destination and origin countries can design and implement policies that further increase the gains and address the downsides (figure O.4).

Destination countries should not let social and cultural controversies overshadow the economic gains of migration

Migrants can contribute much to the destination economy's efficiency and growth, especially over the long term. Low-skilled migrants perform many jobs that locals are unwilling to take, or for which they would ask wages above what consumers are willing to pay.[21] High-skilled migrants—nurses, engineers, scientists—improve productivity across many sectors of an economy, although only four countries—Australia, Canada, the United Kingdom, and the United States—account for over half of all tertiary-educated immigrants.[22] About 17 percent of health care workers in the United States, 12 percent in the United Kingdom, and 79 percent in the Gulf Cooperation Council (GCC) countries are foreign-born.[23] Consumers benefit from lower production costs and the lower prices of some goods and services.[24] The long-term benefits of immigration include increased entrepreneurship and innovation, stronger links for international trade and investment, and better provision of services such as education and health care.[25] Migrants' contributions are larger when they are allowed and able to work formally at the level of their qualifications and experience.

In many countries, however, the controversy is not about economics; it is about the social and cultural impacts of migration. When migrants stay for an extended period of time—or permanently—the question of their integration becomes central. Sociocultural impacts are a function of the size of the migrant group, its origin, its socioeconomic standing, as well as the perceptions of citizens toward migrants—and sometimes their racial prejudices.[26] Sociocultural impacts are also a function of each

Figure O.4 When the match is strong, policies in both destination and origin countries can maximize the gains of migration

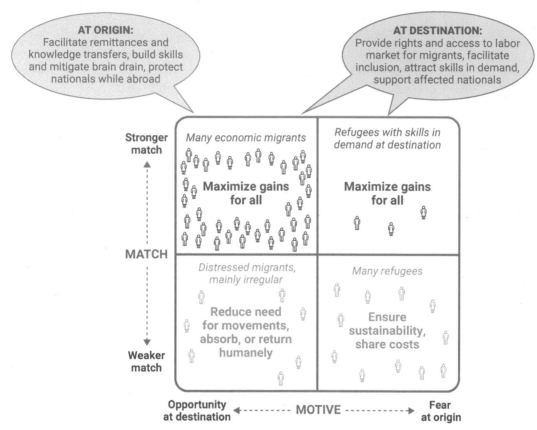

Source: WDR 2023 team.

Note: Match refers to the degree to which a migrant's skills and related attributes meet the demand in the destination country. *Motive* refers to the circumstances under which a person moves—whether in search of opportunity or because of a "well-founded fear" of persecution, armed conflict, or violence in their origin country.

country's sense of identity and social contract.[27] Some countries, such as Canada, define themselves as societies shaped by migrants and their descendants,[28] while others, such as Japan, emphasize their ancient roots.[29]

This debate plays out in a context in which societies and cultures are neither homogeneous nor static. There is no "pre-migration" harmony to return to. In every society, tensions, competition, and cooperation have always existed across a variety of groups that are partly overlapping and constantly changing. Some of these tensions reflect socioeconomic divides: they are not about migration but about poverty and economic opportunity—and large numbers of migrants happen to be poor. Because many of those who moved or their descendants have been naturalized, some of the cultural issues attributed to migration are, in fact, about the inclusion of national minorities. Migration is also just one of many forces transforming societies in an age of rapid change, alongside modernization, secularization, technological progress, shifts in gender roles and family structures, and the emergence of new norms and values, among other trends. Integration happens eventually, and it is facilitated by economic inclusion and nondiscrimination policies.

Destination countries should actively address the actual downsides of migration. The more closely migrants' skills and attributes match the needs of the destination labor market, the smaller are their effects on nationals' wages. Yet even if the average effects are limited, some workers—those whose skills are similar to migrants'—may lose wages or even jobs, and they need support.[30] When a destination country must accommodate large numbers of foreign children, especially if they are not fluent in the local language, additional resources are needed to maintain the quality of education.[31] Public investment should be increased in neighborhoods where migrants live to reduce poverty and discrimination that otherwise can lead to residential segregation and a range of social ills as experienced in France or Sweden.[32] In most countries, migration increases fiscal revenue by expanding the tax-paying workforce, thereby creating space for the necessary spending.[33]

Most migrants benefit greatly—even more so when they have rights in their destination country

Most economic migrants—both low- and high-skilled—fare much better in destination countries than if they had stayed in their origin country. Because migrants aim to maximize the benefits of their movement, they deliberately choose destinations where their skills are in demand. They find opportunities they would not have had in their country of origin, earn higher wages, and often access better services. These gains increase substantially over time, especially if the destination economy is growing and its labor market functions well. Those who return to their country of origin—about 20–50 percent of the total in Organisation for Economic Co-operation and Development (OECD) high-income countries— are better off than before their departure.[34]

Migrants face challenges as well. The financial costs of moving are very high in some situations, and migrants have to work years to repay them.[35] Tens of millions of migrants are separated from their families, and many are at risk of social isolation in unfamiliar settings.[36] The absence of parents raises challenges at home—such as for children's education—with potential long-term consequences.[37]

The benefits of migration are larger when migrants have a legal status and formal employment rights in line with international labor standards. Examples are the right to decent work, to fair recruitment,[38] and to an ability to change employers when new opportunities arise.[39] Once they have such rights, migrants' wages and the quality of their jobs converge with those of nationals much faster than if they are undocumented, and they face less pressure to take on lower-skilled and lower-paying jobs than their skills warrant.[40] They can travel more easily, and, as a result, they can better maintain connections with family members in their country of origin. They are also less vulnerable to abuse and discrimination. By contrast, in destinations where legal protection is inadequate, or where migrants cannot access it because of information and language barriers, they are at increased risk of exploitation.[41]

Origin countries should actively manage migration for its development benefits

In origin countries, emigration can support poverty reduction and development—especially if it is well managed.[42] Remittances are a stable source of income for migrants' families, supporting investments in children's education, health care, housing, and entrepreneurial activities. These benefits could be amplified by lowering the costs of sending remittances.[43] In many cases, migrants, returnees, and diaspora communities transfer ideas, knowledge, and technology, spurring job creation and modernization—just as US Silicon Valley expatriates did when they helped nurture India's information technology sector.[44] This process is easier when the origin country has sound economic policies that foster a favorable business climate, efficient labor market policies, solid institutions, and business ecosystems into which entrepreneurs can tap.

High-skilled emigration from low-income countries—the so-called brain drain—can inflict losses and create development challenges. In Sub-Saharan Africa, the Caribbean, and the Pacific, people with a tertiary education are 30 times more likely to emigrate than those who are less educated.[45] This emigration can aggravate a shortage of skilled workers to provide essential services, such as health care. Because governments cannot prevent people from leaving, they need to expand the training capacity for such skills. This effort could be supported through coordination with destination countries, including to finance higher education and training programs.[46] In essential sectors such as health care, additional measures may be necessary, such as minimum service requirements enforced through bilateral labor agreements with destination countries.[47] Parallel economic and social reforms are needed to ensure that skilled workers have attractive prospects and can be employed at their full capacity in their origin countries.

Origin countries benefit most from labor migration when they make it an explicit part of their poverty reduction strategy. Governments can facilitate orderly movements through labor agreements with destination countries, improved labor market information systems, fair recruitment processes, and consular support to citizens abroad. They can also work to reduce remittance and migration costs and support returning migrants as they reenter the labor market and society. They can adjust education systems to build the low and high skills in demand globally so that their citizens can obtain better jobs if they migrate and thus contribute more through remittances and knowledge transfers. Such initiatives have proved fruitful in several countries such as Bangladesh and the Philippines, although much remains to be done.[48]

When the match is weak, the costs need to be shared—and reduced—multilaterally

When migrants do not bring skills and attributes in demand at their destination, the costs to destination countries exceed the benefits. If there are gains for migrants and origin countries, these gains are not sustainable unless destination countries take action to reduce and manage their own costs (figure O.5). The policy challenges are different for refugees, who under international law must be hosted by the destination countries, and for other migrants who move under distressed circumstances.

Refugee situations should be managed as medium-term development challenges and not just as humanitarian emergencies

Supporting refugee-hosting countries through a succession of emergency responses is both costly and ineffective. On average, the international community spends US$585 a year for each refugee hosted in a low- or lower-middle-income country, in addition to the expenditure incurred by host governments.[49] The way in which international support is delivered often creates incentives for short-term approaches.[50] Yet current refugees have been in exile for an average of 13 years,[51] and millions live in limbo for decades.[52] For example, many Afghans who left their country after the 1979 Soviet invasion are still in exile today, and so are their children and grandchildren. Humanitarian aid is critical to meeting immediate needs, but policy making, from the outset of a crisis, should aim for responses that can be sustained over time, both financially and socially.

Figure O.5 When the match is weaker, policy making involves trade-offs for the destination country between economic gains and migrants' dignity

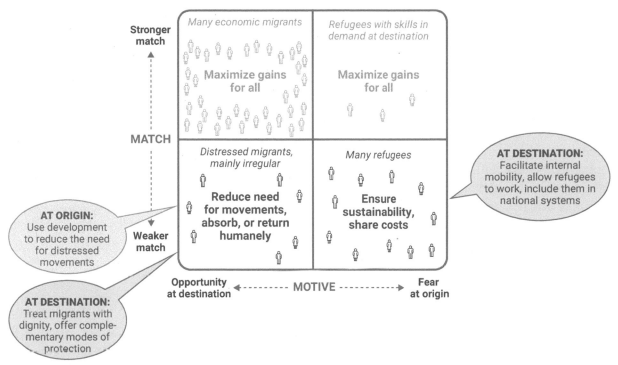

Source: WDR 2023 team.

Note: Match refers to the degree to which a migrant's skills and related attributes meet the demand in the destination country. *Motive* refers to the circumstances under which a person moves—whether in search of opportunity or because of a "well-founded fear" of persecution, armed conflict, or violence in their origin country.

Taking a medium-term approach can both reduce hosting costs and allow refugees to rebuild their lives. The 1951 Refugee Convention obligates states to provide refugees with safety, but also with access to jobs and essential services. Those who flee conflict and persecution often have severe vulnerabilities, including loss of assets and a traumatic experience, which can be compounded by an uncertain status.[53] Many cannot work, such as children or people with disabilities or undergoing trauma. But, if given a chance, most refugees look for ways to improve their lives and contribute to their hosting economies, much in the way other migrants do.[54] This effort can be best supported by giving refugees the right to work, supporting them in accessing jobs, and including them in national education and health systems— with adequate external support. This approach has been adopted in countries as diverse as Colombia,[55] Niger,[56] Poland,[57] Türkiye,[58] and Uganda,[59] among others.

Internal mobility—letting refugees move within destination countries to places where there are jobs and services—can further transform the response to refugee situations. Many refugees are hosted in lagging borderland areas, where opportunities are scarce and where they form a large share of the population. Their presence can impose significant burdens on host communities. But other approaches are possible, as demonstrated by the support some countries have provided to displaced Venezuelans and Ukrainians, for example. In these situations, refugees are allowed, and even encouraged, to move across the entire host country and even within regional blocs. This freedom strengthens their match with the needs of the destination societies because they can access more opportunities. It also lessens pressures on host communities because refugees are more evenly spread across the entire population. Such an approach requires a shift in the way assistance is provided, moving toward adopting predictable medium-term financing, formulating policy support, and strengthening national institutions to provide international protection.[60]

Hosting refugees contributes to a global public good. All nations should therefore help absorb the costs of hosting, but many do not. The vast majority of refugees live in only a dozen countries, typically low- and middle-income countries bordering the countries of origin.[61] For example, in Jordan and Lebanon refugees make up a large share of the total population. Three donors provide almost two-thirds of bilateral financing for assistance to refugees globally,[62] and four countries account for almost three-quarters of all resettlements.[63] This narrow base of support should be broadened by engaging new constituencies, including development organizations, local authorities, the private sector, and civil society. Responsibility-sharing can also be part of broader bilateral negotiations, such as on trade access under the Jordan Compact[64] or investment under the Ethiopia Job Compact.[65] It could be complemented by regional initiatives, including in low-income contexts. For example, in the Horn of Africa the Inter-governmental Authority on Development (IGAD) has helped develop a regional peer-to-peer process to gradually improve the management of refugee situations.[66]

Distressed migration needs to be reduced while respecting people's dignity

The most difficult policy challenges arise when migrants are neither refugees nor a strong match for the destination society. Many of these migrants turn to irregular channels and to the growing smuggling industry and the exploitative labor market it feeds in destination countries.[67] These movements often entail suffering. Since 2014, nearly 50,000 people have died while attempting to migrate.[68] Many have perished while trying to cross the Mediterranean Sea, and deaths on other routes are also increasing. These movements have also created a sense of loss of control over borders, and they undermine the fragile consensus on the treatment of regular migrants and refugees. To deter such movements, some governments have implemented harsh policies, such as family separation at the US southern border in 2018 or externalization of border controls to third countries with dubious human rights records.[69] All of these responses come at a significant cost to the dignity and human rights of migrants and would-be migrants.

Some distressed migrants have protection needs, even though they are not refugees. They take life-threatening risks that suggest they have no viable alternatives in their country of origin, or they fall prey to human trafficking while moving. For example, undocumented migrants on their way to the US southern border face kidnapping, extortion, and sexual and other forms of violence from criminal gangs.[70] In the face of what has become a series of human and political crises, several countries have developed ad hoc legal instruments to provide a form of protection for people who are not recognized as refugees but cannot be safely returned to their country.[71] This approach is sometimes referred to as complementary or subsidiary protection. Such schemes should be extended in a coherent manner, and safe, legal routes should be established to access protection.

Destination countries may choose to return other distressed migrants to their countries of origin. Still, human dignity must remain the yardstick of migration policies. Deportations are a tragedy for the individuals involved, yet they may be necessary to ensure the sustainability of the migration system because they demonstrate to citizens and would-be migrants alike that rules will be enforced. Involuntary returns should be executed in conformity with human rights conventions and in a humane manner.

They should be accompanied by parallel efforts to crack down on both smugglers and those who employ irregular migrants at the destination.

When destination countries adopt restrictive policies, their neighbors can also be affected, especially those through which migrants are transiting. Transit countries become substitute destinations when barriers prevent migrants from moving onward. Distressed migrants stay for months, and at times years, in countries where they did not wish to end up and where they are often vulnerable. This situation raises difficult policy issues for transit countries such as Mexico or Morocco that they cannot address alone. Both the destination and transit countries should work together to absorb distressed migrants or return them humanely (however, return should not apply to refugees for whom the 1951 Refugee Convention applies). This cooperation includes designing mechanisms to determine who should be absorbed in which country—destination or transit—and who should be returned, as well as agreeing on the corresponding processes and financial arrangements to do so effectively. Such arrangements may be complemented by efforts to scale up services and safety in countries in which migrants are merely passing through.

Overall, the main challenge is to reduce the need for such movements (figure O.6). Development plays a critical role in that respect by changing who migrates and under what circumstances.[72] As countries

Figure O.6 Policy actions in both origin and destination countries can reduce distressed migration

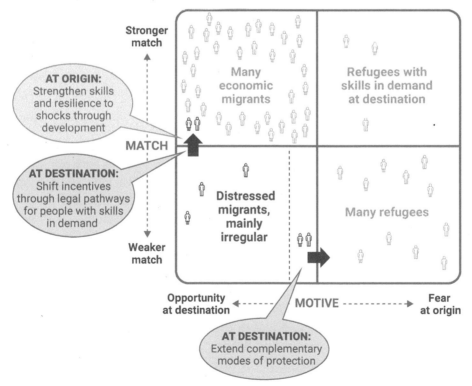

Source: WDR 2023 team.

Note: Match refers to the degree to which a migrant's skills and related attributes meet the demand in the destination country. *Motive* refers to the circumstances under which a person moves—whether in search of opportunity or because of a "well-founded fear" of persecution, armed conflict, or violence in their origin country. The dashed vertical line in the lower-left quadrant highlights the distinction between distressed migrants who have some needs for international protection and those who do not.

develop, people become better educated, and their skills better match the needs of domestic and global labor markets. They also become more resilient to shocks, and the availability of decent work and domestic migration alternatives reduce the need for distressed cross-border movements. But development takes time, and shorter-term responses are also needed. Destination countries can cooperate with origin countries and expand legal pathways for entry to enable or even incentivize movements by people whose skills and attributes match their needs, including lower-skilled workers. In the process, they shape the incentives of would-be migrants and the communities that support them, such as for acquiring specific skills.

Making migration work better requires doing things differently

Now is a difficult time for migration reform. Political debates have become polarized in many countries, at all levels of income. Tensions within the international community increased following the 2022 Russian invasion of Ukraine. The global economic outlook remains uncertain. Yet reforms are needed urgently. Difficult debates lie ahead, but they cannot be avoided or delayed if the gains from migration are to be realized.

Stronger international cooperation is essential: Bilateral to enhance migrants' match and multilateral to respond to movements driven by fear

Both origin and destination countries need to manage migration strategically. For origin countries, the challenge is to maximize the development impacts of labor migration on their own societies. For destination countries, the challenge is to recognize and harness the potential of migration to meet their long-term labor needs, while treating all migrants humanely and addressing social impacts that raise concerns among their citizens.

To increase the benefits they derive from migration, origin and destination countries need to work together (figure O.7). Cooperation can be formalized through bilateral labor agreements that facilitate better matching of skills and provide those who move with legal status,[73] such as between some Pacific Island states and Australia.[74] Bilateral cooperation can help build globally transferable skills in origin countries such as through Global Skills Partnerships.[75] Bilateral cooperation is also critical to process involuntary returns humanely.[76] It can be complemented by regional initiatives—for example, to discuss labor needs across a group of countries of origin and destination or to create regional schemes for recognizing qualifications, such as the Single Market and Economy (CSME) initiative of the Caribbean Community (CARICOM).

Multilateral efforts are also needed to address movements motivated by fear, both to strengthen global norms and to share the costs of hosting refugees. The international legal architecture for migration and forced displacement—and for defining who should receive international protection—has been evolving over the last decades to reflect changes in the patterns of movements. Likely to continue, it should include a strong development perspective. But at a time of renewed tensions in the international community, progress may be slow. Global action should be complemented by regional efforts—in particular, to share responsibility for hosting refugees and other forcibly displaced people—as Latin American countries did by allowing Venezuelan nationals to move across the region.

To make change happen, underrepresented voices must be heard

Migration reform is a political process. Data and evidence are essential for successful reforms, but they are not sufficient. New stakeholder groups need to make their voices heard. This is especially important

Figure O.7 Different types of migration require distinct forms of international cooperation

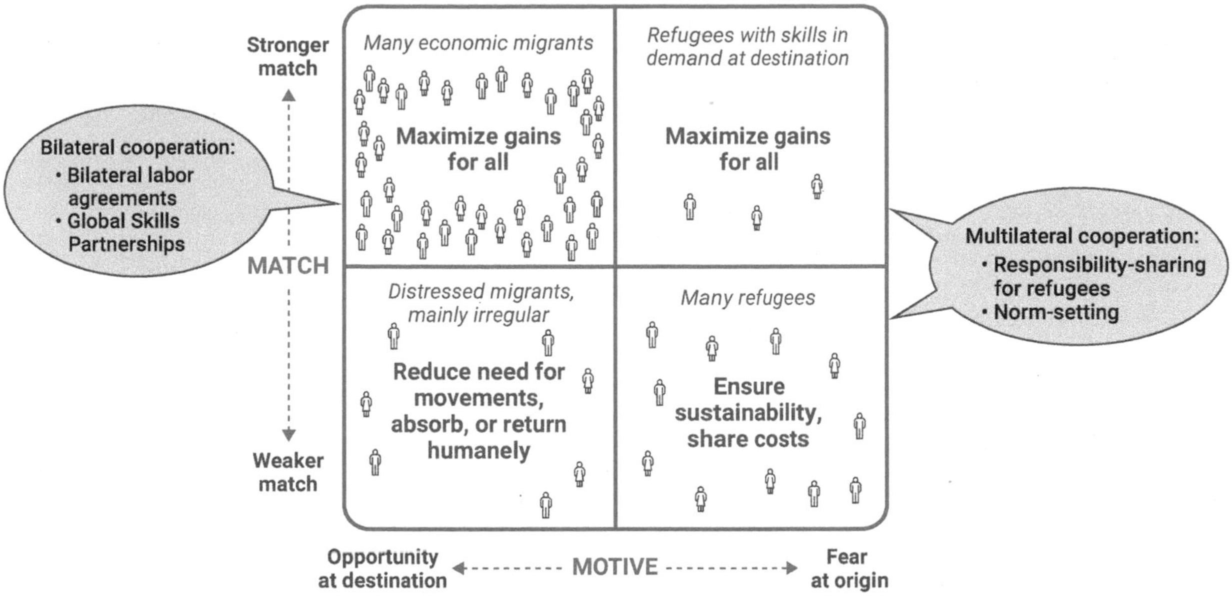

Source: WDR 2023 team.

Note: Match refers to the degree to which a migrant's skills and related attributes meet the demand in the destination country. *Motive* refers to the circumstances under which a person moves—whether in search of opportunity or because of a "well-founded fear" of persecution, armed conflict, or violence in their origin country.

when debates are highly polarized and when there are multiple competing priorities—among them, climate change, food security, and an ongoing global economic slowdown.

In both origin and destination countries, the debates should engage broad segments of society beyond elite circles. This effort can be pursued by taking a whole-of-government approach beyond security agencies, by inviting the private sector and labor unions to assess medium-term labor needs and how to meet them, and by engaging with local authorities, which are often at the forefront of the response and integration challenges. Migrants' and refugees' voices should be heard as well, which requires developing systems to channel them in ways that ensure representation and accountability. Low- and middle-income countries—including origin countries for economic migrants and refugee-hosting countries—can also form constructive coalitions to get their perspectives better heard and defend their interests.

A message of hope

This Report conveys a message of hope. Amid a debate dominated by ideological arguments about whether migration is good or bad, it tries to answer a different question: how can migration work better for global development? The answer requires recognizing both the potential benefits and the challenges—economic, societal, and human—that emerge when people cross borders. Migration is neither universally good nor universally bad. It is complicated and necessary, and it needs to be better managed (table O.1 and see chapter 9 for further details). Whenever and wherever it is well managed, migration is a powerful force for prosperity with benefits for all: economic migrants, refugees, and those who stay behind, and for origin and destination societies.

Table O.1 Main policy recommendations

WHEN MIGRANTS' AND REFUGEES' SKILLS ARE IN DEMAND (STRONG MATCH)		
COUNTRY OF ORIGIN Manage migration for poverty reduction	**COUNTRY OF DESTINATION** Maximize benefits, reduce costs	**BILATERAL COOPERATION** Strengthen match
Strategy. Make emigration part of development strategies. *Remittances.* Leverage remittances for poverty reduction and reduce their costs. *Knowledge.* Work with the diaspora and returnees to spur knowledge transfers and to strengthen integration in the global economy. *Skills development and brain drain mitigation.* Expand education and training in skills that are in demand in both the national and global labor markets. *Protection.* Provide citizens abroad with protection. Support vulnerable family members left behind.	*Strategy.* Acknowledge labor needs. Build a consensus on the role of migration. Ensure policy coherence. *Entry and status.* Incentivize stronger match immigration. Ensure migrants have a formal status and rights. *Economic inclusion.* Facilitate labor market inclusion. Enhance recognition of migrants' qualifications. Combat exploitation and promote decent work. *Social inclusion.* Prevent segregation and facilitate access to services. Combat discrimination. *Support to nationals.* Support citizens who are negatively affected in terms of employment outcomes and public services through social protection and public investments.	*Bilateral labor agreements.* Structure and facilitate win-win movements. Reduce recruitment costs. *Skills development.* Partner to finance the development of skills that are in demand in both the national and global labor markets.

WHEN REFUGEES' SKILLS ARE NOT IN DEMAND (WEAK MATCH, FEAR MOTIVE)	
HOST COUNTRY Manage with a medium-term perspective and enhance the match	**INTERNATIONAL COMMUNITY** Share the costs with hosting countries
Institutions and instruments. Mainstream refugee support through line ministries. Develop sustainable financing frameworks. *Internal mobility.* Facilitate and encourage refugees' movements toward opportunities. *Self-reliance.* Enable refugees to access jobs in the formal labor market. *Inclusion in national services.* Deliver education, health, and social services to refugees through national systems.	*Responsibility-sharing.* Prevent or resolve situations that cause refugees to flee. Provide adequate amounts of medium-term financing. Increase resettlement options. Broaden the base of support beyond current main contributors. Develop regional approaches. *Solutions.* Further work toward "durable solutions" (voluntary return, local integration or resettlement). Develop innovative statuses that provide state protection and access to opportunities over the medium term.

WHEN MIGRANTS' SKILLS ARE NOT IN DEMAND (WEAK MATCH, NO FEAR MOTIVE)		
COUNTRY OF ORIGIN Reduce the need for distressed movements	**COUNTRY OF TRANSIT** Coordinate with countries of destination	**COUNTRY OF DESTINATION** Respect migrants' dignity
Resilience. Enhance social protection. Create domestic alternatives to international migration. *Education.* Build skills that allow people to have more options. *Inclusion.* Promote inclusive and green development. Foster adaptation to climate change.	*Cooperation.* Work with the destination country to absorb migrants or return them humanely (for last transit country).	*Respect.* Treat all migrants humanely. *Complementary protection.* Strengthen the coherence of the current system to protect people at risk who are not refugees. *Legal pathways.* Shift migrants' incentives by establishing legal pathways for workers in demand, including lower-skilled workers. *Enforcement.* Manage necessary returns humanely. Clamp down on smugglers and exploitative employers. Strengthen institutional capacity to process entries.

MAKING MIGRATION POLICY DIFFERENTLY		
DATA AND EVIDENCE	**FINANCIAL INSTRUMENTS**	**NEW VOICES**
Harmonization. Harmonize data collection methods. *Evidence-building.* Invest in new types of surveys to inform policy making. *Open data.* Encourage research by making data widely available, while respecting migrants' and refugees' privacy.	*New or expanded instruments.* Develop medium-term instruments to support refugee-hosting countries. Provide external support to low- and middle-income countries receiving weaker match migrants. *Enhanced use of existing instruments.* Incentivize private sector engagement. Support origin countries in leveraging migration for development. Incentivize bilateral and regional cooperation.	*Affected nations.* Build coalitions among countries facing common challenges. *Domestic stakeholders.* Ensure participation of a broad range of stakeholders in decision-making processes. *Migrants' and refugees' voices.* Develop representation and accountability systems to organize migrants' and refugees' voices.

Source: WDR 2023 team.

Notes

1. Armitage et al. (2011); Beyer et al. (2021).
2. See chapter 2 for further details.
3. See chapters 4–6 for further details.
4. Also see chapter 3 for further details.
5. Black, Kniveton, and Schmidt-Verkerk (2011); Black et al. (2011); McLeman (2016).
6. Global Internal Displacement Database, Internal Displacement Monitoring Centre, Geneva, https://www.internal-displacement.org/database/displacement-data.
7. See chapter 3 for further details.
8. IPCC (2022).
9. Cissé et al. (2022); IPCC (2022, chap. 7).
10. Clement et al. (2021); Rigaud et al. (2018).
11. Refugee Data Finder (dashboard), United Nations High Commissioner for Refugees, Geneva, https://popstats.unhcr.org/refugee-statistics/download/.
12. Melander and Öberg (2006).
13. World Bank (2017).
14. Clemens (2011).
15. Frieden (2019).
16. See chapter 4 for further details.
17. World Bank (2018).
18. OHCHR (1951), article 33.
19. On the Match and Motive Matrix, see chapter 1.
20. See chapter 2 for migrant population numbers.
21. See chapter 6 for further details.
22. Pekkala Kerr et al. (2016).
23. Lafortune, Socha-Dietrich, and Vickstrom (2019).
24. See chapter 6 for further details.
25. See chapter 6 for further details.
26. See chapter 6 and spotlight 6 for further details.
27. See chapter 6 for a discussion on the social and cultural impacts of migration.
28. StatCan (2013).
29. Morris-Suzuki (1995).
30. Dustmann, Glitz, and Frattini (2008).
31. Chin, Daysal, and Imberman (2012); Frattini and Meschi (2019).
32. Auspurg, Schneck, and Hinz (2019); Baldini and Federici (2011); Baptista and Marlier (2019); Bosch, Carnero, and Farré (2010); Fonseca, McGarrigle, and Esteves (2010).
33. Clemens (2021).
34. Bossavie and Özden (2022); Dustmann and Görlach (2016); OECD (2008).
35. See chapter 5 for more on the costs of migration.
36. Graham and Jordan (2011); Mazzucato et al. (2015); Parreñas (2001).
37. Cortés (2015); Jaupart (2019).
38. ILO (2019).
39. Naidu, Nyarko, and Wang (2016); Pan (2012).
40. Damelang, Ebensperger, and Stumpf (2020); Duleep (2015).
41. ILO (2016); ILO, Walk Free, and IOM (2022); UNDP (2020).
42. See chapter 5 for further details.
43. See chapter 5 for further details.
44. Chanda and Sreenivasan (2006); Docquier and Rapoport (2012); Kerr (2008).
45. Pekkala Kerr et al. (2017).
46. Clemens (2015); OECD (2018).
47. See chapter 5 for further details.
48. Ang and Tiongson (2023); Bossavie (2023).
49. OECD (2021).
50. See chapter 7 for further details.
51. Devictor and Do (2017). Based on 2021 data from Refugee Data Finder (dashboard), United Nations High Commissioner for Refugees, Geneva, https://popstats.unhcr.org/refugee-statistics/download/. The average does not include refugees from the Ukraine war.
52. Devictor and Do (2017). For 2020 data, see Refugee Data Finder (searchable data sets), Statistics and Demographics Section, Global Data Service, United Nations High Commissioner for Refugees, Copenhagen, https://www.unhcr.org/refugee-statistics/download/?url=2bxU2f.
53. Porter and Haslam (2005).
54. Hussam et al. (2022).
55. Rossiasco et al. (2023).
56. IDA (2021, 162).
57. EWSI (2022).
58. Tumen (2023).
59. IDA (2021, 9).
60. See chapter 7 for further details.
61. As of the end of 2022, the top 12 refugee-hosting countries by number of refugees hosted were Türkiye, Colombia, Germany, Pakistan, Uganda, the Russian Federation, Poland, Sudan, Bangladesh, Ethiopia, the Islamic Republic of Iran, and Lebanon. See Refugee Data Finder (dashboard), United Nations High Commissioner for Refugees, Geneva, https://popstats.unhcr.org/refugee-statistics/download/.
62. These are European Union institutions, Germany, and the United States (OECD 2021).
63. These are Canada, Germany, Sweden, and the United States (OECD 2021).
64. Government of Jordan (2016).
65. EUTF for Africa (2018).
66. IGAD (2022).
67. See chapter 8, box 8.4, for further details.
68. IOM (2020).
69. See chapter 8, box 8.1, for further details.
70. Infante et al. (2012).
71. Paoletti (2023).
72. See chapter 8 for further details.
73. United Nations Network on Migration (2022).
74. OECD (2018).
75. Clemens (2015).
76. See chapter 8 for further details.

References

Ang, Alvin, and Erwin R. Tiongson. 2023. "Philippine Migration Journey: Processes and Programs in the Migration Life Cycle." Background paper prepared for *World Development Report 2023*, World Bank, Washington, DC.

Armitage, Simon J., Sabah A. Jasim, Anthony E. Marks, Adrian G. Parker, Vitaly I. Usik, and Hans-Peter Uerpmann. 2011. "The Southern Route 'Out of Africa': Evidence for an Early Expansion of Modern Humans into Arabia." *Science* 331 (6016): 453–56.

Auspurg, Katrin, Andreas Schneck, and Thomas Hinz. 2019. "Closed Doors Everywhere? A Meta-Analysis of Field Experiments on Ethnic Discrimination in Rental Housing Markets." *Journal of Ethnic and Migration Studies* 45 (1): 95–114.

Baldini, Massimo, and Marta Federici. 2011. "Ethnic Discrimination in the Italian Rental Housing Market." *Journal of Housing Economics* 20 (1): 1–14.

Baptista, Isabel, and Eric Marlier. 2019. *Fighting Homelessness and Housing Exclusion in Europe: A Study of National Policies*. Synthesis Report, European Social Policy Network. Brussels: European Commission.

Beyer, Robert M., Mario Krapp, Anders Eriksson, and Andrea Manica. 2021. "Climatic Windows for Human Migration Out of Africa in the Past 300,000 Years." *Nature Communications* 12 (1): 4889.

Black, Richard, Stephen R. G. Bennett, Sandy M. Thomas, and John R. Beddington. 2011. "Migration as Adaptation." *Nature* 478 (7370): 447–49.

Black, Richard, Dominic Kniveton, and Kerstin Schmidt-Verkerk. 2011. "Migration and Climate Change: Towards an Integrated Assessment of Sensitivity." *Environment and Planning A: Economy and Space* 43 (2): 431–50.

Bosch, Mariano, M. Angeles Carnero, and Lídia Farré. 2010. "Information and Discrimination in the Rental Housing Market: Evidence from a Field Experiment." *Regional Science and Urban Economics* 40 (1): 11–19.

Bossavie, Laurent Loic Yves. 2023. "Low-Skilled Temporary Migration Policy: The Case of Bangladesh." Background paper prepared for *World Development Report 2023*, World Bank, Washington, DC.

Bossavie, Laurent Loic Yves, and Çağlar Özden. 2022. "Impacts of Temporary Migration on Development in Origin Countries." Policy Research Working Paper 9996, World Bank, Washington, DC.

Chanda, Rupa, and Niranjana Sreenivasan. 2006. "India's Experience with Skilled Migration." In *Competing for Global Talent*, edited by Christiane Kuptsch and Eng Fong Pang, 215–56. Geneva: International Institute for Labour Studies, International Labour Organization.

Chin, Aimee, N. Meltem Daysal, and Scott A. Imberman. 2012. "Impact of Bilingual Education Programs on Limited English Proficient Students and Their Peers: Regression Discontinuity Evidence from Texas." NBER Working Paper 18197, National Bureau of Economic Research, Cambridge, MA.

Cissé, Guéladio, Robert McLeman, Helen Adams, Paulina Aldunce, Kathryn Bowen, Diarmid Campbell-Lendrum, Susan Clayton, et al. 2022. "Health, Wellbeing and the Changing Structure of Communities." In *Climate Change 2022: Impacts, Adaptation, and Vulnerability*, 1041–1170. Sixth Assessment Report. Geneva: Intergovernmental Panel on Climate Change; New York: Cambridge University Press.

Clemens, Michael A. 2011. "Economics and Emigration: Trillion-Dollar Bills on the Sidewalk?" *Journal of Economic Perspectives* 25 (3): 83–106.

Clemens, Michael A. 2015. "Global Skill Partnerships: A Proposal for Technical Training in a Mobile World." *IZA Journal of Labor Policy* 4 (2): 1–18.

Clemens, Michael A. 2021. "The Fiscal Effect of Immigration: Reducing Bias in Influential Estimates." CESifo Working Paper 9464, Munich Society for the Promotion of Economic Research, Center for Economic Studies, Ludwig Maximilian University and Ifo Institute for Economic Research, Munich.

Clement, Viviane, Kanta Kumari Rigaud, Alex de Sherbinin, Bryan Jones, Susana Adamo, Jacob Schewe, Nian Sadiq, and Elham Shabahat. 2021. *Groundswell Part 2: Acting on Internal Climate Migration*. Washington, DC: World Bank.

Cortés, Patricia. 2015. "The Feminization of International Migration and Its Effects on the Children Left Behind: Evidence from the Philippines." *World Development* 65 (January): 62–78.

Damelang, Andreas, Sabine Ebensperger, and Felix Stumpf. 2020. "Foreign Credential Recognition and Immigrants' Chances of Being Hired for Skilled Jobs—Evidence from a Survey Experiment among Employers." *Social Forces* 99 (2): 648–71.

Devictor, Xavier, and Quy-Toan Do. 2017. "How Many Years Have Refugees Been in Exile?" *Population and Development Review* 43 (2): 355–69.

Docquier, Frédéric, and Hillel Rapoport. 2012. "Globalization, Brain Drain, and Development." *Journal of Economic Literature* 50 (3): 681–730.

Duleep, Harriet Orcutt. 2015. "The Adjustment of Immigrants in the Labor Market." In *The Immigrants*, edited by Barry R. Chiswick and Paul W. Miller, 105–82. Vol. 1A of *Handbook of the Economics of International Migration*. Oxford, UK: Elsevier.

Dustmann, Christian, Albrecht Glitz, and Tommaso Frattini. 2008. "The Labour Market Impact of Immigration." *Oxford Review of Economic Policy* 24 (3): 477–94.

Dustmann, Christian, and Joseph-Simon Görlach. 2016. "The Economics of Temporary Migrations." *Journal of Economic Literature* 54 (1): 98–136.

EUTF for Africa (European Union Emergency Trust Fund for Africa). 2018. "Ethiopia Job Compact Sector Reform and Performance Contract." Adoption Date, May 29, 2018, Directorate-General for International Partnerships, European Commission, Brussels. https://ec.europa.eu/trustfundforafrica/region/horn-africa/ethiopia/ethiopia-job-compact-sector-reform-and-performance-contract_en.

EWSI (European Web Site on Integration). 2022. "Poland: Parliament Adopts Law on Assistance to Ukrainian

Refugees." *News*, March 18, 2022. https://ec.europa
.eu/migrant-integration/news/poland-parliament
-adopts-law-assistance-ukrainian-refugees_en.

Fonseca, Maria Lucinda, Jennifer McGarrigle, and Alina Esteves. 2010. "Possibilities and Limitations of Comparative Quantitative Research on Immigrants' Housing Conditions." PROMINSTAT Working Paper 6, Promoting Comparative Quantitative Research in the Field of Migration and Integration in Europe, Directorate-General for Research and Innovation, European Commission, Brussels.

Frattini, Tommaso, and Elena Meschi. 2019. "The Effect of Immigrant Peers in Vocational Schools." *European Economic Review* 113 (April): 1–22.

Frieden, Jeffry. 2019. "The Politics of the Globalization Backlash: Sources and Implications." In *Meeting Globalization's Challenges: Policies to Make Trade Work for All*, edited by Luís A. V. Catão and Maurice Obstfeld, 181–96. Washington, DC: International Monetary Fund; Princeton, NJ: Princeton University Press.

Government of Jordan. 2016. "The Jordan Compact: A New Holistic Approach between the Hashemite Kingdom of Jordan and the International Community to Deal with the Syrian Refugee Crisis." Statement of the Government of Jordan, Supporting Syria and the Region Conference 2016, London, February 4, 2016. https://reliefweb.int
/report/jordan/jordan-compact-new-holistic-approach
-between-hashemite-kingdom-jordan-and.

Graham, Elspeth, and Lucy P. Jordan. 2011. "Migrant Parents and the Psychological Well-Being of Left-Behind Children in Southeast Asia." *Journal of Marriage and the Family* 73 (4): 763–87.

Hussam, Reshmaan N., Erin M. Kelley, Gregory V. Lane, and Fatima T. Zahra. 2022. "The Psychosocial Value of Employment: Evidence from a Refugee Camp." *American Economic Review* 112 (11): 3694–724.

IDA (International Development Association). 2021. *IDA19 Mid-Term Refugee Policy Review*. Washington, DC: IDA. https://documents1.worldbank.org/curated/en
/826851636575674627/pdf/IDA19-Mid-Term-Refugee
-Policy-Review.pdf.

IGAD (Intergovernmental Authority on Development). 2022. "Learning and Experience Sharing between National Refugee Agencies of Ethiopia, Kenya, Somalia, South Sudan, Sudan, and Uganda." *Migration* (post), July 4–8, 2022. https://igad.int/learning-and-experience-sharing
-between-national-refugee-agencies-of-ethiopia-kenya
-somalia-south-sudan-sudan-and-uganda/.

ILO (International Labour Organization). 2016. "Protecting Migrant Domestic Workers: The International Legal Framework at a Glance." Briefing Note, Global Action Programme on Migrant Domestic Workers and Their Families, Research Series, ILO, Geneva.

ILO (International Labour Organization). 2019. "General Principles and Operational Guidelines for Fair Recruitment and Definition of Recruitment Fees and Related Costs." Fundamental Principles and Rights at Work Branch, Labour Migration Branch, ILO, Geneva.

ILO (International Labour Organization), Walk Free, and IOM (International Organization for Migration). 2022. *Global Estimates of Modern Slavery: Forced Labour and Forced Marriage*. Geneva: ILO; Nedlands, WA: Walk Free; Geneva: IOM.

Infante, César, Alvaro J. Idrovo, Mario S. Sánchez-Domínguez, Stéphane Vinhas, and Tonatiuh González-Vázquez. 2012. "Violence Committed against Migrants in Transit: Experiences on the Northern Mexican Border." *Journal of Immigrant and Minority Health* 14 (3): 449–59.

IOM (International Organization for Migration). 2020. "Calculating 'Death Rates' in the Context of Migration Journeys: Focus on the Central Mediterranean." GMDAC Briefing Series: Towards Safer Migration in Africa: Migration and Data in Northern and Western Africa, Global Migration Data Analysis Centre, IOM, Berlin.

IPCC (Intergovernmental Panel on Climate Change). 2022. *Climate Change 2022: Impacts, Adaptation, and Vulnerability*. Sixth Assessment Report. Geneva: IPCC; New York: Cambridge University Press.

Jaupart, Pascal. 2019. "No Country for Young Men: International Migration and Left-Behind Children in Tajikistan." *Economics of Transition and Institutional Change* 27 (3): 579–614.

Kerr, William R. 2008. "Ethnic Scientific Communities and International Technology Diffusion." *Review of Economics and Statistics* 90 (3): 518–37.

Lafortune, Gaétan, Karolina Socha-Dietrich, and Erik Vickstrom. 2019. "Recent Trends in International Mobility of Doctors and Nurses." In *Recent Trends in International Migration of Doctors, Nurses, and Medical Students*, 11–34. Paris: Organisation for Economic Co-operation and Development.

Mazzucato, Valentina, Djamila Schans, Kim Caarls, and Cris Beauchemin. 2015. "Transnational Families between Africa and Europe." *International Migration Review* 49 (1): 142–72.

McLeman, Robert. 2016. "Migration as Adaptation: Conceptual Origins, Recent Developments, and Future Directions." In *Migration, Risk Management and Climate Change: Evidence and Policy Responses*, edited by Andrea Milan, Benjamin Schraven, Koko Warner, and Noemi Cascone, 213–29. Global Migration Issues Series, vol. 6. Geneva: International Organization for Migration; Cham, Switzerland: Springer International.

Melander, Erik, and Magnus Öberg. 2006. "Time to Go? Duration Dependence in Forced Migration." *International Interactions* 32 (2): 129–52.

Morris-Suzuki, Tessa. 1995. "The Invention and Reinvention of 'Japanese Culture.'" *Journal of Asian Studies* 54 (3): 759–80.

Naidu, Suresh, Yaw Nyarko, and Shing-Yi Wang. 2016. "Monopsony Power in Migrant Labor Markets: Evidence from the United Arab Emirates." *Journal of Political Economy* 124 (6): 1735–92.

OECD (Organisation for Economic Co-operation and Development). 2008. *International Migration Outlook 2008*. Paris: OECD.

OECD (Organisation for Economic Co-operation and Development). 2018. "What Would Make Global Skills

Partnerships Work in Practice?" *Migration Policy Debates* 15, OECD, Paris.

OECD (Organisation for Economic Co-operation and Development). 2021. "Financing for Refugee Situations 2018–19." Forced Displacement Series, OECD, Paris.

OHCHR (Office of the United Nations High Commissioner for Human Rights). 1951. "Convention Relating to the Status of Refugees." Adopted July 28, 1951, by the United Nations Conference of Plenipotentiaries on the Status of Refugees and Stateless Persons Convened under General Assembly Resolution 429 (V) of December 14, 1950. OHCHR, Geneva. https://www .ohchr.org/en/instruments-mechanisms/instruments /convention-relating-status-refugees.

Pan, Ying. 2012. "The Impact of Legal Status on Immigrants' Earnings and Human Capital: Evidence from the IRCA 1986." *Journal of Labor Research* 33 (2): 119–42.

Paoletti, Sarah. 2023. "Temporary Protected Status in the United States: An Incomplete and Imperfect Complementary System of Protection." Background paper prepared for *World Development Report 2023*, World Bank, Washington, DC.

Parreñas, Rhacel Salazar. 2001. "Mothering from a Distance: Emotions, Gender, and Intergenerational Relations in Filipino Transnational Families." *Feminist Studies* 27 (2): 361–90.

Pekkala Kerr, Sari, William R. Kerr, Çağlar Özden, and Christopher Robert Parsons. 2016. "Global Talent Flows." *Journal of Economic Perspectives* 30 (4): 83–106.

Pekkala Kerr, Sari, William R. Kerr, Çağlar Özden, and Christopher Robert Parsons. 2017. "High-Skilled Migration and Agglomeration." *Annual Review of Economics* 9 (1): 201–34.

Porter, Matthew, and Nick Haslam. 2005. "Predisplacement and Postdisplacement Factors Associated with Mental Health of Refugees and Internally Displaced Persons: A Meta-Analysis." *JAMA* 294 (5): 602–12.

Rigaud, Kanta Kumari, Alex de Sherbinin, Bryan Jones, Jonas Bergmann, Viviane Clement, Kayly Ober, Jacob Schewe, et al. 2018. *Groundswell: Preparing for Internal Climate Migration.* Washington, DC: World Bank.

Rossiasco, Paula Andrea, Patricia de Narvaez, Ana Aguilera, Greta Granados, Paola Guerra, and Taimur Samad. 2023. "Adapting Public Policies in Response to an Unprecedented Influx of Refugees and Migrants: Colombia Case Study of Migration from Venezuela." Background paper prepared for *World Development Report 2023*, World Bank, Washington, DC.

StatCan (Statistics Canada). 2013. "Immigration and Ethnocultural Diversity in Canada: National Household Survey, 2011." Analytical Document, Catalogue 99-010-X2011001, StatCan, Innovation, Science, and Economic Development Canada, Ottawa. https://www12 .statcan.gc.ca/nhs-enm/2011/as-sa/99-010-x/99-010 -x2011001-eng.pdf.

Tumen, Semih. 2023. "The Case of Syrian Refugees in Türkiye: Successes, Challenges, and Lessons Learned." Background paper prepared for *World Development Report 2023*, World Bank, Washington, DC.

UNDP (United Nations Development Programme). 2020. *Human Mobility, Shared Opportunities: A Review of the 2009 Human Development Report and the Way Ahead.* New York: UNDP.

United Nations. 2018. "Global Compact on Refugees." United Nations, New York. https://www.unhcr.org/5c658aed4.

United Nations. 2019. "Resolution Adopted by the General Assembly on 19 December 2018: Global Compact for Safe, Orderly and Regular Migration." Document A/ RES/73/195, United Nations, New York. https://www.un .org/en/development/desa/population/migration /generalassembly/docs/globalcompact/A_ RES_73_195.pdf.

United Nations Network on Migration. 2022. "Guidance on Bilateral Labour Migration Agreements." United Nations Network on Migration, Geneva.

World Bank. 2017. *Forcibly Displaced: Toward a Development Approach Supporting Refugees, the Internally Displaced, and Their Hosts.* Washington, DC: World Bank.

World Bank. 2018. *Moving for Prosperity: Global Migration and Labor Markets.* Policy Research Report. Washington, DC: World Bank.

1

The Match and Motive Matrix

Key messages

- This Report defines migrants as people who live outside their country of citizenship, regardless of their status and motivations. For practical purposes, the term is used throughout the Report when referring to economic migrants and refugees as a group.

- The Match and Motive Matrix draws from labor economics and international law to develop a unified framework that identifies priority policies for four types of movements based on who moves and under what circumstances (figure 1.1).

- Where a migrant fits in the Match and Motive Matrix depends in part on the policies of the destination countries. Over time, the challenge is to enhance migration outcomes by strengthening the match of all migrants' skills and attributes with their destinations and by reducing the need for so-called distressed movements by migrants who are neither refugees nor whose skills and attributes are a strong match for the destination society.

Figure 1.1 Distinct groups of migrants require distinct policy responses

Maximize gains for all

Strengthen match of all migrants

Stronger match

Many economic migrants

Refugees with skills in demand at destination

Benefits exceed costs

Strengthen match of all migrants

MATCH

Costs exceed benefits

Distressed migrants, mainly irregular

Many refugees

Ensure sustainability, share costs

Weaker match

Reduce need for movements, absorb, or return humanely

Opportunity at destination ◄------- MOTIVE -------► Fear at origin

Choice whether to accept

Obligation to host

Source: WDR 2023 team.

Note: Match refers to the degree to which a migrant's skills and related attributes meet the demand in the destination country. *Motive* refers to the circumstances under which a person moves—whether in search of opportunity or because of a "well-founded fear" of persecution, armed conflict, or violence in their origin country.

A people-centric approach

Migration is about people. It is about those who cross borders, those who stay behind, and those who receive them. When people move to a new country, their decision to move has economic and social consequences for themselves, their communities of origin, and their destinations.

A people-centric approach to migration recognizes that migrants and refugees are men and women who make often difficult choices and deserve fair and decent treatment. They are people with identities, skills, cultures, and preferences. Similarly, destination countries are complex societies with diverse and at times conflicting constituencies, interests, and decision-making processes. As sovereign nations and as members of the international community, they design policies to further their own interests. When people decide to move across borders, their movements affect the development and prosperity of both origin and destination societies.

Migration has proved to be a powerful force for development, improving the lives of hundreds of millions of migrants, their families, and their communities across the world. However, it also entails migrants and refugees, their dependents, and many people in destination communities overcoming a range of issues and vulnerabilities and possibly needing development support to do so. Some of the long-term drivers of mobility have been strengthening, and they are expected to intensify further in coming decades. At the same time, an intense public debate is under way in many destination countries about the costs and benefits of receiving migrants and refugees.

The challenges and tensions associated with cross-border mobility arise because the choices and preferences of stakeholders are often misaligned. They differ between the people moving across borders and the citizens of destination countries; among migrants; and among constituencies in both the origin and destination societies. However, the market mechanisms needed to reconcile these competing interests are often missing. For example, for some categories of workers in high demand, market forces may lead to excess emigration from the standpoint of the origin society (brain drain). Conversely, for other categories, immigration flows may be larger than what destination societies find optimal. Strong development outcomes require policies in both the origin and destination societies to address such mismatches and ensure improved economic and social outcomes for all.

A focus on foreign nationals

This Report defines *migrants* as people who live outside their country of citizenship, regardless of their status and motivations. The distinct challenges migrants face arise from their lack of citizenship in the destination country—and the associated civil, political, and economic rights. In response to migrants' lack of citizenship, destination countries must adopt policies dedicated to defining their status, the rights they can enjoy, and the opportunities they can access. From the perspective of this Report, a person ceases to be a migrant upon returning to his or her country of citizenship or upon naturalization in the destination country (box 1.1).

This Report looks specifically at *international* migration. Domestic and international movements respond to some of the same economic and social forces. In fact, globally the number of internal migrants significantly exceeds that of international migrants. But because people who have crossed an international border lack citizenship at their destination, they find themselves in a situation fundamentally different from that of internal migrants. Governments' policy responses to domestic and international movements, the trade-offs governments face, their ability to regulate movements, and the measures they need to adopt are markedly different.

The debate over migration policies is also separate from the question of how to integrate national minorities. Naturalized migrants may face many challenges in their new country of citizenship, including racism and discrimination. But these issues are not related to their movement or to their lack of citizenship rights. They are instead related to how certain groups of citizens are viewed and treated by the rest of society and to the inclusion challenges faced by national minorities. Recognition of this observation can help to reframe some sensitive issues, such as the cultural impacts of migration. Naturalized citizens, even if they belong to a distinct ethnic group or practice a minority religion, are as much a part of society—and of defining and shaping the national culture—as native-born citizens.

Box 1.1 Foreign nationals or foreign-born?

Many statistical databases and research studies define *migrants* as "foreign-born" people because most censuses, population registers, and surveys include a question on place of birth. By contrast, information on citizenship is not collected systematically, and in some cases respondents may be reluctant to share their legal status if, for example, they are undocumented. In some countries, the census authorities are even prohibited from asking about citizenship status.[a]

Yet defining migrants as "foreign-born" is not equivalent to defining them as foreign nationals. "Foreign-born" implies that being a migrant is a lifelong status that will never change, not even through naturalization or full cultural and political integration. It also implicitly establishes differences among citizens based on their personal history. In countries where the terms *migrant* and *alien* are synonymous, discrimination can be perpetuated or reinforced. By contrast, a focus on foreign nationality makes it possible to better isolate the specific challenges that stem from lack of citizenship.

In practice, use of the "foreign-born" definition results in the categorization of larger numbers of people as migrants, which, in turn, influences perceptions, politics, and policy making in destination countries. For example, even though a relatively large number of migrants are eventually naturalized, under the "foreign-born" definition they are still counted as migrants. In the United States, 54 percent of foreign-born people are naturalized citizens, and the numbers are high as well in many high-income member countries of the Organisation for Economic Co-operation and Development (figure B1.1.1). Large discrepancies between the number of foreign-born and the number of foreign nationals also arise from changes in borders. For example, following the breakup of the Soviet Union and of Yugoslavia, some people who were born in what once was a unified country found themselves counted as "foreign-born" if they ended up living in another part of the country when it became independent. For an older generation, the partition of British India generated significant population movements, and it still accounts for as many as 2 million "foreign-born" people.

The limitations of the "foreign-born" definition of migrants become obvious when considering the many political leaders who happened to be born in a foreign country and yet are prominent citizens of their nation. Among them are former king Juan Carlos of Spain, former presidents Abdelaziz Bouteflika of Algeria, Ian Khama of Botswana, and Toomas Ilves of Estonia, and former prime ministers Tony Abbott of Australia, Manuel Valls of France, Manmohan Singh of India, Shimon Peres of Israel, Boris Johnson of the United Kingdom, and Moana Carcasses Kalosil of Vanuatu, to name just a few.

(Box continues next page)

Box 1.1 Foreign nationals or foreign-born? *(continued)*

Figure B1.1.1 In many high-income OECD countries, over half of foreign-born people have been naturalized

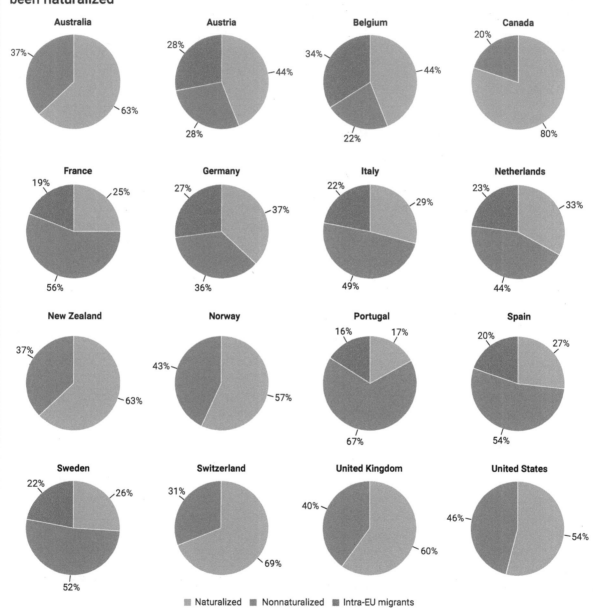

Source: WDR2023 Migration Database, World Bank, Washington, DC, https://www.worldbank.org/wdr2023/data.

Note: Refugees are included in "nonnaturalized" in the calculation of their share of the foreign-born. EU = European Union; OECD = Organisation for Economic Co-operation and Development.

a. For example, the US Supreme Court in Department of Commerce v. New York, 139 S. Ct. 2551; 204 L. Ed. 2d 978 (2019), blocked the Trump administration's intention to ask about citizenship status on the 2020 census form. The citizenship question has been absent from the US Census since the 1950 round.

Two perspectives: Labor economics and international law

Labor economics and international law inform policy making on migration. Their perspectives arise from distinct intellectual and scholarly traditions, and they focus on different aspects of cross-border movements. As a result, each provides important insights, and yet until now there has been no simple framework to integrate them into a coherent whole.

Both labor economics and international law recognize that the policies of destination countries play the primary role in shaping migration patterns and effects. These countries define and regulate, albeit imperfectly, who crosses their borders, who is legally allowed to stay and under which conditions, and what rights those who cross their borders are granted. These policies greatly affect migrants' incentives and decisions before their departure, during their journey, and after their arrival, shaping all aspects of global mobility. By contrast, most origin countries have little sway in regulating movements.

When destination countries set their migration policies, they focus primarily on their own welfare. Through their political process, they consider both the effects of migration on their labor markets and (because they are not just markets) the broader impacts of migration on their society. Only to a much more limited extent do they consider impacts on migrants and origin countries.

Labor economics and cost-benefit calculations

Labor economics views migration as the movement of workers across borders to countries where their labor can be employed more productively than in their origin country. Market forces drive the movement of factors of production—capital and labor—and their allocation across countries. From this perspective, the free movement of people is a key element of the efficient functioning of the global economy, and labor should be allowed to move where it is most productive without the introduction of friction by national borders and other policy restrictions. Nationals of destination countries who are negatively affected by migration—such as workers who compete with migrants in the labor markets—can be supported through distributional policies.

Labor economics focuses on the skills, qualifications, and professional experiences that migrants bring to the destination country and the extent to which these can be used productively. Some migrants bring skills that complement those already available in the labor market. This complementarity increases productivity, with substantial benefits spread across the destination country's economy. In other occupations, migrant workers are substitutes. Their arrival expands the labor supply, thereby lowering wages and overall production costs. Consumers and employers (and the owners of capital) gain, but some existing workers experience lower wages and possibly unemployment. The distinction between complementary and substitute skills is based not on the level of skills, but on how much they match the needs of the labor market: both high skills and low skills can be complements or substitutes.

There is ample empirical evidence that when migrants' skills match the needs of the destination labor market, the migrants benefit as well, as do their countries of origin.[1] Because they can be employed more productively than in their country of origin, migrants earn higher wages. Countries of origin benefit from both financial transfers (remittances) and knowledge transfers. But there are also costs, such as when large numbers of people with scarce skills emigrate (brain drain). However, they tend to be of a smaller order of magnitude.

This perspective has been further developed by recognizing that migrants bring not only skills but also a range of other attributes, including their personal histories and cultural preferences. The match of their skills with the needs of destination economies largely determines labor market effects. Their integration, however, goes beyond the labor market. It may entail financial costs, such as if migrants' families require education and health services. Depending on a migrant's job, age, and family situation, these costs may or may not be fully covered by his or her taxes. Other costs may arise as well, including nonmonetary costs such as for migrants' social integration.

What is considered a strong match depends on both migrants' characteristics and the destination society's preferences. But these characteristics and preferences change over time, such as when economic growth accelerates or slows down. Distinct constituencies in the destination society may also have different views on the costs associated with migrants' integration, especially for social inclusion. Yet both skeptics and supporters agree that some migrants' skills and attributes better match the needs of the destination society than others. The debate is about what constitutes a stronger match and a weaker match. This question is typically arbitrated through political processes, and what is viewed as a desirable outcome evolves over time.

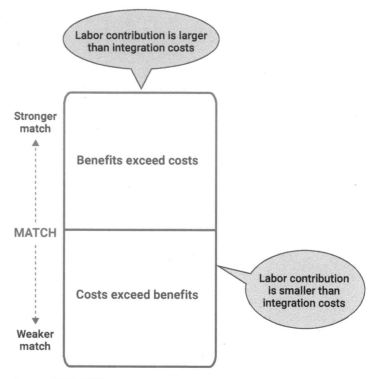

Figure 1.2 When migrants are a strong match, their contributions exceed the costs of their integration

Source: WDR 2023 team.

Note: Match refers to the degree to which a migrant's skills and related attributes meet the demand in the destination country.

Overall, many destination countries derive their migration policies from a cost-benefit calculation. When migrants' profiles match the needs of the destination society, their contributions exceed the costs of their integration (figure 1.2). In this situation, destination societies enjoy a net gain—and in most situations migrants and countries of origin do as well—and they tend to allow or even encourage such movements. By contrast, when migrants' profiles do not match the needs of destination societies, the costs may exceed the benefits from their labor contributions. Migrants themselves may benefit, but destination countries experience a net loss, and therefore they try to discourage these movements.

International law and the obligation to protect

Under international law, the choice of who is admitted into state territory is a matter of state sovereignty. Countries decide who to let in and under what status. This decision can be made unilaterally or through specific agreements between states, such as international conventions, regional free movement agreements, or bilateral labor agreements. Norms are drawn from various sources and fields of law, such as consular and diplomatic protection, the law of state responsibility, international human rights law, international refugee law, and international labor law and standards. They apply differently to distinct groups of migrants,[2] and they are unevenly implemented at national levels.

Human dignity and rights are at the core of international law, including the 1948 Universal Declaration of Human Rights and the 1951 Convention Relating to the Status of Refugees and its 1967 Protocol Relating to the Status of Refugees (the 1951 Refugee Convention), as well as a range of complementary legal instruments. They also underpin key international norms, including the 2018 Global Compact for Safe, Orderly and Regular Migration and the 2018 Global Compact on Refugees, the International Labour Organization Declaration on Fundamental Principles and Rights at Work, and the central promise of the United Nations' 2030 Global Agenda for Development and its Sustainable Development Goals to "leave no one behind." Acknowledging migrants as people implies that these norms fully apply to them whether they are in transit, at a border, or in a destination country. Particular attention should be paid to those facing daunting challenges, such as women and girls in some circumstances, LGBTQ+ individuals, unaccompanied children, and victims of racism, xenophobia, and other forms of discrimination.

In a world of sovereign states, all persons are under the protection of their country of citizenship. Regardless of where a person lives, his or her rights are assured either by the country of citizenship or through an agreement between the country of citizenship and the country of residence. The protection of a state guarantees "the right to have rights," as political philosopher Hannah Arendt famously declared in 1948. But situations can arise in which a country is unwilling or unable to protect the rights of some of its citizens because of, for example, conflict or persecution.

International law defines such people as "refugees." Refugees are people who can demonstrate a "well-founded fear" of harm if they were to return to their country of origin.[3] Their status is protected under the 1951 Refugee Convention as well as regional refugee law instruments. Socioeconomic vulnerability does not enter into this definition. Some refugees are wealthy, although in many cases being a refugee leads to economic deprivation. Conversely, many people who are vulnerable do not require international protection even though they may need material assistance.

At the core of international protection is the principle of *non-refoulement*[4]: refugees shall not be sent back to their country of origin or to another country where they would be at risk of harm (figure 1.3). This principle applies regardless of the costs to the hosting country. International protection also includes a set of specific rights refugees can enjoy in the country in which they are hosted until they regain full protection, as citizens or permanent residents, from either their origin country or another country.

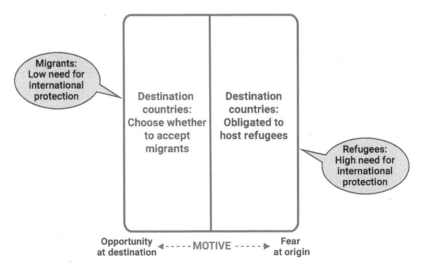

Figure 1.3 When people have a "well-founded fear" of harm if they return to their country of origin, destination countries are obligated to host them

Source: WDR 2023 team.
Note: Motive refers to the circumstances under which a person moves—whether in search of opportunity or because of a "well-founded fear" of persecution, armed conflict, or violence in their origin country.

The Match and Motive Matrix

The perspectives of labor economics and international protection have not been reconciled. Labor economics provides insights into the economics of migration, but it struggles to explain movements that do not follow labor market forces such as forced displacement. The legal protection discourse, with its focus on protecting the life and dignity of refugees, does not fully address the economic and social effects in host countries other than in an instrumental manner to maintain support for refugee protection.

The Match and Motive Matrix provides a unified framework that overlays the distinctions made by labor economics—between movements that represent a net gain and those that represent a net cost for destination countries—and by international law—between situations in which destination countries have the discretion to accept a migrant and situations in which they have an obligation to host a refugee.

Four types of movements

The Match and Motive Matrix distinguishes between four types of movements (figure 1.4):

- *People who are seeking opportunities in the destination country and whose skills and attributes strongly match the needs of the destination society*—the upper-left quadrant in figure 1.4. This category, by far the largest, includes most economic migrants and their families. These migrants can be at all levels of skills—Indian engineers working in California's Silicon Valley as well as South Asian construction workers employed in countries of the Gulf Cooperation Council (GCC). They also include large numbers of undocumented migrants whose skills and attributes fill gaps in the destination labor market even if the migrants do not have a legal status in the country of destination. For all these migrants, labor economics suggests that migration yields net gains—for themselves, their country of origin, and their country of destination.

- *People who are moving out of fear of persecution or serious harm in their country of origin and whose skills and attributes strongly match the needs of the destination society*—the upper-right quadrant in figure 1.4. This group is mainly composed of refugees who have skills in demand at the destination. It is exemplified by theoretical physicist Albert Einstein, who had to flee Europe during World War II and became a refugee. Today, many professionals who left the Syrian Arab Republic, República Bolivariana de Venezuela, or, more recently, Ukraine are part of this group, as well as Afghan truckers in Pakistan or Somali traders in East Africa. Under international law, destination countries are obligated to host these people, but the countries also benefit from their presence.

- *People who are moving out of fear of persecution or serious harm in their country of origin but whose skills and attributes weakly match the needs of the destination society*—the lower-right quadrant in figure 1.4. Most people fleeing conflict or persecution are in this group. Some receive formal refugee status, but others do not, such as the Forcibly Displaced Myanmar Nationals in Bangladesh. The weak match may reflect individual characteristics, such as unaccompanied minors who are too young to work and yet need support. Or it may be a consequence of government policies, such as not allowing some people to work and thus to contribute. Providing these people with international protection is both important and an obligation under international law, but it has a net cost for the destination country. The policy challenge is to manage this cost.

- *People who are seeking opportunities in the destination country but whose skills and attributes weakly match the needs of the destination society*—the lower-left quadrant in figure 1.4. This group is typically composed of migrants who engage in distressed and irregular movements that often involve significant risks and suffering. It includes some of those who arrive at the US southern border

Figure 1.4 The Match and Motive Matrix combines the perspectives of labor economics and international law to distinguish between four types of movements

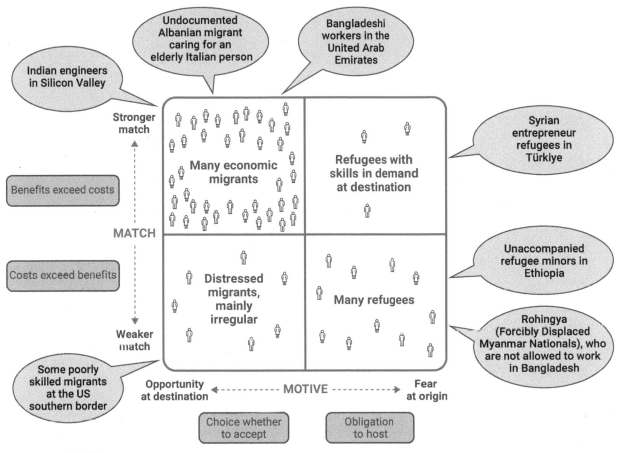

Source: WDR 2023 team.

Note: *Match* refers to the degree to which a migrant's skills and related attributes meet the demand in the destination country. *Motive* refers to the circumstances under which a person moves—whether in search of opportunity or because of a "well-founded fear" of persecution, armed conflict, or violence in their origin country.

or the northern Mediterranean shores, as well as in a host of low- and middle-income countries. Their presence imposes net costs on the destination countries, which have the discretion to accept or return them. This group raises some of the most complex policy trade-offs.

Fluidity between types of movement

Where migrants appear in the Match and Motive Matrix is shaped in part by destination countries' policies (figure 1.5). For example, migrants' ability to contribute to their destination society and the strength of the corresponding match depend on their skills and attributes as well as on the demand in the destination labor market. However, it also depends on whether they are permitted to work at the level of their qualifications. For example, a medical doctor who is not allowed to work in her field—whether because her qualifications were not recognized or because she was altogether prevented from working in the formal sector—will contribute less than if she could work as a doctor. The strength of the match can also evolve over time based on the changing labor needs and social dynamics in the destination country.

Figure 1.5 Destination countries' policies partly determine where migrants fit in the Match and Motive Matrix

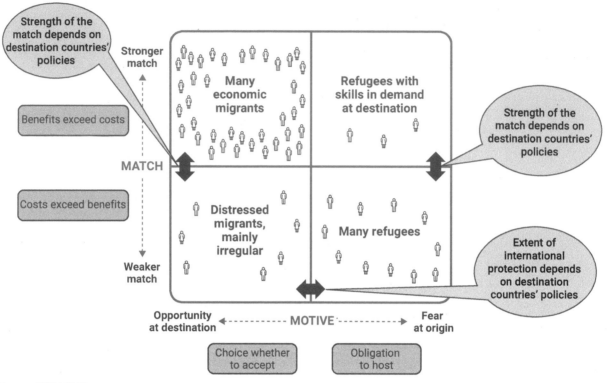

Source: WDR 2023 team.

Note: Match refers to the degree to which a migrant's skills and related attributes meet the demand in the destination country. *Motive* refers to the circumstances under which a person moves—whether in search of opportunity or because of a "well-founded fear" of persecution, armed conflict, or violence in their origin country.

Similarly, the degree to which migrants are provided with protection—and are accepted regardless of the economic benefits of their presence—depends on destination countries' policies. Beyond their obligations under international law, a number of countries have put in place legal frameworks to provide protection to specific groups who are allowed to enter or stay in their territory for humanitarian reasons. Other countries do not have such legal instruments.

Policy priorities

Migration policies can help improve the outcome of cross-border movements for migrants, countries of origin, and countries of destination by adopting approaches tailored to the specifics of each situation. Based on the insights from labor economics and international law, the Match and Motive Matrix identifies policy priorities for all groups (figure 1.6):

- *People whose skills and attributes strongly match the needs of destination societies: Maximize gains at origin and destination.* When migrants and refugees bring skills that are in demand at their destination, the benefits outweigh the costs for the countries of destination, countries of origin, and the migrants and refugees themselves, regardless of status—whether migrants are documented or not. It is also true regardless of motive—whether migrants arrived in search of opportunities or as refugees fleeing persecution and violence. The challenge for both destination and origin

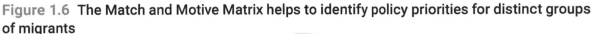

Figure 1.6 The Match and Motive Matrix helps to identify policy priorities for distinct groups of migrants

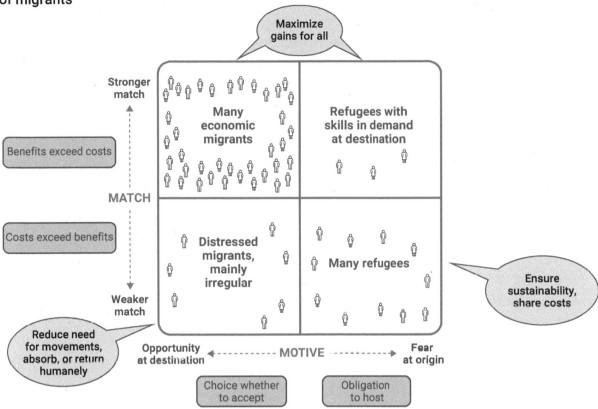

Source: WDR 2023 team.

Note: Match refers to the degree to which a migrant's skills and related attributes meet the demand in the destination country. *Motive* refers to the circumstances under which a person moves—whether in search of opportunity or because of a "well-founded fear" of persecution, armed conflict, or violence in their origin country.

countries is to design and implement measures that further increase the benefits of migration and effectively address its downsides.

- *People who move out of a "well-founded fear" of persecution or conflict but whose skills and attributes are a weak match for the needs of destination societies: Ensure sustainability and share the costs.* When such people's skills and attributes are a weaker match, the socioeconomic costs may exceed the benefits for the destination country. Yet there is an obligation to host refugees. The challenge for the host country is to adopt policies that can reduce the costs. The challenge for the international community is to ensure adequate responsibility-sharing because refugee protection is a global responsibility.

- *People who seek opportunities in the destination country but whose skills and attributes are a weak match for the needs of this country: Absorb or return distressed migrants humanely.* For people whose skills are not a strong match in the destination country and who are not entitled to refugee protection, destination countries face a difficult trade-off. Accepting these migrants entails economic and social burdens, but denying them entry can endanger their basic human rights. The destination country may decide to return them to their origin country. But it should also recognize that some of these migrants have protection needs—for example, if they are fleeing gang violence—and treat them accordingly. In any case, they should be treated humanely.

Making migration better

Over time, the challenge is to strengthen the development outcomes of migration so that all—destination societies, origin societies, and the migrants themselves—can benefit. In a world where migration is increasingly necessary for countries at all levels of income, making migration better requires moving on two complementary fronts (figure 1.7):

- *Strengthen the match of all migrants' skills and attributes with the needs of destination societies.* The benefits of migration—for both origin and destination societies as well as for migrants—are significantly higher when migrants can contribute more to their destination society, when they can earn higher wages, and when they can transfer larger remittances (and knowledge) to their countries of origin. All this requires both providing legal channels for entry of those who have adequate skills—at all levels—and attributes and allowing them to engage in the formal labor market. It may be complemented by building skills in the country of origin—to serve both the global and the domestic labor markets and in the process to mitigate the negative impacts of high-skilled migration (brain drain), which may need international support. Achieving better matching of skills often requires cooperation between the countries of destination and origin.

Figure 1.7 The challenge for countries is to enhance the match of migrants and reduce distressed movements

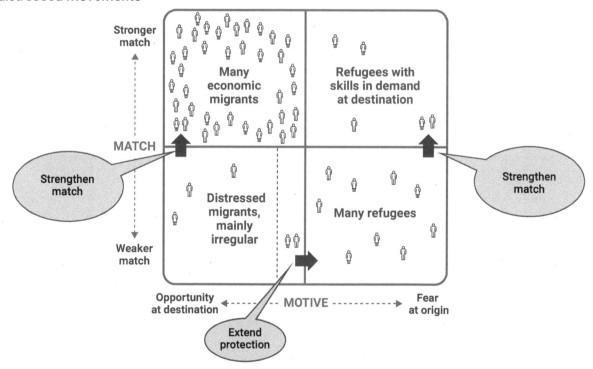

Source: WDR 2023 team.

Note: Match refers to the degree to which a migrant's skills and related attributes meet the demand in the destination country. *Motive* refers to the circumstances under which a person moves—whether in search of opportunity or because of a "well-founded fear" of persecution, armed conflict, or violence in their origin country. The dashed vertical line in the lower-left quadrant highlights the distinction between distressed migrants who have some needs for international protection and those who do not.

- *Reduce the need for distressed movements.* Such movements are often associated with considerable suffering for the migrants themselves. Irregular transit can turn into traumatic ordeals. Upon arrival, migrants face challenges in entering the labor force because their skills do not match the needs of the destination society, and they are often in situations of acute vulnerability. In many countries, distressed movements have polarized the migration debate. Reducing the need for such movements requires strengthening people's resilience in countries of origin; enhancing their skills so they can be better matching the demands in the destination labor market; and recognizing the need of some of these migrants for complementary modes of protection.

Notes

1. World Bank (2018).
2. *Regular migration* is the movement of persons that occurs in compliance with the laws of the countries of origin, transit, and destination. *Irregular migration* is the movement of persons that occurs outside the laws, regulations, or international agreements governing the entry into or exit from the states of origin, transit, and destination.
3. OHCHR (1951, art. 1).
4. OHCHR (1951, art. 33).

References

OHCHR (Office of the United Nations High Commissioner for Human Rights). 1951. "Convention Relating to the Status of Refugees." Adopted July 28, 1951, by the United Nations Conference of Plenipotentiaries on the Status of Refugees and Stateless Persons Convened under General Assembly Resolution 429 (V) of December 14, 1950. OHCHR, Geneva. https://www.ohchr.org/en/instruments-mechanisms/instruments/convention-relating-status-refugees.

World Bank. 2018. *Moving for Prosperity: Global Migration and Labor Markets*. Policy Research Report. Washington, DC: World Bank.

Spotlight 1
History

The history of mobility is the story of humankind—of various groups of people moving out of the African cradle and gradually spreading across all continents.[1] It is a story of contacts and exchanges across groups and of population splits and fusions that resulted in the emergence of distinct ethnicities, languages, and cultures[2] and shaped today's world. Mobility has often driven economic and social progress—for example, by enabling the transmission of ideas and technology.[3] But at times, it has also brought immense suffering. The main causes of these movements are well known to consumers of the daily news and students of history alike: a desire for a better life and fear of persecution or harm.

People's ability to move across borders today varies significantly, depending on which passport and which skills they have. Movements are easing for some people (such as citizens of high-income countries or high-skilled workers), even as they are tightening for others (such as migrants from low-income countries or irregular migrants).[4] The polarization of migration debates is part of a broader backlash against globalization. Similar trends prevailed in the Western world toward the end of the nineteenth century, leading to a similar antiglobalization sentiment and higher barriers to cross-border migration and trade in the run-up to World War I.[5] Yet what is often taken as the "normal" state of affairs—the current understanding of cross-border mobility and the way it is managed—is just a moment in history.

Match: Economic and political considerations

For most of recorded history, migration was not only permitted but often encouraged.[6] The power of rulers was frequently measured by the number of their subjects. But attracting subjects was a challenge. After conquering Constantinople in 1453, Mehmed II strove to repopulate it by attracting people from all over the empire and releasing captured prisoners in the city.[7] His son Bayezid II invited and settled the Sephardic Jews expelled from Spain after the Alhambra Decree in 1492. As late as 1857, the Ottoman sultan issued a decree permitting anyone to immigrate who agreed to be a subject and abide by the Ottoman Empire's laws. This decree was published widely in European newspapers, and the ruler enticed newcomers with guarantees of citizenship, religious liberty, tax concessions, free cattle, plots of agricultural land, and temporary financial aid.[8]

As nation-states developed, systems were gradually put in place to regulate cross-border movements. The arrangements reflected the interests of powerful constituencies or democratic majorities, and they were based on a mix of economic, social, and cultural considerations.[9] These systems were striking in their diversity across regions and countries and in the ways they constantly adjusted to evolving circumstances.[10]

Some countries went so far as to seal themselves from any foreign influence, restricting immigration and even short-term visits. This approach to migration, dominant in Japan between 1630 and 1850 under the Sakoku policy of the Tokugawa shogunate, had lasting consequences for the country's culture and history.[11] Similarly, under the Joseon dynasty, Koreans were forbidden to travel abroad except on diplomatic missions to China or Japan. Some trade with China and Japan was allowed, but the country was closed to other outsiders.[12]

Elsewhere, countries such as the United States have long defined themselves as the lands of immigration. "Give me your tired, your poor, Your huddled masses yearning to breathe free, The wretched refuse of your teeming shore" is inscribed on a plaque affixed to the Statue of Liberty in New York Harbor. Still, the level of openness has varied greatly over time, reflecting both economic conditions and national or racial prejudice. In the United States, the initial inflows of migrants came from a handful of European countries, typically through private enterprises, with little government intervention. With the country's expansion in the nineteenth century, the need for labor and the available opportunities expanded dramatically, while parts of Europe were undergoing political, economic, and social turmoil. Immigration increased 200-fold between 1820 and 1850, primarily from Ireland and Germany, and later from Italy and Central, Eastern, and Northern Europe. This influx was not without controversy, however, and throughout the nineteenth and early twentieth centuries nativist movements emerged.[13] In response, the US federal government sought to restrict the flows. In 1882, with passage of the Chinese Exclusion Act, it curtailed Asian immigration. In 1917, it introduced a literacy requirement to curb low-skilled migration, particularly from Europe.[14] Then in 1924, it imposed national quotas through the Immigration Act.[15] The country reopened to large-scale migration with passage of the 1965 Hart-Celler Act, a by-product of the civil rights movement and an integral part of President Lyndon B. Johnson's Great Society programs. Race-based quotas were replaced by preferential categories based on family relationships and skills. Gradually, immigration from Asia, Latin America, and Africa became more common. Today, the debate remains intense as political controversies over low-skilled and mostly undocumented migration from Central and South America have led to a succession of policies aimed at curbing irregular migration movements.

Many European countries have gone through similar periods of relative openness and restrictions. In premodern Europe, border and immigration control was the exception rather than the rule. The United Kingdom was the first country to introduce an alien law that restricted immigration—in 1793.[16] Yet mobility remained largely unhindered across the continent, and people could move and settle across borders relatively easily until 1914.[17] A system of control was introduced only with the outbreak of World War I—initially for national security considerations, later as part of protectionist efforts in the Great Depression era, and even later to deal with the large movements of refugees during and after World War II, which reshaped the human geography of the continent.[18] Western Europe's reconstruction effort, and the rapid economic growth that followed for almost three decades, led to a rapid increase in the demand for labor. Several "guest worker" programs were put in place to attract people from within and outside Europe, originally on a temporary basis. At the same time, politics—the Cold War and the decolonization process—produced an influx of displaced persons who were rapidly absorbed by receiving countries. These open policies came to a halt, however, with the 1973–74 oil shock and the ensuing economic recession.[19]

Today within Europe, about half of new migrants arrive on a work visa and the other half as family members, students, or asylum-seekers—and some are undocumented.[20] Their integration has been uneven, and it is increasingly controversial, especially where the economy is sluggish and politics are polarized. Although immigration from *outside* the European Union was curtailed, mobility *within* the regional bloc is encouraged, and it increased sharply following the 1985 Schengen Agreement and the expansion of the European Union.[21] This pattern—facilitation of some movements, restriction of others—is an illustration of the two forces at play in setting migration policies: economic forces and political considerations.

Very different patterns prevailed in Persian Gulf countries. In the oil-producing countries of the Gulf Cooperation Council (GCC), migration increased dramatically from 241,000 migrants in 1960 to over

30 million in 2020.[22] Although there had been a long history of permanent trading posts along the Persian Gulf coast and a trickle of South Asian migrants under British colonial rule, movements accelerated from the 1970s on, mainly because of the oil boom and accompanying investments. Governments put in place contractual arrangements with a range of origin countries to attract large numbers of migrant workers on a temporary basis. In just a couple of decades, the region was transformed as migrants became indispensable to the economy.[23] By 2020, migrants accounted for about half the region's population and over 80 percent in Qatar and 90 percent in the United Arab Emirates.[24]

Migration patterns are different in other parts of the world, especially in low-income countries, although they are still heavily influenced by a mix of economic and political considerations.[25] Some South-South migrants move to regional economic hubs in the hope of finding better jobs—hubs such as Angola, Brazil, Chile, Malaysia, Mexico, South Africa, or Thailand.[26] These movements can be temporary or permanent. Other movements take place across borders that do not correspond to ethnic or cultural distinctions but instead to the legacy of colonial administrative boundaries, such as in Africa. In some contexts, such as South Africa, migration has led to social tensions, rejection, and even incidents of violence.[27] In others, migrants are encouraged to come. For example, residents of the former Soviet Union are encouraged to migrate to the Russian Federation.[28] Once again, the patterns reflect a combination of economic forces and political considerations.

Motive: The concept of international refugee protection

Until World War I, people fleeing war or persecution were not regarded as a matter of international concern. Instead, they were generally dealt with on an ad hoc basis by affected states and their allies when problems arose.[29] Because states were traditionally the only subjects of international law, individuals had to rely on their state of nationality to "protect" them in relation to other states—for example, through documentation for international travel, representation in disputes with other states, and other forms of diplomatic protection. However, individuals who had been expelled or displaced from their origin country and had lost their nationality in a de jure or de facto sense were unable to depend on that country to fulfill its protection obligations in relation to other states. These individuals needed protection from a substitute entity.[30]

The first legal framework for international protection was developed by Fridtjof Nansen in the aftermath of the Russian Revolution. A renowned Arctic explorer and a diplomat, Nansen (1861–1930) was appointed High Commissioner for Refugees at the League of Nations in 1921 with a mandate to secure the resettlement of about 2 million Russian refugees. Without legal status in their country of refuge, the refugees were unable to move elsewhere because they could not obtain travel documents from the Soviet Union. In response, Nansen devised a system of international travel documents that became known as the "Nansen passports." It was eventually extended to other groups of people fleeing crises deemed to be "of international concern," including Greek, Bulgarian, Turkish, and Armenian refugees.[31] The Nansen passport provided both a legal status and a form of international protection for its holders, enabling them to cross borders in search of work. It was issued to about 450,000 refugees and was recognized by more than 50 governments.

This approach was transformed after World War II to adjust to new patterns of displacement. The United Nations High Commissioner for Refugees was established with a dual mandate of international protection and solutions, and international standards were codified in the 1951 Convention Relating to the Status of Refugees and its 1967 Protocol.[32] Under these instruments, *refugees* are defined as those who are outside of their country of nationality because of a well-founded fear of persecution[33] against which their country of nationality is unable or unwilling to provide protection. The international refugee protection regime granted to these individuals includes a list of specific rights that signatory states committed to provide. Among those is the principle of *non-refoulement*: countries shall not forcibly return or deport a refugee or asylum-seeker to a country or territory where he or she faces threats to life or freedom because of race, religion, nationality, membership in a particular social group, or political opinion.[34] The refugee protection regime is based on the notion of international responsibility-sharing, even though there is no compulsory mechanism for collective action—a deficiency that is at the root of many of the current challenges.

The international architecture for refugees has continued to adapt to changing circumstances—from the aftermath of decolonization to the end of the Cold War to the emergence of new forms of fragility. The definition of *refugees* has been expanded through regional legal instruments in Africa (the 1969 Organization of African Unity Convention Governing the Specific Aspects of Refugee Problems in Africa) and in Latin America (the 1984 Cartagena Declaration on Refugees) to reflect circumstances specific to these two regions. Other regions and countries, such as the European Union and the United States, have developed arrangements to provide complementary forms of protection to specific groups or individuals who do not meet the traditional refugee criteria. The recent movements of people out of República Bolivariana de Venezuela have raised new questions about who should qualify as a "refugee" or as "in need of international protection." Defining who should be granted international protection—and accepted regardless of society's labor needs—has been an ever-evolving issue, and it continues to drive the public debate in many countries.

Notes

1. Armitage et al. (2011); Beyer et al. (2021).
2. Spolaore and Wacziarg (2016).
3. Goldin, Cameron, and Balarajan (2011); Green (2008); Richerson and Boyd (2008); Rogoff (2016); Skinner (1978).
4. de Haas, Natter, and Vezzoli (2016).
5. Goldin (1994); Rystad (1992); Williamson (1998).
6. Goldin (1994); Rystad (1992); Williamson (1998).
7. Inalcik (2022).
8. Kale (2014).
9. Milner and Tingley (2011); Papademetriou and Kober (2012).
10. de Haas, Natter, and Vezzoli (2016); Stalker (2002).
11. Cullen (2003); Kazui (1982); Takano (2010).
12. "History of Korea: Joseon," *New World Encyclopedia*, Seoul, Republic of Korea, https://www.newworldency-clopedia.org/entry/History_of_Korea#Joseon.
13. Cohn (2000); Giordani and Ruta (2016); Goldin (1994); Menjívar and Enchautegui (2015); Williamson (2006).
14. Goldin (1994).
15. Fairchild (1924); Immigration and Nationality Act, Amendments, Pub. L. No. 89–236, 79 Stat. 911 (1965).
16. Dinwiddy (1968).
17. Keeling (2014).
18. Holborn (1938); Marrus (2002); Rystad (1992).
19. Rystad (1992).
20. Eurostat (2022).
21. Castles (1986); Kennedy (2022); Stalker (2002); Van Mol and de Valk (2016).
22. 1960–2000 data: DataBank: Global Bilateral Migration, World Bank, Washington, DC, https://databank .worldbank.org/databases/migration; 2010–20 data: International Migrant Stock (dashboard), Population Division, Department of Economic and Social Affairs, United Nations, New York, https://www.un.org /development/desa/pd/content/international-migrant -stock.
23. Hameed (2021); Khadria (2016); Naufal (2011); Winckler (1997).
24. WDR2023 Migration Database, World Bank, Washington, DC, https://www.worldbank.org/wdr2023/data.
25. IOM (2013).
26. WDR2023 Migration Database, World Bank, Washington, DC, https://www.worldbank.org/wdr2023/data.
27. *Economist* (2022).
28. Chudinovskikh and Denisenko (2017); Nikiforova and Brednikova (2018).
29. Holborn (1938).
30. Aleinikoff and Zamore (2019); Goodwin-Gill (2020).
31. Goodwin-Gill (2020).
32. UNHCR (2011).
33. "For the purposes of the present Convention, the term 'refugee' shall apply to any person who . . . , owing to well-founded fear of being persecuted for reasons of race, religion, nationality, membership of a particular social group or political opinion, is outside the country of his nationality and is unable or, owing to such fear, is unwilling to avail himself of the protection of that country; or who, not having a nationality and being outside the country of his former habitual residence as a result of such events, is unable or, owing to such fear, is unwilling to return to it" (OHCHR 1951, articles 1.A and 1.A.2).
34. OHCHR (1951, article 33).

References

Aleinikoff, T. Alexander, and Leah Zamore. 2019. *The Arc of Protection: Reforming the International Refugee Regime.* Stanford Briefs Series. Stanford, CA: Stanford University Press.

Armitage, Simon J., Sabah A. Jasim, Anthony E. Marks, Adrian G. Parker, Vitaly I. Usik, and Hans-Peter Uerpmann. 2011. "The Southern Route 'Out of Africa': Evidence for an Early Expansion of Modern Humans into Arabia." *Science* 331 (6016): 453–56.

Beyer, Robert M., Mario Krapp, Anders Eriksson, and Andrea Manica. 2021. "Climatic Windows for Human Migration Out of Africa in the Past 300,000 Years." *Nature Communications* 12 (1): 4889.

Castles, Stephen. 1986. "The Guest-Worker in Western Europe–An Obituary." *International Migration Review* 20 (4): 761–78.

Chudinovskikh, Olga, and Mikhail Denisenko. 2017. "Russia: A Migration System with Soviet Roots." *Migration Information Source: Profile*, May 18, 2017. https://www.migrationpolicy.org/articlerussia-migration-system-soviet-roots.

Cohn, Raymond L. 2000. "Nativism and the End of the Mass Migration of the 1840s and 1850s." *Journal of Economic History* 60 (2): 361–83.

Cullen, Louis Michael. 2003. *A History of Japan, 1582–1941: Internal and External Worlds.* Cambridge, UK: Cambridge University Press.

de Haas, Hein, Katharina Natter, and Simona Vezzoli. 2016. "Growing Restrictiveness or Changing Selection? The Nature and Evolution of Migration Policies." *International Migration Review* 52 (2): 324–67. https://doi.org/10.1111/imre.12288.

Dinwiddy, John Rowland. 1968. "The Use of the Crown's Power of Deportation under the Aliens Act, 1793–1826." *Bulletin of the Institute of Historical Research* 41 (104): 193–211.

Economist. 2022. "South Africa Has Taken a Dangerously Xenophobic Turn." *Scapegoating Africans*, June 9, 2022. https://www.economist.com/leaders/2022/06/09/south-africa-has-taken-a-dangerously-xenophobic-turn.

Eurostat (Statistical Office of the European Communities). 2022. "Residence Permits: Statistics on First Permits Issued during the Year." Version August 3, 2022. Eurostat Explained, Eurostat, European Commission, Luxembourg. https://ec.europa.eu/eurostat/statistics-explained/index.php?title=Residence_permits_-_statistics_on_first_permits_issued_during_the_year.

Fairchild, Henry Pratt. 1924. "The Immigration Law of 1924." *Quarterly Journal of Economics* 38 (4): 653–65.

Giordani, Paolo E., and Michele Ruta. 2016. "Self-Confirming Immigration Policy." *Oxford Economic Papers* 68 (2): 361–78.

Goldin, Claudia. 1994. "The Political Economy of Immigration Restriction in the United States, 1890 to 1921." In *The Regulated Economy: A Historical Approach to Political Economy*, edited by Claudia Goldin and Gary D. Libecap, 223–58. National Bureau of Economic Research Project Report Series. Cambridge, MA: National Bureau of Economic Research; Chicago: University of Chicago Press.

Goldin, Ian, Geoffrey Cameron, and Meera Balarajan. 2011. *Exceptional People: How Migration Shaped Our World and Will Define Our Future.* Princeton, NJ: Princeton University Press.

Goodwin-Gill, Guy S. 2020. "The Lawyer and the Refugee." Talk Given on Receiving the Stefan A. Riesenfeld Memorial Award, Berkeley Law, University of California, Berkeley, February 29, 2020. https://www.kaldorcentre.unsw.edu.au/publication/lawyer-and-refugee.

Green, Nile. 2008. "Islam for the Indentured Indian: A Muslim Missionary in Colonial South Africa." *Bulletin of the School of Oriental and African Studies* 71 (3): 529–53.

Hameed, Sameena. 2021. "India's Labour Agreements with the Gulf Cooperation Council Countries: An Assessment." *International Studies* 58 (4): 442–65.

Holborn, Louise W. 1938. "The Legal Status of Political Refugees, 1920–1938." *American Journal of International Law* 32 (4): 680–703.

Inalcik, Halil. 2022. "Mehmed II: Ottoman Sultan." *Britannica*, November 29, 2022. https://www.britannica.com/biography/Mehmed-II-Ottoman-sultan.

IOM (International Organization for Migration). 2013. *Migration and Development within the South: New Evidence from African, Caribbean and Pacific Countries.* Migration Research Series MRS 46. Geneva: IOM.

Kale, Başak. 2014. "Transforming an Empire: The Ottoman Empire's Immigration and Settlement Policies in the Nineteenth and Early Twentieth Centuries." *Middle Eastern Studies* 50 (2): 252–71.

Kazui, Tashiro. 1982. "Foreign Relations during the Edo Period: Sakoku Reexamined." Translated by Susan Downing Videen. *Journal of Japanese Studies* 8 (2): 283–306.

Keeling, Drew. 2014. "August 1914 and the End of Unrestricted Mass Migration." *VoxEU Column: Migration*, June 23, 2014. https://cepr.org/voxeu/columns/august-1914-and-end-unrestricted-mass-migration.

Kennedy, Aoife. 2022. "Free Movement of Workers." Fact Sheet, September 2022, European Parliament, Strasbourg, France. https://www.europarl.europa.eu/factsheets/en/sheet/41/free-movement-of-workers.

Khadria, Binod. 2016. "Middle East Country Migration Policies." In *Adjusting to a World in Motion: Trends in Global Migration and Migration Policy*, edited by Douglas J. Besharov and Mark H. Lopez, 291–307. International Policy Exchange Series. New York: Oxford University Press.

Marrus, Michael Robert. 2002. *The Unwanted: European Refugees in the Twentieth Century*, 2nd ed. Politics, History, and Social Change Series. Philadelphia: Temple University Press.

Menjívar, Cecilia, and María E. Enchautegui. 2015. "Confluence of the Economic Recession and Immigration Laws in the Lives of Latino Immigrant Workers in the United States." In *Immigrant Vulnerability and Resilience: Comparative Perspectives on Latin American Immigrants during the Great Recession*, edited by María Aysa-Lastra and Lorenzo Cachón, 105–26. International Perspectives on Migration, vol. 11. Cham, Switzerland: Springer International Publishing.

Milner, Helen V., and Dustin H. Tingley. 2011. "The Economic and Political Influences on Different Dimensions of United States Immigration Policy." Working paper, Princeton University, Princeton, NJ. https://doi.org/10.2139/ssrn.2182086.

Naufal, George S. 2011. "Labor Migration and Remittances in the GCC." *Labor History* 52 (3): 307–22.

Nikiforova, Elena, and Olga Brednikova. 2018. "On Labor Migration to Russia: Central Asian Migrants and Migrant Families in the Matrix of Russia's Bordering Policies." *Political Geography* 66 (September): 142–50.

OHCHR (Office of the United Nations High Commissioner for Human Rights). 1951. "Convention Relating to the Status of Refugees." Adopted by United Nations Conference of Plenipotentiaries on the Status of Refugees and Stateless Persons, July 28, 1951, OHCHR, Geneva. https://www.ohchr.org/en/instruments-mechanisms/instruments/convention-relating-status-refugees.

Papademetriou, Demetrios G., and Ulrich Kober. 2012. "Council Statement: Rethinking National Identity in the Age of Migration." In *Rethinking National Identity in the Age of Migration: The Transatlantic Council on Migration*, edited by Bertelsmann Stiftung and Migration Policy Institute. Gütersloh, Germany: Bertelsmann Stiftung.

Richerson, Peter J., and Robert Boyd. 2008. "Migration: An Engine for Social Change." *Nature* 456 (7224): 877.

Rogoff, Kenneth S. 2016. "The Early Development of Coins and Paper Currency." In *The Curse of Cash,* by Kenneth S. Rogoff, 15–30. Princeton, NJ: Princeton University Press.

Rystad, Göran. 1992. "Immigration History and the Future of International Migration." *International Migration Review* 26 (4): 1168–99.

Skinner, David E. 1978. "Mande Settlement and the Development of Islamic Institutions in Sierra Leone." *International Journal of African Historical Studies* 11 (1): 32–62.

Spolaore, Enrico, and Romain Wacziarg. 2016. "Ancestry, Language and Culture." In *The Palgrave Handbook of Economics and Language*, edited by Victor Ginsburgh and Shlomo Weber, 174–211. London: Palgrave Macmillan.

Stalker, Peter. 2002. "Migration Trends and Migration Policy in Europe." *International Migration* 40 (5): 151–79.

Takano, Yayori. 2010. "Foreign Influence and the Transformation of Early Modern Japan." In *Emory Endeavors in World History*. Vol. 3, *Navigating the Great Divergence*, edited by Brian Goodman, 82–93. Atlanta, GA: Department of History, Emory University. http://history.emory.edu/home/documents/endeavors/volume3/Yayori Takano.pdf.

UNHCR (United Nations High Commissioner for Refugees). 2011. "The 1951 Convention Relating to the Status of Refugees and Its 1967 Protocol." UNHCR, Geneva.

Van Mol, Christof, and Helga de Valk. 2016. "Migration and Immigrants in Europe: A Historical and Demographic Perspective." In *Integration Processes and Policies in Europe: Contexts, Levels and Actors*, edited by Blanca Garcés-Mascareñas and Rinus Penninx, 31–55. IMISCOE Research Series. Cham, Switzerland: Springer International Publishing.

Williamson, Jeffrey G. 1998. "Globalization, Labor Markets and Policy Backlash in the Past." *Journal of Economic Perspectives* 12 (4): 51–72.

Williamson, Jeffrey G. 2006. "Global Migration." *Finance and Development* 43 (3). https://www.imf.org/external/pubs/ft/fandd/2006/09/williams.htm.

Winckler, Onn. 1997. "The Immigration Policy of the Gulf Cooperation Council (GCC) States." *Middle Eastern Studies* 33 (3): 480–93.

Part 1

Migration is increasingly necessary for countries at all income levels

Part 1 is an overview of the context in which cross-border movements are taking place and migration policies are being designed and implemented. People have been moving from place to place since the earliest days of civilization. That migration is expected to continue in the decades to come.

Chapter 2 offers an aggregated perspective on key numbers and patterns of movements. Cross-border movements are a response to global imbalances, such as the massive gaps in income and welfare across countries, and to shocks, such as conflicts. The chapter discusses the current trends at both the global and regional levels, pointing out that many economic migrants and refugees live in low- and middle-income countries. It also reviews the evidence on some key characteristics of cross-border movements, both those driven by economic aspirations and those motivated by people's fear for their lives in their country of origin.

Chapter 3 looks ahead. It features two critical issues likely to dramatically alter the drivers of movement. First, demographic changes—including the rapid aging of both high- and middle-income countries—are creating large mismatches in the global labor market that migration can help address. Second, climate change is emerging as a catalyst of other drivers of mobility. Thus far people are moving mainly within their country to escape the outcome of climate-related disasters, but disorderly international movements could ensue if climate action is not taken urgently.

Two spotlights complement this background discussion. Spotlight 2 discusses the challenges and limitations of the available data and the need to dramatically increase efforts in that area. Spotlight 3 presents some of the methodological challenges researchers and practitioners face when trying to determine the effects of cross-border movements on migrants, refugees, and the societies of origin and destination countries.

Overall, the debate over migration should be placed in context and acknowledge the imbalances that shape today's world and the way they are likely to evolve. Whether countries allow migration to help reduce some of the corresponding pressures will largely determine economic and social trajectories in countries at all income levels.

2
The numbers

Understanding who moves, where to, and why

Key messages

- Migration is a mechanism used by people in responding to long-term global imbalances, such as differences in welfare, and in adapting to shocks, such as conflicts.

- Some 184 million people live outside of their country of nationality, about 20 percent of whom are refugees. Patterns of movement differ based on migrants' motives (figure 2.1).

- Migrants and refugees live in countries in all income groups—43 percent in low- and middle-income countries; 40 percent in high-income member countries of the Organisation for Economic Co-operation and Development (OECD); and 17 percent in member countries of the Gulf Cooperation Council (GCC).

- There is no simple dichotomy between migrants' countries of origin and countries of destination. Many countries at all levels of income are both, at the same time.

Figure 2.1 Patterns of movements reflect distinct matches and motives

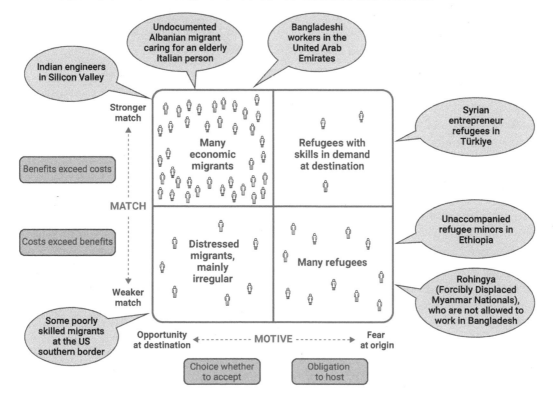

Source: WDR 2023 team.

Note: Match refers to the degree to which a migrant's skills and related attributes meet the demand in the destination country. *Motive* refers to the circumstances under which a person moves—whether in search of opportunity or because of a "well-founded fear" of persecution, armed conflict, or violence in their origin country.

Current trends

This Report focuses on people who live outside their country of nationality, whether they moved in search of better economic opportunities or were displaced by conflict or persecution. There are approximately 184 million such people worldwide, of whom 37 million are refugees, and they constitute about 2.3 percent of the global population. They live in countries in all income groups (figure 2.2):

- *Low- and middle-income countries.* Of the approximately 79 million migrants and refugees who live in these countries, some moved for job opportunities, family, or other reasons under a variety of statuses, including undocumented (detailed data are lacking, however, in most countries). They also include about 27 million refugees.[1] Although migrants represent a relatively small proportion of the population in most low- and middle-income countries, there are exceptions such as Colombia, Côte d'Ivoire, Djibouti, Gabon, Jordan, and Lebanon. Some migrants eventually acquire citizenship in the country of destination.

- *High-income OECD countries.* The approximately 74 million migrants and refugees who live in these countries include both high- and low-skilled workers, migrants on student visas, as well as undocumented migrants. Family reunification with spouses, parents, or children accounts for a

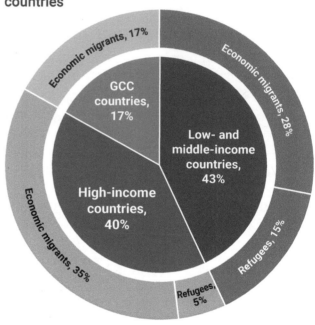

Figure 2.2 A large share of migrants and refugees live in low- and middle-income countries

Source: WDR2023 Migration Database, World Bank, Washington, DC, https://www.worldbank.org/wdr2023/data.

Note: High-income countries exclude Gulf Cooperation Council (GCC) countries.

large share of regular migrants—about 35 percent in the European Union (EU).[2] Among these migrants are people who have extensive residency rights, such as the 11 million EU nationals who live in another EU country and the 13.6 million green card holders in the United States. Also among them are about 10 million refugees, who are receiving international protection. Some migrants to the OECD high-income countries move temporarily, while others intend to settle there. Many are eventually naturalized—about 62 million naturalized citizens are spread across OECD high-income countries (and are not considered to be migrants in this Report).

- *GCC countries.* Of the roughly 31 million migrants living in GCC countries, nearly all have a temporary status, typically a multiyear work visa that can be renewed. They are both high- and low-skilled. Only high-skilled migrants can be accompanied by their families. GCC countries do not host large numbers of refugees. Overall, migrants constitute about half of the GCC population—about 79 percent if Saudi Arabia is excluded (box 2.1).

There is no sharp distinction between countries of origin and countries of destination for migrants. In fact, most countries are both—at the same time. For example, the United Kingdom is home to about 3.5 million immigrants,[3] but it is also the origin of 4.7 million emigrants. At a lower level of income, Nigeria is home to almost 1.3 million immigrants and is the origin for 1.7 million emigrants. Türkiye has a large diaspora of economic migrants in Europe, but also hosts 3.5 million Syrian refugees and over 2 million other migrants. Each society needs a combination of policies to best address the situation of both the people who enter and those who leave.

Box 2.1 Migration data in this Report

Unless otherwise indicated, the data and figures in this Report are based on the WDR2023 Migration Database.[a] The database is constructed from the bilateral immigration data produced by the censuses of individual destination countries. Because of COVID-19 restrictions, only a handful of high-income countries managed to conduct the decadal censuses or nationwide surveys in 2020.[b] Data for member countries of the European Union, as well as for Norway, Switzerland, and the United Kingdom, are based on the European Union Labour Force Survey.[c] Data for all other countries are from the International Migrant Stock estimates of the Population Division of the United Nations Department of Economic and Social Affairs (UN DESA).[d] Most of these data are based on a definition of *migrant* as a person who lives in a country that is different from the country of birth. For the purposes of this Report, the data have been adjusted with citizenship data obtained from a variety of sources or estimations.[e] Data on refugees are based on the Refugee Population Statistics Database of the United Nations High Commissioner for Refugees (UNHCR) and include refugees and asylum-seekers and other people in need of international protection as determined by UNHCR as of mid-year 2022.[f]

a. WDR2023 Migration Database, World Bank, Washington, DC, https://www.worldbank.org/wdr2023/data.
b. They include Australia, Canada, Chile, and the United States.
c. "European Union Labour Force Survey (EU-LFS)," Eurostat, European Commission, Luxembourg, https://ec.europa.eu/eurostat/web/microdata/european-union-labour-force-survey.
d. International Migrant Stock (dashboard), Population Division, Department of Economic and Social Affairs, United Nations, New York, https://www.un.org/development/desa/pd/content/international-migrant-stock.
e. WDR2023 Migration Database, World Bank, Washington, DC, https://www.worldbank.org/wdr2023/data.
f. Refugee Population Statistics Database, United Nations High Commissioner for Refugees, Geneva, https://www.unhcr.org/refugee-statistics/.

Changes over time

Historical data on migration patterns are not available. What is known is that the share of foreign-born people (both migrants and naturalized citizens) has fluctuated between 2.7 percent and 3.5 percent of the world population since 1960.[4] However, the apparent stability of this number is somewhat misleading because, worldwide, demographic growth has been very uneven since 1960. The world population increased by about 156 percent between 1960 and 2020, but high-income countries grew by only 58 percent, while middle-income countries grew by 177 percent and low-income countries by 383 percent.[5] As a result, migration trends vary considerably across country income groups (figures 2.3 and 2.4).

Figure 2.3 Since 1960, the share of emigrants in low-income countries' population has almost doubled

Emigrants as share of population, by country income group, 1960, 1990, 2020

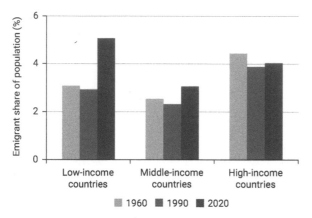

Sources: WDR2023 Migration Database, World Bank, Washington, DC, https://www.worldbank.org/wdr2023 /data; population, 1960–2020: Population Estimates and Projections (database), World Bank, Washington, DC, https://datacatalog.worldbank.org/dataset/population -estimates-and-projections.

Note: The 2020 World Bank income level groups are used for the 1960 and 1990 data (Serajuddin and Hamadeh 2020).

Figure 2.4 Since 1960, the share of immigrants and naturalized citizens in high-income countries' population has tripled

Foreign-born as share of population, by country income group, 1960, 1990, 2020

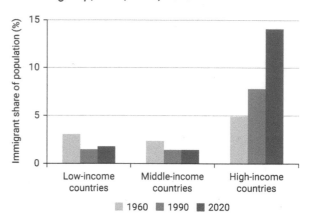

Sources: WDR2023 Migration Database, World Bank, Washington, DC, https://www.worldbank.org/wdr2023 /data; population, 1960–2020: Population Estimates and Projections (database), World Bank, Washington, DC, https://datacatalog.worldbank.org/dataset/population -estimates-and-projections.

Note: The 2020 World Bank income level groups are used for the 1960 and 1990 data (Serajuddin and Hamadeh 2020).

As income levels and demographic trajectories change over time, the directions of migration flows change as well. Some countries or regions emerge as important origins or destinations, while others disappear. For example, the large movements from Europe to Latin America a century ago are no longer happening today. Migration to the GCC countries was almost nonexistent 60 years ago, and yet today these countries are the destination for some of the largest migration corridors. Meanwhile, Ireland and Italy, once countries of origin, have become countries of destination.

Cross-border movements are increasingly distributed across a substantial number of corridors. In 1970, just 150 corridors—out of more than 40,000 possible pairs of origin and destination countries—accounted for 65 percent of the world's migration. By 2020, that share had declined to 50 percent. Today's main corridors include Mexico to the United States; India to the United Arab Emirates and Saudi Arabia; India and China to the United States; Kazakhstan to the Russian Federation and the Russian Federation to Kazakhstan; Bangladesh to India; and the Philippines to the United States. Additional large corridors are associated with the main forced displacement situations, such as between the Syrian Arab Republic and Türkiye, República Bolivariana de Venezuela and Colombia, and Ukraine and Poland.

Origin countries

The largest share of emigrants[6] are from middle-income countries. They are typically among neither the poorest nor the wealthiest in their country of origin; they can afford to move, and they have an incentive to do so. Even in situations of conflict and persecution, those who have more means tend to leave first, although there are exceptions, such as when an entire group is targeted for violence.

Map 2.1 In most countries, only a small share of the population has emigrated to another country

Ratio of persons living abroad to origin country population, 2020

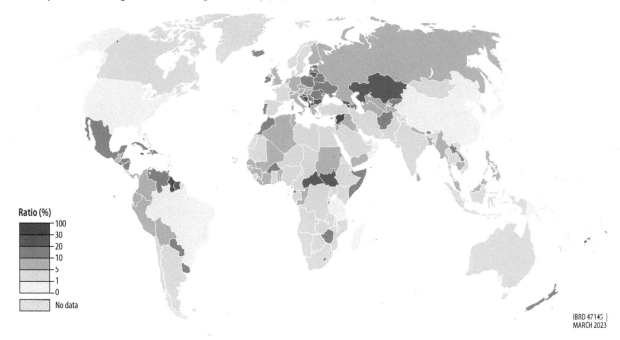

Ratio (%)
100
30
20
10
5
1
0
No data

IBRD 47145 |
MARCH 2023

Source: WDR2023 Migration Database, World Bank, Washington, DC, https://www.worldbank.org/wdr2023/data.

Emigrants constitute a significant share of the population of some origin countries. Many Small Island Developing States have emigration rates well above 25 percent of their population. A number of Central and Eastern European countries also have relatively large emigration rates, typically above 15 percent (their citizens have easier access to Western European countries). The share of refugees to the total population of origin countries is also high in Afghanistan, the Central African Republic, Somalia, South Sudan, Syria, Ukraine, and República Bolivariana de Venezuela (map 2.1). Across all countries, the median emigration rate stands at 7 percent of the population.

Destination countries

Immigrants[7] are spread across the world in countries at all levels of income. The main destination countries (in numbers of migrants) include the United States, Saudi Arabia, the United Arab Emirates, Germany, and France. Other countries, such as Australia, Canada, and the United Kingdom, have naturalized large numbers of migrants over time.

The share of immigrants in the population of destination countries varies (map 2.2). It is largest in the GCC countries—up to 88 percent in the United Arab Emirates. It is also significant in a number of high-income OECD countries, typically 5–15 percent. Part of migration is intraregional, directed to countries that are relatively better-off than their neighbors, such as Costa Rica, Côte d'Ivoire, Gabon, Kazakhstan, Malaysia, or Singapore. The share of immigrants is also large in some countries with a small population, such as Belize, Djibouti, and the Seychelles. Finally, although the share of refugees in the host population is typically small—below 1 percent—there are exceptions. For example, as of mid-2022, one person in six was a refugee in Lebanon; one in 16 in Jordan; and one in 21 in Colombia.[8]

Map 2.2 Immigrants are spread across the world in countries at all levels of income

Ratio of immigrants to destination population, 2020

Source: WDR2023 Migration Database, World Bank, Washington, DC, https://www.worldbank.org/wdr2023/data.

Regional perspectives

Patterns of movements vary widely across regions (figure 2.5):

- In the East Asia and Pacific region, immigration remains limited, except for high-income countries such as Australia and New Zealand. Emigration from the region is directed to a range of destinations, both within the region and outside, such as North America and the GCC countries.
- High-income European countries are home to about 43 million migrants, including 8 million refugees. They are predominantly from other European countries (56 percent) and to a lesser extent from other regions, mainly the Middle East and North Africa (13 percent), Latin America (9 percent), and Sub-Saharan Africa (8 percent). Emigration is mainly directed to other high-income European countries and North America.
- In other European countries and Central Asian countries, the movements mainly take place within the region, totaling about 14 million immigrants. These movements are centered on a few corridors, including between countries of the former Soviet Union. Some people from the region have also migrated to high-income European countries (about 11 million).
- In Latin America and the Caribbean, two main trends are evident. First, relatively large movements occur within the region (about 10.7 million people), including the 4.4 million people who left República Bolivariana de Venezuela. Second, a large number of people originating from the region have emigrated, mainly to North America (about 60 percent) and to a much lesser extent to the European Union (about 10 percent).
- In the Middle East and North Africa, there are three distinct patterns. First, GCC countries receive large numbers of immigrants, mainly but not only from South Asia (60 percent). Second, the rest of the region is the origin of relatively large emigration flows mainly toward high-income European countries (8 million) and to the GCC countries (6 million). And, third, the Syrian crisis and the ongoing insecurity in Iraq have also produced a large number of refugees who are hosted in the region (about 3.5 million).

- In North America, the number of immigrants is about 6 times larger than the number of emigrants. Many of those who come to the region are from Latin America and the Caribbean (about 43 percent). Other large regions of origin are East Asia and Pacific (21 percent), Europe and Central Asia (16 percent), and South Asia (9 percent), with relatively smaller numbers from the Middle East and North Africa. Many of the immigrants to the United States and Canada are eventually naturalized.
- In South Asia, migration is relatively limited considering the demographic size of the region. Three main trends are at play. First, about 19 million people have emigrated to GCC countries. Second, an additional 15 million have emigrated to other regions, mainly North America and high-income European countries. And, third, forced displacement—from Afghanistan to Pakistan and from Myanmar to Bangladesh—accounts for additional movements.
- In Sub-Saharan Africa, most movements take place within the region. Of the approximately 22 million people who live outside of their country, about 35 percent are refugees. These movements are particularly intense along some corridors such as from Burkina Faso to Côte d'Ivoire or to regional economic poles such as Nigeria or South Africa. There are also large refugee movements—for example, out of South Sudan, the Democratic Republic of Congo, Sudan, Somalia, and the Central African Republic. Emigration to other countries is mainly directed to EU countries, the United Kingdom, and the United States—about 10.3 million people.

Motives and patterns

People move for a variety of reasons. Their motives partly determine the socioeconomic outcomes of their migration and their need for international protection. Patterns of movements differ between those who seek economic opportunities in the destination countries and those who move because of a "well-founded fear" of persecution and conflict. In some situations, however, the line is blurred because some people are looking for both opportunities and safety.

The decision to migrate is a complex one, forcing people to weigh their options: staying, moving within their own country, or migrating to a foreign destination. Some migrants decide to move on their own, whereas others do so at the behest and with the support of an entire group—their family or their community. Many factors come into play in making such a decision, including both economic and personal considerations. Economic theory suggests that potential migrants compare their expected welfare in various situations and the corresponding costs of moving—financial and nonfinancial. They eventually settle for the option most likely to let them achieve their objectives in terms of economic prospects, social and psychological well-being, or safety.

Aspirations for a better life

The vast majority of migrants—over 80 percent—move in search of opportunities in the destination country. Their movements are often gradual, with predictable trends that reflect medium-term economic and demographic patterns. These migrants are mainly driven by the potential for higher wages and for access to better services (map 2.3).[9] Although they are not refugees, some people also move to find improved personal safety, a stronger rule of law, and more personal freedoms.

In 2020, the vast majority—about 84 percent—of migrants (and naturalized citizens) lived in a country with an income higher than that of their country of origin. But migration levels are not the highest for corridors where welfare disparities are the largest. Where people are coming from largely determines where they are moving to. Movements are mainly determined by the demands for skills in the labor markets of destination countries, historical and geographic links, and the costs of migration. Most migrants from low-income countries migrate to other low-income countries or to middle-income countries, often because the cost of migration to higher-income destinations is prohibitive. Migrants

Figure 2.5 Cross-border movements vary greatly by region

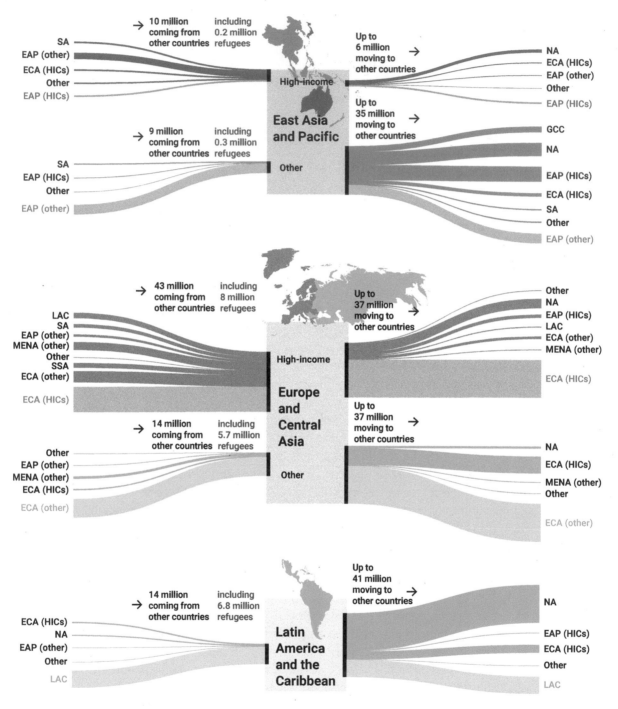

(Figure continues next page)

Figure 2.5 Cross-border movements vary greatly by region *(continued)*

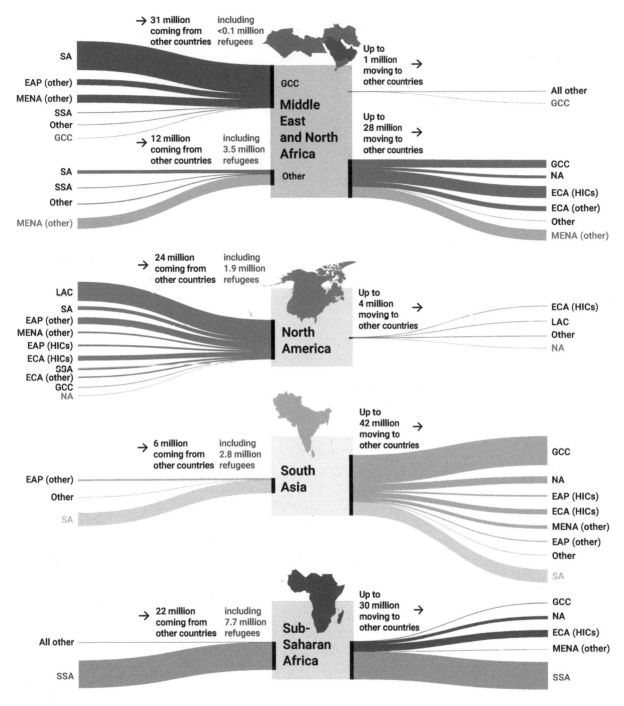

Source: WDR2023 Migration Database, World Bank, Washington, DC, https://www.worldbank.org/wdr2023/data.

Note: Due to limitations on available data, immigration numbers for each region include all of foreign nationals; emigration numbers include foreign-born people (including naturalized). EAP = East Asia and Pacific; ECA = Europe and Central Asia (including Western Europe); GCC = Gulf Cooperation Council (countries); HICs = high-income countries; LAC = Latin America and the Caribbean; MENA = Middle East and North Africa; NA = North America; SA = South Asia; SSA = Sub-Saharan Africa.

Map 2.3 Some of the global imbalances that drive migration movements are reflected in the Human Development Index

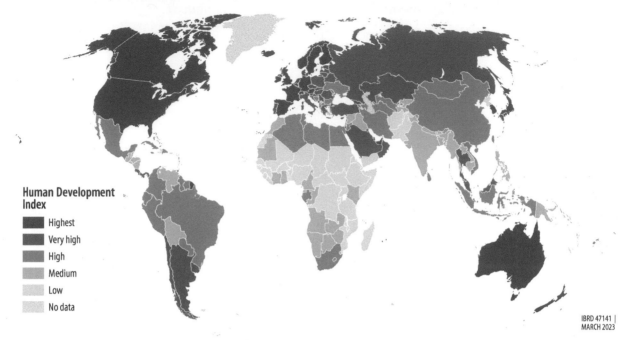

Human Development Index
- Highest
- Very high
- High
- Medium
- Low
- No data

IBRD 47141 |
MARCH 2023

Source: Heat map based on 2021 data, Human Development Insights (table), United Nations Development Programme (UNDP), New York, https://hdr.undp.org/data-center/country-insights#/ranks.

Note: According to UNDP, the Human Development Index is "a summary measure of average achievement in key dimensions of human development: a long and healthy life, being knowledgeable and having a decent standard of living." It ranges between 0 and 1. The categories in the map are defined as follows: low (below 0.55), medium (0.55−0.70), high (0.70−0.80), very high (0.80−0.90), and highest (above 0.90).

from middle-income countries often move to high-income countries. Likewise, many emigrants from high-income countries move to other high-income countries (figure 2.6).

Overall, migration is constrained by challenges and barriers that most migrants face:

- *Uncertainty.* Migration is inherently risky. It involves dealing with unexpected and uncertain outcomes, including the possibility of unemployment, social isolation, psychological stress, or even injuries and death while in transit. People who migrate in search of opportunities tend to be more willing to take risks than others in their communities of origin. They also tend to be more adaptable to new environments and situations, regardless of their skill level or socio-economic background.[10]

- *Unfamiliarity.* Moving to unfamiliar settings entails costs, both monetary and nonmonetary. To succeed, migrants must familiarize themselves with the language, social norms, and culture of their destination society.[11] This may be difficult, and it takes time, although for some people, the social and cultural differences between origin and destination societies are precisely what motivates their movement. Examples are some women and members of ethnic, sexual, and political minorities.[12] The internet and new technologies have enhanced access to information and created both new aspirations and a better awareness of the potential risks and benefits of migration.[13]

- *Job search.* Finding a job in a new country can be challenging. Skills, credentials, or diplomas acquired in one country may not transfer easily to another country. Many migrants end up "downgrading" to a lower-skill occupation, leading to "brain waste."[14] Some migrants rely on information passed through informal networks of friends and family to find decent work.

Figure 2.6 Where migrants go to largely depends on where they come from

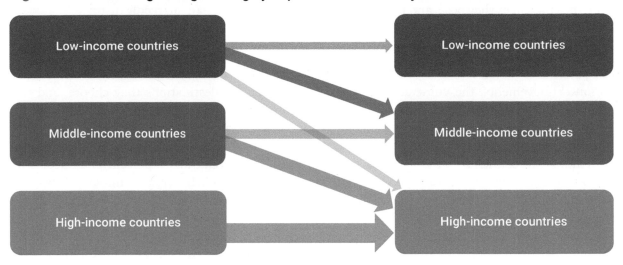

Source: WDR2023 Migration Database, World Bank, Washington, DC, https://www.worldbank.org/wdr2023/data.
Note: The thickness of the arrows reflects the size of the corresponding movements.

They tend to move to areas that are already home to other migrants of their nationality. Other migrants use formal intermediaries—typical for migrants moving from South Asia to the GCC countries—although such intermediation has a high cost.

- *Financing.* The upfront costs of migration can be substantial. They typically include travel and relocation, visas, and processing, as well as payments to intermediaries to find a job or arrange a move. The costs vary widely across corridors. For example, for low-skilled migrants the cost of moving from Central America to Mexico can be as low as US$100, whereas it can reach more than US$4,000 for a move from Pakistan to Saudi Arabia.[15] Irregular migration often requires paying high smugglers' fees. For example, the cost of crossing the southern border of the United States irregularly has been estimated at US$2,000–$10,000, depending on the migrant's point of origin.[16]

These constraints apply differently, depending on skill levels, which largely explains why low- and high-skilled migrants aim for different destinations. A large share of low-skilled migrants move within their region: in 2020, about half of all low-skilled migrants were in a neighboring country.[17] When they go farther, they tend to aim for more familiar places—that is, where they speak the dominant language or where they have access to social networks based on their ethnicity, community, or nationality.[18] They therefore avoid the higher barriers in farther or less familiar destinations—such as higher financing constraints or greater difficulties in finding a job. By contrast, high-skilled individuals are more likely to migrate to high-income countries, and this trend has intensified over time. High-skilled individuals often benefit from a stronger demand for their skills and more-welcoming migration regulations.[19] In some countries, they also have easier access to pathways to residency and citizenship.

Against this backdrop, migration can be both permanent or temporary. Some people, such as many high-skilled migrants in Australia, move with the intention of living permanently in the destination country. Some move with their families, whereas some plan to bring them later. But for others, migration is only temporary. They move for a fixed period of time, to study or to work, with the intention of returning home afterward. This strategy accounts for most movements to GCC countries, the Republic of Korea, and Malaysia. Yet the distinction between temporary and permanent migrants is blurred because many people who initially intended to move for only a few years extend their stay for decades, and sometimes for a lifetime. The impacts of temporary and permanent migration—the benefits they yield, the challenges they pose, and the policy responses they require—are markedly distinct.

Fear in the country of origin

The patterns of forced displacement differ from those of economic migration in terms of the concentration of movements, the vulnerability of those who move, the destinations they choose, and the suddenness and rapid pace under which their movements occur.

Unlike economic migrants who move from a wide range of countries, most refugees come from a limited number of countries of origin—and increasingly so (figure 2.7). Although there are refugees from almost all countries in the world, crises in six countries account for 76 percent of all people in need of international protection: Ukraine (8 million as of February 2023), Syria (6.8 million), República Bolivariana de Venezuela (5.6 million), Afghanistan (2.8 million), South Sudan (2.4 million), and Myanmar (1.2 million Rohingya).[20]

Refugee flows include large numbers of vulnerable people—those a family or a community wants to see out of harm's way—unlike economic migrants, who are primarily working-age adults. In fact, children account for 41 percent of refugees,[21] and some are unaccompanied. For example, as of 2023 more than 70,000 unaccompanied or separated children were in Uganda.[22] Regardless of their situation at origin, many refugees reach their destination in a state of destitution, having left behind their assets and arriving with little or no savings.[23] Some have undergone traumatic ordeals that can make their economic and social inclusion challenging.[24]

Refugees and economic migrants choose their destinations differently. Economic migrants typically move to a place where they believe there is demand for their skills, regardless of the distance from their country of origin.[25] By contrast, refugees prioritize safety and security over labor market considerations, and therefore they tend to move to a safe country that borders their country of origin.

Overall, more than half of all refugees are hosted in just 10 countries[26] that typically border the origin countries (maps 2.4 and 2.5).[27] As of mid-2022, 99 percent of refugees from South Sudan were hosted in neighboring countries, as were 86 percent of refugees from Myanmar; 78 percent of refugees from Syria;

Figure 2.7 Most refugees come from a limited number of countries of origin—and increasingly so

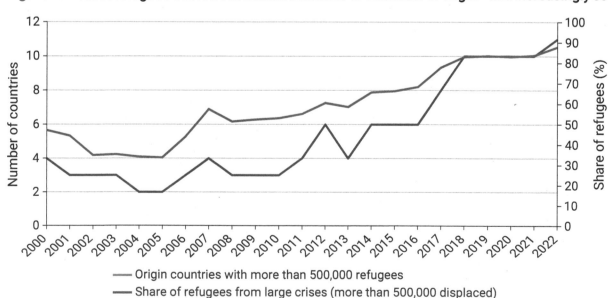

— Origin countries with more than 500,000 refugees

— Share of refugees from large crises (more than 500,000 displaced)

Source: Midyear 2022 data, Refugee Population Statistics Database, United Nations High Commissioner for Refugees, Geneva, https://www.unhcr.org/refugee-statistics/.

Map 2.4 Most refugees flee to neighboring countries

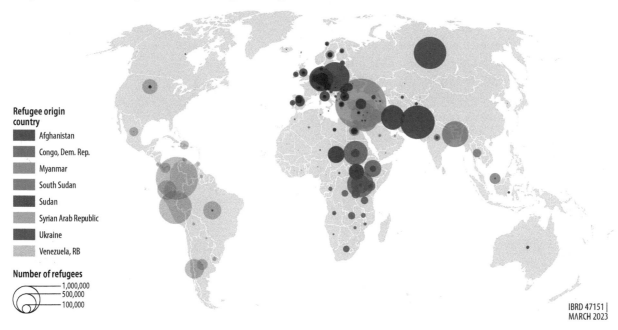

Refugee origin country
- Afghanistan
- Congo, Dem. Rep.
- Myanmar
- South Sudan
- Sudan
- Syrian Arab Republic
- Ukraine
- Venezuela, RB

Number of refugees
- 1,000,000
- 500,000
- 100,000

IBRD 47151 |
MARCH 2023

Source: Midyear 2022 data, Refugee Population Statistics Database, United Nations High Commissioner for Refugees, Geneva, https://www.unhcr.org/refugee-statistics/.

Note: The bubbles indicating the number of refugees are placed at the center of each host country and not over the specific subregions in which refugees are hosted.

Map 2.5 Ten countries host more than half of all refugees

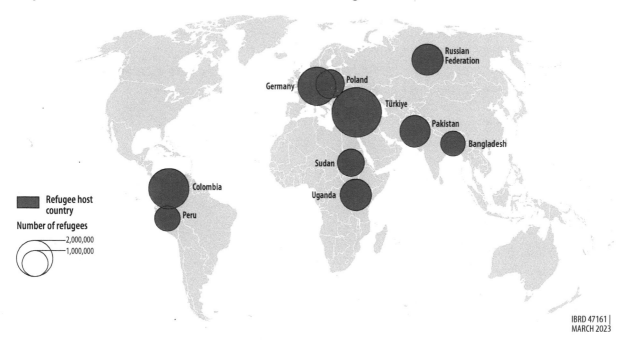

Russian Federation

Germany
Poland
Türkiye
Pakistan
Bangladesh
Sudan
Uganda
Colombia
Peru

Refugee host country

Number of refugees
- 2,000,000
- 1,000,000

IBRD 47161 |
MARCH 2023

Source: Midyear 2022 data, Refugee Population Statistics Database, United Nations High Commissioner for Refugees, Geneva, https://www.unhcr.org/refugee-statistics/.

Note: The bubbles indicating the number of refugees are placed at the center of each host country and not over the specific subregions where refugees are hosted.

and 77 percent of refugees from Afghanistan. In some cases, refugees have moved to other countries within their region—such as those leaving Ukraine and República Bolivariana de Venezuela—but they remain very concentrated. In total, about 74 percent of refugees live in low- and middle-income countries, and 26 percent are in high-income countries, mainly in OECD high-income countries.[28]

Refugees who move beyond neighboring countries are increasingly traveling farther and to a larger number of destinations.[29] They typically have better incomes, assets, education, skills, and access to migration networks than refugees who flee to neighboring countries.[30] Their movements are often influenced by opportunities for better economic benefits, family ties, and political freedoms.[31]

Refugee movements are also often characterized by their suddenness and rapid pace. Some refugee crises build up gradually, giving destination countries and the international community some time to prepare. But many occur suddenly,[32] adding to the challenges of providing adequate assistance to the forcibly displaced and their hosting communities. The number of refugees fleeing a particular conflict may fluctuate as the intensity and geographic spread of violence evolve, triggering successive waves of movements. On average, however, over 40 percent of refugees in a given situation flee in the first year after violence breaks out (figure 2.8).[33] When the numbers are large, hosting countries undergo a significant shock. These spikes often dominate the policy debate and the news headlines because of their intensity and human toll, even though refugees represent a small share of all migrants.

Over the last decade, the nature of refugee movements has begun to change, although it is difficult to assess whether this is part of a longer-term trend. In particular, the countries of origin have changed. Although they were predominantly low-income and low-capacity countries until 2014, they are now increasingly middle-income countries (figure 2.9).

Figure 2.8 Refugee flows spike after a crisis and then slow over time

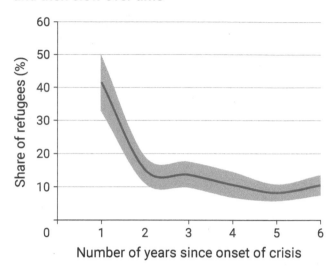

Source: WDR 2023 team calculations, based on October 2022 data from Forced Displacement Flow Dataset (dashboard), Refugee Data Finder, Statistics and Demographics Section, Global Data Service, United Nations High Commissioner for Refugees (UNHCR), Copenhagen, https://www.unhcr.org/refugee-statistics /insights/explainers/forcibly-displaced-flow-data.html.

Note: The figure plots the average flow for refugee "situations" commencing between 1991 and 2017. A "situation" begins when the refugee flow exceeds 25,000. The shaded area indicates the 95 percent confidence interval. The category "refugees" includes refugees, asylum-seekers, and other people in need of international protection as determined by UNHCR.

Figure 2.9 Refugees are increasingly originating from middle-income countries

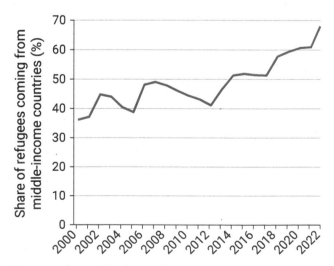

Source: Midyear 2022 data, Refugee Population Statistics Database, United Nations High Commissioner for Refugees, Geneva, https://www.unhcr.org/refugee-statistics/.

This shift is changing some key characteristics of refugee flows. Refugees originating from middle-income countries typically have higher levels of skills than those leaving low-income countries, and their skills and attributes can make for a stronger match with the needs of the destination countries.

A continuum of protection needs

Complex patterns of movements have emerged that blur the distinction between refugees and economic migrants. Some routes, especially to high-income countries, are used by both economic migrants and refugees. Although they travel alongside each other, they still have distinct motivations, prospects, and needs for protection. Yet for destination countries, such "mixed movements" pose particular challenges, requiring significant resources to determine who should be granted entry and under what status. Even on an individual level, movements may be determined by a combination of security threats and other considerations. Although not necessarily direct causes of refugee movements, climate change, environmental degradation, and natural disasters are increasingly interacting with the drivers of such movements.[34]

There is growing recognition that there is a continuum of international protection needs between those who move to seek opportunities and can enjoy the continued protection of their country of citizenship and those who are recognized as refugees under international law. Some people risk harm if they return to their country of origin, even if that risk does not meet the threshold necessary for being granted refugee status—for example, when their country is in deep political crisis or subject to widespread criminal violence. The challenge for both destination countries and the international community is to ensure that all those who need international protection can access it and that the international framework evolves in line with the emergence of new protection needs.

Notes

1. In this Report, unless otherwise stated, the term *refugees* refers to refugees and other people in need of international protection.
2. Data cover all valid permits. They represent all European Union countries for which data were available in 2021. See Eurostat (2022).
3. Sturge (2022, 25).
4. WDR2023 Migration Database, World Bank, Washington, DC, https://www.worldbank.org/wdr2023/data; World Development Indicators (dashboard), World Bank, Washington, DC, https://datatopics.worldbank.org/world-development-indicators/.
5. World Development Indicators (dashboard), World Bank, Washington, DC, https://datatopics.worldbank.org/world-development-indicators/.
6. *Emigrants* are defined as people who have departed from their country of origin to become migrants.
7. *Immigrants* are defined as migrants who have arrived in a destination country.
8. These figures, based on UNHCR (2022b), do not include Palestinian refugees. The government estimate of the number of refugees in Lebanon is more than 1.5 million, including Palestinian refugees. The government estimate of the number of refugees in Jordan is more than 2 million, including Palestinian refugees.
9. Beine, Machado, and Ruyssen (2020); Czaika and Reinprecht (2020).
10. Bütikofer and Peri (2021); Gibson and McKenzie (2012); Jaeger et al. (2010).
11. For a recent review of migration barriers with particular emphasis on familiarity barriers, see McKenzie (2022).
12. For example, in destination countries higher female empowerment—as measured by the political empowerment subindex of *The Global Gender Gap Report 2020* (WEF 2019)—is associated with a higher share of females among migrants. Conversely, higher female empowerment in origin countries is associated with a lower share of females among migrants. The association is much stronger among migrants from low-income countries. In the United States, between 1.2 and 1.7 percent of applicants who applied for asylum because of fear of persecution mentioned gender identities in their asylum interviews (Shaw et al. 2021).
13. Bah et al. (2022).
14. Mattoo, Neagu, and Özden (2008).
15. For the microdata sets, see KNOMAD and ILO (2021a, 2021b). For South Asian migrants to the GCC countries and Malaysia, migration costs ranged from US$600 to US$4,400, which amounted to 2–10 months of migrant earnings. A large share of the migration cost in this

corridor can be attributed to high intermediation fees (Bossavie 2023).

16. See Migrant Smuggling (dashboard), United Nations Office on Drugs and Crime, Vienna, https://www.unodc .org/unodc/en/human-trafficking/migrant-smuggling /migrant-smuggling.html.

17. World Bank (2018).

18. McKenzie and Rapoport (2010).

19. Clemens (2013); de Haas, Natter, and Vezzoli (2016).

20. UNHCR (2022b).

21. Data on refugees are based on Refugee Population Statistics Database, United Nations High Commissioner for Refugees, Geneva, https://www.unhcr.org /refugee-statistics/.

22. Refugee Population Statistics Database, United Nations High Commissioner for Refugees, Geneva, https://www.unhcr.org/refugee-statistics/.

23. World Bank (2017, 80–81).

24. Fazel, Wheeler, and Danesh (2005); Porter and Haslam (2005); Steel et al. (2009).

25. Moore and Shellman (2007).

26. Devictor, Do, and Levchenko (2021); UNHCR (2022b).

27. Devictor, Do, and Levchenko (2021); UNHCR (2022b).

28. The numbers on foreign citizens and foreign-born populations are based on 2020 data of WDR2023 Migration Database, World Bank, Washington, DC, https://www.worldbank.org/wdr2023/data. However, data on refugees are from 2022 and include the movement of refugees stemming from the Russian invasion of Ukraine.

29. Devictor, Do, and Levchenko (2021).

30. Aksoy and Poutvaara (2021).

31. Moore and Shellman (2007); Neumayer (2004).

32. UNHCR (2022a).

33. This result is consistent with the finding of Melander and Öberg (2006) that the rate of forced migration (including both refugees and internally displaced persons) abates rather than escalates over time.

34. United Nations (2018, 4).

References

Aksoy, Cevat Giray, and Panu Poutvaara. 2021. "Refugees' and Irregular Migrants' Self-Selection into Europe." *Journal of Development Economics* 152 (September): 102681.

Bah, Tijan L., Catia Batista, Flore Gubert, and David J. McKenzie. 2022. "Can Information and Alternatives to Irregular Migration Reduce 'Backway' Migration from the Gambia?" Policy Research Working Paper 10146, World Bank, Washington, DC.

Beine, Michel, Joël Machado, and Ilse Ruyssen. 2020. "Do Potential Migrants Internalize Migrant Rights in OECD Host Societies?" *Canadian Journal of Economics* 53 (4): 1429–56.

Bossavie, Laurent. 2023. "Low-Skilled Temporary Migration Policy: The Case of Bangladesh." Background paper prepared for *World Development Report 2023*, World Bank, Washington, DC.

Bütikofer, Aline, and Giovanni Peri. 2021. "How Cognitive Ability and Personality Traits Affect Geographic Mobility." *Journal of Labor Economics* 39 (2): 559–95.

Clemens, Michael A. 2013. "Why Do Programmers Earn More in Houston than Hyderabad? Evidence from Randomized Processing of US Visas." *American Economic Review* 103 (3): 198–202.

Czaika, Mathias, and Constantin Reinprecht. 2020. "Drivers of Migration: A Synthesis of Knowledge." IMI Working Paper 163 (April), International Migration Institute, Amsterdam Institute for Social Science Research, University of Amsterdam, Amsterdam.

de Haas, Hein, Katharina Natter, and Simona Vezzoli. 2016. "Growing Restrictiveness or Changing Selection? The Nature and Evolution of Migration Policies." *International Migration Review* 52 (2): 324–67.

Devictor, Xavier, Quy-Toan Do, and Andrei A. Levchenko. 2021. "The Globalization of Refugee Flows." *Journal of Development Economics* 150 (May): 102605.

Eurostat (Statistical Office of the European Communities). 2022. "Migration and Migrant Population Statistics." Version November 21, 2022. Eurostat Explained, Eurostat, European Commission, Luxembourg. https://ec.europa.eu/eurostat/statistics-explained /index.php?title=Migration_and_migrant_population_ statistics.

Fazel, Mina, Jeremy Wheeler, and John Danesh. 2005. "Prevalence of Serious Mental Disorder in 7000 Refugees Resettled in Western Countries: A Systematic Review." *Lancet* 365 (9467): 1309–14.

Gibson, John, and David J. McKenzie. 2012. "The Economic Consequences of 'Brain Drain' of the Best and Brightest: Microeconomic Evidence from Five Countries." *Economic Journal* 122 (560): 339–75.

Jaeger, David A., Thomas Dohmen, Armin Falk, David Huffman, Uwe Sunde, and Holger Bonin. 2010. "Direct Evidence on Risk Attitudes and Migration." *Review of Economics and Statistics* 92 (3): 684–89.

KNOMAD (Global Knowledge Partnership on Migration and Development) and ILO (International Labour Organization). 2021a. "KNOMAD-ILO Migration Costs Surveys 2015: El Salvador, Ethiopia, Guatemala, Honduras, India, Nepal, Pakistan, Philippines, Vietnam, 2015–2016." Microdata set, version May 24, 2021, World Bank, Washington, DC. https://microdata.worldbank.org/index.php /catalog/2938.

KNOMAD (Global Knowledge Partnership on Migration and Development) and ILO (International Labour Organization). 2021b. "KNOMAD-ILO Migration Costs Surveys 2016: Benin, Burkina Faso, Cabo Verde, Gambia, Ghana, Guinea, Guinea-Bissau, India, Kyrgyz Republic, Liberia, Mali, Mauritania, Nepal, Niger, Nigeria . . . , 2016–2017." Microdata set, version May 24, 2021, World Bank, Washington, DC. https://microdata.worldbank.org/index.php /catalog/2944.

Mattoo, Aaditya, Ileana Cristina Neagu, and Çağlar Özden. 2008. "Brain Waste? Educated Immigrants in the US Labor Market." *Journal of Development Economics* 87 (2): 255–69.

McKenzie, David J. 2022. "Fears and Tears: Should More People Be Moving within and from Developing Countries, and What Stops This Movement?" Policy Research Working Paper 10128, World Bank, Washington, DC.

McKenzie, David J., and Hillel Rapoport. 2010. "Self-Selection Patterns in Mexico-U.S. Migration: The Role of Migration Networks." *Review of Economics and Statistics* 92 (4): 811–21.

Melander, Erik, and Magnus Öberg. 2006. "Time to Go? Duration Dependence in Forced Migration." *International Interactions* 32 (2): 129–52.

Moore, Will H., and Stephen M. Shellman. 2007. "Whither Will They Go? A Global Study of Refugees' Destinations, 1965–1995." *International Studies Quarterly* 51 (4): 811–34.

Neumayer, Eric. 2004. "Asylum Destination Choice: What Makes Some West European Countries More Attractive Than Others?" *European Union Politics* 5 (2): 155–80.

Porter, Matthew, and Nick Haslam. 2005. "Predisplacement and Postdisplacement Factors Associated with Mental Health of Refugees and Internally Displaced Persons: A Meta-Analysis." *JAMA* 294 (5): 602–12.

Serajuddin, Umar, and Nada Hamadeh. 2020. "New World Bank Country Classifications by Income Level: 2020–2021." *Data Blog*, July 1, 2020. https://blogs.worldbank.org/opendata/new-world-bank-country-classifications-income-level-2020-2021.

Shaw, Ari, Winston Luhur, Ingrid Eagly, and Kerith J. Conron. 2021. "LGBT Asylum Claims in the United States." Research That Matters (March), Williams Institute, UCLA School of Law, University of California–Los Angeles, Los Angeles.

Steel, Zachary, Tien Chey, Derrick Silove, Claire Marnane, Richard A. Bryant, and Mark van Ommeren. 2009. "Association of Torture and Other Potentially Traumatic Events with Mental Health Outcomes among Populations Exposed to Mass Conflict and Displacement: A Systematic Review and Meta-Analysis." *JAMA* 302 (5): 537–49.

Sturge, Georgina. 2022. "Migration Statistics." Research Briefing (November 24), House of Commons Library, London.

UNHCR (United Nations High Commissioner for Refugees). 2022a. "Global Trends: Forced Displacement in 2021." June 16, Statistics and Demographics Section, Global Data Service, UNHCR, Copenhagen. https://www.unhcr.org/en-us/publications/brochures/62a9d1494/global-trends-report-2021.html.

UNHCR (United Nations High Commissioner for Refugees). 2022b. "Mid-Year Trends 2022." October 27, Statistics and Demographics Section, Global Data Service, UNHCR, Copenhagen. https://www.unhcr.org/en-us/mid-year-trends.html.

United Nations. 2018. "Global Compact on Refugees." United Nations, New York.

WEF (World Economic Forum). 2019. *Insight Report: The Global Gender Gap Report 2020*. Geneva: WEF.

World Bank. 2017. *Forcibly Displaced: Toward a Development Approach Supporting Refugees, the Internally Displaced, and Their Hosts*. Washington, DC: World Bank.

World Bank. 2018. *Moving for Prosperity: Global Migration and Labor Markets*. Policy Research Report. Washington, DC: World Bank.

Spotlight 2
—
Data

Reliable, timely, comprehensive data are critical to effective policy making, particularly for complex and polarizing issues such as migration. The Global Compact for Safe, Orderly and Regular Migration explicitly states as its first objective collecting and utilizing "accurate and disaggregated data as a basis for evidence-based policies."[1] Yet the current migration data landscape is characterized by divergences and inconsistencies in definitions, data collection methodologies, and dissemination strategies. The available data have large gaps across countries and over time stemming from irregular collection efforts, lack of harmonization, or failures in dissemination. Many of the data sets, including administrative data collected by governments, are beyond the reach of academics and policy makers.

Why data?

Data are needed to inform policy making for all types of movements and at all stages. For example:

- Migration data help policy makers better understand the magnitude of migration, its drivers (including the potential role of climate change), as well as its impacts. High-quality data allow analyses of who moves, with what skills and attributes, and under what circumstances.
- In origin countries, policy makers are interested in measuring how remittances can contribute to poverty reduction—which migrants contribute the most and with what patterns; how remittance flows affect poverty among various households in receiving communities; and how specific policy measures can enhance their effects. Other policy makers are concerned about the downside of emigration: What happens to family members left behind, and how can the issues they are facing best be mitigated? What are the actual effects of a brain drain in a given situation, which professions are most affected, and what is the effect of specific mitigation measures? Yet others look at the impact of emigration—including diaspora and return—on a country's development.
- In destination countries, some policy makers are concerned about economic impacts—migrants' skills and attributes, their participation in the labor market, their effects on productivity, the consequences for various groups of national workers, and the impacts of inclusion policies. Others are interested in social impacts—migrants' abilities to integrate and the pace at which they do so, the effects on the provision of public services, and the differentiated impacts of various policy approaches to manage this process. Information on the subnational distribution of migrants can be critical to informing such discussions.
- Additional data related to forced displacement, transit, undocumented, and "distressed" migration patterns are also important for the relevant countries.

Definitions

Consistency of definitions—across data sources within a country, across countries, and over time—is essential for the effective use of migration- and forced displacement–related data. However, there are wide variations, including in high-income countries with solid statistical systems. For example, the Norwegian authorities and the United Nations High Commissioner for Refugees (UNHCR) noted significant discrepancies between the numbers of refugees in Norway reported for the end of 2013—18,734 by Eurostat; 46,033 by UNHCR; and 132,203 by Statistics Norway—reflecting differences in definitions, time frames, and statistical methods.[2] Similarly, the definition of *migrant* in national censuses varies across countries. It can be based on place of birth, citizenship, time of arrival, or even ethnicity or race (figure S2.1). Countries, government agencies within the same country, and researchers collect data using any one of these definitions, making comparisons and analyses difficult.

Figure S2.1 Many population censuses do not collect basic and consistent data on migration

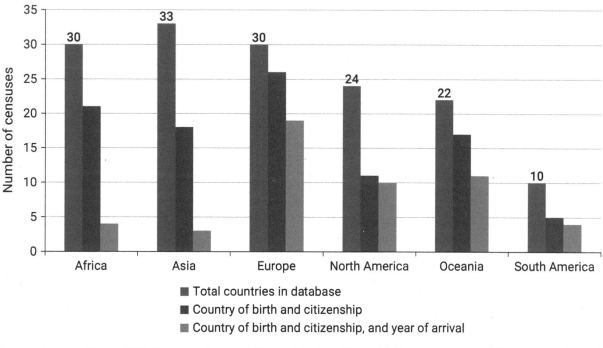

Source: Juran and Snow 2018. Based on data for 149 countries from United Nations Department of Economic and Social Affairs (UN DESA).

Note: The number of censuses refers to censuses in the 2010 round whose questionnaires include two or three core questions on country of birth, citizenship, and year of arrival.

Data sources

Multiple sources of data can inform policy making, each with its strengths and limitations. Each set of instruments is insufficient to fully address the data challenges related to migration. However, each can help provide evidence on specific aspects of cross-border movement. Effective policy making requires using multiple data sources across geographic, disciplinary, and institutional boundaries. Various data sources can complement one another so that, over time, a comprehensive picture emerges:

- *Population censuses* remain the primary data sources on global migration. On the one hand, their extensive coverage and granularity enable measurement of long-term movements of migrants. Population censuses are also conducted in almost every country at all income levels, enabling some level of comparability across countries and time periods. On the other hand, there are challenges related to their timeliness and accessibility. Censuses are most often conducted once every 10 years, and so they cannot capture rapid changes in migration patterns. In destination countries, censuses tend to undercount certain subpopulations, such as undocumented migrants, and other hard-to-reach populations, such as refugees.[3] Even when coverage is not a constraint, information on citizenship is rarely collected, thereby leaving the citizenship of foreign-born people unknown and making it impossible to construct statistics on noncitizens.[4] In origin countries, censuses cannot capture emigrants when the entire household has left.[5] The issues covered in questionnaires are necessarily constrained by issues related to costs and quality, even when extended questionnaires are used for subsample groups. Finally, in some countries, political considerations and financial constraints limit access to census data.

- *Population registers* are another primary source of data on global migration. Similar to censuses, they cover a large part of a country's population and provide long-term data sets. However, they are largely limited to higher-income countries.[6] Population registers often fail to fully account for undocumented migrants and other marginalized populations who have little incentive to register. They may overestimate the numbers of migrants and refugees if those who leave fail to de-register—for example, if registration is tied to receiving benefits. Population registers are often managed by line ministries, which are peripheral to the national statistical system, and this factor limits accessibility. Canada, Spain, and Nordic countries are in the early stages of connecting population registers with a range of administrative databases.[7]

- *Administrative data* are among the most promising yet underutilized sources for migration research and policy making. On the one hand, almost every country collects administrative data, but through different systems. Data are collected on who crosses their borders, taxation, social and welfare programs, pensions, health care, education, and other public services, among other things. On the other hand, ministries and agencies have little incentive to share, harmonize, or integrate their data sources due to national security, privacy, or bureaucratic concerns. The Organisation for Economic Co-operation and Development (OECD) is leading efforts in its member countries and other parts of the world to address some of these issues.[8] However, the true value of these data will be realized only when data sources are integrated, such as through national ID numbers, while ensuring adequate levels of data privacy.

- *Household and labor force surveys* capture rich information on different aspects of migration, such as individual drivers, socioeconomic characteristics, and labor market impacts. Surveys in destination countries provide evidence on the extent to which migrants themselves directly benefit from their movement.[9] Surveys in origin countries help shed light on the development impacts of mobility, particularly on the families and communities of emigrants. However, these surveys are conducted infrequently, and they are rarely conducted among a sample large enough to capture meaningful information about migrants. Expanding coverage is very costly, even more so if coverage is being expanded so that data for the same individuals are collected over multiple periods.[10] In the short term, adjusting existing general survey programs to include more migration-related questions may be a more cost-effective option to improve the availability of data. Experimental approaches (such as impact evaluations) could also solve many of the remaining challenges.

- *Surveys for impact evaluations* can help assess the effects of specific policies on various groups—migrants, refugees, or nationals—and fine-tune policy design and implementation.[11] On the one hand, they provide the more direct evidence that can be used for policy making. On the other, the corresponding data are often costly to collect—if they do not rely directly on administrative data—with possible coverage challenges.
- *New data sources* have been heralded as a solution for the many limitations of traditional sources. Mobile phone call records, geotagged social media data, internet traffic, and Internet Protocol (IP) addresses are being used to track forced displacement, predict migration trends, and analyze remittances.[12] However, these sources suffer from their experimental nature, low statistical rigor, and biases in sampling. Their access for academic and policy research purposes can also raise privacy-related issues.[13]

Additional challenges

Data collection on refugees and other marginalized migrant populations faces particular challenges.[14] The sudden nature of some of these movements and the fact that they are occurring in areas often difficult to access or where administrative capacity is low complicate efforts considerably. At times, security and political considerations hamper data collection efforts as well.[15]

The exclusion of forcibly displaced people from national statistical systems further marginalizes their access to social safety nets, public services, and employment opportunities.[16] Some countries such as Chad have incorporated these populations into existing national data collection efforts.[17] Chad's Refugees and Host Communities Household Survey is fully integrated into its national household surveys as an integral part of the refugee policy dialogues among the government, the West African Economic and Monetary Union (WAEMU), and development partners.[18]

Global efforts to improve the availability and quality of data on refugees and displaced populations have led to some improvements over the last decade. The global survey program on refugees by UNHCR, as well as initiatives such as the World Bank–UNHCR Joint Data Center on Forced Displacement (JDC), have demonstrated the feasibility and benefits of integrated data collection efforts. The Expert Group on Refugee, IDP and Statelessness Statistics (EGRISS), established by the United Nations in 2016, has developed two sets of methodological recommendations—one on refugee statistics and one on internally displaced person (IDP) statistics—that countries should implement to strengthen data collection efforts at national levels.[19]

Data privacy

In a world characterized by a growing need for more reliable statistics and comprehensive, timely data, as well as the emergence of new technologies, data protection is becoming increasingly relevant. The collection of data on migrants, who often lack the legal protections granted to citizens in their country of residence, raises many privacy concerns—and even more so when migrants have an undocumented status. These concerns need to be addressed.[20] Collecting, sharing, and processing data—even if it can help inform policy making—pose privacy risks, including data theft, data loss, and unauthorized use of personal data.[21] In some sensitive contexts such as refugee situations, child migration, human trafficking, and migrant smuggling, confidentiality of personal data is especially important because identification of a data subject can pose life-threatening risks.[22]

Governments and other public authorities should aim to address these concerns by using the best resources available when collecting migration- and forced displacement–related data, while ensuring the fundamental privacy rights and safety of data subjects. They should also ensure that applicable data protection and privacy laws adequately cover noncitizen populations; that they are effectively enforced, including for noncitizen populations; that safe data handling procedures are developed to prevent third parties from accessing potentially harmful data, including through anonymization procedures; and that migrants know their rights and are informed about the purpose of data collection and about data-sharing risks and mitigation measures.[23] Similarly, when using new technologies, governments should ensure that they are transparent about how the data are being used to make decisions about migrants.

Looking ahead

Good data on migration are essential for governments to better manage migration and inform sound and effective policies. Yet there are significant data gaps, and major efforts are needed to collect both timely and granular data in a consistent manner. This will require more financial resources—including funding for long-term data collection—and support to strengthen the technical capacity of each country's statistical agency—including lower-income countries.[24] Dedicated data financing instruments such as the World Bank's Global Data Facility can help address existing funding gaps while promoting greater coherence in investments in migration data.[25]

Within this context, priorities to enhance the availability and quality of data that can inform policy making include:

- *Harmonization.* Efforts are needed to improve the consistency of definitions, or at least to collect data that can make comparisons possible even if countries use distinct definitions. For example, censuses should include at least four core questions: on country of birth, country of citizenship, country of previous residence, and year of arrival. Harmonization efforts undertaken by the United Nations Statistical Commission and OECD are critical. In addition to governments, many international and regional organizations collect data, particularly in areas where government data may be lacking such as on refugees. Coordination among the various actors is needed to prevent duplication, actively seek synergies, and ensure consistency in the methodologies used across surveys, thereby enabling comparability.
- *Innovative surveys.* Beyond traditional data sources, additional surveys can be conducted to inform policy making, including impact evaluations and surveys on the drivers and impacts of different types of movements. For example, longitudinal studies track migrants across borders and over time to understand the impact of migration or integration processes over time.[26] Notable examples include the Mexican Family Life Survey[27] and the Long-Term Impacts of Migration Survey on Tongan Migrants in New Zealand.[28] Agreements across institutions in origin, destination, and transit countries are sometimes needed, such as for the Mexican Migration Project.[29] Similarly, survey instruments are needed to analyze rapid and short-term movements using existing statistical systems, including movements lasting for short periods of time such as those in transit countries.
- *Data accessibility and privacy.* Facilitating access to data while ensuring confidentiality often requires a combination of actions, including strengthening legal and regulatory instruments that regulate data exchanges; enhancing administrative data systems;[30] establishing legal rules, data license agreements, and shared secure architecture to facilitate the exchange of privately owned data;[31] and developing standard data access agreements between the owners and the users of the data, such as the members of the research and policy-making community.

Notes

1. United Nations (2019, 6).
2. World Bank (2017). The UNHCR estimate is based on the total number of asylum-seekers granted a positive decision on their asylum claim over the last 10 years. The Eurostat estimate is based on valid residence permits issued to those granted refugee status or subsidiary protection. Finally, the Statistics Norway estimate is based on the number of "principal applicants"—179,534, when including persons who have been given a residence permit because of a family relationship with refugees.
3. Johnson (2022).
4. Artuc et al. (2015).
5. Indeed, assessing the overall extent of undercounting through demographic analyses and postenumeration surveys is key to determining the credibility and usefulness of population censuses for measuring migrant stocks (Kennel and Jensen 2022).
6. See Poulain and Herm (2013) for a list of population registers available.
7. Careja and Bevelander (2018).
8. OECD (2022).
9. Bilsborrow (2017); Fawcett and Arnold (1987).
10. Bossavie and Wang (2022).
11. Bilsborrow (2016); Bilsborrow et al. (1997); Borjas (1987); de Brauw and Carletto (2012); Eckman and Himelein (2022); Heckathorn (2002); Kish (1965); McKenzie (2012); McKenzie and Mistiaen (2007); McKenzie, Stillman, and Gibson (2010); McKenzie and Yang (2010).
12. Aiken et al. (2021); Hughes et al. (2016); Kim et al. (2020); Laczko and Rango (2014); Sîrbu et al. (2021); Tjaden (2021); UNHCR (2021).
13. Bloemraad and Menjívar (2022).
14. Cirillo et al. (2022); King, Skeldon, and Vullnetari (2008).
15. Sarzin (2017).
16. Baal (2021).
17. Nguyen, Savadogo, and Tanaka (2021).
18. Nguyen, Savadogo, and Tanaka (2021).
19. Baal (2021); EGRIS (2018, 2020).
20. Verhulst and Young (2018).
21. GMDAC (2022).
22. Ganslmeier (2019).
23. Migrants (dashboard), Privacy International, London, https://privacyinternational.org/learn/migrants.
24. GMG (2017).
25. Global Data Facility (dashboard), World Bank, Washington, DC, https://www.worldbank.org/en/programs/global-data-facility.
26. UNECE (2020).
27. Rubalcava et al. (2008).
28. Gibson et al. (2018).
29. Durand and Massey (2006).
30. World Bank (2021).
31. Verhulst and Young (2018). Also see Development Data Partnership (dashboard), World Bank, Washington, DC, https://datapartnership.org/.

References

Aiken, Emily L., Suzanne Bellue, Dean S. Karlan, Christopher R. Udry, and Joshua Evan Blumenstock. 2021. "Machine Learning and Mobile Phone Data Can Improve the Targeting of Humanitarian Assistance." NBER Working Paper 29070 (July), National Bureau of Economic Research, Cambridge, MA.

Artuc, Erhan, Frédéric Docquier, Çağlar Özden, and Christopher Robert Parsons. 2015. "A Global Assessment of Human Capital Mobility: The Role of Non-OECD Destinations." World Development 65 (January): 6–26.

Baal, Natalia Krynsky. 2021. "Including Refugees and IDPs in National Data Systems." Forced Migration Review 66 (March): 52–54.

Bilsborrow, Richard E. 2016. "Concepts, Definitions and Data Collection Approaches." In International Handbook of Migration and Population Distribution, edited by Michael J. White, 109–56. International Handbooks of Population, vol. 6. New York: Springer.

Bilsborrow, Richard E. 2017. "The Global Need for Better Data on International Migration and the Special Potential of Household Surveys." Migration Policy Practice 7 (1): 9–17.

Bilsborrow, Richard E., Graeme Hugo, Amarjit S. Oberai, and Hania Zlotnik. 1997. International Migration Statistics: Guidelines for Improving Data Collection Systems. Geneva: International Labour Office.

Bloemraad, Irene, and Cecilia Menjívar. 2022. "Precarious Times, Professional Tensions: The Ethics of Migration Research and the Drive for Scientific Accountability." International Migration Review 56 (1): 4–32.

Borjas, George J. 1987. "Self-Selection and the Earnings of Immigrants." American Economic Review 77 (4): 531–53.

Bossavie, Laurent, and He Wang. 2022. "Return Migration and Labor Market Outcomes: Evidence from South Asia." Policy Research Working Paper 10180, World Bank, Washington, DC.

Careja, Romana, and Pieter Bevelander. 2018. "Using Population Registers for Migration and Integration Research: Examples from Denmark and Sweden." Comparative Migration Studies 6 (1): 19.

Cirillo, Marinella, Andrea Cattaneo, Meghan Miller, and Ahmad Sadiddin. 2022. "Establishing the Link between Internal and International Migration: Evidence from Sub-Saharan Africa." World Development 157 (September): 105943.

de Brauw, Alan, and Calogero Carletto. 2012. "Improving the Measurement and Policy Relevance of Migration Information in Multi-topic Household Surveys." LSMS Working Paper (May), Living Standards Measurement Study, World Bank, Washington, DC.

Durand, Jorge, and Douglas S. Massey, eds. 2006. *Crossing the Border: Research from the Mexican Migration Project*. New York: Russell Sage Foundation.

Eckman, Stephanie, and Kristen Himelein. 2022. "Innovative Sample Designs for Studies of Refugees and Internally Displaced Persons." In *Migration Research in a Digitized World: Using Innovative Technology to Tackle Methodological Challenges*, edited by Steffen Pötzschke and Sebastian Rinken, 15–34. IMISCOE Research Series. Cham, Switzerland: Springer.

EGRIS (Expert Group on Refugee and Internally Displaced Persons Statistics). 2018. *International Recommendations on Refugee Statistics*. Manuals and Guidelines (March). Luxembourg: Eurostat.

EGRIS (Expert Group on Refugee and Internally Displaced Persons Statistics). 2020. *International Recommendations on Internally Displaced Persons Statistics (IRIS)*. Manuals and Guidelines (March). Luxembourg: Eurostat.

Fawcett, James T., and Fred Arnold. 1987. "The Role of Surveys in the Study of International Migration: An Appraisal." *International Migration Review* 21 (4): 1523–40.

Ganslmeier, Miriam. 2019. "Data Privacy for Migrants: Unrealistic or Simply Neglected?" October 29, Heinrich-Böll-Stiftung, Washington, DC. https://us.boell.org/en/2019/10/29/data-privacy-migrants-unrealistic-or-simply-neglected.

Gibson, John, David J. McKenzie, Halahingano Rohorua, and Steven Stillman. 2018. "The Long-Term Impacts of International Migration: Evidence from a Lottery." *World Bank Economic Review* 32 (1): 127–47.

GMDAC (Global Migration Data Analysis Centre). 2022. "Migration and Data Protection." Immigration and Emigration Statistics, Migration Data Portal, version of June 7, 2022, GMDAC, International Organization for Migration, Berlin. https://www.migrationdataportal.org/themes/migration-and-data-protection.

GMG (Global Migration Group). 2017. Handbook for Improving the Production and Use of Migration Data for Development. Washington, DC: GMG, Global Knowledge Partnership on Migration and Development, World Bank.

Heckathorn, Douglas D. 2002. "Respondent-Driven Sampling II: Deriving Valid Population Estimates from Chain-Referral Samples of Hidden Populations." *Social Problems* 49 (1): 11–34.

Hughes, Christina, Emilio Zagheni, Guy J. Abel, Arkadiusz Wiśniowski, Alessandro Sorichetta, Ingmar Weber, and Andrew J. Tatem. 2016. "Inferring Migrations: Traditional Methods and New Approaches Based on Mobile Phone, Social Media, and Other Big Data." Social Europe (January), European Commission, Brussels.

Johnson, Janna E. 2022. "Does the Census Miss the Native-Born Children of Immigrant Mothers? Evidence from State-Level Undercount by Race and Hispanic Status." *Population Research and Policy Review* 41 (1): 139–95.

Juran, Sabrina, and Rachel C. Snow. 2018. "The Potential of Population and Housing Censuses for International Migration Analysis." *Statistical Journal of the IAOS* 34 (2): 203–13.

Kennel, Timothy, and Eric Jensen. 2022. "Upcoming 2020 Census Coverage Estimates." *Random Samplings* (blog), March 3, 2022. https://www.census.gov/newsroom/blogs/random-samplings/2022/03/upcoming-2020-census-coverage-estimates.html.

Kim, Jisu, Alina Sîrbu, Fosca Giannotti, and Lorenzo. Gabrielli. 2020. "Digital Footprints of International Migration on Twitter." In *Advances in Intelligent Data Analysis XVIII: 18th International Symposium on Intelligent Data Analysis, IDA 2020, Konstanz, Germany, April 27–29, 2020, Proceedings*, edited by Michael R. Berthold, Ad Feelders, and Georg Krempl, 274–86. Berlin: Springer-Verlag.

King, Russell, Ronald Skeldon, and Julie Vullnetari. 2008. "Internal and International Migration: Bridging the Theoretical Divide." Working Paper 52 (December), Sussex Centre for Migration Research, University of Sussex, Brighton, UK.

Kish, Leslie. 1965. "Sampling Organizations and Groups of Unequal Sizes." *American Sociological Review* 30 (4): 564–72.

Laczko, Frank, and Marzia Rango. 2014. "Can Big Data Help Us Achieve a 'Migration Data Revolution'?" *Migration Policy Practice* 4 (2): 20–29.

McKenzie, David J. 2012. "Learning about Migration through Experiments." CReAM Discussion Paper CDP 07/12, Centre for Research and Analysis of Migration, Department of Economics, University College London, London.

McKenzie, David J., and Johan Andre Mistiaen. 2007. "Surveying Migrant Households: A Comparison of Census-Based, Snowball, and Intercept Point Surveys." Policy Research Working Paper 4419, World Bank, Washington, DC.

McKenzie, David J., Steven Stillman, and John Gibson. 2010. "How Important Is Selection? Experimental vs. Non-experimental Measures of the Income Gains from Migration." *Journal of the European Economic Association* 8 (4): 913–45.

McKenzie, David J., and Dean Yang. 2010. "Experimental Approaches in Migration Studies." IZA Discussion Paper 5125 (August), Institute of Labor Economics, Bonn, Germany.

Nguyen, Nga Thi Viet, Aboudrahyme Savadogo, and Tommomi Tanaka. 2021. *Refugees in Chad: The Road Forward*. Washington, DC: World Bank.

OECD (Organisation for Economic Co-operation and Development). 2022. "Recommendation of the Council on Enhancing Access to and Sharing of Data." OECD Legal Instruments OECD/LEGAL/0463, OECD, Paris. https://legalinstruments.oecd.org/en/instruments/OECD-LEGAL-0463.

Poulain, Michel, and Anne Herm. 2013. "Central Population Registers as a Source of Demographic Statistics in Europe." Translated by Roger Depledge. *Population* 68 (2): 183–212.

Rubalcava, Luis N., Graciela M. Teruel, Duncan Thomas, and Noreen Goldman. 2008. "The Healthy Migrant Effect: New Findings from the Mexican Family Life Survey." *American Journal of Public Health* 98 (1): 78–84.

Sarzin, Zara. 2017. "Stocktaking of Global Forced Displacement Data." Policy Research Working Paper 7985, World Bank, Washington, DC.

Sîrbu, Alina, Gennady Andrienko, Natalia Andrienko, Chiara Boldrini, Marco Conti, Fosca Giannotti, Riccardo Guidotti, et al. 2021. "Human Migration: The Big Data Perspective." *International Journal of Data Science and Analytics* 11 (4): 341–60.

Tjaden, Jasper. 2021. "Measuring Migration 2.0: A Review of Digital Data Sources." *Comparative Migration Studies* 9 (1): 59.

UNECE (United Nations Economic Commission for Europe). 2020. *Guidance on the Use of Longitudinal Data for Migration Statistics*. Document ECE/CES/STAT/2020/6. Geneva: United Nations. https://unece.org/sites/default/files/2021-03/ECECESSTAT20206.pdf.

UNHCR (United Nations High Commissioner for Refugees). 2021. "Big (Crisis) Data for Predictive Models: A Literature Review." Statistics and Demographic Section, UNHCR Global Data Services, UNHCR, Geneva.

United Nations. 2019. "Resolution Adopted by the General Assembly on 19 December 2018: Global Compact for Safe, Orderly and Regular Migration." Document A/RES/73/195 (January 11, 2019), United Nations, New York. https://www.un.org/en/development/desa/population/migration/generalassembly/docs/globalcompact/A_RES_73_195.pdf.

Verhulst, Stefaan G., and Andrew Young. 2018. "The Potential and Practice of Data Collaborative for Migration." *Measurement and Evaluation* (blog), March 29, 2018. https://doi.org/10.48558/1D1Q-AM28.

World Bank. 2017. *Forcibly Displaced: Toward a Development Approach Supporting Refugees, the Internally Displaced, and Their Hosts*. Washington, DC: World Bank.

World Bank. 2021. *World Development Report 2021: Data for Better Lives*. Washington, DC: World Bank.

3
The outlook
Changing patterns, needs, and risks

Key messages

- Spurred by two unprecedented forces—rapid demographic transitions and climate change—cross-border movements are becoming both inevitable and necessary for migrants and economies at all levels of income. They will influence where many migrants stand in the Match and Motive Matrix (figure 3.1).

- The populations of high-income and many middle-income countries are aging quickly, while the populations of low-income countries are expected to continue to grow. This trend is creating large mismatches between labor supply and demand across the world. Whether countries allow migration to help reduce some of these mismatches will largely determine economic and social trajectories at all income levels.

- Climate change is compounding other drivers of mobility. So far, most movements induced by climate impacts have been within countries. But climate change has the potential to increase distressed cross-border movements, and the global community urgently needs to limit global warming and support country-level adaptation policies.

Figure 3.1 Demographics and climate change are transforming migration patterns

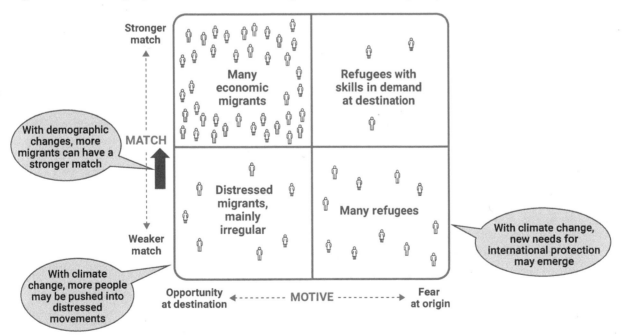

Source: WDR 2023 team.

Note: Match refers to the degree to which a migrant's skills and related attributes meet the demand in the destination country. *Motive* refers to the circumstances under which a person moves—whether in search of opportunity or because of a "well-founded fear" of persecution, armed conflict, or violence in their origin country.

Demographics: The coming competition for workers

Unprecedented demographic changes create more opportunities for "stronger match" movements. Aging countries—both high-income and increasingly middle-income—need large numbers of foreign workers and broad skill sets to sustain their economies and maintain their social contracts. What is considered a strong match between migrants' skills and attributes and the demand of destination countries is changing accordingly. In the decades to come, migration is likely to be driven largely by the needs of destination countries, which will compete for a shrinking pool of qualified workers.

A tale of three countries: Italy, Mexico, and Nigeria

Italy, Mexico, and Nigeria exemplify the divergent demographic forces at play in today's world. One of the main factors affecting the size of a population is the number of children born.[1] Typically measured in terms of the average number of live births per woman over her reproductive years, the fertility rate must exceed 2.1 for replacement of the population. Between 1950 and 2022, Italy's fertility rate fell from 2.4 to 1.3, well below the replacement level. Over the same period, Mexico's fertility rate dropped from 6.7 to 1.8, also below that level. By contrast, Nigeria's fertility rate declined only slightly, from 6.4 to 5.1.[2]

Fertility rates have profound effects that carry through the medium term and are difficult to fully reverse. Based on current trends, Italy's population is expected to shrink from 59 million in 2022 to 32 million by 2100. Mexico's population is also set to decline, from 127 million in 2022 to 116 million by 2100. Nigeria, by contrast, is expected to see its population increase, from 213 million in 2022 to 791 million by 2100, elevating it to the second-most populous country in the world (after India).

Even more striking are the divergences in age distributions. Although all three countries had relatively young populations in 1950, their age pyramids have since assumed different shapes (figure 3.2). In Italy, the share of people over age 50 has more than doubled—from 21.5 percent in 1950 to 46.7 percent in 2022—and the younger population cohorts are significantly smaller than their predecessors. Such an inversion of the age pyramid is unprecedented. Mexico's population is still relatively young, but it is now aging rapidly, at a much faster rate than experienced by Italy. Its demographic pyramid has begun to assume an inverted shape, and it is set to become even more unbalanced by 2050. By contrast, in Nigeria the share of the population over age 50 (about 10 percent) has changed only slightly since the 1950s. The country is likely to remain young well through the middle of the century.

The great divergence: Aging societies and youth bulges

The examples of Italy, Mexico, and Nigeria are reflective of broader trends. Countries at different levels of income are diverging, especially when it comes to population growth and age structures.

As the global population grows, it is rebalancing across regions (figure 3.3). The ongoing growth of the global population—from 2.5 billion in 1950 to 8 billion in 2022 and 9.7 billion in 2050—will largely occur in low- and lower-middle-income countries.[3] Meanwhile, the population is plateauing in high-income countries, and it is beginning to shrink in upper-middle-income countries.

Similarly, while the world as a whole is rapidly aging, low-income countries will remain young throughout the century (figure 3.4). Globally, the number of people over age 65 is already larger than the number of children under age five. By 2050, it will be double that of children under age five and larger than the number of youth ages 15–24.[4] However, this is mainly the result of trends in high- and upper-middle-income countries.

Figure 3.2 Widely different demographic forces are at play in Italy, Mexico, and Nigeria

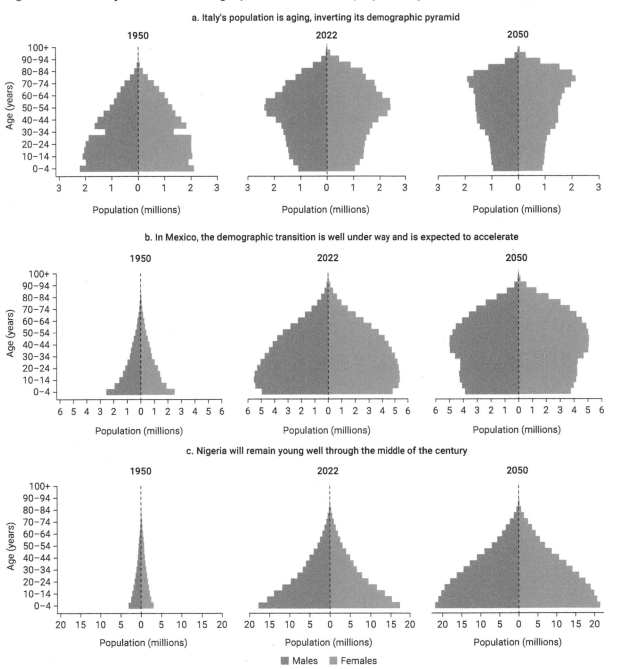

a. Italy's population is aging, inverting its demographic pyramid

b. In Mexico, the demographic transition is well under way and is expected to accelerate

c. Nigeria will remain young well through the middle of the century

Males   Females

Source: 2022 data (medium scenario): World Population Prospects (dashboard), Population Division, Department of Economic and Social Affairs, United Nations, New York, https://population.un.org/wpp/.

Labor needs in high-income countries

High-income countries are aging quickly. The share of people over age 65—already at a historic high of 19 percent in 2022—is expected to increase further, reaching 29 percent by midcentury.[5] In the Republic of Korea—the most rapidly aging country—the share of people over age 80 will quadruple by

Figure 3.3 The population is growing quickly in lower-income countries, whereas it will soon begin to shrink in higher-income countries

Total population, by country income group

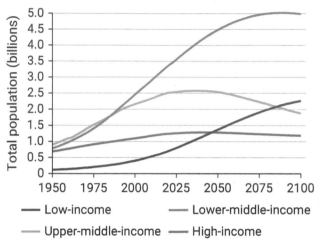

Source: WDR 2023 team calculations, based on the medium fertility scenario, World Population Prospects 2022 (dashboard), Population Division, Department of Economic and Social Affairs, United Nations, New York, https://population.un.org/wpp/, applied to country income groups in Hamadeh et al. (2022).

Figure 3.4 Higher-income countries are aging rapidly, whereas lower-income countries remain young

Number of elderly (65+ years) per child (under five years), by country income group

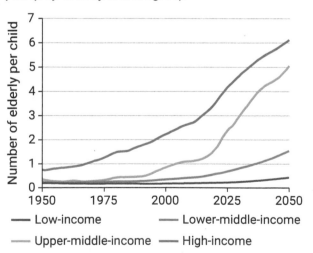

Source: WDR 2023 team calculations, based on the medium fertility scenario, World Population Prospects 2022 (dashboard), Population Division, Department of Economic and Social Affairs, United Nations, New York, https://population.un.org/wpp/, applied to country income groups in Hamadeh et al. (2022).

2050, from the current 4.1 percent to 15.7 percent.[6] Overall, the elderly population in high-income countries is projected to grow by about 118 million by 2050, while the working-age population (ages 20–64) will decline by about 53 million (figure 3.5).[7]

The shrinking labor force is already creating challenges in some countries. In the United States, the number of jobs is projected to increase by 11.9 million between 2020 and 2030, but, short of migration, the labor force will grow by only 8.9 million over the same period. In the European Union, the shortage of health care workers is projected to reach 4.1 million by 2030, including 2.3 million nurses.[8] In Japan, the working-age population peaked in 1998, and it has declined since. In the absence of migration, it is expected to fall by a further 37 percent by 2050.[9] The current demographic trends and the resulting shortages in the labor supply have raised labor costs to the point of compelling a number of Japanese firms to restrict their activities—some even declaring bankruptcy.[10]

Aging is placing unprecedented stress on public finances. Working-age adults are generating the resources needed to support the elderly, but their number is shrinking. In the high-income member countries of the Organisation for Economic Co-operation and Development (OECD), the ratio of working-age adults (20–64 years) to the elderly (65 years and above) went from 7.1 in 1950 to 2.9 in 2022. It is projected to drop to below 2.0 by 2050 (figure 3.6).[11] Yet these countries are projected to increase public expenditures by up to 7.6 percentage points of gross domestic product (GDP) by 2060 to accommodate the costs of their aging populations for pensions,[12] health care, and long-term care.[13] Without major policy reforms, aging could raise the public debt burden of advanced economies in the Group of Twenty (G20) by an average of 180 percent of GDP by 2050.[14] Some countries, such as the United States, have more fiscal space, but in several European countries—such as Austria, Belgium, France, Greece, Italy,

Spain, and the Scandinavian countries[15]—the sustainability of pension systems will already be at risk in the coming decade.

Accelerated transitions in middle-income countries

Most middle-income countries are also well into their demographic transition. In the most populous country, China, the population has begun to shrink. In the second-most populous country, India, the population is projected to fall after midcentury. Fertility rates are plummeting across a range of middle-income countries. In some countries, they are now below the replacement rate (figure 3.7). This transition is happening at a much faster pace than in the past. In the United Kingdom, the rate fell from 5.5 children per woman in 1800 to about 2.0 in 1975—a 175-year period. But it took fewer than 60 years for India's fertility rate to fall from 6.0 children per woman in 1964 to 2.01 in 2022, for Tunisia's to fall from 7.0 in 1964 to 2.06 in 2022, and for Malaysia's to fall from 6.0 to 1.8 over the same period.

Many upper-middle-income countries may grow old before they get rich (figure 3.8).[16] The share of elderly in their population is expected to double by 2050.[17] In upper-middle-income countries, the share of the working-age population (20–64 years) peaked in 2014, and it has since been in decline. It is expected to peak by 2050 in lower-middle-income countries. Considerable policy challenges will confront countries trying, while they are still middle-income, to make up for a shrinking workforce and to finance retirement and care for an aging population. Among the emerging economies in the G20, aging could raise public debt burdens by an average of 130 percent of GDP by 2050 in the absence of policy reforms.[18]

Booming population growth in low-income countries

Low-income countries are in the throes of an ongoing demographic explosion. Niger saw its

Figure 3.5 In high-income countries, the elderly population is growing, whereas the working-age population is declining

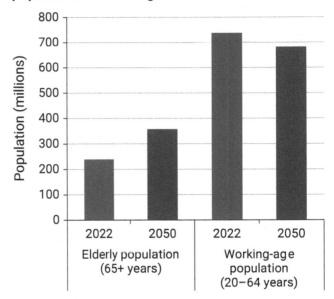

Source: WDR 2023 team calculations, based on the medium fertility scenario, World Population Prospects 2022 (dashboard), Population Division, Department of Economic and Social Affairs, United Nations, New York, https://population.un.org/wpp/, applied to country income groups in Hamadeh et al. (2022).

Figure 3.6 By 2050, in the high-income OECD countries there will be fewer than two working-age individuals to support every elderly person

Ratio of working-age population (20–64 years) to elderly (65+ years)

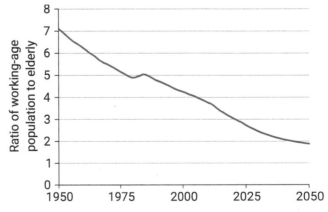

Source: WDR 2023 team calculations, based on the medium fertility scenario, World Population Prospects 2022 (dashboard), Population Division, Department of Economic and Social Affairs, United Nations, New York, https://population.un.org/wpp/, applied to country income groups in Hamadeh et al. (2022).
Note: OECD = Organisation for Economic Co-operation and Development.

Figure 3.7 The number of children born per woman is declining rapidly in middle-income countries

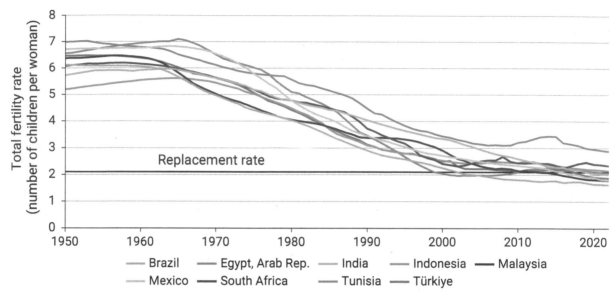

Source: WDR 2023 team calculations, based on the medium fertility scenario, World Population Prospects 2022 (dashboard), Population Division, Department of Economic and Social Affairs, United Nations, New York, https://population.un.org/wpp/.

Figure 3.8 Many upper-middle-income countries are reaching shares of elderly usually seen in higher-income countries

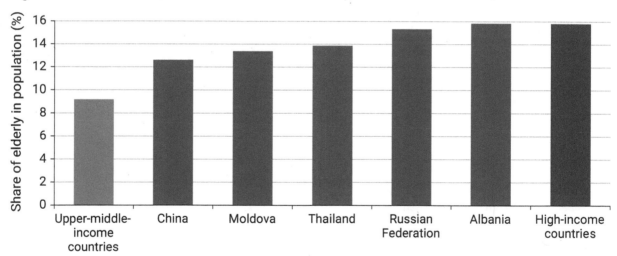

Source: WDR 2023 team calculations, based on the medium fertility scenario, World Population Prospects 2022 (dashboard), Population Division, Department of Economic and Social Affairs, United Nations, New York, https://population.un.org/wpp/, applied to country income groups in Hamadeh et al. (2022).
Note: Elderly are defined as those age 65 and above.

population of 3 million in 1960 rise to 24 million in 2020.[19] In the same period, the population of the Republic of Yemen climbed from 5 million to 30 million.[20] Fertility rates remain very high, with more than six children per woman in Niger, for example.[21] Looking ahead, Sub-Saharan Africa—where most low-income countries are located—is expected to be the only region whose population will continue to grow after 2050, whereas population numbers will gradually decline in the rest of the world (figure 3.9).

Sub-Saharan Africa is also expected to be the only region where the number of children under age five will exceed the number of elderly (age 65 and above) by midcentury.

In the absence of emigration, low- and lower-middle-income countries are expected to add 1.05 billion people to their working-age populations by 2050.[22] Many of these economies are unlikely to grow sufficiently fast to generate the jobs needed to absorb their young and growing populations.[23] They will need additional mechanisms to relieve pressures on the labor market and to offer their youth development opportunities.

Development, prosperity, and the need for migration

Demographic changes are rapidly leading to a global competition for workers. In high- and middle-income countries, the needs for labor are sizable. Low-income countries have large numbers of unemployed or underemployed youth, but only some have the skills in demand in the global labor market. The potential mismatches of labor demand and supply across countries are sizable. Most countries have to face difficult realities if they are to continue to develop or prosper.

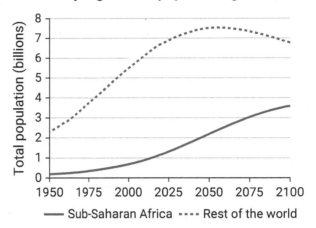

Figure 3.9 By 2050, Sub-Saharan Africa will be the only region with population growth

Source: WDR 2023 team calculations, based on the medium fertility scenario, World Population Prospects 2022 (dashboard), Population Division, Department of Economic and Social Affairs, United Nations, New York, https://population .un.org/wpp/, applied to World Bank regional groups.

Technological change, higher labor force participation, natalist policies, and pension reforms can help meet the labor needs of high- and middle-income countries, but often they will not be sufficient:

- *Technological change.* Automation and technological innovations can improve the productivity of workers and thus compensate for their dwindling numbers. Such changes are profoundly reshaping large swathes of the global economy, but significant needs will remain (box 3.1).
- *Higher labor force participation.* In some countries, labor force participation can be increased, especially for women in aging middle-income countries where participation is lower. For example, Italy, Greece, and Korea could potentially increase the participation of women in their labor markets. Yet the scope for such changes is somewhat limited in many high-income countries, where labor force participation is already high.[24]
- *Natalist policies.* Natalist policies have had a mixed and relatively limited impact across countries.[25] Because the demographic decline is already well advanced, it is not likely to be reversed soon, if at all. Italy, for example, currently has about 2.4 million girls under the age of nine. Each of these girls would need to have 3.3 children if they were to build a generation as large as that of their parents—a dramatic increase in the fertility rate from the current 1.3. Similarly, the fertility rate would have to increase from 1.34 to 3.17 in Thailand and from 0.89 to 4.7 in Korea.
- *Pension reforms.* Several countries have raised or are considering raising the age of retirement. In high-income OECD countries, the working age (20–64 years) to elderly ratio was 2.9 in 2022, and it is likely to fall to 1.85 by 2050. To maintain about the same ratio in 2050, the retirement age would have to increase by an average of seven years. The current public opposition to reform proposals regarding the retirement age and welfare programs in many Western European countries indicates this will not be an easy process.[26]

Box 3.1 Can technology solve labor market mismatches across countries?

Automation and technological innovations have transformed the demand for labor in a process that has led to employment polarization.[a] Automation has largely replaced labor employed in routine tasks that are easy to codify and program. This development has reduced the demand for some intermediate-skilled workers such as bank tellers.

But it has increased the demand for both relatively higher- and lower-skilled workers, such as engineers and construction workers, to carry out tasks that a machine cannot perform—typically nonroutine tasks that are analytical, creative, interpersonal, or physical.

The adoption of technology has also been dependent on the availability of migrant labor in agriculture and manufacturing, for example. Cheap migrant labor reduces the incentives for firms to automate their production processes. In China and the United States, when migrant labor becomes more readily available, firms use less automation and switch to labor-intensive production. Conversely, scarce migrant labor induces firms to automate. When the Bracero program, which arranged agricultural migration between the United States and Mexico, was terminated in 1964, firms switched to greater mechanization in the production of some crops, such as tomatoes and cotton, for which they had relied on migrant labor.[b]

Rapid advances in technology, particularly in artificial intelligence and robotics, are continually changing the frontier of what can be automated. Occupations employing large numbers of people

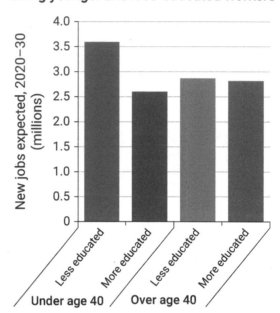

Figure B3.1.1 US employment growth is expected to be higher for occupations having younger and less-educated workers

Sources: WDR 2023 team calculations, based on data from Employment Projections (dashboard), Bureau of Labor Statistics, US Department of Labor, Washington, DC, https://www.bls.gov/emp/, and 2019 one-year estimates from American Community Survey (dashboard), US Census Bureau, Suitland, MD, https://www.census.gov/programs-surveys/acs.

Note: The number of new jobs is calculated based on the current percentage of workers from each demographic category in more than 800 occupations and assumes that shares in each occupation will remain constant.

today will likely be automated in the coming decades. That automation will transform the demand for labor and further push people into tasks that cannot be automated—some of which may not yet exist.[c]

Automation and technological innovations are, however, unlikely to fully offset the increase in demand for workers in aging countries. Aging populations generate demand for personal services that currently are difficult to automate. For example, the top nine occupations in the United States, which account for one-third of the expected net job creation between 2020 and 2030, are all in food services, health care services, freight, or software development, which cannot be easily automated.[d] Many of these occupations require younger and relatively less-educated workers (figure B3.1.1). A number of occupations

(Box continues next page)

Box 3.1 Can technology solve labor market mismatches across countries? *(continued)*

identified by the European Commission as essential during the COVID-19 pandemic also rely heavily on migrant labor.[e]

How much will the COVID-19 pandemic change this picture? It may be too early to tell. During the pandemic, many companies switched to telework and made significant investments in the necessary digital infrastructure. An estimated 30 percent of workers in Europe and 62 percent of workers in the United States have jobs that could eventually be done remotely. The reduction in technological barriers could lead firms to hire more "tele-migrants" in lower-wage countries, providing opportunities for people who otherwise would have migrated. However, this possibility is unlikely to have much impact on a number of occupations in which immigrants are engaged and where a physical presence is required, such as health care services or freight industries.[f]

a. For evidence on the impact of technological change on employment and wage polarization, see Autor, Levy, and Murnane (2003); Goos, Manning, and Salomons (2014); Michaels, Natraj, and Van Reenen (2014). For a review and synthesis, see Autor (2015); World Bank (2012, 2016b).

b. Clemens, Lewis, and Postel (2018).

c. See, for example, Acemoglu and Restrepo (2020); Brynjolfsson and McAfee (2014); Graetz and Michaels (2018).

d. Based on 2022 data of Occupational Outlook Handbook (portal), Office of Occupational Statistics and Employment Projections, Bureau of Labor Statistics, US Department of Labor, Washington, DC, https://www.bls.gov/ooh/.

e. Fasani and Mazza (2020).

f. Brenan (2020); Dingel and Neiman (2020); ILO (2020); Ottaviano, Peri, and Wright (2013).

In many high-income countries, increased immigration will have to be part of the response to demographic changes. German government officials have repeatedly stated that their country's economy needs an annual infusion of 400,000 foreign workers with diverse skills.[27] Japan's decision to admit up to 345,000 foreign workers over a five-year period starting in mid-2019 similarly reflects the country's urgent labor needs.

The needs are growing in middle-income countries as well. Many of these countries were once sources of migration, but with declining fertility rates and rapidly aging populations they will need foreign labor—and even more so if some of their citizens continue to emigrate to high-income countries. For example, Malaysia, Mexico, and Türkiye are becoming destination countries, typically for migrants from lower-income countries in the same region. Policies will have to be adapted to these changing circumstances, thereby requiring a shift of perspective for policy makers and society at large.

Yet to fulfill labor market needs, migrants must possess the skills and attributes needed to match the demand in destination societies. This has proved to be a challenge in some situations. For example, Korea launched a program to temporarily admit migrant workers—the Employment Permit System—but it was able to fill only half of the posted vacancies in 2015 despite an oversupply of applicants from South and Southeast Asia.[28] There may be more opportunities for migration, but only to the extent that would-be migrants can acquire skills that are in demand in destination countries. Countries, especially low-income, urgently need to develop transferable, marketable skills.

Climate change: New risks of distressed movements

Climate change poses an unprecedented and growing threat to human societies. Global warming has already reached approximately 1 degree Celsius above preindustrial levels. At current rates, it is likely to reach 1.5 degrees Celsius between 2030 and 2050.[29] Rising global temperatures have contributed to more frequent and severe extreme weather events around the world, including heat waves, drought, heavy precipitation, floods, and storms. Such disasters can reverse decades of development progress. Climate change is also manifested in slow-onset impacts, such as shifts in temperature and precipitation patterns, sea level rise, and ocean warming.[30] These impacts have documented development effects on a wide range of outcomes such as health, income, food security, water supply, and overall human security.[31] Approximately 40 percent of the world's population—about 3.5 billion people—already live in places highly vulnerable to climate change.[32]

Climate change has emerged as a compounding driver of mobility (figure 3.10). Climate impacts affect the very habitability and income productivity of some regions. But climate impacts can rarely be isolated from other drivers of mobility such as poverty, demographics, or political instability. Many people migrate because of a combination of factors that climate impacts exacerbate rather than climate change alone. Climate impacts often amplify preexisting patterns of movements—circular, seasonal, and rural-to-urban migration.[33]

Figure 3.10 Climate change affects migration through income and habitability

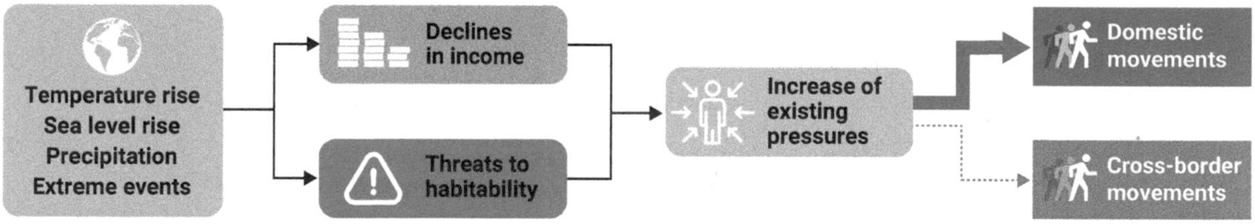

Source: WDR 2023 team.

Climate change is already accelerating internal migration through both sudden- and slow-onset impacts. These effects are expected to grow over time.[34] Sudden-onset extreme weather events displaced over 300 million people within their countries over the last 15 years.[35] In 2022, most new and repeated displacements were recorded in Asia, where tropical cyclones, monsoon rains, and floods hit highly exposed areas that are home to millions of people.[36] Slow-onset climate impacts are also triggering large movements and reshaping where people live in a country because of water stresses and sea level rise, among other things.[37] Projections to 2050 of climate-related internal migration across developing countries range from 44 million to 216 million people under different climate, demographic, and development scenarios.[38]

Climate change also affects the characteristics of who migrates, their skills, and human capital. For example, it can lead to an increase in distressed movements.[39] Climate impacts also affect men and women differently, which, in turn, affects their mobility.[40] Some people, however, may not be able to move because they lack the means to do so, and climate change may actually further impoverish them and trap them in place,[41] especially poorer households who live in highly exposed locations.[42] Finally, migrants from rural regions that experience successive episodes of water scarcity, for example, have lower skills than other migrants, especially where migration tends to be a last resort option such as in Brazil, Indonesia, and Mexico.[43]

So far, climate-related cross-border migration has occurred on a smaller scale than internal move-ments.[44] When they happen, cross-border movements typically take place between neighboring coun-tries or between countries that have agreements governing labor migration, strong diaspora networks, or long-standing economic and cultural ties.[45] For example, migration to the United States from Central America or the Caribbean has increased after climate disasters, especially from countries with larger numbers of US immigrants.[46] When they cannot successfully adapt to climate change in their country of origin, some people have to leave under distressed circumstances (box 3.2).[47]

Box 3.2 Compounded drivers of migration in Sub-Saharan Africa

The various drivers of migration cannot be analyzed independently. Poverty, state fragility, population growth, and climate change often reinforce one another (figure B3.2.1). For example, when climate impacts deplete natural resources, poverty increases. If the population is growing rapidly, the situation becomes worse.[a] In addition, various groups may have to compete for the dwindling resources, which can fuel social tensions and violence and further aggravate poverty. This combination of factors can compel people to move to better locations, either domestically or, if they can mobilize the necessary resources, internationally. Both the drivers and their interplay determine outcomes.

Sub-Saharan Africa is facing pressures on all dimensions at once (map B3.2.1). The region has the lowest average per capita income in the world, the fastest demographic growth, the largest num-ber of fragile and conflict-affected countries, and

Figure B3.2.1 Some intertwined drivers of mobility

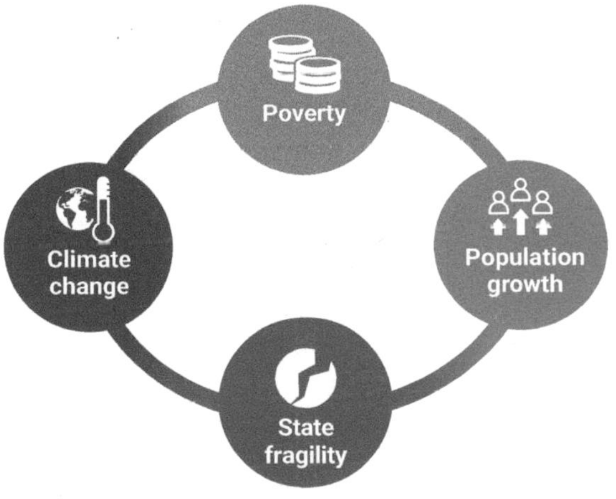

Source: WDR 2023 team.

the highest vulnerability to climate change. The population is expected to grow from 1.2 billion today to 2.5 billion in 2050.[b] Climate change alone has led to a 34 percent reduction in agricultural productivity growth since 1961,[c] with severe consequences for food security.[d] About half of all countries are affected by conflict or institutional fragility. As a result, Sub-Saharan Africa is likely to see further movements in the coming decades, some under distressed circumstances.

The Sahel exemplifies the challenges. Burkina Faso, Chad, Mali, Mauritania, and Niger are among the world's poorest countries. Their fertility rates are among the highest globally—about six births per woman in 2020—and their population doubles every 22 years. At the same time, the region's perennial climate vulnerability has been aggravated by a rise in temperature. Climate change has disrupted traditional trans-humance routes,[e] which has led to clashes between herders and farmers.[f] The region is going through a period of acute fragility, with conflicts in Mali and Burkina Faso, as well as violence in Chad and Niger. Mali experienced coups d'état in 2020 and 2021, and Burkina Faso experienced two in 2022 alone. Millions of people have been forcibly displaced, with about 1 million refugees in the region and over 3 million internally displaced persons.[g] Many others have embarked on irregular and sometimes distressed movements as a coping strategy, either within the region or toward the European Union. The region's many vulnerabilities need to be tackled through a comprehensive development effort if migration is to be managed.

(Box continues next page)

Map B3.2.1 Sub-Saharan Africa is exposed to a combination of vulnerabilities

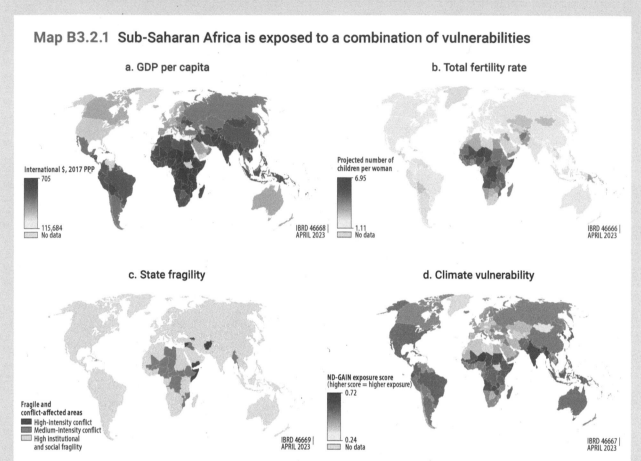

a. GDP per capita

International $, 2017 PPP
705

115,684
No data

IBRD 46668 |
APRIL 2023

b. Total fertility rate

Projected number of
children per woman
6.95

1.11
No data

IBRD 46666 |
APRIL 2023

c. State fragility

Fragile and
conflict-affected areas
High-intensity conflict
Medium-intensity conflict
High institutional
and social fragility

IBRD 46669 |
APRIL 2023

d. Climate vulnerability

ND-GAIN exposure score
(higher score = higher exposure)
0.72

0.24
No data

IBRD 46667 |
APRIL 2023

Sources: Panel a: World Bank 2019. Panel b: projections for 2015–20, World Population Prospects 2022 (dashboard), Population Division, Department of Economic and Social Affairs, United Nations, New York, https://population.un.org /wpp/. Panel c: World Bank 2022. Panel d: 2020 data of University of Notre Dame Global Adaptation Initiative (dashboard), University of Notre Dame, Notre Dame, IN, https://gain.nd.edu/our-work/country-index/.

Note: GDP = gross domestic product; ND-GAIN = Notre Dame Global Adaptation Initiative; PPP = purchasing power parity.

a. World Bank (2010).

b. World Population Prospects 2022 (dashboard), Population Division, Department of Economic and Social Affairs, United Nations, New York, https://population.un.org/wpp/.

c. WMO (2022).

d. IPC Mapping Tool, Integrated Food Security Phase Classification, Rome, https://www.ipcinfo.org/.

e. Liehr, Drees, and Hummel (2016).

f. Benjaminsen (2012); Benjaminsen and Ba (2009); Heinrigs (2010); McGuirk and Nunn (2020); Rigaud et al. (2021); Werz and Conley (2012).

g. R4Sahel Coordination Platform for Forced Displacements in Sahel, United Nations High Commissioner for Refugees, Geneva, https://data.unhcr.org/en/situations/sahelcrisis.

Lower rural productivity and incomes

Higher temperatures and increasingly unpredictable precipitation affect the productivity and viability of rural incomes and thus migration patterns.[48] For example, repeated periods without rainfall affect agricultural yields and income, leading to increased deprivation. Over time, as the options to adapt in place or move within the country are exhausted, some people choose to migrate across borders.[49] Such patterns are especially visible in countries exposed to multiple climate impacts and where incomes are highly dependent on climate patterns and the capacity to adapt is limited.[50] For example, in the Dry Corridor of Central America, which stretches from Panama to southern Mexico, lower precipitation and altered rainfall seasons have increasingly constrained rainfed subsistence farming, incomes, and food security since the 1950s, particularly for smallholder farmers.[51] Some households have used migration to the United States as one of several risk management strategies when other options are not available.[52]

Even with adaptation, certain areas could eventually become unsuitable for food production under high-emission scenarios.[53] In fact, some natural systems have already reached their limits, including some rain forests, coastal wetlands, and subpolar and mountain ecosystems, with dramatic consequences for the people who have relied on them for their sustenance, resources, and income.[54]

Threats to habitability

More than 1 billion people live in low-lying cities and settlements that are at risk from coastal climate impacts by 2050.[55] The global sea level has already risen an average of 0.20 meters since 1900, and the pace has accelerated since the late 1960s.[56] Coastal erosion, submergence of coastal land, losses of coastal habitats and ecosystems, and salinization—compounded by storm surges, floods, and other extreme weather events—are placing increasing numbers of people at risk. Globally, US$7–$14 trillion in coastal infrastructure assets could be at risk by 2100, depending on warming levels and the trajectories of socio-economic development.[57] Large coastal areas across South and Southeast Asia are already at risk, including densely populated regions, both urban and rural.[58] Some governments have begun to implement planned relocation programs away from highly exposed coastal areas, and such responses are becoming more frequent.[59]

Small Island Developing States are among the most threatened. In these states, sea levels are projected to rise by 0.15–0.40 meters by 2050 in worst-case scenarios,[60] thereby doubling the frequency of flooding in much of the Indian Ocean and Pacific islands and worsening the scarcity of freshwater supplies. Some low-lying Pacific atolls could be partly or completely submerged even with warming of 1.5 degrees Celsius.[61] In Kiribati, half of the population of 120,000 is located on the Tarawa atoll, which is at risk of being submerged as temperatures rise. Climate change also continues to put stress on terrestrial and marine ecosystems that are the backbone of key economic sectors, such as fisheries and tourism.[62]

Beyond coastal and low-lying areas, climate change also affects the habitability of vast regions across Africa, Asia, and Latin America. Millions of people are already exposed to acute food insecurity and reduced water security.[63] Human mortality and morbidity are increasing as a result of extreme heat events, aggravated urban air pollution, and the rising incidence of climate-sensitive diseases—whether food-borne, water-borne, or vector-borne.[64] Some cities are already facing water scarcity[65] at the very time large numbers of people are moving to urban areas across low- and middle-income countries.[66] In some parts of South Asia, tropical Sub-Saharan Africa, and Latin America, climate change is expected to reduce people's ability to work outdoors, which will have major economic and social impacts (map 3.1).[67]

Map 3.1 The areas where people can work outdoors are shrinking

Change in the number of days in which the heat index exceeds 35°C by 2050

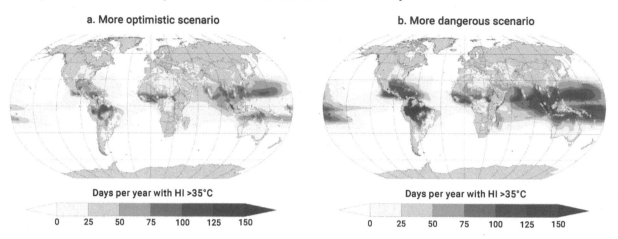

Source: 2022 data, Climate Change Knowledge Portal, World Bank, Washington, DC, https://climateknowledgeportal .worldbank.org/.

Note: The maps depict the change in the number of days (relative to a 1995–2014 reference period) in which the heat index (HI) exceeds 35°C by midcentury under two Intergovernmental Panel on Climate Change climate scenarios (IPCC 2021, 2022a). Panel a corresponds to a scenario in which the goals of the Paris Agreement are met (Shared Socioeconomic Pathway 1-1.9). Panel b corresponds to a scenario under which emissions roughly double from current levels by 2100 (Shared Socioeconomic Pathway 3-7.0).

Risks

Climate change could lead to large, distressed cross-border movements. The extent to which this happens will largely depend on the policies adopted and implemented today at both the global and the national level.

- *Climate mitigation.* The world is not on track to meet the 2 degrees Celsius goal of the Paris Agreement; it is still headed toward 2.8 degrees Celsius of warming by the end of the century.[68] The severity of future climate change impacts depends on the extent to which international collective action is able to curb global warming in the near term.[69] The risks posed to natural and human systems significantly increase with every increment of warming.[70] And past patterns of climate change may not fully predict future impacts. Beyond certain levels of global warming, there may be tipping points and runaway effects that have not yet been experienced.[71]
- *Climate adaptation.* The extent to which vulnerable countries can build resilience and adapt to climate change will largely hinge on the availability of the appropriate financial instruments. Some urban, resource-rich coastal areas may have the resources needed to implement engineering projects and protect themselves against such things as a sea level rise. By contrast, adaptation may be more difficult for poorer rural areas, and the risks of displacement and migration will be higher.[72] The 27th Conference of the Parties to the United Nations Framework Convention on Climate Change, held in 2022, reached a historic agreement on a global fund for losses and damages associated with the adverse effects of climate change. It is a promising example of collective action to help countries increase their adaptive capacity.
- *Migration and protection policies.* Migration can be a critical part of the broader response to climate change. This will, however, depend on destination countries' migration policies.[73] The most

difficult question is whether some of the people whose migration has been partly prompted by the compounding effects of climate change on other drivers of mobility should receive a form of international protection. This question is especially relevant for migrants who bring skills and attributes that only weakly match the demands of destination economies. There is no international legal framework to address this issue comprehensively. Such individuals are not covered by the already stretched system of international protection for refugees, who are fleeing persecution or conflict. Some destination countries have adopted or applied ad hoc protections, such as that offered by the United States to Hondurans after 1998 Hurricane Mitch.[74] The situation of Small Island Developing States may also call for an international response. A comprehensive approach that reflects both the necessary and the distressed nature of some of these movements is urgently needed.

Notes

1. Morland (2019, chap. 2).
2. World Population Prospects 2022 (dashboard), Population Division, Department of Economic and Social Affairs, United Nations, New York, https://population.un.org/wpp/.
3. UN DESA (2022).
4. UN DESA (2019).
5. World Population Prospects 2022 (dashboard), Population Division, Department of Economic and Social Affairs, United Nations, New York, https://population.un.org/wpp/.
6. World Population Prospects 2022 (dashboard), Population Division, Department of Economic and Social Affairs, United Nations, New York, https://population.un.org/wpp/.
7. World Population Prospects 2022 (dashboard), Population Division, Department of Economic and Social Affairs, United Nations, New York, https://population.un.org/wpp/.
8. Michel and Ecarnot (2020).
9. World Population Prospects 2022 (dashboard), Population Division, Department of Economic and Social Affairs, United Nations, New York, https://population.un.org/wpp/.
10. See Jones and Seitani (2019).
11. World Population Prospects 2022 (dashboard), Population Division, Department of Economic and Social Affairs, United Nations, New York, https://population.un.org/wpp/.
12. The fiscal impact of pension systems is expected to vary across countries based on the nature of these systems (such as defined benefits versus defined contributions and automatic adjustment mechanisms).
13. OECD (2019, figure 2.3); Rouzet et al. (2019).
14. Rouzet et al. (2019).
15. This calculation is in accordance with the calibrated overlapping generation life-cycle model of Heer, Polito, and Wickens (2020). See also Naumann (2014).
16. Johnston (2021); World Bank (2016a).
17. World Population Prospects 2022 (dashboard), Population Division, Department of Economic and Social Affairs, United Nations, New York, https://population.un.org/wpp/.
18. Rouzet et al. (2019).
19. World Population Prospects 2022 (dashboard), Population Division, Department of Economic and Social Affairs, United Nations, New York, https://population.un.org/wpp/.
20. World Population Prospects 2022 (dashboard), Population Division, Department of Economic and Social Affairs, United Nations, New York, https://population.un.org/wpp/.
21. "Fertility Rate, Total (Births per Woman): Niger," World Bank, Washington, DC, https://data.worldbank.org/indicator/SP.DYN.TFRT.IN?locations=NE.
22. World Population Prospects 2022 (dashboard), Population Division, Department of Economic and Social Affairs, United Nations, New York, https://population.un.org/wpp/.
23. Kremer, Willis, and You (2022).
24. "Labor Force Participation Rate (% of Population)," Gender Data Portal, World Bank, Washington, DC, https://genderdata.worldbank.org/indicators/sl-tlf-acti-zs/?age=15-64&view=trend.
25. Mills et al. (2011).
26. OECD (2021, chap. 3).
27. Economist (2022).
28. Cho et al. (2018).
29. IPCC (2018).
30. IPCC (2018, 4); WMO (2022, 32).
31. Clement et al. (2021, 2); Hallegatte, Rentschler, and Rozenberg (2020); IPCC (2022b).
32. Global Internal Displacement Database, Internal Displacement Monitoring Centre, Geneva, https://www.internal-displacement.org/database/displacement-data.
33. Black, Kniveton, and Schmidt-Verkerk (2011); Black et al. (2011); McLeman (2016).
34. IDMC (2021, 88); Rigaud et al. (2018, 1).
35. Of the 453.6 million new displacements between 2008 and 2021, 342.3 million were due to disasters, of which 305.6 million stemmed from weather-related disasters, and 111.3 million were due to conflict and violence. Weather-related disasters may consist of extreme temperatures, floods, storms, wildfires, drought, and landslides. Internal displacement refers to the forced

movement of people within the country in which they live. Internal displacements correspond to the estimated number of internal displacements over a given period of time (reporting year). The data may include individuals who have been displaced more than once. See Global Internal Displacement Database, Internal Displacement Monitoring Centre, Geneva, https://www.internal-displacement.org/database/displacement-data.

36. IDMC (2022, 27).
37. Clement et al. (2021, xxiv); Rigaud et al. (2018, chap. 4).
38. Clement et al. (2021, xxvii).
39. Hornbeck (2020).
40. See spotlight 4 for details. See also Gray and Bilsborrow (2013); Holland et al. (2017); Lama, Hamza, and Wester (2021); Miletto et al. (2017); Rigaud et al. (2018, 36); Šedová, Čizmaziová, and Cook (2021).
41. Cattaneo et al. (2019); Hoffmann et al. (2020); Šedová, Čizmaziová, and Cook (2021).
42. Leichenko and Silva (2014).
43. Barrios Puente, Perez, and Gitter (2016); Riosmena, Nawrotzki, and Hunter (2018); Zaveri et al. (2021).
44. Cissé et al. (2022, 1080).
45. Cissé et al. (2022, 1080).
46. Andrade Afonso (2011); Mahajan and Yang (2020); Spencer and Urquhart (2018).
47. Cattaneo and Peri (2016); IPCC (2022a, 1053); McLeman (2019); Veronis et al. (2018).
48. Bezner Kerr et al. (2022, 717); Nawrotzki and Bakhtsiyarava (2017); Wesselbaum (2021).
49. Abel, Muttarak, and Stephany (2022); McLeman (2018); Nawrotzki et al. (2017); Zaveri et al. (2021, 54).
50. Cattaneo et al. (2019); Hoffmann et al. (2020); Šedová, Čizmaziová, and Cook (2021).
51. See Hannah et al. (2017). The Dry Corridor is among the regions most sensitive to climate-related migration and displacement, which have increased in recent years because of a combination of drought, tropical storms and hurricanes, and heavy rains and floods that are interacting with social, political, conflict, violence, and economic drivers. See Bouroncle et al. (2017); Castellanos et al. (2022); Donatti et al. (2019).
52. Bermeo and Leblang (2021); Bouroncle et al. (2017); Donatti et al. (2019); Gray and Bilsborrow (2013); Koubi et al. (2016); Milan and Ruano (2014); Nawrotzki et al. (2016); Thiede, Gray, and Mueller (2016).
53. Bezner Kerr et al. (2022, 725).
54. See IPCC (2019, 235). Several atoll islands could potentially be uninhabitable because of sea level rise, combined with increased aridity and decreased freshwater availability at warming of 1.5 degrees Celsius.
55. Dodman et al. (2022).
56. IPCC (2021, 291).
57. Dodman et al. (2022).
58. Lincke and Hinkel (2021).
59. Cissé et al. (2022); IPCC (2022a, 1117; 2022b, 25).
60. Mycoo et al. (2022).
61. IPCC (2018).
62. Clement et al. (2021, 228).
63. IPCC (2022a).
64. IPCC (2022b, 11).
65. Tuholske et al. (2021).
66. Dodman et al. (2022).
67. Bezner Kerr et al. (2022, 797); de Lima et al. (2021); Foster et al. (2021).
68. UNEP (2022, xvi).
69. IPCC (2022c, 17).
70. IPCC (2018, chap. 3; 2022b, 14).
71. Hoffmann et al. (2020); Šedová, Čizmaziová, and Cook (2021).
72. Glavovic et al. (2022).
73. Benveniste, Oppenheimer, and Fleurbaey (2020); McLeman (2019); Obokata, Veronis, and McLeman (2014).
74. Paoletti (2023).

References

Abel, Guy J., Raya Muttarak, and Fabian Stephany. 2022. "Climatic Shocks and Internal Migration: Evidence from 442 Million Personal Records in 64 Countries." Water Global Practice, World Bank, Washington, DC.

Acemoglu, Daron, and Pascual Restrepo. 2020. "Robots and Jobs: Evidence from US Labor Markets." *Journal of Political Economy* 128 (6): 2188–2244.

Andrade Afonso, Onelica C. 2011. "Natural Disasters and Migration: Storms in Central America and the Caribbean and Immigration to the U.S." *Explorations: The UC Davis Undergraduate Research Journal* 14. https://explorations.ucdavis.edu/docs/2011/andrade.pdf.

Autor, David H. 2015. "Why Are There Still So Many Jobs? The History and Future of Workplace Automation." *Journal of Economic Perspectives* 29 (3): 3–30.

Autor, David H., Frank Levy, and Richard J. Murnane. 2003. "The Skill Content of Recent Technological Change: An Empirical Exploration." *Quarterly Journal of Economics* 118 (4): 1279–1333.

Barrios Puente, Gerónimo, Francisco Perez, and Robert J. Gitter. 2016. "The Effect of Rainfall on Migration from Mexico to the United States." *International Migration Review* 50 (4): 890–909.

Benjaminsen, Tor A. 2012. "The Sahel and the Climate Security Debate." In *Global Security Risks and West Africa: Development Challenges*, edited by Philipp Heinrigs and Marie Trémolières, 77–94. West African Studies Series. Paris: Organisation for Economic Co-operation and Development.

Benjaminsen, Tor A., and Boubacar Ba. 2009. "Farmer-Herder Conflicts, Pastoral Marginalisation, and Corruption: A Case Study from the Inland Niger Delta of Mali." *Geographical Journal* 175 (1): 71–81.

Benveniste, Hélène, Michael Oppenheimer, and Marc Fleurbaey. 2020. "Effect of Border Policy on Exposure and Vulnerability to Climate Change." *PNAS, Proceedings of the National Academy of Sciences* 117 (43): 26692–702.

Bermeo, Sarah, and David Leblang. 2021. "Honduras Migration: Climate Change, Violence, and Assistance." Policy Brief (March), Duke Center for International Development, Sanford School of Public Policy, Duke University, Durham, NC.

Bezner Kerr, Rachel, Toshihiro Hasegawa, Rodel Lasco, Indra Bhatt, Delphine Deryng, Aidan Farrell, Helen Gurney-Smith, et al. 2022. "Food, Fibre, and Other Ecosystem Products." In *Climate Change 2022: Impacts, Adaptation, and Vulnerability*, 713–906. Sixth Assessment Report. Geneva: Intergovernmental Panel on Climate Change; New York: Cambridge University Press.

Black, Richard, Stephen R. G. Bennett, Sandy M. Thomas, and John R. Beddington. 2011. "Migration as Adaptation." *Nature* 478 (7370): 447–49.

Black, Richard, Dominic Kniveton, and Kerstin Schmidt-Verkerk. 2011. "Migration and Climate Change: Towards an Integrated Assessment of Sensitivity." *Environment and Planning A: Economy and Space* 43 (2): 431–50.

Bouroncle, Claudia, Pablo Imbach, Beatriz Rodríguez-Sánchez, Claudia Medellín, Armando Martinez-Valle, and Peter Läderach. 2017. "Mapping Climate Change Adaptive Capacity and Vulnerability of Smallholder Agricultural Livelihoods in Central America: Ranking and Descriptive Approaches to Support Adaptation Strategies." *Climatic Change* 141 (1): 123–37.

Brenan, Megan. 2020. "U.S. Workers Discovering Affinity for Remote Work." *Gallup: Economy*, April 3, 2020. https://news.gallup.com/poll/306695/workers-discovering-affinity-remote-work.aspx.

Brynjolfsson, Erik, and Andrew McAfee. 2014. *The Second Machine Age: Work, Progress, and Prosperity in a Time of Brilliant Technologies*. New York: W. W. Norton.

Castellanos, Edwin Josue, Maria Fernanda Lemos, Laura Astigarraga, Noemi Chacón, Nicolás Cuvi, Christian Huggel, Liliana Raquel Miranda Sara, et al. 2022. "Central and South America." In *Climate Change 2022: Impacts, Adaptation, and Vulnerability*, 1689–1816. Sixth Assessment Report. Geneva: Intergovernmental Panel on Climate Change; New York: Cambridge University Press.

Cattaneo, Cristina, Michel Beine, Christiane J. Fröhlich, Dominic Kniveton, Inmaculada Martinez-Zarzoso, Marina Mastrorillo, Katrin Millock, Etienne Piguet, and Benjamin Schraven. 2019. "Human Migration in the Era of Climate Change." *Review of Environmental Economics and Policy* 13 (2): 189–206.

Cattaneo, Cristina, and Giovanni Peri. 2016. "The Migration Response to Increasing Temperatures." *Journal of Development Economics* 122 (September): 127–46.

Cho, Yoonyoung, Anastasiya Denisova, Soonhwa Yi, and Upasana Khadka. 2018. *Bilateral Arrangement of Temporary Labor Migration: Lessons from Korea's Employment Permit System*. Main Report. Washington, DC: World Bank.

Cissé, Guéladio, Robert McLeman, Helen Adams, Paulina Aldunce, Kathryn Bowen, Diarmid Campbell-Lendrum, Susan Clayton, et al. 2022. "Health, Wellbeing and the Changing Structure of Communities." In *Climate Change 2022: Impacts, Adaptation, and Vulnerability*, 1041–1170. Sixth Assessment Report. Geneva:

Intergovernmental Panel on Climate Change; New York: Cambridge University Press.

Clemens, Michael A., Ethan G. Lewis, and Hannah M. Postel. 2018. "Immigration Restrictions as Active Labor Market Policy: Evidence from the Mexican Bracero Exclusion." *American Economic Review* 108 (6): 1468–87.

Clement, Viviane, Kanta Kumari Rigaud, Alex de Sherbinin, Bryan Jones, Susana Adamo, Jacob Schewe, Nian Sadiq, and Elham Shabahat. 2021. *Groundswell Part 2: Acting on Internal Climate Migration*. Washington, DC: World Bank.

de Lima, Cicero Z., Jonathan R. Buzan, Frances C. Moore, Uris Lantz C. Baldos, Matthew Huber, and Thomas W. Hertel. 2021. "Heat Stress on Agricultural Workers Exacerbates Crop Impacts of Climate Change." *Environmental Research Letters* 16 (4): 044020.

Dingel, Jonathan I., and Brent Neiman. 2020. "How Many Jobs Can Be Done at Home?" NBER Working Paper 26948 (June), National Bureau of Economic Research, Cambridge, MA.

Dodman, David, Bronwyn Hayward, Mark Pelling, Vanesa Castán Broto, Winston Chow, Eric Chu, Richard Dawson, et al. 2022. "Cities, Settlements, and Key Infrastructure." In *Climate Change 2022: Impacts, Adaptation, and Vulnerability*, 907–1040. Sixth Assessment Report. Geneva: Intergovernmental Panel on Climate Change; New York: Cambridge University Press.

Donatti, Camila I., Celia A. Harvey, M. Ruth Martinez-Rodriguez, Raffaele Vignola, and Carlos Manuel Rodriguez. 2019. "Vulnerability of Smallholder Farmers to Climate Change in Central America and Mexico: Current Knowledge and Research Gaps." *Climate and Development* 11 (3): 264–86.

Economist. 2022. "There Are Not Enough Germans to Do the Jobs Germany Needs." *Europe: Willkommen*, October 6, 2022. https://www.economist.com/europe/2022/10/06/there-are-not-enough-germans-to-do-the-jobs-germany-needs.

Fasani, Francesco, and Jacopo Mazza. 2020. "Immigrant Key Workers: Their Contribution to Europe's COVID-19 Response." IZA Policy Paper 155 (April), Institute of Labor Economics, Bonn, Germany.

Foster, Josh, James W. Smallcombe, Simon Hodder, Ollie Jay, Andreas D. Flouris, Lars Nybo, and George Havenith. 2021. "An Advanced Empirical Model for Quantifying the Impact of Heat and Climate Change on Human Physical Work Capacity." *International Journal of Biometeorology* 65 (7): 1215–29.

Glavovic, Bruce, Richard Dawson, Winston Chow, Matthias Garschagen, Marjolijn Haasnoot, Chandni Singh, and Adelle Thomas. 2022. "Cross-Chapter Paper 2: Cities and Settlements by the Sea." In *Climate Change 2022: Impacts, Adaptation, and Vulnerability*, 2163–94. Sixth Assessment Report. Geneva: Intergovernmental Panel on Climate Change; New York: Cambridge University Press.

Goos, Maarten, Alan Manning, and Anna Salomons. 2014. "Explaining Job Polarization: Routine-Biased Technological Change and Offshoring." *American Economic Review* 104 (8): 2509–26.

Graetz, Georg, and Guy Michaels. 2018. "Robots at Work." *Review of Economics and Statistics* 100 (5): 753–68.

Gray, Clark, and Richard Bilsborrow. 2013. "Environmental Influences on Human Migration in Rural Ecuador." *Demography* 50 (4): 1217–41.

Hallegatte, Stéphane, Jun Erik Maruyama Rentschler, and Julie Rozenberg. 2020. *Adaptation Principles: A Guide for Designing Strategies for Climate Change Adaptation and Resilience*. Washington, DC: World Bank.

Hamadeh, Nada, Catherine Van Rompaey, Eric Metreau, and Shwetha Grace Eapen. 2022. "New World Bank Country Classifications by Income Level: 2022–2023." *Data Blog*, July 1, 2022. https://blogs.worldbank.org/open data/new-world-bank-country-classifications-income -level-2022-2023.

Hannah, Lee, Camila I. Donatti, Celia A. Harvey, Eric Alfaro, Daniel Andres Rodriguez, Claudia Bouroncle, Edwin Josue Castellanos, et al. 2017. "Regional Modeling of Climate Change Impacts on Smallholder Agriculture and Ecosystems in Central America." *Climatic Change* 141 (1): 29–45.

Heer, Burkhard, Vito Polito, and Michael R. Wickens. 2020. "Population Aging, Social Security and Fiscal Limits." *Journal of Economic Dynamics and Control* 116 (July): 103913.

Heinrigs, Philipp. 2010. "Security Implications of Climate Change in the Sahel Region: Policy Considerations." Sahel and West Africa Club, Organisation for Economic Co-operation and Development, Boulogne-Billancourt, France.

Hoffmann, Roman, Anna Dimitrova, Raya Muttarak, Jesus Crespo Cuaresma, and Jonas Peisker. 2020. "A Meta-Analysis of Country-Level Studies on Environmental Change and Migration." *Nature Climate Change* 10 (10): 904–12.

Holland, Margaret Buck, Sierra Zaid Shamer, Pablo Imbach, Juan Carlos Zamora, Claudia Medellin Moreno, Efraín J. Leguía Hidalgo, Camila I. Donatti, M. Ruth Martínez-Rodríguez, and Celia A. Harvey. 2017. "Mapping Adaptive Capacity and Smallholder Agriculture: Applying Expert Knowledge at the Landscape Scale." *Climatic Change* 141 (1): 139–53.

Hornbeck, Richard. 2020. "Dust Bowl Migrants: Identifying an Archetype." NBER Working Paper 27656 (August), National Bureau of Economic Research, Cambridge, MA.

IDMC (Internal Displacement Monitoring Centre). 2021. *Global Report on Internal Displacement 2021: Internal Displacement in a Changing Climate*. Geneva: IDMC.

IDMC (Internal Displacement Monitoring Centre). 2022. *Global Report on Internal Displacement 2022: Children and Youth in Internal Displacement*. Geneva: IDMC.

ILO (International Labour Organization). 2020. "Working from Home: Estimating the Worldwide Potential." ILO Policy Brief (April), ILO, Geneva.

IPCC (Intergovernmental Panel on Climate Change). 2018. "Special Report: Global Warming of 1.5 °C; Summary for Policymakers." IPCC, Geneva. https://www.ipcc.ch /sr15/.

IPCC (Intergovernmental Panel on Climate Change). 2019. *Global Warming of 1.5°C*. Geneva: IPCC; New York: Cambridge University Press. https://www.ipcc.ch/site /assets/uploads/sites/2/2022/06/SR15_Full_ Report_LR.pdf.

IPCC (Intergovernmental Panel on Climate Change). 2021. *Climate Change 2021: The Physical Science Basis*. Geneva: IPCC; New York: Cambridge University Press. https://report.ipcc.ch/ar6/wg1/IPCC_AR6_WGI_Full Report.pdf.

IPCC (Intergovernmental Panel on Climate Change). 2022a. *Climate Change 2022: Impacts, Adaptation, and Vulnerability*. Sixth Assessment Report. Geneva: IPCC; New York: Cambridge University Press. https://report.ipcc .ch/ar6/wg2/IPCC_AR6_WGII_FullReport.pdf.

IPCC (Intergovernmental Panel on Climate Change). 2022b. "Climate Change 2022: Impacts, Adaptation, and Vulnerability, Summary for Policymakers." IPCC, Geneva. https://www.ipcc.ch/report/ar6/wg2/.

IPCC (Intergovernmental Panel on Climate Change). 2022c. "Climate Change 2022: Mitigation of Climate Change; Summary for Policymakers." IPCC, Geneva. https:// www.ipcc.ch/report/ar6/wg3/downloads/report /IPCC_AR6_WGIII_SummaryForPolicymakers.pdf.

Johnston, Lauren A. 2021. "'Getting Old before Getting Rich': Origins and Policy Responses in China." *China: An International Journal* 19 (3): 91–111.

Jones, Randall S., and Haruki Seitani. 2019. "Labour Market Reform in Japan to Cope with a Shrinking and Ageing Population." OECD Economics Department Working Paper 1568 (September), Organisation for Economic Co-operation and Development, Paris.

Koubi, Vally, Gabriele Spilker, Lena Schaffer, and Tobias Böhmelt. 2016. "The Role of Environmental Perceptions in Migration Decision-Making: Evidence from Both Migrants and Non-Migrants in Five Developing Countries." *Population and Environment* 38 (2): 134–63.

Kremer, Michael R., Jack Willis, and Yang You. 2022. "Converging to Convergence." In *NBER Macroeconomics Annual*, vol. 36, edited by Martin S. Eichenbaum and Erik Hurst, 337–412. Cambridge, MA: National Bureau of Economic Research; Chicago: University of Chicago Press.

Lama, Phudoma, Mo Hamza, and Misse Wester. 2021. "Gendered Dimensions of Migration in Relation to Climate Change." *Climate and Development* 13 (4): 326–36.

Leichenko, Robin, and Julie A. Silva. 2014. "Climate Change and Poverty: Vulnerability, Impacts, and Alleviation Strategies." *WIREs Climate Change* 5 (4): 539–56.

Liehr, Stefan, Lukas Drees, and Diana Hummel. 2016. "Migration as Societal Response to Climate Change and Land Degradation in Mali and Senegal." In *Adaptation to Climate Change and Variability in Rural West Africa*, edited by Joseph A. Yaro and Jan Hesselberg, 147–69. Cham, Switzerland: Springer International.

Lincke, Daniel, and Jochen Hinkel. 2021. "Coastal Migration due to 21st Century Sea-Level Rise." *Earth's Future* 9 (5): e2020EF001965.

Mahajan, Parag, and Dean Yang. 2020. "Taken by Storm: Hurricanes, Migrant Networks, and US Immigration." *American Economic Journal: Applied Economics* 12 (2): 250–77.

McGuirk, Eoin F., and Nathan Nunn. 2020. "Transhumant Pastoralism, Climate Change, and Conflict in Africa." NBER Working Paper 28243 (December), National Bureau of Economic Research, Cambridge, MA.

McLeman, Robert. 2016. "Migration as Adaptation: Conceptual Origins, Recent Developments, and Future Directions." In *Migration, Risk Management and Climate Change: Evidence and Policy Responses*, edited by Andrea Milan, Benjamin Schraven, Koko Warner, and Noemi Cascone, 213–29. Global Migration Issues Series, vol. 6. Geneva: International Organization for Migration; Cham, Switzerland: Springer International.

McLeman, Robert. 2018. "Thresholds in Climate Migration." *Population and Environment* 39 (4): 319–38.

McLeman, Robert. 2019. "International Migration and Climate Adaptation in an Era of Hardening Borders." *Nature Climate Change* 9 (12): 911–18.

Michaels, Guy, Ashwini Natraj, and John Van Reenen. 2014. "Has ICT Polarized Skill Demand? Evidence from Eleven Countries over Twenty-Five Years." *Review of Economics and Statistics* 96 (1): 60–77.

Michel, Jean-Pierre, and Fiona Ecarnot. 2020. "The Shortage of Skilled Workers in Europe: Its Impact on Geriatric Medicine." *European Geriatric Medicine* 11 (3): 345–47.

Milan, Andrea, and Sergio Ruano. 2014. "Rainfall Variability, Food Insecurity and Migration in Cabricán, Guatemala." *Climate and Development* 6 (1): 61–68.

Miletto, Michela, Martina Angela Caretta, Francesca Maria Burchi, and Giulia Zanlucchi. 2017. "Migration and Its Interdependencies with Water Scarcity, Gender, and Youth Employment." World Water Assessment Programme, United Nations Educational, Scientific, and Cultural Organization, Paris.

Mills, Melinda, Ronald R. Rindfuss, Peter McDonald, Egbert te Velde, and ESHRE Reproduction and Society Task Force. 2011. "Why Do People Postpone Parenthood? Reasons and Social Policy Incentives." *Human Reproduction Update* 17 (6): 848–60.

Morland, Paul. 2019. *The Human Tide: How Population Shaped the Modern World*. New York: PublicAffairs.

Mycoo, Michelle, Morgan Wairiu, Donovan Campbell, Virginie Duvat, Yimnang Golbuu, Shobha Maharaj, Johanna Nalau, Patrick Nunn, John Pinnegar, and Olivia Warrick. 2022. "Small Islands." In *Climate Change 2022: Impacts, Adaptation, and Vulnerability*, 2043–2121. Sixth Assessment Report. Geneva: Intergovernmental Panel on Climate Change; New York: Cambridge University Press.

Naumann, Elias. 2014. "Raising the Retirement Age: Retrenchment, Feedback and Attitudes." In *How Welfare States Shape the Democratic Public: Policy Feedback, Participation, Voting and Attitudes*, edited by Staffan Kumlin and Isabelle Stadelmann-Steffen, 223–43. Globalization and Welfare Series. Cheltenham, UK: Edward Elgar Publishing.

Nawrotzki, Raphael J., and Maryia Bakhtsiyarava. 2017. "International Climate Migration: Evidence for the Climate Inhibitor Mechanism and the Agricultural Pathway." *Population, Space, and Place* 23 (4): e2033.

Nawrotzki, Raphael J., Jack DeWaard, Maryia Bakhtsiyarava, and Jasmine Trang Ha. 2017. "Climate Shocks and Rural-Urban Migration in Mexico: Exploring Nonlinearities and Thresholds." *Climatic Change* 140 (2): 243–58.

Nawrotzki, Raphael J., Daniel M. Runfola, Lori M. Hunter, and Fernando Riosmena. 2016. "Domestic and International Climate Migration from Rural Mexico." *Human Ecology* 44 (6): 687–99.

Obokata, Reiko, Luisa Veronis, and Robert McLeman. 2014. "Empirical Research on International Environmental Migration: A Systematic Review." *Population and Environment* 36 (1): 111–35.

OECD (Organisation for Economic Co-operation and Development). 2019. *OECD Economic Surveys: Switzerland 2019*. Paris: OECD. https://doi.org/10.1787/7e6fd372-en.

OECD (Organisation for Economic Co-operation and Development). 2021. *Pensions at a Glance 2021: OECD and G20 Indicators*. Paris: OECD. https://www.oecd.org/publications/oecd-pensions-at-a-glance-19991363.htm.

Ottaviano, Gianmarco I. P., Giovanni Peri, and Greg C. Wright. 2013. "Immigration, Offshoring, and American Jobs." *American Economic Review* 103 (5): 1925–59.

Paoletti, Sarah. 2023. "Temporary Protected Status in the United States: An Incomplete and Imperfect Complementary System of Protection." Background paper prepared for *World Development Report 2023*, World Bank, Washington, DC.

Rigaud, Kanta Kumari, Alex de Sherbinin, Bryan Jones, Susana Adamo, David Maleki, Nathalie E. Abu-Ata, Anna Taeko Casals Fernandez, et al. 2021. *Groundswell Africa: Internal Climate Migration in West African Countries*. Washington, DC: World Bank.

Rigaud, Kanta Kumari, Alex de Sherbinin, Bryan Jones, Jonas Bergmann, Viviane Clement, Kayly Ober, Jacob Schewe, et al. 2018. *Groundswell: Preparing for Internal Climate Migration*. Washington, DC: World Bank.

Riosmena, Fernando, Raphael J. Nawrotzki, and Lori M. Hunter. 2018. "Climate Migration at the Height and End of the Great Mexican Emigration Era." *Population and Development Review* 44 (3): 455–88.

Rouzet, Dorothée, Aida Caldera Sánchez, Theodore Renault, and Oliver Roehn. 2019. "Fiscal Challenges and Inclusive Growth in Ageing Societies." OECD Economic Policy Paper 27 (September), Organisation for Economic Co-operation and Development, Paris.

Šedová, Barbora, Lucia Čizmaziová, and Athene Cook. 2021. "A Meta-Analysis of Climate Migration Literature." CEPA Discussion Paper 29 (March 18), Center for Economic Policy Analysis, Universität Potsdam, Potsdam, Germany.

Spencer, Nekeisha, and Mikhail-Ann Urquhart. 2018. "Hurricane Strikes and Migration: Evidence from Storms in Central America and the Caribbean." *Weather, Climate, and Society* 10 (3): 569–77.

Thiede, Brian, Clark Gray, and Valerie Mueller. 2016. "Climate Variability and Inter-provincial Migration in South America, 1970–2011." *Global Environmental Change* 41 (November): 228–40.

Tuholske, Cascade, Kelly Caylor, Chris Funk, Andrew Verdin, Stuart Sweeney, Kathryn Grace, Pete Peterson, and Tom Evans. 2021. "Global Urban Population Exposure to Extreme Heat." *PNAS, Proceedings of the National Academy of Sciences* 118 (41): e2024792118.

UN DESA (United Nations Department of Economic and Social Affairs). 2019. "World Population Prospects 2019:

Highlights." Document ST/ESA/SER.A/423, United Nations, New York. https://population.un.org/wpp /publications/files/wpp2019_highlights.pdf.

UN DESA (United Nations Department of Economic and Social Affairs). 2022. "World Population Prospects 2022: Summary of Results." Document UN DESA/POP/2021/ TR/NO. 3, United Nations, New York. https://www.un.org /development/desa/pd/sites/www.un.org.development .desa.pd/files/wpp2022_summary_of_results.pdf.

UNEP (United Nations Environment Programme). 2022. *Emissions Gap Report 2022: The Closing Window, Climate Crisis Calls for Rapid Transformation of Societies.* Nairobi, Kenya: UNEP. https://www.unep.org/resources /emissions-gap-report-2022.

Veronis, Luisa, Bonnie Boyd, Reiko Obokata, and Brittany Main. 2018. "Environmental Change and International Migration: A Review." In *Routledge Handbook of Environmental Displacement and Migration,* edited by Robert McLeman and François Gemenne, 42–70. Routledge Environment and Sustainability Handbooks Series. London: Routledge.

Werz, Michael, and Laura Conley. 2012. "Climate Change, Migration, and Conflict in Northwest Africa: Rising Dangers and Policy Options across the Arc of Tension." Climate Migration Series, Center for American Progress, Washington, DC.

Wesselbaum, Dennis. 2021. "Revisiting the Climate Driver and Inhibitor Mechanisms of International Migration." *Climate and Development* 13 (1): 10–20.

WMO (World Meteorological Organization). 2022. "State of the Climate in Africa 2021." WMO 1300, WMO, Geneva.

World Bank. 2010. "Determinants and Consequences of High Fertility: A Synopsis of the Evidence." Portfolio Review (June), World Bank, Washington, DC.

World Bank. 2012. *World Development Report 2013: Jobs.* Washington, DC: World Bank.

World Bank. 2016a. *Live Long and Prosper: Aging in East Asia and Pacific.* World Bank East Asia and Pacific Regional Report. Washington, DC: World Bank.

World Bank. 2016b. *World Development Report 2016: Digital Dividends.* Washington, DC: World Bank.

World Bank. 2019. *World Development Report 2019: The Changing Nature of Work.* Washington, DC: World Bank.

World Bank. 2022. "Classification of Fragile and Conflict-Affected Situations." *Brief*, July 1, 2022. https://www .worldbank.org/en/topic/fragilityconflictviolence/brief /harmonized-list-of-fragile-situations.

Zaveri, Esha, Jason Russ, Amjad Khan, Richard Damania, Edoardo Borgomeo, and Anders Jägerskog. 2021. *Water, Migration, and Development.* Vol. 1 of *Ebb and Flow.* Washington, DC: World Bank.

Spotlight 3
—
Methodological considerations

The evidence presented in this Report relies on analyses of the effects of migration and migration policies on migrants and refugees, as well as on origin and destination societies. However, a rigorous assessment of such effects is difficult. The difficulties often underpin the debates in the academic community, but even more so among practitioners, policy makers, and political stakeholders. Attributing specific economic or social effects to migration requires resolving complex methodological challenges.

Benchmarking challenges

Determining the effects of migration in a rigorous manner—whether on migrants, refugees, or origin and destination societies—would require comparing two situations: one with a certain set of migration policies and an identical one without those policies. In practice, however, there are no such identical situations. For researchers and practitioners alike, the challenge is to identify situations that can provide suitable comparisons or benchmarks and to correct for possible biases.[1]

A second methodological challenge arises from the diversity of situations among migrants and refugees, as well as among origin and destination societies. Transposing the conclusions of an analysis conducted in a specific context and at a specific point in time to another context and time is not obvious (it is often referred to as assessing the external validity of the results of a study). For example, to what extent are the results of a cash transfer program for Syrian refugees in Türkiye informative when considering similar programs for Somali refugees in the Republic of Yemen? In large part due to the availability of data, most academic studies, including many of those discussed in this Report, have focused on the impacts of migration to high-income countries such as the United States or those in the European Union. Furthermore, some studies were conducted in the recent or distant past. Applying such findings to current low- and middle-income contexts requires careful consideration of their external validity.

Migrants

Migrants differ from nonmigrants in many dimensions such as income, wealth, education, age, and connections abroad, as well as abilities, drive, desires, risk preferences, and motivations. Even when people move under duress, some of these factors matter. Comparing a migrant with a nonmigrant who stayed in the origin country to determine the effect of migration is thus potentially misleading. For example, in some contexts migrants are more willing than nonmigrants to take risks. They may have higher earnings than nonmigrants after they migrate, but is it because they migrated, or is it because they were willing to take risks in the first place? Similarly, comparing a migrant with a citizen, for example, to assess the effects of their distinct status can also be erroneous. Citizens may have distinct characteristics that explain differences in outcomes, such as when young people move to aging countries.

To address such issues, researchers have made various attempts to construct comparison benchmarks that included but were not limited to the following:

- *Learn from a migration lottery that allocates visas randomly among those who apply.* The average characteristics of those who migrated (those who obtained a visa) are similar to the characteristics of those who did not. The differences in their respective outcomes, such as their poverty levels after several years, can thus be attributed to the effects of migration. This approach was used for studies of permanent migration from Tonga to New Zealand;[2] of temporary work migration from Bangladesh to Malaysia;[3] and of skills training and placement in a randomized controlled trial for Indian workers in India interested in hospitality jobs in Gulf Cooperation Council countries.[4]

- *Measure differences in outcomes between migrants and nonmigrants that are comparable.* For example, the Republic of Korea offered visas to migrants whose Korean language test scores were above a given threshold.[5] Those who scored just above the threshold—and who migrated—were largely comparable with those who scored just below. Comparing outcomes between the two groups provides an appropriate benchmark to assess the effects of migration. Similar approaches have leveraged unanticipated changes in migration opportunities stemming from changes in host country policies[6] or fluctuations in exchange rates for remittances.[7] In such instances, those who are less affected can serve as a benchmark for those who are more so.

- *Use available data on migrant and nonmigrant characteristics to disentangle the effects of migration from those of other factors.* For example, individuals—migrants and nonmigrants—with similar education, age, location of origin, household profile, and other features for which data are available can be compared. But interpreting such comparisons can be difficult because some important factors—such as motivation or entrepreneurial spirit—are difficult to observe and quantify. The interpretation of the results thus must account for possible biases.[8]

Societies

The same difficulty applies when examining the impact of migration on origin and destination societies. The questions are similar: to what extent can specific effects be attributed to migration? For example, if regions that receive large numbers of migrants fare better than others economically, is it because of migrants' contributions? Or perhaps it is the other way around—migrants went primarily to regions that were already booming.

In principle, such questions could be addressed by comparing outcomes in migrant-receiving (or migrant-sending) communities with those in identical communities not affected by migration. However, such identical communities rarely exist. Societies or communities that receive migrants may have strong sociocultural or historical ties with migrants (or their origin communities) or thriving economies, compared with those that do not. Likewise, communities of origin may differ from other communities in terms of their economies or networks with potential destinations. The very factors that make them the origins of or destinations for migrants differentiate them from other communities.

To construct benchmarks against which migration effects can be assessed, researchers have used different approaches that include but are not limited to the following:

- *Draw lessons from countries' implementation of dispersal policies that settled migrants or refugees in different localities within the territory in a random manner.* Because the allocation was random, destination communities can be compared with other communities that were candidates to host migrants but ended up with none or only very few. Random dispersal policies adopted in countries such as Denmark or Sweden led to multiple studies on the impact of immigration.[9]

- *Rely on "natural experiments" that may have prompted migration to certain regions such as sudden policy changes (for example, sudden naturalizations), economic shocks, or catastrophic weather events.* An influential early study of the impact of immigration on wages was based on the sudden arrival of Cuban refugees into Miami between April and October 1980, when the Cuban government allowed anyone who wanted to leave the country to do so (the so-called Mariel boatlift).[10] Similar studies were conducted of the immigration of Jews from the Soviet Union to Israel in the 1970s and 1980s.
- *Compare areas with and without preexisting settlement patterns by some ethnic groups.*[11] Immigrants are more likely to move to areas already settled by co-ethnic households. In practice, when implemented correctly[12] this exercise enables comparison of areas that might otherwise be similar in economic terms but have different migration inflows due to earlier settlements. Applications of such an approach include evaluation of the effects of European immigration to US cities between 1910 and 1930 and the effects of Syrian refugee migration on labor markets in Türkiye.[13]
- *Track outcomes over time and evaluate whether localities with more migrants evolved differently than those with fewer or no migrants.* The localities with more migrants should also be compared with ones similar in characteristics for which data are available (such as size of the economy, population, and distance to major trading centers). However, it is still possible that other characteristics—such as governance quality and geography—could explain in part differences in outcomes and development trajectories, irrespective of immigration. Interpretations therefore should take into account such possible distortions.

Notes

1. See McKenzie and Yang (2022) for a detailed review of methodological challenges.
2. Gibson, McKenzie, and Stillman (2011).
3. Mobarak, Sharif, and Shrestha (2021).
4. Gaikwad, Hanson, and Tóth (2021).
5. Clemens and Tiongson (2017).
6. Clemens (2019); Dinkelman and Mariotti (2016).
7. Yang (2008).
8. Clemens and Hunt (2019).
9. For example, see Dahlberg, Edmark, and Lundqvist (2012); Dustmann, Vasiljeva, and Damm (2019).
10. Card (1990). Borjas (2017) revisited Card's findings, and Dustmann, Schönberg, and Stuhler (2016) and Clemens and Hunt (2019) provided an explanation for the divergence in findings between Card (1990) and Borjas (2017). Further discussions of Card (1990) can be found in Angrist and Krueger (1999) and Peri and Yasenov (2019).
11. See Altonji and Card (1991) for a pioneering application of this idea, often referred to as the "shift-share instrument."
12. For a discussion of the methodological challenges of such an approach, see Goldsmith-Pinkham, Sorkin, and Swift (2020); Jaeger, Ruist, and Stuhler (2018).
13. See Altındağ, Bakış, and Rozo (2020); Del Carpio and Wagner (2015); Tabellini (2020).

References

Altındağ, Onur, Ozan Bakış, and Sandra Viviana Rozo. 2020. "Blessing or Burden? Impacts of Refugees on Businesses and the Informal Economy." *Journal of Development Economics* 146 (September): 102490.

Altonji, Joseph G., and David E. Card. 1991. "The Effects of Immigration on the Labor Market Outcomes of Less-Skilled Natives." In *Immigration, Trade, and the Labor Market*, edited by John M. Abowd and Richard B. Freeman, 201–34. National Bureau of Economic Research Project Report. Cambridge, MA: National Bureau of Economic Research; Chicago: University of Chicago Press.

Angrist, Joshua D., and Alan B. Krueger. 1999. "Empirical Strategies in Labor Economics." In *Handbook of Labor Economics*, vol. 3A, edited by Orley C. Ashenfelter and David E. Card, 1277–1366. Handbooks in Economics Series 5. Amsterdam: North-Holland, Elsevier Science.

Borjas, George J. 2017. "The Wage Impact of the *Marielitos*: A Reappraisal." *Industrial and Labor Relations Review* 70 (5): 1077–110.

Card, David E. 1990. "The Impact of the Mariel Boatlift on the Miami Labor Market." *Industrial and Labor Relations Review* 43 (2): 245–57.

Clemens, Michael A. 2019. "Measuring the Spatial Misallocation of Labor: The Returns to India-Gulf Guest Work in a Natural Experiment." CGD Working Paper 501 (January), Center for Global Development, Washington, DC.

Clemens, Michael A., and Jennifer Hunt. 2019. "The Labor Market Effects of Refugee Waves: Reconciling Conflicting Results." *Industrial and Labor Relations Review* 72 (4): 818–57.

Clemens, Michael A., and Erwin R. Tiongson. 2017. "Split Decisions: Household Finance When a Policy Discontinuity Allocates Overseas Work." *Review of Economics and Statistics* 99 (3): 531–43.

Dahlberg, Matz, Karin Edmark, and Heléne Lundqvist. 2012. "Ethnic Diversity and Preferences for Redistribution." *Journal of Political Economy* 120 (1): 41–76.

Del Carpio, Ximena V., and Mathis Christoph Wagner. 2015. "The Impact of Syrians Refugees on the Turkish Labor Market." Policy Research Working Paper 7402, World Bank, Washington, DC.

Dinkelman, Taryn, and Martine Mariotti. 2016. "The Long-Run Effects of Labor Migration on Human Capital Formation in Communities of Origin." *American Economic Journal: Applied Economics* 8 (4): 1–35.

Dustmann, Christian, Uta Schönberg, and Jan Stuhler. 2016. "The Impact of Immigration: Why Do Studies Reach Such Different Results?" *Journal of Economic Perspectives* 30 (4): 31–56.

Dustmann, Christian, Kristine Vasiljeva, and Anna Piil Damm. 2019. "Refugee Migration and Electoral Outcomes." *Review of Economic Studies* 86 (5): 2035–91.

Gaikwad, Nikhar, Kolby Hanson, and Aliz Tóth. 2021. "How Overseas Opportunities Shape Political Preferences: A Field Experiment on International Migration." Paper presented at 2021 American Political Science Association Annual Meeting, Seattle, September 30–October 3, 2021.

Gibson, John, David J. McKenzie, and Steven Stillman. 2011. "The Impacts of International Migration on Remaining Household Members: Omnibus Results from a Migration Lottery Program." *Review of Economics and Statistics* 93 (4): 1297–1318.

Goldsmith-Pinkham, Paul, Isaac Sorkin, and Henry Swift. 2020. "Bartik Instruments: What, When, Why, and How." *American Economic Review* 110 (8): 2586–2624.

Jaeger, David A., Joakim Ruist, and Jan Stuhler. 2018. "Shift-Share Instruments and the Impact of Immigration." NBER Working Paper 24285 (February), National Bureau of Economic Research, Cambridge, MA.

McKenzie, David J., and Dean Yang. 2022. "Field and Natural Experiments in Migration." Policy Research Working Paper 10250, World Bank, Washington, DC.

Mobarak, Ahmed Mushfiq, Iffath Sharif, and Maheshwor Shrestha. 2021. "Returns to International Migration: Evidence from a Bangladesh-Malaysia Visa Lottery." IZA Discussion Paper DP 14232 (March), Institute of Labor Economics, Bonn, Germany.

Peri, Giovanni, and Vasil Yasenov. 2019. "The Labor Market Effects of a Refugee Wave: Synthetic Control Method Meets the Mariel Boatlift." *Journal of Human Resources* 54 (2): 267–309.

Tabellini, Marco. 2020. "Gifts of the Immigrants, Woes of the Natives: Lessons from the Age of Mass Migration." *Review of Economic Studies* 87 (1): 454–86.

Yang, Dean. 2008. "International Migration, Remittances, and Household Investment: Evidence from Philippine Migrants' Exchange Rate Shocks." *Economic Journal* 118 (528): 591–630.

Part 2

When the match is strong, the gains are large

When people bring skills and attributes that are in demand in their destination country, they fill gaps in that country's labor market, with benefits for the destination economy, themselves, and their country of origin. These benefits materialize regardless of migrants' motives for moving, skill levels, or legal status. There are costs as well, both social and economic, but typically they are much smaller than the gains. Both destination and origin countries can design and implement policies that further increase the gains and address the downsides.

This part is an overview of the evidence on the effects that economic migrants and refugees have on a destination economy when their skills and attributes match its labor needs. It also draws lessons from countries' experiences that can inform policy making.

Chapter 4 looks at migration from migrants' perspective. Migration has proved to be a powerful force in reducing poverty by means of enhanced opportunities, higher wages, and access to better services. When they return to their country of origin, many migrants fare better than comparable nonmigrants. But there are challenges as well, including those caused by family separation and, in some cases, social isolation. Some migrants find themselves in dire straits and in situations of exploitation. Policies by both origin and destination countries can help increase the benefits and mitigate the downsides.

Chapter 5 looks at the impact of migration on the countries of origin. A key finding of economic research is that when migrants succeed in their country of destination—when they have skills and attributes that are in demand in that country—their countries of origin gain as well. In a number of countries, emigration has contributed to poverty reduction and development, including through remittances and knowledge transfers. In some cases, however, especially in smaller and poorer economies, emigration of high-skilled individuals—often referred to as a "brain drain"—has had negative effects. Origin countries should therefore actively manage migration to maximize its development benefits.

Chapter 6 presents findings and lessons from destination countries. Migrants contribute to their destination economy's efficiency and growth, especially over the long term, which yields substantial gains. Destination countries' policies—in terms of both determining which migrants are allowed to enter and what status they receive—largely determine the size of these gains. Yet migrants are not just workers, and the question of their social integration has at times become a key part of the public debate. Here, too, success largely depends on destination countries' policies.

Part 2 includes three spotlights featuring important issues that contribute to the overall effects of cross-border movements. Spotlight 4 highlights some of the gender dimensions of cross-border movements, including gender norms, economic participation, and exposure to gender violence. Spotlight 5 examines the challenges in estimating remittances and underlines the need to improve the existing data. Finally, spotlight 6 reviews the effects of racism and xenophobia on migration outcomes.

Overall, the potential benefits of migration—for migrants as well as origin and destination societies—are sizable when people bring skills and attributes that are in demand. The benefits can be further increased by deliberate policy making in both the countries of origin and destination. This is the key message of this part.

4
Migrants
Prospering—and even more so with rights

Key messages

- International migration has proved to be a powerful engine of poverty reduction for people in low- and middle-income countries.

- When migrants' skills and attributes strongly match the needs of their destination society, they reap significant benefits (figure 4.1). Many migrants earn higher wages and enjoy access to better public services in the destination country than in their country of origin.

- Formal access to the labor market—documented status, the right to work and to change employers, recognition of professional licenses and qualifications—leads to better outcomes for migrants. Undocumented migrants fare significantly worse, and they are more vulnerable to exploitation.

- Migration is often not a one-way move; return migration is a significant phenomenon. Migrants who return voluntarily typically fare better than before they left—and better than nonmigrants.

Figure 4.1 When migrants' skills and attributes match the needs of destination societies, the gains are large

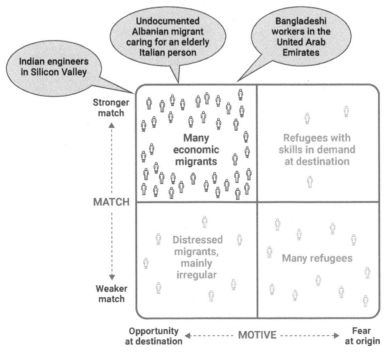

Source: WDR 2023 team.

Note: Match refers to the degree to which a migrant's skills and related attributes meet the demand in the destination country. *Motive* refers to the circumstances under which a person moves—whether in search of opportunity or because of a "well-founded fear" of persecution, armed conflict, or violence in their origin country.

Receiving higher wages

Migration leads to large wage increases for most people whose skills and attributes are a strong match with the needs of the destination society. These gains often exceed what could be achieved in the country of origin, even from internal migration to relatively better-off locations (figure 4.2). The gains are so large that at current rates of economic growth it would take decades for the average low-skilled person working in some countries of origin to earn the income they achieve by migrating to a high-income country (figure 4.3). These gains are then shared with families and communities in the countries of origin through remittances. For many migrants and their families, the income gains mean better living conditions and a greater ability to save and invest in businesses, housing, education, or health care.

Wage gaps between destination and origin countries are a key driver of economic migration. Even after adjusting for the differences in the cost of living, a truck driver in Canada earns over five times more than a truck driver in Mexico.[1] Nurses in Germany earn nearly seven times more than nurses in the Philippines.[2] A physician in Canada earns 20 times more than a physician in Zambia, around 10 times more than a physician in Côte d'Ivoire or Malawi, and about four times more than a physician in South Africa.[3] The potential gains are highest for people who move from low- to high-income countries.

The labor demand at the destination also shapes outcomes.[4] Gains depend on migrants' skills, gender, age, and language ability. Although the absolute gains are larger for high-skilled workers than for low-skilled workers, low-skilled workers experience a multifold increase in their income as well (figure 4.4, panel a). For example, low-skilled

Figure 4.2 In Bangladesh, Ghana, and India, income gains from international migration are many times greater than those from internal migration

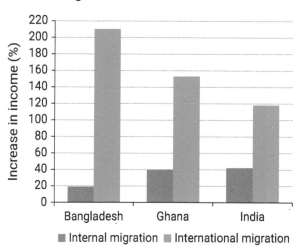

Sources: WDR 2023 team calculations, based on Akram, Chowdhury, and Mobarak (2017); Dercon, Krishnan, and Krutikova (2013); Gaikwad, Hanson, and Tóth (2023); Gibson and McKenzie (2012); Lagakos et al. (2020); Mobarak, Sharif, and Shrestha (2021).

Note: The income gains from international migration are based on experimental evidence from low-skilled migration to Malaysia from Bangladesh and to Gulf Cooperation Council (GCC) countries from India, as well as a survey of high-skilled migrants from Ghana to various destinations.

Figure 4.3 Decades of economic growth are needed in the country of origin for non-migrants to achieve the economic gains of migrants who moved to high-income countries

Number of years of economic growth in origin country needed to match economic gains of migrants in high-income countries

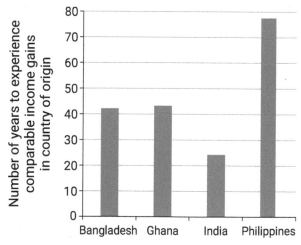

Sources: WDR 2023 team calculations. Gains from international migration: Clemens and Tiongson (2017); Gaikwad, Hanson, and Tóth (2023); Gibson and McKenzie (2012); Mobarak, Sharif, and Shrestha (2021). GDP per capita: World Development Indicators (dashboard), World Bank, Washington, DC, https://datatopics.worldbank.org/world-development-indicators/.

Note: Number of years of growth is calculated by dividing the income gains from international migration by the average annual growth in gross domestic product (GDP) per capita (in constant international dollars) from 2002 to 2021.

Yemenis and Nigerians moving to the United States increase their earnings by about 15 times (figure 4.4, panel b).[5] The gains achieved by low-skilled workers are higher when they move from a society with high socioeconomic inequalities to a country with fewer inequalities and where the difference in wages between low- and high-skilled workers is lower.[6]

Figure 4.4 **For low-skilled migrants, incomes surge at the destination**

a. Income gains for low-skilled workers, by migration corridor

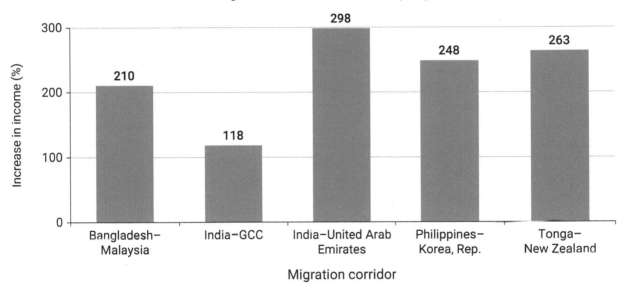

b. Income gains for low-skilled workers migrating to the United States, by origin country

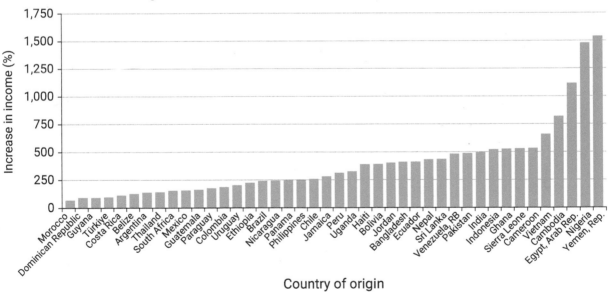

Sources: Panel a: Bangladesh–Malaysia: Mobarak, Sharif, and Shrestha (2021); India–Gulf Cooperation Council (GCC) countries: Gaikwad, Hanson, and Tóth (2023); India–United Arab Emirates (UAE): Clemens (2019); Philippines–Republic of Korea: Clemens and Tiongson (2017); Tonga–New Zealand: McKenzie, Stillman, and Gibson (2010). Panel b: Clemens, Montenegro, and Pritchett (2019).

Note: In panel a, income gains are taken from experimental studies. Percentage increases in income reflect comparisons in local currency. Incomes are not typically adjusted for purchasing power parity (PPP) because most spending continues to occur in the origin country through remittances, and in some cases expenses in destinations are covered under contractual agreements. One such estimate for the India–UAE corridor suggests that 85 percent of the earnings of Indian migrant workers in the UAE are spent in India. In panel b, percentage increases are calculated as real income gains for observably equivalent low-skilled male workers and adjusted for potential differences in unobservable characteristics.

Financial costs

Income gains are at times partly offset by the financial costs of moving, especially for the low-skilled.[7] Migrants incur a range of expenses before their departure, from the job information and job matching fees they pay to intermediary agents to the regulatory compliance or documentation fees (for a visa/sponsorship, medical tests, and security clearance), transportation costs, and predeparture training costs they must pay. For low-skilled migration, these costs tend to be borne by the workers, thereby contravening the principles of fair recruitment.[8] These costs tend to increase with the duration of contracts, and they limit the ability of many low-skilled workers to benefit from migration opportunities. Credit-constrained young and low-skilled workers are especially affected. For example, in Bangladesh halving the migration cost increases the migration rate of these workers by 29 percent.[9] In Pakistan, a 1 percent increase in recruitment costs resulted in a 0.15 percent reduction in remittances.[10]

Migration costs are particularly high along some corridors, especially for low-skilled South Asian workers moving to some Gulf Cooperation Council (GCC) countries. These costs can reach as much as 10 months of expected earnings, although they are also highly variable across corridors (figure 4.5). Migrant households tend to finance these costs by selling their assets or by borrowing money from informal lenders at above-market interest rates, thereby significantly diminishing the economic gains of their migration for themselves and their families.

The high costs incurred by low-skilled migrants moving to some GCC countries reflect not only direct costs but also payments to intermediaries who link them up with employers. By contrast, the costs of migrating from Southeast Asia to the Republic of Korea are significantly lower—about one month of expected earnings for low-skilled workers, thanks to bilateral labor agreements and government-led

Figure 4.5 South Asian workers moving to Gulf Cooperation Council countries face some of the highest migration costs

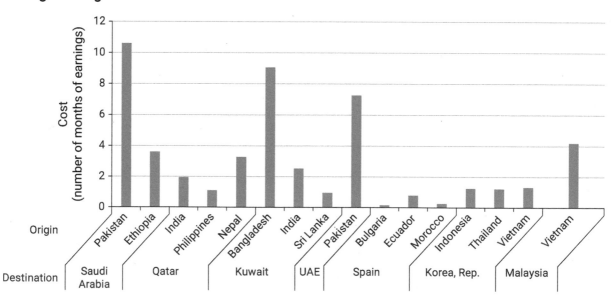

Source: WDR 2023 team calculations, based on World Bank KNOMAD migration cost database, https://www.knomad.org/data/recruitment-costs.

Note: All surveyed Sri Lankan workers in Kuwait were females engaged in domestic help services. UAE = United Arab Emirates.

job matching services that reduce recruitment fees. Some countries of origin, such as the Philippines, mandate that migrants pay no recruitment costs out of pocket, but their ability to enforce such arrangements is limited, and some migrant workers are charged through deductions in their salaries.

The importance of human capital

Many migrants do not realize income gains immediately, even when their skills and attributes match the needs of the destination society.[11] Those who move often differ from the average worker in the origin and destination labor markets in skills and personal characteristics such as risk tolerance, ambition, and entrepreneurship. However, they may lack the needed professional certifications, language skills, or social capital to enter the labor market at the destination at the average wage level. As a result, many migrants earn less than nationals with comparable education and professional characteristics, at least initially.[12] In a range of high-income countries, migrants are overrepresented in the location-based gig economy, which is easy to enter on arrival,[13] but the pay is low, and the prospects for advancement are limited.[14]

Some migrants face occupational or professional downgrading—that is, they cannot work in occupations commensurate with the diplomas or credentials they received outside of the destination country. This inability typically weakens the match between their skills and attributes and the needs of the destination economy. The extent of such "brain waste" depends on the quality of the education migrants received and on the transferability of the credentials they obtained.[15] Meanwhile, the longer migrants work in occupations below their skill level, the greater is the loss of skills and the more difficulty they face in catching up. Disruptions caused by migration and policies that restrict migrants' access to the labor market can further erode their human capital.

Over time, however, migrants' gains increase as they acquire human capital on and off the job,[16] and the match between their skills and attributes and the needs of the destination economy strengthens. Migrants who are better prepared before departure reap these larger gains more quickly. In the United States, those who start from a relatively lower basis—notably, those from low-income countries—enjoy faster wage growth and improvements in occupational quality than nationals or migrants from higher-income origin countries.[17] Through their engagement in the labor force, migrants acquire new skills and develop social networks that increase their income and open doors for professional advancement. Many migrants further invest in formal training while employed, especially if their credentials from their origin country are not fully recognized or are not relevant.[18] These opportunities are additional incentives for the highly skilled to migrate to higher-income destinations.[19]

Dedicated policies adapted to migrants' specific needs can help accelerate their inclusion in the labor market.[20] Recognition and certification of migrants' skills and experience influence how quickly they find a job and the extent of skill downgrading they experience. Training has positive impacts in the longer term, especially if combined with clear job prospects and interventions targeting other obstacles.[21] In high-income countries, counseling and wage subsidies have proved effective.[22]

The importance of rights

When migrants have legal and socioeconomic rights, their wages, employment levels, and job quality increase faster and gradually converge with those of nationals.[23] Migrants' gains—and their ability to contribute—depend on labor market conditions and the strength of the match of their skills and attributes with the needs of the destination economy, but also on the rights they receive in terms of labor market access.[24]

Secure prospects of stay, access to formal jobs, and complementary legal rights are critical to better labor market outcomes. To succeed, migrants often need to make certain investments specific to the destination country, such as learning a new language, establishing social and professional connections, or acquiring relevant skills. Secure prospects of stay and legal employment rights increase their incentives to do so.[25] Naturalization goes hand in hand with further enhanced economic outcomes.[26] It allows access to a wider set of jobs in the labor market (such as in civil service and regulated professions) and has positive signaling effects for employers. Moreover, those who are offered a chance to be naturalized are often among the most successful migrants. To best contribute to the destination economy, migrants also need access to a range of complementary rights such as to move across the country, to open a bank account and obtain credit, or to create a business. The faster migrants gain legal status and access to the labor market, the better are their labor market outcomes.[27]

Undocumented migrants fare significantly worse than other migrants in the labor markets, even when their skills and other attributes are needed in the destination country (figure 4.6). They cannot access most formal jobs because either they fear being detected or they lack the required licenses and credentials. Relegation to the informal sector means lower wages and fewer opportunities for advancement. Because undocumented migrants cannot readily report abuses to the police or access court systems, they are more easily exploited and underpaid. When they return to their country of origin, undocumented migrants fare worse relative to documented migrants, especially if they have been deported.[28]

Figure 4.6 **In the United States, migrants' wages are close to those of nationals—when migrants have documented status**

Age earnings profiles, by legal status

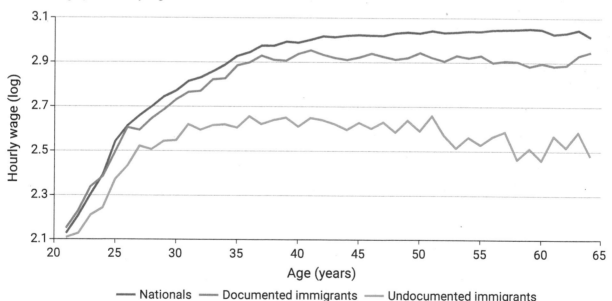

Source: WDR 2023 team calculations, based on Borjas (2017) using data from American Community Survey (dashboard), US Census Bureau, Suitland, MD, https://www.census.gov/programs-surveys/acs.

Note: Earnings profiles are constructed at each year of age by calculating the average hourly wage for workers of each legal status. Undocumented immigrants are identified based on the methodology outlined in Borjas (2017).

Undocumented migrants may still earn an income higher than what they would have earned in their own country, but the increase is smaller than if they are documented. Regularization programs for undocumented migrants have shown positive impacts on wages—notably, for those with more education—in the United States and European countries.[29] In Colombia, the 2018 regularization of Venezuelan nationals led to an average 35 percent increase in migrants' income and an average 10 percent increase in formal employment.[30]

A much-discussed aspect of migrants' rights has been their ability to change employers. Some migrants' work permits are tied to an employer whom they cannot change. An example is the sponsorship (*kafala*) system in GCC countries. Such systems confer disproportionate power on these employers, which, in turn, reduces migrant wages[31] and potentially leads to other abuses or exploitative work conditions.[32]

Some GCC countries, such as Qatar in 2020 and Saudi Arabia in 2021, have begun to relax their sponsorship system, allowing migrant workers to seek other employers once their initial contract has expired and thereby increasing labor market flexibility and improving workers' welfare.[33] An earlier reform in the United Arab Emirates (2011) that allowed some workers to change employer revealed the impact of such changes. Prior to the reform, workers renewing their initial contract were forced to accept a 5 percent reduction in their wage. After the reform, they could renew their contract with the same or a slightly higher wage[34] (figure 4.7). Additional reforms are under way, including the introduction of a minimum wage in Qatar in 2021 and of unemployment insurance for migrant workers in the United Arab Emirates in 2022,[35] although much remains to be done to fully enforce these new regulations and to cover all sectors of the economies, including domestic workers.

The question of migrants' rights cannot be addressed separately from broader migration objectives. Migration policies and the rights granted to migrants determine the outcomes of existing migrants, but they also largely determine who migrates, where to, and for how long.[36] For example, the policies of some destination countries directly or indirectly incentivize the migration of higher-skilled people who come with the intention to stay and integrate.[37] Other policies encourage temporary migration by lower-skilled workers. Still others *de facto* create perverse incentives for workers to enter the country through irregular channels if, for example, there is a demand for their labor but no legal route. Broader social norms can play a role as well (box 4.1). The challenge for a destination country is to look at migration policies not only as a way to regulate the status of those who are already in the country, but also as a means of incentivizing movements that strongly match its needs.

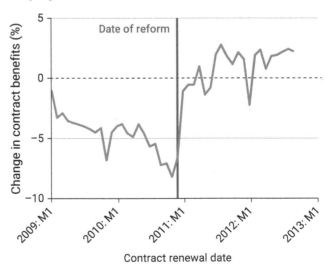

Figure 4.7 **In the United Arab Emirates, workers received higher benefits upon contract renewal after a reform allowing them to change employers**

Source: Naidu, Nyarko, and Wang 2016.

Note: The vertical line indicates the announcement date of the reform. Contract benefits include both earnings and benefits as defined in the contract. M1 = month 1.

A growing number of women with a tertiary education are migrating on their own to work or pursue further education. They tend to favor destinations with smaller gender gaps and less gender discrimination.[a] Migration allows these women to circumvent labor market obstacles in their origin countries.

The propensity of highly educated women to migrate is highest when they come from countries that are in the midrange of gender discrimination—that is, from countries where they have both the possibility and the incentives to move (figure B4.1.1). By contrast, lower-educated women migrate less frequently on their own, regardless of the level of gender discrimination in their origin countries.

Figure B4.1.1 **Emigration rates of high-skilled women are highest in countries in the midrange of gender-based discrimination**

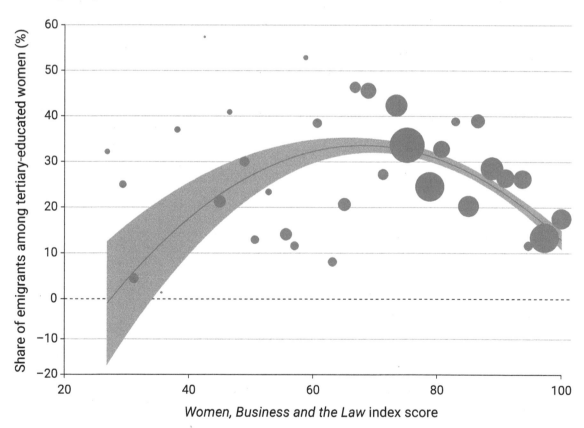

Women, Business and the Law index score

Source: WDR 2023 team calculations, based on World Bank (2022) and WDR2023 Migration Database, World Bank, Washington, DC, https://www.worldbank.org/wdr2023/data.

Note: The World Bank's *Women, Business and the Law* index measures the legal differences between the access of men and women to economic opportunities across phases of a woman's career. Scores (1–100) are based on a set of binary questions on eight indicators: Mobility, Workplace, Pay, Marriage, Parenthood, Entrepreneurship, Assets, and Pension. The size of the bubbles is proportional to the total combined number of high-skilled female emigrants in countries with the same index scores. The shaded area represents the 95 percent confidence interval. The dashed line represents a 0 percent emigration rate for tertiary-educated women.

a. Ferrant and Tuccio (2015); Ruyssen and Salomone (2018).

Accessing better services

Education

Worldwide, there are more than 6 million international students. The top destinations are the United States, the United Kingdom, and Australia, but France, South Africa, and the United Arab Emirates, among other countries, are important destinations as well for students from specific regions (figure 4.8). By migrating to study, people can acquire more human capital than they would have in their country of origin.

Student migration can be beneficial to both migrants and their destination countries in several ways. Some students stay after finishing their studies, as many countries provide easier access to work visas and give graduates time to find a job after graduation. Because employers in migrants' destination countries are familiar with the tertiary degrees offered there, migrants who have received such degrees can earn wages similar to those of nationals with the same qualifications.[38] When they return to their country of origin, foreign students may receive a wage premium as well as facilitate economic or other relations between their country and the one in which they studied.[39]

Many migrants move to provide a better future for their families, including better opportunities for education and health care.[40] Indeed, children may benefit more from a move than their parents.[41] In European member countries of the Organisation for Economic Co-operation and Development (OECD), children with parents born abroad obtain, on average, 1.3 more years of schooling than their parents.[42] In the United States, the children of lower-income immigrants are more likely to be wealthier than the children of US-born parents at similar income levels.[43] In the European Union (EU), the upward economic mobility of children with parents born in other EU countries is similarly higher than for nationals, although it is lower for those with parents born outside the EU.[44]

Figure 4.8 Destination countries attract international students from distinct parts of the world

Share of international students in select destinations, by region of origin

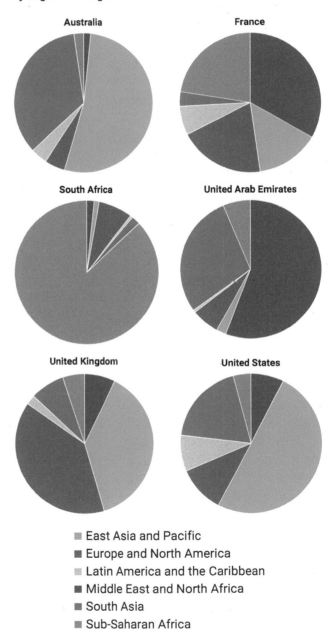

- ■ East Asia and Pacific
- ■ Europe and North America
- ▨ Latin America and the Caribbean
- ■ Middle East and North Africa
- ■ South Asia
- ■ Sub-Saharan Africa

Source: WDR 2023 team calculations, based on UIS.Stat (dashboard), Institute for Statistics, United Nations Educational, Scientific, and Cultural Organization, Montreal, http://data.uis.unesco.org/.

Education policies matter. Outcomes are better if school systems promote intergenerational economic and social mobility, accommodate children from other cultural and linguistic backgrounds, and provide them with additional support. Migrants' children should also have access to schools of the same quality as those attended by the children of nationals.[45] The age of children on arrival and their ability to adapt to a new environment also play an important role. The younger migrant children are on arrival and the closer the destination environment is to the country of origin, the easier it is for them to adapt.[46]

Children of undocumented migrants face specific challenges. Some of these children do not have access to education, or they are able to access only education of lower quality. When enforcement of immigration laws increases in the United States, the number of children of undocumented migrants repeating a grade or dropping out of school increases.[47] These children are less likely to attend preschool where they could develop their English language skills because of their parents' fear of being detected.[48] However, once their parents legalize their status, the children of undocumented parents are able to improve their educational outcomes.[49]

Health care

Migrants' health outcomes depend on their working and living conditions and access to health care services. Economic migrants tend to arrive in their country of destination in relatively good health.[50] But if they have poor living conditions or little access to health care services, or if they have jobs in which the likelihood of occupational injuries is high, their health and well-being tend to deteriorate over time.[51] In Europe, for example, many migrants live in low-quality housing and in areas underserved by public services.[52] More than one in three migrants in Italy and Greece report living in overcrowded housing. Living conditions are also a challenge for temporary migrants. Many workers in GCC countries live in crowded compounds far from where nationals live.[53]

The COVID-19 pandemic underscored the importance of access to health care systems. The health of some migrants was compromised because of their living conditions—overcrowded spaces, limited availability of waste disposal facilities, and poor hygienic conditions—which drew public attention.[54] In other cases, migrants' health was compromised because they worked in essential jobs that required face-to-face contact.[55] At times, migrants with COVID-19 symptoms did not seek medical care because of financial constraints or lack of access.[56]

For migrants who move with their families, the ability to access better health care services, especially for young children, is an important part of their gains. The younger a child is at the time of immigration and the safer and quicker the immigration journey, the higher are the potential health gains.[57] Among Ethiopian Jews who were airlifted to Israel in 1991, mothers benefited at the destination from earlier access to prenatal care, which was not available in their country of origin, and their children had better educational and labor market outcomes later in life.[58]

Because access to health care depends on migrants' legal status and destination countries' regulations, undocumented migrants are at a severe disadvantage. In fact, they are less likely to have access to health care services than education services.[59] Fearing detection, they are also less likely to use health services for their children even when the children are covered by public health insurance.[60] Health outcomes for children in migrant families improve when their legal status is secure. For example, an amnesty for undocumented migrants in Italy reduced the incidence of low birthweight among their children.[61]

Dealing with social costs

One of the many challenges migrants face in a foreign social environment and far away from families and social networks is isolation. Women who move to join their spouse are often affected if they have no access to a job where they can meet people or to social networks of co-nationals.

Discriminatory policies and attitudes can heighten these difficulties. In some countries, darker skin color and foreign-sounding names affect migrants' ability to enter the labor market[62] and to access housing, education, health care, and social services,[63] with significant negative effects on their well-being.[64] Discrimination can lower the performance of migrant workers, as well as their acquisition of human capital.[65]

Undocumented migrants face particular challenges because of the constant fear of deportation and separation from loved ones. They cannot report abuses, which increases their likelihood of being victimized.[66] These restrictions impair their physical and mental health and that of their children.[67]

Family separation, even when expected or planned, is often difficult. The policies of destination countries—such as whether they allow migrants to bring their families with them or to visit them regularly—largely determine the costs in well-being. Undocumented migrants are especially affected because they cannot easily reenter the destination country if they visit their families in their origin country. By contrast, policies that allow migrants to move with their families, to reunite with them at a later stage, or at least to be able to visit them regularly have proved important for the well-being of migrants.

Social inclusion and social support programs help reduce the risks of social isolation. The formation of social networks in the destination society—not only with co-nationals but also with citizens—helps migrants develop a feeling of belonging, while facilitating labor market and social integration. Destination countries can encourage the creation of such networks by adopting policies that incentivize and enable migrants to learn the local language and culture and to choose where to settle.[68]

Family members left in the country of origin also suffer from the absence of parents, spouses, or children, especially when the separation is prolonged.[69] Migrants' absence can have negative effects, even if family members benefit from the financial remittances sent by them.[70] For example, the absence of migrant parents is associated with a range of issues affecting the children left behind—such as lower school attendance in Albania,[71] poor psychological well-being in both Albania and Ecuador,[72] conduct problems in Thailand, and adverse emotional symptoms in Indonesia.[73]

Creating formal and informal social support systems for migrant families in the countries of origin is critical. Networks of migrant households can provide informal social services. Examples are the seafarer migrant household networks in the Philippines, the village-level Desmigratif support program in Indonesia, and the migrant support networks in Mozambique. Risks to the well-being of the migrant family can also be reduced when other relatives step in as caregivers and when remittances allow families to seek paid care services.

Returning

Worldwide, an estimated 40 percent of all migrants eventually return to their country of origin. There are, however, large variations across destination countries.[74] Nearly all migrants to GCC countries return eventually to their country of origin because all migration to those countries is temporary by design.[75] In OECD countries, between 20 and 50 percent of immigrants leave their destination within five to 10 years after their arrival to return to their origin country or to move on to a third country. However, there are significant differences between, for example, the United States and Western Europe (figures 4.9 and 4.10).[76]

Migrants who expect to return behave differently than those who intend to stay permanently. The latter have stronger incentives to invest in human and social capital specific to the destination, including learning the language. By contrast, those planning to return tend to be less willing to make such medium-term investments, even if it means working for lower wages. Migrants who plan to return have higher rates of savings and of sending remittances.[77]

Figure 4.9 Only a minority of migrants to the United States return to their countries of origin, mainly those from other high-income OECD countries

Percentage of migrants leaving the United States, by gender and region of origin

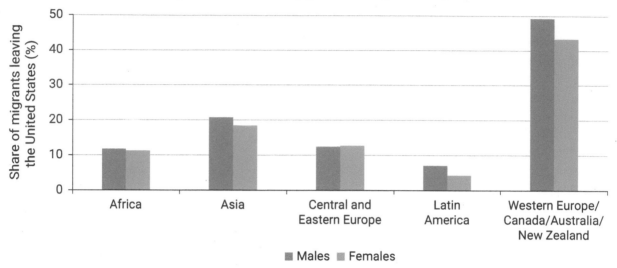

Source: Bossavie and Özden 2022, based on data from American Community Survey (dashboard), US Census Bureau, Suitland, MD, https://www.census.gov/programs-surveys/acs.

Note: OECD = Organisation for Economic Co-operation and Development.

Figure 4.10 Many migrants to Western Europe return to their country of origin, but less so women from Eastern Europe

Percentage of migrants leaving Western Europe, by gender and region of origin

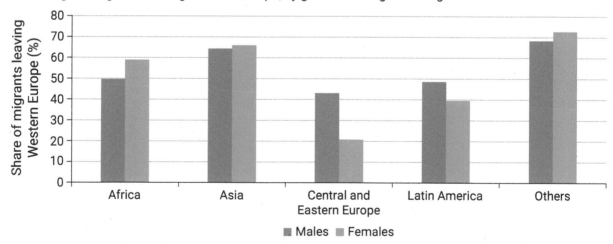

Source: Bossavie and Özden 2022, based on data from Employment and Unemployment (LFS): Overview (European Union Labour Force Survey, Overview) (dashboard), Eurostat, European Commission, Luxembourg, https://ec.europa.eu/eurostat/web/lfs.

The intent to stay or return may change over time. Return decisions depend on socioeconomic conditions in both the origin and destination societies. The return of Turkish migrants from Germany to Türkiye has been influenced by the extent of their engagement while abroad with their community back at home, as well as the economic difficulties or xenophobia faced in Germany.[78] Similarly, for Moroccan migrants, having investment opportunities and social ties in Morocco has played a key role in their decision to return.[79] Knowing that if they leave the destination country they may not be able to come back lessens migrants' incentives to return to their origin country.[80] Conversely, when migrants have the option to return, and especially if they have citizenship, they engage more frequently in circular migration between their countries of origin and destination, especially those who have relatively lower levels of education.[81]

Many migrants return to their origin countries voluntarily; they are legally able to stay but choose to return because, for example, they have saved the intended resources. In the Netherlands, migrants who have met their savings target are more likely to return to their origin country, and it is both the highest- and lowest-skilled migrants who are the most likely to return voluntarily to their origin country.[82] In Bangladesh and the Philippines, migrants who have been able to accumulate sufficient assets tend to return to the domestic labor market after several episodes of temporary migration.[83]

At times, sudden economic shocks, family pressure, or other social factors precipitate a decision to return, even when migrants have the legal right to stay longer. During the COVID-19 pandemic, many migrant workers, especially those on temporary contracts, were forced to return to their origin country either because they lost their jobs or because the destination countries deported them.[84]

Temporary migrants who return voluntarily after a successful stay abroad often end up better off than before they left.[85] They usually benefit from a wage premium on return, especially if they are higher-skilled.[86] This premium depends on whether the work experience and human capital gained at the destination are in demand in the origin country, on the development level of migrants' destination country, and on how long they stayed abroad. Successful migrants also have more access to capital than before they left, and they are more likely than nonemigrants to invest in housing and other assets and to become entrepreneurs.[87] Higher savings and a longer stay are positively associated with entrepreneurship after return.[88]

Legally, however, some migrants are not able to stay even if they would like to do so. Their visas may have expired; their asylum application may have been rejected; or they never had the legal right to stay. They return by themselves; they are assisted in their return; or they are deported. The number of forced returns (assisted returns or deportations) is much lower than the number of voluntary, spontaneous returns. On average, less than 2 percent of migrants are forced to return from the United States, Canada, European Union, Japan, and Korea every year.[89]

Those forced to return, however, have worse socioeconomic outcomes after their return.[90] They are less likely to have prepared for their return, and they often have not stayed long enough to accumulate sufficient savings and social and human capital. Undocumented migrants are similarly less likely to be able to accumulate the financial, human, and social capital needed for a successful return. As a result, after their return, undocumented migrants face a wage penalty, compared with both documented migrants and those who never migrated, as has been documented in the case of the Arab Republic of Egypt.[91]

For destination countries, the policy challenge is twofold. First, they can support those who return voluntarily—for example, by means of labor market policies that enable migrants to accumulate savings or by enabling them to move back and forth between the countries of origin and destination, especially if they have skills and attributes that match the needs of the destination economy. Second, they must treat humanely those who are deported, and in some cases they can assist some in their reintegration in the country of origin.[92]

Failing, sometimes

For some migrants, migration does not work out as expected—even if their skills and attributes were a strong match for the needs of the destination society—because of conditions faced either during transit or at their destination.

Transit can be dangerous—and sometimes deadly—even for migrants whose skills and attributes are a strong match for the needs of the destination country, and especially the undocumented. In Italy, 45 percent of undocumented migrants reported experiencing physical violence in transit through African countries.[93] During their transit, they had to work without pay and were detained by authorities or criminal networks. Many undocumented migrants on their way from Central America to the United States, as well as those who attempted to reach Saudi Arabia via the Gulf of Aden and the Republic of Yemen, have been kidnapped and confronted with extortion and other forms of violence by criminal gangs and other actors.[94] Those who cannot pay for the whole trip in advance are at particular risk. Women and adolescent girls face sexual violence and exploitation.[95]

Once at their destination, some migrants face exploitative labor conditions. Even if they are documented, migrants do not always benefit from the labor protections given citizens or permanent residents. They are not always included in minimum wage legislation or allowed to join trade unions and participate in collective bargaining.[96] Migrant workers also often lack adequate information about their rights and may not have the social networks or language skills needed to claim them. Lack of documentation, unethical recruitment practices, and lack of protection or enforcement of migrant rights heighten the risks.

Long working hours and higher incidences of work-related injuries are more common among migrants.[97] This situation can arise when work and residency permits are tied to a specific employer, leaving a migrant with limited options for changing jobs. The employer's dominant position not only reduces a migrant's wages,[98] but also may lead to the illegal extraction of forced labor.[99] For low-skilled migrants to GCC countries, the aggregate losses resulting from wage shortfalls, excessive hours, and occupational safety and health issues amount, on average, to an estimated 27 percent of total actual wages.[100] Some migrants face pressure to accept poor working conditions because they lack other options and need to repay the cost of migration and send the expected remittances to their origin country. Others are victims of deception and end up in forced labor with little or no recourse.

In some extreme situations, migrants are exposed to crime, violence, and exploitation by abusive employers, traffickers, and recruitment agents.[101] Migrants' passports may be confiscated; they may be threatened with being reported to the police; or they may be held in debt bondage and forced to repay their loans. As a result, migrants are three times more likely than citizens to experience forced labor—which has been called a form of modern slavery[102]—especially in the construction and domestic work sectors.[103] Domestic workers are at special risk because they are often isolated and less protected by labor laws.[104] The prosecution of human traffickers is hampered when victims are not protected and not allowed to stay in the destination country after reporting their traffickers.[105]

Outbreaks of violence against foreigners threaten migrants across the globe. Many have been insulted and threatened because of their status, their skin color, their religion, among other things. In some instances, migrants' shops, houses, and group accommodations have been attacked by mobs, and they have been physically harmed or killed.[106] In Germany, foreigners experienced more than 5,000 politically motivated crimes at the height of the influx of refugees in 2015 and 2016 and more than 2,000 such crimes in 2021.[107] In South Africa, riots against foreign nationals (mostly from other African countries), as well as attacks on them and their businesses, have occurred in several waves since 2008.[108] In the United States, there was a strong rise in anti-Muslim sentiments and hate crimes after the terrorist attacks of September 11, 2001.[109]

Destination countries can reduce some of these negative impacts by ensuring that migrants have access to fair recruitment and decent work in line with international standards. They are also responsible for enforcing their laws and regulations, including to prevent forced labor and exploitation. Strong antidiscrimination initiatives are needed in some countries, as well as efforts to ensure migrants' security and safety. Overall, migrants—even when they fail—must be treated humanely.

Notes

1. Occupational Wages around the World (dashboard), World Bank, Washington, DC, https://datacatalog.worldbank.org/search/dataset/0041465.
2. Occupational Wages around the World (dashboard), World Bank, Washington, DC, https://datacatalog.worldbank.org/search/dataset/0041465.
3. Vujicic et al. (2004).
4. Åslund and Rooth (2007); Azlor, Damm, and Schultz-Nielsen (2020); Barth, Bratsberg, and Raaum (2004); Braun and Dwenger (2020); Fasani, Frattini, and Minale (2021); Godøy (2017).
5. In the studies cited in figure 4.4, panel a, migrants are randomly selected among applicants.
6. Borjas (1987).
7. Ahmed and Bossavie (2022); KNOMAD and ILO (2021a, 2021b).
8. ILO (2019).
9. Bossavie et al. (2021).
10. Ahmed and Bossavie (2022).
11. The wage differentials by occupation are not the same as the potential income gains through migration because those who move are not the same as those who stay in the origin country (selection effects), and migrants may earn less than nationals, at least in the short term. Figure 4.4, which compares the income gains of migrants at the destination with the wages of those who stay behind, presents more exact estimates. It only compares the migrants and those who stayed behind who have similar observable and unobservable characteristics—for example, where migrants were selected through a lottery—or they compare individuals with similar observable characteristics and adjust for potential differences in unobservable characteristics (Clemens, Montenegro, and Pritchett 2019).
12. Amo-Agyei (2020).
13. Jeon, Liu, and Ostrovsky (2021); Madariaga et al. (2019); McDonald et al. (2020); Urzi Brancati, Pesole, and Férnandéz-Macías (2020); WDR 2023 team, based on Current Population Survey, May 2017: Contingent Worker Supplement (dashboard), Bureau of the Census and Bureau of Labor Statistics, US Department of Labor, Washington, DC, ICPSR 37191, Inter-university Consortium for Political and Social Research, 2021-04-29, https://doi.org/10.3886/ICPSR37191.v2. The part of the gig economy in which gigs are mediated through digital platforms but the work is carried out in a specific location has disproportionately attracted migrant workers. Migrants can sign up easily; there is less discrimination against newcomers; little social or financial capital is required; language is less of a hindrance; and migration regulations that restrict formal employment possibilities are not applied in the same way (van Doorn, Ferrari, and Graham 2022). Some countries have recently begun to collect quantitative data on the size of (employment in) the gig economy (OECD 2019). But, given the growth of the gig economy, data collection efforts should be stepped up and further unified.
14. van Doorn, Ferrari, and Graham (2022).
15. Damelang, Ebensperger, and Stumpf (2020); Duleep (2015); Mattoo, Neagu, and Özden (2008).
16. Duleep (2015).
17. Mattoo, Neagu, and Özden (2012).
18. Duleep (2015).
19. Astor et al. (2005); Luboga et al. (2011).
20. See literature reviews by Butschek and Walter (2014); Schuettler and Caron (2020).
21. Card, Kluve, and Weber (2018); Clausen et al. (2009); Foged et al. (2022); Lochmann, Rapoport, and Speciale (2019).
22. Battisti, Giesing, and Laurentsyeva (2019); Butschek and Walter (2014); Card, Kluve, and Weber (2018); Clausen et al. (2009); Foged, Hasager, and Peri (2022); Foged, Kreuder, and Peri (2022); Joona and Nekby (2012); Sarvimäki and Hämäläinen (2016).
23. Because of poor data availability, evidence is based on high-income countries. For refugees, see Dustmann et al. (2017); Fasani, Frattini, and Minale (2021). For European Union destination countries, see the following: Belgium: Dries, Ive, and Vujić (2019); Canada: Aydemir (2011); Finland: Sarvimäki (2017); Italy: Ortensi and Ambrosetti (2022); the Netherlands: Bakker, Dagevos, and Engbersen (2017); Sweden: Åslund, Forslund, and Liljeberg (2017); Baum, Lööf, and Stephan (2018); Baum et al. (2020); Switzerland: Spadarotto et al. (2014). For the United Kingdom, see Ruiz and Vargas-Silva (2018). For East African Asians in the United Kingdom, see Anders, Burgess, and Portes (2018). For the United States, see Connor (2010); Cortes (2004); Evans and Fitzgerald (2017). For migrants, see the literature review by Duleep (2015) covering high-income destination countries, including Australia, European countries, Israel, New Zealand, and the United States. For migrants in the United Arab Emirates, see Joseph, Nyarko, and Wang (2018).
24. Dustmann (2000); Dustmann and Görlach (2016); Slotwinski, Stutzer, and Uhlig (2019).
25. Dustmann (2000); Dustmann et al. (2017).
26. Bakker, Dagevos, and Engbersen (2014); Bevelander and Pendakur (2014); Bevelander and Veenman (2006); Helgertz, Bevelander, and Tegunimataka (2014); OECD (2011); Peters, Schmeets, and Vink (2020); Steinhardt (2012).
27. Aksoy, Poutvaara, and Schikora (2020); Azlor, Damm, and Schultz-Nielsen (2020); Bansak et al. (2018); Bertoli, Özden, and Packard (2021); Fasani, Frattini, and Minale (2021); Ginn et al. (2022); Hainmueller, Hangartner, and Lawrence (2016); Marbach, Hainmueller, and Hangartner (2018); Martén, Hainmueller, and Hangartner (2019); Müller, Pannatier, and Viarengo (2022); Zetter and Ruaudel (2016).
28. Beauchemin et al. (2022).
29. Baker (2015); Orrenius and Zavodny (2014); Pan (2012); Pinotti (2017).
30. Ibáñez et al. (2022). A second wave of regularization in 2021 increased income by a third (JDC 2023).

31. Examples include the impacts of H1B visas in the United States (Kim and Pei 2022) and work permits in the United Arab Emirates (Naidu, Nyarko, and Wang 2016).
32. ILO (2017).
33. Kagan and Cholewinski (2022).
34. Naidu, Nyarko, and Wang (2016).
35. ILO (2021); UAE (2023).
36. Abramitzky and Boustan (2017); Aksoy and Poutvaara (2021); Lazear (2021).
37. Abramitzky and Boustan (2017); Czaika and Parsons (2017); Lazear (2021).
38. Mattoo, Neagu, and Özden (2008).
39. Bound et al. (2015); World Bank (2018b).
40. The impacts on children left behind in the country of origin are discussed in chapter 5.
41. Nakamura, Sigurdsson, and Steinsson (2022).
42. OECD (2017).
43. Abramitzky and Boustan (2022); Abramitzky et al. (2021).
44. OECD (2017).
45. Alesina et al. (2018).
46. Kırdar, Koç, and Dayıoğlu Tayfur (2021).
47. Amuedo-Dorantes and Lopez (2015); Arenas-Arroyo and Schmidpeter (2022).
48. Arenas-Arroyo and Schmidpeter (2022); Santillano, Potochnick, and Jenkins (2020).
49. Felfe, Rainer, and Saurer (2020); Orrenius and Zavodny (2014).
50. While economic migrants tend to be healthier at arrival than the population at destination, refugees tend to have poorer health outcomes. The difference between refugees and other migrants stems from selection and the impact of conflict and displacement, as well as explicit policies (Chin and Cortes 2015; Giuntella and Mazzonna 2015; Giuntella et al. 2018; McDonald and Kennedy 2004).
51. Garcés, Scarinci, and Harrison (2006); Giuntella and Mazzonna (2015); Grove and Zwi (2006); Hacker et al. (2015); Hasager and Jørgensen (2021); Nwadiuko et al. (2021); Orrenius and Zavodny (2009); Pega, Govindaraj, and Tran (2021).
52. Baptista and Marlier (2019); Fonseca, McGarrigle, and Esteves (2010).
53. Asi (2020).
54. Testaverde and Pavilon (2022).
55. Testaverde and Pavilon (2022).
56. WHO (2022).
57. Alacevich and Tarozzi (2017); van den Berg et al. (2014).
58. Lavy, Schlosser, and Shany (2021).
59. WDR 2023 team calculations based on data of MIPEX (Migrant Integration Policy Index 2020) (dashboard), Migration Policy Group and Barcelona Centre for International Affairs, Barcelona, https://www.mipex .eu/. MIPEX measures policies to integrate migrants in 56 countries, including all EU Member States; other European countries (Albania, Iceland, Moldova, North Macedonia, Norway, Serbia, Switzerland, the Russian Federation, Türkiye, Ukraine, the United Kingdom); Asian countries (China, India, Indonesia, Israel, Japan, Jordan, Korea, Saudi Arabia, United Arab Emirates); North American countries (Canada, Mexico, the United States); South American countries (Argentina, Brazil, Chile); South Africa; and Australia and New Zealand in Oceania.
60. Hacker et al. (2015); Watson (2014); WHO (2022).
61. Salmasi and Pieroni (2015).
62. Abel (2017); Adida, Laitin, and Valfort (2010); Carlsson (2010); Dávila, Mora, and Stockly (2011); Duguet et al. (2010); Hersch (2008); Oreopoulos (2011); Quillian and Midtbøen (2021); Quillian et al. (2019); Weichselbaumer (2020).
63. Auspurg, Schneck, and Hinz (2019); Baldini and Federici (2011); Bosch, Carnero, and Farré (2010).
64. de Coulon, Radu, and Steinhardt (2016); Gould and Klor (2016); Pascoe and Richman (2009); Steinhardt (2018); Suleman, Garber, and Rutkow (2018); Weichselbaumer (2020); WHO (2022).
65. Bertrand and Duflo (2016); Glover, Pallais, and Parienté (2017).
66. Juárez et al. (2019); Martinez et al. (2015); Wang and Kaushal (2019).
67. Giuntella and Lonsky (2020); Giuntella et al. (2021); Hainmueller et al. (2017); Ibáñez et al. (2022); Venkataramani et al. (2017).
68. Bailey et al. (2022).
69. Parreñas (2001).
70. Ivlevs, Nikolova, and Graham (2019).
71. Giannelli and Mangiavacchi (2010).
72. Cortina (2014); Giannelli and Mangiavacchi (2010).
73. Graham and Jordan (2011).
74. Chen et al. (2022).
75. Bossavie and Özden (2022).
76. Bossavie and Özden (2022); Dustmann and Görlach (2016); OECD (2008).
77. Adda, Dustmann, and Görlach (2022); Dustmann and Görlach (2016); Dustmann and Mestres (2010); Merkle and Zimmermann (1992).
78. Tezcan (2018).
79. de Haas, Fokkema, and Fihri (2015).
80. Czaika and de Haas (2017); Flahaux (2017).
81. Constant and Zimmermann (2011).
82. Bijwaard and Wahba (2014).
83. Dustmann and Görlach (2016).
84. Testaverde and Pavilon (2022).
85. Beauchemin et al. (2022); David (2017); Gubert and Nordman (2008); Mezger Kveder and Flahaux (2013).
86. Wahba (2015).
87. Bossavie and Özden (2022).
88. Bossavie et al. (2021).
89. WDR 2023 team calculations, based on data from Office of the Auditor General of Canada, Canada Border Services Agency, Eurostat, Immigration Services Agency of Japan, Korean Ministry of Justice Immigration Service, and US Department of Homeland Security.
90. David (2017); Gubert and Nordman (2008); Mezger Kveder and Flahaux (2013).
91. Elmallakh and Wahba (2021).

92. See chapter 8 for details.
93. World Bank (2018a).
94. Albuja (2014); DRC and RMMS (2012); HRW (2014).
95. WHO (2022).
96. Amo-Agyei (2020); Faraday (2022); KNOMAD (2022). A minimum wage has been in place in Qatar since March 2021. In 2022, the United Arab Emirates introduced unemployment insurance for migrant workers (ILO 2021; UAE 2023).
97. Aleksynska, Kazi Aoul, and Petrencu (2017); Hargreaves et al. (2019); Moyce and Schenker (2018).
98. Examples include the impacts of H1B visas in the United States (Kim and Pei 2022) and work permits in the United Arab Emirates (Naidu, Nyarko, and Wang 2016).
99. ILO (2017).
100. Aleksynska, Kazi Aoul, and Petrencu (2017).
101. ILO, Walk Free, and IOM (2022); WHO (2022).
102. David, Bryant, and Joudo Larsen (2019).
103. ILO, Walk Free, and IOM (2022).
104. ILO (2016); UNDP (2020).
105. UNODC (2008).
106. Benček and Strasheim (2016); HRW (2020); Steinhardt (2018).
107. BKA (2021).
108. Xenowatch Dashboard: Incidents of Xenophobic Discrimination in South Africa, 1994−29 January 2023, Xenowatch, University of the Witwatersrand, Johannesburg, https://www.xenowatch.ac.za/statistics-dashboard/.
109. Gould and Klor (2016).

References

Abel, Martin D. 2017. "Labor Market Discrimination and Sorting: Evidence from South Africa." Policy Research Working Paper 8180, World Bank, Washington, DC.

Abramitzky, Ran, and Leah Platt Boustan. 2017. "Immigration in American Economic History." *Journal of Economic Literature* 55 (4): 1311–45.

Abramitzky, Ran, and Leah Platt Boustan. 2022. *Streets of Gold: America's Untold Story of Immigrant Success.* New York: PublicAffairs.

Abramitzky, Ran, Leah Platt Boustan, Elisa Jácome, and Santiago Pérez. 2021 "Intergenerational Mobility of Immigrants in the US over Two Centuries." *American Economic Review* 111 (2): 580–608.

Adda, Jérôme, Christian Dustmann, and Joseph-Simon Görlach. 2022. "The Dynamics of Return Migration, Human Capital Accumulation, and Wage Assimilation." *Review of Economic Studies* 89 (6): 2841–71.

Adida, Claire L., David D. Laitin, and Marie-Anne Valfort. 2010. "Identifying Barriers to Muslim Integration in France." *Proceedings of the National Academy of Sciences* 107 (52): 22384–90.

Ahmed, S. Amer, and Laurent Bossavie, eds. 2022. *Toward Safer and More Productive Migration for South Asia.* International Development in Focus Series. Washington, DC: World Bank.

Akram, Agha Ali, Shyamal K. Chowdhury, and Ahmed Mushfiq Mobarak. 2017. "Effects of Emigration on Rural Labor Markets." NBER Working Paper 23929 (October), National Bureau of Economic Research, Cambridge, MA.

Aksoy, Cevat Giray, and Panu Poutvaara. 2021. "Refugees' and Irregular Migrants' Self-Selection into Europe." *Journal of Development Economics* 152 (September): 102681.

Aksoy, Cevat Giray, Panu Poutvaara, and Felicitas Schikora. 2020. "First Time Around: Local Conditions and Multi-Dimensional Integration of Refugees." IZA Discussion Paper DP 13914 (November), Institute of Labor Economics, Bonn, Germany.

Alacevich, Caterina, and Alessandro Tarozzi. 2017. "Child Height and Intergenerational Transmission of Health: Evidence from Ethnic Indians in England." *Economics and Human Biology* 25 (May): 65–84.

Albuja, Sebastián. 2014. "Criminal Violence, Displacement, and Migration in Mexico and Central America." In *Humanitarian Crises and Migration: Causes, Consequences and Responses,* edited by Susan F. Martin, Sanjula Weerasinghe, and Abbie Taylor, 113–37. Abingdon, UK: Routledge.

Aleksynska, Mariya, Samia Kazi Aoul, and Veronica Petrencu. 2017. "Deficiencies in Conditions of Work as a Cost to Labor Migration: Concepts, Extent, and Implications." KNOMAD Working Paper 28 (August), Global Knowledge Partnership on Migration and Development, World Bank, Washington, DC.

Alesina, Alberto Francesco, Michela Carlana, Eliana La Ferrara, and Paolo Pinotti. 2018. "Revealing Stereotypes: Evidence from Immigrants in Schools." NBER Working Paper 25333 (December), National Bureau of Economic Research, Cambridge, MA.

Amo-Agyei, Silas. 2020. *The Migrant Pay Gap: Understanding Wage Differences between Migrants and Nationals.* Geneva: International Labour Organization.

Amuedo-Dorantes, Catalina, and Mary J. Lopez. 2015. "Falling through the Cracks? Grade Retention and School Dropout among Children of Likely Unauthorized Immigrants." *American Economic Review* 105 (5): 598–603.

Anders, Jake, Simon Burgess, and Jonathan Portes. 2018. "The Long-Term Outcomes of Refugees: Tracking the Progress of the East African Asians." IZA Discussion Paper DP 11609 (June), Institute of Labor Economics, Bonn, Germany.

Arenas-Arroyo, Esther, and Bernhard Schmidpeter. 2022. "Spillover Effects of Immigration Policies on Children's Human Capital." IZA Discussion Paper DP 15624 (October), Institute of Labor Economics, Bonn, Germany.

Asi, Yara M. 2020. "Migrant Workers' Health and COVID-19 in GCC Countries." *Policy Analysis*, July 7, 2020. https://arabcenterdc.org/resource/migrant-workers-health-and-covid-19-in-gcc-countries/.

Åslund, Olof, Anders Forslund, and Linus Liljeberg. 2017. "Labour Market Entry of Non-Labour Migrants—Swedish Evidence." IFAU Working Paper 2017:15, Institute for Evaluation of Labour Market and Education Policy, Uppsala, Sweden.

Åslund, Olof, and Dan-Olof Rooth. 2007. "Do When and Where Matter? Initial Labour Market Conditions and Immigrant Earnings." *Economic Journal* 117 (518): 422–48.

Astor, Avraham, Tasleem Akhtar, María Alexandra Matallana, Vasantha Muthuswamy, Folarin A. Olowu, Veronica Tallo, and Reidar K. Lie. 2005. "Physician Migration: Views from Professionals in Colombia, Nigeria, India, Pakistan and the Philippines." *Social Science and Medicine* 61 (12): 2492–2500.

Auspurg, Katrin, Andreas Schneck, and Thomas Hinz. 2019. "Closed Doors Everywhere? A Meta-Analysis of Field Experiments on Ethnic Discrimination in Rental Housing Markets." *Journal of Ethnic and Migration Studies* 45 (1): 95–114.

Aydemir, Abdurrahman. 2011. "Immigrant Selection and Short-Term Labor Market Outcomes by Visa Category." *Journal of Population Economics* 24 (2): 451–75.

Azlor, Luz, Anna Piil Damm, and Marie Louise Schultz-Nielsen. 2020. "Local Labour Demand and Immigrant Employment." *Labour Economics* 63 (April): 101808.

Bailey, Michael, Drew M. Johnston, Martin Koenen, Theresa Kuchler, Dominic Russel, and Johannes Stroebel. 2022. "The Social Integration of International Migrants: Evidence from the Networks of Syrians in Germany." NBER Working Paper 29925 (April), National Bureau of Economic Research, Cambridge, MA.

Baker, Scott R. 2015. "Effects of Immigrant Legalization on Crime." *American Economic Review* 105 (5): 210–13.

Bakker, Linda, Jaco Dagevos, and Godfried Engbersen. 2014. "The Importance of Resources and Security in the Socio-Economic Integration of Refugees: A Study on the Impact of Length of Stay in Asylum Accommodation and Residence Status on Socio-Economic Integration for the Four Largest Refugee Groups in the Netherlands." *Journal of International Migration and Integration* 15 (3): 431–48.

Bakker, Linda, Jaco Dagevos, and Godfried Engbersen. 2017. "Explaining the Refugee Gap: A Longitudinal Study on Labour Market Participation of Refugees in the Netherlands." *Journal of Ethnic and Migration Studies* 43 (11): 1775–91.

Baldini, Massimo, and Marta Federici. 2011. "Ethnic Discrimination in the Italian Rental Housing Market." *Journal of Housing Economics* 20 (1): 1–14.

Bansak, Kirk, Jeremy Ferwerda, Jens Hainmueller, Andrea Dillon, Dominik Hangartner, Duncan Lawrence, and Jeremy Weinstein. 2018. "Improving Refugee Integration through Data-Driven Algorithmic Assignment." *Science* 359 (6373): 325–29.

Baptista, Isabel, and Eric Marlier. 2019. *Fighting Homelessness and Housing Exclusion in Europe: A Study of National Policies.* Synthesis Report, European Social Policy Network. Brussels: European Commission.

Barth, Erling, Bernt Bratsberg, and Oddbjørn Raaum. 2004. "Identifying Earnings Assimilation of Immigrants under Changing Macroeconomic Conditions." *Scandinavian Journal of Economics* 106 (1): 1–22.

Battisti, Michele, Yvonne Giesing, and Nadzeya Laurentsyeva. 2019. "Can Job Search Assistance Improve the Labour Market Integration of Refugees? Evidence from a Field Experiment." *Labour Economics* 61 (December): 101745.

Baum, Christopher F., Hans Lööf, and Andreas Stephan. 2018. "Economic Impact of STEM Immigrant Workers." GLO Discussion Paper 257, Global Labor Organization, Maastrict, the Netherlands.

Baum, Christopher F., Hans Lööf, Andreas Stephan, and Klaus F. Zimmermann. 2020. "Occupational Sorting and Wage Gaps of Refugees." UNU-MERIT Working Paper 2020–023 (May 27), United Nations University–Maastricht Economic and Social Research Institute on Innovation and Technology, Maastricht, the Netherlands.

Beauchemin, Cris, Adrien Vandenbunder, Tanguy Mathon Cécillon, Zélia Goussé-Breton, Mourtada Dieng, and Myriam Yahyaoui. 2022. "Socioeconomic Reintegration of Return Migrants and the Varieties of Legal Status Trajectory in Europe." *Population, Space and Place* 28 (7): e2565.

Benček, David, and Julia Strasheim. 2016. "Refugees Welcome? A Dataset on Anti-Refugee Violence in Germany." *Research and Politics* 3 (4): 2053168016679590.

Bertoli, Simone, Çağlar Özden, and Michael Packard. 2021. "Segregation and Internal Mobility of Syrian Refugees in Turkey: Evidence from Mobile Phone Data." *Journal of Development Economics* 152 (September): 102704.

Bertrand, Marianne, and Esther Duflo. 2016. "Field Experiments on Discrimination." NBER Working Paper 22014 (February), National Bureau of Economic Research, Cambridge, MA.

Bevelander, Pieter, and Ravi Pendakur. 2014. "The Labour Market Integration of Refugee and Family Reunion Immigrants: A Comparison of Outcomes in Canada and Sweden." *Journal of Ethnic and Migration Studies* 40 (5): 689–709.

Bevelander, Pieter, and Justus Veenman. 2006. "Naturalisation and Socioeconomic Integration: The Case of the Netherlands." IZA Discussion Paper DP 2153 (May), Institute of Labor Economics, Bonn, Germany.

Bijwaard, Govert, and Jackline Wahba. 2014. "Do High-Income or Low-Income Immigrants Leave Faster?" *Journal of Development Economics* 108 (May): 54–68.

BKA (Bundeskriminalamt). 2021. "Kriminalität im Kontext von Zuwanderung: Bundeslagebild 2021." June, BKA, Wiesbaden, Germany.

Borjas, George J. 1987. "Self-Selection and the Earnings of Immigrants." *American Economic Review* 77 (4): 531–53.

Borjas, George J. 2017. "The Labor Supply of Undocumented Immigrants." *Labour Economics* 46 (June): 1–13.

Bosch, Mariano, M. Angeles Carnero, and Lídia Farré. 2010. "Information and Discrimination in the Rental Housing Market: Evidence from a Field Experiment." *Regional Science and Urban Economics* 40 (1): 11–19.

Bossavie, Laurent, Joseph-Simon Görlach, Çağlar Özden, and He Wang. 2021. "Temporary Migration for

Long-Term Investment." Policy Research Working Paper 9740, World Bank, Washington, DC.

Bossavie, Laurent, and Çağlar Özden. 2022. "Impacts of Temporary Migration on Development in Origin Countries." Policy Research Working Paper 9996, World Bank, Washington, DC.

Bound, John, Murat Demirci, Gaurav Khanna, and Sarah Turner. 2015. "Finishing Degrees and Finding Jobs: US Higher Education and the Flow of Foreign IT Workers." *Innovation Policy and the Economy* 15 (January): 27–72.

Braun, Sebastian T., and Nadja Dwenger. 2020. "Settlement Location Shapes the Integration of Forced Migrants: Evidence from Post-War Germany." *Explorations in Economic History* 77 (July): 101330.

Butschek, Sebastian, and Thomas Walter. 2014. "What Active Labour Market Programmes Work for Immigrants in Europe? A Meta-Analysis of the Evaluation Literature." *IZA Journal of Migration* 3 (1): 1–18.

Card, David E., Jochen Kluve, and Andrea Weber. 2018. "What Works? A Meta Analysis of Recent Active Labor Market Program Evaluations." *Journal of the European Economic Association* 16 (3): 894–931.

Carlsson, Magnus. 2010. "Experimental Evidence of Discrimination in the Hiring of First- and Second-Generation Immigrants." *Labour* 24 (3): 263–78.

Chen, Chen, Aude Bernard, Ryan Rylee, and Guy Abel. 2022. "Brain Circulation: The Educational Profile of Return Migrants." *Population Research and Policy Review* 41 (1): 387–99.

Chin, Aimee, and Kalena E. Cortes. 2015. "The Refugee/Asylum Seeker." In *The Immigrants*, edited by Barry R. Chiswick and Paul W. Miller, 585–658. Vol. 1A of *Handbook of the Economics of International Migration*. Oxford, UK: Elsevier.

Clausen, Jens, Eskil Heinesen, Hans Hummelgaard, Leif Husted, and Michael Rosholm. 2009. "The Effect of Integration Policies on the Time until Regular Employment of Newly Arrived Immigrants: Evidence from Denmark." *Labour Economics* 16 (4): 409–17.

Clemens, Michael A. 2019. "Measuring the Spatial Misallocation of Labor: The Returns to India-Gulf Guest Work in a Natural Experiment." CGD Working Paper 501 (January), Center for Global Development, Washington, DC.

Clemens, Michael A., Claudio E. Montenegro, and Lant H. Pritchett. 2019. "The Place Premium: Bounding the Price Equivalent of Migration Barriers." *Review of Economics and Statistics* 101 (2): 201–13.

Clemens, Michael A., and Erwin R. Tiongson. 2017. "Split Decisions: Household Finance When a Policy Discontinuity Allocates Overseas Work." *Review of Economics and Statistics* 99 (3): 531–43.

Connor, Phillip. 2010. "Explaining the Refugee Gap: Economic Outcomes of Refugees versus Other Immigrants." *Journal of Refugee Studies* 23 (3): 377–97.

Constant, Amelie F., and Klaus F. Zimmermann. 2011. "Circular and Repeat Migration: Counts of Exits and Years Away from the Host Country." *Population Research and Policy Review* 30 (4): 495–515.

Cortes, Kalena E. 2004. "Are Refugees Different from Economic Immigrants? Some Empirical Evidence on the Heterogeneity of Immigrant Groups in the United States." *Review of Economics and Statistics* 86 (2): 465–80.

Cortina, Jeronimo. 2014. "Beyond the Money: The Impact of International Migration on Children's Life Satisfaction: Evidence from Ecuador and Albania." *Migration and Development* 3 (1): 1–19.

Czaika, Mathias, and Hein de Haas. 2017. "The Effect of Visas on Migration Processes." *International Migration Review* 51 (4): 893–926.

Czaika, Mathias, and Christopher R. Parsons. 2017. "The Gravity of High-Skilled Migration Policies." *Demography* 54 (2): 603–30.

Damelang, Andreas, Sabine Ebensperger, and Felix Stumpf. 2020. "Foreign Credential Recognition and Immigrants' Chances of Being Hired for Skilled Jobs: Evidence from a Survey Experiment among Employers." *Social Forces* 99 (2): 648–71.

David, Anda Mariana. 2017. "Back to Square One: Socioeconomic Integration of Deported Migrants." *International Migration Review* 51 (1): 127–54.

David, Fiona, Katharine Bryant, and Jacqueline Joudo Larsen. 2019. *Migrants and Their Vulnerability to Human Trafficking, Modern Slavery, and Forced Labour*. Geneva: International Organization for Migration.

Dávila, Alberto, Marie T. Mora, and Sue K. Stockly. 2011. "Does Mestizaje Matter in the US? Economic Stratification of Mexican Immigrants." *American Economic Review* 101 (3): 593–97.

de Coulon, Augustin, Dragos Radu, and Max Friedrich Steinhardt. 2016. "Pane E Cioccolata: The Impact of Native Attitudes on Return Migration." *Review of International Economics* 24 (2): 253–81.

de Haas, Hein, Tineke Fokkema, and Mohamed Fassi Fihri. 2015. "Return Migration as Failure or Success? The Determinants of Return Migration Intentions among Moroccan Migrants in Europe." *Journal of International Migration and Integration* 16 (2): 415–29.

Dercon, Stefan, Pramila Krishnan, and Sofya Krutikova. 2013. "Changing Living Standards in Southern Indian Villages 1975–2006: Revisiting the ICRISAT Village Level Studies." *Journal of Development Studies* 49 (12): 1676–93.

DRC (Danish Refugee Council) and RMMS (Regional Mixed Migration Secretariat). 2012. "Desperate Choices: Conditions, Risks, and Protection Failures Affecting Ethiopian Migrants in Yemen." October, Regional Office for the Horn of Africa and Yemen, DRC; RMMS, Nairobi, Kenya.

Dries, Lens, Marx Ive, and Sunčica Vujić. 2019. "Double Jeopardy: How Refugees Fare in One European Labor Market." *IZA Journal of Development and Migration* 10 (1): 1–29.

Duguet, Emmanuel, Noam Leandri, Yannick L'Horty, and Pascale Petit. 2010. "Are Young French Jobseekers of Ethnic Immigrant Origin Discriminated Against? A Controlled Experiment in the Paris Area." *Annals of Economics and Statistics* 2019 (99–100): 187–215.

Duleep, Harriet Orcutt. 2015. "The Adjustment of Immigrants in the Labor Market." In *The Immigrants*, edited by Barry R. Chiswick and Paul W. Miller, 105–82. Vol. 1A of *Handbook of the Economics of International Migration*. Oxford, UK: Elsevier.

Dustmann, Christian. 2000. "Temporary Migration and Economic Assimilation." *Swedish Economic Policy Review* 7 (2): 213–44.

Dustmann, Christian, Francesco Fasani, Tommaso Frattini, Luigi Minale, and Uta Schönberg. 2017. "On the Economics and Politics of Refugee Migration." *Economic Policy* 32 (91): 497–550.

Dustmann, Christian, and Joseph-Simon Görlach. 2016. "The Economics of Temporary Migrations." *Journal of Economic Literature* 54 (1): 98–136.

Dustmann, Christian, and Josep Mestres. 2010. "Savings, Asset Holdings, and Temporary Migration." *Annals of Economics and Statistics* 97/98 (January/June): 289–306.

Elmallakh, Nelly, and Jackline Wahba. 2021. "Return Migrants and the Wage Premium: Does the Legal Status of Migrants Matter?" IZA Discussion Paper DP 14492 (June), Institute of Labor Economics, Bonn, Germany.

Evans, William N., and Daniel Fitzgerald. 2017. "The Economic and Social Outcomes of Refugees in the United States: Evidence from the ACS." NBER Working Paper 23498 (June), National Bureau of Economic Research, Cambridge, MA.

Faraday, Fay. 2022. "The Empowerment of Migrant Workers in a Precarious Situation: Labor Inspection." KNOMAD Paper 43 (September), Global Knowledge Partnership on Migration and Development, World Bank, Washington, DC.

Fasani, Francesco, Tommaso Frattini, and Luigi Minale. 2021. "Lift the Ban? Initial Employment Restrictions and Refugee Labour Market Outcomes." *Journal of the European Economic Association* 19 (5): 2803–54.

Felfe, Christina, Helmut Rainer, and Judith Saurer. 2020. "Why Birthright Citizenship Matters for Immigrant Children: Short- and Long-Run Impacts on Educational Integration." *Journal of Labor Economics* 38 (1): 143–82.

Ferrant, Gaëlle, and Michele Tuccio. 2015. "South-South Migration and Discrimination against Women in Social Institutions: A Two-Way Relationship." *World Development* 72 (August): 240–54.

Flahaux, Marie-Laurence. 2017. "The Role of Migration Policy Changes in Europe for Return Migration to Senegal." *International Migration Review* 51 (4): 868–92.

Foged, Mette, Linea Hasager, and Giovanni Peri. 2022. "Comparing the Effects of Policies for the Labor Market Integration of Refugees." NBER Working Paper 30534 (October), National Bureau of Economic Research, Cambridge, MA.

Foged, Mette, Linea Hasager, Giovanni Peri, Jacob Nielsen Arendt, and Iben Bolvig. 2022. "Language Training and Refugees' Integration." *Review of Economics and Statistics*. Published ahead of print, June 23, 2022. https://doi.org/10.1162/rest_a_01216.

Foged, Mette, Janis Kreuder, and Giovanni Peri. 2022. "Integrating Refugees by Addressing Labor Shortages?

A Policy Evaluation." NBER Working Paper 29781 (February), National Bureau of Economic Research, Cambridge, MA.

Fonseca, Maria Lucinda, Jennifer McGarrigle, and Alina Esteves. 2010. "Possibilities and Limitations of Comparative Quantitative Research on Immigrants' Housing Conditions." PROMINSTAT Working Paper 6, Directorate-General for Research and Innovation, European Commission, Brussels.

Gaikwad, Nikhar, Kolby Hanson, and Aliz Tóth. 2023. "Exit Options: How International Migration Opportunities Shape Economic Standing and Political Preferences." Working paper, January 31. http://dx.doi.org/10.2139/ssrn.3816464.

Garcés, Isabel C., Isabel C. Scarinci, and Lynda Harrison. 2006. "An Examination of Sociocultural Factors Associated with Health and Health Care Seeking among Latina Immigrants." *Journal of Immigrant and Minority Health* 8 (4): 377–85.

Giannelli, Gianna Claudia, and Lucia Mangiavacchi. 2010. "Children's Schooling and Parental Migration: Empirical Evidence on the 'Left Behind' Generation in Albania." *Labour* 24 (s1): 76–92.

Gibson, John, and David J. McKenzie. 2012. "The Economic Consequences of 'Brain Drain' of the Best and Brightest: Microeconomic Evidence from Five Countries." *Economic Journal* 122 (560): 339–75.

Ginn, Thomas, Reva Resstack, Helen Dempster, Emily Arnold-Fernández, Sarah Miller, Martha Guerrero Ble, and Bahati Kanyamanza. 2022. *2022 Global Refugee Work Rights Report*. Washington, DC: Center for Global Development.

Giuntella, Osea, Zovanga L. Kone, Isabel Ruiz, and Carlos Vargas-Silva. 2018. "Reason for Immigration and Immigrants' Health." *Public Health* 158 (May): 102–09.

Giuntella, Osea, and Jakub Lonsky. 2020. "The Effects of DACA on Health Insurance, Access to Care, and Health Outcomes." *Journal of Health Economics* 72 (July): 102320.

Giuntella, Osea, Jakub Lonsky, Fabrizio Mazzonna, and Luca Stella. 2021. "Immigration Policy and Immigrants' Sleep: Evidence from DACA." *Journal of Economic Behavior and Organization* 182 (February): 1–12.

Giuntella, Osea, and Fabrizio Mazzonna. 2015. "Do Immigrants Improve the Health of Natives?" *Journal of Health Economics* 43 (September): 140–53.

Glover, Dylan, Amanda Pallais, and William Parienté. 2017. "Discrimination as a Self-Fulfilling Prophecy: Evidence from French Grocery Stores." *Quarterly Journal of Economics* 132 (3): 1219–60.

Godøy, Anna S. 2017. "Local Labor Markets and Earnings of Refugee Immigrants." *Empirical Economics* 52 (1): 31–58.

Gould, Eric D., and Esteban F. Klor. 2016. "The Long-Run Effect of 9/11: Terrorism, Backlash, and the Assimilation of Muslim Immigrants in the West." *Economic Journal* 126 (597): 2064–2114.

Graham, Elspeth, and Lucy P. Jordan. 2011. "Migrant Parents and the Psychological Well-Being of Left-Behind Children in Southeast Asia." *Journal of Marriage and the Family* 73 (4): 763–87.

Grove, Natalie J., and Anthony B. Zwi. 2006. "Our Health and Theirs: Forced Migration, Othering, and Public Health." *Social Science and Medicine* 62 (8): 1931–42.

Gubert, Flore, and Christophe Jalil Nordman. 2008. "Return Migration and Small Enterprise Development in the Maghreb." Analytical Report MIREM-AR 2008/02, Robert Schuman Centre for Advanced Studies, European University Institute, San Domenico di Fiesole (FI), Italy.

Hacker, Karen, Maria Anies, Barbara L. Folb, and Leah Zallman. 2015. "Barriers to Health Care for Undocumented Immigrants: A Literature Review." *Risk Management and Healthcare Policy* 8 (October): 175–83.

Hainmueller, Jens, Dominik Hangartner, and Duncan Lawrence. 2016. "When Lives Are Put on Hold: Lengthy Asylum Processes Decrease Employment among Refugees." *Science Advances* 2 (8): e1600432.

Hainmueller, Jens, Duncan Lawrence, Linna Martén, Bernard Black, Lucila Figueroa, Michael Hotard, Tomás R. Jiménez, et al. 2017. "Protecting Unauthorized Immigrant Mothers Improves Their Children's Mental Health." *Science* 357 (6355): 1041–44.

Hargreaves, Sally, Kieran Rustage, Laura B. Nellums, Alys McAlpine, Nicola Pocock, Delan Devakumar, Robert W. Aldridge, et al. 2019. "Occupational Health Outcomes among International Migrant Workers: A Systematic Review and Meta-Analysis." *Lancet Global Health* 7 (7): e872–e882.

Hasager, Linea, and Mia Jørgensen. 2021. "Sick of Your Poor Neighborhood? Quasi-Experimental Evidence on Neighborhood Effects on Health." CEBI Working Paper 02/21, Center for Economic Behavior and Inequality, Department of Economics, University of Copenhagen, Copenhagen.

Helgertz, Jonas, Pieter Bevelander, and Anna Tegunimataka. 2014. "Naturalization and Earnings: A Denmark–Sweden Comparison." *European Journal of Population* 30 (3): 337–59.

Hersch, Joni. 2008. "Profiling the New Immigrant Worker: The Effects of Skin Color and Height." *Journal of Labor Economics* 26 (2): 345–86.

HRW (Human Rights Watch). 2014. "Yemen's Torture Camps: Abuse of Migrants by Human Traffickers in a Climate of Impunity." May, HRW, New York.

HRW (Human Rights Watch). 2020. "'They Have Robbed Me of My Life': Xenophobic Violence against Non-Nationals in South Africa." September, HRW, New York.

Ibáñez, Ana María, Andrés Moya, María Adelaida Ortega, Sandra Viviana Rozo, and María José Urbina. 2022. "Life Out of the Shadows: Impacts of Amnesties in the Lives of Refugees." Policy Research Working Paper 9928, World Bank, Washington, DC.

ILO (International Labour Organization). 2016. "Protecting Migrant Domestic Workers: The International Legal Framework at a Glance." Briefing Note, Global Action Programme on Migrant Domestic Workers and Their Families, Research Series, ILO, Geneva.

ILO (International Labour Organization). 2017. "Migrant Domestic and Garment Workers in Jordan: A Baseline Analysis of Trafficking in Persons and Related Laws and Policies." ILO, Geneva.

ILO (International Labour Organization). 2019. "General Principles and Operational Guidelines for Fair Recruitment and Definition of Recruitment Fees and Related Costs." Fundamental Principles and Rights at Work Branch, Labour Migration Branch, ILO, Geneva.

ILO (International Labour Organization). 2021. "Qatar's New Minimum Wage Enters into Force." *ILO News: Labour Reforms*, March 19, 2021. https://www.ilo.org/beirut/countries/qatar/WCMS_775981/lang--en/index.htm.

ILO (International Labour Organization), Walk Free, and IOM (International Organization for Migration). 2022. *Global Estimates of Modern Slavery: Forced Labour and Forced Marriage.* September. Geneva: ILO; Nedlands, WA: Walk Free; Geneva: IOM.

Ivlevs, Artjoms, Milena Nikolova, and Carol Lee Graham. 2019. "Emigration, Remittances, and the Subjective Well-Being of Those Staying Behind." *Journal of Population Economics* 32 (1): 113–51.

JDC (Joint Data Center on Forced Displacement). 2023. "Labor Market Access and Outcomes for Refugees." *JDC Quarterly Digest* 7 (January), JDC, World Bank and United Nations High Commissioner for Refugees, Washington, DC.

Jeon, Sung-Hee, Huju Liu, and Yuri Ostrovsky. 2021. "Measuring the Gig Economy in Canada Using Administrative Data." *Canadian Journal of Economics* 54 (4): 1638–66.

Joona, Pernilla Andersson, and Lena Nekby. 2012. "Intensive Coaching of New Immigrants: An Evaluation Based on Random Program Assignment." *Scandinavian Journal of Economics* 114 (2): 575–600.

Joseph, Thomas, Yaw Nyarko, and Shing-Yi Wang. 2018. "Asymmetric Information and Remittances: Evidence from Matched Administrative Data." *American Economic Journal: Applied Economics* 10 (2): 58–100.

Juárez, Sol Pía, Helena Honkaniemi, Andrea C. Dunlavy, Robert W. Aldridge, Mauricio L. Barreto, Srinivasa Vittal Katikireddi, and Mikael Rostila. 2019. "Effects of Non–Health-Targeted Policies on Migrant Health: A Systematic Review and Meta-Analysis." *Lancet Global Health* 7 (4): e420–e435.

Kagan, Sophia, and Ryszard Cholewinski. 2022. "Reforming the Sponsorship System in the Gulf Cooperation Council Countries: Opportunities and Challenges as a Result of COVID-19 and the Fiscal Crisis." Explanatory Note, Gulf Labour Markets, Migration, and Population 1/2022, Gulf Research Center, Jeddah, Saudi Arabia.

Kim, Seohee, and Alison Pei. 2022. "Monopsony in the High-Skilled Migrant Labor Market: Evidence from H-1B Petition Data." Paper presented at the Environmental, Social, and Governance Initiative's Migration and Organizations Conference, Political Risk and Identity Lab, Wharton School, University of Pennsylvania, Philadelphia, October 21–22, 2022. https://esg.wharton.upenn.edu/events/2022-migration-and-organizations-conference/.

Kirdar, Murat Güray, İsmet Koç, and Meltem Dayıoğlu Tayfur. 2021. "School Integration of Refugee Children: Evidence from the Largest Refugee Group in Any Country." IZA Discussion Paper DP 14716 (September), Institute of Labor Economics, Bonn, Germany.

KNOMAD (Global Knowledge Partnership on Migration and Development). 2022. "Migration and the Law Project: From Immigration to Integration." KNOMAD Study (February), KNOMAD, World Bank, Washington, DC.

KNOMAD (Global Knowledge Partnership on Migration and Development) and ILO (International Labour Organization). 2021a. "KNOMAD-ILO Migration Costs Surveys 2015: El Salvador, Ethiopia, Guatemala, Honduras, India, Nepal, Pakistan, Philippines, Vietnam, 2015–2016." Microdata set, version May 24, 2021, World Bank, Washington, DC. https://microdata.worldbank .org/index.php/catalog/2938.

KNOMAD (Global Knowledge Partnership on Migration and Development) and ILO (International Labour Organization). 2021b. "KNOMAD-ILO Migration Costs Surveys 2016: Benin, Burkina Faso, Cabo Verde, Gambia, Ghana, Guinea, Guinea-Bissau, India, Kyrgyz Republic, Liberia, Mali, Mauritania, Nepal, Niger, . . . , 2016–2017." Microdata set, version May 24, 2021, World Bank, Washington, DC. https://microdata.worldbank .org/index.php/catalog/2944.

Lagakos, David, Samuel Marshall, Ahmed Mushfiq Mobarak, Corey Vernot, and Michael E. Waugh. 2020. "Migration Costs and Observational Returns to Migration in the Developing World." NBER Working Paper 26868 (March), National Bureau of Economic Research, Cambridge, MA.

Lavy, Victor, Analia Schlosser, and Adi Shany. 2021. "Immigration and the Short- and Long-Term Impact of Improved Prenatal Conditions." IZA Discussion Paper DP 14576 (July), Institute of Labor Economics, Bonn, Germany.

Lazear, Edward P. 2021. "Why Are Some Immigrant Groups More Successful Than Others?" *Journal of Labor Economics* 39 (1): 115–33.

Lochmann, Alexia, Hillel Rapoport, and Biagio Speciale. 2019. "The Effect of Language Training on Immigrants' Economic Integration: Empirical Evidence from France." *European Economic Review* 113 (April): 265–96.

Luboga, Samuel, Amy Hagopian, John Ndiku, Emily Bancroft, and Pamela McQuide. 2011. "Satisfaction, Motivation, and Intent to Stay among Ugandan Physicians: A Survey from 18 National Hospitals." *International Journal of Health Planning and Management* 26 (1): 2–17.

Madariaga, Javier, César Buenadicha, Erika Molina, and Christoph Ernst. 2019. *Economía de plataformas y empleo ¿Cómo es trabajar para una app en Argentina?* [in Spanish]. IDB Monograph 718 (May). Washington, DC: Inter-American Development Bank.

Marbach, Moritz, Jens Hainmueller, and Dominik Hangartner. 2018. "The Long-Term Impact of Employment Bans on the Economic Integration of Refugees." *Science Advances* 4 (9): eaap9519.

Martén, Linna, Jens Hainmueller, and Dominik Hangartner. 2019. "Ethnic Networks Can Foster the Economic Integration of Refugees." *Proceedings of the National Academy of Sciences* 116 (33): 16280–85.

Martinez, Omar, Elwin Wu, Theo Sandfort, Brian Dodge, Alex Carballo-Dieguez, Rogeiro Pinto, Scott D. Rhodes, Eva Moya, and Silvia Chavez-Baray. 2015. "Evaluating the Impact of Immigration Policies on Health Status among Undocumented Immigrants: A Systematic Review." *Journal of Immigrant and Minority Health* 17 (3): 947–70.

Mattoo, Aaditya, Ileana Cristina Neagu, and Çağlar Özden. 2008. "Brain Waste? Educated Immigrants in the US Labor Market." *Journal of Development Economics* 87 (2): 255–69.

Mattoo, Aaditya, Ileana Cristina Neagu, and Çağlar Özden. 2012. "Performance of Skilled Migrants in the U.S.: A Dynamic Approach." *Regional Science and Urban Economics* 42 (5): 829–43.

McDonald, James Ted, and Steven Kennedy. 2004. "Insights into the 'Healthy Immigrant Effect': Health Status and Health Service Use of Immigrants to Canada." *Social Science and Medicine* 59 (8): 1613–27.

McDonald, Paula, Penny Williams, Andrew Stewart, Robyn Mayes, and Damian Oliver. 2020. *Digital Platform Work in Australia: Prevalence, Nature and Impact.* Brisbane, Australia: Queensland University of Technology.

McKenzie, David J., Steven Stillman, and John Gibson. 2010. "How Important Is Selection? Experimental vs. Non-experimental Measures of the Income Gains from Migration." *Journal of the European Economic Association* 8 (4): 913–45.

Merkle, Lucie, and Klaus F. Zimmermann. 1992. "Savings, Remittances, and Return Migration." *Economics Letters* 38 (1): 77–81.

Mezger Kveder, Cora Leonie, and Marie-Laurence Flahaux. 2013. "Returning to Dakar: A Mixed Methods Analysis of the Role of Migration Experience for Occupational Status." *World Development* 45 (May): 223–38.

Mobarak, Ahmed Mushfiq, Iffath Sharif, and Maheshwor Shrestha. 2021. "Returns to International Migration: Evidence from a Bangladesh-Malaysia Visa Lottery." IZA Discussion Paper DP 14232 (March), Institute of Labor Economics, Bonn, Germany.

Moyce, Sally, and Marc Schenker. 2018. "Migrant Workers and Their Occupational Health and Safety." *Annual Review of Public Health* 39 (April): 351–65.

Müller, Tobias, Pia Pannatier, and Martina Viarengo. 2022. "Labor Market Integration, Local Conditions, and Inequalities: Evidence from Refugees in Switzerland." Policy Research Working Paper 9914, World Bank, Washington, DC.

Naidu, Suresh, Yaw Nyarko, and Shing-Yi Wang. 2016. "Monopsony Power in Migrant Labor Markets: Evidence from the United Arab Emirates." *Journal of Political Economy* 124 (6): 1735–92.

Nakamura, Emi, Jósef Sigurdsson, and Jón Steinsson. 2022. "The Gift of Moving: Intergenerational Consequences of a Mobility Shock." *Review of Economic Studies* 89 (3): 1557–92.

Nwadiuko, Joseph, Jashalynn German, Kavita Chapla, Frances Wang, Maya Venkataramani, Dhananjay Vaidya, and Sarah Polk. 2021. "Changes in Health Care Use among Undocumented Patients, 2014–2018." *JAMA Network Open* 4 (3): e210763.

OECD (Organisation for Economic Co-operation and Development). 2008. *International Migration Outlook 2008.* Paris: OECD.

OECD (Organisation for Economic Co-operation and Development). 2011. *Naturalisation: A Passport for the Better Integration of Immigrants?* Paris: OECD.

OECD (Organisation for Economic Co-operation and Development). 2017. *Catching Up? Intergenerational Mobility and Children of Immigrants.* Paris: OECD.

OECD (Organisation for Economic Co-operation and Development). 2019. "Measuring Platform Mediated Workers." OECD Digital Economy Paper 282 (April), OECD, Paris.

Oreopoulos, Philip. 2011. "Why Do Skilled Immigrants Struggle in the Labor Market? A Field Experiment with Thirteen Thousand Resumes." *American Economic Journal: Economic Policy* 3 (4): 148–71.

Orrenius, Pia M., and Madeline Zavodny. 2009. "Do Immigrants Work in Riskier Jobs?" *Demography* 46 (3): 535–51.

Orrenius, Pia M., and Madeline Zavodny. 2014. "How Do E-Verify Mandates Affect Unauthorized Immigrant Workers?" IZA Discussion Paper DP 7992 (February), Institute of Labor Economics, Bonn, Germany.

Ortensi, Livia Elisa, and Elena Ambrosetti. 2022. "Even Worse than the Undocumented? Assessing the Refugees' Integration in the Labour Market of Lombardy (Italy) in 2001–2014." *International Migration* 60 (3): 20–37.

Pan, Ying. 2012. "The Impact of Legal Status on Immigrants' Earnings and Human Capital: Evidence from the IRCA 1986." *Journal of Labor Research* 33 (?): 119–42.

Parreñas, Rhacel Salazar. 2001. "Mothering from a Distance: Emotions, Gender, and Intergenerational Relations in Filipino Transnational Families." *Feminist Studies* 27 (2): 361–90.

Pascoe, Elizabeth A., and Laura Smart Richman. 2009. "Perceived Discrimination and Health: A Meta-Analytic Review." *Psychological Bulletin* 135 (4): 531–54.

Pega, Frank, Srinivasan Govindaraj, and Nguyen Toan Tran. 2021. "Health Service Use and Health Outcomes among International Migrant Workers Compared with Non-Migrant Workers: A Systematic Review and Meta-Analysis." *PlOS One* 16 (6): e0252651.

Peters, Floris, Hans Schmeets, and Maarten Vink. 2020. "Naturalisation and Immigrant Earnings: Why and to Whom Citizenship Matters." *European Journal of Population* 36 (3): 511–45.

Pinotti, Paolo. 2017. "Clicking on Heaven's Door: The Effect of Immigrant Legalization on Crime." *American Economic Review* 107 (1): 138–68.

Quillian, Lincoln, Anthony Heath, Devah Pager, Arnfinn H. Midtbøen, Fenella Fleischmann, and Ole Hexel. 2019. "Do Some Countries Discriminate More than Others? Evidence from 97 Field Experiments of Racial Discrimination in Hiring." *Sociological Science* 6 (June): 467–96.

Quillian, Lincoln, and Arnfinn H. Midtbøen. 2021. "Comparative Perspectives on Racial Discrimination in Hiring: The Rise of Field Experiments." *Annual Review of Sociology* 47 (1): 391–415.

Ruiz, Isabel, and Carlos Vargas-Silva. 2018. "Differences in Labour Market Outcomes between Natives, Refugees, and Other Migrants in the UK." *Journal of Economic Geography* 18 (4): 855–85.

Ruyssen, Ilse, and Sara Salomone. 2018. "Female Migration: A Way Out of Discrimination?" *Journal of Development Economics* 130 (January): 224–41.

Salmasi, Luca, and Luca Pieroni. 2015. "Immigration Policy and Birth Weight: Positive Externalities in Italian Law." *Journal of Health Economics* 43 (September): 128–39.

Santillano, Robert, Stephanie Potochnick, and Jade Jenkins. 2020. "Do Immigration Raids Deter Head Start Enrollment?" *AEA Papers and Proceedings* 110 (May): 419–23.

Sarvimäki, Matti. 2017. "Labor Market Integration of Refugees in Finland." VATT Research Report 185, VATT Institute for Economic Research, Helsinki, Finland.

Sarvimäki, Matti, and Kari Hämäläinen. 2016. "Integrating Immigrants: The Impact of Restructuring Active Labor Market Programs." *Journal of Labor Economics* 34 (2): 479–508.

Schuettler, Kirsten, and Laura Caron. 2020. "Jobs Interventions for Refugees and Internally Displaced Persons." Jobs Working Paper 47, World Bank, Washington, DC.

Slotwinski, Michaela, Alois Stutzer, and Roman Uhlig. 2019. "Are Asylum Seekers More Likely to Work with More Inclusive Labor Market Access Regulations?" *Swiss Journal of Economics and Statistics* 155 (1): 1–15.

Spadarotto, Claudio, Maria Bieberschulte, Katharina Walker, Michael Morlok, and Andrea Oswald. 2014. *Studie: Erwerbsbeteiligung von anerkannten Flüchtlingen und vorläufig Aufgenommenen auf dem Schweizer Arbeitsmarkt.* Wabern bei Bern, Switzerland: Abteilung Integration, Bundesamt für Migration.

Steinhardt, Max Friedrich. 2012. "Does Citizenship Matter? The Economic Impact of Naturalizations in Germany." *Labour Economics* 19 (6): 813–23.

Steinhardt, Max Friedrich. 2018. "The Impact of Xenophobic Violence on the Integration of Immigrants." IZA Discussion Paper DP 11781 (August), Institute of Labor Economics, Bonn, Germany.

Suleman, Shazeen, Kent D. Garber, and Lainie Rutkow. 2018. "Xenophobia as a Determinant of Health: An Integrative Review." *Journal of Public Health Policy* 39 (4): 407–23.

Testaverde, Mauro, and Jacquelyn Pavilon. 2022. *Building Resilient Migration Systems in the Mediterranean Region: Lessons from COVID-19.* Washington, DC: World Bank.

Tezcan, Tolga. 2018. "On the Move in Search of Health and Care: Circular Migration and Family Conflict amongst Older Turkish Immigrants in Germany." *Journal of Aging Studies* 46 (September): 82–92.

UAE (United Arab Emirates' Government Portal). 2023. "Unemployment Insurance Scheme." *Jobs*, January 9, 2023. https://u.ae/en/information-and-services/jobs/unemployment-insurance-scheme.

UNDP (United Nations Development Programme). 2020. "Human Mobility, Shared Opportunities: A Review of the 2009 Human Development Report and the Way Ahead." New York: UNDP.

UNODC (United Nations Office on Drugs and Crime). 2008. "Human Trafficking: An Overview." United Nations, New York.

Urzi Brancati, Maria Cesira, Annarosa Pesole, and Enrique Férnandéz-Macías. 2020. "New Evidence on Platform Workers in Europe." Science for Policy Report, European Union, Luxembourg.

van den Berg, Gerard J., Petter Lundborg, Paul Nystedt, and Dan-Olof Rooth. 2014. "Critical Periods during Childhood and Adolescence." *Journal of the European Economic Association* 12 (6): 1521–57.

van Doorn, Niels, Fabian Ferrari, and Mark Graham. 2022. "Migration and Migrant Labour in the Gig Economy: An Intervention." *Work, Employment and Society.* Published ahead of print, July 5, 2022. https://journals .sagepub.com/doi/full/10.1177/09500170221096581.

Venkataramani, Atheendar S., Sachin J. Shah, Rourke O'Brien, Ichiro Kawachi, and Alexander C. Tsai. 2017. "Health Consequences of the US Deferred Action for Childhood Arrivals (DACA) Immigration Programme: A Quasi-Experimental Study." *Lancet Public Health* 2 (4): e175–e181.

Vujicic, Marko, Pascal Zurn, Khassoum Diallo, Orvill Adams, and Mario R. Dal Poz. 2004. "The Role of Wages in the Migration of Health Care Professionals from Developing Countries." *Human Resources for Health* 2, 3. https://human-resources-health.biomedcentral.com /articles/10.1186/1478-4491-2-3.

Wahba, Jackline. 2015. "Selection, Selection, Selection: The Impact of Return Migration." *Journal of Population Economics* 28 (3): 535–63.

Wang, Julia Shu-Huah, and Neeraj Kaushal. 2019. "Health and Mental Health Effects of Local Immigration Enforcement." *International Migration Review* 53 (4): 970–1001.

Watson, Tara. 2014. "Inside the Refrigerator: Immigration Enforcement and Chilling Effects in Medicaid Participation." *American Economic Journal: Economic Policy* 6 (3): 313–38.

Weichselbaumer, Doris. 2020. "Multiple Discrimination against Female Immigrants Wearing Headscarves." *ILR Review* 73 (3): 600–27.

WHO (World Health Organization). 2022. *World Report on the Health of Refugees and Migrants.* Geneva: WHO.

World Bank. 2018a. "Asylum Seekers in the European Union: Building Evidence to Inform Policy Making." World Bank, Washington, DC.

World Bank. 2018b. *Moving for Prosperity: Global Migration and Labor Markets.* Policy Research Report. Washington, DC: World Bank.

World Bank. 2022. *Women, Business and the Law 2022.* Washington, DC: World Bank.

Zetter, Roger, and Héloïse Ruaudel. 2016. "Refugees' Right to Work and Access to Labor Markets: An Assessment, Part 1: Synthesis." KNOMAD Study (September), Global Knowledge Partnership on Migration and Development, World Bank, Washington, DC.

Spotlight 4

Gender

The features and implications of cross-border mobility differ by gender, gender identity, and sexual orientation. Women migrate for many reasons and in many ways, depending on whether they are labor migrants, refugees, or reuniting with their family; whether they are traveling alone, with children, or with their entire family; and whether they have skills in demand at their destination. Risks associated with fragility, conflict, and violence, coupled with legal frameworks that criminalize same-sex conduct, are steadily driving forced displacement for sexual and gender minorities. Because data and empirical evidence on sexual and gender minorities are scarce, this spotlight focuses primarily on the migration of women.

Patterns of male and female migration vary widely across countries. The feminization of migration flows has been increasing since well before the 1960s.[1] This shift reflects a combination of factors, including the feasibility of travel by women[2] and the nature of the demand for migrant labor (construction versus domestic work, for example). The percentage of female migrants is particularly high in certain migration corridors, such as from Indonesia, the Philippines, and Thailand to Hong Kong SAR, China, and from Sri Lanka to Jordan.[3]

Women and girls are overrepresented among some groups of migrants. For example, in 2022, 86 percent of adult Ukrainian refugees arriving in Europe were women,[4] as were 62 percent of Ethiopian adult refugees present in South Sudan.[5] Many of these women came with children, while the men stayed behind. Women also constitute a large part of those who migrate for family reunification. Typically, a wife and children move to join a migrant male family member who has already settled at the destination. This is the main long-term immigration flow in many member countries of the Organisation for Economic Co-operation and Development (OECD), including the United States.[6]

Climate change brings new dynamics to affected communities, and women face specific challenges. In many low- and lower-middle-income countries, women are often engaged in agriculture, frequently at the small, independent production level.[7] These activities can be disproportionately affected by slow-onset climate change. Yet when they do not have other skills that are in demand in the labor market or when they are constrained by family obligations, women may not be able to move,[8] and they are trapped in a situation of "maladaptation." Still, patterns vary across countries and contexts. For example, in Bangladesh women are more likely to migrate than men in cases of crop failure and flooding[9] because of insecurity in land tenure. By contrast, in Mali and Nigeria males are more likely to migrate in the event of climate shocks.

Overall, women and girls make up a relatively large share of emigrants from some regions and countries, such as Latin America, the Russian Federation and Central Asia, Central and Northern Europe, and the Philippines and Thailand (map S4.1). In other regions, such as South Asia, the Middle East, and large parts of Africa, men and boys predominate.

Similarly, some regions and countries receive relatively larger shares of female immigrants, such as Eastern Europe, the Balkans, and Argentina and, to a lesser degree, the United States, Australia, and some Western European countries (map S4.2). Others receive a larger share of male immigrants, such as the Gulf Cooperation Council (GCC) countries, Germany, and most of Scandinavia.

Map S4.1 **Some countries send more female migrants; others send more male migrants**

Share of females among emigrants from origin countries where migrants constitute at least 2 percent of the total population

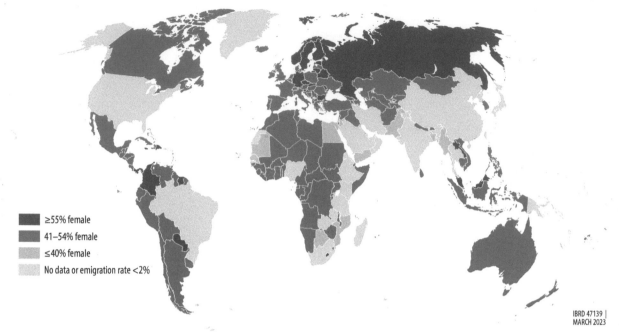

- ≥55% female
- 41–54% female
- ≤40% female
- No data or emigration rate <2%

IBRD 47139 |
MARCH 2023

Source: WDR2023 Migration Database, World Bank, Washington, DC, https://www.worldbank.org/wdr2023/data.

Map S4.2 **Some countries receive more female migrants; others receive more male migrants**

Share of females among immigrants in destination countries where migrants constitute at least 2 percent of the total population

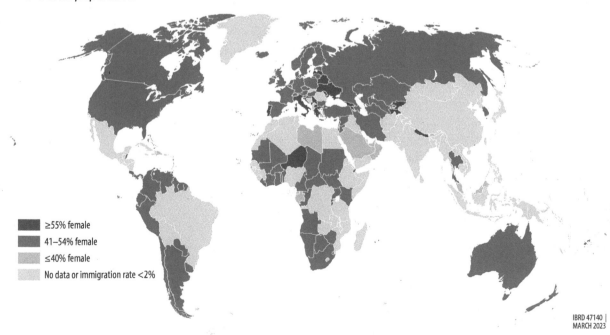

- ≥55% female
- 41–54% female
- ≤40% female
- No data or immigration rate <2%

IBRD 47140 |
MARCH 2023

Source: WDR2023 Migration Database, World Bank, Washington, DC, https://www.worldbank.org/wdr2023/data.

Migration and gender norms

Gender norms affect cross-border mobility at all stages, from the decision to migrate to the decision to settle or return. Gender norms often determine the options available to women and girls in the country of origin, including in terms of education and jobs. In some countries, women also face higher barriers to accessing the labor market.[10] Even when legal norms are not as restrictive, such as in Brazil, Guatemala, India, and Lebanon, laws do not mandate equal remuneration for work of equal value.[11] These factors affect women's choices to migrate and seek better opportunities. Restrictive gender norms are also driving women, especially high-skilled women, to emigrate. Many highly skilled women are choosing to migrate on their own to work, and they tend to favor destinations with lower gender gaps and less discrimination, such as OECD countries.[12] Between 2000 and 2020, the rate of migration from low- and middle-income countries to high-income countries increased 163 percent among tertiary-educated women (figure S4.1). This rate is faster than the increase in tertiary-educated male migrants (138 percent), as well

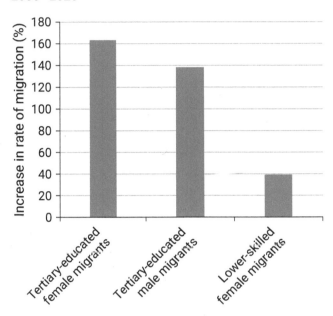

Figure S4.1 **The rate of migration of tertiary-educated female migrants is increasing faster than that of tertiary-educated male migrants and lower-skilled female migrants**

Increase in the rate of migration from low- and middle-income countries to high-income countries, 2000–2020

Sources: IOM and OECD 2014; WDR2023 Migration Database, World Bank, Washington, DC, https://www.worldbank.org/wdr 2023/data.

as the increase in lower-skilled female migrants (39 percent).[13] The rate of single women with a college education migrating to the United States has been growing steadily, particularly for women from South Asia and certain countries in the Middle East and North Africa.

Restrictive gender norms can be an incentive for migration, but they can also be an obstacle.[14] For example, in Iraq, Jordan, Sudan, and the Syrian Arab Republic women cannot travel outside of their countries under the same conditions as men.[15] In other countries, social expectations place higher burdens on women—for example, when it comes to fulfilling family duties or making decisions independently. These burdens may limit women's options for migration.

Access to the labor market at the destination

Many migrant women face challenges in accessing the labor market in the destination country. Some immigrant women have few labor market opportunities outside the informal and service sectors, and so they often work as domestic or care workers in precarious conditions.[16] For example, in Colombia, Venezuelan women are more likely than men to work in the informal sector; recent women migrants are more than twice as likely as men with similar education levels to be unemployed; and even when migrant women have higher levels of education, they earn less than migrant men.[17] Targeted policies are needed to leverage women's economic potential and tackle issues of gender and labor discrimination.

Many of the women who move for family reunification—about one-third of migrant women in Europe[18]—need support to access labor markets. This support includes childcare, skills matching, language courses, and vocational training. Several municipalities in Germany have implemented the *Mama lernt Deutsch* (Mom is learning German) initiative, which provides German-language courses for migrant women and childcare while mothers attend class.[19] Torino, Italy, has offered courses in language, mathematics, civic education, and migration rights to less-educated Arab-speaking women from North Africa, who often live in isolation because they lack jobs and social networks.[20] Indeed, for women and girls, being able to work helps reduce social isolation and improve the prospects of social integration.

Women refugees often face additional challenges. In situations of forced displacement, families are often torn apart, frequently leaving women with the full responsibility for their children. When they do not have support networks or childcare, women face extreme difficulties in accessing the labor force. They also may face discrimination as they look for full-time employment. Some Syrian refugee women, for example, have to juggle jobs, childcare, and household duties in fulfilling their role as the main or sole breadwinner.[21]

Policies and support programs can help address gender differences in labor market access for migrant women. Civil society organizations and local governments have developed a range of initiatives, and additional efforts are under way at the national level. For example, Portugal implemented an initiative at the municipal level to provide women who had immigrated from Brazil and Cabo Verde with skills and job training.[22] In Jordan, recent changes in work regulations allow home-based businesses to be registered. This new policy is expected to benefit both Syrian refugee women and Jordanian women whose ability to work outside their home is limited because of childcare responsibilities.[23] In parallel, origin countries such as the Philippines have established a set of requirements to protect the rights of migrant domestic workers—mostly female—at their destination.[24] But such protective measures must be balanced with other economic considerations so that migrants are not denied jobs or opportunities.[25]

Education at their destination can help women access careers that were not available in their origin countries. It is even more important for girls. Migrant girls in OECD countries perform better than boys at all education levels,[26] suggesting there are high returns on investments in their education. One crucial component of scaling up education and access to the labor market is the availability of language courses.

Gender-based violence

Some women and girls, both refugees and nonrefugees, migrate to escape sexual and gender-based violence (GBV) in their origin country. Women and girls are especially affected by GBV in contexts of armed conflict. For example, in the Democratic Republic of Congo women and girls have been raped on an alarming scale.[27] Between 2003 and 2006, the International Rescue Committee registered 40,000 cases of GBV in the country.[28] In fact, between 2005 and 2007 more than 32,000 cases of conflict-related sexual violence were registered in the province of South Kivu alone, and the actual numbers are believed to be even higher.[29] Other forms of GBV are also common in situations of conflict, forced displacement, and humanitarian crises, including early marriage.[30]

Women are often subject to intimate partner violence in both conflict-affected and safer settings, even though such violence often goes unreported because of trauma, fear of retaliation, and lack of laws addressing the issue.[31] Several countries affected by fragility, conflict, or violence, such as Afghanistan, Guinea, Haiti, Libya, Sudan, and Syria, do not have specific legislation addressing domestic violence.[32]

Women and girls encounter great risks of GBV at all stages of migration, as do sexual and gender minorities. Migrants in general—but especially women, girls, and sexual and gender minorities—face a very high risk of sexual and gender-based violence along migration routes. Forced migrants and those who are smuggled are particularly affected.[33] The risks are exacerbated when victims have a limited ability to report crime to local authorities—such as if they are undocumented.[34] Women are about three times more likely than men to be subjected to sexual violence along the western and central Mediterranean routes.[35] Unaccompanied women and girls are 71 percent more likely to be victims of human trafficking,[36] sexual exploitation, and abuse than those who are accompanied.

Gender-based violence urgently requires dedicated, holistic policies. Origin and destination countries have begun to tackle this issue. For example, Slovenia has placed specialized staff in asylum facilities to mitigate GBV risks. In Sweden, staff at reception centers are trained to identify possible GBV victims at all stages of processing applications for asylum.[37] Since 2019, the Vietnamese government has been regularly informing embassy and consular officials about GBV, labor migration, and trafficking, and it instructed them to respond to GBV through direct service provision and referrals.[38] More needs to be done, however, including increasing funding and investment in women's groups, widening access to sustained services for survivors, investing in efforts to prevent GBV in situations of forced displacement, and improving understanding of local settings through better data.[39]

A path toward empowerment

People leave their countries in a quest for a better life. This is a particularly important option for women and girls and sexual and gender minorities when local gender norms may hamper their mobility, access to justice, safety, and fair access to the labor market. Migration can lead to empowerment, financial independence, better opportunities for education, safety, family reunification, and employment. However, migration brings additional challenges, which can add to existing vulnerabilities. To maximize the benefits of migration for women and their families, discrimination should be addressed by increasing the access of women and children to educational opportunities, fighting against labor market discrimination, preventing and tackling GBV, and working toward social integration. To better inform policy making, more—and disaggregated—data on gender and migration are needed.

Notes

1. Donato and Gabaccia (2015).
2. Ferrant et al. (2014).
3. WDR2023 Migration Database, World Bank, Washington, DC, https://www.worldbank.org/wdr2023/data.
4. 2022 data of Ukraine Refugee Situation (dashboard), Operational Data Portal, United Nations High Commissioner for Refugees, Geneva, https://data.unhcr.org/en/situations/ukraine.
5. 2022 data of Refugee Data Finder (dashboard), United Nations High Commissioner for Refugees, Geneva, https://popstats.unhcr.org/refugee-statistics/download/.
6. Ferrant et al. (2014).
7. Udry (1996).
8. Šedová, Čizmaziová, and Cook (2021).
9. Miletto et al. (2017).
10. Women, Business and the Law (dashboard), World Bank, Washington, DC, https://wbl.worldbank.org/en/wbl.
11. Women, Business and the Law (dashboard), World Bank, Washington, DC, https://wbl.worldbank.org/en/wbl.
12. Ferrant and Tuccio (2015); IOM and OECD (2014); Ruyssen and Salomone (2018); WDR2023 Migration Database, World Bank, Washington, DC, https://www.worldbank.org/wdr2023/data.
13. IOM and OECD (2014); WDR2023 Migration Database, World Bank, Washington, DC, https://www.worldbank.org/wdr2023/data.
14. Ferrant et al. (2014).
15. See Women, Business and the Law (dashboard), World Bank, Washington, DC, https://wbl.worldbank.org/en/wbl.
16. Testaverde et al. (2017).
17. Woldemikael et al. (2022).
18. OECD (2020).
19. EIGE (2019).
20. EIGE (2019).
21. Ibesh et al. (2021); UNHCR (2014).
22. GRASE (2021).
23. UNHCR and Blumont (2019); World Bank (2019).
24. Testaverde et al. (2017). These requirements include a minimum age (23) for migration, regulation of recruitment, mandatory training before departure, and a

minimum wage that migrant domestic workers should receive at their destination.
25. Testaverde et al. (2017).
26. OECD (2020).
27. Banwell (2020).
28. Dallman (2009).
29. Shannon (2010).
30. Girls Not Brides (2020).
31. Ekhator-Mobayode (2020).
32. *Women, Business and the Law* (dashboard), World Bank, Washington, DC, https://wbl.worldbank.org/en/wbl.
33. Tan and Kuschminder (2022).
34. UNODC (2021).
35. UNODC (2021).
36. UNODC (2016).
37. See "Thematic Focus: Gender-Based Violence," European Union Agency for Fundamental Rights, Vienna, https://fra.europa.eu/en/content/thematic-focus-gender-based-violence.
38. ILO and UN Women (2020).
39. Arango et al. (2021).

References

Arango, Diana Jimena, Jocelyn Thalassa Deverall Kelly, Jeni Klugman, and Elena Judith Ortiz. 2021. "Forced Displacement and Violence against Women: A Policy Brief." Gender Dimensions of Forced Displacement Research Program, World Bank, Washington, DC.

Banwell, Stacy. 2020. "Conflict-Related Sexual Violence in the DRC." In *Gender and the Violence(s) of War and Armed Conflict: More Dangerous to Be a Woman?*, edited by Stacy Banwell, 43–64. Emerald Studies in Criminology, Feminism, and Social Change. Bingley, UK: Emerald Publishing.

Dallman, Ashley. 2009. "Prosecuting Conflict-Related Sexual Violence at the International Criminal Court." SIPRI Insights on Peace and Security 2009/1, Stockholm International Peace Research Institute, Solna, Sweden.

Donato, Katherine M., and Donna Gabaccia. 2015. *Gender and International Migration: From the Slavery Era to the Global Age*. New York: Russell Sage Foundation.

EIGE (European Institute for Gender Equality). 2019. "Gender-Sensitive Education and Training for the Integration of Third-Country Nationals." EIGE, Vilnius, Lithuania.

Ekhator-Mobayode, Uche. 2020. "Does Armed Conflict Increase a Woman's Risk of Suffering Intimate Partner Violence?" *Development for Peace* (blog), May 19, 2020. https://blogs.worldbank.org/dev4peace/does-armed-conflict-increase-womans-risk-suffering-intimate-partner-violence.

Ferrant, Gaëlle, and Michele Tuccio. 2015. "South-South Migration and Discrimination against Women in Social Institutions: A Two-Way Relationship." *World Development* 72 (August): 240–54.

Ferrant, Gaëlle, Michele Tuccio, Estelle Loiseau, and Keiko Nowacka. 2014. "The Role of Discriminatory Social Institutions in Female South-South Migration." Issues Paper, OECD Development Centre, Organisation for Economic Co-operation and Development, Paris. https://www.oecd.org/dev/development-gender/SIGI%20and%20Female%20Migration_final.pdf.

Girls Not Brides. 2020. "Child Marriage in Humanitarian Contexts." Thematic Brief, Girls Not Brides, London. https://www.girlsnotbrides.org/documents/959/Child-marriage-in-humanitarian-contexts_August-2020.pdf.

GRASE (Gender and Race Stereotypes Eradication in Labor Market Access). 2021. "Policies and Practices of Labour Inclusion of Migrant Women." Fondazione Iniziative e Studi sulla Multietnicità, Milan.

Ibesh, Rasem, Wael Ahmad, Rachid Chikhou, Razan Jumah, Hayat Sankar, and Allen Thurston. 2021. "The Educational Experiences of Syrian Women in Countries of Safety/Asylum." *International Journal of Educational Research Open* 2 (2): 100027.

ILO (International Labour Organization) and UN Women (United Nations Entity for Gender Equality and the Empowerment of Women). 2020. "Safe and Fair: Realizing Women Migrant Workers' Rights and Opportunities in the ASEAN Region." Policy Brief: Coordinated Quality Services for Ending Violence against Women Migrant Workers, Spotlight Initiative, ILO Regional Office for Asia and the Pacific, Bangkok, Thailand.

IOM (International Organization for Migration) and OECD (Organisation for Economic Co-operation and Development). 2014. "Harnessing Knowledge on the Migration of Highly Skilled Women: Overview of Key Findings." IOM, Geneva.

Miletto, Michaela, Martina Angela Caretta, Francesca Maria Burchi, and Giulia Zanlucchi. 2017. *Migration and Its Interdependencies with Water Scarcity, Gender and Youth Employment*. World Water Assessment Programme, United Nations Educational, Scientific, and Cultural Organization, Paris.

OECD (Organisation for Economic Co-operation and Development). 2020. "How to Strengthen the Integration of Migrant Women?" Migration Policy Debates 25, OECD, Paris. https://www.oecd.org/migration/mig/migration-policy-debates-25.pdf.

Ruyssen, Ilse, and Sara Salomone. 2018. "Female Migration: A Way Out of Discrimination?" *Journal of Development Economics* 130 (January): 224–41.

Šedová, Barbora, Lucia Čizmaziová, and Athene Cook. 2021. "A Meta-Analysis of Climate Migration Literature." CEPA Discussion Paper 29, Center for Economic Policy Analysis, Universität Potsdam, Potsdam, Germany. https://doi.org/10.25932/publishup-49982.

Shannon, Lisa J. 2010. *A Thousand Sisters: My Journey into the Worst Place on Earth to Be a Woman*. Berkeley, CA: Seal Press.

Tan, Sze Eng, and Katie Kuschminder. 2022. "Migrant Experiences of Sexual and Gender Based Violence: A Critical

Interpretative Synthesis." *Globalization and Health* 18 (June 28): 68.

Testaverde, Mauro, Henry Moroz, Claire H. Hollweg, and Achim Schmillen. 2017. *Migrating to Opportunity: Overcoming Barriers to Labor Mobility in Southeast Asia*. Washington, DC: World Bank.

Udry, Christopher R. 1996. "Gender, Agricultural Production, and the Theory of the Household." *Journal of Political Economy* 104 (5): 1010–46. https://www.jstor.org/stable/2138950.

UNHCR (United Nations High Commissioner for Refugees). 2014. "Woman Alone: The Fight for Survival by Syria's Refugee Women." UNHCR, Geneva. https://www.unhcr.org/ar/53bb8d006.pdf.

UNHCR (United Nations High Commissioner for Refugees) and Blumont. 2019. "First Syrian Refugee-Owned Home-Based Business Registered in Jordan." UNHCR, Amman, Jordan. https://www.unhcr.org/jo/12391-first-syrian-refugee-owned-home-based-business-registered-in-jordan.html.

UNODC (United Nations Office on Drugs and Crime). 2016. *Global Report on Trafficking in Persons 2016*. New York: United Nations.

UNODC (United Nations Office on Drugs and Crime). 2021. *Abused and Neglected: A Gender Perspective on Aggravated Migrant Smuggling Offences and Response*. Vienna: UNODC.

Woldemikael, Olivia, Stephanie López Villamil, María Alejandra Uribe, and Julio Daly. 2022. "Overcoming Barriers to Venezuelan Women's Inclusion and Participation in Colombia." CGD Policy Paper, Center for Global Development, Washington, DC.

World Bank. 2019. "Jordan: Improving Women Economic Opportunities: Select Entry Points for Policy Dialogue and Operational Interventions." Report AUS0000935, World Bank, Washington, DC.

5
Origin countries

Managing migration for development

Key messages

- When migrants' skills and attributes are a strong match with the needs of destination countries, origin countries benefit as well. Benefits include remittances, knowledge transfers, and positive impacts on the labor market. These benefits accrue to both regular and irregular migrants, although migrants' gains, and how much they can share with their families in their origin countries, are larger when they have regular status.

- However, the absence of migrants also has a downside for their families and origin countries, including the impacts of the brain drain when high-skilled workers emigrate. Although the costs tend to be smaller in magnitude than the gains, they are significant in some countries.

- Origin countries benefit most when they make labor emigration an integral part of their development strategy. In doing so, they can adopt policies and engage in bilateral cooperation with destination countries to increase the net impact of migration on poverty reduction (figure 5.1).

Figure 5.1 **The policies of origin countries can maximize the impacts of migration on poverty reduction**

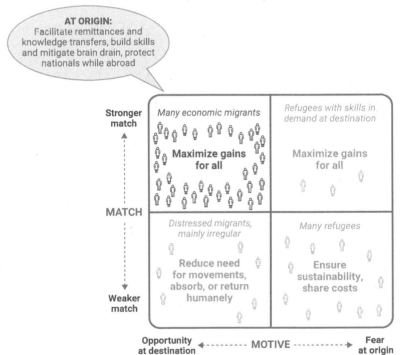

Source: WDR 2023 team.

Note: Match refers to the degree to which a migrant's skills and related attributes meet the demand in the destination country. *Motive* refers to the circumstances under which a person moves—whether in search of opportunity or because of a "well-founded fear" of persecution, armed conflict, or violence in their origin country.

Reaping the full development benefits of remittances

Remittances to low- and middle-income countries have increased dramatically over the last two decades. They were estimated at US$605 billion in 2021,[1] even though their measurement raises technical difficulties (spotlight 5). In 2021, India, Mexico, China, the Philippines, and the Arab Republic of Egypt were the main recipient countries, in that order. Remittances account for about one-third of the total recorded capital inflows to low- and middle-income countries (figure 5.2). They also account for a large share of the gross domestic product (GDP) in several countries in Central America and Central Asia, in small low-income economies, and in countries with a large diaspora, such as Lebanon (figure 5.3).

The remittances they can send their families is often a primary motivation for people to migrate.[2] Many families decide together on the optimal migration strategy—who migrates, where, how long, and how remittances will be spent.[3] Some migrants send remittances to their broader community, especially when the community is in need.

The size of remittance inflows depends on migrants' characteristics. Many low-skilled workers migrate alone and regularly remit a large share of their income to support the families they left behind.[4] For example, Indian migrants in Gulf Cooperation Council (GCC) countries send, on average, nearly 70 percent of their earnings to their families.[5] Among low-skilled migrants, women are more likely to remit higher amounts. By contrast, high-skilled migrants are more likely to come from wealthier families, migrate with their immediate families, and move permanently. Although they may remit higher amounts, they tend to do so sporadically.[6]

Figure 5.2 **Remittances represent a large and growing share of external financing flows to low- and middle-income countries**

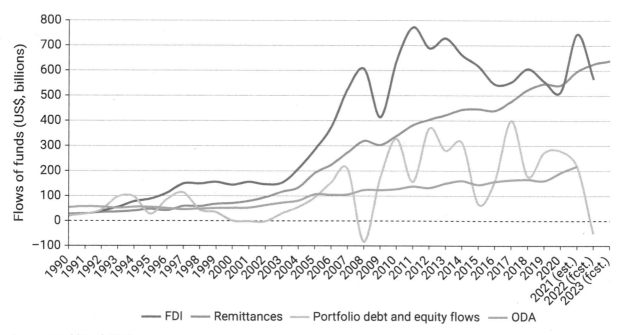

Source: World Bank 2022a.

Note: The figure covers low- and middle-income countries as classified by the World Bank. The data for 2021 are estimates; the data for 2022 and 2023 are forecasts. Portfolio flows include both debt and equity investments. If China were excluded, trends would show remittance flows exceeding FDI flows over the last five years. FDI = foreign direct investment; ODA = official development assistance.

Figure 5.3 In some countries, remittances account for over one-fifth of national income

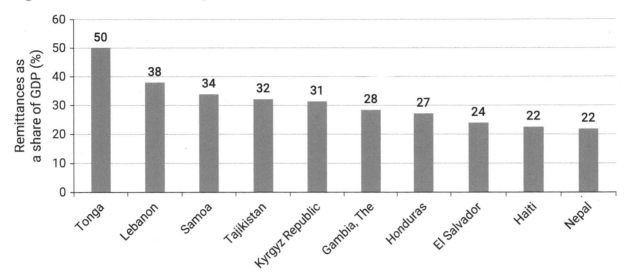

Sources: Remittances: KNOMAD Remittances Data (dashboard), Global Knowledge Partnership on Migration and Development, World Bank, Washington, DC, https://www.knomad.org/data/remittances; World Bank 2022a. GDP (current US dollars): World Economic Outlook Databases (dashboard), International Monetary Fund, Washington, DC, https://www.imf.org/en/Publications/SPROLLS/world-economic-outlook-databases#sort=%40imfdate%20descending.

Note: Remittances as a share of gross domestic product (GDP) are based on 2022 estimates.

Remittance flows depend as well on how successful migrants are in the destination country, whether they have a job, and how much they earn. Remittances are larger when migrants' skills and attributes are a stronger match with the needs of the destination society—which is why origin countries benefit more from such movements. Remittances are also larger when migrants have a documented status. Irregular migrants face greater exposure to job insecurity and income fluctuations and are thus less able to remit in a regular and predictable manner.[7]

Effects on poverty reduction

Remittances have proved to be a powerful instrument for reducing poverty in origin countries. In Nepal, remittances from GCC countries and Malaysia accounted for 40 percent of the decline in poverty rates between 2001 and 2011 (figure 5.4).[8] In 2018, remittances were found to reduce the poverty rate in the Kyrgyz Republic from 30.6 percent to 22.4 percent of households.[9] In Central America and the Caribbean, large reductions in poverty were experienced between 1970 and 2000 in areas where migrants came from the bottom 40 percent of the income distribution.[10] Similar positive impacts on poverty reduction have been found in Indonesia and the Philippines.[11]

Remittances contribute to poverty reduction across a variety of dimensions:

- *Remittances increase household income.* For example, in Bangladesh remittances from low-skilled migrants double their families' income.[12] In Albania, remittances nearly double the daily per capita income of households in the bottom 30th percentile.[13] In some households, remittances function as lifelines, especially in conflict-afflicted countries such as Somalia. Internally displaced persons living outside settlement areas receive an average of US$876 a year in international remittances, or almost twice the level of GDP per capita.[14]

Figure 5.4 In **Nepal, poverty levels declined between 2001 and 2011 in villages with higher emigration**

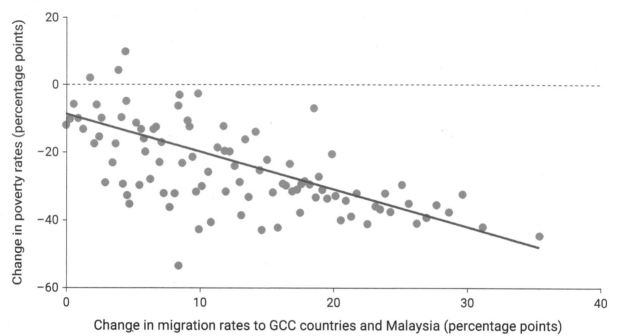

Source: Shrestha 2017.

Note: The figure was constructed using Nepal's Housing and Population Census data for 2001 and 2011. Villages were first sorted based on the change in migration rates to member countries of the Gulf Cooperation Council (GCC) and Malaysia. They were then grouped into 100 bins, each containing 1 percent of Nepal's population. Each point in the figure indicates the average change in migration rate (horizontal axis) and average change in poverty rate (vertical axis) of each bin.

- *Remittances increase consumption and food security.* For example, Indonesian households receiving remittances spend about 16 percent more on food than they would without remittances.[15] In Ethiopia, farm households receiving remittances are less worried about procuring sufficient food and are at lower risk of malnutrition.[16]

- *Remittances allow households to spend more on education and health care*—human capital investments with important long-term benefits. For example, in Colombia households receiving remittances spend 10 percent more on education.[17] In Malawi, migration to South Africa has increased the educational attainment of children in rural communities.[18] In many other countries, children in households that receive remittances tend to stay in school longer[19] and reach higher levels of education and lifetime income.[20]

- *Remittances enable some household members to reduce their working hours.*[21] In rural Nepal, remittances allow women to spend less time in agricultural and informal work.[22] In some Latin American countries, thanks to remittances female household members in rural areas were able to reduce the number of hours they spent in informal and nonpaid work. However, male household members were not similarly affected.[23] The effects, though, are uneven. In Nigeria[24] and Mexico,[25] some household members have to replace the labor and income of the person who left, such as when the family is operating an enterprise.

- *Remittances help close some gender gaps.* In some countries, such as Pakistan, remittances contribute to closing the gender gap in primary education.[26] In Morocco, parents with low levels of education in households that receive remittances postpone their daughters' entry into the labor market so they can stay in school longer.[27] But social norms play a key role. For example, in rural Tajikistan the main beneficiaries of remittances are boys because they are expected to be more productive than girls in the labor market.[28]

In addition to their immediate effects on available income, remittances contribute to poverty reduction through a variety of channels:

- *Remittances protect households from shocks.* Remittances increase when migrants' families face economic downturns, and they smooth consumption, especially for families with limited access to formal financial markets. In the Philippines, remittances have made up, on average, 60 percent of household income lost from typhoons and other natural disasters.[29] In Ethiopia, households that receive remittances use cash reserves to cope with drought instead of selling livestock.[30] Although permanent migrants do not send remittances frequently, they tend to increase their remittances when their families in their home countries face adverse economic shocks.[31] In times of crises, remittances can be directed to entire communities. For example, migrants from the Pacific Islands residing in New Zealand sent goods and remittances through nongovernmental organizations to rebuild village livelihoods and wider communities after Cyclone Winston hit their region of origin in 2016.[32]

- *Remittances can facilitate entrepreneurship by easing financial constraints.* In Morocco and Tunisia[33] and in the Sahel,[34] households that receive remittances are more likely to engage in commercial agriculture (rather than subsistence farming) and purchase modern agricultural equipment. In Nigeria, households that receive remittances invest more in agrochemicals and planting materials, and thus their farms have larger yields.[35] In Ecuador, remittances increase the probability of being self-employed among men and of microenterprise ownership among females.[36]

- *Remittances reduce poverty even in households that do not receive them.* Households that receive remittances increase their spending, which boosts local economic activity and the incomes of other households in the community.[37] Spending from remittances creates local jobs in nontradable sectors such as construction.[38] In Albania, international migrants tend to invest in businesses and housing in the capital city, Tirana, instead of their home villages, fueling urban job creation and internal migration.[39] In the midst of the Asian financial crisis in 1997–98, remittances increased in some regions in the Philippines and protected them from the downturn.[40] The development impacts were long-lasting in these regions, mainly through higher investments in education.[41]

Despite the benefits, remittances have mixed effects on inequality.[42] In some countries, remittances boost the economic and social mobility of the poor, such as in Morocco.[43] But the dynamics can be complex. The effect of remittances on inequality depends on which households receive them and how much they receive.[44] For example, remittances were found to increase inequality in Kosovo while lowering it in Mexico and Pakistan.[45] Remittances can initially increase inequality because wealthier households can more easily afford to send migrants abroad and thus earn higher remittances. But equality will decline over time when emigration becomes easier through migrant networks and lower costs, making it possible for less wealthy households to benefit as well. Remittances may also create new equalities—between households that receive remittances and become relatively wealthier and those that do not in the same community.

Some policies further increase the impacts of remittances on poverty reduction. For example, making it easier for migrants and their families to open savings accounts in origin countries linked to remittances helps them accumulate assets.[46] Some countries are also providing financial literacy training for migrants before their departure and for their families, which leads to higher savings rates, lower debt levels, and ownership of more assets.[47] In Mexico, regulatory reforms to enable land ownership by women have improved the entrepreneurial activities of female members of households that receive remittances in rural areas.[48] Other interventions shown to increase the development impact of migration include matching grants that incentivize households to direct remittances for education purposes. Two pilot activities—EduRemesa (2011–12), aimed at El Salvadorian migrants in Washington, DC,[49] and EduPay (2012–13), aimed at Filipinos in Rome[50]—increased education expenditures without crowding out other expenditure categories.

Macroeconomic stability

Remittances are a stable source of foreign exchange, which supports macroeconomic stability. Unlike official development assistance (ODA) flows—government to government—or profit-seeking foreign direct investment (FDI) and other capital flows, remittances are transfers between private individuals based on family relationships. In contributing to foreign exchange inflows, remittances increase the foreign exchange reserves available to pay for imports and to service the external debt.[51] In the Philippines, they are the largest source of external financing, covering the trade deficit and keeping the current account balance in surplus.[52]

Because they are mostly used to finance household consumption, remittances tend to be less volatile than FDI and other capital flows. From 1980 to 2015, official capital flows were twice as volatile as remittances, and private capital flows were almost three times more volatile than remittances (figure 5.5).[53] Remittances tend to be resilient even in times of crises. For example, during the global financial crisis of 2008–10 they remained relatively stable while other capital inflows suddenly stopped.[54] During the COVID-19 pandemic, after initially dropping, they recovered rapidly following the adoption of fiscal stimulus packages in destination countries.[55] The availability of large amounts of foreign exchange provided by remittances and their relative stability help anchor market confidence and contain borrowing costs for governments and businesses.[56]

The ability of migrants to send remittances is not affected by business cycle fluctuations in countries of origin, which can help smooth these fluctuations. For example, remittance inflows increase after natural disasters. In Latin America and the Caribbean, remittances were found to rise from 4 percent to 4.6 percent of GDP after hurricanes and other natural disasters,[57] and remittances to El Salvador rose following harsh agricultural conditions.[58]

However, remittance flows can be affected by business cycle fluctuations in the countries of destination. For example, in 2015 and 2020 weak oil prices reduced the economic activities

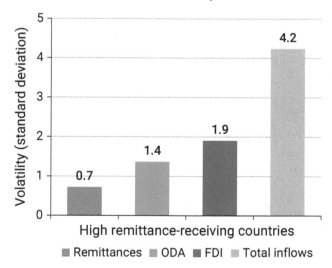

Figure 5.5 Between 1980 and 2015, remittances were less volatile than other capital inflows

Source: De et al. 2019.

Note: Financial flows are measured relative to each country's gross domestic product (GDP). Their volatility is measured as the deviation of annual data from the average over the period 1980–2015. If annual flows remain very close to the average—that is, if they do not vary much from one year to the next—volatility is low. But if they change significantly from year to year, their dispersion and volatility increase. "High remittance-receiving countries" refers to countries for which remittances were greater than 1 percent of GDP during 2003–12. FDI = foreign direct investment; ODA = official development assistance.

Figure 5.6 From 2007 to 2020, remittance outflows from the Russian Federation were more correlated with oil prices than those from Saudi Arabia

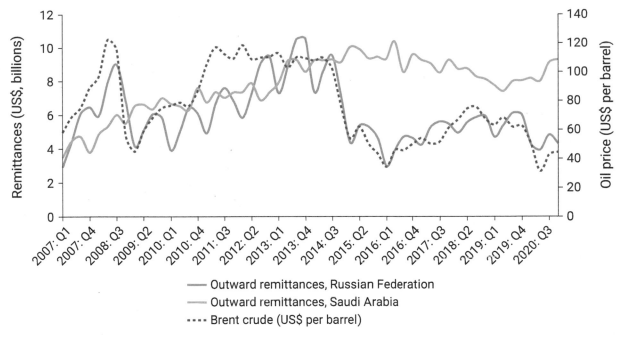

Source: World Bank 2021b.
Note: Q = quarter.

and employment of migrant workers in countries dependent on oil exports, thereby affecting remittance outflows. Yet the decline was less pronounced in countries that managed to better smooth macroeconomic fluctuations. For example, outward remittances from the Russian Federation experienced a bigger decline than those from Saudi Arabia (figure 5.6).[59]

Countries that receive remittances from a diversified set of destination countries are less exposed to business cycle fluctuations in these countries.[60] This is illustrated by the diverging experiences of the Philippines and Mexico following the 2008–10 global financial crisis. Filipino migrants have global footprints, and they work across a range of sectors such as health care, manufacturing, construction, and seafaring industries. At the peak of the global financial crisis, their remittances rose by 5.6 percent. By contrast, Mexican migrants are concentrated in the United States, and they work primarily in the construction and services sectors, which contracted severely during the financial crisis.[61] Remittances to Mexico fell by 16 percent.

The cost of sending remittances

Sending money across international borders remains expensive, despite technological advances. Remittance costs averaged 6 percent (of a remittance) during the second quarter of 2022, or twice the 3 percent target of the United Nations' Sustainable Development Goals (SDGs). Costs include various fees and foreign exchange margins in both the sending and receiving countries.[62] They are highest for transfers to Sub-Saharan Africa, at 8.8 percent in the second quarter of 2022.

Remittances are channeled through a range of operators—including banks, money transfer operators, post offices, and mobile operators—as well as through informal systems, such as the *hawala* used in parts of Africa, the Middle East, and South Asia. On average, banks tend to charge higher fees, and their delivery times are longer than other means of transfer. Post offices are less expensive, although volume and demand are often low.[63] In cost, money transfer operators, such as Western Union or MoneyGram, are third. Mobile operators, such as M-Pesa (from Kenya to Tanzania and Uganda, from Rwanda to Kenya, and from Tanzania to Kenya) and Orange Money (from France to Côte d'Ivoire and Mali and from Senegal to Mali), are the cheapest channel, and their costs are close to the SDG target (figure 5.7). Typically, informal transfers are more expensive than mobile payment services.[64]

The costs of sending remittances reflect a variety of factors. Countries with large remittance inflows such as India and the Philippines generally enjoy low costs—even "no fees" for certain corridors and transaction amounts. But low-income countries face costlier options, especially for poorer households receiving smaller and irregular amounts. Corridors with higher fees tend to be those in which competition is limited in either the sending or receiving countries,[65] where migrants are fewer,[66] and where access to financial institutions is more difficult, once again in both sending and receiving countries.[67]

The use of mobile digital money, regardless of operators, is lowering costs. However, its potential growth and availability are constrained by regulations aimed at money laundering and the financing of terrorism. These operators face strict scrutiny when partnering with international money transfer networks and accessing domestic payment systems.[68]

Lowering the cost of remittances will require increasing competition in both the sending and receiving countries and ensuring that migrants and their families can compare the costs of all the channels available to them.[69] Expanding the use of mobile payment services could also help lower costs within the context of a well-regulated market. The Group of Twenty (G20) has developed a road map to that effect. It calls for (1) a commitment to a joint public and private sector vision; (2) coordination of regulatory,

Figure 5.7 Money transfers via mobile operators are less expensive than through other channels

Average cost of sending a US$200 remittance, 2011–22

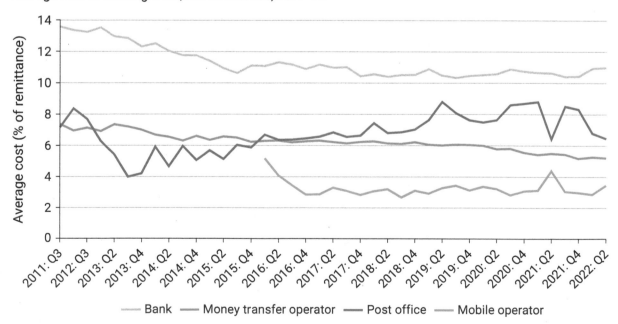

Source: WDR 2023 team calculations, based on data from Remittance Prices Worldwide (portal), World Bank, Washington, DC, https://remittanceprices.worldbank.org.

Note: Q = quarter.

supervisory, and oversight frameworks; (3) improvements in existing payment infrastructure and arrangements to support the requirements of cross-border payments; (4) increased data quality and standardized data exchange; and (5) new payment infrastructure and arrangements.[70] In some countries, reforms aimed at strengthening the financial sector can also encourage senders to transfer money through formal financial channels.

Leveraging knowledge transfers

Migration benefits countries of origin through knowledge transfers from diasporas and returning migrants. These effects are larger when migrants are successfully employed in the destination country—that is, when their skills and attributes are a strong match with the needs of the destination economy. Knowledge transfers can also include the transfer of institutional and social norms to the country of origin (box 5.1).

Box 5.1 Migrants can transfer institutional and social norms to their origin country

Migrants can be agents of institutional change in their countries of origin. The shorter their stay in destination countries (that is, the stronger the links with their origin countries), the greater is the diffusion of ideas from destination to origin countries.[a] The transfer of "social remittances" has largely occurred in three areas.

Institutional quality. The migration of high-skilled individuals has a positive effect on institutional quality if the origin country has policies that allow diaspora members and returning migrants to take part in social and economic activities. In such contexts, institutional quality can benefit from the knowledge and experience acquired in the destination country. These effects are blunted, however, when large-scale emigration leads to a dearth of qualified professionals in local government and political parties, which delays political and social change.[b]

Demand for accountability. Migrant households tend to be more politically active, and they may demand greater political accountability in communities of origin, such as in Cabo Verde and the Philippines. Remittances from Filipino migrants are related positively to government effectiveness at the provincial level.[c] As education increases thanks to remittances, residents call for more political accountability, and rent-seeking activity in local governments becomes less likely. Networks connecting migrants to residents in their origin villages have shaped political attitudes and empowered village residents in countries such as in Mozambique.

Gender norms. Migration affects the evolution of gender norms but in different ways. For example, Moroccan and Turkish migrants to Europe have transmitted liberal views on gender roles to their communities of origin, and they tend to have fewer children. By contrast, migrants to the Gulf Cooperation Council (GCC) countries, such as those from Jordan and the Arab Republic of Egypt, tend to adopt and transmit more conservative gender norms[d] and to have more children than comparable households without migrants.[e] Migration to countries with female political empowerment is associated with higher female parliamentary participation in origin countries.

a. Docquier et al. (2016); Levitt (1998); Tran, Cameron, and Poot (2017).
b. Anelli and Peri (2017); Horvat (2004).
c. Tusalem (2018).
d. Chattopadhyay, White, and Debpuur (2006); Ferrant and Tuccio (2015), studying South-South migration; Hadi (2001); Sakka, Dikaiou, and Kiosseoglou (1999); Tuccio and Wahba (2018).
e. Bertoli and Marchetta (2015); Fargues (2013).

Migration contributes to the integration of origin countries into global networks. Some migrants have served as catalysts for increasing international trade between origin and destination countries.[71] They have provided information on laws, regulations, markets, and products and have linked sellers and buyers across these countries. An increase in demand for goods and services produced in origin countries has also been linked to migrants from those countries.[72] Migration has been linked as well to an increase in FDI flows from destination to origin countries[73] and a reduction of the corresponding transaction costs.

Migrants—especially if they are highly educated and are in high-skilled occupations—have also helped to develop industries in their countries of origin by transferring knowledge and fostering innovation.[74] For example, Indian migrants in California's Silicon Valley have launched large information technology–related firms in India.[75] In 2006, firms established by returnees accounted for some 90 percent of firms in software technology parks in Bangalore.[76] Citations in patent applications reveal that ethnic networks facilitate knowledge transfer, raising the labor productivity of manufacturing in origin countries.[77] Some diasporas are contributing to the national debates on economic policy making. For example, Vietnam[78] and the Republic of Korea have programs to invite their diasporas to take part in formulating their economic development plans.

Some temporary migrants acquire skills abroad and return home better equipped with skills and assets.[79] They command higher wages than nonmigrant workers with similar education levels, especially those who have a tertiary education.[80] They are also more likely than nonmigrants to engage in self-employment and entrepreneurship, especially because migrants tend to have a relatively high risk tolerance and an entrepreneurial appetite.[81] For example, in Bangladesh more than two-thirds of returning temporary migrants engage in some form of entrepreneurial or self-employment activity after returning, as opposed to only one-third of similarly educated nonmigrant workers (figure 5.8).[82]

Figure 5.8 **In Bangladesh, returning migrants are more likely than nonmigrants to be self-employed or entrepreneurs**

Share of population self-employed or engaged in entrepreneurial activity, by age and migration status

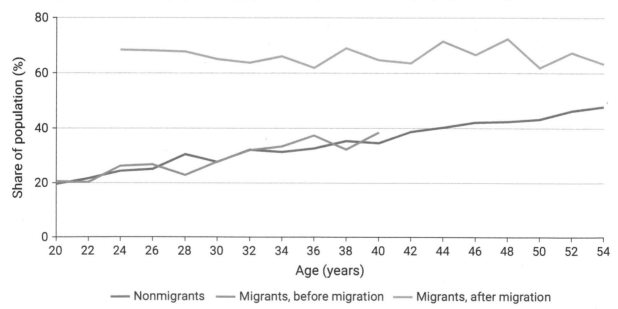

Source: Bossavie et al. 2021.

Knowledge transfers can be supported by government policies in the country of origin. The extent of transfers depends on political stability, institutional quality, the investment climate, human capital, and export capacity. Some countries have also adopted measures to facilitate diaspora engagement, including to foster collaboration in research and development.[83] Others, like the Philippines, offer temporary emigrants entrepreneurial training to ease their return to the domestic labor force and improve the odds that they can contribute to national development.[84]

Managing labor market impacts

Employment and wages

The emigration of large numbers of workers reduces the size of the labor force in origin countries. In the Philippines, approximately 2 million workers (or about 5 percent of the labor force) leave for temporary foreign jobs each year—on average for seven years. In Tajikistan, nearly half of the labor force works abroad on a seasonal basis, primarily in Russia. Such outward migration alleviates the pressures of unemployment and underemployment, especially in lower-income countries with younger populations.[85] However, this effect is partly blunted if migrants return and reenter the domestic labor force.

In origin countries, the effects of migration on the labor force are uneven across regions because migrants come disproportionately from some regions, such as in Mexico (map 5.1). In parts of the Philippines, the rate of emigration is twice higher than the national average. In Bangladesh, emigration rates can reach 10 percent of the labor force in some areas. Labor market effects are greater in regions with large outflows.[86]

At times, emigration creates tight labor market conditions and, in turn, generates movement by workers within a country. For example, in India emigration from the state of Kerala created relocation opportunities for workers from Kolkata.[87] In Bangladesh, the government has subsidized internal transportation costs to facilitate such labor reallocations within the country.[88]

The effects of migration on domestic wages are often more complex—and they largely depend on who migrates. If migrants were unemployed before moving, migration increases labor force participation without significantly changing wages.[89] If, on the other hand, migrants were working before moving, their departure may increase wages for those who have similar skills and who stay in the country of origin. For example, in the early 2000s, outflows of young and low-skilled workers improved wages for other low-skilled people in Pakistan and the Philippines.[90] But migration can also depress wages for those whose skills are complementary to those of the migrants.

Map 5.1 Emigration from Mexico is uneven across regions

Share of households with emigrant(s), by municipality

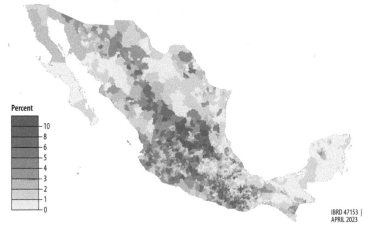

Percent
- 10
- 8
- 6
- 5
- 4
- 3
- 2
- 1
- 0

IBRD 47153 |
APRIL 2023

Source: WDR 2023 team calculations, based on data from Censo de Población y Vivienda 2020 (dashboard), Instituto Nacional de Estadística y Geografía, Aguascalientes, Mexico, https://www.inegi.org.mx/programas/ccpv/2020/.

Note: The map shows the share of households in each municipality with at least one person who emigrated from 2014 to 2019.

For example, emigration of high-skilled workers reduces the wages of low-skilled workers if a substantial part of the service industry serves clients with high incomes who are no longer in the country.[91]

Brain drain

Migrants whose skills and attributes are a strong match with the needs of the destination economy can also be critical workers in their country of origin. Thus their emigration can create situations in which the interests of the countries of origin and destination are not aligned.

The emigration of highly skilled people from lower-income countries is often referred to as a "brain drain." It is an impediment to development when the costs to the origin society from losing a highly qualified worker outweigh the benefits from the remittances and the knowledge spillovers the worker generates. These adverse effects are especially relevant when workers are in occupations deemed essential for the origin society such as health care.

The emigration of high-skilled workers is a global phenomenon. It stands at about 4 percent of the high-skilled population of high-income member countries of the Organisation for Economic Co-operation and Development (OECD), slightly over 10 percent for middle-income countries, and around 20 percent for low-income countries.[92] High-level skills tend to be in greater demand in many destination countries, and these migrants have better access to foreign employment opportunities. Accordingly, tertiary-educated workers tend to be overrepresented among emigrants from lower- and middle-income countries (figure 5.9).[93] The emigration rate for individuals with a tertiary education is 7.3 times that of individuals with only a primary education and 3.5 times that of individuals with only secondary schooling. For example, 25.6 percent of Cambodians (age 25 and over) with a tertiary education live abroad, compared with 6.7 percent of those with a primary or secondary education.[94]

The emigration rates of highly skilled and educated workers is especially high in low-income and smaller countries. In Sub-Saharan Africa and in Small Island Developing States in the Caribbean and the Pacific, the emigration rates of the tertiary-educated are 30 times higher than those of the less-educated.[95] More than 40 percent of all tertiary-educated people born in Small Island Developing States have emigrated to another country. About 70 percent of highly educated Cabo Verdeans live abroad.[96] In 2018, about 25,000 doctors trained in Sub-Saharan Africa—that is, nearly one-quarter of the total number of physicians in Africa—were working in OECD countries.[97]

For origin countries, the brain drain raises two policy questions. First, how do they mitigate the brain drain's effects, especially on sectors such as health care? Second, when the losses in origin countries translate into gains in destination countries, can mechanisms be established to redistribute some of the gains from destination to origin countries? This issue is particularly relevant when the education of the emigrants is financed publicly, either in part or in full.

High-skilled emigration often stems from the economic limitations and resource constraints in the origin countries. Some high-skilled workers are not employed at their full productive capacity domestically.[98] For example, challenges in providing basic health care services in some countries arise not only from the absence of health professionals, but also from the shortage of inputs, medicines, and facilities in the health care system. Some shortages have stemmed from doctors' preference for working in urban areas to the detriment of rural areas,[99] such as in Benin, Côte d'Ivoire, Mali, and Senegal. At times, the decision to migrate is linked not only to income but also to professional advancement prospects, better facilities, and family safety.[100]

In many small countries, the domestic market is too limited for some sectors to be profitable. Seeking to give high-skilled professionals incentives to stay rather than migrate, some countries have specialized in niche activities that can also serve the global market. For example, medical tourism

Figure 5.9 On average, migrants are more educated than the labor force in their origin countries

Share of the tertiary-educated among emigrants and labor force in origin countries, 2020

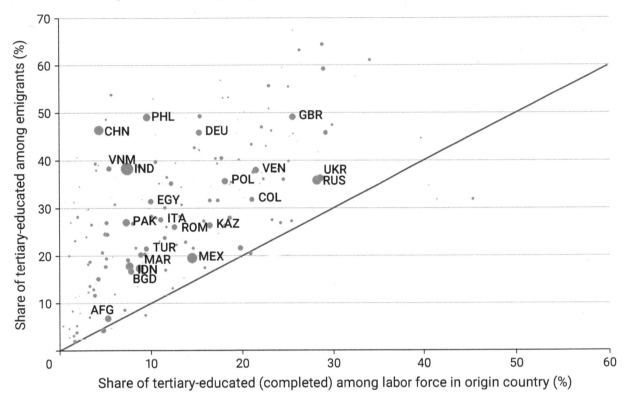

Sources: WDR 2023 team compilations. WDR2023 Migration Database, World Bank, Washington, DC, https://www.world bank.org/wdr2023/data. Data on skill structure of population: census data, 2014–20; updated Barro and Lee (2013); Data (portal), Wittgenstein Centre for Demography and Global Human Capital, Vienna, https://www.wittgensteincentre.org/en /data.htm.

Note: The size of the circles is relative to the number of emigrants from the country. The diagonal line represents equal levels of tertiary education between emigrants and the labor force in the origin country. For country abbreviations, see International Organization for Standardization (ISO), https://www.iso.org/obp/ui/#search.

not only can serve as a source of additional revenue in the health care sector, but also can give medical workers opportunities to stay as well as respond to the domestic demand.[101] For smaller economies, regional cooperation could also make it possible to expand domestic markets and sustain specialized activities that would otherwise not be viable, thereby reducing the incentives of high-skilled professionals to emigrate.

To reduce the impact of brain drain, origin countries need to expand their capacity for training high-skilled workers. Greater capacity increases the likelihood that a sufficient number of high-skilled workers stay, even if others migrate. The challenge, however, is how to finance such an expansion.

When high-skilled workers who leave have been educated with public funding from the origin country, their migration becomes a de facto subsidy from the origin country (typically lower-income) to the destination country (typically higher-income). Almost one-third of college-educated emigrants, however, have obtained their education after they migrate—at no cost to their country of origin.[102] This proportion is particularly high among some migrant groups. For example, more than 50 percent of college-educated Jamaicans who live in the United States studied there (figure 5.10), and 90 percent of Micronesians and 95 percent of Tongans with tertiary education received their degrees abroad.[103]

In some countries, private education can complement public efforts. For example, in response to the rising demand in destination countries for nurses, the Philippines rapidly expanded its nursing education programs in private institutions.[104] For every new emigrant nurse, nine new nurses were licensed, ultimately boosting the net number of nurses in the country.[105]

International cooperation can enhance the match between workers' skills and attributes and the needs of the destination economy while reducing some of the adverse effects of the brain drain. For example, the Global Skills Partnerships (GSPs) and other bilateral and regional agreements between origin and destination countries facilitate expansion of training.[106] In a GSP, the country of destination—either the government or the private sector—underwrites the training of potential migrants so that they acquire the qualifications needed by its labor market. The training is held in the country of origin prior to migration. It also benefits students who will stay home and enter the domestic labor force.

To be effective, however, such schemes must be market-driven with substantive involvement by the private sector. The Australia Pacific Training Coalition (APTC) learned this lesson. It established technical and vocational training campuses on five Pacific Island countries and had by 2019 graduated over 15,000 students.[107] However, only a small fraction of these students moved to Australia or New Zealand for work, despite a majority aspiring to do so. This outcome was attributed to weak links with prospective employers and inadequate mechanisms for recognizing skills and experience obtained in the country of origin.[108]

Figure 5.10 **Many high-skilled migrants who migrate to the United States from Latin America and the Caribbean and Sub-Saharan Africa receive their tertiary education in the United States**

Share of high-skilled migrants in the United States who received their tertiary degree in the United States

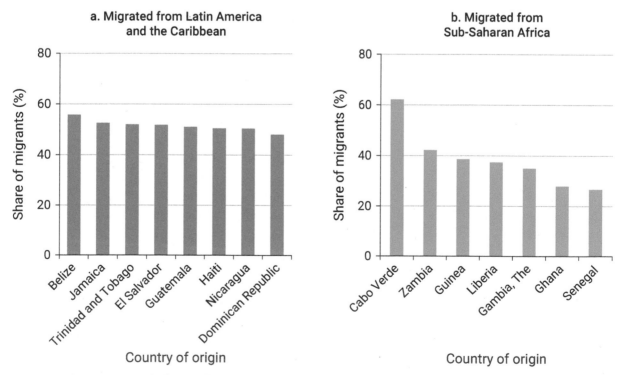

Source: WDR 2023 team calculations, based on 2019 five-year estimates of American Community Survey (dashboard), US Census Bureau, Suitland, MD, https://www.census.gov/programs-surveys/acs.

The additional measures needed to retain essential workers in critical sectors such as health care would require cooperation between origin and destination countries. For example, some origin countries have considered requiring essential workers to undertake a minimum period of national service. The enforcement of such schemes that go against market forces is challenging and more likely to succeed when supported by both origin and destination countries—for example, if destination countries mandate a minimum period of service as a condition for receiving a visa within the broader context of bilateral labor arrangements.[109] But such measures can only be complements, not substitutes, for other policies that make domestic labor markets more attractive for the targeted workers.[110]

Taking a strategic approach

Migration of workers whose skills and attributes are a strong match in destination economies can be a powerful driver of poverty reduction in countries of origin. Some origin countries, such as the Philippines, have managed it as an integral component of their development strategies, with noticeable results (box 5.2).

Box 5.2 The Philippines: A case study of how origin countries can benefit from migration

The Philippines offers an instructive example of a proactive, integrated policy approach to migration. Its migration system evolved from the 1970s to its current structure spanning the entire migration life cycle—from pre-deployment to eventual return and reintegration. Its elements include the following:

- *Bilateral labor agreements.* The Philippines entered into 54 bilateral labor agreements (BLAs) to provide better conditions for emigrants. For example, the BLA with Saudi Arabia and other Gulf Cooperation Council (GCC) countries for household service workers abolished placement fees to reduce migration costs and included a model contract enshrining certain rights and protections. It permitted the establishment of a minimum wage. The BLA also accompanied broader reforms to better equip workers with technical skills and knowledge. Enforcement of these agreements requires ongoing efforts by both destination countries and the Philippines.[a]
- *Preparation of migrants.* The government has put in place programs to develop potential migrants' skills in line with the demands in the global market. The Technical Skills and Development Authority (TESDA) trains more than 800,000 graduates a year. Education in selected occupations in high demand globally, such as nursing, has also been expanded. This approach has positive spillovers for the domestic labor market because some graduates from these programs do not migrate. In parallel, the government provides pre-departure orientation programs to inform migrants about the risks and benefits of migration and labor rights and safety measures, as well as information specific to the destination. Recently, the Philippine government began requiring financial literacy training for all prospective overseas workers. The recent inclusion of this pilot financial literacy class in the orientation programs increased the likelihood of having a bank account among some migrants.[b] Lessons from these pilots will need to be reflected in broader efforts beyond the pilot phase.
- *Protection of migrants.* The Philippines aims to engage with workers while they are overseas through its Philippine Overseas Labor Offices (POLOs). These offices assist with labor protection, training, and general support. In addition, the Philippines has established a Post Arrival Orientation Seminar that

(Box continues next page)

imparts information about the destination country and, in some exceptional circumstances, resource centers that can serve as shelters for women migrant workers in need. To further protect workers and their households, the government requires that they be covered by insurance, which is generally the responsibility of the employer or recruiter, but there are gaps in such health insurance coverage as exposed during the COVID-19 pandemic.[c]

- *Cost of remittances.* Remittances are important determinants of investment in health and education in the Philippines, especially for children. The costs of sending remittances to the Philippines from other countries in the region are among the world's lowest because of efforts by the government and the private sector to develop digital platforms and expand information on remittance services. Investments in education have also increased thanks to private sector innovations that allow lenders to designate remittances for specific purposes. And yet despite the significant development impacts of remittances, gaps remain, particularly for children whose parent or caregiver goes abroad. Households relying on remittances may face uninsured shocks from abroad, such as a pandemic.[d]

- *Support to returning migrants.* To maximize the economic potential of returning migrants, the government implements programs to support their reintegration into the labor market, which includes providing information about return and opportunities to gain skills while abroad. The government also offers business training and loans or grants for entrepreneurship. However, uptake of these supportive efforts has been low—just 4 percent of returnees. Seventy percent of returning migrants still report having difficulty finding a satisfactory job. The government has continued to expand these efforts, especially during the COVID-19 pandemic.[e]

- *Institutional arrangements.* The Philippine Development Plan 2017–2022 aimed to mainstream migration, facilitate temporary movements, and support migrants' return.[f] The new Philippine Development Plan (2023–28) focuses on returning migrants' reentry into the economy, and on the management of social impacts, including through health and psychosocial services to migrants' children. To ensure coherence among all interventions, the government has merged several agencies to form the cabinet-level Department of Migrant Workers to support migrants and their families prior to departure, while abroad, and upon return.[g] In addition, the government recently resuscitated the right of migrants overseas to vote for senators and party-list representatives as a way to get their voice heard.

Source: Ang and Tiongson (2023).

a. Arriola (2022); Chilton and Woda (2021); ILO (2019); Rivera, Serrano, and Tullao (2013); Ruhunage (2014); Wickramasekara (2015); Yagi et al. (2014).

b. Abarcar and Theoharides (2021); Barsbai et al. (2022); Cabanda (2017); OECD (2017, 105). See also the various entries on the Philippines in the Good Practices Database: Labour Migration Policies and Programmes, International Labour Organization, Geneva, https://www.ilo.org/dyn/migpractice/migmain.home.

c. Ang and Tiongson (2023); DOLE (2015).

d. Asis (2006); Clemens and Tiongson (2017); Cortes (2015); De Arcangelis et al. (2015); Dominguez and Hall (2022); Edillon (2008); NEDA (2021); Pajaron, Latinazo, and Trinidad (2020); World Bank (2022b); Yang (2008).

e. Ang and Tiongson (2023); Asis (2020); OECD (2017, 83).

f. NEDA (2021).

g. "About DMW," Department of Migrant Workers, Mandaluyong City, the Philippines, https://www.dmw.gov.ph/about-dmw.

To manage emigration for poverty reduction, countries have adopted measures in areas that often reinforce one another:

- *Remittance costs.* Reducing remittance costs and incentivizing migrants to channel such transactions through the formal financial sector. For example, Mexico does not charge income tax on remittances received under a certain amount (about US$30,000).[111] Vietnam and Tajikistan have also removed taxes on incoming remittances and saw increased flows as a result.[112] These efforts can also be complemented by partnerships in destination countries. For example, the Tonga Development Bank has created the 'Ave Pa'anga Pau initiative, a digital service supporting remittances received from New Zealand and Australia for a fee of about 4.5 percent.[113]
- *Knowledge transfers.* Strengthening the business environment to maximize the effects of knowledge transfers and engaging with the diaspora to further encourage knowledge flows. For example, Korea and Vietnam have programs to invite their diasporas to take part in formulating their economic development plans.
- *Supporting return.* Supporting return migrants as they reenter the domestic labor force, such as in Malaysia. To entice migrant workers to come back, Malaysia offers benefits that include a 15 percent flat income tax for five years, permanent status eligibility for foreign spouses and children, and various duty exemptions.
- *Skills building.* Providing workers with skills that are a strong match with the needs of both the domestic market and potential destination countries and even specializing in some skill sets, such as in Bosnia and Herzegovina, the Philippines, Tunisia, Indonesia, and India in the context of the Triple Win Program with Germany. The program is designed to facilitate migration to Germany. The process comprises foreign credential recognition processes, language and professional courses, and job placements. Beneficiaries are then entitled to a residence permit.
- *Supporting nationals abroad.* Strengthening consular services to support migrants while they are abroad, which the Philippines did so migrants would be better protected against abuse and exploitation.

Efforts like these have been institutionalized in some countries, both at the national level and through bilateral cooperation. Many origin countries have established specialized agencies to design and implement emigration-related policies and coordinate with other government departments. Some countries, such as Bangladesh, Pakistan, and the Philippines, have established dedicated ministries for effective coordination. In parallel, some origin countries have entered into formal bilateral labor agreements with destination countries as a way to regulate and steer labor migration in a manner that is mutually beneficial.

Notes

1. World Bank (2022b).
2. Migrants' reasons for sending remittances depend on the conditions in their origin countries and the type of migration. On the one hand, the countercyclicality of remittances suggests migrants' altruism—that is, they send money to improve the well-being of their families (Frankel 2011; Lucas and Stark 1985; Osili 2004). On the other hand, remitting behavior can be motivated by migrants' self-interest, such as to increase the probability that it will lead to an inheritance (Hoddinott 1994; Osili 2004) or to invest in assets in the origin country (Garip 2012). Whatever the motivation, it is difficult to test for altruism or self-interest because remittances reflect diverse factors and reasons—such as to compensate a family member caring for a migrant's children (Cox 1987). Or perhaps altruism and self-interest coexist. Lucas and Stark (1985, 904) assert: "In the end, one cannot probe whether the true motive is one of caring or more selfish wishing to enhance prestige by being perceived as caring."
3. Adams (2009); Fischer, Martin, and Straubhaar (1997); Stark and Bloom (1985). When remitting part of their

income, migrants may conceal their true earnings from their family members back home to, for example, avoid pressure from family members to remit. See McKenzie, Gibson, and Stillman (2013); Seshan and Zubrickas (2017).

4. Brown and Poirine (2005); Delpierre and Verheyden (2014).
5. According to the KNOMAD–International Labour Organization (ILO) migration cost survey (KNOMAD and ILO 2021a, 2021b).
6. World Bank (2018, chap. 5).
7. The positive impacts of remittances may be weaker for families of refugees. Finding employment in the host country takes refugees longer, and their potential to earn and remit to their families back home may be lower as family ties become stretched. Sending remittances may also be complicated by sanctions and the impact of conflict on the origin country's financial system.
8. Shrestha (2017).
9. Bossavie and Garrote-Sánchez (2022, 24).
10. Acosta et al. (2008).
11. See Cuecuecha and Adams (2016) for Indonesia; Ducanes (2015) for the Philippines.
12. Mobarak, Sharif, and Shrestha (2021).
13. Frasheri and Dushku (2021).
14. World Bank (2019, 123).
15. Cuecuecha and Adams (2016).
16. Abadi et al. (2018).
17. Medina and Cardona-Sosa (2010).
18. Dinkelman and Mariotti (2016).
19. McKenzie and Rapoport (2011) found this to be true in Mexico, especially among younger adolescents ages 13–15.
20. Bansak, Chezum, and Giri (2015).
21. Chami et al. (2018), using 177 cross-country data at the aggregate level for 1991–2015. The term *reservation wage* refers to the least amount of money a person would accept to work in a particular position or type of employment.
22. Lokshin and Glinskaya (2009).
23. For El Salvador, see Acosta (2006). For Mexico, see Amuedo-Dorantes and Pozo (2006).
24. Urama et al. (2017).
25. Cox-Edwards and Rodríguez-Oreggia (2006).
26. Mansuri (2006).
27. Bouoiyour and Miftah (2015).
28. Jaupart (2019).
29. Yang and Choi (2007).
30. Mohapatra, Joseph, and Ratha (2009).
31. Taylor et al. (2005). The longer migrants stay abroad, the weaker are the ties to the origin country and the less frequent are the remittances.
32. Pairama and Le Dé (2018).
33. de Haas (2001).
34. Konseiga (2004).
35. Iheke (2014).
36. Acosta, Fajnzylber, and López (2007).
37. It is not empirically simple to properly measure the relationship between remittances and overall poverty because they mutually reinforce one another. For

example, increased poverty may induce migrants to send more remittances.
38. Chami et al. (2018).
39. Chami et al. (2018); Gedeshi and Jorgoni (2012).
40. Yang and Martínez (2006).
41. Khanna et al. (2022).
42. On positive effects, see Acosta et al. (2008); Gubert, Lassourd, and Mesplé-Somps (2010); Margolis et al. (2013); Mughal and Anwar (2012); Taylor and Dyer (2009). On negative effects, see Adams (2006); Möllers and Meyer (2014). On no effects, see Yang and Martínez (2006).
43. de Haas (2009).
44. Koczan et al. (2021).
45. Koczan et al. (2021, 21).
46. Chin, Karkoviata, and Wilcox (2015). For Albania, see Piracha and Vadean (2010). For Egypt, see Mahé (2022); McCormick and Wahba (2001); Wahba and Zenou (2012). For the Kyrgyz Republic, see Brück, Mahé, and Naudé (2018). For returnees from Germany to Türkiye, see Dustmann and Kirchkamp (2002).
47. McKenzie and Yang (2014).
48. IOM (2015).
49. Ambler, Aycinena, and Yang (2015).
50. De Arcangelis et al. (2015).
51. Hosny (2020); Le Dé et al. (2015).
52. IMF (2017) and various other Article IV Consultations reports.
53. Chami et al. (2008).
54. Le Dé et al. (2015).
55. Kpodar et al. (2021); Quayyum and Kpodar (2020); World Bank (2021a).
56. Ahsan, Kellett, and Karuppannan (2014).
57. Beaton et al. (2017).
58. Halliday (2006).
59. Russia is a key destination for low-skilled migrants from Central Asian countries such as the Kyrgyz Republic and Tajikistan, while Saudi Arabia and other Gulf Cooperation Council countries attract many low-skilled migrants from South Asian countries, Egypt, Indonesia, and the Philippines.
60. Barajas et al. (2012).
61. Villareal (2010).
62. A transaction fee charged by a recipient's bank for cash transferred via a wire transfer is often referred to as a lifting fee.
63. World Bank (2021b). The World Bank's Remittance Prices Worldwide (RPW) monitors the cost incurred by remitters when sending money through the major remittance corridors. RPW is used as a reference for measuring progress toward global cost reduction objectives, including SDG 10.c and the Group of Twenty (G20) commitment to reducing the global average transfer cost to 5 percent. Since the second quarter of 2016, RPW has been tracking 48 remittance-sending countries and 105 remittance-receiving countries, for a total of 367 country corridors worldwide. RPW tracks the cost of sending remittances for four main types of remittance service providers: banks, money transfer operators (MTOs), post offices, and mobile operators. MTOs include

64. See, for example, Munyegera and Matsumoto (2016, 2018).
65. Beck, Janfils, and Kpodar (2022).
66. Beck and Martínez Pería (2011).
67. Beck, Janfils, and Kpodar (2022).
68. UNCTAD (2014).
69. A World Bank indicator, the Smart Remitter Target (SmaRT), benchmarks the average of the three lowest-cost remittance service providers in each corridor to inform customers of cheaper options available (World Bank 2016).
70. FSB (2020).
71. Lucas (2014).
72. Fagiolo and Mastrorillo (2014); Felbermayr and Jung (2009); Genç (2014).
73. Javorcik et al. (2011); Mayda et al. (2022); Parsons and Vézina (2018).
74. Docquier and Rapoport (2012); Kerr (2008).
75. Chanda and Sreenivasan (2006).
76. Chanda and Sreenivasan (2006).
77. Kerr (2008).
78. "Decree No. 74-CP on the 30th of July, 1994 of the Government on the Tasks, Authority and Organization of the Apparatus of the Committee for Overseas Vietnamese," Legal Normative Documents (database), Government of Vietnam, Hanoi, https://vbpl.vn/TW/Pages/vbpqen-toanvan.aspx?ItemID=2831.
79. Gaillard and Gaillard (1998); Johnson and Regets (1998).
80. Wahba (2015).
81. OECD (2008).
82. Bossavie et al. (2021).
83. Gamlen, Cummings, and Vaaler (2019); Newland (2010); Tabar (2020).
84. Ang and Tiongson (2023).
85. OECD (2016).
86. The regional concentration highlights that social networks influence the decision to migrate. Extensive networks of migrants who are immediate family members, relatives, and friends encourage those who would otherwise remain to emigrate. Giulietti, Wahba, and Zenou (2018) estimate that if 50 percent of someone's weak ties have migrated, his/her probability of migrating increases by 155 percent if his/her strong ties have migrated compared to the case in which the strong ties have not migrated.
87. Viswanathan and Kumar (2014).
88. See Bryan, Chowdhury, and Mobarak (2014).
89. Lucas (2004).
90. Gazdar (2003); Majid (2000); World Bank (2005).
91. Docquier, Özden, and Peri (2014).
92. Artuc et al. (2015).
93. Dao et al. (2018).
94. Gibson and McKenzie (2011); WDR2023 Migration Database, World Bank, Washington, DC, https://www.worldbank.org/wdr2023/data.
95. Pekkala Kerr et al. (2017).
96. Batista, Lacuesta, and Vicente (2012); Kone and Özden (2017).
97. Socha-Dietrich and Dumont (2021).
98. Pekkala Kerr et al. (2017).
99. The Joint Learning Initiative–World Health Organization benchmark defines such a shortage as 2.28 health workers (including doctors, nurses, and midwives) per 1,000 inhabitants.
100. Clemens (2009).
101. Chanda (2015); Stephany et al. (2021).
102. Beine, Docquier, and Rapoport (2008).
103. Gibson and McKenzie (2011).
104. Abarcar and Theoharides (2021).
105. Abarcar and Theoharides (2021).
106. Clemens (2015); OECD (2018).
107. Curtain and Howes (2021a).
108. Curtain and Howes (2021b).
109. Clemens (2015); OECD (2018).
110. Restricting migration could reduce the incentives for individuals to invest in and accumulate human capital (World Bank 2019). Restrictions on outflows of workers have often lasted only a short time and can harm workers. Clemens (2015) asserts that obstructing outflows of skilled workers harms the workers themselves, substantially eliminating their earning power—for example, by 60–90 percent for a professor, engineer, or doctor.
111. GPFI (2021).
112. Mohapatra, Moreno-Dodson, and Ratha (2012).
113. GSMA (2021); TDB (2012).

References

Abadi, Nigussie, Ataklti Techane, Girmay Tesfay, Daniel Maxwell, and Bapu Vaitla. 2018. "The Impact of Remittances on Household Food Security: A Micro Perspective from Tigray, Ethiopia." WIDER Working Paper 40/2018, United Nations University–World Institute for Development Economics Research, Helsinki, Finland.

Abarcar, Paolo, and Caroline B. Theoharides. 2021. "Medical Worker Migration and Origin-Country Human Capital: Evidence from U.S. Visa Policy." *Review of Economics and Statistics*. Published ahead of print, October 15, 2021. https://doi.org/10.1162/rest_a_01131.

Acosta, Pablo Ariel. 2006. "Labor Supply, School Attendance, and Remittances from International Migration: The Case of El Salvador." Policy Research Working Paper 3903, World Bank, Washington, DC.

Acosta, Pablo Ariel, César Calderón, Pablo Fajnzylber, and J. Humberto López. 2008. "What Is the Impact of International Remittances on Poverty and Inequality in Latin America?" *World Development* 36 (1): 89–114.

Acosta, Pablo Ariel, Pablo Fajnzylber, and J. Humberto López. 2007. "The Impact of Remittances on Poverty and Human Capital: Evidence from Latin American

Household Surveys." Policy Research Working Paper 4247, World Bank, Washington, DC.

Adams, Richard H., Jr. 2006. "Remittances and Poverty in Ghana." Policy Research Working Paper 3838, World Bank, Washington, DC.

Adams, Richard H., Jr. 2009. "The Determinants of International Remittances in Developing Countries." *World Development* 37 (1): 93–103.

Ahsan, Reazul, Jon Kellett, and Sadasivam Karuppannan. 2014. "Climate Induced Migration: Lessons from Bangladesh." *International Journal of Climate Change: Impacts and Responses* 5 (2): 1–15.

Ambler, Kate, Diego Aycinena, and Dean Yang. 2015. "Channeling Remittances to Education: A Field Experiment among Migrants from El Salvador." *American Economic Journal: Applied Economics* 7 (2): 207–32.

Amuedo-Dorantes, Catalina, and Susan Pozo. 2006. "Migration, Remittances, and Male and Female Employment Patterns." *American Economic Review* 96 (2): 222–26.

Anelli, Massimo, and Giovanni Peri. 2017. "Does Emigration Delay Political Change? Evidence from Italy during the Great Recession." *Economic Policy* 32 (91): 551–96.

Ang, Alvin, and Erwin R. Tiongson. 2023. "Philippine Migration Journey: Processes and Programs in the Migration Life Cycle." Background paper prepared for *World Development Report 2023*, World Bank, Washington, DC.

Arriola, Sarah Lou Y. 2022. "Philippines' Submission of the Voluntary National Review for the Implementation of the Global Compact for Safe, Orderly and Regular Migration." Office of the Undersecretary for Migrant Workers Affairs, Department of Foreign Affairs, Pasay City, Philippines. https://www.un.org/sites/un2.un.org /files/imrf-philippines.pdf.

Artuc, Erhan, Frédéric Docquier, Çağlar Özden, and Christopher Robert Parsons. 2015. "A Global Assessment of Human Capital Mobility: The Role of Non-OECD Destinations." *World Development* 65 (January): 6–26.

Asis, Maruja M. B. 2006. "Living with Migration: Experiences of Left-Behind Children in the Philippines." *Asian Population Studies* 2 (1): 45–67.

Asis, Maruja M. B. 2020. "Repatriating Filipino Migrant Workers in the Time of the Pandemic." Migration Research Series 63, International Organization for Migration, Geneva.

Bansak, Cynthia, Brian Chezum, and Animesh Giri. 2015. "Remittances, School Quality, and Household Education Expenditures in Nepal." *IZA Journal of Migration* 4 (1): 16.

Barajas, Adolfo, Ralph Chami, Christian H. Ebeke, and Sampawende J. A. Tapsoba. 2012. "Workers' Remittances: An Overlooked Channel of International Business Cycle Transmission?" IMF Working Paper WP12/251 (October), International Monetary Fund, Washington, DC.

Barro, Robert J., and Jong-Wha Lee. 2013. "A New Data Set of Educational Attainment in the World, 1950–2010." *Journal of Development Economics* 104 (September): 184–98.

Barsbai, Toman, Andreas Steinmayr, Dean Yang, Erwin R. Tiongson, and Victoria Licuanan. 2022. "Harnessing the Development Benefits of International Migration: A Randomized Evaluation of Enhanced Pre-Departure Orientation Seminars for Migrants from the Philippines to Hong Kong and Saudi Arabia." 3ie Impact Evaluation, Ongoing Study, International Initiative for Impact Evaluation, New Delhi.

Batista, Catia, Aitor Lacuesta, and Pedro C. Vicente. 2012. "Testing the 'Brain Gain' Hypothesis: Micro Evidence from Cape Verde." *Journal of Development Economics* 97 (1): 32–45.

Beaton, Kimberly, Svetlana Cerovic, Misael Galdamez, Metodij Hadzi-Vaskov, Franz Loyola, Zsoka Koczan, Bogdan Lissovolik, et al. 2017. "Migration and Remittances in Latin America and the Caribbean: Engines of Growth and Macroeconomic Stabilizers?" IMF Working Paper WP/17/144 (June), International Monetary Fund, Washington, DC.

Beck, Thorsten, Mathilde Janfils, and Kangni Roland Kpodar. 2022. "What Explains Remittance Fees? Panel Evidence." IMF Working Paper WP/22/63 (April), International Monetary Fund, Washington, DC.

Beck, Thorsten, and María Soledad Martínez Pería. 2011. "What Explains the Price of Remittances? An Examination Across 119 Country Corridors." *World Bank Economic Review* 25 (1): 105–31.

Beine, Michel, Frédéric Docquier, and Hillel Rapoport. 2008. "Brain Drain and Human Capital Formation in Developing Countries: Winners and Losers." *Economic Journal* 118 (528): 631–52.

Bertoli, Simone, and Francesca Marchetta. 2015. "Bringing It All Back Home: Return Migration and Fertility Choices." *World Development* 65 (January): 27–40.

Bossavie, Laurent, and Daniel Garrote-Sánchez. 2022. *Safe and Productive Migration from the Kyrgyz Republic: Lessons from the COVID-19 Pandemic*. International Development in Focus Series. Washington, DC: World Bank.

Bossavie, Laurent, Joseph-Simon Görlach, Çağlar Özden, and He Wang. 2021. "Temporary Migration for Long-Term Investment." Policy Research Working Paper 9740, World Bank, Washington, DC.

Bouoiyour, Jamal, and Amal Miftah. 2015. "The Impact of Remittances on Children's Human Capital Accumulation: Evidence from Morocco." *Journal of International Development* 28 (2): 266–80.

Brown, Richard P. C., and Bernard Poirine. 2005. "A Model of Migrants' Remittances with Human Capital Investment and Intrafamilial Transfers." *International Migration Review* 39 (2): 407–38.

Brück, Tilman, Clotilde Mahé, and Wim Naudé. 2018. "Return Migration and Self-Employment: Evidence from Kyrgyzstan." IZA Discussion Paper DP 11332 (February), Institute of Labor Economics, Bonn, Germany.

Bryan, Gharad T., Shyamal Chowdhury, and Ahmed Mushfiq Mobarak. 2014. "Underinvestment in a Profitable Technology: The Case of Seasonal Migration in Bangladesh." *Econometrica* 82 (5): 1671–1748.

Cabanda, Exequiel. 2017. "Higher Education, Migration and Policy Design of the Philippine Nursing Act of 2002." *Higher Education Policy* 30 (4): 555–75.

Chami, Ralph, Adolfo Barajas, Thomas Cosimano, Connel Fullenkamp, Michael Gapen, and Peter Montiel. 2008.

"Macroeconomic Consequences of Remittances." Occasional Paper 259, International Monetary Fund, Washington, DC.

Chami, Ralph, Ekkehard Ernst, Connel Fullenkamp, and Anne Oeking. 2018. "Are Remittances Good for Labor Markets in LICs, MICs and Fragile States? Evidence from Cross-Country Data." IMF Working Paper WP18/102 (May), International Monetary Fund, Washington, DC.

Chanda, Rupa. 2015. "Medical Tourism and Outward FDI in Health Services: India in South Asia." In *Handbook on Medical Tourism and Patient Mobility*, edited by Neil Lunt, Daniel Horsfall, and Johanna Hanefeld, 296–306. Cheltenham, UK: Edward Elgar.

Chanda, Rupa, and Niranjana Sreenivasan. 2006. "India's Experience with Skilled Migration." In *Competing for Global Talent*, edited by Christiane Kuptsch and Eng Fong Pang, 215–56. Geneva: International Institute for Labour Studies.

Chattopadhyay, Arpita, Michael J. White, and Cornelius Debpuur. 2006. "Migrant Fertility in Ghana: Selection versus Adaptation and Disruption as Causal Mechanisms." *Population Studies* 60 (2): 189–203.

Chilton, Adam S., and Bartosz Woda. 2021. "The Effects of Bilateral Labor Agreements: Evidence from the Philippines." *Immigration, Refugee, and Citizenship Law eJournal* 22 (51). https://facultyblog.law.ucdavis.edu/post/immigration-refugee-citizenship-law-ejournal-vol-22 no-51.aspx.

Chin, Aimee, Léonie Karkoviata, and Nathaniel Wilcox. 2015. "Impact of Bank Accounts on Migrant Savings and Remittances: Evidence from a Field Experiment." Working paper (April), University of Houston. https://uh.edu/~achin/research/ckw_banking_april2015.pdf.

Clemens, Michael A. 2009. "Skill Flow: A Fundamental Reconsideration of Skilled-Worker Mobility and Development." CGD Working Paper 180 (August), Center for Global Development, Washington, DC.

Clemens, Michael A. 2015. "Global Skill Partnerships: A Proposal for Technical Training in a Mobile World." *IZA Journal of Labor Policy* 4 (2): 1–18.

Clemens, Michael A., and Erwin R. Tiongson. 2017. "Split Decisions: Household Finance When a Policy Discontinuity Allocates Overseas Work." *Review of Economics and Statistics* 99 (3): 531–43.

Cortes, Patricia. 2015. "The Feminization of International Migration and Its Effects on the Children Left Behind: Evidence from the Philippines." *World Development* 65 (January): 62–78.

Cox, Donald. 1987. "Motives for Private Income Transfers." *Journal of Political Economy* 23 (3): 508–46.

Cox-Edwards, Alejandra, and Eduardo Rodríguez-Oreggia. 2006. "The Effect of Remittances on Labor Force Participation: An Analysis Based on Mexico's 2002 ENET." Paper prepared for Institute of Labor Economics–World Bank Conference on "Employment and Development," Berlin, May 25–27.

Cuecuecha, Alfredo, and Richard H. Adams, Jr. 2016. "Remittances, Household Investment and Poverty in Indonesia." *Journal of Finance and Economics* 4 (3): 12–31.

Curtain, Richard, and Stephen Howes. 2021a. "Helping APTC Trades Graduates to Migrate to Australia under the TSS." Policy Brief 20 (February), Development Policy Centre, Crawford School of Public Policy, College of Asia and the Pacific, Australian National University, Canberra, Australia.

Curtain, Richard, and Stephen Howes. 2021b. "Worsening Employment Outcomes for Pacific Technical Graduate Job-Seekers." Development Policy Center Discussion Paper DP 91, Development Policy Centre, Crawford School of Public Policy, College of Asia and the Pacific, Australian National University, Canberra, Australia.

Dao, Thu Hien, Frédéric Docquier, Christopher Robert Parsons, and Giovanni Peri. 2018. "Migration and Development: Dissecting the Anatomy of the Mobility Transition." *Journal of Development Economics* 132 (May): 88–101.

De, Supriyo, Ergys Islamaj, M. Ayhan Kose, and S. Reza Yousefi. 2019. "Remittances over the Business Cycle: Theory and Evidence." *Economic Notes* 48 (3): e12143.

De Arcangelis, Giuseppe, Majlinda Joxhe, David J. McKenzie, Erwin R. Tiongson, and Dean Yang. 2015. "Directing Remittances to Education with Soft and Hard Commitments: Evidence from a Lab-in-the-Field Experiment and New Product Take-Up among Filipino Migrants in Rome." *Journal of Economic Behavior and Organization* 111 (March): 197–208.

de Haas, Hein. 2001. "Migration and Agricultural Transformations in the Oases of Morocco and Tunisia." Geographical Studies of Development and Resource Use Series 3, Royal Dutch Geographical Society, Utrecht, the Netherlands.

de Haas, Hein. 2009. "Remittances and Social Development." In *Financing Social Policy: Mobilizing Resources for Social Development*, edited by Katja Hujo and Shea McClanahan, 293–318. Social Policy in a Development Context Series. Geneva: United Nations Research Institute for Social Development; Basingstoke, UK: Palgrave Macmillan.

Delpierre, Matthieu, and Bertrand Verheyden. 2014. "Remittances, Savings and Return Migration under Uncertainty." *IZA Journal of Migration and Development* 3 (1): 22.

Dinkelman, Taryn, and Martine Mariotti. 2016. "The Long-Run Effects of Labor Migration on Human Capital Formation in Communities of Origin." *American Economic Journal: Applied Economics* 8 (4): 1–35.

Docquier, Frédéric, Elisabetta Lodogiani, Hillel Rapoport, and Maurice Schiff. 2016. "Emigration and Democracy." *Journal of Development Economics* 120 (May): 209–23.

Docquier, Frédéric, Çağlar Özden, and Giovanni Peri. 2014. "The Labour Market Effects of Immigration and Emigration in OECD Countries." *Economic Journal* 124 (579): 1106–45.

Docquier, Frédéric, and Hillel Rapoport. 2012. "Globalization, Brain Drain, and Development." *Journal of Economic Literature* 50 (3): 681–730.

DOLE (Department of Labor and Employment, the Philippines). 2015. "Resource Centers to Provide Welfare and Assistance to Migrant Filipinos." *Official Gazette*, August 18, 2015. https://www.officialgazette.gov.ph /2015/08/18/resource-centers-to-provide-welfare -and-assistance-to-migrant-filipinos/.

Dominguez, Georgia B., and Brian J. Hall. 2022. "The Health Status and Related Interventions for Children Left behind Due to Parental Migration in the Philippines: A Scoping Review." *Lancet Regional Health, Western Pacific* 28 (November): 100566.

Ducanes, Geoffrey. 2015. "The Welfare Impact of Overseas Migration on Philippine Households: Analysis Using Panel Data." *Asian and Pacific Migration Journal* 24 (1): 79–106. https://doi.org/10.1177/0117196814565166.

Dustmann, Christian, and Oliver Kirchkamp. 2002. "The Optimal Migration Duration and Activity Choice after Re-Migration." *Journal of Development Economics* 67 (2): 351–72.

Edillon, Rosemarie. 2008. "The Effects of Parent's Migration on the Rights of Children Left behind in the Philippines." Working paper (August), Policy, Advocacy and Knowledge Management Section, Division of Policy and Practice, United Nations Children's Fund, New York.

Fagiolo, Giorgio, and Marina Mastrorillo. 2014. "Does Human Migration Affect International Trade? A Complex-Network Perspective." *PLOS ONE* 9 (5): e97331.

Fargues, Philippe. 2013. "International Migration and the Nation State in Arab Countries." *Middle East Law and Governance* 5 (1–2): 5–35.

Felbermayr, Gabriel J., and Benjamin Jung. 2009. "The Pro-Trade Effect of the Brain Drain: Sorting Out Confounding Factors." *Economics Letters* 104 (2): 72–75.

Ferrant, Gaëlle, and Michele Tuccio. 2015. "South-South Migration and Discrimination against Women in Social Institutions: A Two-Way Relationship." *World Development* 72 (August): 240–54.

Fischer, Peter, Reiner Martin, and Thomas Straubhaar. 1997. "Should I Stay or Should I Go?" In *International Migration, Immobility and Development: Multidisciplinary Perspectives*, edited by Tomas Hammar, Grete Brochmann, Kristof Tamas, and Thomas Faist, 49–90. London: Routledge.

Frankel, Jeffrey Alexander. 2011. "Are Bilateral Remittances Countercyclical?" *Open Economies Review* 22 (1): 1–16.

Frasheri, Argita, and Elona Dushku. 2021. "Remittances and Their Impact of Poverty: The Case of Albania." Paper presented at International Statistical Institute's 63rd World Statistics Congress, The Hague, the Netherlands, July 12.

FSB (Financial Stability Board). 2020. "Enhancing Cross-Border Payments: Stage 3 Roadmap." FSB, Basel, Switzerland. https://www.fsb.org/2020/10/enhancing -cross-border-payments-stage-3-roadmap/.

Gaillard, Anne Marie, and Jacques Gaillard. 1998. *International Migration of the Highly Qualified: A Bibliographic and Conceptual Itinerary*. CMS Occasional Paper 23, Bibliographies and Documentation Series. New York: Center for Migration Studies.

Gamlen, Alan, Michael E. Cummings, and Paul M. Vaaler. 2019. "Explaining the Rise of Diaspora Institutions." *Journal of Ethnic and Migration Studies* 45 (4): 492–516.

Garip, Filiz. 2012. "An Integrated Analysis of Migration and Remittances: Modeling Migration as a Mechanism for Selection." *Population Research and Policy Review* 31 (5): 637–63.

Gazdar, Haris. 2003. "A Review of Migration Issues in Pakistan." Paper presented at Regional Conference on Migration, Development, and Pro-Poor Policy Choices in Asia, Dhaka, Bangladesh, June 22–24.

Gedeshi, Ilir, and Elira Jorgoni. 2012. "Social Impact of Emigration and Rural-Urban Migration in Central and Eastern Europe: Final Country Report, Albania." Directorate-General for Employment, Social Affairs, and Inclusion, European Commission, Brussels.

Genç, Murat. 2014. "The Impact of Migration on Trade." IZA World of Labor (June), Institute of Labor Economics, Bonn, Germany.

Gibson, John, and David J. McKenzie. 2011. "Eight Questions about Brain Drain." *Journal of Economic Perspectives* 25 (3): 107–28.

Giulietti, Corrado, Jackline Wahba, and Yves Zenou. 2018. "Strong versus Weak Ties in Migration." *European Economic Review* 104 (May): 111–37.

GPFI (Global Partnership for Financial Inclusion). 2021. "G20 National Remittance Plan, Mexico 2021: Biennial Update." GPFI, World Bank, Washington, DC. https:// www.gpfi.org/sites/gpfi/files/sites/default/files /Mexico.pdf.

GSMA (GSM Association). 2021. "Using Mobile Technology to Improve Remittances to the Pacific." July, GSMA, London. https://www.gsma.com/mobilefor development/wp-content/uploads/2021/07/CIU_ PacificRemittances_R_WebSingles1.pdf.

Gubert, Flore, Thomas Lassourd, and Sandrine Mesplé-Somps. 2010. "Do Remittances Affect Poverty and Inequality? Evidence from Mali." Working Paper DT/2010/08, Unité Mixte de Recherche DIAL (Développement, Institutions et Mondialisation), Institut de Recherche pour le Développement, Université Paris-Dauphine, Paris.

Hadi, Abdullahel. 2001. "International Migration and the Change of Women's Position among the Left-Behind in Rural Bangladesh." *International Journal of Population Geography* 7 (1): 53–61.

Halliday, Timothy. 2006. "Migration, Risk, and Liquidity Constraints in El Salvador." *Economic Development and Cultural Change* 54 (4): 893–925.

Hoddinott, John F. 1994. "A Model of Migration and Remittances Applied to Western Kenya." *Oxford Economic Papers* 46 (3): 459–76.

Horvat, Vedran. 2004. "Brain Drain: Threat to Successful Transition in South East Europe?" *Southeast European Politics* 5 (1): 76–93.

Hosny, Amr. 2020. "Remittance Concentration and Volatility: Evidence from 72 Developing Countries." *International Economic Journal* 34 (4): 553–70.

Iheke, Onwuchekwa Raphael. 2014. "Impact of Migrant Remittances on the Output of Arable Crop of Farm Households in South Eastern Nigeria." *American Journal of Experimental Agriculture* 4 (10): 1209–18.

ILO (International Labour Organization). 2019. "Philippines, Hong Kong SAR, China, Agencies Ink Fair Recruitment Code." Press release, June 14, 2019. http://www .ilo.org/manila/public/pr/WCMS_710556/lang--en /index.htm.

IMF (International Monetary Fund). 2017. "Philippines: 2017 Article IV Consultation: Press Release, Staff Report." IMF Country Report 17/334, IMF, Washington, DC.

IOM (International Organization for Migration). 2015. "Gender, Migration and Remittances." Factsheet, June 23, 2015. https://www.iom.int/sites/g/files/tmzbdl486 /files/2018-07/Gender-migration-remittances -infosheet.pdf.

Jaupart, Pascal. 2019. "No Country for Young Men: International Migration and Left-Behind Children in Tajikistan." *Economics of Transition and Institutional Change* 27 (3): 579–614.

Javorcik, Beata Smarzynska, Çağlar Özden, Mariana Spatareanu, and Cristina Neagu. 2011. "Migrant Networks and Foreign Direct Investment." *Journal of Development Economics* 94 (2): 231–41.

Johnson, Jean M., and Mark C. Regets. 1998. "International Mobility of Scientists and Engineers to the United States: Brain Drain or Brain Circulation?" SRS Issue Brief NSF 98-316, June 22 (revised November 10), Division of Science Resources Studies, Directorate for Social, Behavioral, and Economic Sciences, National Science Foundation, Arlington, VA.

Kerr, William R. 2008. "Ethnic Scientific Communities and International Technology Diffusion." *Review of Economics and Statistics* 90 (3): 518–37.

Khanna, Gaurav, Emir Murathanoglu, Caroline B. Theoharides, and Dean Yang. 2022. "Abundance from Abroad: Migrant Income and Long Run Economic Development." NBER Working Paper 29862 (March), National Bureau of Economic Research, Cambridge, MA.

KNOMAD (Global Knowledge Partnership on Migration and Development) and ILO (International Labour Organization). 2021a. "KNOMAD-ILO Migration Costs Surveys 2015: El Salvador, Ethiopia, Guatemala, Honduras, India, Nepal, Pakistan, Philippines, Vietnam, 2015–2016." Microdata set, version May 24, 2021, World Bank, Washington, DC. https://microdata .worldbank.org/index.php/catalog/2938.

KNOMAD (Global Knowledge Partnership on Migration and Development) and ILO (International Labour Organization). 2021b. "KNOMAD-ILO Migration Costs Surveys 2016: Benin, Burkina Faso, Cabo Verde, Gambia, Ghana, Guinea, Guinea-Bissau, India, Kyrgyz Republic, Liberia, Mali, Mauritania, Nepal, Niger, . . . , 2016–2017." Microdata set, version May 24, 2021, World Bank, Washington, DC. https://microdata .worldbank.org/index.php/catalog/2944.

Koczan, Zsoka, Giovanni Peri, Magali Pinat, and Dmitriy L. Rozhkov. 2021. "The Impact of International Migration on Inclusive Growth: A Review." IMF Working Paper WP/21/88 (March), International Monetary Fund, Washington, DC.

Kone, Zovanga L., and Çağlar Özden. 2017. "Brain Drain, Gain and Circulation." In *Handbook of Globalisation and Development*, edited by Kenneth Reinert, 349–70. Handbooks on Globalisation Series. Cheltenham, UK: Edward Elgar.

Konseiga, Adama. 2004. "Adoption of Agricultural Innovations in the Sahel: The Role of Migration in Food Security." Paper presented at 38th Annual Meetings of the Canadian Economics Association, Toronto, June 3–6.

Kpodar, Kangni Roland, Montfort Mlachila, Saad Noor Quayyum, and Vigninou Gammadigbe. 2021. "Defying the Odds: Remittances during the COVID-19 Pandemic." IMF Working Paper WP/21/186 (July), International Monetary Fund, Washington, DC.

Le Dé, Loïc, J. C. Gaillard, Wardlow Friesen, and Fagalua Matautia Smith. 2015. "Remittances in the Face of Disasters: A Case Study of Rural Samoa." *Environment, Development and Sustainability* 17 (3): 653–72.

Levitt, Peggy. 1998. "Social Remittances: Migration Driven Local-Level Forms of Cultural Diffusion." *International Migration Review* 32 (4): 926–48.

Lokshin, Michael M., and Elena Glinskaya. 2009. "The Effect of Male Migration on Employment Patterns of Women in Nepal." *World Bank Economic Review* 23 (3): 481–507.

Lucas, Robert E. B., Jr. 2004. "Life Earnings and Rural-Urban Migration." *Journal of Political Economy* 112 (Supplement 1): S29–S59.

Lucas, Robert E. B., Jr. 2014. "The Migration–Trade Link in Developing Economies: A Summary and Extension of Evidence." In *International Handbook on Migration and Economic Development*, edited by Robert E. B. Lucas, Jr., 288–326. Cheltenham, UK: Edward Elgar.

Lucas, Robert E. B., Jr., and Oded Stark. 1985. "Motivations to Remit: Evidence from Botswana." *Journal of Political Economy* 93 (5): 901–18.

Mahé, Clotilde. 2022. "Return Migration and Self-Employment: Is There a 'Jack-of-All-Trades' Effect?" *Oxford Economic Papers* 74 (1): 62–84.

Majid, Nomaan. 2000. "Pakistan: Employment, Output and Productivity." Issues in Development Discussion Paper 33, International Labour Organization, Geneva.

Mansuri, Ghazala. 2006. "Migration, School Attainment, and Child Labor: Evidence from Rural Pakistan." Policy Research Working Paper 3945, World Bank, Washington, DC.

Margolis, David N., Egidio Luis Miotti, El Mouhoub Mouhoud, and Joël Oudinet. 2013. "'To Have and Have Not': Migration, Remittances, Poverty and Inequality in Algeria." IZA Discussion Paper DP 7747 (November), Institute of Labor Economics, Bonn, Germany.

Mayda, Anna-Maria, Christopher Robert Parsons, Han Pham, and Pierre-Louis Vézina. 2022. "Refugees and Foreign Direct Investment: Quasi-experimental Evidence from US Resettlements." *Journal of Development Economics* 156 (May): 102818.

McCormick, Barry, and Jackline Wahba. 2001. "Overseas Work Experience, Savings and Entrepreneurship amongst Return Migrants to LDCs." *Scottish Journal of Political Economy* 48 (2): 164–78.

McKenzie, David J., John Gibson, and Steven Stillman. 2013. "A Land of Milk and Honey with Streets Paved with Gold: Do Emigrants Have Over-Optimistic Expectations about Incomes Abroad?" *Journal of Development Economics* 102 (May): 116–27.

McKenzie, David J., and Hillel Rapoport. 2011. "Can Migration Reduce Educational Attainment? Evidence from Mexico." *Journal of Population Economics* 24 (4): 1331–58.

McKenzie, David J., and Dean Yang. 2014. "Evidence on Policies to Increase the Development Impacts of International Migration." Policy Research Working Paper 7057, World Bank, Washington, DC.

Medina, Carlos, and Lina Cardona-Sosa. 2010. "The Effects of Remittances on Household Consumption, Education Attendance and Living Standards: The Case of Colombia." *Lecturas de Economía* 72 (January–June): 11–34.

Mobarak, Ahmed Mushfiq, Iffath Sharif, and Maheshwor Shrestha. 2021. "Returns to International Migration: Evidence from a Bangladesh-Malaysia Visa Lottery." IZA Discussion Paper DP 14232 (March), Institute for Labour Economics, Bonn, Germany.

Mohapatra, Sanket, George Joseph, and Dilip Ratha. 2009. "Remittances and Natural Disasters: Ex-post Response and Contribution to Ex-ante Preparedness." Policy Research Working Paper 4972, World Bank, Washington, DC.

Mohapatra, Sanket, Blanca Moreno-Dodson, and Dilip Ratha. 2012. "Migration, Taxation, and Inequality." Economic Premise 80 (May), Poverty Reduction and Economic Management Network, World Bank, Washington, DC. https://documents1.worldbank.org/curated/en/257461468337203140/pdf/684860BRI0EP8000502020120Box367936B.pdf.

Möllers, Judith, and Wiebke Meyer. 2014. "The Effects of Migration on Poverty and Inequality in Rural Kosovo." *IZA Journal of Labor and Development* 3 (1): 16.

Mughal, Mazhar, and Amar Iqbal Anwar. 2012. "Remittances, Inequality and Poverty in Pakistan: Macro and Microeconomic Evidence." Working Paper CATT WP 2 (August), Centre d'Analyse Théorique et de Traitement des données économiques, UFR Droit, Economie et Gestion, Université de Pau et des Pays de l'Adour, Pau, France.

Munyegera, Ggombe Kasim, and Tomoya Matsumoto. 2016. "Mobile Money, Remittances, and Household Welfare: Panel Evidence from Rural Uganda." *World Development* 79 (March): 127–37.

Munyegera, Ggombe Kasim, and Tomoya Matsumoto. 2018. "ICT for Financial Access: Mobile Money and the Financial Behavior of Rural Households in Uganda." *Review of Development Economics* 22 (1): 45–66.

NEDA (National Economic and Development Authority). 2021. *Updated Philippine Development Plan 2017–2022*. Pasig City, the Philippines: NEDA. https://pdp.neda.gov.ph/updated-pdp-2017-2022/.

Newland, Kathleen. 2010. "Voice after Exit: Diaspora Advocacy." Diasporas and Development Policy Project (November), Migration Policy Institute, Washington, DC.

OECD (Organisation for Economic Co-operation and Development). 2008. *International Migration Outlook 2008*. Paris: OECD.

OECD (Organisation for Economic Co-operation and Development). 2016. *International Migration Outlook 2016*. Paris: OECD.

OECD (Organisation for Economic Co-operation and Development). 2017. *Interrelations between Public Policies, Migration and Development in the Philippines*. OECD Development Pathways Series. Quezon City, the Philippines: Scalabrini Migration Center; Paris: OECD.

OECD (Organisation for Economic Co-operation and Development). 2018. "What Would Make Global Skills Partnerships Work in Practice?" Migration Policy Debates 15 (May), OECD, Paris.

Osili, Una Okonkwo. 2004. "Migrants and Housing Investments: Theory and Evidence from Nigeria." *Economic Development and Cultural Change* 52 (4): 821–49.

Pairama, Jenna, and Loïc Le Dé. 2018. "Remittances for Disaster Risk Management: Perspectives from Pacific Island Migrants Living in New Zealand." *International Journal of Disaster Risk Science* 9 (3): 331–43.

Pajaron, Marjorie, Cara T. Latinazo, and Enrico G. Trinidad. 2020. "The Children Are Alright: Revisiting the Impact of Parental Migration in the Philippines." GLO Discussion Paper 507, Global Labor Organization, Essen, Germany.

Parsons, Christopher Robert, and Pierre-Louis Vézina. 2018. "Migrant Networks and Trade: The Vietnamese Boat People as a Natural Experiment." *Economic Journal* 128 (612): F210–F234.

Pekkala Kerr, Sari, William R. Kerr, Çağlar Özden, and Christopher Robert Parsons. 2017. "High-Skilled Migration and Agglomeration." *Annual Review of Economics* 9 (1): 201–34.

Piracha, Matloob, and Florin Vadean. 2010. "Return Migration and Occupational Choice: Evidence from Albania." *World Development* 38 (8): 1141–55.

Quayyum, Saad Noor, and Kangni Roland Kpodar. 2020. "Supporting Migrants and Remittances as COVID-19 Rages On." *COVID-19* (IMF blog), September 11, 2020. https://www.imf.org/en/Blogs/Articles/2020/09/11/blog-supporting-migrants-and-remittances-as-covid19-rages-on.

Rivera, John Paolo R., Denise Jannah D. Serrano, and Tereso S. Tullao. 2013. "Bilateral Labor Agreements and Trade in Services: The Experience of the Philippines." In *Let Workers Move: Using Bilateral Labor Agreements to Increase Trade in Services*, edited by Sebastián Sáez, 109–28. Directions in Development: Trade Series. Washington, DC: World Bank.

Ruhunage, Leelananda Kumara. 2014. "Consolidated Report on Assessing Labour Migration Related Bilateral Agreements (BLAs), Memorandum of Understandings (MOUs) and Other Similar Arrangement in the Asian Region." Draft report (July 16), International Labour

Organization–Global Knowledge Partnership on Migration and Development Thematic Working Group on Low Skilled Migration, International Migration Branch, International Labour Organization, Geneva.

Sakka, Despina, Maria Dikaiou, and Grigoris Kiosseoglou. 1999. "Return Migration: Changing Roles of Men and Women." *International Migration* 37 (4): 741–64.

Seshan, Ganesh, and Robertas Zubrickas. 2017. "Asymmetric Information about Migrant Earnings and Remittance Flows." *World Bank Economic Review* 31 (1): 24–43.

Shrestha, Maheshwor. 2017. "Push and Pull: A Study of International Migration from Nepal." Policy Research Working Paper 7965, World Bank, Washington, DC.

Socha-Dietrich, Karolina, and Jean-Christophe Dumont. 2021. "International Migration and Movement of Doctors to and within OECD Countries, 2000 to 2018: Developments in Countries of Destination and Impact on Countries of Origin." OECD Health Working Paper 126 (February 19), Organisation for Economic Co-operation and Development, Paris.

Stark, Oded, and David E. Bloom. 1985. "The New Economics of Labor Migration." *American Economic Review* 75 (2): 173–78.

Stephany, Fabian, Otto Kässi, Uma Rani, and Vili Lehdonvirta. 2021. "Online Labour Index 2020: New Ways to Measure the World's Remote Freelancing Market." *Big Data and Society* 8 (2): 20539517211043240.

Tabar, Paul. 2020. "Transnational Is Not Diasporic: A Bourdieucian Approach to the Study of Modern Diaspora." *Journal of Sociology* 56 (3): 455–71.

Taylor, J. Edward, and George A. Dyer. 2009. "Migration and the Sending Economy: A Disaggregated Rural Economy-Wide Analysis." *Journal of Development Studies* 45 (6): 966–89.

Taylor, J. Edward, Jorge Mora, Richard H. Adams, Jr., and Alejandro López-Feldman. 2005. "Remittances, Inequality, and Poverty: Evidence from Rural Mexico." Agriculture and Resource Economics Working Paper 05-003, Department of Agricultural and Resource Economics, University of California. https://escholarship.org/uc/item/9s14452d.

TDB (Tonga Development Bank). 2015. "'Ave Pa'anga Pau." Press release. https://www.tdb.to/ave-paanga-pau.html.

Tran, Ngoc Thi Minh, Michael P. Cameron, and Jacques Poot. 2017. "International Migration and Institutional Quality in the Home Country: It Matters Where You Go and How Long You Stay!" IZA Discussion Paper DP 10945 (August), Institute of Labor Economics, Bonn, Germany.

Tuccio, Michele, and Jackline Wahba. 2018. "Return Migration and the Transfer of Gender Norms: Evidence from the Middle East." *Journal of Comparative Economics* 46 (4): 1006–29.

Tusalem, Rollin F. 2018. "Do Migrant Remittances Improve the Quality of Government? Evidence from the Philippines." *Asian Journal of Comparative Politics* 3 (4): 336–66.

UNCTAD (United Nations Conference on Trade and Development). 2014. "Impact of Access to Financial Services, Including by Highlighting Remittances on Development: Economic Empowerment of Women and Youth." Note by the UNCTAD Secretariat (November), UNCTAD, Geneva. https://unctad.org/system/files/official-document/ciem6d2_en.pdf.

Urama, Nathaniel E., Emmanuel O. Nwosu, Denis N. Yuni, and Stephen E. Aguegboh. 2017. "International Migrant Remittances and Labour Supply in Nigeria." *International Migration* 55 (1): 37–50.

Villareal, M. Angeles. 2010. "The Mexican Economy after the Global Financial Crisis." CRS Report for Congress, September 16, Congressional Research Service, Washington, DC.

Viswanathan, Brinda, and K. S. Kavi Kumar. 2014. "Weather Variability, Agriculture and Rural Migration: Evidence from State and District Level Migration in India." SANDEE Working Paper 83–14, South Asian Network for Development and Environmental Economics, Kathmandu, Nepal.

Wahba, Jackline. 2015. "Selection, Selection, Selection: The Impact of Return Migration." *Journal of Population Economics* 28 (3): 535–63.

Wahba, Jackline, and Yves Zenou. 2012. "Out of Sight, Out of Mind: Migration, Entrepreneurship and Social Capital." *Regional Science and Urban Economics* 42 (5): 890–903.

Wickramasekara, Piyasiri. 2015. "Bilateral Agreements and Memoranda of Understanding on Migration of Low Skilled Workers: A Review." Labour Migration Branch, International Labour Office, Geneva.

World Bank. 2005. *World Development Report 2006: Equity and Development*. Washington, DC: World Bank; New York: Oxford University Press.

World Bank. 2016. "Getting SmaRT about Remittance Price Monitoring." Payment Systems Development Group, World Bank, Washington, DC.

World Bank. 2018. *Moving for Prosperity: Global Migration and Labor Markets*. Washington, DC: World Bank.

World Bank. 2019. *Leveraging Economic Migration for Development: A Briefing for the World Bank Board*. Washington, DC: World Bank.

World Bank. 2021a. "Recovery: COVID-19 Crisis through a Migration Lens." Migration and Development Brief 35 (November), Global Knowledge Partnership on Migration and Development, World Bank, Washington, DC.

World Bank. 2021b. *Remittance Prices Worldwide Quarterly*. Issue 40. Washington, DC: World Bank.

World Bank. 2022a. "Remittances Brave Global Headwinds, Special Focus: Climate Migration." Migration and Development Brief 37 (November), Global Knowledge Partnership on Migration and Development (KNOMAD), World Bank, Washington, DC.

World Bank. 2022b. "A War in a Pandemic: Implications of the Ukraine Crisis and COVID-19 on Global Governance of Migration and Remittance Flows." Migration and Development Brief 36 (May), Global Knowledge Partnership on Migration and Development, World Bank, Washington, DC.

Yagi, Nozomi, Tim K. Mackey, Bryan A. Liang, and Lorna Gerlt. 2014. "Policy Review: Japan–Philippines Economic Partnership Agreement (JPEPA), Analysis of a Failed Nurse Migration Policy." *International Journal of Nursing Studies* 51 (2): 243–50.

Yang, Dean. 2008. "International Migration, Remittances and Household Investment: Evidence from Philippine Migrants' Exchange Rate Shocks." *Economic Journal* 118 (528): 591–630.

Yang, Dean, and HwaJung Choi. 2007. "Are Remittances Insurance? Evidence from Rainfall Shocks in the Philippines." *World Bank Economic Review* 21 (2): 219–48.

Yang, Dean, and Claudia A. Martínez. 2006. "Remittances and Poverty in Migrants' Home Areas: Evidence from the Philippines." In *International Migration, Remittances, and the Brain Drain,* edited by Çağlar Özden and Maurice Schiff, 81–121. Washington, DC: World Bank; New York: Palgrave Macmillan.

Spotlight 5
Measurement of remittances

Properly estimating and monitoring personal remittance flows have become critical for many countries of origin because of the macroeconomic effects of such flows and their potential contribution to poverty reduction and development. Yet there are significant issues surrounding the remittance data currently available.[1]

Discrepancies

Remittance data are based on information provided by countries—both sending and receiving—in their annual balance of payments (BoP) reports. Estimating remittances, however, is a complex endeavor, and countries use different methods. Most BoP reports are based on some combination of direct reporting from commercial banks and other financial intermediaries; household surveys to account for transfers through informal channels, among other things; and estimation models.[2]

There are, however, significant inconsistencies in estimates of remittances. In principle, the total received (remittance inflows, as reported by countries that received them) should be equal to the total sent (remittance outflows, as reported by countries from which they are sent).[3] But there is a significant gap, which has widened since the early 2000s. In 2020, the reported remittances received exceeded the remittances sent by almost 40 percent (figure S5.1). Such inconsistencies can also be observed in bilateral remittances data (box S5.1).

Figure S5.1 **In 2020, the gap between global estimates of remittances received and sent reached 40 percent**

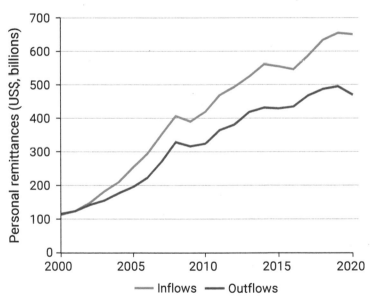

Source: Balance of Payments and International Investment Position Statistics (dashboard), International Monetary Fund, Washington, DC, https://data.imf.org/?sk=7A51304B-6426-40C0-83DD-CA473CA1FD52.

Note: The figure includes remittances for all countries reporting balance of payments data to the International Monetary Fund (IMF). Inflows are reported by the countries to which remittances are sent. Outflows are reported by the countries from which remittances are sent. As per the IMF's *Balance of Payments and International Investment Position Manual*, 6th edition (IMF 2009a), personal remittances include only the standard components of personal transfers and employee compensation. Missing data for Vietnam and the United Arab Emirates are replaced with estimates from KNOMAD Data, Global Knowledge Partnership on Migration and Development, World Bank, Washington, DC, https://www.knomad.org/data.

Box S5.1 Testing the inflow-outflow gap at the country level

The most commonly used remittances database, the Bilateral Remittances Matrix,[a] contains data on remittance inflows and outflows, as well as estimated bilateral flows by corridor.[b] However, the estimated amounts are not fully consistent because of the gap between reported inflows and outflows in balance of payments (BoP) reports. For example, the total outflow reported by a country in its BoP should, in principle, equal the sum of all bilateral outflows originating from that country, but often it does not (figure SB5.1.1). The difference is sometimes positive, sometimes negative; there is no clear pattern. Although many of these discrepancies could be attributed to normal estimation errors, large gaps—such as in the United Kingdom, Spain, and Canada, as well as in Luxembourg and Switzerland—suggest broader issues. For the United States, the gap suggests an underreporting of remittance outflows in the BoP by a staggering US$125 billion.

Figure SB5.1.1 Remittance estimation gaps are significant in many economies

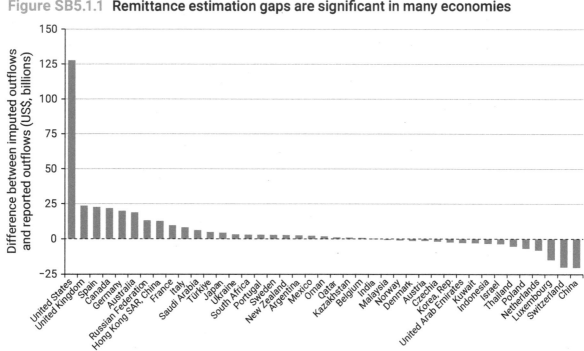

Sources: Balance of Payments and International Investment Position Statistics (dashboard), International Monetary Fund, Washington, DC, https://data.imf.org/?sk=7A51304B-6426-40C0-83DD-CA473CA1FD52; KNOMAD Remittances Data (dashboard), Global Knowledge Partnership on Migration and Development, World Bank, Washington, DC, https://www.knomad.org/data/remittances.

Note: Imputed outflows represent the sum of all bilateral outflows originating from a country based on Bilateral Remittances Matrix estimates. Reported outflows are based on balance of payments data. Only economies with at least US$3 billion in either recorded or imputed outflows are included.

a. KNOMAD Remittances Data (dashboard), Global Knowledge Partnership on Migration and Development, World Bank, Washington, DC, https://www.knomad.org/data/remittances.
b. Ratha and Shaw (2007). The breakdown by bilateral corridor is based on the total amount of remittances received by a given country, the share of workers from that country in each destination country, and the difference in gross domestic product per capita between origins and destinations.

Inconsistency with other economic measures

The observed gaps in the measurement of remittances raise a question: in the face of large discrepancies, which estimates are more reliable—inflows data from remittance recipients or outflows data from remittance-sending countries? One way to address this question is to compare the trends in remittance inflows and outflows with the underlying economic fundamentals.[4]

Economic fundamentals are based on changes in the main factors that drive remittances: (1) the number of migrant workers; (2) their average income; and (3) the share of that income they send back to their country of origin. Assuming that the share of income remitted by migrants was constant between 2000 and 2020, the economic fundamental estimates increased by 84 percent between 2000 and 2020; the reported outflows increased by 96 percent; and the reported inflows increased by 177 percent (figure S5.2). In other words, at the global level the economic fundamentals are consistent with the observed growth in reported remittance outflows, but they cannot explain the increase in reported inflows.

Global trends, however, mask significant variations across countries, where both inflows and outflows can be inconsistent with economic fundamentals and fluctuate dramatically (figure S5.3). In Guatemala, for example, the reported remittance inflows grew over four times faster than what the economic fundamentals would suggest. In Nigeria, remittance inflows jumped by almost 10 times in one year and then declined, even though economic fundamentals suggest they should have increased steadily. Remittance outflows from China overall follow the economic fundamentals, but with large annual variations. Remittance outflows from the euro area also increased much faster than economic fundamentals and then declined, once again suggesting measurement issues.

Figure S5.2 At the global level, outflow remittance reports are closer than inflow remittance reports to economic fundamentals

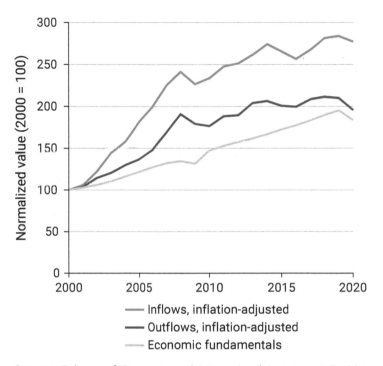

Legend:
— Inflows, inflation-adjusted
— Outflows, inflation-adjusted
— Economic fundamentals

Sources: Balance of Payments and International Investment Position Statistics (dashboard), International Monetary Fund, Washington, DC, https://data.imf.org/?sk=7A51304B-6426-40C0-83DD-CA473CA1FD52; KNOMAD Remittances Data (dashboard), Global Knowledge Partnership on Migration and Development, World Bank, Washington, DC, https://www.knomad.org/data/remittances; World Development Indicators (dashboard), World Bank, Washington, DC, https://datatopics.worldbank.org/world-development-indicators/; WDR2023 Migration Database, World Bank, Washington, DC, https://www.worldbank.org/wdr2023/data.

Note: As per the International Monetary Fund's *Balance of Payments and International Investment Position Manual*, 6th edition (IMF 2009a), personal remittances include only the standard components of personal transfers and employee compensation for both inflows and outflows. Missing data for Vietnam and the United Arab Emirates are replaced with estimates from KNOMAD Data, Global Knowledge Partnership on Migration and Development, World Bank, Washington, DC, https://www.knomad.org/data. Economic fundamentals are estimated based on (1) the global number of migrants; (2) migrants' income as proxied by the global gross domestic product (GDP) per capita weighted by the number of migrants in each country; and (3) a stable share of income remitted. Weights for the year 2000 are used for 2001–09, and weights for the year 2010 are used for 2011–19.

Figure S5.3 At the country level, reports of both inflows and outflows can be inconsistent with economic fundamentals

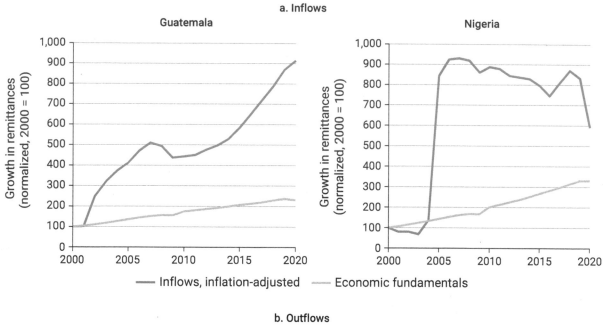

a. Inflows

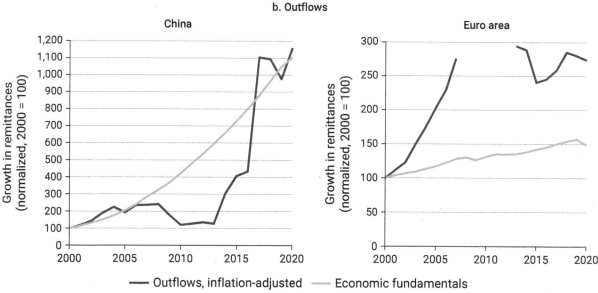

b. Outflows

Sources: Balance of Payments and International Investment Position Statistics (dashboard), International Monetary Fund, Washington, DC, https://data.imf.org/?sk=7A51304B-6426-40C0-83DD-CA473CA1FD52; KNOMAD Remittances Data (dashboard), Global Knowledge Partnership on Migration and Development, World Bank, Washington, DC, https://www.knomad .org/data/remittances; World Development Indicators (dashboard), World Bank, Washington, DC, https://datatopics.world bank.org/world-development-indicators/.

Note: As per the International Monetary Fund's *Balance of Payments and International Investment Position Manual*, 6th edition (IMF 2009a), personal remittances include only the standard components of personal transfers and employee compensation for both inflows and outflows. Economic fundamentals are the product of real gross domestic product (GDP) per capita (constant US$) and the total number of migrants. For Guatemala and Nigeria (inflows), economic fundamentals are the total number of emigrants multiplied by a composite real GDP per capita of destination countries, weighted by migrant share. For China and the euro area (outflows), they are a product of the total number of immigrants and real GDP per capita. Data on personal transfers are not available in the balance of payments for the euro area between 2008 and 2012.

Underlying challenges

The gaps in remittance estimates reflect challenges many countries are facing in compiling data from various sources:

- *Measurement of informal flows.* Large amounts of remittances are transferred via informal channels, such as *hawala*,[5] or carried by hand across borders, typically because of lower fees, more favorable exchange rates, or better accessibility. Most countries use surveys and models to estimate such transfers, but doing so accurately is notoriously challenging. When large amounts shift from informal to formal channels—or vice versa—large variations in reported flows sometimes occur, even though the actual amounts transferred did not change to the same extent. For example, during the COVID-19 pandemic, lockdowns and border closures between the United States and Mexico raised the costs of informal channels prohibitively. Some migrants thus shifted from informal channels to formal channels, such as banks or mobile operators, which are easier to capture in official statistics.[6] This shift led, in turn, to an increase in formal remittances, in spite of the economic slowdown.

- *Inconsistent estimation methods.* Many countries use a combination of instruments to estimate remittances, including financial institution reports, household surveys, and econometric models. For example, Mexico's central bank relies on monthly reports by remittance firms and surveys of incoming Mexican nationals at the US border. Similarly, the Philippine central bank tracks amounts transferred through the banking sector and uses surveys to estimate transfers through informal channels. By contrast, the US government relies on an economic model to assess the amounts of remittances sent to other countries. The model uses data on the number of foreign-born residents, their income, the share of their income remitted,[7] and other demographic indicators. Although based on similar principles, these approaches rely on different instruments, yielding results that are not fully consistent.

- *Classification issues.* As per the International Monetary Fund (IMF) guidelines, personal remittances include only the standard components of personal transfers and employee compensation for both inflows and outflows.[8] However, some small cross-country transactions are often classified in the BoP as remittances, even though they may be payments for international trade in goods or services or the repatriation of savings.[9] For example, when Pakistani migrants in Dubai repatriated their savings in the wake of the 2008–09 Great Recession, these flows were counted as remittances.[10]

- *Administrative capacity.* In some low- and middle-income countries, statistical offices have limited administrative capacity, which compounds the remittance estimation issues. The quality of financial reporting from banking institutions and mobile operators also varies across countries. Complementary sources of information, such as household and enterprise surveys or administrative data, can be expensive, and many countries do not use them in a systematic manner. This practice limits the universal applicability of sophisticated estimation methodologies.

Looking forward, improving the measurement of remittance flows is critical to enable countries of origin and destination to manage them at both the macroeconomic and microeconomic levels. The current discrepancies and inconsistencies across countries suggest the need for a significant effort to improve the accuracy and comparability of remittance data. This effort will require enhancing the implementation of shared guidelines, as provided by the IMF;[11] encouraging the widespread use of both complementary sources of information, such as household and enterprise surveys, as well as administrative data; and strengthening statistical capacity where needed, including in low- and middle-income countries.[12] Such efforts are urgent because the emergence of new money transfer operators and the diversification in the way person-to-person transactions are conducted are transforming the ways in which migrant workers are sending remittances.

Notes

1. The sixth edition of the International Monetary Fund's *Balance of Payments and International Investment Position Manual* (BPM6) and its "International Transactions in Remittances: Guide for Compilers and Users," both released in 2009, as well as its *BPM6 Compilation Guide,* released in 2014, provide the statistical framework, methodology, and practical guidance needed to record and compile the components of personal remittances (IMF 2009a, 2009b, 2014).
2. IMF (2009a).
3. Each cross-border financial transaction should be recorded as both an inflow in the remittance-receiving-country's BoP and an outflow in the remittance-sending country's BoP.
4. Clemens and McKenzie (2018).
5. *Hawala* is an informal method of transferring remittances. A payment is made by the remitter to an intermediary in the remitting country. The intermediary asks his or her partner in the country to which the remittance is sent to arrange a payment in local currency to the beneficiary. The debt between the partners is then settled at a later time through other mechanisms (Afram 2012).
6. Dinarte-Diaz et al. (2022).
7. GAO (2006).
8. IMF (2009a).
9. Amjad, Irfan, and Arif (2013).
10. Amjad, Irfan, and Arif (2013).
11. IMF (2009a, 2009b, 2014).
12. Ambler, Aycinena, and Yang (2015); Clemens and McKenzie (2018).

References

Afram, Gabi G. 2012. "The Remittance Market in India: Opportunities, Challenges, and Policy Options." World Bank, Washington, DC.

Ambler, Kate, Diego Aycinena, and Dean Yang. 2015. "Channeling Remittances to Education: A Field Experiment among Migrants from El Salvador." *American Economic Journal: Applied Economics* 7 (2): 207–32.

Amjad, Rashid, Mohammad Irfan, and G. M. Arif. 2013. "How to Increase Formal Inflows of Remittances: An Analysis of the Remittance Market in Pakistan." IGC Working Paper S-37046-PAK-1 (May), International Growth Centre, London School of Economics and Political Science, London.

Clemens, Michael A., and David J. McKenzie. 2018. "Why Don't Remittances Appear to Affect Growth?" *Economic Journal* 128 (612): F179–F209.

Dinarte-Diaz, Lelys, David Jaume, Eduardo Medina-Cortina, and Hernán Jorge Winkler. 2022. "Neither by Land nor by Sea: The Rise of Electronic Remittances during COVID-19." Policy Research Working Paper 10057, World Bank, Washington, DC.

GAO (Government Accountability Office, United States). 2006. "International Remittances: Different Estimation Methodologies Produce Different Results." Report to the Committee on Banking, Housing, and Urban Affairs, US Senate, Report GAO-06-210 (March 28), GAO, Washington, DC. https://www.gao.gov/assets/gao-06-210.pdf.

IMF (International Monetary Fund). 2009a. *Balance of Payments and International Investment Position Manual,* 6th ed. Washington, DC: IMF. https://www.imf.org/external/pubs/ft/bop/2007/bopman6.htm.

IMF (International Monetary Fund). 2009b. "International Transactions in Remittances: Guide for Compilers and Users." IMF, Washington, DC. https://www.imf.org/external/np/sta/bop/2008/rcg/pdf/guide.pdf.

IMF (International Monetary Fund). 2014. *BPM6 Compilation Guide: Companion Document to the Sixth Edition of the Balance of Payments and International Investment Position Manual.* Washington, DC: IMF. https://www.imf.org/external/pubs/ft/bop/2014/pdf/GuideFinal.pdf.

Ratha, Dilip, and William Shaw. 2007. "South-South Migration and Remittances." Working Paper 102, World Bank, Washington, DC.

6

Destination countries

Maximizing gains through economic and social policies

Key messages

- Destination countries gain significantly from the contributions of migrants whose skills and attributes strongly match their needs, irrespective of migrants' legal status or motivation.
- Benefits arise from migrants' contributions in the labor market and to higher productivity and greater availability and lower prices for some goods and services, as well as their fiscal contributions. These benefits are larger if migrants are allowed and able to work formally at the level of their qualifications.
- Costs are associated with the use of public services and the negative wage or employment effects on some nationals (typically among the lower-skilled). Social integration can have a cost as well, but the debate must be placed in context: destination societies are not identical, culturally uniform, or static.
- Destination countries can adopt policies that improve how well migrants' skills and attributes match countries' needs—and thus their gains—by creating adequate legal pathways for entry and by facilitating economic and social inclusion (figure 6.1).

Figure 6.1 When migrants' skills and attributes are a strong match with the needs of their destination countries, the countries benefit and can increase their benefits through policy actions

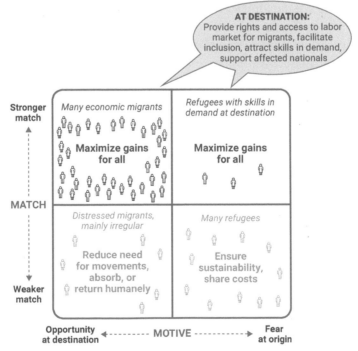

Source: WDR 2023 team.

Note: Match refers to the degree to which a migrant's skills and related attributes meet the demand in the destination country. *Motive* refers to the circumstances under which a person moves—whether in search of opportunity or because of a "well-founded fear" of persecution, armed conflict, or violence in their origin country.

Benefiting from migrants' labor

About 30 percent of Australia's population has migrated from another country, and two-thirds of them are now citizens. The country has a market-driven immigration policy that, with inputs from employers, prioritizes the skill sets and occupations in high demand. It also has programs aimed at family reunification, students in tertiary (postsecondary) education, and investors. This approach has attracted qualified individuals from many countries, with the result that 55 percent of adult migrants have a tertiary education.[1] Australia has also expanded its temporary migration programs, such as for agricultural workers, making it possible for migrants to convert to a longer-term status and, in some cases, citizenship.[2] These policies aim to ensure that economic immigrants' skills and attributes are a strong match with the needs of the labor market, thereby improving labor productivity and responding to the needs of particular regions and industries.

In the European Union (EU), all nationals of EU Member States have the right to enter and reside in any Member State with the same socioeconomic rights as citizens.[3] Some movements within the bloc are even encouraged through programs supported by the European Commission, such as Erasmus+ for students.[4] About 3 percent of EU citizens live in an EU country other than their own, and the proportion is higher among younger and more educated citizens.[5] Indeed, free movement is a cornerstone of the European construction and "convergence machine."[6] It has transformed the European economy and improved productivity, and it has allowed income levels to rise rapidly across the regional bloc, especially among the new Member States.[7]

Other countries rely on temporary migration to meet their labor needs, including the Gulf Cooperation Council (GCC) countries. Millions of immigrant workers from all over the world are employed in construction, engineering, banking, health care, and almost every other low-, medium-, and high-skilled occupation. In fact, the GCC receives significantly larger numbers of low-skilled workers than other high-income countries, although there has also been widespread criticism of their treatment.[8] Today, about two-thirds of the labor force in Bahrain, Oman, and Saudi Arabia and 80–90 percent in Kuwait, Qatar, and the United Arab Emirates consist of temporary migrants whose stays range from a few months to several decades. For these destination economies, migrants' contributions are indispensable, and migration is largely behind the region's modernization.

Many middle- and upper-middle-income countries are also important destinations, especially for relatively lower-skilled migrants from neighboring countries and lower-income countries. In Malaysia, 11.9 percent of the labor force is composed of migrants, with the vast majority from Indonesia, the Philippines, and Thailand.[9] As the education and income levels of citizens rose in Malaysia over the last three decades, labor demand in construction, agriculture, low-tech manufacturing, and services were met by lower-skilled migrants from these countries, supporting and enabling the country's further development.

The experience of high-income countries is relevant to the development debate for two main reasons. First, the success of migrants in high-income destination societies contributes to development outcomes in countries of origin and therefore is of interest to the development efforts in these countries.

Second, because data and research have predominantly focused on high-income countries, they provide insight into both the short- and long-term economic effects of migration (box 6.1), which will be helpful to policy makers in middle- and low-income countries that receive large numbers of migrants.

Demand for skills and labor in destination countries

Today, entire industries are relying on immigrant labor—construction and high-tech in the United States, oil and energy in the Middle East, mining in South Africa, plantations in Malaysia, childcare in Singapore, finance in the United Kingdom, transportation in Germany, and agriculture in almost every

Box 6.1 The longer-term economic effects of migration

Long-term data underscore the aggregate economic gains of "strong match" immigration. In Argentina, counties that received higher shares of migrants during the age of mass migration (1850–1914) had higher gross domestic product (GDP) per capita a century later. For example, an average Argentinian county that increased its share of immigrants from 20 percent to 25 percent in 1914 had GDP per capita almost 40 percent higher at the turn of the twenty-first century.[a] Massive inflows of immigrants to neighboring Brazil in 1850 had similar impacts. Municipalities that received a higher share of migrants experienced higher per capita income and higher levels of schooling than the national average, and this outcome persisted 100 years after the migration episode.[b] Population inflows during the age of great migration to the United States (1850–1920) increased overall prosperity through higher incomes, lower poverty and unemployment, faster rates of urbanization, and greater educational attainment that are still evident today. The economic gains enjoyed by the counties that received more immigrants did not come at the expense of nearby counties that received fewer immigrants.[c]

Even when people move under duress, the long-term benefits can be significant. In India, districts that received large numbers of people displaced during the 1947 Partition were more likely to adopt new agricultural technologies in the decades that followed, and they experienced significantly higher agricultural yields than other parts of the country.[d] Similarly, in Greece municipalities that received large numbers of people who were forcibly displaced following the Greco-Turkish War of 1919–22 benefited from new skills, especially in textile production and commercial agriculture. Seventy years later, they still had larger manufacturing sectors and higher average earnings than the rest of the country.[e] However, where newcomers were segregated in separate villages, the economic benefits were smaller, which illustrates the importance of social integration.[f]

a. Droller (2018).
b. Rocha, Ferraz, and Soares (2017).
c. Sequeira, Nunn, and Qian (2020); Tabellini (2020).
d. Bharadwaj and Ali Mirza (2019).
e. Murard and Sakalli (2020).
f. Murard and Sakalli (2020).

high-income country. In many countries, migrants are a significant addition to the labor force for both high- and low-skilled occupations.

In high-income countries, migrant workers are usually concentrated at opposite ends of the education distribution—among the highly educated and among those with only a primary education or less—which reflects labor market demands. By contrast, the share of migrants and naturalized citizens with an intermediate level of education—high school (upper-secondary) and postsecondary—is much lower (figure 6.2). Nationals with intermediate-skilled jobs act as complements to both high- and low-skilled migrant workers and benefit from their presence.

Fewer data are available on the skills complementarity of migrants in low- and middle-income destination countries. Most migrants are predominantly lower-skilled workers, and the complementarity of their skills with those already in the labor market is possibly weaker than in high-income countries. Many low- and middle-income countries also have relatively large informal economies. In the informal sector, migrants, irrespective of their skills, typically act as competitors with other informal workers.[10] When they can engage in the formal sector, migrants are more likely to be complementary to other workers.[11]

Figure 6.2 In the United States and Western Europe, migrants and naturalized citizens are overrepresented at both ends of the education spectrum

Difference between share of migrants and naturalized citizens and share of native-born citizens, by education level

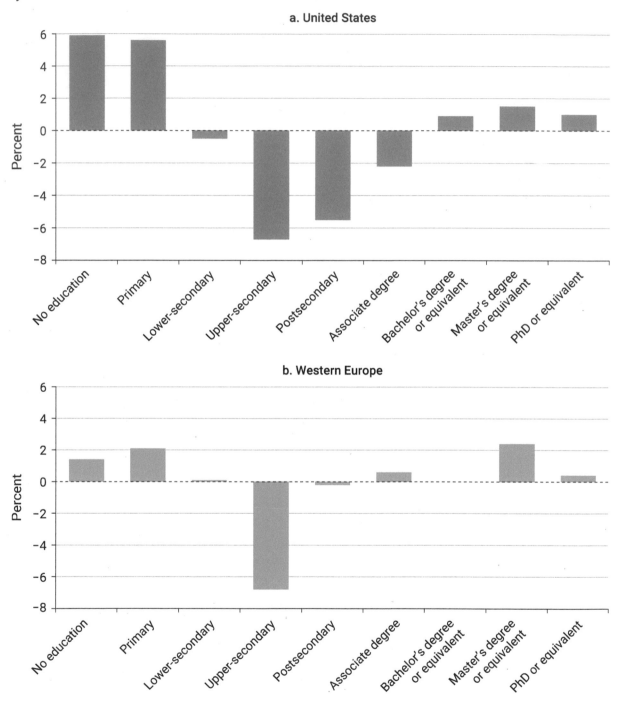

Sources: WDR 2023 team compilations, based on education data from American Community Survey (dashboard), US Census Bureau, Suitland, MD, https://www.census.gov/programs-surveys/acs; European Union Labour Force Survey (database), Eurostat, European Commission, Luxembourg, https://ec.europa.eu/eurostat/statistics-explained/index.php/EU_labour_force_survey.

Note: A postsecondary education includes those who have completed one year or more of college education without receiving a full degree. Western Europe is composed of Austria, Belgium, Denmark, Finland, France, Germany, Ireland, Italy, Luxembourg, Netherlands, Norway, Portugal, Spain, Sweden, and the United Kingdom. The data include all workers over age 15.

Skills complementarity reflects not only migrants' qualifications but also the response by national workers. For example, when low-skilled immigrants arrive, the incentives for young nationals to acquire higher skills increase. This has been documented in Western Europe from 1996 to 2010. Younger nationals who had just entered or were about to enter the labor force invested in additional education that allowed them to take on jobs requiring more abstract thinking and communication and commanding higher wages.[12] Likewise, in Denmark the settlement programs of low-skilled refugees across municipalities between 1986 and 1998 prompted young and less-educated nationals to strengthen their skills so that they could pursue occupations that were less intensive in manual labor and that offered better wages, employment prospects, and occupational mobility.[13]

Broader economic effects: Higher productivity, lower consumer prices, and stronger business links

The economic effects of migration stem from the complementarity of migrants' skills with those of national workers. When migrants' skills complement those already in the labor market, productivity increases, spreading substantial benefits across the destination country's economy.

High-skilled migrants generate productivity gains and spillovers that create opportunities for workers at lower levels of skills—both migrants and nationals.[14] In 18 Organisation for Economic Co-operation and Development (OECD) member countries taken together, foreign-born individuals accounted for 27 percent of all doctors and 16 percent of all nurses in 2018.[15] In the United States, over a third of current medical residents completed their medical degree abroad. And almost two-thirds of the US winners of the Nobel Prize are foreign-born.[16] High degrees of skill complementarity result in agglomeration economies and geographic concentration in many sectors—such as technology in California's Silicon Valley and finance in London, New York, and Singapore.[17]

Migrants in low-skilled occupations can also provide complementary skills. As education levels have increased and the workforce has aged rapidly in many high- and upper-middle-income economies, the share of national workers without a high school degree has declined. Immigration is making it possible for employers to hire the low-skilled workers they need to keep their businesses sustainable. Migrant workers represent 12 percent of agricultural workers across the European Union and over 40 percent in Spain.[18] They account for 64 percent of agricultural workers in the United States.[19] Similarly, the vast majority of the construction workers in the GCC countries and plantation workers in Malaysia are also migrants.[20]

The presence of low-skilled workers has additional effects. The cost of domestic household services declines when immigrants perform housework and childcare in higher-income countries. Women nationals, released from these tasks, can then join the labor force in larger numbers—especially high-skilled married women—leading to overall economic gains. This pattern has been observed in a wide range of economies, such as Germany; Hong Kong SAR, China; Italy; Spain; Switzerland; the United Kingdom; and the United States.[21]

Migrants also facilitate trade, investment, and other economic flows between destination and origin countries.[22] They bring their social capital and business networks to the destination country, along with their knowledge of the origin country's language, regulations, market opportunities, and institutions, thereby creating opportunities for trade and investment in the origin country and lowering the corresponding transaction costs. For example, the United States received large numbers of Vietnamese refugees in the 1970s who settled across the country. When trade restrictions between the United States and Vietnam were lifted 29 years later, US states with larger Vietnamese populations experienced the most significant growth in exports to Vietnam.[23] The return of Bosnian refugees from Germany also resulted in higher exports from Germany to Bosnia and Herzegovina in sectors in which refugees previously had a higher presence.[24] Ethnic Chinese networks established via historical migration patterns facilitated foreign direct investment (FDI) in Southeast Asia.[25]

How migration gains are shared within the destination society varies across countries and sectors of activity. In addition to the migrants themselves, two groups stand to potentially gain from migrants' labor: consumers, if migrants' contributions result in greater availability and lower prices for some domestically produced goods and services, and employers or owners of capital, if migrants' contributions are reflected in higher profits.

Policy choices made by the destination society—including the degree to which markets are competitive—determine the outcome. A 2014 study found that in the United Kingdom immigration had no effect on the prices of tradable goods, but it did result in lower prices for nontraded services, such as construction, restaurants, and hairdressers.[26] In the United States, a 10 percent increase in the share of low-skilled immigrants in the labor force reduced the price of some services, such as housekeeping, and construction by 2 percent.[27] Similarly, after large numbers of immigrants from the former Soviet Union arrived in Israel during the 1990s, a 1 percentage point increase in the ratio of immigrants to nationals in a region was associated with a 0.5 percentage point decrease in the price of a basket of consumer goods.[28]

Mixed effects on wages and employment

Despite economywide gains, migration can be disruptive at the local level for some groups, even if migrants' skills and attributes strongly match the needs of the destination economy. Impacts are often felt in the geographic areas and occupations in which migrants are concentrated. The economic adjustment can affect nationals' wages and employment levels, at least in the short term. It affects some groups negatively—typically those whose skills are similar to those of the migrants[29]—while benefiting complementary workers.[30] Cross-country variations reflect a range of factors, including the state of the destination economy, the share of migrants in the labor force, and the complementarity of skills between migrants and nationals.

As for other shocks, markets eventually adjust through a reallocation of capital and the movement of workers to other occupations, sectors, and regions. Over time, the adverse impacts of migration tend to decline, especially when product and labor markets are flexible[31] and social protection mechanisms are effective. Still, the adjustment costs can be significant for some workers and their families. For many workers, it is difficult to switch jobs, firms, or geographic locations to adjust to the presence of immigrant workers.[32]

In terms of wage gains (or losses) experienced by existing workers, a review of 111 studies in 29 countries reveals different outcomes (figure 6.3) when immigration increases the labor force by 1 percentage point. They range from a net loss of 6 percent for low-skilled workers in Colombia to a net gain of about 5 percent for high-skilled workers in Türkiye.[33]

When wages are relatively rigid, the short-term effects of migration may include higher unemployment for nationals at the local level.[34] For example, in the early 1990s Germany received about 2.8 million ethnic Germans from the former Soviet bloc (not including the former Democratic Republic of Germany), settling them randomly across the country. Although wages remained largely stable, for every 10 new workers who arrived in a certain region three German workers lost their jobs. Similarly, a 1990 policy gave workers from the Czech Republic employment rights—but not residency—in some German border municipalities. By 1993, wages had declined by only 0.13 percent, but the influx of Czech workers had led to almost one-to-one job losses for Germans in that area.[35] Some affected workers chose to withdraw from the labor force or to relocate to other regions.[36] In South Africa, the arrival of migrant workers led to lower wages and prompted nationals to move to areas with better employment prospects.[37] In Europe, immigration-related job losses among nationals are lower in labor markets with smaller hiring costs, less rigid wages, and lower business entry costs.[38]

Overall, lower-skilled workers tend to be negatively affected more often—and more severely—by immigration than higher-skilled workers because their skills tend to be closer to those of migrants.

Figure 6.3 The impacts of immigration on wages vary across countries

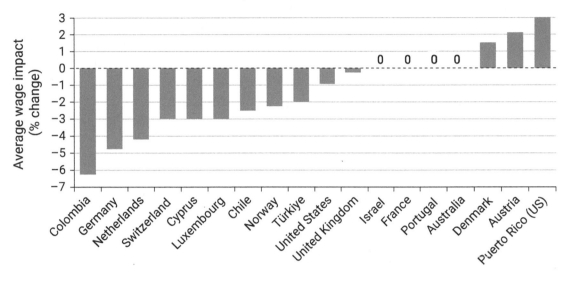

a. Impacts on low-skilled workers

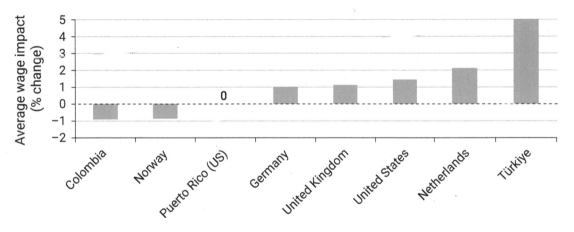

b. Impacts on high-skilled workers

Source: WDR 2023 team calculations, based on a review of 111 studies in 29 countries.
Note: The average wage impact is the percentage wage gain or loss experienced by existing workers when the local labor force increases by 1 percentage point due to immigration.

For example, in Colombia, although both low- and high-skilled workers are negatively affected, lower-skilled are more so. In Germany, the Netherlands, Türkiye, and the United Kingdom, lower-skilled workers experience negative wage impacts, while high-skilled workers see gains.[39] In Colombia and Türkiye, the arrival of refugees in the labor market has negative effects on informal workers and positive effects on formal workers.[40] Migration to low- and middle-income countries, when it is a close substitute for low-skilled workers and a strong complement for high-skilled workers, also disproportionately affects low-skilled and thus low-income individuals.[41]

In many countries, previous waves of migrants are the most affected by new inflows because their skills are most similar to the skills that new migrants bring. In the United States, new migration between 1990 and 2006 reduced the wages of previous cohorts of migrant workers by 7.6 percent, whereas the impact on nationals was a marginal gain of 0.6 percent.[42] The pattern was similar in Malaysia, where a

10 percent increase in the number migrants reduced the wages of existing migrants by about 3.9 percent, with no observable impacts on the wages of nationals.[43]

Fiscal contributions

The fiscal impacts of migration are usually positive. In OECD countries, the net fiscal contributions of migrants—measured as the tax revenue and social security contributions collected from migrants minus the social transfers they receive[44]—are often even higher than those of nationals (figure 6.4).[45] The net fiscal contribution is higher when migrants arrive with skills and attributes that strongly match the needs of the destination country. They can, however, be reduced when migrants face labor market discrimination or do not work at the level of their skills and qualifications and thus earn lower wages than comparable nationals.

Differences in the age distribution of immigrants and naturalized citizens relative to the native-born account for a large part of the difference in their net fiscal contribution—70 percent in the OECD countries (figure 6.5).[46] This finding stems from the fact that immigrants are overrepresented among prime-age individuals—the age group that contributes more and draws relatively fewer benefits—and underrepresented among children and the elderly—the age groups that consume the most education, health, and old-age benefits, while not contributing much.[47] Most immigrants arrive in the host country

Figure 6.4 **On average, the net fiscal contributions of migrants and naturalized citizens in OECD countries are higher than those of native-born citizens**

Ratio of individual-level government revenue to expenditure (per capita), 2006–18 average

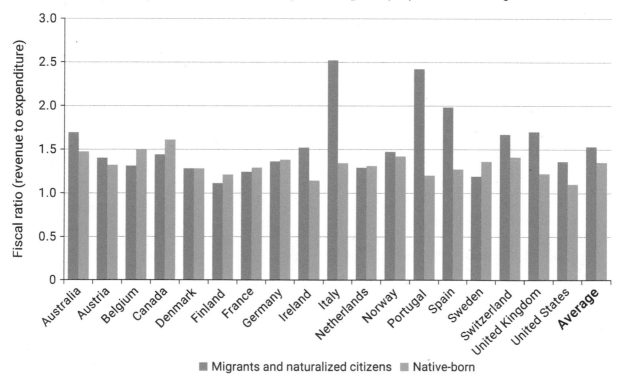

Source: Damas de Matos 2021.

Note: Data include only individual-level government expenditures and revenue. Expenditures are on health, education, and social protection. Revenue is from direct and indirect taxes, as well as social contributions. Expenditures on pure public goods, such as national defense, are excluded. OECD = Organisation for Economic Co-operation and Development.

Figure 6.5 Migrants' fiscal contributions are larger when they are working age

Correlation between the relative fiscal ratio (foreign-born to native-born) and the relative share of the population ages 15–64, 2006–18 average

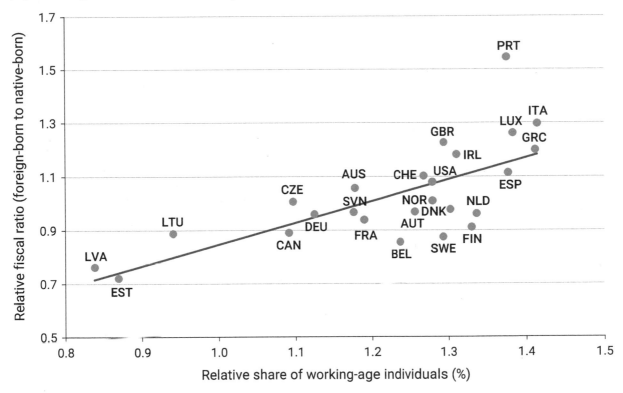

Source: OECD 2021.

Note: For country abbreviations, see International Organization for Standardization (ISO), https://www.iso.org/obp/ui /#search.

having completed their education.[48] Between 1995 and 2011, European immigrants brought skills and training into the United Kingdom that would have cost almost US$17 billion if produced through the British education system.[49] As they engage in the labor force, prime-aged immigrants contribute three times more than the government spends on them.[50] Overall, the average recent immigrant to the United States with less than a high school education delivers an estimated net present value contribution of US$128,000 over the course of their employment—almost twice the median annual income level.[51]

Other factors also matter. The fiscal effects of temporary and permanent migration differ. Temporary workers typically return to their countries of origin before needing the public expenditures associated with old age—health care and pensions. Many migrate without their families and thus do not use the education system. By contrast, permanent migrants need full access to health care, education, and pension systems, and they typically generate smaller fiscal gains for the destination country.[52] Education and skill levels also affect migrants' net fiscal contributions. Individual government expenditures on migrants are similar across education levels,[53] but migrants' fiscal contributions are not; higher-skilled migrants contribute more than those with lower skills.

Migrants' legal status and formal employment are the single most important determinant of a migrant's net fiscal contribution.[54] Whereas all migrants—whether documented or undocumented— pay consumption and value added taxes, only documented migrants pay income or social security taxes. Having the right to work allows documented migrants to earn higher wages, which, in turn, increases their fiscal contributions.[55] In Colombia, a large amnesty program that granted job permits to about half a million Venezuelan migrants in 2018 increased formalization rates by 10 percentage points—and many of these migrants are now paying taxes.[56]

The overall fiscal impact of immigration also includes indirect contributions. Indirect and long-run fiscal impacts are generally harder to quantify. They are based on assumptions about productivity, growth, capital allocation, and other adjustment mechanisms in the economy. But it is clear that migrant labor increases the revenue and profits of the firms that employ them and thus the taxes these firms have to pay. In the United States, such taxes are over three times larger than the direct (net) fiscal effects of migrants.[57]

Maximizing economic gains

Destination countries' policies largely affect the size of their economic gains. Policies include those affecting entry—determining who is allowed to come into a country—as well as policies affecting migrants' stay—determining the rights they can enjoy and the opportunities they can access. Migrants' contributions are larger in countries where migration policies ensure a high complementarity between migrants and nationals across all skill levels. Specifically, those are countries in which it is possible for migrants to work formally and at their level of qualification and in which the business environment enables capital and labor to be allocated swiftly across regions and sectors of the economy.

Entry policies

To meet their economic needs, most countries need multiple legal migration channels, including for both permanent and temporary migration. For example, the United States has as many as 185 visa categories, among them those for high-skilled workers and for agricultural seasonal laborers, for family reunification, and for temporary stay on humanitarian grounds. Similarly, numerous criteria provide grounds for obtaining a green card (permanent residency), such as family ties, employment, refugee status, and protection from abuse or human trafficking.[58] Multiple channels make for a cumbersome system, but they also allow nuanced and comprehensive responses to a wide variety of situations and needs.

Entry policies need to acknowledge market forces. Where there is a demand, restrictions on immigrant labor come at a high economic cost and generate adverse effects, such as increases in undocumented migration and declines in output and productivity.[59] For example, the US Bracero program provided Mexican farm workers with temporary work permits, and its termination in 1964 closed legal paths to employment for almost half a million temporary workers. Closure of the program was intended to benefit domestic workers. However, employers replaced migrant labor with machines, or they hired undocumented migrants, who simply replaced the legal temporary workers. More recently, several oil-rich GCC countries imposed hiring quotas on immigrants to promote employment of nationals in the private sector. In Saudi Arabia, the employment of Saudi nationals increased, but the affected firms were 7 percentage points less likely to export; the value of their exports was likely to fall by 14 percent; and they were 1.5 percentage points more likely to exit the market.[60] In response to government restrictions, an irregular market then emerged, with migrants working illegally for an employer other than their visa sponsor.[61]

Measures to deter irregular migration can have unintended consequences. For example, the Secure Communities program implemented in the United States between 2008 and 2013 deterred irregular migration of one person for every person deported.[62] However, the policy also had negative consequences for US citizens. It reduced the employment and wages of low-skilled workers[63] because of a reduction in local consumption and an increase in labor costs that reduced job creation. And it curtailed the labor force participation of high-skilled citizens, especially women.[64]

To ensure the effectiveness and sustainability of legal pathways, some countries have developed consultative processes with employers, labor unions, and other stakeholders. For example, in the United Kingdom the Migration Advisory Committee reviews labor needs in selected sectors to advise the government on the potential use of immigration as a response to those needs.[65] Similar schemes have been developed in Australia and Singapore, among others. Some countries also engage with local authorities or civil society as a way to build and strengthen a consensus on migration objectives. Such processes aim to ensure better matching of the potential pool of incoming migrants with the needs of the destination labor market.

Permanent schemes

When designing pathways for permanent migration, some destination countries focus on migrants' potential for integration. Canada and New Zealand have organized their permanent migration pathways using a points system. Applicants are scored based on a set of criteria, such as skills, language, or demographics, and those who accrue a sufficient number of points are allowed entry on a path that typically leads to naturalization. Canada's points system is based on a migrant's potential to succeed, whereas New Zealand mostly gives preference to skilled migrants.[66] Australia has also implemented a points-based system. Until the mid-1990s, it offered skilled migrants permanent migration opportunities, but it has evolved to focus on people with strong employment prospects.[67] Austria, Germany, Portugal, Sweden, and the United Arab Emirates have also established job search visas; foreign workers who meet specific criteria are allowed entry for the purpose of finding employment.

In fact, most destination countries have adopted policies aimed at attracting high-skilled migrants. These policies include employment rights and residency privileges comparable to those of nationals, as well as a greater ability than lower-skilled migrants to migrate with their families.[68] Consequently, in many destination countries the share of immigrants and naturalized citizens with a tertiary education is higher than that of nationals (figure 6.6).

Almost half of all tertiary-educated migrants live in just four destination countries: the United States, the United Kingdom, Canada, and Australia.[69] For example, almost half of all doctoral students in science, technology, engineering, and mathematics (STEM) in the United States and Canada are from other countries—and a large share of these students stay after graduation.[70] Overall, high-income OECD countries receive almost 75 percent of all tertiary-educated migrants.

Some legal entry pathways have been designed to reflect the economic and social objectives of destination countries. For example, in the United States some channels aim to strengthen the country's diversity by allocating a certain number of green cards (permanent residency) through an annual lottery system that gives preference to people from origin countries underrepresented among migrants.[71] Other legal pathways also encourage and facilitate longer-term integration. For example, admissions on family reunification grounds have become the largest migration channel to OECD countries.[72]

Temporary pathways

Temporary migration pathways are used by a range of destination countries. They account for almost all migrants in the GCC countries, Malaysia, and Singapore. And they are used in EU countries to fulfill labor demands across the skills spectrum.[73] They have also been introduced in the Republic of Korea,

Figure 6.6 In many destination countries, the share of immigrants and naturalized citizens with a tertiary education exceeds the average for the labor force

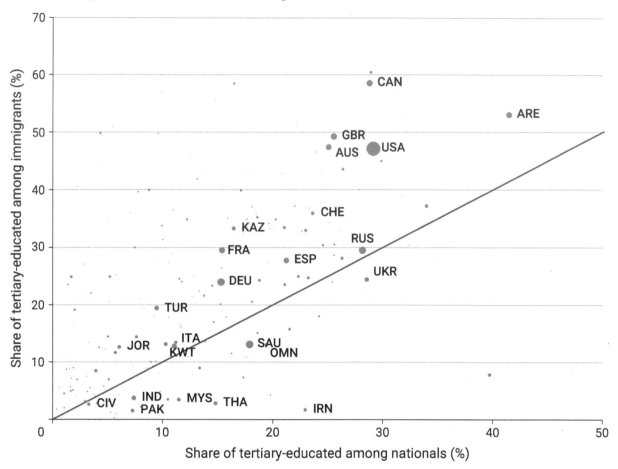

Sources: WDR 2023 team compilations, based on migration data for 2020 from DataBank: Global Bilateral Migration, World Bank, Washington, DC, https://databank.worldbank.org/source/global-bilateral-migration; data on skill structure of the population from census data (2014–20); updated Barro and Lee (2013); and Data (portal), Wittgenstein Centre for Demography and Global Human Capital, Vienna, https://www.wittgensteincentre.org/en/data.htm.

Note: The size of the circles is relative to the number of immigrants and naturalized citizens in the country. For country abbreviations, see International Organization for Standardization (ISO), https://www.iso.org/obp/ui/#search.

which in 2003 established an Employment Permit System to address the labor demand of small and medium enterprises.

Several OECD countries are turning increasingly to temporary forms of migration, including as a first stage of permanent migration.[74] In Australia, for example, until the mid-1990s almost all foreign workers admitted into the country were arriving as permanent settlers. Today, three-quarters of migrants are entering under a temporary work visa.[75] This visa serves as a "trial period" before migrants apply for permanent status.[76] In Canada, temporary migration has also overtaken permanent movements (figure 6.7). Similarly, Germany has gradually developed a path to a permanent stay for temporary migrants.[77] Korea permits low-skilled foreign workers to change their visa category to a semiskilled one, subject to passing skills qualification tests. Thus far, a quarter of migrants with

Figure 6.7 Temporary migration has overtaken permanent migration in Canada

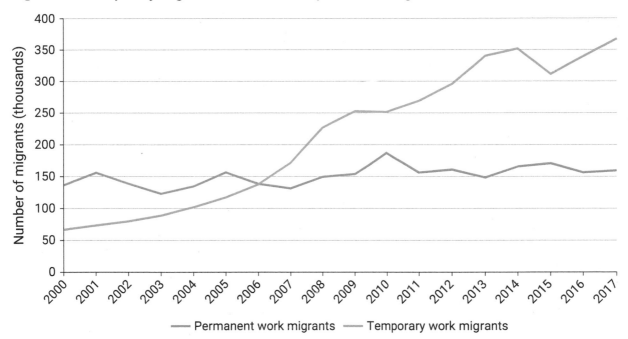

Source: WDR 2023 team, based on data from Open Government (dashboard), Strategic Communications and Ministerial Affairs, Treasury Board of Canada Secretariat, Ottawa, https://open.canada.ca/en.

Note: Temporary work migrants include those who entered Canada through the Temporary Foreign Worker Program (TFWP) and the International Mobility Program (IMP). Permanent work migrants are permanent residents under the economic class of immigrants.

semi- to high-skilled visas have benefited from such a conversion, which, in some cases, also provides a pathway to residence and family reunion.[78]

Many countries use seasonal migration programs to fill labor shortfalls in certain sectors, and this approach has proved mutually beneficial for migrants, origin countries, and destination countries in many contexts.[79] For example, Spain and Morocco signed a bilateral agreement in 2001 that allowed Moroccans to work in Spain's agriculture sector for up to nine months a year.[80] Spain has similar programs with countries in Latin America such as Honduras, Colombia, and Ecuador.[81] Poland is issuing seasonal work permits for up to nine months at the request of employers in the agriculture and tourism sectors.[82] Similar seasonal worker programs are also common in Australia, Canada, New Zealand, and the United States. In Canada, the Seasonal Agricultural Worker Program brings in 20,000 workers a year from Mexico and participating Caribbean countries for between six weeks and eight months.[83] To ensure that seasonal workers do not overstay their visas, some countries allow workers to return the following season if they comply with a stated return rule. Compliance rates have been high in Canada, New Zealand, and Spain.[84]

Temporary migration is indeed a suitable channel to address temporary labor needs. For destination countries, temporary migration meets labor needs while reducing medium-term social impacts. For example, under such programs migrants are typically not allowed to bring their families. In other words, these arrangements separate the migrant's labor from other traits and characteristics that could make long-term inclusion more complex.

Temporary migration, however, is less suitable to address longer-term labor needs. When temporary work permits are extended or renewed over long periods of time, the integration challenges may be heightened. Temporary visas lower incentives to acquire languages and invest in country-specific human capital and social networks,[85] and the destination country usually does not implement measures to support integration.[86] For example, in the 1960s in Europe foreign workers—such as the *Gastarbeiter* (guest workers) in Germany—were expected to stay for only a few years, but many never left.

Stay policies

Skills recognition and skills building

Recognition of degrees and skill certifications is important to make the best of labor migration. To do so, destination countries must develop mechanisms to determine whether origin countries' standards for each skill are equivalent to their own.[87] International standards may help facilitate such assessments,[88] but they have proved difficult to put in place. Regional cooperation and the development of regional qualification frameworks are promising. Examples are the European Qualifications Framework and the Association of Southeast Asian Nations (ASEAN) Qualifications Reference Framework.[89] Although such certification efforts are heavily technical and time-consuming, they are critical to maximizing the benefits of cross-border labor movements for migrants and destination economies alike.[90]

Better command of the local language and language training programs are also associated with higher productivity and the labor force participation of migrants,[91] which, in turn, benefit the destination society economically. Access to language training and some integration support have had positive impacts in high-income countries such as Denmark, France, and Germany.[92]

Student visas offer an alternative route for migrants to obtain the skills needed in destination labor markets. By accepting migrant students, countries are able to offer them qualifications that will be easily recognized by their employers—often more effective than an ex post certification of degrees and experiences obtained elsewhere. Accepting migrants as students also gives them both the opportunity and the incentive to invest in learning the local language and accumulate other forms of social capital specific to the destination country, thereby facilitating their social integration.

Global Skills Partnerships are another model. By means of partnerships, destination countries finance the training of potential migrants in their origin countries and provide them with entry upon graduation. This approach aims to ensure that the skills and attributes of potential migrants match the labor needs at destination and to reduce the negative brain drain impacts because some program participants eventually choose not to migrate. Pilot programs have been launched by Belgium and Morocco in the information and communication technology sector and by Germany and Tunisia in the nursing sector,[93] but this approach has not yet been scaled up. Early lessons highlight the need to ensure active employers' participation in the design of the training programs, the importance of ensuring the social acceptability of these programs in the origin country, and the complexity of multilateral partnerships involving training institutes and public authorities in both origin and destination countries, as well as employers at the destination.

Legal status and labor rights

Providing migrants with a secure legal status and formal employment rights facilitates their inclusion in the labor market and makes it possible for them to engage in formal activities at the level of their skills and qualifications. Having a secure legal status—whether it involves having a valid employment visa, asylum or residency status, or citizenship—means predictable prospects of stay, protection of the rule of law, and other legal rights.[94] Migrants then have greater incentives to invest in their destination community, workplace, or country, and they learn a new language, engage in entrepreneurial activities, acquire additional educational degrees, and become part of social networks.[95] With secure legal status, migrants can move more freely within the economy and society, increase their income and personal ties, and further integrate socially and economically.

Support for affected nationals

Labor market flexibility is key to supporting nationals whose skills are similar to those of migrants and who are negatively affected because of a decline in wages or employment. Flexibility allows complementary workers and capital to move to areas and sectors that migrants entered, and it allows workers with similar skills to move to other regions, sectors, or occupations.[96] Similarly, flexible capital markets can facilitate the entry of new firms in a sector or the expansion of existing firms, both of which increase the demand for labor and reduce the negative impacts of migration on wages and employment.[97] By contrast, market rigidities that hamper capital or labor market adjustments increase the negative effects of immigration. These restrictions are particularly pervasive in low- and middle-income countries where migrants are concentrated in the informal economy, the mobility of nationals is low, and firms' capacity to expand is limited because of lack of access to financial markets and low productivity,[98] as documented in Colombia,[99] Ecuador,[100] and Peru.[101]

Workers who face job losses and mobility costs may also need support as they search for employment in other regions or sectors. Social protection programs and active labor market policies reduce the adverse effects of immigration. In high-income countries where the aggregate gains from migration create the necessary fiscal resources, it is possible to support those who are temporarily affected by job loss. However, experience with the adjustment to trade liberalization reveals the complexity of such efforts if, for example, people are unwilling or unable to move to new areas or activities. In lower- and middle-income destination countries, where the skills of nationals and migrants are more similar and fiscal resources are more limited, implementing such social protection programs may be even more challenging.

Fostering social inclusion

In many countries, the political debate on migration has shifted from economics to the challenges associated with migrants' social inclusion. When migrants stay for an extended period of time—or permanently—the question of their integration becomes central. The findings on integration outcomes are mainly limited to high-income countries, but they can help inform migration policies in other destination countries, both middle- and low-income, while adjusting to local circumstances.

Successful integration benefits both migrants and destination societies. Migrants gain significantly through better outcomes in the labor market,[102] as well as stronger engagement in society. Destination countries benefit through migrants' stronger economic contributions[103] and by avoiding the emergence of a marginalized population. Within a society, trust and cohesion between groups are associated with higher economic growth.[104] But when social tensions are particularly strong, divisions along the lines of ethnicity, race, religion, or national origin can worsen productivity by reducing cooperation between workers.[105]

Residential segregation

Migrants and their families tend to settle in certain regions, municipalities, or even neighborhoods in a community from their country of origin that can help them find a job and adjust to a new social and cultural environment (maps 6.1 and 6.2).[106] For example, Mexican migrants to the United States

Map 6.1 In the United States, immigrant households are largely concentrated along the southern border and in major metropolitan areas

Percentage of households with at least one foreign-born member

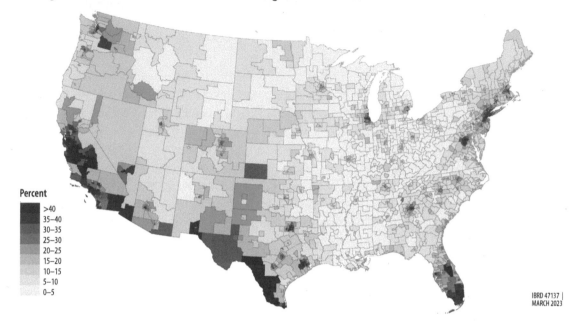

Percent
>40
35–40
30–35
25–30
20–25
15–20
10–15
5–10
0–5

IBRD 47137 |
MARCH 2023

Source: WDR 2023 team calculations, based on 2019 five-year estimates of American Community Survey (dashboard), US Census Bureau, Suitland, MD, https://www.census.gov/programs-surveys/acs.

with limited English-language skills tend to live in communities with high concentrations of Mexican migrants.[107] In Denmark, refugees often prefer to live in areas with higher proportions of migrants from their origin countries.[108] These preferences may be reinforced when discrimination affects migrants' ability to access the housing market in some areas, as has been documented in France.[109] Because of residential segregation, migrants may represent a large share of the population in some areas, even when national averages are relatively low.

Migrants' concentration may be exacerbated when nationals relocate to avoid sharing public spaces with those who differ from them in, for example, ethnicity or religion—a phenomenon called "native flight."[110] Such relocation further affects a neighborhood's desirability for other

Map 6.2 In the New York City metropolitan area, migrants are concentrated in certain neighborhoods

Percentage of households with at least one foreign-born member

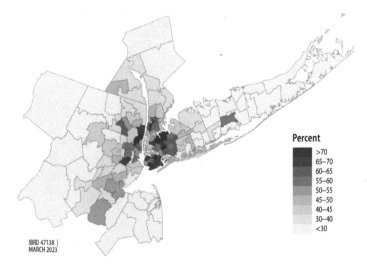

Percent
>70
65–70
60–65
55–60
50–55
45–50
40–45
30–40
<30

IBRD 47138 |
MARCH 2023

Source: WDR 2023 team calculations, based on 2019 five-year estimates of American Community Survey (dashboard), US Census Bureau, Suitland, MD, https://www.census.gov/programs-surveys/acs.

nationals. These effects can be significant in some situations. For example, in France municipalities that opened new refugee centers saw an average of three to six residents leave for each refugee who arrived within two years of the opening.[111]

Residential segregation affects housing prices. In most high-income countries, where the immigration inflow is gradual and responds to local economic opportunities, the housing market adjusts—unless it is constrained by zoning laws.[112] In Canada and the United States, an immigration inflow of 1 percent of a city's population increases rents, but by less than 1 percent as new construction takes place.[113]

In some cases, native flight contributes to lowering housing prices in neighborhoods with a large share of migrants. In the largest 20 cities in Italy, between 2000 and 2010 a 10 percent increase in the immigrant population led to a 2 percent decline in housing prices relative to other parts of the cities as the locals moved out.[114] Similar effects have been documented in the United States, the United Kingdom, and Germany.[115] When a refugee shelter opened in Berlin, the listed prices for new rentals near the shelter declined by 3–4 percent, and satisfaction with the neighborhood's amenities fell.[116] Native flight can also affect housing prices in neighboring areas with a lower share of migrants. For example, in the United States housing demand and prices increase in the areas to which natives are moving.[117]

Residential segregation tends to be associated with lower public investment, further aggravating the situation. The priority that public authorities give to serving the needs of migrant communities may depend on migrants' voting rights.[118] Nationals may react to the arrival of migrants by supporting less redistributive policies.[119] In the early decades of the twentieth century, public spending per capita declined in areas of the United States that received large numbers of immigrants.[120] However, this effect may depend on a country's current socioeconomic condition[121] or on migrants' legal status.[122]

Education and health care

The impact of immigrants on education systems depends on the size, composition, and concentration of the immigrant population. Larger numbers lead to larger adverse effects when investments in infrastructure, teachers, and resources do not adjust in a timely manner or when the neighborhoods in which migrants live are not prioritized.[123] In Spain, provinces with the largest shares of migrants have higher student-teacher ratios (figure 6.8).[124]

Educational outcomes for nationals also reflect peer effects, which encompass social interactions and group learning, among other things.[125] In some situations, the presence of migrant children in a classroom negatively affects average learning and test scores. However, the number of migrants' children in the classroom, whether their parents are highly or less educated and whether these children have a solid command of the local language, can make a significant difference.[126] Such negative effects have also been observed in low-income countries such as Colombia and Uganda.[127] In the Netherlands, the effects are the strongest if immigrant children are recent arrivals, suggesting that increasing levels of integration can lessen the negative impacts.[128] Still, many other factors come into play to explain learning outcomes, such as class size or cultural background in the communities.[129]

Native flight compounds the situation in many communities. Evidence of families changing school districts in response to large migrant inflows has been documented in several countries, such as in the United States when students must transition from relatively homogeneous primary schools to more mixed high schools.[130] Similarly, in Spain and Türkiye in response to higher numbers of immigrant children in public schools, the enrollment of native-born children in private education tends to increase,[131] especially if those students are from higher-income households.[132] That increase raises the ratio of migrants to nationals in public schools, amplifying negative perceptions. It can also reduce support for disadvantaged public schools.[133]

Figure 6.8 Student-teacher ratios in Spain increase with higher shares of migrant students

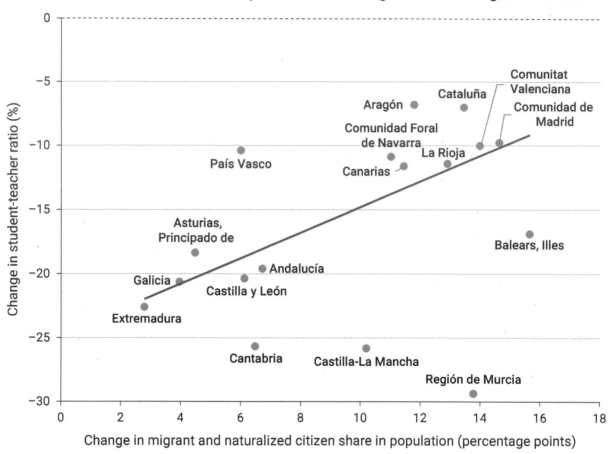

Source: Tanaka, Farré, and Ortega 2018.

Note: The figure depicts the change in the student-teacher ratio for 17 provinces in Spain over the period 2000–2010. The regression line is weighted by population in each province.

Immigration has similar effects on the access to and delivery of health care, especially in communities with limited public resources, but these effects are ambiguous. In some countries, migrants account for a relatively large share of health care workers, thereby providing the national population with additional services. The impact of migrants' consumption of health care services on nationals depends on migrants' geographic concentration, their age profile and health status, and the share of patients who need specialized services. In the United Kingdom, waiting times for health care have increased in disadvantaged areas with large inflows of immigrants. However, migrants have a lower propensity to use health care services than nationals, in part because they tend to be younger and healthier[134] and in part because they may face discrimination and barriers to accessing health care.[135]

Crime and insecurity

The relationship between immigration and crime has been the subject of intense public debates. In most OECD countries, foreign nationals make up a larger share of the incarcerated population than their share of the overall population, often by a significant margin.[136] Yet empirical investigations of the link between immigration and crime have been largely inconclusive. Some studies find no significant effect of immigration on overall crime rates, as in Italy.[137] Others document a lower propensity to commit crime among migrants, as in Malaysia.[138] And yet others find a positive effect on crimes that are motivated by monetary gains, as in the United States.[139] Crime rates also reflect reactions from nationals. For example, when the presence of immigrants induces a sense of insecurity, nationals may relocate or preemptively invest in security measures.[140]

Criminal behavior mainly arises from the conditions in which migrants live, work, and interact with others in the destination country. In any population, unemployment increases the likelihood of committing crimes, as does social marginalization.[141] In many countries, migrants are overrepresented in the poorer and excluded segments of society—that is, those in which criminal behavior is more prevalent. Economic and social inclusion go a long way in reducing the risk of migrants committing crime. For example, lifting the legal barriers to employment for irregular migrants and asylum-seekers reduces the incidence of crime.[142] In Italy, irregular migrants are less likely to commit crimes when they have a legal status that allows them to access the formal labor market.[143] The regularization of nearly 3 million immigrants in the United States in 1986 led to a 3–5 percent decrease in crime.[144]

In some countries, the presence of migrants has also raised national security concerns. These concerns span a range of issues from spying to terrorism, which typically involve a small number of individuals but are broadly feared. When terrorist events occur,[145] fear can drive negative sentiments toward entire communities,[146] such as those experienced by members of Muslim communities since the rise of Islamic terrorism in the 1990s.[147]

Beyond inclusion: Social integration

The notion of social integration varies significantly across societies. In some destination societies, migrants are expected to rapidly embrace the cultural heritage of the majority of the population, whereas other countries are more open to the long-term persistence of migrants' cultural preferences. Some of the "cultural" issues attributed to migrants reflect, in fact, a lack of progress toward the inclusion of national minorities—and especially the descendants of naturalized migrants. These attitudes are reflected in the criteria used for naturalization, which can range from blood lineages, as in Germany until 2000; to command of the dominant language, as in France; to knowledge of the constitution and government institutions, as in the United States. Countries that define or perceive themselves as multiethnic or multireligious often embrace a greater degree of cultural diversity.

Most destination societies and cultures are neither homogeneous nor static (box 6.2). Algeria and Canada have two official languages, Belgium three, Switzerland four, and South Africa 11. Some countries officially recognize additional languages: four minority languages in Sweden, 22 scheduled languages in India, and various indigenous languages in countries as diverse as Mexico, Nigeria, and the Russian Federation. In some countries, including several in Western Europe, regional political movements are seeking independence or greater autonomy, challenging the narrative of a unified national culture. In various parts of the world, including Sub-Saharan Africa, political borders do not always correspond to linguistic or cultural boundaries, blurring the distinction between "national" and (some) "foreign" cultures. In every country, tensions, competition, and cooperation across a variety of groups that are partly overlapping and constantly changing have always existed.

Integration requires a degree of change by both migrants and nationals.[148] The US National Academies of Sciences, Engineering, and Medicine defines *integration* as "the process by which members of immigrant groups and host societies come to resemble one another. . . . Integration is a two-fold process: it happens both because immigrants experience changes once they arrive and because native-born [individuals] . . . change in response to immigration."[149]

Box 6.2 Profound cultural changes are under way

In the realm of social integration, migration is just one of many forces rapidly reshaping societies, many of which have little to do with migration:

- *Aging.* Many societies are rapidly aging. The share of people over age 65 rose from 7.9 percent to 20.1 percent between 1950 and 2022. This development poses threats to the social contract—including in terms of care for the elderly and pension systems—which could be very disruptive.
- *Urbanization.* The share of the world population that lives in cities rose from 37 percent to 56 percent over the last 50 years, transforming the way people connect with one another and their perspectives and expectations.[a]
- *Technology.* The rise of the internet—like television before it—has transformed almost every aspect of lives, including values, social interactions, entertainment, and business practices.[b] In 2020, people in the United States spent an average of 1,300 hours on social media—almost four hours a day.[c] A 2022 survey found the average screen time among adults in the United Kingdom to be five hours a day, in addition to any screen-related work. Relatively higher use was observed among younger cohorts.[d]
- *Education levels.* In France, the share of those who have a high school degree (*baccalaureat*) increased from 29 percent in 1985 to 80 percent in 2020,[e] which has transformed both culture and society. In the United States, the number of people with a master's degree doubled to 21 million from 2000 to 2018.[f]
- *Gender relations.* Access to contraception has deeply transformed gender relations, with effects on fertility, women's professional engagement, and patterns of cohabitation.[g] In the United States, women have consistently earned the majority of doctoral degrees since academic year 2008/09.[h] And in Colombia, the share of women ages 25–29 cohabiting increased from about 20 percent in 1973 to almost 50 percent in 1993 and to over 65 percent in 2005.[i]
- *Family structures.* The share of married adults has drastically fallen across a range of countries. In the Republic of Korea, the number of marriages per 1,000 inhabitants fell from 9.2 in 1970 to 5.2 in 2018, and in Argentina from 7.5 to 2.7 over the same period.[j] In the United States, the share of children living in a "traditional" nuclear family—two married heterosexual parents in their first marriage—dropped from 73 percent in 1960 to less than half, 46 percent, in 2022. About 40 percent of children were born out of wedlock in 2020, up from 5 percent in 1960.[k] In Chile, where divorce was only legalized in 2014, about 70 percent of children were born out of wedlock that year, up from almost none in 1964.[l]
- *Religious practice.* The share of self-declared French Catholics fell from 70 percent in 1981 to 32 percent in 2018 (of whom only 6.6 percent were practicing Catholics), while those who indicate they do not belong to any religion increased from 26 percent to 58 percent over the same period.[m]
- *New ways of working.* The COVID-19 pandemic, with its social distancing and shift toward remote work, changed people's relationships to their jobs and their social relations.[n] In the United States, less than 10 percent of the workforce telecommuted before the pandemic. In June 2022, 80 percent were working full-time or part-time remotely.[o]

a. Data: Rural Population (% of Total Population) (dashboard), World Bank, Washington, DC, https://data.worldbank.org/indicator/SP.RUR.TOTL.ZS.
b. Castells (2002); DiMaggio et al. (2001); Gauntlett and Hill (1999); La Ferrara, Chong, and Duryea (2012); Olken (2009).
c. Suciu (2021).
d. Hiley (2022).
e. INSEE (2021).
f. America Counts Staff (2019).
g. Bailey (2006); Bailey, Hershbein, and Miller (2012); Christensen (2012); Goldin and Katz (2002); Marcén (2021); Miller (2011).
h. Perry (2021).
i. Esteve et al. (2016).
j. Ortiz-Ospina and Roser (2020).
k. Livingston (2014); Pew Research Center (2015).
l. Chamie (2017).
m. Fourquet and Jardon (2021).
n. Hayes et al. (2021); Irawanto, Novianti, and Roz (2021); McDermott and Hansen (2021).
o. Paulise (2022).

Specifically:

- Migrants and their descendants converge toward the culture of the destination society, becoming more likely to identify as members of their destination society.[150] In the United States, migrants' attitudes toward divorce and women's work tend to converge faster than attitudes toward family structure and relatives[151] or attitudes toward redistribution, social assistance, political orientation, sexual morality, and religion.[152] And yet the path to integration is not necessarily one in which migrants have to forgo all elements of their origin culture to fit in destination societies. In fact, in some situations forcing migrants to give up elements of their culture has negative effects.[153]

- Local cultures also integrate some elements of migrants' heritage and values. The present-day political ideology and preferences for redistribution in the United States were historically affected by European values and ideas of the welfare state brought by migrants during the nineteenth and early twentieth centuries.[154] More recently, the influence of the Hispanic community has been seen across the United States, with more and more states translating laws and various applications into Spanish. Today, driver's license exams are offered in Spanish in all but five states.[155]

Unless specific steps are taken to prevent it, integration happens. Many migrants and their descendants once described as irreducibly different—such as Irish immigrants in the United States or Italian and Polish migrants in France—are now unquestionably part of the mainstream. The challenge is to make integration happen quickly and in a way that results in positive outcomes for all.

The success of social integration depends on a range of factors specific to each context: migrants' personal characteristics, backgrounds, skill levels, and expectations; destination societies' social contract, norms, and understanding of what it takes to be a citizen; and government policies (figure 6.9).[156]

Overall, several factors affect migrants' prospects for social integration:

- *Migrants' number and concentration.* Social integration is more challenging when the number of migrants is larger at the national or the local level.[157] Some nationals find the presence of large numbers of immigrants a threat to their sense of nationhood or to their relative position in society.[158] Meanwhile, when migrants can rely on a large community of co-nationals, they have fewer incentives to establish links outside of their group. The community provides an effective

Figure 6.9 **The determinants of social integration**

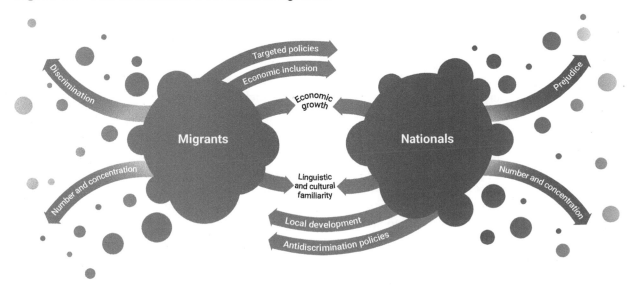

Source: WDR 2023 team.

social network and helps with finding employment and meeting the other challenges faced by migrants, as has been shown in Denmark, Sweden, and the United States.

- *Economic conditions.* Social integration is easier during times of economic growth and low unemployment. By contrast, economic shocks create insecurity, which may prompt those who are affected to identify more strongly with the values and traditions associated with stability.[159] In such times, some nationals feel a greater sense of belonging to their cultural group and are more likely to see migrants and naturalized citizens as outsiders.[160] In Europe, the attitudes toward immigrants are most positive among workers in the occupational sectors that are growing, and the rising number of immigrants has no impacts on attitudes when the economy is performing well.[161]

- *Linguistic and cultural familiarity.* Familiarity with the language and culture of the country of destination can facilitate migrants' social integration—but not in all situations. All else being equal, migrants tend to prefer to move to countries that are culturally or at least linguistically more familiar.[162] Yet even where migrants share an ethnic background, race, or culture with most native-born citizens, social integration can be challenging.[163] For example, Burkinabe migrants to Côte d'Ivoire and Zimbabwean migrants to South Africa have been subjected to discrimination.[164]

- *Perceptions and prejudice.* When migrants do not share the dominant cultural expectations or fully embrace the societal norms of their destination country, their presence may be resented.[165] Racial, cultural, or social differences can result in stereotyping and misperceptions[166] and can be amplified by media coverage,[167] political narratives and framing,[168] or social media.[169] The presence of migrants may even lead to a realignment of nationals' group identities away from social class and along cultural or racial lines.[170] This effect may depend on a country's or community's culture.[171] In Denmark, for example, opposition to migrants increased in rural municipalities but not in the most urban ones,[172] a pattern that reflects a greater emphasis on group identity in rural areas.[173] In some contexts, migrants adjust by choosing "native-sounding" names for their children—such as in the United States, Canada, and Europe[174]—or by adopting local languages or styles of clothing—such as in urban West Africa.[175] However, discrimination may become self-reinforcing by leading migrants to "disidentify" and disengage with the destination culture, which, in turn, increases marginalization and discrimination.[176]

Government policies can support migrants' social integration (box 6.3). What is needed depends on the specific circumstances of each country, but often it includes several elements:

- *Economic inclusion.* Migrants' economic integration is often a prelude—and a precondition—of their social integration. Economic inclusion provides migrants with both the financial resources that allow settling stably in the destination society and access to networks, including connections with national workers. In turn, economic inclusion is made easier by social integration. Still, the policies aimed at facilitating labor market inclusion should be understood as a critical element of the social integration agenda. Such policies include providing a legal status and secure terms of stay, which allow and incentivize migrants to make investments in the destination society such as in language acquisition, cultural familiarization, and establishment of social connections with those who are not co-nationals.

- *Dispersion policies.* Some countries have attempted to disperse newly arrived migrants across their entire territory to mitigate the difficulties arising from an overconcentration. The results, however, have been mixed. For example, in Sweden migrants and refugees who were settled in less dynamic regions had less access to jobs, which negatively affected their prospects for social integration. Similarly, the dispersion of asylum-seekers across Germany in 2015–16 did not consider the match between their skills and aspirations and the training and employment prospects in their regions of settlement. This approach led to disappointing results.[177] By contrast, the integration model in other countries, such as the United States, allows the formation of strong ethnic communities. Policies should reflect the specific social dynamic of each country, but also should accompany—rather than oppose—market forces to find an adequate balance between concentration and dispersion.

- *Local development.* Public and private investments in areas where migrants are heavily concentrated are often necessary to provide additional services and prevent the emergence of pockets of poverty. It is also important to prevent or mitigate native flight and support nationals in those areas, including through investments in housing, public transportation, education, and health care services.
- *Antidiscrimination efforts.* Discrimination negatively affects migrants, and it also hampers their eventual integration. Influencing nationals' perceptions of migrants—such as through public campaigns—has produced some success in certain settings[178] but mixed results in others.[179] Interactions between migrants and nationals can reduce stereotyping and influence the attitudes that people form toward one another. For example, in Austria support for parties that promote more restrictive migration policies grew in municipalities that refugees passed by without settling in, but they declined in municipalities where they settled and had the opportunity to interact with locals.[180] Political leadership is critical to antidiscrimination efforts.
- *Targeted integration policies.* Policies fostering the development of human and social capital have succeeded in encouraging and enabling integration, but policies that require migrants to renounce their cultural identity have usually proved ineffective.[181] Furthermore, policies targeting a specific group can have ambiguous effects when they accentuate group boundaries and thus reinforce rather than mitigate cultural and social differences.[182] Integration policies should be carefully designed and implemented to avoid unintended consequences.

Box 6.3 Lessons from Germany: The successful integration of asylum-seekers and refugees

Between July 2015 and February 2016, nearly 1 million Syrian refugees and other asylum-seekers entered Germany seeking international protection, thereby stretching the capacity of the government and civil society organizations. Emotions ran high. Large segments of society came together under Chancellor Angela Merkel's mantra "Wir schaffen das" ("We can do this") and embraced the notion of Germany as an open and welcoming country. But others felt alienated by the large numbers of new arrivals. In the medium term, the country's efforts to integrate the newcomers into German society were largely successful, albeit not without challenges.

Labor market integration
Asylum-seekers and refugees in Germany quickly integrated into the labor market, with over half (55 percent) employed within five years of their arrival. Specifically, 9 percent were employed within the first two years, rising to 22 percent, 32 percent, and 46 percent in each subsequent year. Critical factors included:

- *Secure terms of stay.* Migrants who were granted protection were also granted a secure residence status.
- *Decentralization.* Each federal state was allowed to implement labor market integration schemes tailored to its own environment and constraints.
- *Firms structure.* The prevalence of dynamic medium-size enterprises in the economy facilitated labor market integration outside the major metropolitan hubs. For example, the "Wir zusammen" ("We together") network brought together more than 230 individual companies and facilitated the employment of more than 33,000 asylum-seekers and refugees.

(Box continues next page)

- *Skills-building systems.* Germany's well-established system of vocational training enabled the newcomers to acquire the skills they needed to enter the labor market. Significant investments were made in German language and integration courses throughout the country.

Yet challenges remain. Significant gender gaps persist in terms of employment, which are partly attributable to lower levels of education and work experience, lower or later participation in integration programs, and cultural norms related to women's entry into the labor market. During the COVID-19 pandemic, the unemployment rate of asylum-seekers and refugees also increased by 4 percentage points—considerably higher than the 1.1 percent increase for German citizens and permanent residents—and language and integration measures, as well as schooling and vocational training, were largely suspended or slowed.

Accommodation, education, and health care
Beyond the labor market, several lessons emerged in other areas:

- Decentralization played a key role in the reception and integration of the newcomers. Despite being under significant stress, subnational governments proved to be best placed to address the new challenges[a] and more effective in addressing the concerns of local communities affected by temporary housing arrangements for asylum-seekers.
- Investing in language acquisition was a success factor throughout all stages of education and in terms of entry into the labor market.[b] However, placing teenage refugees who lacked German language skills in separate classes proved to be counterproductive in the long term.[c]
- The introduction of electronic health care cards for asylum-seekers in some federal states and individual districts made health care services more accessible and resulted in beneficial health outcomes without any significant drawbacks or higher costs.[d]
- In both education and health care delivery, the sudden and rapid inflow of migrants highlighted some long-standing shortcomings, triggering new efforts to improve data collection and gather knowledge about the specific needs of asylum-seekers and to identify gaps in targeted service provision and find ways to address them. The Federal Office for Migration and Refugees (Bundesamt für Migration und Flüchtlinge, BAMF) improved its data collection efforts and launched a concerted effort to improve its data management system and digitalize working processes.

Resentment and new restrictive policy measures
From the outset of the refugee influx, the government balanced its relative openness with several restrictive policy measures, including the requirement that refugees remain in their assigned states during asylum procedures, reductions in the social benefits granted to asylum-seekers, restrictions on family reunification options for beneficiaries of subsidiary protection,[e] and ramped-up return efforts for those who did not have legal status. While working domestically on processing new arrivals, the government also supported European Union (EU) policies that reduced pathways for legal entry, including the EU-Turkey Agreement.[f]

Overall lessons learned
Several overarching lessons can be drawn from Germany's experience:

- *Political leadership and communication.* Political leadership played a key role, as well as clear, informative, and solution-oriented communications. These proved crucial for bringing people together and mobilizing support. Candor was critical to maintaining trust in state institutions, including by recognizing short-term negative effects and describing the steps taken to implement sustainable long-term solutions.

(Box continues next page)

Box 6.3 Lessons from Germany: The successful integration of asylum-seekers and refugees *(continued)*

- *Comprehensive responses.* All policy areas are invariably linked, and the successful integration of a large number of asylum-seekers within a short period of time requires an integrated approach. Labor market integration is linked not only to language and vocational training and skills recognition, but also to child-care, teacher training, and the provision of secure residency statuses. Although some of these areas can be addressed through legislative changes, others require financing and adequate burden-sharing arrangements between levels of government.
- *Engagement of civil society.* Civil society is a crucial resource for the short-, medium-, and long-term integration of refugees. These efforts can be supported financially, as well as sustained, through trust-based cooperation between civil society and state authorities.

Source: Based on Koch et al. (2023).
a. Thränhardt (2020).
b. Brücker, Rother, and Schupp (2016).
c. Morris-Lange (2018).
d. Lindner (2022).
e. Subsidiary protection is international protection for persons seeking asylum who do not qualify as refugees.
f. European Council (2016).

Notes

1. WDR2023 Migration Database, World Bank, Washington, DC, https://www.worldbank.org/wdr2023/data.
2. Doan et al. (2023).
3. EU (2008).
4. Erasmus+: EU Programme for Education, Training, Youth and Sport (dashboard), Directorate-General for Education, Youth, Sport and Culture, European Commission, Brussels, https://erasmus-plus.ec.europa.eu/.
5. EU-LFS (European Union Labour Force Survey) (database), Eurostat, European Commission, Luxembourg, https://ec.europa.eu/eurostat/statistics-explained/index.php/EU_labour_force_survey.
6. Gill and Raiser (2012).
7. Gill and Raiser (2012).
8. HRW (2015); ILO (2017).
9. Testaverde et al. (2017).
10. Fallah, Krafft, and Wahba (2019).
11. Del Carpio et al. (2015); Hiller and Rodríguez Chatruc (2020).
12. D'Amuri and Peri (2014).
13. Foged and Peri (2016).
14. Borjas (2014).
15. OECD (2019).
16. Pekkala Kerr et al. (2016).
17. Kerr (2018).
18. European Union Labour Force Survey (database), Eurostat, European Commission, Luxembourg, https://ec.europa.eu/eurostat/statistics-explained/index.php/EU_labour_force_survey.
19. National Agricultural Workers Survey (dashboard), Employment and Training Administration, US Department of Labor, Washington, DC, https://www.dol.gov/agencies/eta/national-agricultural-workers-survey.
20. Testaverde et al. (2017).
21. See Cortés and Tessada (2011); Freire (2011); and Hiller and Rodríguez Chatruc (2020).
22. See the examples offered by Bahar, Ibáñez, and Rozo (2021); Burchardi, Chaney, and Hassan (2018); Cohen, Gurun, and Malloy (2017); Foley and Kerr (2013); Gould (1994); Javorcik et al. (2011); Kugler, Levintal, and Rapoport (2018); Kugler and Rapoport (2007); Mayda, Peri, and Steingress (2022); Ottaviano, Peri, and Wright (2018); Parsons and Vézina (2018); Rauch (1999); Rauch and Trindade (2002).
23. Parsons and Vézina (2018).
24. Bahar, Ibáñez, and Rozo (2021).
25. Tong (2005).
26. Frattini (2014).
27. Cortés (2008).
28. Lach (2007).
29. Dustmann, Glitz, and Frattini (2008).
30. Altonji and Card (2001).
31. Angrist and Kugler (2003).
32. Longhi, Nijkamp, and Poot (2010).
33. Banerjee and Duflo (2019, 267); NASEM (2017); National Research Council (1997). In synthesizing the consensus of the research about the impacts of immigration, the National Academies of Sciences, Engineering, and Medicine (NASEM 2017, 267) conclude: "Empirical research in recent decades suggest that findings remain by and large consistent with those in *The New Americans* (National Research Council 1997) in that, when measured over a period of more than

10 years, the impact of immigration on the wages of natives overall is very small."

34. D'Amuri and Peri (2014).
35. Dustmann, Schönberg, and Stuhler (2017).
36. Glitz (2012).
37. Biavaschi et al. (2018).
38. Angrist and Kugler (2003).
39. For Colombia, see Caruso, Canon, and Mueller (2021); Lebow (2022). For Germany, see Brücker and Jahn (2011). For the Netherlands and the United Kingdom, see Zorlu and Hartog (2005). For Türkiye, see Altındağ, Bakış, and Rozo (2020); Del Carpio and Wagner (2015).
40. Altındağ and Kaushal (2021); Del Carpio and Wagner (2015); Lombardo et al. (2021).
41. Lombardo et al. (2021).
42. Ottaviano and Peri (2012).
43. Özden and Wagner (2014).
44. Net direct fiscal transfers exclude the expenses for public goods, such as defense or environment. They only account for direct personal payments, such as welfare payments.
45. Damas de Matos (2021).
46. Damas de Matos (2021).
47. Lee and Miller (2000).
48. Damas de Matos (2021).
49. Dustmann and Frattini (2014).
50. Damas de Matos (2021).
51. Clemens (2022b).
52. OECD (2013).
53. Damas de Matos (2021).
54. NASEM (2017).
55. OECD (2013).
56. Ibáñez et al. (2022).
57. Clemens (2022a).
58. Green Card Eligibility Categories (dashboard), US Citizenship and Immigration Services, US Department of Homeland Security, Camp Springs, MD, https://www.uscis.gov/green-card/green-card-eligibility-categories.
59. Benhabib and Jovanovic (2012); Bradford (2012); Clemens and Pritchett (2016); di Giovanni, Ortega, and Levchenko (2015); Kennan (2013).
60. Cortés, Kasoolu, and Pan (2021).
61. Shah (2009, 12).
62. Medina-Cortina (2023).
63. East et al. (2022).
64. East and Velásquez (2018).
65. Migration Advisory Committee (dashboard), MAC, London, https://www.gov.uk/government/organisations/migration-advisory-committee.
66. IOM (2002).
67. Crock and Parsons (2023).
68. World Bank (2018).
69. WDR2023 Migration Database, World Bank, Washington, DC, https://www.worldbank.org/wdr2023/data.
70. See Survey of Earned Doctorates (dashboard), National Science Foundation, Alexandria, VA, https://www.nsf.gov/statistics/srvydoctorates/.
71. Diversity Immigrant Visa Program (Green Card Lottery) (dashboard), USA.gov, https://www.usa.gov/green-cards#item-34962.
72. OECD (2017).
73. IOM (2002); Triandafyllidou, Bartolini, and Guidi (2019).
74. IOM (2002).
75. Gregory (2015).
76. Crock and Parsons (2023).
77. Finotelli and Kolb (2017); Laubenthal (2014); Schneider (2023).
78. Cho et al. (2018).
79. Gibson and McKenzie (2014).
80. AEBOE (2021); EU (2014).
81. AEBOE (2001a, 2001b, 2023).
82. EMNPL (2020).
83. "Hire a Temporary Worker through the Seasonal Agricultural Worker Program," Employment and Social Development Canada, Ottawa, Canada, https://www.canada.ca/en/employment-social-development/services/foreign-workers/agricultural/seasonal-agricultural.html.
84. Gibson and McKenzie (2014); González Enríquez and Reynés Ramón (2011); Newland, Agunias, and Terrazas (2008).
85. Dustmann (2000); Görlach and Kuske (2022).
86. Dustmann (2000).
87. Nielson (2004).
88. Correia de Brito, Kauffmann, and Pelkmans (2016).
89. Cedefop (2019). The EU developed the European Qualifications Framework (EQF) as a translation tool to make national qualifications easier to understand and more comparable. The EQF seeks to support cross-border mobility of learners and workers and promote lifelong learning and professional development across Europe. See European Qualifications Framework (dashboard), Europass, Directorate-General for Education, Youth, Sport and Culture, European Commission, Brussels, https://europa.eu/europass/en/europass-tools/european-qualifications-framework#:~:text=The%20EU%20developed%20the%20European,and%20professional%20development%20across%20Europe. The ASEAN Qualifications Reference Framework (AQRF) is a common reference framework that enables comparisons of education qualifications across participating ASEAN member states. See ASEAN Qualifications Reference Framework (dashboard), Secretariat, Association of Southeast Asian Nations, Jakarta, Indonesia, https://asean.org/our-communities/economic-community/services/aqrf/.
90. See further discussion on skills recognition in the context of Global Skills Partnership (chapter 5).
91. Bleakley and Chin (2004); Chiswick and Miller (2010); Foged et al. (2022); Lochmann, Rapoport, and Speciale (2019).
92. Bailey et al. (2022); Foged et al. (2022); Lochmann, Rapoport, and Speciale (2019).
93. Maunganidze and Abebe (2020).
94. Borjas (2014); Trachtman (2009).
95. Amuedo-Dorantes and Bansak (2011).
96. Altonji and Card (2001); Borjas (2014); Card (2001); Ottaviano and Peri (2012).
97. Ottaviano and Peri (2008).

98. Altındağ, Bakış, and Rozo (2020); Bahar, Ibáñez, and Rozo (2021); Ibáñez et al. (2022); Rozo and Winkler (2019).
99. Caruso, Canon, and Mueller (2021).
100. Olivieri et al. (2022).
101. Morales and Pierola (2020).
102. Bleakley and Chin (2004); Chiswick and Miller (2010); Danzer and Ulku (2011); Dustmann (1994); Foged et al. (2022); Kanas et al. (2012); Lochmann, Rapoport, and Speciale (2019); Meng and Gregory (2005).
103. Danzer and Ulku (2011); Dustmann (1994); Kanas et al. (2012).
104. Bjørnskov (2012); Gradstein and Justman (2002); Pervaiz and Chaudhary (2015).
105. Hjort (2014).
106. Beaman (2012); Damm (2009b, 2014); Edin, Fredriksson, and Åslund (2003); Martén, Hainmueller, and Hangartner (2019); Patel and Vella (2013).
107. Bauer, Epstein, and Gang (2005).
108. Damm (2009a, 2014).
109. Acolin, Bostic, and Painter (2016).
110. Betts and Fairlie (2003).
111. Batut and Schneider-Strawczynski (2022).
112. Degen and Fischer (2017); Gonzalez and Ortega (2013); Saiz (2007); Verme and Schuettler (2021).
113. Akbari and Aydede (2012); Saiz (2007).
114. Accetturo et al. (2014).
115. Lastrapes and Lebesmuehlbacher (2020); Sá (2015); Saiz and Wachter (2011).
116. Hennig (2019).
117. Mussa, Nwaogu, and Pozo (2017).
118. Ferwerda (2021).
119. Alesina, Miano, and Stantcheva (2018).
120. Tabellini (2020).
121. Banting and Soroka (2020); Wilkes, Guppy, and Farris (2008).
122. Bloemraad, Silva, and Voss (2016); Voss, Silva, and Bloemraad (2020).
123. Assaad, Ginn, and Saleh (2018); Bilgili et al. (2019); Kebede and Özden (2021); Morales (2022).
124. Tanaka, Farré, and Ortega (2018).
125. Sacerdote (2011).
126. Bossavie (2020); Chin, Daysal, and Imberman (2012); Frattini and Meschi (2019); Tonello (2016).
127. For effects in Colombia, see Namen et al. (2021). For effects in Uganda, see Sakaue and Wokadala (2022).
128. Bossavie (2020).
129. Ammermueller and Pischke (2009); Angrist and Lavy (1999); Frattini and Meschi (2019).
130. Betts and Fairlie (2003).
131. Farré, Ortega, and Tanaka (2018); Tumen (2019). More examples of native flight are presented in Farré and Tanaka (2016).
132. Betts and Fairlie (2003); Farré, Ortega, and Tanaka (2018).
133. Alesina, Miano, and Stantcheva (2018); Tabellini (2020).
134. Giuntella, Nicodemo, and Vargas-Silva (2018).
135. Gelatt (2016); Omenka, Watson, and Hendrie (2020).
136. "Highest to Lowest: Foreign Prisoners (Percentage of Prison Population)," World Prison Brief, Institute for Crime and Justice Policy Research, School of Law, Birkbeck, University of London, London (accessed January 25, 2023). https://www.prisonstudies.org/highest-to-lowest/foreign-prisoners?field_region_taxonomy_tid=All.
137. Bianchi, Buonanno, and Pinotti (2012).
138. Özden, Testaverde, and Wagner (2018).
139. Spenkuch (2014).
140. Ajzenman, Domínguez, and Undurraga (2020); Bove, Elia, and Ferraresi (2021).
141. Becker (1993); Fasani (2018); Mastrobuoni and Pinotti (2015); Özden, Testaverde, and Wagner (2018); Pinotti (2017).
142. Baker (2015); Bell, Fasani, and Machin (2013); Fasani (2018); Mastrobuoni and Pinotti (2015); Pinotti (2016, 2017).
143. Fasani (2018); Mastrobuoni and Pinotti (2015); Pinotti (2017).
144. Baker (2015).
145. Gaibulloev and Sandler (2019).
146. Couttenier et al. (2021); Das et al. (2009); Giavazzi et al. (2020).
147. Echebarria-Echabe and Fernández-Guede (2006).
148. Rapoport, Sardoschau, and Silve (2021); Shayo (2020).
149. NASEM (2015, 19).
150. Casey and Dustmann (2010); Giavazzi, Petkov, and Schiantarelli (2019); Manning and Roy (2010).
151. Blau, Kahn, and Papps (2011); Giavazzi, Petkov, and Schiantarelli (2019).
152. Giavazzi, Petkov, and Schiantarelli (2019). A large body of empirical work documents the role of cultural heritage in the persistence of attitudes related to living arrangements (Giuliano 2007); gender norms and fertility outcomes (Alesina, Giuliano, and Nunn 2013; Antecol 2000; Fernández 2007; Fernández and Fogli 2006, 2009); trust (Algan and Cahuc 2010; Butler, Giuliano, and Guiso 2016); preference for redistribution (Luttmer and Singhal 2011); corruption (Fisman and Miguel 2007); aggression (Miguel, Saiegh, and Satyanath 2011); and religion (Bisin, Topa, and Verdier 2004; Bisin and Verdier 2000).
153. Berry (2005); Fouka (2020); Nguyen and Benet-Martínez (2013).
154. Giuliano and Tabellini (2020).
155. The five exceptions are Alaska, Louisiana, Oklahoma, Utah, and Wyoming.
156. For a more detailed discussion on issues of social integration, see Bloemraad et al. (2023).
157. Bonomi, Gennaioli, and Tabellini (2021); Shayo (2020).
158. Ceobanu and Escandell (2010).
159. Rodrik (2021).
160. Bonomi, Gennaioli, and Tabellini (2021); Guriev and Papaioannou (2022); Rodrik (2021).
161. Dancygier and Donnelly (2013).
162. Belot and Ederveen (2012); Bredtmann, Nowotny, and Otten (2020); Lanati and Venturini (2021).
163. Adida (2014); Gagnon and Khoudour-Castéras (2011); Zhou (2021).
164. Charman and Piper (2012); Crush et al. (2017).
165. Esses (2021).
166. Alesina and Tabellini (2022); Bonomi, Gennaioli, and Tabellini (2021).

167. Abrajano and Singh (2009); Blinder and Allen (2016); Couttenier et al. (2019); Dunaway, Branton, and Abrajano (2010); Kerevel (2011).
168. Bloemraad, Silva, and Voss (2016); Bursztyn, Egorov, and Fiorin (2020); Gaucher et al. (2018); Whitaker and Giersch (2015).
169. Allcott et al. (2020); Halberstam and Knight (2016); Müller and Schwarz (2022); Zhuravskaya, Petrova, and Enikolopov (2020).
170. Bonomi, Gennaioli, and Tabellini (2021); Shayo (2020).
171. Enke (2020).
172. Dustmann, Vasiljeva, and Damm (2019).
173. Enke (2020).
174. Abramitzky, Boustan, and Eriksson (2020); Algan et al. (2022); Arai and Skogman Thoursie (2009); Biavaschi, Giulietti, and Siddique (2017); Carneiro, Lee, and Reis (2020).

175. Adida (2014).
176. Jaschke, Sardoschau, and Tabellini (2022); Jasinskaja-Lahti, Liebkind, and Solheim (2009).
177. BAMF (2022).
178. Facchini, Margalit, and Nakata (2022); Grigorieff, Roth, and Ubfal (2020); Haaland and Roth (2023); Rodríguez Chatruc and Rozo (2021).
179. Adida, Lo, and Platas (2018); Alesina et al. (2018); Hopkins, Sides, and Citrin (2019); Lergetporer, Piopiunik, and Simon (2018); Shayo (2020); Sides and Citrin (2007); Williamson (2020).
180. Steinmayr (2021).
181. Fouka (2020); Lleras-Muney and Shertzer (2015).
182. Lehmann and Masterson (2020); Valli, Peterman, and Hidrobo (2019); Zhou (2019).

References

Abrajano, Marisa A., and Simran Singh. 2009. "Examining the Link between Issue Attitudes and News Source: The Case of Latinos and Immigration Reform." *Political Behavior* 31 (1): 1–30.

Abramitzky, Ran, Leah Platt Boustan, and Katherine Eriksson. 2020. "Do Immigrants Assimilate More Slowly Today Than in the Past?" *American Economic Review: Insights* 2 (1): 125–41.

Accetturo, Antonio, Francesco Manaresi, Sauro Mocetti, and Elisabetta Olivieri. 2014. "Don't Stand So Close to Me: The Urban Impact of Immigration." *Regional Science and Urban Economics* 45 (March): 45–56.

Acolin, Arthur, Raphael W. Bostic, and Gary Painter. 2016. "A Field Study of Rental Market Discrimination across Origins in France." *Journal of Urban Economics* 95 (September): 49–63.

Adida, Claire L. 2014. *Immigrant Exclusion and Insecurity in Africa: Coethnic Strangers*. New York: Cambridge University Press.

Adida, Claire L., Adeline Lo, and Melina R. Platas. 2018. "Perspective Taking Can Promote Short-Term Inclusionary Behavior toward Syrian Refugees." *Proceedings of the National Academy of Sciences* 115 (38): 9521–26.

AEBOE (Agencia Estatal Boletín Oficial del Estado, State Agency of Official State Gazette, Spain). 2001a. "13269: Aplicación provisional del Acuerdo entre el Reino de España y la República del Ecuador relativo a la regulación y ordenación de los flujos migratorios, hecho en Madrid, el 29 de mayo de 2001." *Boletín Oficial del Estado* 164 (July 10): 24909–12. https://www.boe.es/boe/dias/2001/07/10/pdfs/A24909-24912.pdf.

AEBOE (Agencia Estatal Boletín Oficial del Estado, State Agency of Official State Gazette, Spain). 2001b. "12853: Aplicación provisional del Acuerdo entre España y Colombia relativo a la regulación y ordenación de los flujos migratorios laborales, hecho en Madrid el 21 de mayo de 2001." *Boletín Oficial del Estado* 159 (July 4): 23724–26, AEBOE, Madrid.

https://www.boe.es/boe/dias/2001/07/04/pdfs/A23724-23726.pdf.

AEBOE (Agencia Estatal Boletín Oficial del Estado, State Agency of Official State Gazette, Spain). 2021. "21795: Orden ISM/1485/2021, de 24 de diciembre, por la que se regula la gestión colectiva de contrataciones en origen para 2022." *Boletín Oficial del Estado* 313 (December 30): 166978–167034, AEBOE, Madrid. https://www.boe.es/boe/dias/2021/12/30/pdfs/BOE-A-2021-21795.pdf.

AEBOE (Agencia Estatal Boletín Oficial del Estado, State Agency of Official State Gazette, Spain). 2023. "2936: Acuerdo entre el Reino de España y la República de Honduras relativo a la regulación y ordenación de los flujos migratorios laborales entre ambos Estados, hecho en Madrid el 28 de mayo de 2021." *Boletín Oficial del Estado* 30 (February 4): 16108–14, AEBOE, Madrid. https://www.boe.es/boe/dias/2023/02/04/pdfs/BOE-A-2023-2936.pdf.

Ajzenman, Nicolás, Patricio Domínguez, and Raimundo Undurraga. 2020. "Immigration, Crime, and Crime (Mis)Perceptions." Discussion Paper IDB-DP-00808 (September), Inter-American Development Bank, Washington, DC.

Akbari, Ather H., and Yigit Aydede. 2012. "Effects of Immigration on House Prices in Canada." *Applied Economics* 44 (13): 1645–58.

Alesina, Alberto Francesco, Michela Carlana, Eliana La Ferrara, and Paolo Pinotti. 2018. "Revealing Stereotypes: Evidence from Immigrants in Schools." NBER Working Paper 25333 (December), National Bureau of Economic Research, Cambridge, MA.

Alesina, Alberto Francesco, Paola Giuliano, and Nathan Nunn. 2013. "On the Origins of Gender Roles: Women and the Plough." *Quarterly Journal of Economics* 128 (2): 469–530.

Alesina, Alberto Francesco, Armando Miano, and Stefanie Stantcheva. 2018. "Immigration and Redistribution." NBER Working Paper 24733 (June), National Bureau of Economic Research, Cambridge, MA.

Alesina, Alberto Francesco, and Marco Tabellini. 2022. "The Political Effects of Immigration: Culture or Economics?" NBER Working Paper 30079 (May), National Bureau of Economic Research, Cambridge, MA.

Algan, Yann, and Pierre Cahuc. 2010. "Inherited Trust and Growth." *American Economic Review* 100 (5): 2060–92.

Algan, Yann, Clément Malgouyres, Thierry Mayer, and Mathias Thoenig. 2022. "The Economic Incentives of Cultural Transmission: Spatial Evidence from Naming Patterns across France." *Economic Journal* 132 (642): 437–70.

Allcott, Hunt, Luca Braghieri, Sarah Eichmeyer, and Matthew Gentzkow. 2020. "The Welfare Effects of Social Media." *American Economic Review* 110 (3): 629–76.

Altındağ, Onur, Ozan Bakış, and Sandra Viviana Rozo. 2020. "Blessing or Burden? Impacts of Refugees on Businesses and the Informal Economy." *Journal of Development Economics* 146 (September): 102490.

Altındağ, Onur, and Neeraj Kaushal. 2021. "Do Refugees Impact Voting Behavior in the Host Country? Evidence from Syrian Refugee Inflows to Turkey." *Public Choice* 186 (1): 149–78.

Altonji, Joseph G., and David E. Card. 2001. "The Effects of Immigration on the Labor Market Outcomes of Less-Skilled Natives." In *Interdisciplinary Perspectives on the New Immigration*, vol. 2 *The New Immigrant in the American Economy*, edited by Marcelo M. Suárez-Orozco, Carola Suárez-Orozco, and Desirée Qin-Hilliard, 137–70. New York: Routledge.

America Counts Staff. 2019. "Number of People with Master's and Doctoral Degrees Doubles since 2000: About 13.1 Percent Have a Master's, Professional Degree, or Doctorate." *America Counts: Stories*, February 21, 2019. https://www.census.gov/library/stories/2019/02/number-of-people-with-masters-and-phd-degrees-double-since-2000.html.

Ammermueller, Andreas, and Jörn-Steffen Pischke. 2009. "Peer Effects in European Primary Schools: Evidence from the Progress in International Reading Literacy Study." *Journal of Labor Economics* 27 (3): 315–48.

Amuedo-Dorantes, Catalina, and Cynthia Bansak. 2011. "The Impact of Amnesty on Labor Market Outcomes: A Panel Study Using the Legalized Population Survey." *Industrial Relations* 50 (3): 443–71.

Angrist, Joshua D., and Adriana D. Kugler. 2003. "Protective or Counter-Productive? Labour Market Institutions and the Effect of Immigration on EU Natives." *Economic Journal* 113 (488): F302–F331.

Angrist, Joshua D., and Victor Lavy. 1999. "Using Maimonides' Rule to Estimate the Effect of Class Size on Scholastic Achievement." *Quarterly Journal of Economics* 114 (2): 533–75.

Antecol, Heather. 2000. "An Examination of Cross-Country Differences in the Gender Gap in Labor Force Participation Rates." *Labour Economics* 7 (4): 409–26.

Arai, Mahmood, and Peter Skogman Thoursie. 2009. "Renouncing Personal Names: An Empirical Examination of Surname Change and Earnings." *Journal of Labor Economics* 27 (1): 127–47.

Assaad, Ragui A., Thomas Ginn, and Mohamed Saleh. 2018. "Impact of Syrian Refugees on Education Outcomes in Jordan." CEPR Discussion Paper 14056, Centre for Economic Policy Research, London.

Bahar, Dany, Ana María Ibáñez, and Sandra Viviana Rozo. 2021. "Give Me Your Tired and Your Poor: Impact of a Large-Scale Amnesty Program for Undocumented Refugees." *Journal of Development Economics* 151 (June): 102652.

Bailey, Martha J. 2006. "More Power to the Pill: The Impact of Contraceptive Freedom on Women's Life Cycle Labor Supply." *Quarterly Journal of Economics* 121 (1): 289–320.

Bailey, Martha J., Brad Hershbein, and Amalia R. Miller. 2012. "The Opt-In Revolution? Contraception and the Gender Gap in Wages." *American Economic Journal: Applied Economics* 4 (3): 225–54.

Bailey, Michael, Drew M. Johnston, Martin Koenen, Theresa Kuchler, Dominic Russel, and Johannes Stroebel. 2022. "The Social Integration of International Migrants: Evidence from the Networks of Syrians in Germany." NBER Working Paper 29925 (April), National Bureau of Economic Research, Cambridge, MA.

Baker, Scott R. 2015. "Effects of Immigrant Legalization on Crime." *American Economic Review* 105 (5): 210–13.

BAMF (Bundesamt für Migration und Flüchtlinge, Federal Office for Migration and Refugees, Germany). 2022. "Initial Distribution of Asylum-Seekers (EASY)." *Article: Asylum and Refugee Protection*, February 2, 2022. https://www.bamf.de/EN/Themen/AsylFluechtlingsschutz/AblaufAsylverfahrens/Erstverteilung/erstverteilung-node.html.

Banerjee, Abhijit Vinayak, and Esther Duflo. 2019. *Good Economics for Hard Times*. New York: PublicAffairs.

Banting, Keith, and Stuart Soroka. 2020. "A Distinctive Culture? The Sources of Public Support for Immigration in Canada, 1980–2019." *Canadian Journal of Political Science* 53 (4): 821–38.

Barro, Robert J., and Jong-Wha Lee. 2013. "A New Data Set of Educational Attainment in the World, 1950–2010." *Journal of Development Economics* 104 (September): 184–98.

Batut, Cyprien, and Sarah Schneider-Strawczynski. 2022. "Rival Guests or Defiant Hosts? The Local Economic Impact of Hosting Refugees." *Journal of Economic Geography* 22 (2): 327–50.

Bauer, Thomas, Gil S. Epstein, and Ira N. Gang. 2005. "Enclaves, Language, and the Location Choice of Migrants." *Journal of Population Economics* 18 (4): 649–62.

Beaman, Lori A. 2012. "Social Networks and the Dynamics of Labour Market Outcomes: Evidence from Refugees Resettled in the U.S." *Review of Economic Studies* 79 (1): 128–61.

Becker, Gary S. 1993. "The Economic Way of Looking at Life." Coase-Sandor Working Paper in Law and Economics 12, Coase-Sandor Institute for Law and Economics, University of Chicago Law School, Chicago.

Bell, Brian, Francesco Fasani, and Stephen Machin. 2013. "Crime and Immigration: Evidence from Large

Immigrant Waves." *Review of Economics and Statistics* 95 (4): 1278–90.

Belot, Michèle, and Sjef Ederveen. 2012. "Cultural Barriers in Migration between OECD Countries." *Journal of Population Economics* 25 (3): 1077–1105.

Benhabib, Jess, and Boyan Jovanovic. 2012. "Optimal Migration: A World Perspective." *International Economic Review* 53 (2): 321–48.

Berry, John W. 2005. "Acculturation: Living Successfully in Two Cultures." *International Journal of Intercultural Relations* 29 (6): 697–712.

Betts, Julian R., and Robert W. Fairlie. 2003. "Does Immigration Induce 'Native Flight' from Public Schools into Private Schools?" *Journal of Public Economics* 87 (5–6): 987–1012.

Bharadwaj, Prashant, and Rinchan Ali Mirza. 2019. "Displacement and Development: Long Term Impacts of Population Transfer in India." *Explorations in Economic History* 73 (July): 101273.

Bianchi, Milo, Paolo Buonanno, and Paolo Pinotti. 2012. "Do Immigrants Cause Crime?" *Journal of the European Economic Association* 10 (6): 1318–47.

Biavaschi, Costanza, Giovanni Facchini, Anna Maria Mayda, and Mariapia Mendola. 2018. "South-South Migration and the Labor Market: Evidence from South Africa" *Journal of Economic Geography* 18 (4): 823–53.

Biavaschi, Costanza, Corrado Giulietti, and Zahra Siddique. 2017. "The Economic Payoff of Name Americanization." *Journal of Labor Economics* 35 (4): 1089–1116.

Bilgili, Özge, Craig Loschmann, Sonja Fransen, and Melissa Siegel. 2019. "Is the Education of Local Children Influenced by Living Near a Refugee Camp? Evidence from Host Communities in Rwanda." *International Migration* 57 (4): 291–309.

Bisin, Alberto, Giorgio Topa, and Thierry Verdier. 2004. "Religious Intermarriage and Socialization in the United States." *Journal of Political Economy* 112 (3): 615–64.

Bisin, Alberto, and Thierry Verdier. 2000. " 'Beyond the Melting Pot': Cultural Transmission, Marriage, and the Evolution of Ethnic and Religious Traits." *Quarterly Journal of Economics* 115 (3): 955–88.

Bjørnskov, Christian. 2012. "How Does Social Trust Affect Economic Growth?" *Southern Economic Journal* 78 (4): 1346–68.

Blau, Francine D., Lawrence M. Kahn, and Kerry L. Papps. 2011. "Gender, Source Country Characteristics, and Labor Market Assimilation among Immigrants." *Review of Economics and Statistics* 93 (1): 43–58.

Bleakley, Hoyt, and Aimee Chin. 2004. "Language Skills and Earnings: Evidence from Childhood Immigrants." *Review of Economics and Statistics* 86 (2): 481–96.

Blinder, Scott, and William L. Allen. 2016. "Constructing Immigrants: Portrayals of Migrant Groups in British National Newspapers, 2010–2012." *International Migration Review* 50 (1): 3–40.

Bloemraad, Irene, Victoria M. Esses, Will Kymlicka, and Yang-Yang Zhou. 2023. "Unpacking Immigrant Integration: Concepts, Mechanisms, and Context." Background paper prepared for *World Development Report 2023*, World Bank, Washington, DC.

Bloemraad, Irene, Fabiana Silva, and Kim Voss. 2016. "Rights, Economics, or Family? Frame Resonance, Political Ideology, and the Immigrant Rights Movement." *Social Forces* 94 (4): 1647–74.

Bonomi, Giampaolo, Nicola Gennaioli, and Guido Tabellini. 2021. "Identity, Beliefs, and Political Conflict." *Quarterly Journal of Economics* 136 (4): 2371–2411.

Borjas, George J. 2014. *Immigration Economics.* Cambridge, MA: Harvard University Press.

Bossavie, Laurent Loic Yves. 2020. "The Effect of Immigration on Natives' School Achievement: Does Length of Stay in the Host Country Matter?" *Journal of Human Resources* 55 (2): 733–66.

Bove, Vincenzo, Leandro Elia, and Massimiliano Ferraresi. 2021. "Immigration, Fear of Crime, and Public Spending on Security." *Journal of Law, Economics, and Organization.* Published ahead of print, November 9, 2021. https://doi.org/10.1093/jleo/ewab021.

Bradford, Scott. 2012. "The Global Welfare and Poverty Effects of Rich Nation Immigration Barriers." Paper presented at the Global Trade Analysis Project's 15th Annual Conference on Global Economic Analysis, "New Challenges for Global Trade and Sustainable Development," Geneva, June 27–29, 2012.

Bredtmann, Julia, Klaus Nowotny, and Sebastian Otten. 2020. "Linguistic Distance, Networks and Migrants' Regional Location Choice." *Labour Economics* 65 (August): 101863.

Brücker, Herbert, and Elke J. Jahn. 2011. "Migration and Wage-Setting: Reassessing the Labor Market Effects of Migration." *Scandinavian Journal of Economics* 113 (2): 286–317.

Brücker, Herbert, Nina Rother, and Jürgen Schupp. 2016. "IAB-BAMF-SOEP-Befragung von Geflüchteten: *Überblick* und erste Ergebnisse." Forschungsbericht 29 (December), Bundesamt für Migration und Flüchtlinge, Nürnberg.

Burchardi, Konrad B., Thomas Chaney, and Tarek Alexander Hassan. 2018. "Migrants, Ancestors, and Foreign Investments." *Review of Economic Studies* 86 (4): 1448–86.

Bursztyn, Leonardo, Georgy Egorov, and Stefano Fiorin. 2020. "From Extreme to Mainstream: The Erosion of Social Norms." *American Economic Review* 110 (11): 3522–48.

Butler, Jeff, Paola Giuliano, and Luigi Guiso. 2016. "Trust and Cheating." *Economic Journal* 126 (595): 1703–38.

Card, David E. 2001. "Immigrant Inflows, Native Outflows, and the Local Labor Market Impacts of Higher Immigration." *Journal of Labor Economics* 19 (1): 22–64.

Carneiro, Pedro Manuel, Sokbae Lee, and Hugo Reis. 2020. "Please Call Me John: Name Choice and the Assimilation of Immigrants in the United States, 1900–1930." *Labour Economics* 62 (January): 101778.

Caruso, Germán Daniel, Christian Gomez Canon, and Valerie Mueller. 2021. "Spillover Effects of the Venezuelan Crisis: Migration Impacts in Colombia." *Oxford Economic Papers* 73 (2): 771–95.

Casey, Teresa, and Christian Dustmann. 2010. "Immigrants' Identity, Economic Outcomes and the Transmission of Identity across Generations." *Economic Journal* 120 (542): F31–F51.

Castells, Manuel. 2002. *The Internet Galaxy: Reflections on the Internet, Business, and Society.* Clarendon Lectures in Management Studies Series. Oxford, UK: Oxford University Press.

Cedefop (European Center for the Development of Vocational Training). 2019. "Overview of National Qualifications Framework Developments in Europe 2019." Cedefop, Thessaloniki, Greece.

Ceobanu, Alin M., and Xavier Escandell. 2010. "Comparative Analyses of Public Attitudes toward Immigrants and Immigration Using Multinational Survey Data: A Review of Theories and Research." *Annual Review of Sociology* 36 (August): 309–28.

Chamie, Joseph. 2017. "Out-of-Wedlock Births Rise Worldwide." *YaleGlobal Online*, March 17, 2017. https://archive-yaleglobal.yale.edu/content/out-wedlock-births-rise-worldwide.

Charman, Andrew, and Laurence Piper. 2012. "Xenophobia, Criminality and Violent Entrepreneurship: Violence against Somali Shopkeepers in Delft South, Cape Town, South Africa." *South African Review of Sociology* 43 (3): 81–105.

Chin, Aimee, N. Meltem Daysal, and Scott A. Imberman. 2012. "Impact of Bilingual Education Programs on Limited English Proficient Students and Their Peers: Regression Discontinuity Evidence from Texas." NBER Working Paper 18197 (June), National Bureau of Economic Research, Cambridge, MA.

Chiswick, Barry R., and Paul W. Miller. 2010. "Occupational Language Requirements and the Value of English in the US Labor Market." *Journal of Population Economics* 23 (1): 353–72.

Christensen, Finn. 2012. "The Pill and Partnerships: The Impact of the Birth Control Pill on Cohabitation." *Journal of Population Economics* 25 (1): 29–52.

Cho, Yoonyoung, Anastasiya Denisova, Soonhwa Yi, and Upasana Khadka. 2018. *Bilateral Arrangement of Temporary Labor Migration: Lessons from Korea's Employment Permit System.* Washington, DC: World Bank.

Clemens, Michael A. 2022a. "The Economic and Fiscal Effects on the United States from Reduced Numbers of Refugees and Asylum Seekers." *Oxford Review of Economic Policy* 38 (3): 449–86.

Clemens, Michael A. 2022b. "The Fiscal Effect of Immigration: Reducing Bias in Influential Estimates." IZA Discussion Paper DP 15592 (September), Institute of Labor Economics, Bonn, Germany.

Clemens, Michael A., and Lant H. Pritchett. 2016. "The New Economic Case for Migration Restrictions: An Assessment." CGD Working Paper 423 (February), Center for Global Development, Washington, DC.

Cohen, Lauren, Umit G. Gurun, and Christopher Malloy. 2017. "Resident Networks and Corporate Connections: Evidence from World War II Internment Camps." *Journal of Finance* 72 (1): 207–48.

Correia de Brito, Anabela, Céline Kauffmann, and Jacques Pelkmans. 2016. "The Contribution of Mutual Recognition to International Regulatory Co-operation." OECD Regulatory Policy Working Paper 2, Organisation for Economic Co-operation and Development, Paris.

Cortés, Patricia. 2008. "The Effect of Low-Skilled Immigration on U.S. Prices: Evidence from CPI Data." *Journal of Political Economy* 116 (3): 381–422.

Cortés, Patricia, Semiray Kasoolu, and Carolina Pan. 2021. "Labor Market Nationalization Policies and Exporting Firm Outcomes: Evidence from Saudi Arabia." NBER Working Paper 29283 (September), National Bureau of Economic Research, Cambridge, MA.

Cortés, Patricia, and José Tessada. 2011. "Low-Skilled Immigration and the Labor Supply of Highly Skilled Women." *American Economic Journal: Applied Economics* 3 (3): 88–123.

Couttenier, Mathieu, Sophie Hatte, Mathias Thoenig, and Stephanos Vlachos. 2019. "The Logic of Fear: Populism and Media Coverage of Immigrant Crimes." CEPR Discussion Paper DP13496 (January), Centre for Economic Policy Research, London.

Couttenier, Mathieu, Sophie Hatte, Mathias Thoenig, and Stephanos Vlachos. 2021. "Anti-Muslim Voting and Media Coverage of Immigrant Crimes." *Review of Economics and Statistics.* Published ahead of print, December 20, 2021. https://doi.org/10.1162/rest_a_01152.

Crock, Mary, and Christopher Parsons. 2023. "Australia as a Modern Migration State: Past and Present." Background paper prepared for *World Development Report 2023*, World Bank, Washington, DC.

Crush, Jonathan, Godfrey Tawodzera, Abel Chikanda, and Daniel Tevara. 2017. "Living with Xenophobia: Zimbabwean Informal Enterprise in South Africa." SAMP Migration Policy Series 77, Southern African Migration Programme, Wilfrid Laurier University, Waterloo, Ontario, Canada. https://scholars.wlu.ca/samp/21/.

Damas de Matos, Ana. 2021. "The Fiscal Impact of Immigration in OECD Countries since the Mid-2000s." In *International Migration Outlook 2021*, 111–62. Paris: Organisation for Economic Co-operation and Development.

Damm, Anna Piil. 2009a. "Determinants of Recent Immigrants' Location Choices: Quasi-Experimental Evidence." *Journal of Population Economics* 22 (1): 145–74.

Damm, Anna Piil. 2009b. "Ethnic Enclaves and Immigrant Labor Market Outcomes: Quasi-Experimental Evidence." *Journal of Labor Economics* 27 (2): 281–314.

Damm, Anna Piil. 2014. "Neighborhood Quality and Labor Market Outcomes: Evidence from Quasi-Random Neighborhood Assignment of Immigrants." *Journal of Urban Economics* 79 (January): 139–66.

D'Amuri, Francesco, and Giovanni Peri. 2014. "Immigration, Jobs, and Employment Protection: Evidence from Europe before and during the Great Recession." *Journal of the European Economic Association* 12 (2): 432–64.

Dancygier, Rafaela M., and Michael J. Donnelly. 2013. "Sectoral Economies, Economic Contexts, and Attitudes toward Immigration." *Journal of Politics* 75 (1): 17–35.

Danzer, Alexander M., and Hulya Ulku. 2011. "Integration, Social Networks and Economic Success of

Immigrants: A Case Study of the Turkish Community in Berlin." *Kyklos* 64 (3): 342–65.

Das, Enny, Brad J. Bushman, Marieke D. Bezemer, Peter Kerkhof, and Ivar E. Vermeulen. 2009. "How Terrorism News Reports Increase Prejudice against Outgroups: A Terror Management Account." *Journal of Experimental Social Psychology* 45 (3): 453–59.

Degen, Kathrin, and Andreas Fischer. 2017. "Immigration and Swiss House Prices." *Swiss Journal of Economics and Statistics* 153 (1): 15–36.

Del Carpio, Ximena V., Çağlar Özden, Mauro Testaverde, and Mathis Christoph Wagner. 2015. "Local Labor Supply Responses to Immigration." *Scandinavian Journal of Economics* 117 (2): 493–521.

Del Carpio, Ximena V., and Mathis Christoph Wagner. 2015. "The Impact of Syrian Refugees on the Turkish Labor Market." Policy Research Working Paper 7402, World Bank, Washington, DC.

di Giovanni, Julian, Francesc Ortega, and Andrei A. Levchenko. 2015. "A Global View of Cross-Border Migration." *Journal of the European Economic Association* 13 (1): 168–202.

DiMaggio, Paul, Eszter Hargittai, W. Russell Neuman, and John P. Robinson. 2001. "Social Implications of the Internet." *Annual Review of Sociology* 27 (August): 307–36.

Doan, Dung, Matthew Dornan, Jesse Doyle, and Kirstie Petrou. 2023. "Migration and Labor Mobility from Pacific Island Countries." Background paper prepared for *World Development Report 2023*, World Bank, Washington, DC.

Droller, Federico. 2018. "Migration, Population Composition and Long Run Economic Development: Evidence from Settlements in the Pampas." *Economic Journal* 128 (614): 2321–52.

Dunaway, Johanna, Regina P. Branton, and Marisa A. Abrajano. 2010. "Agenda Setting, Public Opinion, and the Issue of Immigration Reform." *Social Science Quarterly* 91 (2): 359–78.

Dustmann, Christian. 1994. "Speaking Fluency, Writing Fluency and Earnings of Migrants." *Journal of Population Economics* 7 (2): 133–56.

Dustmann, Christian. 2000. "Temporary Migration and Economic Assimilation." *Swedish Economic Policy Review* 7 (2): 213–44.

Dustmann, Christian, and Tommaso Frattini. 2014. "The Fiscal Effects of Immigration to the UK." *Economic Journal* 124 (580): F593–F643.

Dustmann, Christian, Albrecht Glitz, and Tommaso Frattini. 2008. "The Labour Market Impact of Immigration." *Oxford Review of Economic Policy* 24 (3): 477–94.

Dustmann, Christian, Uta Schönberg, and Jan Stuhler. 2017. "Labor Supply Shocks, Native Wages, and the Adjustment of Local Employment." *Quarterly Journal of Economics* 132 (1): 435–83.

Dustmann, Christian, Kristine Vasiljeva, and Anna Piil Damm. 2019. "Refugee Migration and Electoral Outcomes." *Review of Economic Studies* 86 (5): 2035–91.

East, Chloe N., Annie Laurie Hines, Philip Luck, Hani Mansour, and Andrea Velásquez. 2022. "The Labor Market Effects of Immigration Enforcement." *Journal of Labor Economics*. Published ahead of print, June 6, 2022. https://www.journals.uchicago.edu/doi/10.1086/721152.

East, Chloe N., and Andrea Velásquez. 2018. "The Effect of Increasing Immigration Enforcement on the Labor Supply of High-Skilled Citizen Women." IZA Discussion Paper, Institute of Labor Economics, Bonn, Germany.

Echebarria-Echabe, Agustin, and Emilia Fernández-Guede. 2006. "Effects of Terrorism on Attitudes and Ideological Orientation." *European Journal of Social Psychology* 36 (2): 259–65.

Edin, Per-Anders, Peter Fredriksson, and Olof Åslund. 2003. "Ethnic Enclaves and the Economic Success of Immigrants: Evidence from a Natural Experiment." *Quarterly Journal of Economics* 118 (1): 329–57.

EMNPL (European Migration Network in Poland). 2020. "Attracting Seasonal Workers from Third Countries and Their Protection in Poland." National Report, Ministry of the Interior and Administration, Coordinator of the National Contact Point, EMNPL, Warsaw.

Enke, Benjamin. 2020. "Moral Values and Voting." *Journal of Political Economy* 128 (10): 3679–3729.

Esses, Victoria M. 2021. "Prejudice and Discrimination toward Immigrants." *Annual Review of Psychology* 72 (January): 503–31.

Esteve, Albert, Ron J. Lesthaeghe, Antonio López-Gay, and Joan García-Román. 2016. "The Rise of Cohabitation in Latin America and the Caribbean, 1970–2011." In *Cohabitation and Marriage in the Americas: Geohistorical Legacies and New Trends*, edited by Albert Esteve and Ron J. Lesthaeghe, 25–57. Cham, Switzerland: Springer.

EU (European Union). 2008. "Consolidated Version of the Treaty on the Functioning of the European Union; Part Two: Non-Discrimination and Citizenship of the Union, Article 21 (ex-Article 18 TEC)." *Official Journal of the European Union* C 115 1 (May 9): 057. https://eur-lex.europa.eu/eli/treaty/tfeu_2008/art_21/oj.

EU (European Union). 2014. "Directive 2014/36/EU of the European Parliament and of the Council of 26 February 2014 on the Conditions of Entry and Stay of Third-Country Nationals for the Purpose of Employment as Seasonal Workers." *Official Journal of the European Union* L 94 (March 28): 375. https://eur-lex.europa.eu/legal-content/EN/TXT/PDF/?uri=CELEX:32014L0036.

European Council. 2016. "EU-Turkey Statement, 18 March 2016." Press Release, March 18, 2016. https://www.consilium.europa.eu/en/press/press-releases/2016/03/18/eu-turkey-statement/.

Facchini, Giovanni, Yotam Margalit, and Hiroyuki Nakata. 2022. "Countering Public Opposition to Immigration: The Impact of Information Campaigns." *European Economic Review* 141 (January): 103959.

Fallah, Belal, Caroline Krafft, and Jackline Wahba. 2019. "The Impact of Refugees on Employment and Wages in Jordan." *Journal of Development Economics* 139 (June): 203–16.

Farré, Lídia, Francesc Ortega, and Ryuichi Tanaka. 2018. "Immigration and the Public–Private School Choice." *Labour Economics* 51 (April): 184–201.

Farré, Lídia, and Ryuichi Tanaka. 2016. "Education Policy and Migration." In *Refugees and Economic Migrants: Facts, Policies, and Challenges*, edited by Francesco Fasani, 81–97. Vox.EU.org Book (October). London: CEPR Press.

Fasani, Francesco. 2018. "Immigrant Crime and Legal Status: Evidence from Repeated Amnesty Programs." *Journal of Economic Geography* 18 (4): 887–914.

Fernández, Raquel. 2007. "Women, Work, and Culture." *Journal of the European Economic Association* 5 (2–3): 305–32.

Fernández, Raquel, and Alessandra Fogli. 2006. "Fertility: The Role of Culture and Family Experience." *Journal of the European Economic Association* 4 (2–3): 552–61.

Fernández, Raquel, and Alessandra Fogli. 2009. "Culture: An Empirical Investigation of Beliefs, Work, and Fertility." *American Economic Journal: Macroeconomics* 1 (1): 146–77.

Ferwerda, Jeremy. 2021. "Immigration, Voting Rights, and Redistribution: Evidence from Local Governments in Europe." *Journal of Politics* 83 (1): 321–39.

Finotelli, Claudia, and Holger Kolb. 2017. " 'The Good, the Bad, and the Ugly' Reconsidered: A Comparison of German, Canadian, and Spanish Labour Migration Policies." *Journal of Comparative Policy Analysis: Research and Practice* 19 (1): 72–86.

Fisman, Raymond, and Edward Miguel. 2007. "Corruption, Norms, and Legal Enforcement: Evidence from Diplomatic Parking Tickets." *Journal of Political Economy* 115 (6): 1020–48.

Foged, Mette, Linea Hasager, Giovanni Peri, Jacob N. Arendt, and Iben Bolvig. 2022. "Intergenerational Spillover Effects of Language Training for Refugees." NBER Working Paper 30341 (August), National Bureau of Economic Research, Cambridge, MA.

Foged, Mette, and Giovanni Peri. 2016. "Immigrants' Effect on Native Workers: New Analysis on Longitudinal Data." *American Economic Journal: Applied Economics* 8 (2): 1–34.

Foley, C. Fritz, and William R. Kerr. 2013. "Ethnic Innovation and U.S. Multinational Firm Activity." *Management Science* 59 (7): 1529–44.

Fouka, Vasiliki. 2020. "Backlash: The Unintended Effects of Language Prohibition in U.S. Schools after World War I." *Review of Economic Studies* 87 (1): 204–39.

Fourquet, Jérôme, and Gautier Jardon. 2021. "Le Rapport des Français à la Religion." Institut français d'opinion publique, Paris. https://www.ifop.com/wp-content/uploads/2021/09/118372-Rapport.pdf.

Frattini, Tommaso. 2014. "Impact of Migration on UK Consumer Prices." Independent Report, Migration Advisory Committee, Home Office, London.

Frattini, Tommaso, and Elena Meschi. 2019. "The Effect of Immigrant Peers in Vocational Schools." *European Economic Review* 113 (April): 1–22.

Freire, Tiago. 2011. "Maids and School Teachers: Low Skill Migration and High Skill Labor Supply." ERSA Conference Paper ersa10p160 (September), European Regional Science Association, Vienna.

Gagnon, Jason, and David Khoudour-Castéras. 2011. *Tackling the Policy Challenges of Migration: Regulation, Integration, Development*. Development Centre Studies Series. Paris: Organisation for Economic Co-operation and Development.

Gaibulloev, Khusrav, and Todd Sandler. 2019. "What We Have Learned about Terrorism since 9/11." *Journal of Economic Literature* 57 (2): 275–328.

Gaucher, Danielle, Justin P. Friesen, Katelin H. S. Neufeld, and Victoria M. Esses. 2018. "Changes in the Positivity of Migrant Stereotype Content: How System-Sanctioned Pro-Migrant Ideology Can Affect Public Opinions of Migrants." *Social Psychological and Personality Science* 9 (2): 223–33.

Gauntlett, David, and Annette Hill. 1999. *TV Living: Television, Culture and Everyday Life*. Abingdon, UK: Routledge.

Gelatt, Julia. 2016. "Immigration Status and the Healthcare Access and Health of Children of Immigrants." *Social Science Quarterly* 97 (3): 540–54.

Giavazzi, Francesco, Felix Iglhaut, Giacomo Lemoli, and Gaia Rubera. 2020. "Terrorist Attacks, Cultural Incidents and the Vote for Radical Parties: Analyzing Text from Twitter." NBER Working Paper 26825 (November), National Bureau of Economic Research, Cambridge, MA.

Giavazzi, Francesco, Ivan Petkov, and Fabio Schiantarelli. 2019. "Culture: Persistence and Evolution." *Journal of Economic Growth* 24 (2): 117–54.

Gibson, John, and David J. McKenzie. 2014. "The Development Impact of a Best Practice Seasonal Worker Policy." *Review of Economics and Statistics* 96 (2): 229–43.

Gill, Indermit Singh, and Martin Raiser. 2012. *Golden Growth: Restoring the Lustre of the European Economic Model*. With Andrea Mario Dall'Olio, Truman Packard, Kaspar Richter, Naotaka Sugawara, Reinhilde Veugelers, and Juan Zalduendo. Washington, DC: World Bank.

Giuliano, Paola. 2007. "Living Arrangements in Western Europe: Does Cultural Origin Matter?" *Journal of the European Economic Association* 5 (5): 927–52.

Giuliano, Paola, and Marco Tabellini. 2020. "The Seeds of Ideology: Historical Immigration and Political Preferences in the United States." NBER Working Paper 27238 (May), National Bureau of Economic Research, Cambridge, MA.

Giuntella, Osea, Catia Nicodemo, and Carlos Vargas-Silva. 2018. "The Effects of Immigration on NHS Waiting Times." *Journal of Health Economics* 58 (March): 123–43.

Glitz, Albrecht. 2012. "The Labor Market Impact of Immigration: A Quasi-Experiment Exploiting Immigrant Location Rules in Germany." *Journal of Labor Economics* 30 (1): 175–213.

Goldin, Claudia, and Lawrence F. Katz. 2002. "The Power of the Pill: Oral Contraceptives and Women's Career and

Marriage Decisions." *Journal of Political Economy* 110 (4): 730–70.

Gonzalez, Libertad, and Francesc Ortega. 2013. "Immigration and Housing Booms: Evidence from Spain." *Journal of Regional Science* 5 (1): 37–59.

González Enríquez, Carmen, and Miquel Reynés Ramón. 2011. "Circular Migration between Spain and Morocco: Something More than Agricultural Work?" METOI-KOS Project Case Study, Robert Schuman Centre for Advanced Studies, European University Institute, San Domenico di Fiesole (FI), Italy. https://cadmus.eui.eu/handle/1814/19721.

Görlach, Joseph-Simon, and Katarina Kuske. 2022. "Temporary Migration Entails Benefits, but Also Costs, for Sending and Receiving Countries." IZA World of Labor 503 (November), Institute of Labor Economics, Bonn, Germany.

Gould, David Michael. 1994. "Immigrant Links to the Home Country: Empirical Implications for U.S. Bilateral Trade Flows." *Review of Economics and Statistics* 76 (2): 302–16.

Gradstein, Mark, and Moshe Justman. 2002. "Education, Social Cohesion, and Economic Growth." *American Economic Review* 92 (4): 1192–1204.

Gregory, Robert G. 2015. "The Two-Step Australian Immigration Policy and Its Impact on Immigrant Employment Outcomes." In *The Immigrants*, edited by Barry R. Chiswick and Paul W. Miller, 1421–43. Vol. 1A of *Handbook of the Economics of International Migration*. Oxford, UK: Elsevier.

Grigorieff, Alexis, Christopher Roth, and Diego Javier Ubfal. 2020. "Does Information Change Attitudes toward Immigrants?" *Demography* 57 (3): 1117–43.

Guriev, Sergei, and Elias Papaioannou. 2022. "The Political Economy of Populism." *Journal of Economic Literature* 60 (3): 753–832.

Haaland, Ingar, and Christopher Roth. 2023. "Beliefs about Racial Discrimination and Support for Pro-Black Policies." *Review of Economics and Statistics* 105 (1): 40–53.

Halberstam, Yosh, and Brian G. Knight. 2016. "Homophily, Group Size, and the Diffusion of Political Information in Social Networks: Evidence from Twitter." *Journal of Public Economics* 143 (November): 73–88.

Hayes, Sherrill W., Jennifer L. Priestley, Brian A. Moore, and Herman E. Ray. 2021. "Perceived Stress, Work-Related Burnout, and Working from Home before and during COVID-19: An Examination of Workers in the United States." *SAGE Open* 11 (4): 21582440211.

Hennig, Jakob. 2019. "Refugee Shelters, Neighbourhood Quality and Electoral Outcomes in Germany." Paper presented at the ifoCEMIR and CESifo Junior Economist Workshop on Migration Research, Munich, July 4–5, 2019. https://www.ifo.de/sites/default/files/cemir19_Hennig.pdf.

Hiley, Catherine. 2022. "Screen Time Report 2022." *How Much of Your Time Is Screen Time?* (blog), September 13, 2022. https://www.uswitch.com/mobiles/screentime-report/.

Hiller, Tatiana, and Marisol Rodríguez Chatruc. 2020. "South-South Migration and Female Labor Supply in the Dominican Republic." IDB Working Paper IDB-WP-1136 (July), Inter-American Development Bank, Washington, DC.

Hjort, Jonas. 2014. "Ethnic Divisions and Production in Firms." *Quarterly Journal of Economics* 129 (4): 1899–1946.

Hopkins, Daniel J., John Sides, and Jack Citrin. 2019. "The Muted Consequences of Correct Information about Immigration." *Journal of Politics* 81 (1): 315–20.

HRW (Human Rights Watch). 2015. "Guidelines for a Better Construction Industry in the GCC: A Code of Conduct for Construction Companies." HRW, New York. https://www.hrw.org/sites/default/files/supporting_resources/2015.12.21.gcc_brochure_dec_2015.pdf.

Ibáñez, Ana María, Andrés Moya, María Adelaida Ortega, Sandra Viviana Rozo, and María José Urbina. 2022. "Life Out of the Shadows: Impacts of Amnesties in the Lives of Refugees." Policy Research Working Paper 9928, World Bank, Washington, DC.

ILO (International Labour Organization). 2017. "Employer-Migrant Worker Relationships in the Middle East: Exploring Scope for Internal Labour Market Mobility and Fair Migration." White Paper (March), Regional Office for Arab States, ILO, Beirut.

INSEE (Institut national de la statistique et des études économiques). 2021. *France: Portrait Social*. 2020 ed. (January 8, 2021). Montrouge, France: INSEE.

IOM (International Organization for Migration). 2002. *International Comparative Study of Migration Legislation and Practice*. Dublin: Stationary Office.

Irawanto, Dodi Wirawan, Khusnul Rofida Novianti, and Kenny Roz. 2021. "Work from Home: Measuring Satisfaction between Work-Life Balance and Work Stress during the COVID-19 Pandemic in Indonesia." *Economies* 9 (3): 1–13.

Jaschke, Philipp, Sulin Sardoschau, and Marco Tabellini. 2022. "Scared Straight? Threat and Assimilation of Refugees in Germany." NBER Working Paper 30381 (August), National Bureau of Economic Research, Cambridge, MA.

Jasinskaja-Lahti, Inga, Karmela Liebkind, and Erling Solheim. 2009. "To Identify or Not to Identify? National Disidentification as an Alternative Reaction to Perceived Ethnic Discrimination." *Applied Psychology* 58 (1): 105–28.

Javorcik, Beata Smarzynska, Çağlar Özden, Mariana Spatareanu, and Cristina Neagu. 2011. "Migrant Networks and Foreign Direct Investment." *Journal of Development Economics* 94 (2): 231–41.

Kanas, Agnieszka, Barry R. Chiswick, Tanja van der Lippe, and Frank van Tubergen. 2012. "Social Contacts and the Economic Performance of Immigrants: A Panel Study of Immigrants in Germany." *International Migration Review* 46 (3): 680–709.

Kebede, Hundanol Atnafu, and Çağlar Özden. 2021. "The Effects of Refugee Camps on Children of Host Communities: Evidence from Ethiopia." Working paper (December 28), Development Research Group, World Bank, Washington, DC.

Kennan, John. 2013. "Open Borders." *Review of Economic Dynamics* 16 (2): L1–L13.

Kerevel, Yann P. 2011. "The Influence of Spanish-Language Media on Latino Public Opinion and Group Consciousness." *Social Science Quarterly* 92 (2): 509–34.

Kerr, William R. 2018. *The Gift of Global Talent: How Migration Shapes Business, Economy and Society.* Stanford, CA: Stanford University Press.

Koch, Anne, Nadine Biehler, Nadine Knapp, and David Kipp. 2023. "Integrating Refugees: Lessons from Germany since 2015/2016." Background paper prepared for *World Development Report 2023*, World Bank, Washington, DC.

Kugler, Maurice, Oren Levintal, and Hillel Rapoport. 2018. "Migration and Cross-Border Financial Flows." *World Bank Economic Review* 32 (1): 148–62.

Kugler, Maurice, and Hillel Rapoport. 2007. "International Labor and Capital Flows: Complements or Substitutes?" *Economics Letters* 94 (2): 155–62.

Lach, Saul. 2007. "Immigration and Prices." *Journal of Political Economy* 115 (4): 548–87.

La Ferrara, Eliana, Alberto Chong, and Suzanne Duryea. 2012. "Soap Operas and Fertility: Evidence from Brazil." *American Economic Journal: Applied Economics* 4 (4): 1–31.

Lanati, Mauro, and Alessandra Venturini. 2021. "Cultural Change and the Migration Choice." *Review of World Economics* 157 (4): 799–852.

Lastrapes, William D., and Thomas Lebesmuehlbacher. 2020. "Asylum Seekers and House Prices: Evidence from the United Kingdom." *Journal of Housing Economics* 49 (September): 101712.

Laubenthal, Barbara. 2014. "Europeanization and the Negotiation of a New Labour Migration Policy in Germany: The Goodness of Fit Approach Revisited." *Comparative Migration Studies* 2 (4): 469–92.

Lebow, Jeremy. 2022. "The Labor Market Effects of Venezuelan Migration to Colombia: Reconciling Conflicting Results." *IZA Journal of Development and Migration* 13 (1): 1–49.

Lee, Ronald Demos, and Timothy Miller. 2000. "Immigration, Social Security, and Broader Fiscal Impacts." *American Economic Review* 90 (2): 350–54.

Lehmann, M. Christian, and Daniel T. R. Masterson. 2020. "Does Aid Reduce Anti-Refugee Violence? Evidence from Syrian Refugees in Lebanon." *American Political Science Review* 114 (4): 1335–42.

Lergetporer, Philipp, Marc Piopiunik, and Lisa Simon. 2018. "Does the Education Level of Refugees Affect Natives' Attitudes?" CESifo Working Paper 6832 (November), Munich Society for the Promotion of Economic Research, Center for Economic Studies, Ludwig Maximilian University and Ifo Institute for Economic Research, Munich.

Lindner, Katja. 2022. "Gesundheitsversorgung von Asylsuchenden in den Bundesländern: Rahmenbedingungen und Reformbedarfe." MIDEM Policy Paper 2022-1, Mercator Forum Migration und Demokratie, Technische Universität Dresden, Dresden, Germany.

Livingston, Gretchen. 2014. "Fewer Than Half of U.S. Kids Today Live in a 'Traditional' Family." *Marriage and Divorce* (blog), December 22, 2014. https://www.pewresearch.org/fact-tank/2014/12/22/less-than-half-of-u-s-kids-today-live-in-a-traditional-family/.

Lleras-Muney, Adriana, and Allison Shertzer. 2015. "Did the Americanization Movement Succeed? An Evaluation of the Effect of English-Only and Compulsory Schooling Laws on Immigrants." *American Economic Journal: Economic Policy* 7 (3): 258–90.

Lochmann, Alexia, Hillel Rapoport, and Biagio Speciale. 2019. "The Effect of Language Training on Immigrants' Economic Integration: Empirical Evidence from France." *European Economic Review* 113 (April): 265–96.

Lombardo, Carlo, Julian Martinez-Correa, Leonardo Peñaloza-Pacheco, and Leonardo Gasparini. 2021. "The Distributional Effect of a Massive Exodus in Latin America and the Role of Downgrading and Regularization." CEDLAS Documento de Trabajo 290, Centro de Estudios Distributivos, Laborales y Sociales, Facultad de Ciencias Económicas, Universidad Nacional de La Plata, La Plata, Argentina.

Longhi, Simonetta, Peter Nijkamp, and Jacques Poot. 2010. "Joint Impacts of Immigration on Wages and Employment: Review and Meta-Analysis." *Journal of Geographical Systems* 12 (4): 355–87.

Luttmer, Erzo F. P., and Monica Singhal. 2011. "Culture, Context, and the Taste for Redistribution." *American Economic Journal: Economic Policy* 3 (1): 157–79.

Manning, Alan, and Sanchari Roy. 2010. "Culture Clash or Culture Club? National Identity in Britain." *Economic Journal* 120 (542): F72–F100.

Marcén, Miriam. 2021. "Gender, Time Allocation, and Birth Controls." In *Handbook of Labor, Human Resources and Population Economics*, edited by Klaus F. Zimmermann, 1–14. Cham, Switzerland: Springer.

Martén, Linna, Jens Hainmueller, and Dominik Hangartner. 2019. "Ethnic Networks Can Foster the Economic Integration of Refugees." *Proceedings of the National Academy of Sciences* 116 (33): 16280–85.

Mastrobuoni, Giovanni, and Paolo Pinotti. 2015. "Legal Status and the Criminal Activity of Immigrants." *American Economic Journal: Applied Economics* 7 (2): 175–206.

Maunganidze, Ottilia Anna, and Tsion Tadesse Abebe. 2020. "Implications of the COVID-19 Pandemic for the Africa–EU Partnership Agenda on Migration and Mobility: A Continental Perspective." IAI Paper 20 (43), December, Istituto Affari Internazionali, Rome.

Mayda, Anna Maria, Giovanni Peri, and Walter Steingress. 2022. "The Political Impact of Immigration: Evidence from the United States." *American Economic Journal: Applied Economics* 14 (1): 358–89.

McDermott, Grant R., and Benjamin Hansen. 2021. "Labor Reallocation and Remote Work during COVID-19: Real-Time Evidence from Github." NBER Working Paper 29598 (December), National Bureau of Economic Research, Cambridge, MA.

Medina-Cortina, Eduardo. 2023. "Deportations, Network Disruptions, and Undocumented Migration." Job Market Paper, University of Illinois at Urbana-Champaign. https://www.emedina.net/job-market-paper.

Meng, Xin, and Robert G. Gregory. 2005. "Intermarriage and the Economic Assimilation of Immigrants." *Journal of Labor Economics* 23 (1): 135–76.

Miguel, Edward, Sebastián M. Saiegh, and Shanker Satyanath. 2011. "Civil War Exposure and Violence." *Economics and Politics* 23 (1): 59–73.

Miller, Laura M. 2011. "Emergency Contraceptive Pill (ECP) Use and Experiences at College Health Centers in the Mid-Atlantic United States: Changes since ECP Went Over-the-Counter." *Journal of American College Health* 59 (8): 683–89.

Morales, Camila. 2022. "Do Refugee Students Affect the Academic Achievement of Peers? Evidence from a Large Urban School District." *Economics of Education Review* 89 (August): 102283.

Morales, Fernando, and Martha Denisse Pierola. 2020. "Venezuelan Migration in Peru: Short-Term Adjustments in the Labor Market." IDB Working Paper IDP-WP-1146 (August), Inter-American Development Bank, Washington, DC.

Morris-Lange, Simon. 2018. "Schule als Sackgasse? Jugendliche Flüchtlinge an segregierten Schulen." SVR Studie 2018-1, Forschungsbereich beim Sachverständigenrat deutscher Stiftungen für Integration und Migration, Berlin. https://www.svr-migration.de/wp-content/uploads/2018/02/SVR-FB_Bildungsintegration.pdf.

Müller, Karsten, and Carlo Schwarz. 2022. "From Hashtag to Hate Crime: Twitter and Anti-Minority Sentiment." CEPR Discussion Paper DP17647 (November), Center for Economic Policy Research, London.

Murard, Elie, and Seyhun Orcan Sakalli. 2020. "Mass Refugee Inflow and Long-Run Prosperity: Lessons from the Greek Population Resettlement." CReAm Discussion Paper CDP 05/20, Centre for Research and Analysis of Migration, Department of Economics, University College London, London.

Mussa, Abeba, Uwaoma G. Nwaogu, and Susan Pozo. 2017. "Immigration and Housing: A Spatial Econometric Analysis." *Journal of Housing Economics* 35 (March): 13–25.

Namen, Olga, Mounu Prem, Sandra Viviana Rozo, and Juan F. Vargas. 2021. "The Effects of Venezuelan Migration on Educational Outcomes in Colombia." Working paper, Inter-American Development Bank, Washington, DC.

NASEM (National Academies of Sciences, Engineering, and Medicine). 2015. *The Integration of Immigrants into American Society.* Washington, DC: National Academies Press.

NASEM (National Academies of Sciences, Engineering, and Medicine). 2017. *The Economic and Fiscal Consequences of Immigration.* Washington, DC: National Academies Press.

National Research Council. 1997. *The New Americans: Economic, Demographic, and Fiscal Effects of Immigration.* Washington, DC: National Academies Press.

Newland, Kathleen, Dovelyn Rannveig Agunias, and Aaron Terrazas. 2008. "Learning by Doing: Experiences of Circular Migration." MPI Insight (September), Migration Policy Institute, Washington, DC.

Nguyen, Angela-MinhTu D., and Verónica Benet-Martínez. 2013. "Biculturalism and Adjustment: A Meta-Analysis." *Journal of Cross-Cultural Psychology* 44 (1): 122–59.

Nielson, Julia. 2004. "Trade Agreements and Recognition." In *Quality and Recognition in Higher Education,* 155–203. Paris: Organisation for Economic Co-operation and Development.

OECD (Organisation for Economic Co-operation and Development). 2013. *International Migration Outlook 2013.* Paris: OECD.

OECD (Organisation for Economic Co-operation and Development). 2017. *International Migration Outlook 2017.* Paris: OECD.

OECD (Organisation for Economic Co-operation and Development). 2019. *Recent Trends in International Migration of Doctors, Nurses and Medical Students.* Paris: OECD.

OECD (Organisation for Economic Co-operation and Development). 2021. *International Migration Outlook 2021.* Paris: OECD.

Olivieri, Sergio, Francesc Ortega, Ana Rivadeneira, and Eliana Carranza. 2022. "The Labour Market Effects of Venezuelan Migration in Ecuador." *Journal of Development Studies* 58 (4): 713–29.

Olken, Benjamin A. 2009. "Do Television and Radio Destroy Social Capital? Evidence from Indonesian Villages." *American Economic Journal: Applied Economics* 1 (4): 1–33.

Omenka, Ogbonnaya Issac, Dennis P. Watson, and Hugh C. Hendrie. 2020. "Understanding the Healthcare Experiences and Needs of African Immigrants in the United States: A Scoping Review." *BMC Public Health* 20 (1): 27.

Ortiz-Ospina, Esteban, and Max Roser. 2020. "Marriages and Divorces." Our World in Data, Global Change Data Lab and Oxford Martin Program on Global Development, University of Oxford, Oxford, UK. https://ourworldindata.org/marriages-and-divorces#.

Ottaviano, Gianmarco I. P., and Giovanni Peri. 2008. "Immigration and National Wages: Clarifying the Theory and the Empirics." NBER Working Paper 14188 (July), National Bureau of Economic Research, Cambridge, MA.

Ottaviano, Gianmarco I. P., and Giovanni Peri. 2012. "Rethinking the Effect of Immigration on Wages." *Journal of the European Economic Association* 10 (1): 152–97.

Ottaviano, Gianmarco I. P., Giovanni Peri, and Greg C. Wright. 2018. "Immigration, Trade and Productivity in Services: Evidence from U.K. Firms." *Journal of International Economics* 112 (May): 88–108.

Özden, Çağlar, Mauro Testaverde, and Mathis Christoph Wagner. 2018. "How and Why Does Immigration Affect Crime? Evidence from Malaysia." *World Bank Economic Review* 32 (1): 183–202.

Özden, Çağlar, and Mathis Christoph Wagner. 2014. "Immigrant versus Natives? Displacement and Job Creation." Policy Research Working Paper 6900, World Bank, Washington, DC.

Parsons, Christopher Robert, and Pierre-Louis Vézina. 2018. "Migrant Networks and Trade: The Vietnamese Boat People as a Natural Experiment." *Economic Journal* 128 (612): F210–F234.

Patel, Krishna, and Francis Vella. 2013. "Immigrant Networks and Their Implications for Occupational Choice and Wages." *Review of Economics and Statistics* 95 (4): 1249–77.

Paulise, Luciana. 2022. "The 2022 Status of Remote Work and Top Future Predictions." *Careers* (blog), December 8, 2022. https://www.forbes.com/sites/luciana paulise/2022/12/08/the-2022-status-of-remote -work-and-top-future-predictions/?sh=413bf4791310.

Pekkala Kerr, Sari, William R. Kerr, Çağlar Özden, and Christopher Robert Parsons. 2016. "Global Talent Flows." *Journal of Economic Perspectives* 30 (4): 83–106.

Perry, Mark J. 2021. "Women Earned the Majority of Doctoral Degrees in 2020 for the 12th Straight Year and Outnumber Men in Grad School 148 to 100." *Post* (blog), October 14, 2021. https://www.aei .org/carpe-diem/women-earned-the-majority-of -doctoral-degrees-in-2020-for-the-12th-straight-year -and-outnumber-men-in-grad-school-148-to-100/.

Pervaiz, Zahid, and Amatul R. Chaudhary. 2015. "Social Cohesion and Economic Growth: An Empirical Investigation." *Australian Economic Review* 48 (4): 369–81.

Pew Research Center. 2015. *Parenting in America: Outlook, Worries, Aspirations Are Strongly Linked to Financial Situation*. December 17. Washington, DC: Pew Research Center.

Pinotti, Paolo. 2016. "Immigrants and Crime." In *Refugees and Economic Migrants: Facts, Policies, and Challenges*, edited by Francesco Fasani, 115–23. Vox. EU.org Book (October). London: CEPR Press.

Pinotti, Paolo. 2017. "Clicking on Heaven's Door: The Effect of Immigrant Legalization on Crime." *American Economic Review* 107 (1): 138–68.

Rapoport, Hillel, Sulin Sardoschau, and Arthur Silve. 2021. "Migration and Cultural Change." IZA Discussion Paper DP 14772 (October), Institute of Labor Economics, Bonn, Germany.

Rauch, James E. 1999. "Networks versus Markets in International Trade." *Journal of International Economics* 48 (1): 7–35.

Rauch, James E., and Vitor Trindade. 2002. "Ethnic Chinese Networks in International Trade." *Review of Economics and Statistics* 84 (1): 116–30.

Rocha, Rudi, Claudio Ferraz, and Rodrigo Reis Soares. 2017. "Human Capital Persistence and Development." *American Economic Journal: Applied Economics* 9 (4): 105–36.

Rodríguez Chatruc, Marisol, and Sandra Viviana Rozo. 2021. "In Someone Else's Shoes: Promoting Prosocial Behavior through Perspective Taking." Policy Research Working Paper 9866, World Bank, Washington, DC.

Rodrik, Dani. 2021. "Why Does Globalization Fuel Populism? Economics, Culture, and the Rise of Right-Wing Populism." *Annual Review of Economics* 13 (1): 133–70.

Rozo, Sandra Viviana, and Hernán Jorge Winkler. 2019. "Is Informality Good for Business? The Impacts of Inflows of Internally Displaced Persons on Formal Firms." *Journal of Human Resources* 56 (4): 1141–86.

Sá, Filipa. 2015. "Immigration and House Prices in the UK." *Economic Journal* 125 (587): 1393–1424.

Sacerdote, Bruce I. 2011. "Peer Effects in Education: How Might They Work, How Big Are They, and How Much Do We Know Thus Far?" In *Handbook of the Economics of Education*, edited by Eric Alan Hanushek, Stephen J. Machin, and Ludger Woessmann, 249–77. Handbooks in Economics Series. Amsterdam: North-Holland.

Saiz, Albert. 2007. "Immigration and Housing Rents in American Cities." *Journal of Urban Economics* 61 (2): 345–71.

Saiz, Albert, and Susan Wachter. 2011. "Immigration and the Neighborhood." *American Economic Journal: Economic Policy* 3 (2): 169–88.

Sakaue, Katsuki, and James Wokadala. 2022. "Effects of Including Refugees in Local Government Schools on Pupils' Learning Achievement: Evidence from West Nile, Uganda." *International Journal of Educational Development* 90 (April): 102543.

Schneider, Jan. 2023. "Labor Migration Schemes, Pilot Partnerships and Skills Mobility Initiatives in Germany." Background paper prepared for *World Development Report 2023*, World Bank, Washington, DC.

Sequeira, Sandra, Nathan Nunn, and Nancy Qian. 2020. "Immigrants and the Making of America." *Review of Economic Studies* 87 (1): 382–419.

Shah, Nasra. 2009. "The Management of Irregular Migration and Its Consequences for Development: GCC." Working Paper 19, Asia Regional Programme on Governance of Labour Migration, International Labour Organization, Bangkok.

Shayo, Moses. 2020. "Social Identity and Economic Policy." *Annual Review of Economics* 12 (1): 355–89.

Sides, John, and Jack Citrin. 2007. "European Opinion about Immigration: The Role of Identities, Interests and Information." *British Journal of Political Science* 37 (3): 477–504.

Spenkuch, Jörg L. 2014. "Understanding the Impact of Immigration on Crime." *American Law and Economics Review* 16 (1): 177–219.

Steinmayr, Andreas. 2021. "Contact versus Exposure: Refugee Presence and Voting for the Far Right." *Review of Economics and Statistics* 103 (2): 310–27.

Suciu, Peter. 2021. "Americans Spent on Average More Than 1,300 Hours on Social Media Last Year." *Social Media* (blog), June 24, 2021. https://www.forbes .com/sites/petersuciu/2021/06/24/americans -spent-more-than-1300-hours-on-social-media /?sh=220ee77d2547.

Tabellini, Marco. 2020. "Gifts of the Immigrants, Woes of the Natives: Lessons from the Age of Mass Migration." *Review of Economic Studies* 87 (1): 454–86.

Tanaka, Ryuichi, Lídia Farré, and Francesc Ortega. 2018. "Immigration, Assimilation, and the Future of Public Education." *European Journal of Political Economy* 52 (March): 141–65.

Testaverde, Mauro, Henry Moroz, Claire H. Hollweg, and Achim Schmillen. 2017. *Migrating to Opportunity: Overcoming Barriers to Labor Mobility in Southeast Asia*. Washington, DC: World Bank.

Thränhardt, Dietrich. 2020. "Integrationspolitik im deutschen Föderalismus: eine Implementationsanalyse." In *Reformbaustelle Bundesstaat*, edited by Felix

Knüpling, Mario Kölling, Sabine Kropp, and Henrik Scheller, 485–515. Wiesbaden, Germany: Springer VS.

Tonello, Marco. 2016. "Peer Effects of Non-Native Students on Natives' Educational Outcomes: Mechanisms and Evidence." *Empirical Economics* 51 (1): 383–414.

Tong, Sarah Y. 2005. "Ethnic Networks in FDI and the Impact of Institutional Development." *Review of Development Economics* 9 (4): 563–80.

Trachtman, Joel P. 2009. *The International Law of Economic Migration: Toward the Fourth Freedom*. Kalamazoo, MI: W. E. Upjohn Institute for Employment.

Triandafyllidou, Anna, Laura Bartolini, and Caterina Francesca Guidi. 2019. "Exploring the Links between Enhancing Regular Pathways and Discouraging Irregular Migration: A Discussion Paper to Inform Future Policy Deliberations." International Organization for Migration, Geneva. https://cadmus.eui.eu/handle/1814/61251.

Tumen, Semih. 2019. "Refugees and 'Native Flight' from Public to Private Schools." *Economics Letters* 181 (August): 154–59.

Valli, Elsa, Amber Peterman, and Melissa Hidrobo. 2019. "Economic Transfers and Social Cohesion in a Refugee-Hosting Setting." *Journal of Development Studies* 55 (Supplement 1): 128–46.

Verme, Paolo, and Kirsten Schuettler. 2021. "The Impact of Forced Displacement on Host Communities: A Review of the Empirical Literature in Economics." *Journal of Development Economics* 150 (May): 102606.

Voss, Kim, Fabiana Silva, and Irene Bloemraad. 2020. "The Limits of Rights: Claims-Making on Behalf of Immigrants." *Journal of Ethnic and Migration Studies* 46 (4): 791–819.

Whitaker, Beth Elise, and Jason Giersch. 2015. "Political Competition and Attitudes towards Immigration in Africa." *Journal of Ethnic and Migration Studies* 41 (10): 1536–57.

Wilkes, Rima, Neil Guppy, and Lily Farris. 2008. " 'No Thanks, We're Full': Individual Characteristics, National Context, and Changing Attitudes toward Immigration." *International Migration Review* 42 (2): 302–29.

Williamson, Scott. 2020. "Countering Misperceptions to Reduce Prejudice: An Experiment on Attitudes toward Muslim Americans." *Journal of Experimental Political Science* 7 (3): 167–78.

World Bank. 2018. *Moving for Prosperity: Global Migration and Labor Markets*. Policy Research Report. Washington, DC: World Bank.

Zhou, Yang-Yang. 2019. "How Refugee Resentment Shapes National Identity and Citizen Participation in Africa." PhD dissertation, Department of Politics, Princeton University, Princeton, NJ.

Zhou, Yang-Yang. 2021. "Studying Migrant Exclusion within the Global South." American Political Science Association–Comparative Politics ARSA-CP Newsletter 31 (1): 66–75. American Political Science Association, Washington, DC.

Zhuravskaya, Ekaterina, Maria Petrova, and Ruben Enikolopov. 2020. "Political Effects of the Internet and Social Media." *Annual Review of Economics* 12 (1): 415–38.

Zorlu, Aslan, and Joop Hartog. 2005. "The Effect of Immigration on Wages in Three European Countries." *Journal of Population Economics* 18 (1): 113–51.

Spotlight 6

Racism, xenophobia, and discrimination

Migration policies and impacts cannot be fully understood without acknowledging how race and ethnicity shape individual and community experiences at all stages of cross-border movements—in normative frameworks, as drivers of movement, in explicit and tacit criteria for entry, and in treatment at the destination. The factors driving discrimination include racism, xenophobia, ethnic animosities, and religious prejudice.[1] Playing out in countries at all income levels, they aggravate human distress and result in inequitable opportunities and outcomes.

Normative frameworks and policies

Some migration policies have been designed with an explicit racialized intent, even though international human rights law precludes discrimination on the basis of race, nationality, or ethnic origin.[2] For example, with passage of the 1882 Chinese Exclusion Act and the 1924 Immigration Act, the United States aimed to restrict or ban immigrants of non-European descent.[3] Likewise, the "White Australia" policy aimed to maintain racial homogeneity, and it was not revoked until 1973.[4]

Some migration systems have been less explicit in their attempt to exclude people with certain racial backgrounds, typically non-White, but they have been similarly intentional. For example, in 1908 Canada enacted the "continuous journey regulation" in response to an influx of Asian laborers, mostly Japanese and Indian. The regulation required whoever immigrated to Canada to make a continuous journey from their country of citizenship, but there were no direct routes from Japan or India. The government could then restrict immigration from these countries without specifying exclusion on the basis of race, nationality, or ethnic origin.[5]

Immigration measures that provide preferential visas based on descent may not be as intentional, but they have racialized impacts. For example, in the United Kingdom an Ancestry Visa is available to South Africans with a grandparent, and in some cases a great-grandparent, born in the United Kingdom, and it grants the bearer five years of work authorization with a pathway to citizenship.[6] This visa has the effect of allowing access for predominantly White South Africans that their Black co-nationals do not enjoy.

The international refugee system has long been applied in a racialized manner as well. The 1951 Geneva Convention restricted the definition of *refugees* to persons fleeing events in Europe before 1951, leaving out the 14–18 million people who were displaced in the aftermath of the 1947 partition of British India and the 5 million people who fled from the Korean War in the early 1950s.[7] The 1967 Protocol to the Convention lifted these restrictions and somewhat relaxed the "Eurocentric" definition of a refugee in international law. Still, the number of non-European people recognized as refugees remained very low throughout the 1960s and early 1970s, even though war was raging in Vietnam and tens of millions were displaced during the Bangladesh Liberation War. It is only from the mid-1970s on that the international system began to recognize large numbers of refugees outside of the European context.[8]

The very definition of *migrant* in many countries has exclusionary undertones. Unlike this Report, many data sources on migration define a *migrant* as a foreign-born individual rather than a foreign national. This definition implies that integration or assimilation is not sufficient to be no longer considered an alien: migrant is a lifelong status. In countries where most migrants have a different racial or ethnic background from the majority population of the destination country, expressions such as "second-generation immigrants" can carry the distinction between citizens even further, and they can compound other forms of discrimination.

Drivers of movement out of origin societies

Racial, ethnic, or religious discrimination in the origin society determines in part who decides to migrate or to flee. It also underpins many situations of statelessness. Discrimination is severest when specific groups are targeted for violence or persecution because of their race, ethnicity, or religion. The experience of Jewish people forced to flee Nazi Germany and other occupied countries during World War II exemplifies such situations. Later, and under less extreme circumstances, Jewish minorities disproportionately fled the Soviet Union and other countries. In the early 1970s, people of South Asian descent were disenfranchised and persecuted in Uganda, which led to their massive exodus.[9] More recently, the Muslim Rohingya in Myanmar and the Shi'a Hazara in Afghanistan had to leave their respective countries because of targeted violence. Discrimination also may spur migration when specific groups are no longer able to access economic opportunities in their country of origin, such as those of South Asian descent in Fiji following a regime change in 1987.[10] When members of these groups have the necessary resources, they often migrate to more open environments.

Perceptions in destination societies

Racism and other prejudices play a central role in the perceptions of migrants and refugees in destination societies, particularly when race is regarded as a key part of the destination country's national identity.[11] In North America and Europe, many citizens' positions on immigration depend on the race or ethnicity of the migrants.[12] For example, polls in both the United Kingdom and the United States reveal that their citizens were more welcoming to Ukrainians fleeing violence than to other populations such as Syrians or Afghans.[13] In the Russian Federation, attitudes toward immigrants from the South Caucasus and Central Asia are more negative than attitudes toward immigrants from other regions of the former Soviet Union with a predominantly White population.[14]

Political leaders may reflect or further fuel popular misgivings. In January 2018, US president Donald Trump asked why more people from "shithole countries" should be allowed into the United States, reportedly referring to African countries. He then suggested that, instead, the United States should allow more entrants from countries such as Norway. In July 2022, Hungarian prime minister Viktor Orbán expressed concern about non-European migration: "This is why we have always fought: we are willing to mix with one another, but we do not want to become peoples of mixed-race."[15]

Ethnic differences can also negatively affect the perception of migrants and refugees in destination societies. In South Africa, for example, attitudinal surveys suggest a degree of xenophobia (figure S6.1). Somali and Zimbabwean migrants and refugees have been subject to violent xenophobic attacks.[16] Such attacks against foreigners and their businesses have predominantly occurred in townships and informal settlements where marginalized South Africans feel they are competing with migrants for scarce employment opportunities and a better quality of life.

Figure S6.1 Attitudes toward migrants in South Africa are more negative than positive

Percentage of responses to 2019 survey question "Do you agree/disagree with the statements about cross-border migrants?"

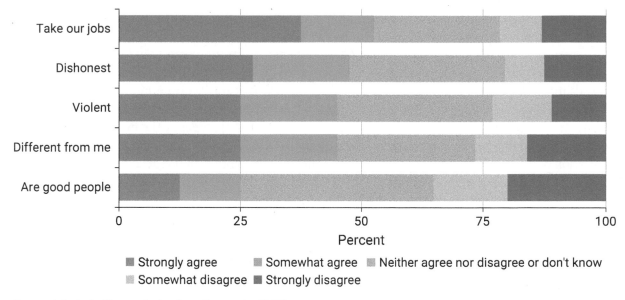

Source: Adapted with permission from *Economist* 2022b.

Differences in religious and cultural backgrounds are also often invoked to justify prejudice. Even in European countries where religious practice is low, citizens usually express a preference for migrants originating from traditionally Christian countries,[17] and they are less welcoming to migrants with a Muslim background.[18] In some Swiss municipalities where citizenship applications used to be decided by referendum, the country of origin was a critical determinant. Turkish applicants were found to receive a higher rate of "No" votes than applicants from Northern or Western Europe, even when other factors such as their language ability, age, education, and number of years since arrival were the same.[19]

Effects on migration policies

Perceptions of and racial attitudes toward migrants affect the conditions under which they can enter a country. For example, in the United States undocumented immigrants, who are largely from Latin America, face harsher consequences than White Europeans faced in years past for the same offense—unauthorized entry.[20] For refugees and asylum-seekers, racism and prejudice against certain ethnicities sometimes drive who is granted status, even though the asylum regime is explicitly intended to protect individuals who have faced persecution based on race and ethnicity.[21] In 2022, for example, many African immigrants living in Ukraine experienced discrimination when trying to flee the war.[22]

Perceptions and attitudes also affect how migrants and refugees are treated in the destination country.[23] Darker skin color is associated with lower call-back rates for interviews in at least nine European and North American countries.[24] Women with a Turkish name but with a résumé otherwise identical to those of women with a German name are less likely to be invited to a job interview in Germany, especially if they wear a headscarf.[25] Employers in Uganda are also less likely to hire refugees than citizens,[26] and the policy in Ethiopia that permitted refugees to leave camps was initially limited to Eritrean refugees. In some countries, migrants and refugees also face ethnic discrimination in the workplace and in the housing market,[27] as well as in their access to social services. They are subject to harassment, and in some extreme cases to racially motivated hate crimes.[28]

Racial and ethnic discrimination affect migrants' economic outcomes and compromise the benefits that accrue to host societies.[29] Darker skin color is associated with worse economic outcomes among immigrants in the United States.[30] Besides making it more difficult to obtain a job, discrimination can lower the actual performance of migrant workers as well as their acquisition of human capital.[31] Faced with discrimination in hiring, migrants search for jobs farther from where they live, and the higher transportation costs reduce their earnings, as experienced in South Africa.[32]

Discrimination also affects migrants' social integration and overall well-being.[33] Anti-immigration attitudes and perceived discrimination are closely associated with worsened mental health for migrants.[34] Social integration is hindered or facilitated by the perceptions and attitudes of the host community.[35] In Germany, attitudes toward immigrants are as important as local unemployment rates in shaping refugees' integration outcomes.[36] Openness toward migrants affects their ability to build social networks with their hosts, which are important for integration.

* * *

Migrants have the right to fair and decent treatment regardless of their race, ethnicity, religion, or cultural origin. This principle should be at the center of all policy making. It implies that countries need to adopt policies *explicitly* aimed at combating all racial and other forms of discrimination. Global normative frameworks can also help ensure that racism and other forms of discrimination do not negatively influence policy making.

Notes

1. For a discussion of discrimination against women and girls, as well as sexual and gender minorities, see spotlight 4.
2. See UNHRC (2018); United Nations (1965).
3. "Chinese Exclusion Act (1882)," National Archives and Records Administration, Washington, DC, https://www.archives.gov/milestone-documents/chinese-exclusion-act#:~:text=That%20any%20person%20who%20shall,be%20deemed%20guilty%20of%20a; Immigration Act of 1924, United States Statutes at Large (68th Cong., Sess. I, Chap. 190, pp. 153–169), https://loveman.sdsu.edu/docs/1924ImmigrationAct.pdf.
4. See Immigration Restriction Act 1901, C1901A00017 (December 23, 1901), Federal Register of Legislation, Australia, https://www.legislation.gov.au/Details/C1901A00017.
5. See "Continuous Journey Regulation, 1908," Canadian Museum of Immigration at Pier 21, Halifax, Nova Scotia, Canada, https://pier21.ca/research/immigration-history/continuous-journey-regulation-1908.
6. "UK Ancestry Visa," GOV.UK, https://www.gov.uk/ancestry-visa.
7. See OHCHR (1951), Article 1, Paragraph B.(1).
8. Achiume (2022).
9. Jamal (1976).
10. Chand and Clemens (2019).
11. Devos and Banaji (2005); Devos and Heng (2009).
12. Card, Dustmann, and Preston (2005); Valentino et al. (2019).
13. *Economist* (2022a); Kirk (2022).
14. Yuri Levada Analytical Center (2017).
15. Embassy of Hungary (2022).
16. Charman and Piper (2012); Crush et al. (2017).
17. Adida, Lo, and Platas (2019); Bansak, Hainmueller, and Hangartner (2016).
18. Heath and Richards (2016).
19. Hainmueller and Hangartner (2013).
20. Ngai (2014).
21. Achiume (2022).
22. OHCHR (2022).
23. Kamasaki (2021); Li (2019).
24. Quillian and Midtbøen (2021); Quillian et al. (2019).
25. Weichselbaumer (2020).
26. Loiacono and Silva-Vargas (2019).
27. Auspurg, Schneck, and Hinz (2019); Baldini and Federici (2011); Bosch, Carnero, and Farré (2010).
28. Kirkwood, McKinlay, and McVittie (2013); Kusuma, York, and Wibowo (2015).
29. Esses, Bennett-AbuAyyash, and Lapshina (2014).
30. Dávila, Mora, and Stockly (2011); Hersch (2008).
31. Bertrand and Duflo (2016); Glover, Pallais, and Pariente (2017); Steinhardt (2018).
32. Abel (2017).
33. de Coulon, Radu, and Steinhardt (2016); Steinhardt (2018); Suleman, Garber, and Rutkow (2018); WHO (2022).
34. Pascoe and Richman (2009); Steinhardt (2018).
35. Bailey et al. (2022); Gould and Klor (2016).
36. Aksoy, Poutvaara, and Schikora (2020).

References

Abel, Martin D. 2017. "Labor Market Discrimination and Sorting: Evidence from South Africa." Policy Research Working Paper 8180, World Bank, Washington, DC.

Achiume, E. Tendayi. 2022. "Racial Borders." *Georgetown Law Journal* 110 (3): 445–508.

Adida, Claire L., Adeline Lo, and Melina R. Platas. 2019. "Americans Preferred Syrian Refugees Who Are Female, English-Speaking, and Christian on the Eve of Donald Trump's Election." *PLOS One* 14 (10): e0222504.

Aksoy, Cevat Giray, Panu Poutvaara, and Felicitas Schikora. 2020. "First Time Around: Local Conditions and Multi-Dimensional Integration of Refugees." IZA Discussion Paper DP 13914, Institute of Labor Economics, Bonn, Germany.

Auspurg, Katrin, Andreas Schneck, and Thomas Hinz. 2019. "Closed Doors Everywhere? A Meta-Analysis of Field Experiments on Ethnic Discrimination in Rental Housing Markets." *Journal of Ethnic and Migration Studies* 45 (1): 95–114.

Bailey, Michael, Drew M. Johnston, Martin Koenen, Theresa Kuchler, Dominic Russel, and Johannes Stroebel. 2022. "The Social Integration of International Migrants: Evidence from the Networks of Syrians in Germany." NBER Working Paper 29925, National Bureau of Economic Research, Cambridge, MA.

Baldini, Massimo, and Marta Federici. 2011. "Ethnic Discrimination in the Italian Rental Housing Market." *Journal of Housing Economics* 20 (1): 1–14.

Bansak, Kirk, Jens Hainmueller, and Dominik Hangartner. 2016. "How Economic, Humanitarian, and Religious Concerns Shape European Attitudes toward Asylum Seekers." *Science* 354 (6309): 217–22.

Bertrand, Marianne, and Esther Duflo. 2016. "Field Experiments on Discrimination." NBER Working Paper 22014, National Bureau of Economic Research, Cambridge, MA.

Bosch, Mariano, M. Angeles Carnero, and Lídia Farré. 2010. "Information and Discrimination in the Rental Housing Market: Evidence from a Field Experiment." *Regional Science and Urban Economics* 40 (1): 11–19.

Card, David E., Christian Dustmann, and Ian Preston. 2005. "Understanding Attitudes to Immigration: The Migration and Minority Module of the First European Social Survey." CReAM Discussion Paper CDP 03/05, Centre for Research and Analysis of Migration, Department of Economics, University College London, London.

Chand, Satish, and Michael A. Clemens. 2019. "Human Capital Investment under Exit Options: Evidence from a Natural Quasi-Experiment." IZA Discussion Paper DP 12173, Institute of Labor Economics, Bonn, Germany.

Charman, Andrew, and Laurence Piper. 2012. "Xenophobia, Criminality and Violent Entrepreneurship: Violence against Somali Shopkeepers in Delft South, Cape Town, South Africa." *South African Review of Sociology* 43 (3): 81–105.

Crush, Jonathan, Godfrey Tawodzera, Abel Chikanda, and Daniel Tevara. 2017. "Living with Xenophobia: Zimbabwean Informal Enterprise in South Africa." SAMP Migration Policy Series 77, Southern African Migration Programme, Wilfrid Laurier University, Waterloo, Ontario, Canada. https://scholars.wlu.ca/samp/21/.

Dávila, Alberto, Marie T. Mora, and Sue K. Stockly. 2011. "Does Mestizaje Matter in the US? Economic Stratification of Mexican Immigrants." *American Economic Review* 101 (3): 593–97.

de Coulon, Augustin, Dragos Radu, and Max Friedrich Steinhardt. 2016. "Pane e Cioccolata: The Impact of Native Attitudes on Return Migration." *Review of International Economics* 24 (2): 253–81.

Devos, Thierry, and Mahzarin R. Banaji. 2005. "American = White?" *Journal of Personality and Social Psychology* 88 (3): 447–66.

Devos, Thierry, and Leakhena Heng. 2009. "Whites Are Granted the American Identity More Swiftly than Asians: Disentangling the Role of Automatic and Controlled Processes." *Social Psychology* 40 (4): 192–201.

Economist. 2022a. "Americans Are More Willing to Welcome Ukrainians Than Others Fleeing Violence." *Graphic Detail: Daily Chart*, March 25, 2022. https://www.economist.com/graphic-detail/2022/03/25/americans-are-more-willing-to-welcome-ukrainians-than-others-fleeing-violence.

Economist. 2022b. "South African Xenophobes Run Amok." *Middle East and Africa*, June 9, 2022. https://www.economist.com/middle-east-and-africa/2022/06/09/south-african-xenophobes-run-amok.

Embassy of Hungary, Bucharest. 2022. "Speech by Prime Minister Viktor Orbán at the 31st Bálványos Summer Free University and Student Camp, 23 July 2022, Tusnádfürdő (Băile Tuşnad)." Ministry of Foreign Affairs and Trade, Budapest. https://bukarest.mfa.gov.hu/eng/news/speech-by-prime-minister-viktor-orban-at-the-31st-balvanyos-summer-free-university-and-student-camp-23-july-2022-tusnadfuerdo-baile-tusnad.

Esses, Victoria M., Caroline Bennett-AbuAyyash, and Natalia Lapshina. 2014. "How Discrimination against Ethnic and Religious Minorities Contributes to the Underutilization of Immigrants' Skills." *Policy Insights from the Behavioral and Brain Sciences* 1 (1): 55–62.

Glover, Dylan, Amanda Pallais, and William Pariente. 2017. "Discrimination as a Self-Fulfilling Prophecy: Evidence from French Grocery Stores." *Quarterly Journal of Economics* 132 (3): 1219–60.

Gould, Eric D., and Esteban F. Klor. 2016. "The Long-Run Effect of 9/11: Terrorism, Backlash, and the Assimilation of Muslim Immigrants in the West." *Economic Journal* 126 (597): 2064–2114.

Hainmueller, Jens, and Dominik Hangartner. 2013. "Who Gets a Swiss Passport? A Natural Experiment in Immigrant Discrimination." *American Political Science Review* 107 (1): 159–87.

Heath, Anthony, and Lindsay Richards. 2016. "Attitudes towards Immigration and Their Antecedents: Topline Results from Round 7 of the European Social Survey." *ESS Topline Results Series* 7 (7): 3–14.

Hersch, Joni. 2008. "Profiling the New Immigrant Worker: The Effects of Skin Color and Height." *Journal of Labor Economics* 26 (2): 345–86.

Jamal, Vali. 1976. "Asians in Uganda, 1880–1972: Inequality and Expulsion." *Economic History Review* 29 (4): 602–16.

Kamasaki, Charles. 2021. "US Immigration Policy: A Classic, Unappreciated Example of Structural Racism." *How We Rise* (blog), March 26, 2021. https://www.brookings.edu/blog/how-we-rise/2021/03/26/us-immigration-policy-a-classic-unappreciated-example-of-structural-racism/.

Kirk, Isabelle. 2022. "Are Attitudes to Ukrainian Refugees Unique?" *Politics and Current Affairs* (blog), July 12, 2022. https://yougov.co.uk/topics/politics/articles-reports/2022/07/12/are-attitudes-ukrainian-refugees-unique.

Kirkwood, Steve, Andrew McKinlay, and Chris McVittie. 2013. "'They're More than Animals': Refugees' Accounts of Racially Motivated Violence." *British Journal of Social Psychology* 52 (4): 747–62.

Kusuma, Ardli Johan, Michael Ryan York, and Rizki Hari Wibowo. 2015. "Violence against Indonesian Migrant Workers: A Causal Analysis." *Jurnal Hubungan Internasional* 4 (1): 47–57.

Li, Yao-Tai. 2019. "'It's Not Discrimination': Chinese Migrant Workers' Perceptions of and Reactions to Racial Microaggressions in Australia." *Sociological Perspectives* 62 (4): 554–71.

Loiacono, Francesco, and Mariajose Silva-Vargas. 2019. "Improving Access to Labour Markets for Refugees: Evidence from Uganda." Policy Brief 43445, International Growth Centre, London School of Economics and Political Science, London. https://www.theigc.org/wp-content/uploads/2019/10/Loiacono-and-Vargas-2019-final-paper_revision-1.pdf.

Ngai, Mae M. 2014. *Impossible Subjects: Illegal Aliens and the Making of Modern America*. Rev. ed. Politics and Society in Modern America Series, 105. Princeton, NJ: Princeton University Press.

OHCHR (Office of the United Nations High Commissioner for Human Rights). 1951. "Convention Relating to the Status of Refugees." Adopted July 28, 1951, by United Nations Conference of Plenipotentiaries on the Status of Refugees and Stateless Persons Convened under General Assembly Resolution 429 (V) of December 14, 1950. OHCHR, Geneva. https://www.ohchr.org/en/instruments-mechanisms/instruments/convention-relating-status-refugees.

OHCHR (Office of the United Nations High Commissioner for Human Rights). 2022. "Ukraine: UN Experts Concerned by Reports of Discrimination against People of African Descent at Border." Press release, March 3, 2022. https://www.ohchr.org/en/press-releases/2022/03/ukraine-un-experts-concerned-reports-discrimination-against-people-african.

Pascoe, Elizabeth A., and Laura Smart Richman. 2009. "Perceived Discrimination and Health: A Meta-Analytic Review." *Psychological Bulletin* 135 (4): 531–54.

Quillian, Lincoln, Anthony Heath, Devah Pager, Arnfinn H. Midtbøen, Fenella Fleischmann, and Ole Hexel. 2019. "Do Some Countries Discriminate More than Others? Evidence from 97 Field Experiments of Racial Discrimination in Hiring." *Sociological Science* 6 (June): 467–96.

Quillian, Lincoln, and Arnfinn H. Midtbøen. 2021. "Comparative Perspectives on Racial Discrimination in Hiring: The Rise of Field Experiments." *Annual Review of Sociology* 47 (1): 391–415.

Steinhardt, Max Friedrich. 2018. "The Impact of Xenophobic Violence on the Integration of Immigrants." IZA Discussion Paper DP 11781, Institute of Labor Economics, Bonn, Germany.

Suleman, Shazeen, Kent D. Garber, and Lainie Rutkow. 2018. "Xenophobia as a Determinant of Health: An Integrative Review." *Journal of Public Health Policy* 39 (4): 407–23.

UNHRC (United Nations Human Rights Council). 2018. "Report of the Special Rapporteur on Contemporary Forms of Racism, Racial Discrimination, Xenophobia and Related Intolerance." Document A/HRC/38/52, General Assembly, United Nations, New York. https://documents-dds-ny.un.org/doc/UNDOC/GEN/G18/117/79/PDF/G1811779.pdf?OpenElement.

United Nations. 1965. "Resolution Adopted by the General Assembly: International Convention on the Elimination of All Forms of Racial Discrimination." Document A/RES/20/, United Nations, New York. https://treaties.un.org/pages/ViewDetails.aspx?src=IND&mtdsg_no=IV-2&chapter=4&clang=_en.

Valentino, Nicholas A., Stuart N. Soroka, Shanto Iyengar, Toril Aalberg, Raymond Duch, Marta Fraile, Kyu S. Hahn, et al. 2019. "Economic and Cultural Drivers of Immigrant Support Worldwide." *British Journal of Political Science* 49 (4): 1201–26.

Weichselbaumer, Doris. 2020. "Multiple Discrimination against Female Immigrants Wearing Headscarves." *ILR Review* 73 (3): 600–27.

WHO (World Health Organization). 2022. *World Report on the Health of Refugees and Migrants*. Geneva: WHO.

Yuri Levada Analytical Center. 2017. "Attitudes toward Migrants." Press release, May 29, 2017. https://www.levada.ru/en/2017/05/29/attitudes-toward-migrant.

Part 3

When the match is weak, the costs need to be shared— and reduced—multilaterally

When people do not bring skills and attributes that are in demand at their destination, the costs to destination countries often exceed the benefits of migration. Moreover, any gains for migrants and their origin countries are not sustainable unless the destination countries are able to reduce and manage their own costs. The policy challenges are different for refugees, who under international law must be hosted by the destination countries, and for other migrants. This part is an overview of the evidence on the effects of such movements. It also reviews countries' experiences to draw lessons for policy makers.

Chapter 7 focuses on refugees. Under international law, destination countries are obligated to host those who have a "well-founded fear" of persecution and violence in their country of origin, regardless of the costs. But refugee situations should be managed as medium-term challenges and not just as humanitarian emergencies because they tend to extend over time. The economic outcomes for both refugees and their host communities are largely determined by host countries' policies, as well as by the international community's ability to share responsibilities equitably.

Chapter 8 looks at the situation in which migrants who are not refugees bring skills and attributes that are only a weak match with the needs of the destination economy. Such movements—referred to in this Report as distressed migration—are often irregular and harrowing, and they pose difficult policy challenges for destination countries. The effects of such movements are largely determined by destination countries' responses, including their cooperation with transit countries. Overall, human dignity should be the yardstick of migration policies. Over time, the main challenge is to reduce the need for such movements. Development in the countries of origin can play a critical role.

Two spotlights complement this discussion. Spotlight 7 discusses both internally displaced persons (IDPs)— that is, those fleeing conflict and violence but remaining in their own country—and stateless persons. Spotlight 8 examines the evidence on the impact of development on cross-border movements in terms of both numbers and destinations for countries at different levels of income.

Overall, the potential costs of forced displacement and distressed migration—for migrants as well as destination societies—can be managed through effective policy making and international cooperation. That is the key message of this part.

7 Refugees
Managing with a medium-term perspective

Key messages

- Because refugees move for safety, they are not always able to reach destinations where their skills are in demand. Providing international protection often comes with costs for the host country, and yet it is an obligation under international law.

- Responsibility-sharing is key to managing these costs, and it requires complementing global efforts with regional action.

- Host countries' policies can also help reduce the costs, while maintaining high protection standards. Refugee situations tend to last for years, and managing them exclusively through emergency and humanitarian programs is ineffective. Policies should be geared toward financial and social sustainability by means of internal mobility, self-reliance, and inclusion in national services (figure 7.1).

- Innovative approaches are also needed to facilitate the achievement of durable solutions by combining legal and development perspectives.

Figure 7.1 Refugee situations are best managed with a medium-term perspective, with costs shared across countries

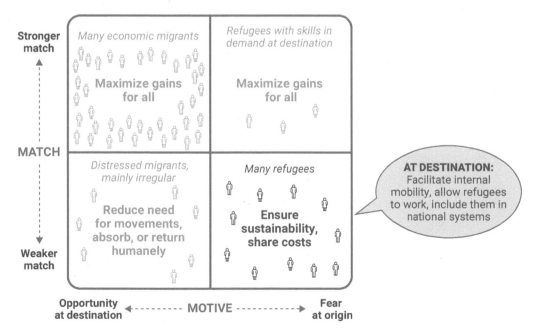

Source: WDR 2023 team.

Note: Match refers to the degree to which a migrant's skills and related attributes meet the demand in the destination country. *Motive* refers to the circumstances under which a person moves—whether in search of opportunity or because of a "well-founded fear" of persecution, armed conflict, or violence in their origin country.

Recognizing the development challenge

Under international law, international protection is required when people crossing borders are "unable or unwilling to return to their country of origin owing to a well-founded fear" for their life, physical integrity, or freedom as a result of persecution, armed conflict, or other forms of violence—that is, they are refugees.[1] This definition was codified in the 1951 Convention Relating to the Status of Refugees, its 1967 Protocol,[2] and subsequent international refugee law. As of 2022, more than 149 states were parties to the convention or the protocol, or both, although almost half of them have reservations about specific articles.

Central to the Refugee Convention is the binding legal norm of *non-refoulement*—that is, the prohibition on sending refugees back to their country of origin or other places "where [their] life or freedom would be threatened."[3] The convention also provides certain socioeconomic rights that are essential for refugees to reestablish themselves. Although implementation has been uneven across countries, this system has been praised for saving tens of millions of lives over the last several decades.[4]

A growing crisis

The number of refugees has more than doubled over the last decade (figure 7.2).[5] As of mid-2022, there were about 37.8 million refugees worldwide: 26.7 million refugees (and people in refugee-like situations) under the mandate of the United Nations High Commissioner for Refugees (UNHCR); 5.8 million Palestine refugees under the mandate of the United Nations Relief and Works Agency for Palestine Refugees

Figure 7.2 The number of refugees has more than doubled over the last decade

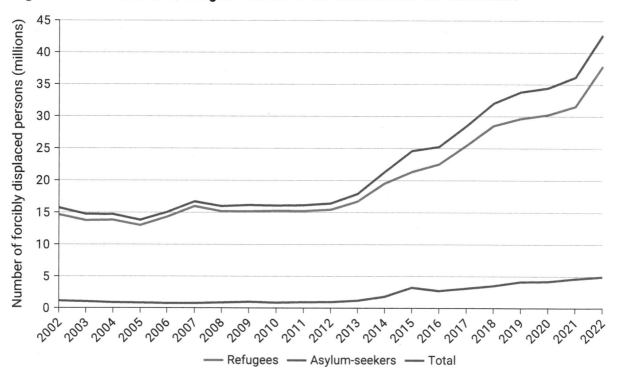

Source: WDR 2023 team, based on 2022 data from Refugee Data Finder (dashboard), United Nations High Commissioner for Refugees, Geneva, https://popstats.unhcr.org/refugee-statistics/download/.

Note: Refugees include all those under the mandate of the United Nations High Commissioner for Refugees (UNHCR), Palestine refugees under the mandate of the United Nations Relief and Works Agency for Palestine Refugees in the Near East (UNRWA), and other people in need of international protection. Data for 2022 are as of mid-2022, when the latest figures were available.

in the Near East (UNRWA); and 5.3 million other people in need of international protection. An additional 4.9 million people have requested asylum (asylum-seekers) and are awaiting a decision on whether they will be granted refugee status. These numbers have since increased, including with the flight of over 8 million Ukrainians as of February 2023 (box 7.1).[6]

Box 7.1 Ukrainian refugee crisis

The Russian Federation's invasion of Ukraine has triggered the largest humanitarian and displacement crisis in Europe since World War II. Nearly a third of Ukraine's prewar population was displaced by late February 2023,[a] including over 8 million refugees registered across Europe[b] and 5.4 million internally displaced persons within the country.[c]

Most Ukrainian refugees initially fled to neighboring countries (Poland, the Slovak Republic, Hungary, Romania, and Moldova) before moving on to higher-income countries in the European Union. In 2023, Poland and Germany are hosting the largest numbers of Ukrainian refugees (1.6 million and 1 million, respectively), whereas Czechia, Estonia, Latvia, and Lithuania are hosting the largest numbers of refugees as a percentage of their population (map B7.1.1).[d]

Map B7.1.1 Ukrainian refugees are hosted across the European Union and neighboring countries

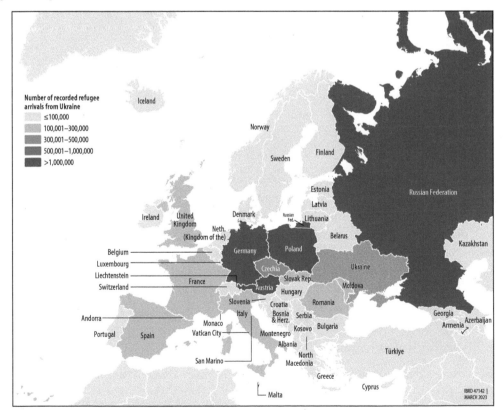

Source: Ukraine Refugee Situation (dashboard), Operational Data Portal, data version of February 22, 2023, United Nations High Commissioner for Refugees, Geneva, https://data.unhcr.org/en/situations/ukraine.

(Box continues next page)

Women and children account for 86 percent of Ukrainian refugees, and 78 percent of refugees have been separated from immediate family members, mainly because of restrictions on men leaving Ukraine.[e] A recent survey found that 40 percent of refugees have already found employment or are self-employed, although about half still rely on social protection or cash assistance (or both).

Refugee-hosting countries swiftly established temporary protection regimes that now cover more than 4.8 million Ukrainian refugees, providing a legal basis for them to work and access services across the European Union and in Moldova. To provide refugees with protection and assistance, national and municipal authorities have generally coordinated local responses involving national and local nongovernmental organizations, civil society groups, volunteers, Ukrainian diaspora communities, and refugee-led organizations.

The Ukrainian government is supportive of these efforts—in particular, to prepare refugees for an eventual return to Ukraine. At least 80 percent of refugees plan to stay in their current host countries until hostilities subside and the situation improves in Ukraine.[f] Although for refugees peace in Ukraine is the main condition for their return, adequate access to electricity and water, health care services, housing, and livelihoods in Ukraine also significantly influence return intentions.[g]

a. Ukraine's population was 43.3 million as of January 1, 2022.
b. As of February 21, 2023, 8,087,952 refugees from Ukraine were recorded across Europe, of whom 4,863,513 were registered for temporary protection or similar national protection schemes in Europe. See Ukraine Refugee Situation (dashboard), Operational Data Portal, data version of February 22, 2023, United Nations High Commissioner for Refugees, Geneva, https://data.unhcr.org/en/situations/ukraine.
c. Ukraine Refugee Situation (dashboard), Operational Data Portal, data version of February 22, 2023, United Nations High Commissioner for Refugees, Geneva, https://data.unhcr.org/en/situations/ukraine.
d. UNHCR (2023b).
e. UNHCR (2023c).
f. UNHCR (2023c).
g. UNHCR (2023a).

Refugee situations—traditionally seen as humanitarian emergencies—are also increasingly lasting many years (figure 7.3)[7] because conflicts are often protracted, and durable solutions are lacking. Of the large refugee crises since the end of the Cold War, only one—Kosovo in 1999—was resolved in a matter of weeks. In all other crises, refugees have found themselves in a lengthy, intractable state of limbo.[8] For example, many of the Afghans who left their country following the 1979 Soviet invasion are still out of their country, and many of the current Afghan refugees are, in fact, the grandchildren of those who initially fled. At the end of 2021, there were 51 protracted refugee situations[9] that accounted for 15.9 million refugees, or more than 40 percent of all refugees.[10]

Refugees' specific vulnerabilities

The plight of refugees poses challenges for development efforts aimed at eradicating extreme poverty, boosting shared prosperity, and achieving the United Nations' Sustainable Development Goals.[11] As extreme poverty has receded across the globe, it has become increasingly concentrated among vulnerable groups, including refugees.[12]

Many refugees have specific vulnerabilities that distinguish them from other poor populations and require dedicated support.[13] Many of them have also lost assets and have undergone traumatic ordeals.[14] The challenges they face are often compounded by a status that gives them limited rights, limited access

Figure 7.3 The number of refugees in protracted situations has more than doubled over the last decade

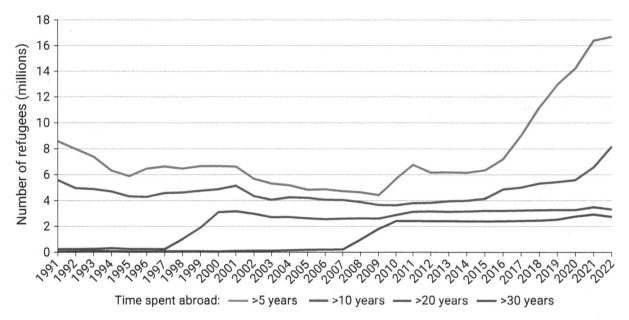

Source: Refugee Population Statistics Database, United Nations High Commissioner for Refugees, Geneva, https://www .unhcr.org/refugee-statistics/, based on the methodology outlined in Devictor and Do (2017).
Note: Data for 2022 are as of mid-2022, when the latest figures were available.

to opportunities, and a short planning horizon.[15] As a result, they tend to be disproportionately affected by poverty. In Uganda, for example, in spite of progressive refugee policies, 46 percent of refugees lived in poverty in 2018, compared with 17 percent of the host population.[16] Some refugees also have higher protection needs (box 7.2). An example is unaccompanied minors, who accounted for about 15 percent of those who sought asylum in the European Union in 2020.[17]

Box 7.2 Among refugees, some have higher protection needs

Women and girls experience forced displacement differently than men and boys and often face special challenges. Displaced populations have large shares of women and children and a high prevalence of female-headed households.[a] In some situations, it has been suggested that displacement provides space for "positive" change and empowerment, such as when gender norms are more progressive at the destination than in the place of origin, or when traditional divisions of labor are disrupted in ways that are favorable to women.[b] But women's access to the labor market, as well as to education and adequate health services, is not always guaranteed. For example, a recent study found that the employment rates for displaced men were at least 90 percent higher than for displaced women in Ethiopia, Nigeria, Somalia, South Sudan, and Sudan.[c]

  Women and girls are also often at risk of rape, sexual abuse, and other forms of gender-based violence throughout the displacement cycle—during flight, in transit, and in exile.[d] Early marriage, sexual exploitation, or engagement in survival sex to provide for families are common occurrences in many forced displacement situations.

(Box continues next page)

Refugees need safety and security, but they also need an opportunity to rebuild their lives while in exile and in the expectation of a durable solution. This requires addressing their specific vulnerabilities so they can be back on a level playing field with other members of their community. Under the 1951 Refugee Convention and its 1967 Protocol, international refugee protection is not limited to providing a temporary legal status that prevents people from being subjected to violence and harm. It also entails granting rights that enable refugees to recover and contribute to their host society, such as the right to move freely within the host country, to work, and to access services.[18] Indeed, once they have reached safety, many refugees, like other people in their host society, seek jobs and access to services—at least where they are allowed to do so.

A transformed environment for the development of host communities

By creating new challenges and new opportunities, the presence of refugees transforms the environment in which host communities are pursuing their own development efforts.[19] A combination of policy measures and investments is needed to mitigate the downside of hosting refugees, while taking advantage of the benefits their presence may generate.

The arrival of large numbers of refugees is often a disruptive shock for host communities. The consequences of this shock depend largely on the preexisting conditions, the number and composition of new arrivals, and the policy responses. The presence of refugees may exacerbate some preexisting challenges such as unemployment or inadequate services, or it may increase competition for natural resources.[20] It can also disproportionately affect some groups within the host society, including those who have similar qualifications or spending patterns and find themselves in competition with the refugees.[21]

The effects can be significant, depending on the initial conditions and on the government's and the international community's ability to respond at scale. For example, in Tanzania, following the arrival of half a million survivors of the Rwanda genocide in 1994, adverse health impacts were apparent in neighboring communities more than a year later, including a worsening of children's height, weight, body mass, and other anthropometrics; an increase in the incidence of infectious diseases (by 15–20 percentage points); and an increase in mortality for children under five (by 7 percentage points).[22] These impacts were caused in part by the spread of vector-borne and infectious diseases, combined with the overcrowding of sanitation infrastructure and health care facilities.

And yet the presence of refugees can also benefit host communities. For example, in Tanzania the abundance of refugee labor enabled farmers in host communities to double their cultivated areas between 1993 and 1996.[23] Some refugees use their assets to create enterprises and jobs, such as in Türkiye.[24] An influx of external assistance in previously underserved regions can also transform the economy. In northeast Kenya, local wages around the Dadaab refugee camp are reportedly 60 percent higher than in comparable parts of the country because of the greater economic activity generated in the camp by external assistance.[25]

Hosting costs that need to be managed

Because they move to seek safety, refugees do not always bring skills in demand at the destination. Most economic migrants seek a place where there is a demand for their work, but the logic of forced displacement is different: people flee to a safe place, often without regard for labor market considerations. If refugees have skills in demand in the host economy—and if they are allowed to work—their presence provides benefits that are similar to those offered by regular labor migrants,[26] and hosting them is beneficial to the host country. But many refugees do not have such skills or simply cannot work, such as children, persons with disabilities, or those suffering from trauma. Moreover, many end up in places where job opportunities are limited, usually in economically lagging areas of low- or middle-income economies close to the border. In some cases, refugees are even compelled to flee to other conflict-affected countries, such as Somali refugees to the Republic of Yemen. Refugees are denied the right to work in a number of host countries because these countries prioritize access to the labor market for citizens or want to deter further arrivals. In these situations, the economic benefits of labor mobility cannot materialize. Host societies thus need to absorb, even temporarily, large groups of people who cannot easily contribute to their economy.

Hosting refugees therefore often has costs, even though it is an obligation under international law. The challenge for the host country is to manage such costs. It can be achieved through a combination of efforts, such as (1) sharing the costs across the international community using effective responsibility-sharing arrangements; (2) reducing the costs (while preserving high standards of protection) by adopting and implementing adequate policies that go beyond emergency responses; and (3) making progress toward durable solutions—when refugees no longer have protection needs—including by exploring innovative schemes that combine both legal status and access to opportunities.

Such actions should be complemented by international action in the countries of origin to help mitigate the drivers of fragility and address the root causes of forced displacement. International actions include supporting peace, human rights, and the rule of law, as well as supporting durable solutions such as voluntary repatriation and reintegration.

Enhancing responsibility-sharing through regional solidarity

The costs—and potential benefits—of hosting are both economic and fiscal.[27] Hosting costs typically are short-term costs related to absorption of the shock caused by a large influx of people, as well as medium-term costs related to hosting refugees in more protracted situations. Economic costs emerge when large numbers of refugees are not able to engage in the host economy—for example, when a large share of the refugees are children, when refugees' skills are not consistent with the needs of the labor market, or when refugees are not allowed to work. Fiscal costs—government expenditures that must be financed through taxes or external aid—arise when refugees benefit from public services to which they are not contributing. Both economic and fiscal costs are closely linked to hosting policies.

These costs should not be borne by the host countries alone. The preamble of the 1951 Refugee Convention recognizes "that the grant of asylum may place unduly heavy burdens on certain countries" and that, due to the "international scope and nature" of the refugee problem, it could not be solved "without international co-operation."[28] It recommends "that Governments . . . act in concert in a true spirit of international co-operation in order that these refugees may find asylum and the possibility of resettlement."[29] This nonbinding framework does not *require* cooperation between states, but its objectives cannot be met without responsibility-sharing.

Addressing the challenge of responsibility-sharing is at the core of the 2018 Global Compact on Refugees (GCR). The GCR aims to "provide a basis for predictable and equitable burden- and responsibility-sharing" among states and other stakeholders.[30] Yet the lack of explicit legally binding rules defining the way in which states should fulfill the obligation to share responsibilities for hosting refugees creates uncertainty about how this global public good can be adequately provided.[31] This problem is at the core of the international refugee protection system.

The current limitations of responsibility-sharing

The responsibility-sharing challenge is acute because most refugees are hosted in a small number of countries—typically low- and middle-income countries bordering the countries of origin. As of mid-2022, about 52 percent of the world's refugees and other people in need of international protection were hosted in middle-income countries and 22 percent in low-income countries (figure 7.4).[32] Because of the protracted nature of forced displacement crises, many of the largest host countries have been hosting refugees for extended periods of time—for some, such as the Islamic Republic of Iran and Pakistan, more than four decades.

Over the years, an elaborate system of external assistance has been developed for high-income countries to support refugee-hosting low- and middle-income countries. As the numbers of refugees increase, however, this system has been challenged on multiple fronts:

- *Resource availability.* International financing in support of refugees and host communities has been estimated at 12.3 percent of all bilateral official development assistance (ODA) and 3.2 percent of multilateral development bank financing, for a total of US$46.7 billion over 2018 and 2019.[33] In light of the competing demands on external financing needs—on issues such as climate change, food security, and other development needs—these amounts are unlikely to be increased dramatically.
- *Narrow donor base.* External assistance rests on a small number of donors—with three (European Union institutions, Germany, and the United States) accounting for almost two-thirds of the total (figure 7.5).[34]
- *Effectiveness.* For the international community, the cost of supporting refugee-hosting in low- and middle-income countries is, on average, about US$585 per refugee per year—in addition to what these countries are spending directly. This is a substantial amount in view of the average

Figure 7.4 More than half of the world's refugees are hosted in middle-income countries

Share of refugees hosted, by country income group

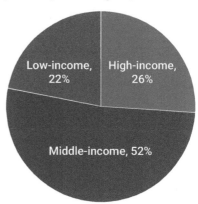

Source: UNHCR 2022b.

annual income per capita in 2019 of US$743 in low-income countries and US$5,499 in middle-income countries.[35]

- *Cross-country allocations.* External aid has also been unevenly distributed across refugee situations.[36] In 2018–19, about 43 percent of these resources was used for hosting refugees in high-income donor countries. Nearly all of the remaining amount was earmarked for specific countries or regions, of which almost half was directed to the Middle East. Some other host countries, such as Colombia, the Islamic Republic of Iran, Pakistan, and Sudan, were facing a "responsibility-sharing gap."

- *Emergency focus.* About 71 percent of external financing was provided through humanitarian financing in 2019, typically as a short-term response to urgent demands and often through a cycle of annual budgets.[37] This approach creates a mismatch between the needs—which are medium term and require predictable streams of resources—and the available funding. The reallocation of resources in 2022 to accommodate Ukrainian refugees following the Russian invasion is an example of the volatility of programming that leaves many host countries ambivalent about making medium-term commitments to improving refugee situations.

Resettlement, the other traditional form of responsibility-sharing, remains marginal in terms of numbers, even though it is politically important.[38] Refugees are "resettled" when they are offered a chance to move from a low- or middle-income host country to a high-income country where they will be integrated.[39] These programs have undeniably resulted in positive outcomes for refugees, but very few countries are involved in resettling refugees. In fact, almost three-quarters of all resettlement activity occurs in just four countries: Canada, Germany, Sweden, and the United States (figure 7.6).[40] Only 57,500 refugees were resettled in 2021, whereas more than 1.4 million refugees needed to be, according to UNHCR.[41] The low 2021 numbers partially reflected border and travel restrictions in response to the COVID-19 pandemic, but also a downward trend in resettlement options offered by states.

Figure 7.5 Three donors contribute almost two-thirds of all bilateral ODA to refugees

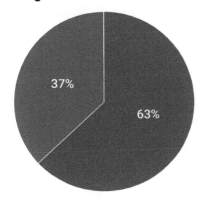

■ United States, Germany, EU institutions
■ All other countries

Source: OECD 2021.
Note: EU = European Union; ODA = official development assistance.

Figure 7.6 Four countries receive almost three-quarters of resettled refugees

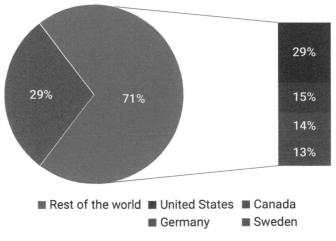

■ Rest of the world ■ United States ■ Canada
■ Germany ■ Sweden

Source: OECD 2021.

Beyond global approaches

Looking ahead, the priority is to strengthen aid effectiveness because the share of ODA available for refugee-related programs is unlikely to increase dramatically. This effort will require developing instruments that can provide medium-term resources in line with the protracted nature of many forced displacement situations (box 7.3). It can build on ongoing efforts to track financing, such as through the Development Assistance Committee (DAC) of the Organisation for Economic Co-operation and Development (OECD), thereby taking stock of spending and facilitating an informed allocation of funds across countries over time. This effort should support hosting policies that provide adequate international protection but also aim to lower the medium-term costs of doing so.

Meanwhile, the base of support for refugees and host communities must be broadened. Under the Global Compact on Refugees framework, responsibility-sharing can be implemented in various ways. They include addressing the underlying causes of displacement, enabling the resettlement of refugees, creating paths for the self-sufficiency of refugees and asylum-seekers, financing assistance and international protection programs, investing in technical assistance and capacity-building in host countries, hosting refugees and asylum-seekers, and improving internal and regional migratory policies.[42] The GCR also aims to broaden the range of partners involved, including development organizations, local authorities, the private sector, and civil society.[43] For example, leveraging new resources for support in refugee-hosting areas in the form of targeted private sector interventions can complement ODA. It is too early to assess how successful such arrangements will be, especially in view of the disruptions

Box 7.3 An example of development financing: IDA's Window for Host Communities and Refugees

Since 2017, the World Bank's financing arm for low-income countries, the International Development Association (IDA), has been providing low-income refugee-hosting countries with development resources over and above their country allocations. These resources, totaling about US$6 billion, help refugee-hosting countries (1) mitigate the shocks stemming from refugee inflows and create social and economic development opportunities for refugees and host communities; (2) facilitate sustainable solutions to protracted refugee situations, including through the sustainable socioeconomic inclusion of refugees in the host country or their return to the origin country; and (3) strengthen country preparedness for increased or new refugee flows. The resources have been deployed in over 17 low-income refugee-hosting countries across a variety of sectors, such as community development, education, health, and social protection.

The IDA Window for Host Communities and Refugees (WHR) provides predictable resources over a multiyear horizon, with a focus on supporting sound hosting policies. The WHR is closely linked to the international protection agenda. To be eligible for these resources, a refugee-hosting country must maintain an adequate protection framework, which is assessed in partnership with the United Nations High Commissioner for Refugees. The WHR also seeks to support and create incentives for government leadership by requiring authorities to develop a strategy for addressing refugee situations. In several countries, the WHR has been instrumental in expanding the policy dialogue to a range of sectoral ministries, such as health or education, beyond dedicated refugee agencies. It has also introduced the Refugee Policy Review Framework (RPRF), which takes stock of key refugee-related policies and provides a basis for coordination on policy reforms.

Source: IDA 2022.

produced by the COVID-19 pandemic. However, the first GCR "Indicator Report," issued in late 2021, noted that progress has been slow, and it may be further aggravated by the current fractures in the international community.[44]

Complementary forms of cooperation at the regional level are more promising. Most Latin American countries have worked together (including in the context of the Quito Process[45]) to develop a region-wide approach that can provide consistency across national responses in the face of the Venezuelan crisis. This approach has helped to lessen pressures on first-line countries, especially Colombia. A similar approach has been adopted by the European Union for refugees from Ukraine, helping to reduce the load on countries such as Moldova, Poland, and Romania.[46] Regional efforts are not limited to middle- or high-income contexts. In Africa, the Intergovernmental Authority on Development (IGAD) has helped develop a regional peer-to-peer process to gradually improve the management of refugee situations in the broader Horn of Africa.[47]

Responsibility-sharing can also be advanced through broader bilateral or multilateral negotiations, such as on trade access.[48] In Jordan, the government agreed to provide more than 200,000 Syrian refugees with access to job opportunities in the form of work permits and grant them the right to access public education. As part of a responsibility-sharing scheme—the Jordan Compact—the European Union provided the country with grants, loans, and preferential trade and investment agreements for certain products from Jordanian businesses in which at least 15 percent of workers were Syrian refugees. However, the actual amount of new investments and the actual number of work permits delivered were somewhat below expectations, in part because of the need to ramp up administrative delivery mechanisms (for example, Syrians were working even without work permits) and in part because refugees were limited to formally working only in designated low-skilled sectors.[49] The Jordan Compact was followed by a similar scheme in Ethiopia in which the country received significant external financing to develop new industrial zones as part of an effort to create jobs also accessible to refugees.[50] Such initiatives can help improve the social and political environment for refugee protection.

Going beyond emergency responses

Because refugee situations almost always last for years, "hosting policies" should be financially and socially sustainable. Decisions made at the onset of a refugee crisis—such as where to accommodate refugees and what status to give them—often set a dependency path that can have long-term implications for both the refugees and the host communities. Tanzania is an extreme case. In the initial rush to accommodate large numbers of Burundi refugees in the 1970s, Tanzania established camps miles away from water sources. As a result, water had to be trucked to the camps for almost 40 years at a considerable cost.[51] There is no evidence that hosting policies that take a medium-term planning horizon create incentives for refugees to extend their stay. In fact, they provide a way to minimize costs if the situation becomes protracted.

Successful responses to an influx of refugees enable them to find jobs and obtain services. Examples of responses that reduced the host country's medium-term needs for financial support as well as major social tensions include Türkiye's hosting of Syrian refugees,[52] the welcoming of large numbers of Venezuelans by Colombia and other countries in Latin America,[53] and the efforts of the European Union to respond to the flight of millions of Ukrainians.[54]

These responses have three main elements (figure 7.7): (1) permitting internal mobility for refugees to lessen pressures on host regions and foster self-reliance (the more refugees are dispersed, the smaller their impact on communities in areas of first arrival); (2) supporting self-reliance and access to the labor market to reduce the financial and social costs of "enforced idleness" (the more refugees can work, the

Figure 7.7 In responding to refugee inflows, host countries should aim for medium-term sustainability—financial and social

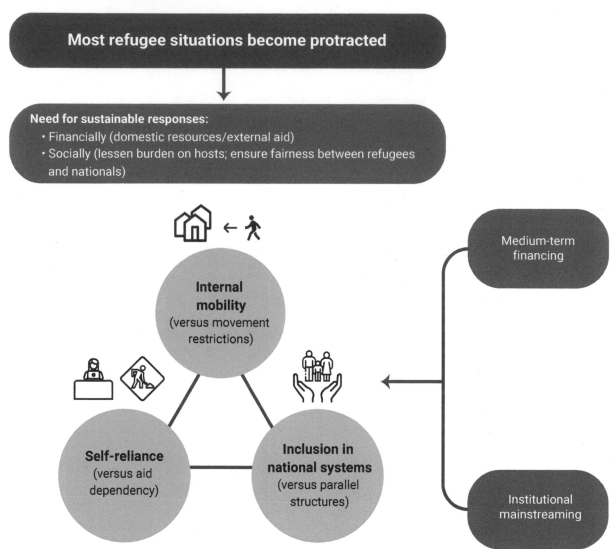

Most refugee situations become protracted

Need for sustainable responses:
- Financially (domestic resources/external aid)
- Socially (lessen burden on hosts; ensure fairness between refugees and nationals)

Internal mobility (versus movement restrictions)

Self-reliance (versus aid dependency)

Inclusion in national systems (versus parallel structures)

Medium-term financing

Institutional mainstreaming

Source: WDR 2023 team.

less they need assistance and the lower the costs);[55] and (3) delivering services through national systems (such as health and education) to ensure refugees' welfare and fair treatment between refugees and nationals while minimizing costs (parallel structures are typically costlier than national ones).

Why are such medium-term approaches not being used more often? The problem may be a lack of incentives and a bias toward the short term. Most international assistance is delivered in the form of humanitarian aid, which has short-term horizons for planning and delivery. But a medium-term approach often requires medium-term financial commitments from donors and host communities to, notably, include refugees in national health and education systems. Financing instruments that can provide predictable resources over a long horizon are thus critical.[56]

Institutional arrangements matter as well. For example, autonomous "refugee agencies" set up at the request of international partners and attached to a country's security apparatus may have a vested interest in adopting a short-term perspective centered on legal and security considerations.[57] By contrast, some countries have established light coordination structures to promote a comprehensive socioeconomic approach implemented across sectoral ministries. That is, for example, the approach used by the Border Management Office, Gerencia de la Frontera, in Colombia, which works with sectoral ministries to provide refugees with services within the scope of their sectors, such as education or health care. Institutional arrangements have to be adapted to each context, including in view of the host country's overall administrative capacity. In some contexts, institutional arrangements can also include a preparedness element (box 7.4).

Box 7.4 Preparedness is critical when refugee situations are predictable or chronic

Refugee movements are not always unpredictable crises. In some countries, refugee inflows have, unfortunately, become regular events. For example, in 23 of the last 30 years Chad has received new refugee inflows from its neighbors. Ethiopia and Uganda are similarly experiencing frequent episodes of large-scale arrivals. And Pakistan and the Islamic Republic of Iran have seen a succession of partial returns and new arrivals of Afghan refugees since 1979. In other countries such as República Bolivariana de Venezuela, the crises that generate displacements build slowly, and so do their effects.

In such situations, medium-term planning can help countries better prepare for possible refugee movements by putting in place institutional and financial arrangements to better absorb the shocks. For example, countries can make contingency plans to deploy civil servants and medical staff to affected areas should a refugee crisis arise. They can identify possible locations and solutions to accommodate large numbers of people in ways that would minimize the long-term financial and social impacts should the refugee situation last. They can also consider prearranged mechanisms that can be activated in crises to transfer additional resources to affected municipalities.

Experience with the management of other crises has shown that preparedness—planning, institutional arrangements, and prepositioned resources—can yield disproportionate benefits. Examples are Japan's and Mexico's programs to mitigate the impacts of earthquakes[a] and Ethiopia's scalable safety net to respond to drought.[b] The preparedness agenda has remained relatively less developed in the context of refugee movements, but some countries, such as Uganda, have begun to consider the steps they could take to better plan and respond to possible movements.

a. Takemoto, Shibuya, and Sakoda (2021).
b. Productive Safety Net Programme in Ethiopia (dashboard), Capacity4dev, European Commission, Brussels, https://europa .eu/capacity4dev/project_psnp_ethiopia.

Internal mobility

Despite provisions for freedom of movement in the 1951 Refugee Convention, one-third of refugees cannot move freely in their host country.[58] Some 22 percent live in camps, where they are often subject to significant restrictions on their movements, such as being barred from leaving the camp or having to submit an administrative request to do so.[59] Even when refugees live outside of camps, their movements can be restricted—for example, if they live in remote regions.

Such mobility restrictions hurt refugees and host communities alike. For refugees, being able to move to locations where there are opportunities is critical to finding a job. Denmark, Sweden, and other European countries learned that placing refugees or asylum-seekers in areas with fewer economic opportunities and restricting their ability to relocate to other areas curtailed employment outcomes.[60] A lack of economic opportunities where refugees reside makes self-reliance an elusive goal, and they remain largely dependent on external assistance at a high cost for the host government and the donor community.

Host communities are negatively affected as well. Mobility restrictions concentrate refugees in relatively small areas, where they typically make up a large share of the population. Such arrangements amplify the impacts on host communities, and they significantly increase the need for government and external assistance. For example, the Rohingya in Bangladesh (referred to as Forcibly Displaced Myanmar Nationals) account for less than 0.6 percent of the country's population but about a third of the total population in the Cox's Bazar district where they are hosted.[61]

In the face of such realities, some countries have, with promising results, introduced a "hosting model" that permits internal mobility. For example, Ethiopia recently adopted "out of camp" policies intended to permit and facilitate movements by refugees in protracted situations. Many of the recent large inflows are managed along similar lines. In Türkiye, Syrian refugees have been granted the right to move freely across large parts of the country, and they have moved to economically stronger regions where they can sustain themselves with minimal assistance and contribute to the economy (map 7.1). In some cases, mobility has also been allowed across entire regions, such as for Venezuelans across Latin American countries[62] and more recently for Ukrainians within the European Union.[63]

Internal mobility has the potential to dramatically change the way refugee crises are managed. It reduces the mismatches between the skills that refugees bring and the demands of the labor market by allowing refugees to access more opportunities. And it allows them to make larger contributions to

Map 7.1 By allowing refugees to move within Türkiye, the government reduced the impact on communities in areas of first arrival along the border with Syria

Ratio of refugees to nationals, by region

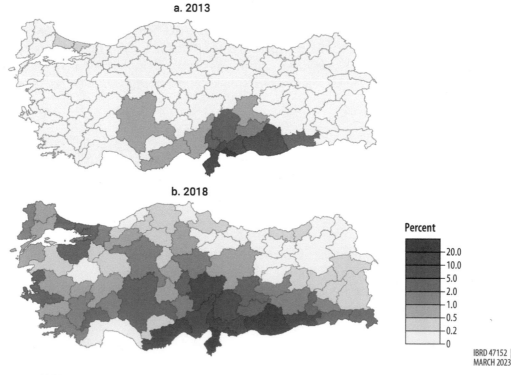

Source: Tumen 2023.

the local economy. Meanwhile, it dramatically reduces the adverse impacts on the communities in areas of first arrival—in terms of jobs, prices, services, infrastructure,[64] and social cohesion—by reducing the share of refugees in their population.[65]

Internal mobility also has implications for the way international support is provided. External financing continues to be needed, but often in the form of policy support rather than investment projects as refugees are dispersed across a larger area.[66] At times, the very definition of *host community* needs to be reconsidered—from a typically rural area where refugees account for a large share of the community to an urban neighborhood where they represent only a fraction of the population. Providing legal protection to refugees when they are living across the host country's entire territory may also require strengthening capacity in the executive and judiciary as the ability of national institutions to implement legal protection provisions becomes crucial.

Self-reliance and access to the labor market

Refugees' self-reliance and access to the labor market are critical elements of sustainability—both financially and socially. When refugees remain dependent on aid programs, there are high costs in terms of aid, social tensions, and dignity, whether the aid is financed by host governments or foreign donors. Some host countries have thus encouraged refugees to become self-sustaining. For example, in Uganda refugee households with a farming background are given a plot of land to cultivate, although the size of such plots has become smaller as refugee numbers have grown over time.

Medium-term economic outcomes for refugees depend on how quickly they receive a legal status after arrival. Many host countries have processes to deal with new asylum claims and to determine who should be granted refugee status, while others do not. In some contexts, refugee status is immediately granted *prima facie*—that is, to all persons coming from a specific country of origin regardless of their individual circumstances. But in many other contexts asylum-seekers must go through a years-long process to be recognized as refugees—or not. The wait has adverse development consequences. Indeed, extended periods of forced unemployment impede refugees' longer-term integration into the labor market.[67] In Switzerland, for example, between 1994 and 2004 one additional year of waiting reduced refugees' subsequent employment rate by 16–23 percent, compared with the average.[68] Enabling refugees' labor market participation from a very early stage—even while they are applying for asylum—can yield positive long-term results.[69]

For those who receive refugee status, the duration of the status is important. Secure, predictable terms of stay accelerate refugees' path to self-reliance. They provide a degree of stability that facilitates their getting a job and incentivizes them to make investments—such as in learning a new language or opening a business—that benefit host communities as well.[70] In Colombia, for example, in 2018 a large amnesty program granted legal status, including access to an employment permit, to approximately half a million undocumented Venezuelans. The program increased their income by 31 percent, consumption by 60 percent, and labor formalization rates by 10 percentage points,[71] with minimal effects on the formal employment of Colombian workers (also see box 7.6 later in this chapter).[72] By contrast, in Pakistan Afghan refugees must renew their Proof of Registration Card (their certification of refugee status) every year, which creates significant uncertainty.[73]

The right to work is necessary—but often not sufficient. Although the 1951 Refugee Convention upholds the importance of giving refugees the legal right to work on the same basis as other foreign nationals, only 75 of the 145 signatories grant this right without reservations.[74] Even then, refugees can face administrative or practical barriers in many countries such as the need for work permits,[75] caps on the percentage of foreign workers, exclusion from some sectors, wait periods, and limited access to financial services. As a result, more than 55 percent of refugees live in a country that restricts their right to work,[76] and many can only access informal jobs.[77]

Those countries that grant refugees the right *to work* typically also grant them rights *at work,* including minimum standards and conditions.[78] Yet because refugees often have an insecure legal status and lack knowledge of local regulations and language skills, they may still be subject to exploitation, harassment, abuse, or underpayment in the workplace. Complementary measures will, then, be needed for refugees to access economic opportunities. Among other things, being able to access personal identification documents, to open a bank account, to have a driver's license, or to purchase cellular phone service are critical to labor market participation.[79] Some countries have also put in place programs dedicated to supporting refugees' economic inclusion, such as direct job matching, counseling by public employment services, language instruction, acquisition of soft skills, or technical training.[80]

Yet even where refugees are allowed to work, it takes them years to close the employment or wage gaps with nationals, as well as with economic migrants.[81] Refugees often start behind economic migrants in employment outcomes and wages.[82] Because they move primarily for safety reasons, many are hosted in areas where their skills and attributes poorly match the labor needs. Some refugees must also overcome trauma experienced in their country of origin and during their journey, which affects their ability to thrive in the labor market.[83] They therefore tend to have more precarious working conditions and to rely more on unearned income in the form of public transfers or remittances in host countries such as Ethiopia, Jordan, and Uganda (figure 7.8).

Figure 7.8 Refugees depend more on transfers and work under more precarious conditions than their hosts

Comparison of primary income sources for refugees and their hosts

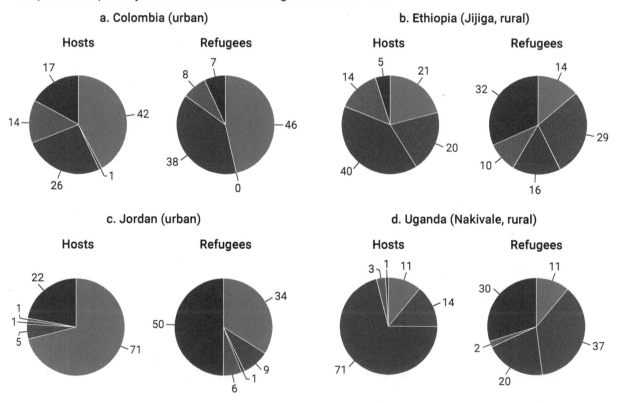

■ Wage work ■ Casual, precarious labor ■ Self-employment ■ Remittances ■ Aid, other official transfers

Sources: von der Goltz and Schuettler 2022; World Bank 2023.

Note: The figure compares the primary income sources of refugees and their hosts. The findings for Colombia are for those displaced from República Bolivariana de Venezuela, and the findings for Jordan are for Syrian refugees.

The private sector has the potential to create jobs and other income-generating activities for refugees and host communities. Various private actors, however, have distinct incentives, capacities, and limitations in refugee-hosting situations. For example, large multinational firms can command sizable investments, but they also require infrastructure and a sound business climate. National companies, which may also be able to invest large resources, typically concentrate on regions where they are already present or that have a demonstrated potential to grow. By contrast, small and medium enterprises are often more nimble and able to adapt in refugee-hosting environments, but they also often find it more difficult to access financing. Support of the private sector's engagement in refugee settings thus needs to be tailored to the specifics of each situation.

Overall, in many countries the private sector's engagement is still at a nascent stage.[84] Large private investments in lagging refugee-hosting areas have yet to materialize at scale. Often these areas have little infrastructure, access to energy, or markets. The potential of the private sector is higher in countries where the business environment is strong and where refugees can move and have unhindered access to jobs, such as in Colombia and Poland. Targeted interventions, such as those to attract Kenyan banks to the Kakuma refugee camp and neighboring towns[85] or to enroll refugees in microfinance programs of "graduation," have yet to be scaled up. To attract additional resources, support may be needed, possibly in the form of blended finance for risk-sharing facilities, performance-based incentives, or other de-risking instruments to make investment in refugee-hosting areas profitable.

Inclusion in national services

The COVID-19 pandemic demonstrated the importance of refugees' access to social services.[86] It especially highlighted the public health benefits of ensuring that refugees can access adequate health services for prevention and care.[87] The spread of infectious diseases in overcrowded refugee settlements can indeed impair the health of the host population as well.[88]

The pandemic also revealed the impacts that interruptions in schooling can have on learning, particularly for vulnerable groups—long a reality for many refugee children.[89] Indeed, although children make up almost half of all refugees, only 77 percent are enrolled in primary schools and only 31 percent in secondary school, which is well below global averages.[90] Consequently, the literacy and learning outcomes for refugee children tend to be low.[91] The risk is that many children will become part of a "lost generation," with possible destabilizing effects on their countries of origin or destination.

Overall, many refugees are extremely vulnerable and need social assistance over longer periods.[92] For example, one in four Syrian refugees in Sultanbeyli, Türkiye, has a disability, and 60 percent of households include at least one person with a disability.[93] Even with access to the labor market, these refugees are unlikely to become fully self-reliant in the short to medium term. Financial resources and dedicated institutional structures are needed to support them and other highly vulnerable groups, such as unaccompanied and separated children, victims of trafficking, and survivors of gender-based violence. Support needs to be provided in financially sustainable ways, but also with a view toward ensuring that the treatment of refugees and nationals with similar vulnerabilities does not differ unfairly.

The modalities of service delivery for refugees vary significantly across host countries, whether national systems, parallel structures, or a combination. In some countries such as the Islamic Republic of Iran, South Africa, Sweden, and Uganda, refugees can access national health systems and services under the same conditions as nationals. In other countries, refugees obtain basic health care services through parallel health care systems funded and run by external actors such as charities, nongovernmental organizations (NGOs), and international organizations such as UNHCR and the International Organization for Migration.[94] Similarly, country models that deliver services in the education sector or social support to the most vulnerable refugees also differ. These services are often provided through externally financed systems that are not part of national structures—typically through NGOs.

Integrating refugees into functioning national systems—for education, health, and social protection—can improve financial sustainability and fairness with nationals in access and quality. In some countries, typically lower-income, the externally financed services offered to refugees may be superior to those that can be accessed by nationals, although at a high cost. In other countries, refugees have access only to inferior systems.[95] Such differences result in unequal outcomes, and they may create tensions between refugees and their hosts. Dependence on external financing has also raised concerns about the sustainability of such approaches. External financing is typically provided through emergency assistance with a one-year time horizon and can be withdrawn as new emergencies arise. A more sustainable approach entails including refugees in national service delivery systems, as well as strengthening these systems and establishing dedicated programs where needed such as for trauma recovery or language acquisition.[96] This approach is being implemented in Colombia[97] and Türkiye,[98] as well as in the European Union.[99]

Inclusion in national systems implies medium-term commitments for the host country. It has two key requirements: predictable financing and mainstreamed institutional arrangements. Governments need to have access to financing arrangements that provide a degree of predictability and confidence that resources will be available beyond the short term. Sizable amounts of external financing may be needed to scale up and maintain national systems in refugee-hosting regions, especially in countries where services are already strained for nationals.[100] But these amounts may not be out of reach, especially when compared with the potential social and economic benefits. For example, a recent report estimated the global cost of including refugee children in national education systems at US$4.9 billion a year.[101] In addition, institutional arrangements are needed to allow engagement of the relevant technical ministries—education, health, and social protection—in support of refugees. However, such arrangements are often not easy to put in place, especially when they entail transferring to sectoral ministries responsibilities and competencies that belong to specialized agencies connected to the national security apparatus.

Making progress toward durable solutions by combining legal status and access to opportunities

The ultimate objective of international support is to help refugees find durable solutions that will end their need for international protection. Many refugee-hosting countries are willing to provide international protection, but with the understanding that the protection will be time-limited. For that reason, political leaders in refugee-hosting countries often emphasize the need for durable solutions at scale, and any discussion of durable solutions to forced displacement ought to incorporate the concerns of host countries.

A dearth of durable solutions

A durable solution—the point at which refugees no longer need international protection—is often defined from a legal viewpoint. Put simply, refugees are entitled to international protection because they cannot rely on the protection of their country of citizenship, typically because of conflict or persecution. They are refugees until they can regain guarantees of sustainable, long-term protection by a state. This state can be (1) the state of origin (return or voluntary repatriation and reintegration); (2) the state of asylum (local integration and, in some cases, naturalization); or (3) a third state (resettlement). To conform to international law, each of these solutions, including return, needs to be achieved on a voluntary basis in line with human rights norms.[102]

Figure 7.9 The share of refugees who achieve a durable solution has been very low over the last 15 years

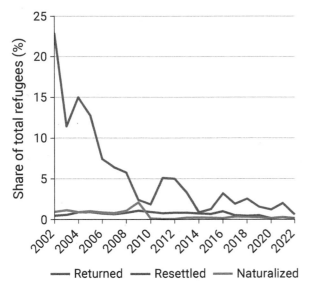

Source: WDR 2023 team, based on 2022 data from Refugee Data Finder (dashboard), United Nations High Commissioner for Refugees, Geneva, https://popstats.unhcr.org/refugee-statistics/download/.

Note: Refugees include those under the mandate of the United Nations High Commissioner for Refugees (UNHCR).

Figure 7.10 The number of refugees continues to grow as new entries (recognitions) outpace exits

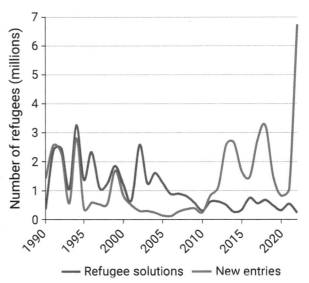

Source: WDR 2023 team, based on 2022 data from Refugee Data Finder (dashboard), United Nations High Commissioner for Refugees, Geneva, https://popstats.unhcr.org/refugee-statistics/download/.

Note: Refugees include those under the mandate of the United Nations High Commissioner for Refugees (UNHCR).

The share of refugees who have attained a durable solution in recent years is extremely low. From 2012 to 2022, it averaged 2 percent and never exceeded 4 percent of the total number of refugees. In 2021, in part because of COVID-19 restrictions, the average share fell to 1 percent (figure 7.9). As UNHCR has noted, "durable solutions have . . . become an option for fewer and fewer refugees."[103] In fact, the number of new refugees has outpaced solutions every year since 2010 (figure 7.10).

The dearth of durable solutions is a reason behind the steady increase in the number of refugees and in the number of years people spend in exile with little hope of reestablishing themselves. It has also resulted in some refugees engaging in high-risk irregular movements. In 2017, for example, 21 percent of asylum-seekers entering Italy and 25 percent of those entering Greece were onward movers—people who moved because of the lack of prospects for a resolution of their situation and the lack of opportunity in their initial host country.[104]

The complexity of decision-making

The conceptual simplicity of the durable solutions framework does not fully account for the complexity of refugees' lives and decision-making. Any change in their situation, especially if associated with a new movement, can be risky for refugees. With their memories of past trials and their limited resources, they are unlikely to take such risks readily or easily.[105]

The simple notion of return or voluntary repatriation (box 7.5) or of local integration does not align neatly with some patterns of forced displacement. For example, in some cases large numbers of refugees

Box 7.5 Return: Homecoming or new movement?

Return is often regarded as the most natural solution for forced displacement. Refugees are viewed as "out of place," and so return to their origin country is thought to be a way of restoring the natural order of things. Meanwhile, it is often assumed that refugees want to repatriate.[a] Return is discussed in terms of a return "home," even after a generation in exile and although descendants of the original refugees may never have seen their "homeland." For example, about three-quarters of Afghan refugees in Pakistan were born there.[b]

The decision to repatriate is more complex than just contemplating a homecoming or a return to a pre-existing order.[c] The place of origin has often undergone wrenching social, economic, and political changes since a refugee's departure. Refugees may have changed as well. Women may have acquired more rights; children born in exile may not be literate in the language of the country of origin; and youth may have adopted new norms and values. For some refugees, memories of the conflict that prompted their exile and of a time in which the government, neighbors, and friends became their most feared enemies remain overwhelming. Under such circumstances, the "reconnecting" is often complex, and return may be experienced as a new movement rather than as going back to the status quo ante. Some returns resemble more a new movement than a homecoming.

Not all returns have a happy ending. Many returning refugees continue to struggle for a long time after their return. Women and girls often face particular challenges on return, especially when they have fewer opportunities, fewer resources, lower status, and less power and influence than men in their country of origin.[d] For example in Afghanistan large numbers of returnees have become internally displaced persons (IDPs)—that is, not only did they not return to their place of origin, but their new situation is so insecure that they need continued assistance and protection. Between 2000 and 2015, 46 percent of large-scale returns were matched by a sizable increase in the number of IDPs.[e] Returnees may even have to flee again, as refugees or irregular migrants, after returning to their country of origin. Multiple instances of repeated back-and-forth movements have been observed in and from, for example, Afghanistan, Myanmar, Somalia, and South Sudan.[f] Of the 15 largest instances of return since 1991, about one-third were followed within a couple of years by a new round of conflict.[g]

Policy makers should therefore focus not just on migrants' return, but on their *successful* or *sustainable* return—that is, ensuring that people can reestablish themselves in a stable manner that precludes the need for further movement. Such an approach is in the interest of refugee-hosting countries as well. Although the prevailing security, legal, and economic conditions in areas of return are an important factor,[h] individual circumstances also matter greatly. Refugees are more likely to repatriate successfully where they have portable assets (such as capital to rebuild their homes and to provide a cushion in case of adverse developments) and marketable skills.[i] The extent to which life in exile provides space to build assets and skills can therefore be critical to a successful return.

Source: Adapted from World Bank (2017).

a. Lomax (2018).
b. Bakewell (2000); Hammond (1999, 2014).
c. Black and Koser (1999); Monsutti (2008); Omata (2013).
d. Bascom (2005); Harild, Christensen, and Zetter (2015).
e. Calculations are based on United Nations High Commissioner for Refugees (UNHCR) data for refugees and Internal Displacement Monitoring Centre (IDMC) data for IDPs. See Global Internal Displacement Database, Internal Displacement Monitoring Centre, Geneva, https://www.internal-displacement.org/database/displacement-data; Refugee Data Finder (dashboard), United Nations High Commissioner for Refugees, Geneva, https://popstats.unhcr.org/refugee-statistics/download/.
f. World Bank (2017).
g. This estimate is based on UNHCR return data as of the end of 2014. Examples of return followed by renewed bouts of conflict include Afghanistan (returns in 2001–05); Burundi (returns in 1996–97); Democratic Republic of Congo (returns in 1997–98); Iraq (returns in 2003–05); and Somalia (returns in 1993–95). See Refugee Data Finder (dashboard), United Nations High Commissioner for Refugees, Geneva, https://popstats.unhcr.org/refugee-statistics/download/.
h. Alrababa'h et al. (2023); Beaman, Onder, and Onder (2022).
i. Omata (2013); Stepputat (2004).

were temporary migrants in the host country before the conflict broke out in their country of origin, such as some Syrian workers in Lebanon. What changed with the conflict was not their location, but their ability to return to their country of origin safely and the arrival of their families. Some refugee movements are also part of complex family strategies or iterative processes,[106] including split families or cyclical return, with some household members moving back and forth between their place of origin and a place of exile. This practice is, for example, adopted by some Somali refugees.[107]

Trade-offs and tensions

In looking for a durable solution, many refugees may behave in part like economic migrants. Refugees have distinct needs for international protection and specific vulnerabilities, but they share migrants' desire and economic need for a better life. Accessing economic opportunities—jobs and services—is critical to reconstituting lost assets, overcoming trauma, and restoring a planning horizon, which are essential to people's recovery. Thus for many refugees, accessing a durable solution means securing two essentials—a durable legal status and effective access to economic opportunities. The difficulty in combining these two elements may be at the root of the difficulties encountered in resolving many forced displacement situations (figure 7.11).

For many refugees, it can be hard to both acquire a durable (nonrefugee) legal status and access economic opportunities in the same country. In the absence of naturalization or resettlement at scale, the only way to obtain a durable legal status is often to return to the country of origin. But where conflicts or political crises are protracted, return may not be possible. Even when the security situation has settled, there are often few economic opportunities for returning refugees. On the other hand, staying in their host country or moving on (even irregularly) may provide refugees with economic opportunities, but not necessarily a longer-term formal legal status.

In some situations, then, refugees may have to choose between achieving a durable solution from a legal perspective and accessing economic opportunities. At least in some cases, some refugees may prioritize access to economic opportunities over legal status, in the same way that many irregular migrants do.

Figure 7.11 **The tension between legal status and economic opportunities lies at the root of the difficulties in resolving refugee situations**

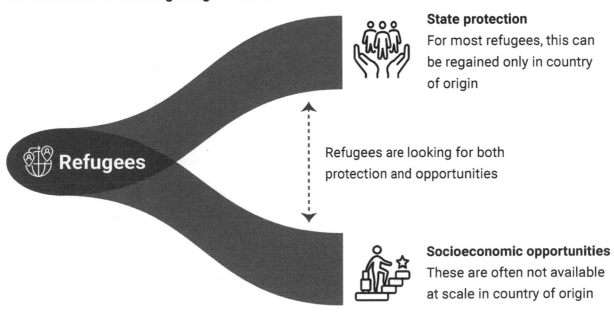

State protection
For most refugees, this can be regained only in country of origin

Refugees are looking for both protection and opportunities

Socioeconomic opportunities
These are often not available at scale in country of origin

Source: WDR 2023 team.

Innovative approaches

Policy makers could ease this tension by emphasizing more intermediate solutions that fall short of permanent state protection (citizenship with formal political membership and associated rights) but provide long-term residency (economic and social inclusion) in places with economic opportunities. In other words, citizenship in one country is combined with residency in another to form an intermediate solution. This arrangement could alleviate some of the host countries' concerns about national identity and the political implications of a long-term stay.[108]

Several approaches offer some innovative ways of moving forward, including for some of the ongoing protracted situations, although responses must ensure access to protection and rights and be tailored to each set of circumstances and support provided where needed:

- *Regional freedom of movement.* In West Africa, the Economic Community of West African States (ECOWAS) adopted a protocol in 1979 that granted citizens of ECOWAS countries the right to enter and live in any of the member states under some conditions.[109] Although implementation has lagged because of a host of institutional, political, economic, and legal challenges,[110] the arrangement is an alternative for some of those who flee conflict and violence, and it allows them to secure residence without naturalization and for as long as they deem it necessary.[111]

- *Shift to labor migration status.* Offering the option to access a labor migration status that falls short of naturalization but provides socioeconomic rights in a predictable manner may allow progress in some situations. For Afghans, for example, the only option for residing legally in Pakistan is refugee status, even for those whose motivations are mainly economic. Before the Taliban takeover of Afghanistan in 2021, the government of Pakistan was on its way to adopting a reform to enable Afghan nationals to access labor migration status instead of having to request refugee status.[112] External monitoring would be needed to ensure that such arrangements do not undermine the provision of international protection for those who need it.

- *Complementary pathways.* These legal channels allow refugees to obtain regular entry to and residency in third countries as complementary channels to the refugee resettlement process.[113] This option may involve education or labor mobility programs (such as for Syrian students in Portugal under the Global Platform for Syrian Students),[114] as well as private sector or community sponsorship. For example, for over 40 years Canada has allowed private groups (composed of Canadian citizens or residents or community sponsors such as associations or corporations) to identify and sponsor refugees for their settlement in Canada.[115] Sponsors provide refugees with settlement and financial support, in partnership with local service providers, for at least 12 months.[116] The process of identifying complementary pathways could be accelerated by helping refugees build skills that can be transferred globally so they can better match the labor needs of destination economies, possibly through Global Skills Partnerships.[117]

- *Long-term nonrefugee status.* The government of Colombia recently adopted a host of measures aimed at providing Venezuelan nationals with a 10-year horizon during which they can enjoy extensive socioeconomic rights.[118] They could then achieve a degree of recovery and contribute to the economy of the host community, even in the absence of a long-term durable solution (box 7.6).

Box 7.6 Creating better outcomes through integration: Lessons from Colombia

Over the last few years, Colombia has become the primary destination for Venezuelans fleeing their country. As of August 2022, an estimated 2.8 million Venezuelans (51 percent of whom were women) were living in Colombia.[a] They accounted for about one-third of all Venezuelans hosted across Latin America. In the face of a large-scale influx, the Colombian government gradually implemented a range of measures to manage the situation.

How did the government respond?

After the expulsion and return of 22,000 Colombians from República Bolivariana de Venezuela in 2015, the government provided humanitarian support, such as shelters, emergency health care, pediatrics, and vaccination services. In parallel, it developed institutional arrangements to ensure the coherence of local and national interventions.

From 2017 on, as increasing numbers of Venezuelans crossed the border, the government introduced several regulatory schemes. The Tarjeta de Movilidad Fronteriza (TMF), Border Mobility Card, was established to give access to border areas for up to seven days. It has been used by Venezuelans who cross the border in search of food or consumption goods not available at home. Five humanitarian assistance routes (Ruta del Caminante) were established for those who sought to transit through Colombia to more distant destinations. A special regularization scheme was launched to grant a temporary permit of stay and access to social services to Venezuelans residing in Colombia.

The 2018 Strategy for the Response to Migration from Venezuela (CONPES 3950)[b] confirmed the government's commitment to improving institutional mobilization and coordination across the relevant ministries and agencies. The Border Management Office (Gerencia de Frontera) was established within the presidency to coordinate efforts. Roundtables were set up with local authorities. In parallel, children born in Colombia to Venezuelan parents were granted Colombian citizenship so they would not be stateless (an estimated 78,000 minors had benefited as of May 2022). The government also granted Venezuelans access to the national health and education systems irrespective of their migration status, and it extended services provided by the Colombian Institute for Family Welfare (ICBF) to Venezuelan households.

The July 2022 Strategy for the Integration of the Venezuelan Population (CONPES 4100)[c] goes one step further by aiming to support the social and economic integration of Venezuelans and to harness their contribution to Colombia's development and prosperity over the next 10 years. For example, the government began to grant temporary protected status to Venezuelans. Estatuto Temporal de Protección para Migrantes Venezolanos (ETPV) is a process for the accelerated registration and regularization of migrants. Venezuelans possessing ETPV status are eligible for national subsidies and services under the same conditions as Colombians, such as access to health care and social security services. More than 814,000 Venezuelans were registered to receive such services as of July 2022. This process has helped to equalize opportunities for medium- and long-term integration.

Although many challenges remain to fully implementing these policies, they have already had positive effects. Consumption per capita among regularized Venezuelans is between 31 and 60 percent higher than among those who are irregular. Once regularized, Venezuelans' employment in the formal sector increased by 10 percent and incomes by up to 31 percent. Meanwhile, mass regularization has had only negligible effects on the formal employment of national workers.[d]

(Box continues next page)

Box 7.6 Creating better outcomes through integration: Lessons from Colombia *(continued)*

What has worked?

Many lessons have emerged from Colombia's experience:

- *Multitier approach*. The parallel execution of measures that follow different time frames and objectives—short term to provide humanitarian aid; medium term to provide access to basic social services; and long term to support regularization and socioeconomic integration—has allowed the government to respond to the needs of displaced persons within its limited capacity and resources.
- *Status and inclusion*. Granting regular migratory status using clear terms and procedures—whether through refugee status, regular migration pathways, or extraordinary regularization schemes—has proved critical and beneficial to both Venezuelans and Colombia. Similarly, the integration of Venezuelans in the regular labor force and in national systems for service delivery has been positive.
- *Institutional arrangements*. The establishment of institutional, legal, and policy frameworks that enable systematic and integrated responses has allowed rapid progress.
- *Proactive support of social cohesion*. Promoting social cohesion and addressing xenophobia and discrimination though a communications strategy have yielded positive results.
- *Responsibility-sharing*. Responsibility-sharing—in particular, across Latin America—has proved key, including through regional approaches.

Source: Rossiasco et al. 2023.

a. Alvarez et al. (2022).

b. DNP (2018).

c. DNP (2022).

d. Ibáñez et al., "Salir de la sombra" (2022).

Notes

1. UNHCR (2010, 3).
2. UNHCR (2011).
3. United Nations (1952, 29).
4. UNHCR (2021e).
5. Refugee Data Finder (dashboard), United Nations High Commissioner for Refugees, Geneva, https://popstats.unhcr.org/refugee-statistics/download/.
6. Ukraine Refugee Situation (dashboard), Operational Data Portal, data version of February 22, 2023, United Nations High Commissioner for Refugees, Geneva, https://data.unhcr.org/en/situations/ukraine.
7. Devictor and Do (2017).
8. UNHCR (2004, 2022b).
9. UNHCR Master Glossary of Terms (dashboard), United Nations High Commissioner for Refugees, Geneva, https://www.unhcr.org/glossary/. *Protracted refugee situations* are defined as those in which 25,000 or more refugees from the same country of origin have been in exile for at least five consecutive years.
10. UNHCR (2022b).
11. World Bank (2017).
12. World Bank (2017).
13. World Bank (2017).
14. For physical health, see Cuadrado, Libuy, and Moreno-Serra (2023); Giuntella et al. (2018); Verme et al. (2016); WHO (2022). For mental health, see Blackmore et al. (2020); Fazel, Wheeler, and Danesh (2005); Lindert et al. (2009); Porter and Haslam (2005).
15. Becker and Ferrara (2019); Brell, Dustmann, and Preston (2020); Schuettler and Caron (2020).
16. See World Bank (2019).
17. "Share of Unaccompanied Minors in the Total Number of First-Time Applicant Children in the EU, 2011–2021," Statistical Office of the European Communities, Luxembourg, https://ec.europa.eu/eurostat/statistics-explained/images/3/31/F9_Share_of_unaccompanied_minors_in_the_total_number_of_first-time_applicant_children_in_the_EU%2C_2011-2021_%28%25%29.png.

18. 1951 Convention: Chapter III (right to work), Chapter IV (access to public services), Article 26 (freedom of movement). See United Nations (1952).
19. Becker and Ferrara (2019); Verme and Schuettler (2021); World Bank (2017).
20. Rozo and Sviatschi (2021).
21. Aksu, Erzan, and Kırdar (2022); Becker and Ferrara (2019); Olivieri et al. (2022); Verme and Schuettler (2021).
22. Báez (2011).
23. World Bank (2017, 49).
24. Altındağ, Bakış, and Rozo (2020).
25. World Bank (2017, 49).
26. Verme and Schuettler (2021).
27. World Bank and UNHCR (2021).
28. United Nations (1952, 13).
29. United Nations (1952, 9).
30. United Nations (2018, 1).
31. Lutz, Stünzi, and Manser-Egli (2021).
32. UNHCR (2022b).
33. OECD (2021). The data used in OECD (2021) are the most comprehensive publicly available and include 28 Development Assistance Committee (DAC) countries, four non-DAC members, and four multilateral development banks.
34. OECD (2021).
35. World Development Indicators (dashboard), World Bank, Washington, DC, https://datatopics.worldbank .org/world-development-indicators/.
36. OECD (2021).
37. OECD (2021).
38. Kneebone and Macklin (2021).
39. Kneebone and Macklin (2021).
40. UNHCR (2021h, 2022b).
41. UNHCR (2022b).
42. United Nations (2018).
43. United Nations (2018).
44. UNHCR (2021d).
45. The International Technical Meeting on Human Mobility of Venezuelan Citizens in the Region (Quito Process) was launched in 2018 to promote communication and coordination among countries in Latin America and the Caribbean receiving Venezuelan refugees and migrants. One of the main objectives is to exchange information and good practices and articulate regional coordination to respond to the influx of Venezuelan refugees and migrants in the region. For more information, see Proceso de Quito (dashboard), https://www.procesodequito.org/en.
46. "Migration Management: Welcoming Refugees from Ukraine," Migration and Home Affairs, European Commission, Brussels, https://home-affairs.ec.europa .eu/policies/migration-and-asylum/migration -management/migration-management-welcoming -refugees-ukraine_en.
47. UNHCR (2021d).
48. Barbelet, Hagen-Zanker, and Mansour-Ille (2018); Ginn et al. (2022); Gray Meral (2020).
49. Gray Meral (2020).
50. EU (2023).
51. UNHCR (2017).
52. Tumen (2023).
53. Rossiasco et al. (2023).
54. "Migration Management: Welcoming Refugees from Ukraine," Migration and Home Affairs, European Commission, Brussels, https://home-affairs.ec.europa .eu/policies/migration-and-asylum/migration -management/migration-management-welcoming -refugees-ukraine_en.
55. Hussam et al. (2022).
56. Clarke and Dercon (2016).
57. Kagan (2011); Naseem (2022).
58. UNHCR (2022a).
59. UNHCR (2021f).
60. Azlor, Damm, and Schultz-Nielsen (2020); Eckert, Hejlesen, and Walsh (2022); Edin, Fredriksson, and Åslund (2004); Fasani, Frattini, and Minale (2022).
61. According to the Bangladesh Bureau of Statistics (BBS 2022, 27), the population of the Cox's Bazar district is 2,823,265, and the government and UNHCR estimate that 954,707 Rohingya refugees were hosted in Kutupalong and Nayapara refugee camps as of the end of January 2023 (Government of Bangladesh and UNHCR 2023).
62. Chaves-González and Echeverría-Estrada (2020).
63. "Migration Management: Welcoming Refugees from Ukraine," Migration and Home Affairs, European Commission, Brussels, https://home-affairs.ec.europa .eu/policies/migration-and-asylum/migration -management/migration-management-welcoming -refugees-ukraine_en.
64. Access to safe, affordable, and reliable energy is essential, but it has posed challenges for destination countries and has strained local resources and capacity. It also presents considerable political challenges for host countries. See World Bank and ESMAP (2022).
65. See chapter 6 for further details.
66. World Bank (2022b).
67. Edin, Fredriksson, and Åslund (2004); Hainmueller, Hangartner, and Lawrence (2016).
68. Hainmueller, Hangartner, and Lawrence (2016).
69. Fasani, Frattini, and Minale (2021); Marbach, Hainmueller, and Hangartner (2018); Slotwinski, Stutzer, and Uhlig (2019).
70. Cortes (2004); Dustmann et al. (2017).
71. Ibáñez et al., "Life Out of the Shadows" (2022); World Bank (2023).
72. Bahar, Ibáñez, and Rozo (2021).
73. "Frequently Asked Questions," Commissionerate for Afghan Refugees Punjab, Ministry of States and Frontier Regions, Lahore, Pakistan, https://car.punjab .gov.pk/faqs.
74. Zetter and Ruaudel (2016b).
75. Ginn et al. (2022); Zetter and Ruaudel (2016a, 2016b).
76. Ginn et al. (2022).
77. Zetter and Ruaudel (2016a).
78. Ginn et al. (2022); UNHCR (2021g).

79. Ginn et al. (2022).
80. Arendt (2022); Battisti, Giesing, and Laurentsyeva (2019); Clausen et al. (2009); Lochmann, Rapoport, and Speciale (2019); Schuettler and Caron (2020).
81. For European Union countries, see Dustmann et al. (2017); Fasani, Frattini, and Minale (2022). For Belgium, see Dries, Ive, and Vujić (2019). For Finland, see Sarvimäki (2017). For Sweden, see Åslund, Forslund, and Liljeberg (2017); Baum, Lööf, and Stephan (2018); Baum et al. (2020). For Switzerland, see Spadarotto et al. (2014). For the United Kingdom, see Ruiz and Vargas-Silva (2018). For East African Asians in the United Kingdom, see Anders, Burgess, and Portes (2018). For the United States, see Connor (2010); Cortes (2004); Evans and Fitzgerald (2017).
82. Brell, Dustmann, and Preston (2020); Fasani, Frattini, and Minale (2022); Schuettler and Caron (2020).
83. Brell, Dustmann, and Preston (2020); Schuettler and Do (2023).
84. Bridgespan Group and IFC (2019); Wang, Cakmak, and Hagemann (2021).
85. IFC (2018).
86. UNHCR (2021a, 2021b, 2021c, 2022a). See also Atamanov et al. (2021); World Bank (2022a).
87. Testaverde and Pavilon (2022).
88. Ibáñez, Rozo, and Urbina (2021).
89. Azevedo et al. (2020).
90. UNHCR (2020).
91. Piper et al. (2020).
92. Porter and Haslam (2005); World Bank (2017).
93. Polack et al. (2021).
94. WHO (2021).
95. WHO (2021).
96. Abu-Ghaida and Silva (2020); Bilgili et al. (2019); Piper et al. (2020); UNHCR (2020).
97. Rossiasco et al. (2023).
98. Tumen (2021).
99. Woodman (2022).
100. Abu-Ghaida and Silva (2020).
101. World Bank and UNHCR (2021).
102. UNHCR Master Glossary of Terms (dashboard), United Nations High Commissioner for Refugees, Geneva, https://www.unhcr.org/glossary/.
103. UNHCR (2022b, 9).
104. World Bank (2018a, 38).
105. Hammond (2014).
106. Black and Koser (1999); Vancluysen (2022).
107. Lindley (2013).
108. Alrababa'h et al. (2023); Beaman, Onder, and Onder (2022); Hannafi and Marouani (2022).
109. ECOWAS (1979).
110. Adepoju, Boulton, and Levin (2010).
111. Adepoju, Boulton, and Levin (2010).
112. EUAA (2022).
113. UNHCR (2019); van Selm (2020).
114. Global Platform for Syrian Students (website), Global Platform for Higher Education in Emergencies, Lisbon, https://www.globalplatformforsyrianstudents.org/.
115. Reynolds and Clark-Kazak (2019).
116. Reynolds and Clark-Kazak (2019).
117. Clemens (2015).
118. Bahar, Ibáñez, and Rozo (2021).

References

Abu-Ghaida, Dina, and Karishma Silva. 2020. "Forced Displacement and Educational Outcomes: Evidence, Innovations, and Policy Indications." *JDC Quarterly Digest on Forced Displacement* 2 (December): 2–10.

Adepoju, Aderanti, Alistair Boulton, and Mariah Levin. 2010. "Promoting Integration through Mobility: Free Movement under ECOWAS." *Refugee Survey Quarterly* 29 (3): 120–44.

Aksu, Ege, Refik Erzan, and Murat Güray Kırdar. 2022. "The Impact of Mass Migration of Syrians on the Turkish Labor Market." *Labour Economics* 76 (June): 102183.

Alrababa'h, Ala', Daniel Masterson, Marine Casalis, Dominik Hangartner, and Jeremy M. Weinstein. 2023. "The Dynamics of Refugee Return: Syrian Refugees and Their Migration Intentions." *British Journal of Political Science*. Published ahead of print, February 16, 2023. doi:10.1017/S0007123422000667.

Altındağ, Onur, Ozan Bakış, and Sandra Viviana Rozo. 2020. "Blessing or Burden? Impacts of Refugees on Businesses and the Informal Economy." *Journal of Development Economics* 146 (September): 102490.

Alvarez, Jorge A., Marco Arena, Alain Brousseau, Hamid Faruqee, Emilio Fernandez-Corugedo, Jaime Guajardo, Gerardo Peraza, and Juan Yépez Albornoz. 2022. "Regional Spillovers from the Venezuelan Crisis: Migration Flows and Their Impact on Latin America and the Caribbean." IMF Departmental Paper DP/2022/019 (December), International Monetary Fund, Washington, DC.

Anders, Jake, Simon Burgess, and Jonathan Portes. 2018. "The Long-Term Outcomes of Refugees: Tracking the Progress of the East African Asians." IZA Discussion Paper DP 11609 (June), Institute of Labor Economics, Bonn, Germany.

Arendt, Jacob Nielsen. 2022. "Labor Market Effects of a Work-First Policy for Refugees." *Journal of Population Economics* 35 (1): 169–96.

Åslund, Olof, Anders Forslund, and Linus Liljeberg. 2017. "Labour Market Entry of Non-Labour Migrants: Swedish Evidence." IFAU Working Paper 2017:15, Institute for Evaluation of Labour Market and Education Policy, Uppsala, Sweden.

Atamanov, Aziz, Theresa Beltramo, Benjamin Christopher Reese, Laura Abril Rios Rivera, and Peter Waita. 2021. "One Year in the Pandemic: Results from the High-Frequency Phone Surveys for Refugees in Uganda." Poverty and Equity Practice 2021 Policy Brief, World Bank, Washington, DC.

Azevedo, João Pedro, Amer Hasan, Diana Goldemberg, Syedah Aroob Iqbal, and Koen Geven. 2020.

"Simulating the Potential Impacts of COVID-19 School Closures on Schooling and Learning Outcomes: A Set of Global Estimates." Conference edition (June), World Bank, Washington, DC.

Azlor, Luz, Anna Piil Damm, and Marie Louise Schultz-Nielsen. 2020. "Local Labour Demand and Immigrant Employment." *Labour Economics* 63 (April): 101808.

Báez, Javier E. 2011. "Civil Wars beyond Their Borders: The Human Capital and Health Consequences of Hosting Refugees." *Journal of Development Economics* 96 (2): 391–408.

Bahar, Dany, Ana María Ibáñez, and Sandra Viviana Rozo. 2021. "Give Me Your Tired and Your Poor: Impact of a Large-Scale Amnesty Program for Undocumented Refugees." *Journal of Development Economics* 151 (June): 102652.

Bakewell, Oliver. 2000. "Repatriation and Self-Settled Refugees in Zambia: Bringing Solutions to the Wrong Problems." *Journal of Refugee Studies* 13 (4): 356–73.

Barbelet, Veronique, Jessica Hagen-Zanker, and Dina Mansour-Ille. 2018. "The Jordan Compact: Lessons Learnt and Implications for Future Refugee Compacts." ODI Policy Briefing (February 8), Overseas Development Institute, London. https://cdn.odi.org/media/documents/12058.pdf.

Bascom, Johnathan. 2005. "The Long, 'Last Step'? Reintegration of Repatriates in Eritrea." *Journal of Refugee Studies* 18 (2): 165–80.

Battisti, Michele, Yvonne Giesing, and Nadzeya Laurentsyeva. 2019. "Can Job Search Assistance Improve the Labour Market Integration of Refugees? Evidence from a Field Experiment." *Labour Economics* 61 (December): 101745.

Baum, Christopher F., Hans Lööf, and Andreas Stephan. 2018. "Economic Impact of STEM Immigrant Workers." GLO Discussion Paper 257, Global Labor Organization, Maastricht, the Netherlands.

Baum, Christopher F., Hans Lööf, Andreas Stephan, and Klaus F. Zimmermann. 2020. "Occupational Sorting and Wage Gaps of Refugees." UNU-MERIT Working Paper 2020–023 (May 27), United Nations University–Maastricht Economic and Social Research Institute on Innovation and Technology, Maastricht, the Netherlands.

BBS (Bangladesh Bureau of Statistics). 2022. "Population and Housing Census 2022: Preliminary Report." August, Bangladesh Bureau of Statistics, Statistics and Informatics Division, Ministry of Planning, Dhaka, Bangladesh.

Beaman, Lori A., Harun Onder, and Stefanie Onder. 2022. "When Do Refugees Return Home? Evidence from Syrian Displacement in Mashreq." *Journal of Development Economics* 155 (March): 102802.

Becker, Sascha O., and Andreas Ferrara. 2019. "Consequences of Forced Migration: A Survey of Recent Findings." *Labour Economics* 59 (August) 1–16.

Bilgili, Özge, Craig Loschmann, Sonja Fransen, and Melissa Siegel. 2019. "Is the Education of Local Children Influenced by Living Near a Refugee Camp? Evidence from Host Communities in Rwanda." *International Migration* 57 (4): 291–309.

Black, Richard, and Khalid Koser, eds. 1999. *The End of the Refugee Cycle? Refugee Repatriation and Reconstruction.* Vol. 4 of *Refugee and Forced Migration Studies.* Oxford, UK: Berghahn Books.

Blackmore, Rebecca, Jacqueline A. Boyle, Mina Fazel, Sanjeeva Ranasinha, Kylie M. Gray, Grace Fitzgerald, Marie Misso, and Melanie Gibson-Helm. 2020. "The Prevalence of Mental Illness in Refugees and Asylum Seekers: A Systematic Review and Meta-Analysis." *PLOS Medicine* 17 (9): e1003337.

Brell, Courtney, Christian Dustmann, and Ian Preston. 2020. "The Labor Market Integration of Refugee Migrants in High-Income Countries." *Journal of Economic Perspectives* 34 (1): 94–121.

Bridgespan Group and IFC (International Finance Corporation). 2019. "Private Sector and Refugees: Pathways to Scale." April, IFC, Nairobi, Kenya.

Chaves-González, Diego, and Carlos Echeverría-Estrada. 2020. "Venezuelan Migrants and Refugees in Latin America and the Caribbean: A Regional Profile." Fact Sheet (August), International Organization for Migration, Panama City, Panama; Migration Policy Institute, Washington, DC.

Clarke, Daniel J., and Stefan Dercon. 2016. *Dull Disasters? How Planning Ahead Will Make a Difference.* Washington, DC: World Bank; New York: Oxford University Press.

Clausen, Jens, Eskil Heinesen, Hans Hummelgaard, Leif Husted, and Michael Rosholm. 2009. "The Effect of Integration Policies on the Time until Regular Employment of Newly Arrived Immigrants: Evidence from Denmark." *Labour Economics* 16 (4): 409–17.

Clemens, Michael A. 2015. "Global Skill Partnerships: A Proposal for Technical Training in a Mobile World." *IZA Journal of Labor Policy* 4 (2): 1–18.

Connor, Phillip. 2010. "Explaining the Refugee Gap: Economic Outcomes of Refugees Versus Other Immigrants." *Journal of Refugee Studies* 23 (3): 377–97.

Cortes, Kalena E. 2004. "Are Refugees Different from Economic Immigrants? Some Empirical Evidence on the Heterogeneity of Immigrant Groups in the United States." *Review of Economics and Statistics* 86 (2): 465–80.

Cuadrado, Cristóbal, Matías Libuy, and Rodrigo Moreno-Serra. 2023. "What Is the Impact of Forced Displacement on Health? A Scoping Review." *Health Policy and Planning* 38 (3): 394–408.

Devictor, Xavier, and Quy-Toan Do. 2017. "How Many Years Have Refugees Been in Exile?" *Population and Development Review* 43 (2): 355–69.

DNP (National Planning Department, Colombia). 2018. *Estrategia para la atención de la migración desde Venezuela.* Documento CONPES 3950. Bogotá: National Council for Economic and Social Policy, DNP. https://colaboracion.dnp.gov.co/CDT/Conpes/Econ%C3%B3micos/3950.pdf.

DNP (National Planning Department, Colombia). 2022. *Estrategia para la integración de la población migrante Venezolana como factor de desarrollo para el país.* Documento CONPES 4100. Bogotá: National Council for Economic and Social Policy, DNP. https://

colaboracion.dnp.gov.co/CDT/Conpes/Econ%C3%B3micos/4100.pdf.

Dries, Lens, Marx Ive, and Sunčica Vujić. 2019. "Double Jeopardy: How Refugees Fare in One European Labor Market." *IZA Journal of Development and Migration* 10 (1): 1–29.

Dustmann, Christian, Francesco Fasani, Tommaso Frattini, Luigi Minale, and Uta Schönberg. 2017. "On the Economics and Politics of Refugee Migration." *Economic Policy* 32 (91): 497–550.

Eckert, Fabian, Mads Hejlesen, and Conor Walsh. 2022. "The Return to Big-City Experience: Evidence from Refugees in Denmark." *Journal of Urban Economics* 130 (July): 103454.

ECOWAS (Economic Community of West African States). 1979. "Protocol Relating to Free Movement of Persons, Residence and Establishment." Protocol A/P 1/5/79 (May 29), *Official Journal of the ECOWAS* 1 (June 15): 3–5. https://www.unhcr.org/49e47c9238.pdf.

Edin, Per-Anders, Peter Fredriksson, and Olof Åslund. 2004. "Settlement Policies and the Economic Success of Immigrants." *Journal of Population Economics* 17 (1): 133–55.

EU (European Union). 2023. "Ethiopia Job Compact Sector Reform and Performance Contract." EU Emergency Trust Fund for Africa, Brussels. https://trust-fund-for-africa.europa.eu/our-programmes/ethiopia-job-compact-sector-reform-and-performance-contract_fr.

EUAA (European Union Agency for Asylum). 2022. *Pakistan: Situation of Afghan Refugees.* Country of Origin Information Report (May). Luxembourg: Publications Office of the European Union.

Evans, William N., and Daniel Fitzgerald. 2017. "The Economic and Social Outcomes of Refugees in the United States: Evidence from the ACS." NBER Working Paper 23498 (June), National Bureau of Economic Research, Cambridge, MA.

Fasani, Francesco, Tommaso Frattini, and Luigi Minale. 2021. "Lift the Ban? Initial Employment Restrictions and Refugee Labour Market Outcomes." *Journal of the European Economic Association* 19 (5): 2803–54.

Fasani, Francesco, Tommaso Frattini, and Luigi Minale. 2022. "(The Struggle for) Refugee Integration into the Labour Market: Evidence from Europe." *Journal of Economic Geography* 22 (2): 351–93.

Fazel, Mina, Jeremy Wheeler, and John Danesh. 2005. "Prevalence of Serious Mental Disorder in 7000 Refugees Resettled in Western Countries: A Systematic Review." *Lancet* 365 (9467): 1309–14.

Fiddian-Qasmiyeh, Elena. 2014. "Gender and Forced Migration." In *The Oxford Handbook of Refugee and Forced Migration Studies*, edited by Elena Fiddian-Qasmiyeh, Gil Loescher, Katy Long, and Nando Sigona, 395–408. Oxford Handbooks Series. Oxford, UK: Oxford University Press.

Fincham, Kathleen. 2022. "Syrian Refugee Women's Negotiation of Higher Education Opportunities in Jordan and Lebanon." *International Journal of Educational Development* 92 (July): 102629.

Ginn, Thomas, Reva Resstack, Helen Dempster, Emily Arnold-Fernández, Sarah Miller, Martha Guerrero Ble, and Bahati Kanyamanza. 2022. *2022 Global Refugee Work Rights Report.* Washington, DC: Center for Global Development.

Giuntella, Osea, Zovanga L. Kone, Isabel Ruiz, and Carlos Vargas-Silva. 2018. "Reason for Immigration and Immigrants' Health." *Public Health* 158 (May): 102–09.

GIWPS (Georgetown Institute for Women, Peace, and Security) and PRIO (Peace Research Institute Oslo). 2021. "Women, Peace, and Security Index 2021/22: Tracking Sustainable Peace through Inclusion, Justice, and Security for Women." Washington, DC: GIWPS and PRIO.

Government of Bangladesh and UNHCR (United Nations High Commissioner for Refugees). 2023. "Rohingya Refugee Response/Bangladesh: Joint Government of Bangladesh–UNHCR Population Factsheet (as of January 2023)." February 10, UNHCR, Geneva. https://data.unhcr.org/en/documents/details/98702.

Gray Meral, Amanda Louise. 2020. "Assessing the Jordan Compact One Year On: An Opportunity or a Barrier to Better Achieving Refugees' Right to Work." *Journal of Refugee Studies* 33 (1): 42–61.

Habash, Dunya, and Naohiko Omata. 2022. "The 'Private' Sphere of Integration? Reconfiguring Gender Roles within Syrian Refugee Families in the UK." *Journal of International Migration and Integration.* Published ahead of print, September 19, 2022. https://doi.org/10.1007/s12134-022-00982-x.

Hainmueller, Jens, Dominik Hangartner, and Duncan Lawrence. 2016. "When Lives Are Put on Hold: Lengthy Asylum Processes Decrease Employment among Refugees." *Science Advances* 2 (8): e1600432.

Hammond, Laura. 1999. "Examining the Discourse of Repatriation: Towards a More Proactive Theory of Return Migration." In *Refugee and Forced Migration Studies.* Vol. 4, *The End of the Refugee Cycle? Refugee Repatriation and Reconstruction,* edited by Richard Black and Khalid Koser, 227–44. Oxford, UK: Berghahn Books.

Hammond, Laura. 2014. "'Voluntary' Repatriation and Reintegration." In *The Oxford Handbook of Refugee and Forced Migration Studies*, edited by Elena Fiddian-Qasmiyeh, Gil Loescher, Katy Long, and Nando Sigona, 499–511. Oxford Handbooks Series. Oxford, UK: Oxford University Press.

Hannafi, Cyrine, and Mohamed Ali Marouani. 2022. "Social Integration of Syrian Refugees and Their Intention to Stay in Germany." *Journal of Population Economics* 36 (2): 581–607.

Harild, Niels, Asger Christensen, and Roger Zetter. 2015. *Sustainable Refugee Return: Triggers, Constraints, and Lessons on Addressing the Development Challenges of Forced Displacement.* GPFD Issue Note (August), Global Program on Forced Displacement. Washington, DC: World Bank.

Hussam, Reshmaan, Erin M. Kelley, Gregory V. Lane, and Fatima T. Zahra. 2022. "The Psychosocial Value of Employment: Evidence from a Refugee Camp." *American Economic Review* 112 (11): 3694–724.

Ibáñez, Ana María, Andrés Moya, María Adelaida Ortega, Marisol Rodríguez Chatruc, Sandra Viviana Rozo, and María José Urbina. 2022. "Salir de la sombra: Cómo un programa de regularización mejoró la vida de los migrantes Venezolanos en Colombia." Monografía del BID IDB-MG-992, Inter-American Development Bank, Washington, DC.

Ibáñez, Ana María, Andrés Moya, María Adelaida Ortega, Sandra Viviana Rozo, and María José Urbina. 2022. "Life Out of the Shadows: Impacts of Amnesties in the Lives of Migrants." IZA Discussion Paper DP 15049 (January), Institute of Labor Economics, Bonn, Germany.

Ibáñez, Ana María, Sandra Viviana Rozo, and María José Urbina. 2021. "Forced Migration and the Spread of Infectious Diseases." Journal of Health Economics 79 (September): 102491.

IDA (International Development Association). 2022. Building Back Better from the Crisis: Toward a Green, Resilient, and Inclusive Future; Additions to IDA Resources: Twentieth Replenishment. Report from the Executive Directors of the International Development Association to the Board of Governors, February 17. Washington, DC: IDA, World Bank.

IFC (International Finance Corporation). 2018. "Kakuma as a Marketplace: A Consumer and Market Study of a Refugee Camp and Town in Northwest Kenya." April, IFC, Washington, DC.

Kagan, Michael. 2011. "'We Live in a Country of UNHCR': The UN Surrogate State and Refugee Policy in the Middle East." Research Paper 201 (February), Policy Development and Evaluation Service, United Nations High Commissioner for Refugees, Geneva.

Klugman, Jeni. 2021. "The Gender Dimensions of Forced Displacement: Findings from New Empirical Analysis." JDC Quarterly Digest 4 (December): 3–12.

Kneebone, Susan, and Audrey Macklin. 2021. "Resettlement." In The Oxford Handbook of International Refugee Law, edited by Cathryn Costello, Michelle Foster, and Jane McAdam, 1080–98. Oxford Handbooks Series. Oxford, UK: Oxford University Press.

Lindert, Jutta, Ondine S. von Ehrenstein, Stefan Priebe, Andreas Mielck, and Elmar Brähler. 2009. "Depression and Anxiety in Labor Migrants and Refugees: A Systematic Review and Meta-Analysis." Social Science and Medicine 69 (2): 246–57.

Lindley, Anna. 2013. "Displacement in Contested Places: Governance, Movement and Settlement in the Somali Territories." Journal of Eastern African Studies 7 (2): 291–313.

Lochmann, Alexia, Hillel Rapoport, and Biagio Speciale. 2019. "The Effect of Language Training on Immigrants' Economic Integration: Empirical Evidence from France." European Economic Review 113 (April): 265–96.

Lomax, Gisella. 2018. "Afghan Refugees Share Hopes and Fears with UN Refugee and Relief Chiefs." News (blog), September 9, 2018. https://www.unhcr.org/en-us /news/latest/2018/9/5b940bf24/afghan-refugees -share-hopes-fears-un-refugee-relief-chiefs.html.

Lutz, Philipp, Anna Stünzi, and Stefan Manser-Egli. 2021. "Responsibility-Sharing in Refugee Protection: Lessons from Climate Governance." International Studies Quarterly 65 (2): 476–87.

Marbach, Moritz, Jens Hainmueller, and Dominik Hangartner. 2018. "The Long-Term Impact of Employment Bans on the Economic Integration of Refugees." Science Advances 4 (9): eaap9519.

Monsutti, Alessandro. 2008. "Afghan Migratory Strategies and the Three Solutions to the Refugee Problem." Refugee Survey Quarterly 27 (1): 58–73.

Naseem, Noorulain. 2022. "A Balancing Act: Challenges to Pakistan's Refugee Management." Defense and Security (blog), October 14, 2022. https://southasian voices.org/a-balancing-act-challenges-to-pakistans -refugee-management/.

OECD (Organisation for Economic Co-operation and Development). 2021. "Financing for Refugee Situations 2018–19." Forced Displacement Series, OECD, Paris.

Olivieri, Sergio, Francesc Ortega, Ana Rivadeneira, and Eliana Carranza. 2022. "The Labour Market Effects of Venezuelan Migration in Ecuador." Journal of Development Studies 58 (4): 713–29.

Omata, Naohiko. 2013. "Repatriation and Integration of Liberian Refugees from Ghana: The Importance of Personal Networks in the Country of Origin." Journal of Refugee Studies 26 (2): 265–82.

Piper, Benjamin, Sarah Dryden-Peterson, Vidur Chopra, Cella Reddick, and Arbogast Oyanga. 2020. "Are Refugee Children Learning? Early Grade Literacy in a Refugee Camp in Kenya." Journal on Education in Emergencies 5 (2): 71–107.

Polack, Sarah, Nathaniel Scherer, Hisem Yonso, Selin Volkan, Isotta Pivato, Ahmad Shaikhani, Dorothy Boggs, et al. 2021. "Disability among Syrian Refugees Living in Sultanbeyli, Istanbul: Results from a Population-Based Survey." PLOS ONE 16 (11): e0259249.

Porter, Matthew, and Nick Haslam. 2005. "Predisplacement and Postdisplacement Factors Associated with Mental Health of Refugees and Internally Displaced Persons: A Meta-Analysis." JAMA 294 (5): 602–12.

Reynolds, Johanna, and Christina Clark-Kazak. 2019. "Introduction: Special Issue on Private Sponsorship in Canada." Refuge 35 (2): 3–8.

Rossiasco, Paula Andrea, Patricia de Narvaez, Ana Aguilera, Greta Granados, Paola Guerra, and Taimur Samad. 2023. "Adapting Public Policies in Response to an Unprecedented Influx of Refugees and Migrants: Colombia Case Study of Migration from Venezuela." Background paper prepared for World Development Report 2023, World Bank, Washington, DC.

Rozo, Sandra Viviana, and Micaela Sviatschi. 2021. "Is a Refugee Crisis a Housing Crisis? Only If Housing Supply Is Unresponsive." Journal of Development Economics 148 (January): 102563.

Ruiz, Isabel, and Carlos Vargas-Silva. 2018. "Differences in Labour Market Outcomes between Natives, Refugees, and Other Migrants in the UK." Journal of Economic Geography 18 (4): 855–85.

Sarvimäki, Matti. 2017. "Labor Market Integration of Refugees in Finland." VATT Research Report 185, VATT Institute for Economic Research, Helsinki, Finland.

Schuettler, Kirsten, and Laura Caron. 2020. "Jobs Interventions for Refugees and Internally Displaced Persons." Jobs Working Paper 47, World Bank, Washington, DC.

Schuettler, Kirsten, and Quy-Toan Do. 2023. "Outcomes for Internally Displaced Persons and Refugees in Low- and Middle-Income Countries." Policy Research Working Paper 10278, World Bank, Washington, DC.

Slotwinski, Michaela, Alois Stutzer, and Roman Uhlig. 2019. "Are Asylum Seekers More Likely to Work with More Inclusive Labor Market Access Regulations?" *Swiss Journal of Economics and Statistics* 155 (1): 1–15.

Spadarotto, Claudio, Maria Bieberschulte, Katharina Walker, Michael Morlok, and Andrea Oswald. 2014. *Studie: Erwerbsbeteiligung von anerkannten Flüchtlingen und vorläufig Aufgenommenen auf dem Schweizer Arbeitsmarkt*. April. Wabern bei Bern, Switzerland: Abteilung Integration, Bundesamt für Migration.

Stepputat, Finn. 2004. "Refugees, Security, and Development: Current Experience and Strategies of Protection and Assistance in 'the Region of Origin.'" DIIS Working Paper 2004/11, Danish Institute for International Studies, Copenhagen.

Takemoto, Shoko, Naho Shibuya, and Keiko Sakoda. 2021. "Learning from Megadisasters: A Decade of Lessons from the Great East Japan Earthquake." *Feature Story* (blog), March 11, 2021. https://www.worldbank.org/en/news/feature/2021/03/11/learning-from-mega disasters-a-decade-of-lessons-from-the-great-east-japan-earthquake-drmhubtokyo.

Testaverde, Mauro, and Jacquelyn Pavilon. 2022. *Building Resilient Migration Systems in the Mediterranean Region: Lessons from COVID-19*. Washington, DC: World Bank.

Tumen, Semih. 2021. "The Effect of Refugees on Native Adolescents' Test Scores: Quasi-Experimental Evidence from PISA." *Journal of Development Economics* 150 (May): 102633.

Tumen, Semih. 2023. "The Case of Syrian Refugees in Türkiye: Successes, Challenges, and Lessons Learned." Background paper prepared for *World Development Report 2023*, World Bank, Washington, DC.

UNHCR (United Nations High Commissioner for Refugees). 2004. "Protracted Refugee Situations." Document EC/54/SC/CRP.14 (June 10), Executive Committee of the High Commissioner's Programme, UNHCR, Geneva. https://www.unhcr.org/en-us/excom/standcom/40c982172/protracted-refugee-situations.html.

UNHCR (United Nations High Commissioner for Refugees). 2010. "Convention and Protocol Relating to the Status of Refugees." 60th anniversary edition, December, with an introduction by UNHCR, Geneva. https://www.unhcr.org/en-us/protection/basic/3b66c2aa10/convention-protocol-relating-status-refugees.html.

UNHCR (United Nations High Commissioner for Refugees). 2011. "The 1951 Convention Relating to the Status of Refugees and Its 1967 Protocol." September, UNHCR, Geneva. https://www.unhcr.org/en-us/about-us/background/4ec262df9/1951-convention-relating-status-refugees-its-1967-protocol.html.

UNHCR (United Nations High Commissioner for Refugees). 2017. "United Republic of Tanzania: Refugees (Camps) and Asylum-Seekers." Global Focus, UNHCR, Geneva.

UNHCR (United Nations High Commissioner for Refugees). 2019. "Three-Year Strategy (2019–2021) on Resettlement and Complementary Pathways." June, UNHCR, Geneva.

UNHCR (United Nations High Commissioner for Refugees). 2020. "Coming Together for Refugee Education." Education Report 2020, September 3, UNHCR, Geneva.

UNHCR (United Nations High Commissioner for Refugees). 2021a. "Assessing the Socioeconomic Impact of COVID-19 on Forcibly Displaced Populations: The Case of Kenya." Thematic Brief 1 (September), UNHCR, Geneva.

UNHCR (United Nations High Commissioner for Refugees). 2021b. "Assessing the Socioeconomic Impact of COVID-19 on Forcibly Displaced Populations: The Case of Lebanon." Thematic Brief 3 (April), UNHCR, Geneva.

UNHCR (United Nations High Commissioner for Refugees). 2021c. "Assessing the Socioeconomic Impact of COVID-19 on Forcibly Displaced Populations: The Case of Nigeria." Thematic Brief 2 (June), UNHCR, Geneva.

UNHCR (United Nations High Commissioner for Refugees). 2021d. "Global Compact on Refugees: Indicator Report 2021." UNHCR, Geneva.

UNHCR (United Nations High Commissioner for Refugees). 2021e. "The 1951 Refugee Convention: 70 Years of Life-Saving Protection." Press release, July 28, 2021. https://www.unhcr.org/en-us/news/press/2021/7/6100199a4/1951-refugee-convention-70-years-life-saving-protection.html.

UNHCR (United Nations High Commissioner for Refugees). 2021f. "Refugee Camps Explained." *News* (blog), April 6, 2021. https://www.unrefugees.org/news/refugee-camps-explained/.

UNHCR (United Nations High Commissioner for Refugees). 2021g. *UNHCR Guidelines on International Legal Standards Relating to Decent Work for Refugees*. UNHCR, Geneva. https://www.refworld.org/docid/60e5cfd74.html.

UNHCR (United Nations High Commissioner for Refugees). 2021h. *UNHCR Projected Global Resettlement Needs 2022*. Geneva: UNHCR.

UNHCR (United Nations High Commissioner for Refugees). 2022a. *Global Report 2021: The Stories behind the Numbers*. Geneva: UNHCR.

UNHCR (United Nations High Commissioner for Refugees). 2022b. "Global Trends: Forced Displacement in 2021." June 16, Statistics and Demographics Section, Global Data Service, UNHCR, Copenhagen. https://www.unhcr.org/en-us/publications/brochures/62a9d1494/global-trends-report-2021.html.

UNHCR (United Nations High Commissioner for Refugees). 2023a. "Lives on Hold: Intentions and Perspectives of Refugees from Ukraine." Regional Intentions Report 3 (February), Data, Identity Management and Analysis Unit, Regional Bureau for Europe, UNHCR, Geneva. https://reliefweb.int/report/poland/lives-hold-intentions-and-perspectives-refugees-ukraine-3-february-2023.

UNHCR (United Nations High Commissioner for Refugees). 2023b. "Ukraine Situation Flash Update #40 (10 February 2023)." https://reliefweb.int/report/ukraine/ukraine-situation-flash-update-40-10-february-2023.

UNHCR (United Nations High Commissioner for Refugees). 2023c. *Ukraine Situation: Regional Refugee Response Plan, January–December 2023*. Regional Refugee Response for the Ukraine Situation (January). Geneva: Regional Bureau for Europe, UNHCR. https://reliefweb.int/report/poland/ukraine-situation-regional-refugee-response-plan-january-december-2023.

UNHCR (United Nations High Commissioner for Refugees) and World Bank. 2019. "Kalobeyei Settlement: Results from the 2018 Kalobeyei Socioeconomic Survey." Vol. A of *Understanding the Socioeconomic Conditions of Refugees in Kenya*. World Bank, Washington, DC.

United Nations. 1952. "Final Act of the United Nations Conference of Plenipotentiaries on the Status of Refugees and Stateless Persons." Document A/CONF.2/108/Rev.1 (November 26), United Nations, Geneva.

United Nations. 2018. "Global Compact on Refugees." United Nations, New York. https://www.unhcr.org/5c658aed4.

Vancluysen, Sarah. 2022. "Deconstructing Borders: Mobility Strategies of South Sudanese Refugees in Northern Uganda." *Global Networks* 22 (1): 20–35.

van Selm, Joanne. 2020. "Complementary Pathways to Protection: Promoting the Integration and Inclusion of Refugees in Europe?" *Annals of the American Academy of Political and Social Science* 690 (1): 136–52.

Verme, Paolo, Chiara Gigliarano, Christina Wieser, Kerren Hedlund, Marc Petzoldt, and Marco Santacroce. 2016. *The Welfare of Syrian Refugees: Evidence from Jordan and Lebanon*. Washington, DC: World Bank.

Verme, Paolo, and Kirsten Schuettler. 2021. "The Impact of Forced Displacement on Host Communities: A Review of the Empirical Literature in Economics." *Journal of Development Economics* 150 (May): 102606.

von der Goltz, Jan, and Kirsten Schuettler. 2022. "Jobs and Forced Displacement: Labor Market Impacts and Cost of Jobs Support." PowerPoint presentation, Copenhagen, November 28, 2022. https://www.jointdatacenter.org/wp-content/uploads/2022/12/JDC-slides-Jobs-and-FD-November-28-2022.pdf.

Vu, Alexander, Atif Adam, Andrea L. Wirtz, Kiemanh Pham, Leonard Rubenstein, Nancy Glass, Chris Beyrer, and Sonal Singh. 2014. "The Prevalence of Sexual Violence among Female Refugees in Complex Humanitarian Emergencies: A Systematic Review and Meta-Analysis." *PLOS Currents* 6 (March 18).

Wang, Weiyi, Ozan Cakmak, and Kurt Hagemann. 2021. "Private Sector Initiatives in Forced Displacement Contexts: Constraints and Opportunities for Market-Based Approaches." EM Compass Note 103 (May), International Finance Corporation, Washington, DC.

WHO (World Health Organization). 2021. "Mapping Health Systems' Responsiveness to Refugee and Migrant Health Needs." Health and Migration Programme, WHO, Geneva.

WHO (World Health Organization). 2022. *World Report on the Health of Refugees and Migrants*. Health and Migration Programme. Geneva: WHO.

Woodman, Mike. 2022. "More Countries Are Including Refugees in National Health Systems, and Development Partnerships Are Key to the Process." *UNHCR Blogs* (blog), December 7, 2022. https://www.unhcr.org/blogs/more-countries-are-including-refugees-in-national-health-systems-development-partnerships-are-key/.

World Bank. 2013. *Lebanon: Economic and Social Impact Assessment of the Syrian Conflict*. Report 81098-LB (September 20). Washington, DC: World Bank.

World Bank. 2017. *Forcibly Displaced: Toward a Development Approach Supporting Refugees, the Internally Displaced, and Their Hosts*. Washington, DC: World Bank.

World Bank. 2018a. "Asylum Seekers in the European Union: Building Evidence to Inform Policy Making." World Bank, Washington, DC.

World Bank. 2018b. "Informing Durable Solutions by Micro-Data: A Skills Survey for Refugees in Ethiopia." July 10, World Bank, Washington, DC.

World Bank. 2019. "Informing the Refugee Policy Response in Uganda: Results from the Uganda Refugee and Host Communities 2018 Household Survey." World Bank, Washington, DC.

World Bank. 2022a. "Phone Survey Data: Monitoring COVID-19 Impact on Firms and Households in Ethiopia." *Ethiopia Brief*, February 10, 2022. https://www.worldbank.org/en/country/ethiopia/brief/phone-survey-data-monitoring-covid-19-impact-on-firms-and-households-in-ethiopia.

World Bank. 2022b. "Supporting Fiscal Sustainability, Competitiveness, and Migration Policy in Colombia." Results Brief, April 28, 2022. https://www.worldbank.org/en/results/2022/04/28/supporting-fiscal-sustainability-competitiveness-and-migration-policy-in-colombia.

World Bank. 2023. "Labor Market Impacts of Forced Displacement." Unpublished report, World Bank, Washington, DC.

World Bank and ESMAP (Energy Sector Management Assistance Program). 2022. "Leaving No One Behind: Rethinking Energy Access in Displacement Settings." World Bank, Washington, DC.

World Bank and UNHCR (United Nations High Commissioner for Refugees). 2021. "The Global Cost of Inclusive Refugee Education." Report (January), World Bank, Washington, DC.

Zetter, Roger, and Héloïse Ruaudel. 2016a. "Refugees' Right to Work and Access to Labor Markets: An Assessment, Part 1: Synthesis." KNOMAD Study (September), Global Knowledge Partnership on Migration and Development, World Bank, Washington, DC.

Zetter, Roger, and Héloïse Ruaudel. 2016b. "Refugees' Right to Work and Access to Labor Markets: An Assessment, Part 2: Country Case Studies." KNOMAD Study (September), Global Knowledge Partnership on Migration and Development, World Bank, Washington, DC.

Spotlight 7
—
Internal displacement and statelessness

Internal displacement

Whereas some people are forced to move across international borders, others are forced to move within their own country in response to, among other things, conflict, violence, persecution, or natural disasters. They are referred to as *internally displaced persons* (IDPs). Internal displacement raises particular development challenges.[1]

The number of IDPs has increased rapidly over the last decade.[2] Aggregate estimates are based on national definitions that are not directly comparable, but the Internal Displacement Monitoring Centre has assessed that 59.1 million people were internally displaced as of the end of 2021, up from 26.4 million at the end of 2012.[3] Of these, 53.2 million were internally displaced by conflict and violence and 5.9 million by natural disasters across 59 countries and territories (map S7.1). Ten countries account for more than two-thirds of the total.[4]

Although some IDPs leave their homes for only a short period, others remain displaced for years. In the Syrian Arab Republic, for example, an estimated four out of five displaced households have been in that situation for more than five years, and in Sudan an estimated 56 percent of IDPs have been displaced

Map S7.1 Internal displacement occurs worldwide

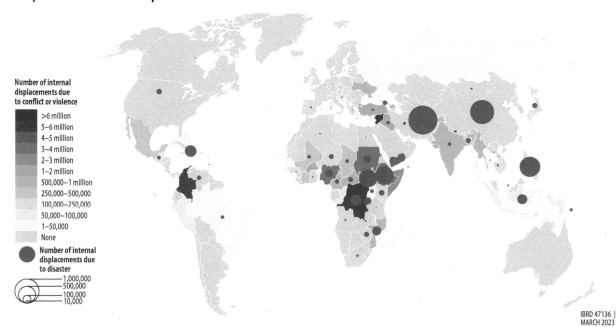

IBRD 47136 |
MARCH 2023

Source: Global Internal Displacement Database (GIDD), Internal Displacement Monitoring Centre, Geneva, https://www.internal-displacement.org/database/displacement-data.

for more than 10 years.[5] In other situations, displacement is repeated or even cyclical, with devastating impacts on affected individuals and households. Many IDPs experience trauma and losses similar to those experienced by refugees (box S7.1).[6] Internal displacement has long-lasting economic effects, including increased poverty and vulnerability.[7]

Like refugees, IDPs are often concentrated in particular geographic areas, and their host communities are substantially affected.[8] Many IDPs move from rural to urban areas, particularly in low- and middle-income countries. Most IDPs live in cities and towns, often in informal settlements alongside other poor urban dwellers.[9]

Normative frameworks and the need for a typology

The 1998 United Nations Guiding Principles on Internal Displacement are the main normative framework for IDPs, although the Guiding Principles are not legally binding.[10] Based on human rights law and international humanitarian law, they recognize IDPs as persons endowed with human rights who, because of their displacement, need dedicated attention.[11] They also draw on international refugee law, including for notions such as protection and "durable solutions." The Guiding Principles underpin a range of legally binding instruments, including the 2009 African Union Convention for the Protection and Assistance of Internally Displaced Persons in Africa (Kampala Convention) as well as laws and regulations in several countries.[12]

Yet definitions of an IDP vary significantly across countries. Of the 72 countries that have IDP-specific legal frameworks, only 21 use the definition in the Guiding Principles.[13] More frequently, IDP definitions are limited to specific groups, geographic areas, or causes of displacement.[14] For example, Bosnia and Herzegovina considers IDPs as only those who were displaced within a particular time period, and the Kurdistan Region of Iraq ties displacement to specific conflict events. Georgia and Ukraine have at various times restricted IDPs to citizens and a few other select groups. There is also no consensus on how far a person must flee to be considered internally displaced or for how long (it can be brief in the case of natural disasters); what it means for nomadic groups; and whether children born to IDPs in displacement are themselves IDPs, as in Azerbaijan and Colombia.[15]

Internal displacement encompasses a broad range of situations that are hardly comparable: a US family affected by flooding in the state of Maine; Ukrainians displaced by the Russian invasion of their country; returning Afghan refugees who settled in the suburbs of Kabul; and villagers evicted from their homes in Ethiopia to make space for agroindustrial projects. The necessary responses vary considerably across such situations. Distinguishing between various types of internal displacements is key to addressing the corresponding challenges effectively.

The solutions conundrum

Defining what constitutes a satisfactory endpoint to internal displacement is critical. The aim of support for IDPs is not only to help them survive while in displacement but also to enable them to reestablish their lives as contributing members of society and to reach a point where dedicated assistance is no longer needed. Thus support of IDPs is not just temporary relief; it needs to be designed and delivered throughout the displacement cycle in a manner that facilitates achievement of a durable solution.

What constitutes a durable solution to IDP situations is not easily articulated. In some debates, durable solutions are modeled on the refugee paradigm. They focus on three possibilities for a solution that are derived from the experience with refugees: return to the place of origin; local integration in areas of displacement; or integration elsewhere in the country.[16] However, as displacement becomes protracted, the definition of what is considered a durable solution becomes increasingly ambiguous. For example, at what point should urban IDPs (who are unlikely to return to rural areas) no longer considered IDPs? And how does one determine whether sustainable integration has been achieved?

The Inter-Agency Standing Committee (IASC) has elaborated on these definitions with a focus on socioeconomic vulnerabilities. A durable solution is considered achieved when, based on a set of criteria, IDPs no longer have needs arising from their forced displacement.[17] Yet, in practice, some of these criteria are difficult to achieve in countries and regions where even nondisplaced households face dire development challenges. As a result, many people continue to be considered IDPs with no solution in sight, which is in part behind the steady increase in global IDP numbers.

The Expert Group on Refugee, IDP and Statelessness Statistics (EGRISS) under the United Nations Statistical Commission has proposed a practical way forward.[18] It recommends using a comparison with the general population, rather than global standards, to assess the persistence of displacement-related vulnerabilities among IDPs. It suggests that IDPs form a distinct population of concern to the extent that they have specific vulnerabilities and cannot seize economic opportunities available to other nationals. Under this approach, they are no longer IDPs when they are back on a level playing field with those who have not been displaced.

Internal displacement and vulnerability

Many people are affected by conflicts or disasters, but those who have been internally displaced are the subject of special attention. Why? In many contexts, internal displacement has become a proxy to identify those who should benefit from specific forms of assistance (box S7.2).

The nature of such assistance varies across countries and contexts. For example, internal displacement can be a proxy for vulnerability to violence or abuses and for the need for protection against such harm, such as in Ukraine. It can be a proxy as well for war-induced destitution and humanitarian assistance needs, such as in Somalia and the Republic of Yemen. It can also be used to assess and signal the severity of a conflict situation and help steer the allocation of scarce aid resources across countries.

The focus on IDPs can also be grounded in more political rationales. For example, in the Caucasus the insistence that IDPs have the right to return to their places of origin—even if they are under the

Box S7.2 Internal displacement and assistance targeting

Assistance targeting is critical to the effectiveness of development programs in resource-constrained settings.[a] Targeting systems provide tools to identify those who should receive priority for specific programs or policies. Identification of those most in need is typically based on a range of proxy indicators that can be collected at reasonably low cost and closely correlated with the objectives of the programs. For example, income levels or asset ownership are used as proxies to identify those most in need of support under antipoverty initiatives.

Internal displacement has become such a proxy indicator in some contexts. It is used to determine those who need specific forms of support and to identify individuals and households who will benefit. Statistics on internally displaced persons (IDPs) may provide a visible metric to prioritize scarce resources when there are logistical challenges in collecting data on alternative measures of vulnerability, such as in a conflict setting. This approach, however, raises two questions. First, in a given context what specific program or policy does the IDP category help target? And, second, is being an IDP the best proxy for defining those who should be targeted by this specific program or policy? The availability of data and evidence is key to informing the response to such questions and to determining the optimal use of resources.

a. Brown, Ravallion, and van de Walle (2018); Coady, Grosh, and Hoddinott (2004); Grosh et al. (2008); Lindert et al. (2020).

de facto control of another country—is an important part of a political discourse aimed at asserting territorial claims. In other contexts, such as in Colombia, the IDP status is linked to expectations of future compensation processes for war victims.

Internal displacement should be approached in the context of a broader discussion on vulnerability. In a context of conflict, persecution, or natural disaster, IDPs are often not the only highly vulnerable group. The new widows and widowers arising from a war or disaster, for example, may also be highly vulnerable, even though they are not the subject of a distinct international framework.

Prioritizing IDPs over other groups of citizens may not always be an effective way to frame policies or deliver aid, especially in resource-constrained environments.[19] In some cases, other indicators of vulnerability, such as income or household composition or belonging to certain social groups, may be better proxies to focus the limited assistance on those who need it most. For example, in Georgia IDPs who live in the capital, Tbilisi, are less likely to be poor than non-IDPs in rural areas. In the Sahel, some ethnic groups are deliberately targeted by armed factions and need protection, regardless of whether they have been displaced.

In any event, IDP status should not become a source of vulnerability in its own right. This has happened when the mere use of the IDP category creates forms of discrimination, such as when IDPs are required to live in specific settlements or to send their children to dedicated IDP schools, especially if the situation becomes protracted.[20]

Key principles for intervention

Governments can consider several key principles for intervention:

Government leadership. National governments retain the primary responsibility for IDPs in their territory consistent with their international human rights obligations, including when IDPs are stateless. Sustainable improvements in the situation of IDPs and their host communities often depend on policies adopted by their governments.

Political economy. Governments' decisions are often influenced by political considerations that go beyond the interests of those who have been displaced. In a conflict context, for example, governments may focus on how internal displacement affects conflict dynamics and potential drivers of future unrest. They manage IDPs with a view toward reducing social tensions and violence nationwide instead of a sole focus on IDPs' needs. Politics play an even larger role when IDPs have fled violence instigated by the government itself or when their loyalty is questioned. Even in natural disasters, government decisions may be steered by political considerations based, for example, on the ethnicity or perceived political affiliations of the IDP population.[21] Because political considerations are so central and because IDP situations vary widely—including in war-torn regions, stable middle-income environments, or places affected by natural disaster—government and international responses must be adjusted to each context.

Holistic perspective and inclusion. Once they have reached a safe place, many IDPs behave like other internal (voluntary) migrants and look for opportunities to improve their welfare. If well managed, the resolution of internal displacement can generate some of the positive benefits of economic mobility. This can benefit both IDPs, as well as the rest of the country. Promoting IDPs' economic and social inclusion is crucial, including improving their self-reliance and incorporating them into national health and education systems.[22] Facilitating IDPs' movements to areas where they can find socioeconomic opportunities may also ease their recovery and lessen adverse impacts on host communities.

Statelessness

At least 4.3 million people in 95 countries are stateless or of undetermined nationality.[23] Under international law, states set the rules for the acquisition, change, and withdrawal of nationality. A stateless person is defined as someone who is not considered to be a national by any state.[24]

Among those for whom data are publicly available, stateless persons or those with undetermined nationality are currently found mainly in Côte d'Ivoire (about 930,000 persons); among Forcibly Displaced Myanmar Nationals hosted by Bangladesh (about 920,000 persons); in Myanmar (about 600,000 Rohingya in Rakhine State); in Thailand (about 560,000 persons); in Syria (about 160,000 persons); in Malaysia (about 100,000 persons); in Kuwait (about 92,000 persons); and in Cambodia (about 75,000 ethnic Vietnamese).[25]

Statelessness arises from a variety of reasons: discrimination against particular ethnic or religious groups (such as that against the Rohingya in Myanmar) or on the basis of gender; the emergence or breakup of states (a situation that left some Roma minorities stateless following the dissolution of the former Yugoslavia); or incomplete nationality laws or conflicts between them (for example, when a child is unable to access the nationality of his or her parents or the nationality of the country of birth, which can happen in forced displacement or irregular migration). Other people are not stateless by law but find themselves unable to obtain documentation that would prove their nationality. For all practical purposes, they are in a situation similar to that of stateless persons.[26]

Regardless of its causes, statelessness has adverse development consequences. Stateless persons are often denied a range of socioeconomic rights: to enter the labor market, access public services, own property, or simply move within the country. These can be both formal legal interdictions or unpassable administrative hurdles, such as if family members must present identification papers or a birth certificate to register a child in school.[27] Even when stateless persons are granted a protected status, they often do not have clear pathways to acquiring nationality for themselves and their children. Detailed data on their circumstances are often missing, but most stateless persons live on the margins of society with high degrees of vulnerability.

Over the last few decades, some countries have taken steps to resolve major situations of statelessness. Sri Lanka passed legislation in 2003 allowing about 200,000 Hill Tamils to acquire nationality.

Bangladesh confirmed the citizenship of Urdu-speaking or "Bihari" persons in 2008.[28] The Russian Federation naturalized about 650,000 former Soviet nationals between 2003 and 2012. And in 2017, Kenya offered citizenship to about 6,000 ethnic Makonde—the descendants of Mozambican migrants who had arrived in the 1930s.

Resolving statelessness is part of achieving the United Nations' Sustainable Development Goals. Some situations may be politically difficult. But others arise mainly from legal inconsistencies that could be corrected with relatively few political costs if there are incentives to do so. For example, ensuring that no child is born stateless and adopting universal birth registration; removing gender discrimination from nationality laws; preventing denial, loss, or deprivation of nationality on discriminatory grounds; and issuing nationality documentation to those who are entitled to it.[29]

Notes

1. World Bank (2021).
2. Global Internal Displacement Database (GIDD), Internal Displacement Monitoring Centre, Geneva, https://www.internal-displacement.org/database/displacement-data.
3. IDMC (2022).
4. The 10 countries are the Syrian Arab Republic (6.7 million IDPs), the Democratic Republic of Congo (5.3 million), Colombia (5.2 million), Afghanistan (4.3 million), the Republic of Yemen (4.3 million), Ethiopia (3.6 million), Nigeria (3.2 million), Sudan (3.2 million), Somalia (3.0 million), and Burkina Faso (1.6 million). Numbers are based on IDMC (2022).
5. IDMC (2022).
6. While both refugee and IDP populations have higher rates of mental health issues than the nondisplaced populations (Porter and Haslam 2005; Steel et al. 2009), IDPs have been shown to have higher rates of morbidity than refugees and returned refugees in several settings (Al Ibraheem et al. 2017; Mels et al. 2010; Tekeli-Yesil et al. 2018). In Colombia, the psychological effects of IDPs' traumatic experiences have been shown to lead to risk aversion and hopelessness, affecting their economic decisions and contributing to their vulnerability (Moya 2018; Moya and Carter 2019).
7. Gimenez-Nadal, Molina, and Silva-Quintero (2019); Ivlevs and Veliziotis (2018); Kondylis (2010); Torosyan, Pignatti, and Obrizan (2018).
8. Alix-Garcia, Bartlett, and Saah (2012, 2013); Bohnet, Cottier, and Hug (2018); Bozzoli, Brück, and Wald (2013); Calderón-Mejía and Ibáñez (2016); Depetris-Chauvin and Santos (2018); Morales (2018).
9. World Bank (2017).
10. OCHA (2004).
11. OCHA (2004).
12. African Union (2012); UNHCR and Global Protection Cluster (2022).
13. EGRIS (2020).
14. Adeola and Orchard (2020).
15. EGRIS (2020).
16. Since the introduction of the Inter-Agency Standing Committee's Framework on Durable Solutions for IDPs in 2010 (IASC 2010), there has been a progressive shift away from a refugee paradigm of durable solutions to the IASC (2010, A1) definition of the end of internal displacement ("when internally displaced persons no longer have any specific assistance and protection needs that are linked to their displacement and can enjoy their human rights without discrimination on account of their displacement"), whereby (re)integration in places of origin/refuge/elsewhere in the country is a gradual path to a durable solution. The debate has shifted to how to operationalize the IASC definition and criteria for durable solutions.
17. The Framework on Durable Solutions for Internally Displaced Persons of the IASC suggests eight criteria for determining whether durable solutions have been achieved: (1) safety and security, including freedom of movement; (2) an adequate standard of living, including access to essential food and water, basic housing, essential health care, and basic education; (3) access to employment and livelihoods; (4) restoration of housing, land, and property; (5) access to documentation; (6) family reunification; (7) participation in public affairs; and (8) access to effective remedies and justice (IASC 2010).
18. EGRIS (2020). EGRIS was recently renamed EGRISS to include statelessness—that is, the Expert Group on Refugee, IDP and Statelessness Statistics.
19. Grosh et al. (2022).
20. Kazimzade (2013).
21. Sobel and Leeson (2006).
22. World Bank (2011, 2013, 2019).
23. UNHCR (2022a).
24. The 1954 Convention Relating to the Status of Stateless Persons is the cornerstone of the international protection regime for stateless people (OHCHR 1954). The 1961 Convention on the Reduction of Statelessness establishes specific obligations to prevent and reduce statelessness (OHCHR 1961).
25. UNHCR (2022a, 2022b).
26. UNHCR (2014, 2017).
27. UNHCR (2014).
28. Wijetunga (2004).
29. UNHCR (2014).

References

Adeola, Romola, and Phil Orchard. 2020. "The Role of Law and Policy in Fostering Responsibility and Accountability of Governments towards Internally Displaced Persons." *Refugee Survey Quarterly* 39 (4): 412–24.

African Union. 2012. "African Union Convention for the Protection and Assistance of Internally Displaced Persons in Africa (Kampala Convention)." Text of December 6, 2012, African Union, Addis Ababa, Ethiopia. https://au.int/en/treaties/african-union-convention-protection-and-assistance-internally-displaced-persons-africa.

Al Ibraheem, Boshra, Ibrahim Aref Kira, Jakoub Aljakoub, and Ahmad Al Ibraheem. 2017. "The Health Effect of the Syrian Conflict on IDPs and Refugees." *Peace and Conflict: Journal of Peace Psychology* 23 (2): 140–52.

Alix-Garcia, Jennifer, Anne Bartlett, and David Saah. 2012. "Displaced Populations, Humanitarian Assistance and Hosts: A Framework for Analyzing Impacts on Semi-Urban Households." *World Development* 40 (2): 373–86.

Alix-Garcia, Jennifer, Anne Bartlett, and David Saah. 2013. "The Landscape of Conflict: IDPs, Aid and Land-Use Change in Darfur." *Journal of Economic Geography* 13 (4): 589–617.

Bohnet, Heidrun, Fabien Cottier, and Simon Hug. 2018. "Conflict-Induced IDPs and the Spread of Conflict." *Journal of Conflict Resolution* 62 (4): 691–716.

Bozzoli, Carlos Guillermo, Tilman Brück, and Nina Wald. 2013. "Self-Employment and Conflict in Colombia." *Journal of Conflict Resolution* 57 (1): 117–42.

Brown, Caitlin S., Martin Ravallion, and Dominique van de Walle. 2018. "A Poor Means Test? Econometric Targeting in Africa." *Journal of Development Economics* 134 (September): 109–24.

Calderón-Mejía, Valentina, and Ana María Ibáñez. 2016. "Labour Market Effects of Migration-Related Supply Shocks: Evidence from Internal Refugees in Colombia." *Journal of Economic Geography* 16 (3): 695–713.

Coady, David P., Margaret E. Grosh, and John F. Hoddinott. 2004. *Targeting of Transfers in Developing Countries: Review of Lessons and Experience.* World Bank Regional and Sectoral Studies Series. Washington, DC: World Bank.

Depetris-Chauvin, Emilio, and Rafael J. Santos. 2018. "Unexpected Guests: The Impact of Internal Displacement Inflows on Rental Prices in Colombian Host Cities." *Journal of Development Economics* 134 (September): 289–309.

EGRIS (Expert Group on Refugee and Internally Displaced Persons Statistics). 2020. *International Recommendations on Internally Displaced Persons Statistics (IRIS).* Manuals and Guidelines. Luxembourg: Eurostat.

Gimenez-Nadal, Jose Ignacio, José Alberto Molina, and Edgar Silva-Quintero. 2019. "On the Relationship between Violent Conflict and Wages in Colombia." *Journal of Development Studies* 55 (4): 473–89.

Grosh, Margaret E., Carlo del Ninno, Emil D. Tesliuc, and Azedine Ouerghi. 2008. *For Protection and Promotion: The Design and Implementation of Effective Safety Nets.* Washington, DC: World Bank.

Grosh, Margaret E., Phillippe George Leite, Matthew Wai-Poi, and Emil D. Tesliuc, eds. 2022. *Revisiting Targeting in Social Assistance: A New Look at Old Dilemmas.* Human Development Perspectives Series. Washington, DC: World Bank.

IASC (Inter-Agency Standing Committee). 2010. "IASC Framework on Durable Solutions for Internally Displaced Persons." Brookings Institution–University of Bern Project on Internal Displacement, Washington, DC.

IDMC (Internal Displacement Monitoring Centre). 2022. *Global Report on Internal Displacement 2022: Children and Youth in Internal Displacement.* Geneva: IDMC.

Ivlevs, Artjoms, and Michail Veliziotis. 2018. "Beyond Conflict: Long-Term Labour Market Integration of Internally Displaced Persons in Post-Socialist Countries." *Journal of Vocational Behavior* 105 (April): 131–46.

Kazimzade, Elmina. 2013. "IDP Education in Azerbaijan: Overcoming Isolation and Stigma." Paper presented at CIES2013, the 57th Annual Conference of the Comparative and International Education Society, New Orleans, March 10–15, 2013.

Kondylis, Florence. 2010. "Conflict Displacement and Labor Market Outcomes in Post-War Bosnia and Herzegovina." *Journal of Development Economics* 93 (2): 235–48.

Lindert, Kathy, Tina George Karippacheril, Inés Rodríguez Caillava, and Kenichi Nishikawa Chávez, eds. 2020. *Sourcebook on the Foundations of Social Protection Delivery Systems.* Washington, DC: World Bank.

Mels, Cindy, Ilse Derluyn, Eric Broekaert, and Yves Rosseel. 2010. "The Psychological Impact of Forced Displacement and Related Risk Factors on Eastern Congolese Adolescents Affected by War." *Journal of Child Psychology and Psychiatry* 51 (10): 1096–1104.

Morales, Juan S. 2018. "The Impact of Internal Displacement on Destination Communities: Evidence from the Colombian Conflict." *Journal of Development Economics* 131 (March): 132–50.

Moya, Andrés. 2018. "Violence, Psychological Trauma, and Risk Attitudes: Evidence from Victims of Violence in Colombia." *Journal of Development Economics* 131 (March): 15–27.

Moya, Andrés, and Michael R. Carter. 2019. "Violence and the Formation of Hopelessness: Evidence from Internally Displaced Persons in Colombia." *World Development* 113 (January): 100–115.

OCHA (United Nations Office for the Coordination of Humanitarian Affairs). 2004. "Guiding Principles on Internal Displacement, Second Edition." Document OCHA/IDP/2004/01, United Nations, Geneva.

OHCHR (Office of the United Nations High Commissioner for Human Rights). 1954. "Convention Relating to the Status of Stateless Persons." Adopted September 28, 1954, by the Conference of Plenipotentiaries Convened by Economic and Social Council Resolution 526 A (XVII) of 26 April 1954. OHCHR, Geneva. https://www.ohchr.org/en/instruments-mechanisms/instruments/convention-relating-status-stateless-persons.

OHCHR (Office of the United Nations High Commissioner for Human Rights). 1961. "Convention on the Reduction of Statelessness." Adopted August 30, 1961, by the Conference of Plenipotentiaries Which Met in 1959 and Reconvened in 1961 in Pursuance of General Assembly Resolution 896 (IX). OHCHR, Geneva. https://www.ohchr.org/en/instruments-mechanisms/instruments/convention-reduction-statelessness.

Porter, Matthew, and Nick Haslam. 2005. "Predisplacement and Postdisplacement Factors Associated with Mental Health of Refugees and Internally Displaced Persons: A Meta-Analysis." *JAMA* 294 (5): 602–12.

Sobel, Russell S., and Peter T. Leeson. 2006. "Government's Response to Hurricane Katrina: A Public Choice Analysis." *Public Choice* 127 (1): 55–73.

Steel, Zachary, Tien Chey, Derrick Silove, Claire Marnane, Richard A. Bryant, and Mark van Ommeren. 2009. "Association of Torture and Other Potentially Traumatic Events with Mental Health Outcomes among Populations Exposed to Mass Conflict and Displacement: A Systematic Review and Meta-Analysis." *JAMA* 302 (5): 537–49.

Tekeli-Yesil, Sidika, Esra Isik, Yesim Unal, Fuad Aljomaa Almossa, Hande Konsuk Ünlü, and Ahmet Tamer Aker. 2018. "Determinants of Mental Disorders in Syrian Refugees in Turkey versus Internally Displaced Persons in Syria." *American Journal of Public Health* 108 (7): 938–45.

Torosyan, Karine, Norberto Pignatti, and Maksym Obrizan. 2018. "Job Market Outcomes for IDPs: The Case of Georgia." *Journal of Comparative Economics* 46 (3): 800–820.

Turkoglu, Oguzhan. 2022. "Look Who Perpetrates Violence: Explaining the Variation in Forced Migration." *Political Geography* 94 (April): 102558.

UNHCR (United Nations High Commissioner for Refugees). 2014. "Global Action Plan to End Statelessness, 2014–2024." November 4, Division of International Protection, UNHCR, Geneva.

UNHCR (United Nations High Commissioner for Refugees). 2017. " 'This Is Our Home': Stateless Minorities and Their Search for Citizenship." Division of International Protection, UNHCR, Geneva.

UNHCR (United Nations High Commissioner for Refugees). 2022a. "Action 1: Resolving Existing Major Situations of Statelessness." UNHCR Good Practice Paper (August), UNHCR, Geneva.

UNHCR (United Nations High Commissioner for Refugees). 2022b. "Mid-Year Trends 2022." October 27, Statistics and Demographics Section, Global Data Service, UNHCR, Copenhagen.

UNHCR (United Nations High Commissioner for Refugees) and Global Protection Cluster. 2022. *Global Report on Law and Policy on Internal Displacement: Implementing National Responsibility.* Geneva: UNHCR.

Wijetunga, Chetani Priyanga. 2004. "Feature: Sri Lanka Makes Citizens Out of Stateless Tea Pickers." *News* (blog), October 7, 2004. https://www.unhcr.org/news/latest/2004/10/416564cd4/feature-sri-lanka-makes-citizens-stateless-tea-pickers.html.

World Bank. 2011. "Azerbaijan: Building Assets and Promoting Self Reliance; The Livelihoods of Internally Displaced Persons." Report AAA64-AZ, World Bank, Washington, DC.

World Bank. 2013. "Supporting the Livelihoods of Internally Displaced Persons in Georgia: A Review of Current Practices and Lessons Learned." World Bank, Washington, DC.

World Bank. 2017. "Cities of Refuge in the Middle East: Bringing an Urban Lens to the Forced Displacement Challenge." Policy Note, World Bank, Washington, DC.

World Bank. 2019. *Country Case Studies.* Vol. B of *Informing Durable Solutions for Internal Displacement in Nigeria, Somalia, South Sudan, and Sudan.* Washington, DC: World Bank.

World Bank. 2021. "A Development Approach to Conflict-Induced Internal Displacement." World Bank, Washington, DC.

8

Distressed migrants

Preserving dignity

Key messages

- The circumstances surrounding distressed migration are often irregular and painful. This type of migration also entails costs for destination countries, but these countries have no international legal obligation to host distressed migrants. Many countries seek to prevent the entry of distressed migrants, but restrictive policies often undermine migrants' dignity, which creates difficult policy trade-offs.

- In this context, the challenge is to reduce the need for distressed migration, including by extending the scope of international protection, shifting incentives through the establishment of legal entry pathways, and strengthening the match of migrants' skills and attributes with the needs of destination economies through development.

- Transit countries face particular issues, which can be addressed only through bilateral and multilateral cooperation.

- Overall, migrants' inherent dignity should be the yardstick of migration policies (figure 8.1).

Figure 8.1 **The policy challenge is to reduce distressed movements while treating migrants humanely**

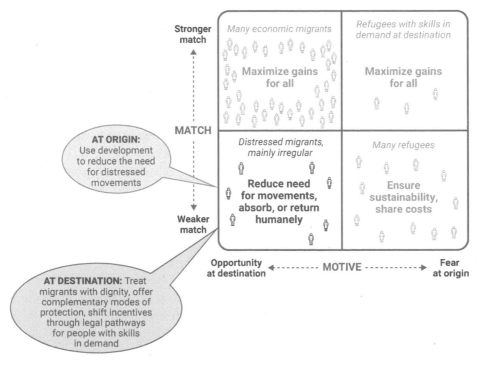

Source: WDR 2023 team.

Note: Match refers to the degree to which a migrant's skills and related attributes meet the demand in the destination country. *Motive* refers to the circumstances under which a person moves—whether in search of opportunity or because of a "well-founded fear" of persecution, armed conflict, or violence in their origin country.

Acknowledging policy trade-offs

Some of the most difficult challenges for immigration policy arise when migrants do not bring skills and attributes that match the needs of the destination country, nor are they entitled to international refugee protection. An example is people who leave a low-income country where their life is not at risk, but who do not have the basic literacy skills that would enable them to contribute to a middle- or high-income economy. In such cases, the costs of accommodating them often exceed the benefits for the destination country. International law gives this country a large degree of discretion about whether to accept such migrants in its territory.

Because the movements of many such migrants are irregular and harrowing, those movements are referred to here as *distressed migration*. Indeed, many distressed migrants are very vulnerable and at risk of marginalization, both while in transit and once at their destination. They therefore pose important development issues, including in the context of the 2030 Agenda for Sustainable Development and its central pledge to "leave no one behind."

Such movements are also causing political controversies in middle- and high-income countries. Although they represent only a fraction of people crossing borders, distressed movements are relatively visible. They contribute to shaping perceptions in destination countries,[1] including concerns that some migrants are abusing the immigration system or that the authorities have "lost control." These perceptions may, in turn, translate into xenophobic narratives and discriminatory practices.[2] In some cases, they could undermine the entire architecture of sound migration management and so reduce the development benefits of mutually beneficial movements.

Difficult trade-offs at the border

At the root of many distressed migrations are the vast economic differences between countries of origin and possible countries of destination. When these differences—and the corresponding drivers of migration—are acute, some people try to move even if they face high risks.[3]

Many destination countries do not allow entry of distressed migrants. In crafting their immigration policies, they prioritize their own interests, considering the labor market effects of migration as well as the broader effects on society. They typically give preference to migrants who have skills and attributes that match their needs.[4]

The conflation of high pressures to move, on the one hand, and severe entry restrictions, on the other, has led to the emergence of an illegal market for people smuggling and irregular movements. Most visible are the irregular entries—for example, at the US southern border, on the northern shores of the Mediterranean Sea, or at the border between Haiti and the Dominican Republic. Yet in many countries the majority of irregular migrants enter legally and overstay their visas.[5] In the United States, from 2010 to 2016 there were twice as many visa overstayers as irregular border crossings.[6] Similarly, in the United Kingdom the number of visa overstays exceeds illegal entries, even in 2021 when irregular inflows across the English Channel were at an all-time high.[7]

In the absence of legal pathways, some distressed migrants, upon entering their destination country, ask for asylum—that is, to be recognized as refugees (a status granted to those who have a "well-founded fear" of persecution or violence in their countries of origin). This request generally prevents their immediate deportation because it initiates a review process of the merits of their application for international protection. A large share of such requests are rejected, but the adjudication process takes time, allowing some distressed migrants to disappear into the fringes of society[8] so they cannot be identified and deported. Indeed, many asylum and reception systems are ill-equipped to process large numbers of people efficiently.[9] The delays create large backlogs, with extended waiting times. In the European Union, for example, more than 950,000 asylum cases were pending at the end of November 2022.[10] Such delays prolong the uncertainty under which all asylum-seekers live—including those who will eventually be recognized as refugees—and thus their vulnerability.[11]

Against this backdrop, many destination countries face difficult challenges in maintaining effective control of their borders. To deter distressed migration, some countries have adopted approaches that aim to make the movements less attractive to potential migrants. They include intentional policy measures, as well as toleration of situations—both in transit and at destination—that discourage unlawful entry and stay. However, when human distress becomes the modulator of migration flows, many destination countries have adopted policies that reflect the difficult trade-offs between their migration objectives and their commitments to respecting migrants' human rights:

- *Many destination countries have taken measures to deter irregular migration, especially of migrants who do not bring skills and attributes that match their labor market's needs.*[12] Such measures include penalties such as fines and imprisonment.[13] Some countries maintain provisions in their laws that include corporal punishment, such as judicial caning in Malaysia and Singapore.[14] In 2018, the US government implemented a program at its border with Mexico that separated children and infants from their parents or guardians with whom they had entered the United States in an explicit effort to deter irregular movements. In recent years, several high-income destination countries have entered into arrangements with third countries to "externalize" border control (box 8.1).[15]
- *When distressed migrants manage to enter, most destination countries do not provide them with any status, often as part of an explicit effort to reduce incentives for such movements.* As a result, distressed migrants are exposed to higher risk of abuse and marginalization. Migrants are three times as likely as citizens to work in situations of forced labor[16]—especially in sectors such as construction and domestic work[17]—and this particularly affects distressed migrants. Undocumented distressed migrants typically have only limited or no recourse in such situations. Moreover, in some countries undocumented status restricts migrants from access to education or health care services.[18]
- *In some cases, destination countries tolerate situations that aggravate migrants' distress and discourage their movements.* Nearly 50,000 migrants have died while in transit since 2014. Half of them perished while trying to cross the Mediterranean Sea,[19] but the deaths on other routes are also increasing (figure 8.2).[20] Distressed migrants are taking increasingly dangerous routes, and some have become victims of kidnapping, trafficking, sexual violence, and exploitation.[21] About 45 percent of those arriving in Italy in 2018 reported experiencing physical violence while in transit through African countries.[22] Some worked without pay, and some were held captive by criminal gangs.[23] Many undocumented migrants on their way to the US border through Central America face similar risks from criminal gangs.[24]

Harsh policies against migrants may effectively deter irregular migration, but they also undermine the fundamental principle that all migrants deserve fair and humane treatment. The challenges are particularly pressing for high-income destination countries—such as the United States and the southern European Union countries—that are in the immediate geographical vicinity of low- and middle-income origin countries. They are less urgent in destination countries farther removed such as Australia and Canada because of the significantly smaller numbers involved.

Box 8.1 The externalization of migration policy

In response to irregular migration pressures, several high-income destination countries have entered into agreements with other countries—typically low- or middle-income countries—to shift border control or asylum processing functions away from their physical borders.[a] This externalization of border control takes various forms,[b] as described in these examples:

- Italy entered into a series of bilateral agreements with Libya to cooperate on coast guard patrols and to provide development financing and technical and material support to combat irregular migration in the Mediterranean and in Libya.[c]
- Australia entered into an agreement with Papua New Guinea and Nauru in which these countries would process the claims of people seeking asylum in Australia and would settle those whose claims were successful (the agreement with Papua New Guinea ended at the end of 2021).[d] Under this arrangement, Australia provided a "package of assistance and other bilateral cooperation."[e]
- Türkiye and the European Union agreed on the return of irregular migrants who had crossed from Türkiye into the Greek islands, while the European Union committed to (1) resettling some Syrian refugees; (2) providing financial support for Syrian refugees in Türkiye; and (3) facilitating the issuance of Schengen visas to Turkish citizens.[f]
- The United States and Mexico entered into an arrangement in 2019 in which Mexico would take "unprecedented steps" to increase border enforcement to curb irregular migration and would hold asylum-seekers who had crossed the border from Mexico while their asylum claims were being adjudicated in the United States.[g]
- The United Kingdom established a partnership with Rwanda whereby asylum-seekers who reached the United Kingdom irregularly would be sent to Rwanda to lodge their asylum claims there. The arrangement also included financial commitments to supporting Rwanda's development.[h] This partnership is currently under legal review.

Such arrangements have been controversial. In the absence of sufficient safeguards, their implementation can contravene countries' legal obligations related to due process and the nonpenalization of asylum-seekers (*non-refoulement*) and human rights. For example, Italy's arrangement with Libya was condemned by the European Court of Human Rights in 2012[i] and denounced by the United Nations Special Rapporteur on the Human Rights of Migrants as exposing distressed migrants to death, torture, sexual and gender-based violence, labor exploitation, and other forms of contemporary slavery.[j]

Similarly, in 2016 the Supreme Court of Papua New Guinea found that detention of migrants and asylum-seekers transferred from Australia contravened Papua New Guinea's constitution.[k] Ongoing debates in the United Kingdom and the United States, among others, have yet to be settled.

a. FitzGerald (2019); Gammeltoft-Hansen (2011); Longo (2018); Sandven (2022); Shachar (2019, 2020).

b. Hatton (2017); Kaufmann (2021); Lutz, Kaufmann, and Stünzi (2020); UNHCR (2021).

c. See, for example, the Treaty of Friendship, Partnership, and Cooperation between the Italian Republic and the Great Socialist People's Libyan Arab Jamahiriya, 2008 (MPISOC 2014); Memorandum of Understanding on Cooperation in the Fields of Development, the Fight against Illegal Immigration, Human Trafficking and Fuel Smuggling and on Reinforcing the Security of Borders between the State of Libya and the Italian Republic, 2017 (Odysseus Network 2017).

d. Andrews (2021).

e. See, for example, the 2013 Australia–Papua New Guinea Memorandum of Understanding (DFAT 2013).

f. EC (2015); European Council (2016).

g. US State Department (2019).

h. Home Office (2022).

i. Hirsi Jamaa and Others v. Italy, Application 27765/09 (Judgment, European Court of Human Rights, November 16, 2016). See also Haitian Centre for Human Rights et al. v. United States, Case 10.675 (Inter-American Commission on Human Rights, Report 51/96, March 13, 1997).

j. OHCHR (2017).

k. Namah v. Pato, SCA 84 (Supreme Court of Justice of Papua New Guinea, 2013).

Figure 8.2 Thousands of migrants die every year in transit

Number of migrants dead or missing, by origin region

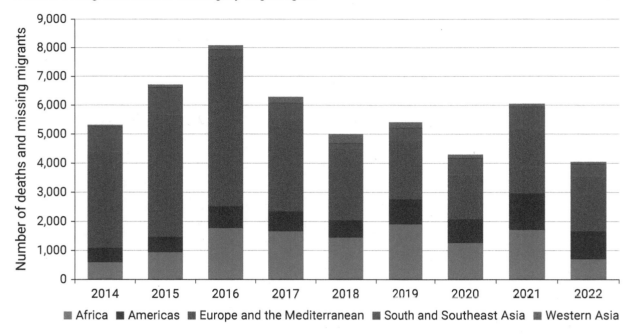

Source: Missing Migrants Project (dashboard), International Organization for Migration, Geneva, https://missingmigrants .iom.int/.

The peculiar situation of transit countries

Some distressed migrants travel through several countries before reaching their destination. In some cases, they merely pass through for a few days or a few weeks. In others, they stay longer—a few months or a few years—for a variety of reasons, including at times to earn the income needed to pay for the next stage of their journey. In still other cases, they try to settle, and only when they fail do they engage in further movements.[25] These distinct situations call for various responses by transit countries.

Most transit countries are part of broader corridors, with the longest corridors leading to high-income countries (map 8.1). These routes are highly dynamic, responding to legal restrictions and border controls by the transit and destination countries. Among those are the following:

- *The corridor from Latin America to the southern border of the United States through the Darien Gap and Central America.*[26] This corridor is primarily used by irregular migrants originating from Latin America, although there are increasing numbers of distressed migrants from other parts of the world.[27] The share of children and unaccompanied minors along this corridor has fluctuated according to the US policies affecting undocumented migrants' families.[28]
- *The corridors leading from Sub-Saharan Africa to the European Union.*[29] These corridors are composed of a set of distinct routes across the Sahara and the Mediterranean Sea that originate in West Africa and East Africa. The use of these routes is also fluctuating in the face of circumstances in countries of origin and restrictive measures adopted by destination countries. Irregular crossings on the Western Mediterranean route, through Morocco and Algeria, peaked in 2018 and are now declining, but irregular crossings on the Central Mediterranean route have been picking up since 2019 after a period of decline.[30]
- *The corridors leading from South Asia and the Middle East to the European Union through Türkiye.* This route was used extensively by refugees and distressed migrants in the mid-2010s, but it is now less significant.

Map 8.1 Main transit migration routes

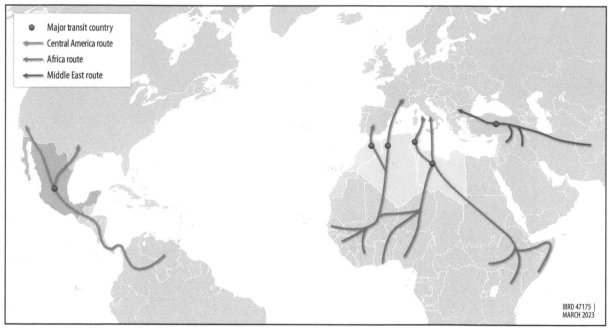

Sources: WDR 2023 team calculations based on Conant (2015) and World Bank (2018b).

Additional corridors include convoluted routes to high-income countries, such as the Arctic route used by over 5,000 migrants in 2016 that involved traveling through the Russian Federation and crossing its border with Norway.[31] They also include some relatively less visible corridors leading to middle-income destination countries such as South Africa and Thailand. In some cases, transit countries have actively encouraged migrants to come and cross from their territory to a destination country with which they have poor relations. For example, in 2021–22 Belarus provoked a crisis at its border with Poland in a situation referred to as the "instrumentalization" or the "weaponization" of migration.[32]

Some transit countries—the last countries before the border with attractive high-income destinations—face special challenges. When high-income destinations restrict entry into their territory, some distressed migrants end up stranded in the "last border" countries of transit. Some choose to return or are deported to their country of origin, but others stay—either to establish themselves in a second-best destination or, more commonly, to prepare for another attempt at border crossing.[33] Such stays can last for years.

For last border transit countries, accommodating an often-vulnerable population of distressed migrants comes at a cost. The distressed migrants' skills and attributes are not a strong match with the needs of their intended destination country, but they also may not meet the labor market needs of the last border transit country. Distressed migrants intending to continue their journey from the last border transit country also have limited incentives to integrate in its economy and in the broader society. Moreover, their demand for the services of smugglers fuels criminal networks and organizations, with heightened risks for the migrants and negative impacts on public safety.

The challenges faced by last border transit countries and the intended destination countries are inextricably linked. The situation of the last border transit countries is the result of restrictive policies adopted by the intended destination countries. However, the effectiveness of these restrictive policies depends on the ability of last border transit countries to manage distressed movements across their territory.

Thus the management of distressed migration cannot be resolved through unilateral approaches by destination countries; it requires cooperation. Most pressing is bilateral cooperation between the intended destination countries and the last border transit countries to ensure that the respective entry and asylum policies, and their implementation, are consistent (although not necessarily identical). Such coordinated policies must be grounded in the central tenets of international human rights law and recognize the inherent dignity of all migrants. In some situations, cooperation may also entail arrangements to ensure that the costs generated by high-income countries' policies and incurred by last border transit countries are shared adequately.

But what happens when the intended destination country and the last border transit country create a coordinated migration area? The border of this area then becomes the last border and another country finds itself in a difficult situation. Ultimately, then, for such an approach to achieve its full intent, a broader set of multilateral cooperation arrangements must be adopted along the entirety of a corridor.

Beyond the trade-offs

Distressed migration often entails much suffering—in transit and at destination—for those who undertake such movements. That leads to difficult trade-offs between managing borders and respecting human rights that frequently are not resolved satisfactorily. Reducing the need for such movements is thus critical. Progress will require short-term action to expand protection to the most at risk among irregular migrants, to develop legal channels for entry that can shift migrants' incentives, and to use development to provide alternatives to cross-border movement and strengthen the match of migrants' skills and attributes with the needs of destination economies (figure 8.3).

Figure 8.3 Coordinated policy action in origin and destination countries can reduce distressed migration

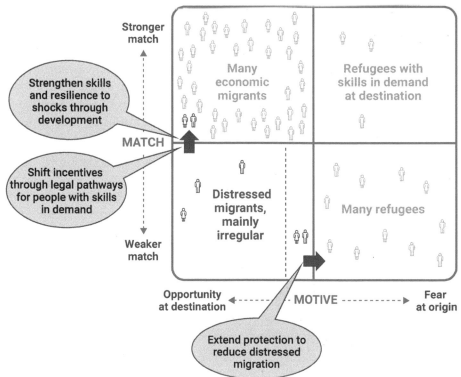

Source: WDR 2023 team.

Note: Match refers to the degree to which a migrant's skills and related attributes meet the demand in the destination country. *Motive* refers to the circumstances under which a person moves—whether in search of opportunity or because of a "well-founded fear" of persecution, armed conflict, or violence in their origin country. The dashed vertical line in the lower-left quadrant highlights the distinction between distressed migrants who have some needs for international protection and those who do not.

Extending international protection

Some distressed migrants are facing high risks if they return—or are deported—to their countries of origin. For example, they may be moving to escape gang violence, severe economic deprivation, or other forms of harm. The simple dichotomy between refugees and nonrefugees masks, in fact, a continuum of international protection needs (figure 8.4). International law distinguishes between refugees (who are entitled to international protection and its associated rights) and other migrants (who are not entitled to any particular rights or status beyond what national legislation may provide).[34] Yet the degree of harm to which people would be exposed if they were to return—or be sent back—to their country of origin varies, along a range of possible threats with different levels of severity.

In this context, some distressed migrants have international protection needs but not to a level that would qualify them as refugees. The risks they are willing to take to cross borders reveals a degree of despair and suggests that the conditions in their country of origin are worth risking their life to escape. These migrants may need some form of protection, but for reasons that fall outside of the 1951 Refugee Convention such as acute humanitarian crises. Others may not receive international refugee protection because of different interpretations of the 1951 Refugee Convention and other applicable legal instruments (box 8.2).[35]

There is no consensus, however, on how to precisely identify or define those who fall between the cracks of the international protection system. Several terms and concepts have emerged to serve a variety of academic, institutional, advocacy, and statistical purposes, although they do not determine legal status. Some categorizations are based on legal protection needs (whether people would be at risk of serious harm if returned and whether their country of origin is willing and able to mitigate such risks). This approach is exemplified by the term *persons in need of international protection* used by the United Nations High Commissioner for Refugees.[36] Other categorizations focus on the vulnerabilities of migrants in a specific situation, such as the references in the Global Compact on Migration to "migrants who face situations of vulnerability" and "missing migrants" or the concept of "migrants in vulnerable situations," which is used by the International Organization for Migration and other international organizations.[37] Still other categorizations reflect the motivations for movements, proposing terms such as *climate refugees*,[38] *survival migrants*,[39] or *flee-ers of necessity*.[40]

Amid pressing situations, some destination countries have acknowledged that some distressed migrants, although not refugees, still need a form of international protection, even if it comes at a cost. They have developed instruments to provide complementary protection for these people[41] and to regularize their entry or stay.[42] These instruments are defined by national or regional laws and include a variety

Figure 8.4 A continuum of needs falls under international protection

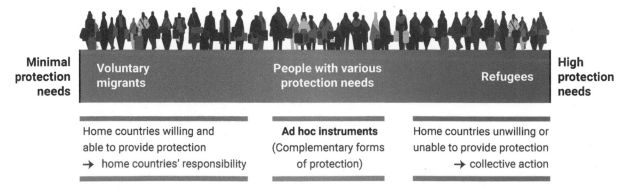

Source: WDR 2023 team.

Box 8.2 The evolving definition of *refugee*

Although the 1951 Refugee Convention provides the overarching legal framework for international refugee protection, there are substantive variations in the way the corresponding principles are implemented:

- Within the framework of international refugee law, states exercise discretion in how they process and adjudicate asylum claims. A person whose claim for international protection would succeed in one destination country may not succeed in another, as evidenced by the wide variations in the recognition rates for Afghan asylum-seekers across European Union countries in 2021 (figure B8.2.1). Although some of the differences are due to the way these rates are computed, they also stem from the different legal instruments, interpretations, and priorities in these countries.
- The definition of *refugee* also varies across regions, reflecting historical circumstances and the varied nature of displacement crises. For example, the 1969 Organisation of African Unity (OAU) Convention Governing the Specific Aspects of Refugee Problems in Africa expanded the definition of *refugee* to include those who flee due to "external aggression, occupation, foreign domination, or events seriously disturbing public order."[a] This definition was drafted not only to protect those in Africa not covered by the individualized, persecution-based refugee definition of the 1951 Refugee Convention,[b] but also to ensure that refugee issues would not be a source of friction between states and that individuals fleeing colonial and apartheid rules would receive refugee protection.[c] Similarly, in Latin America the 1984 Cartagena Declaration on Refugees extended international protection to several groups,[d] including

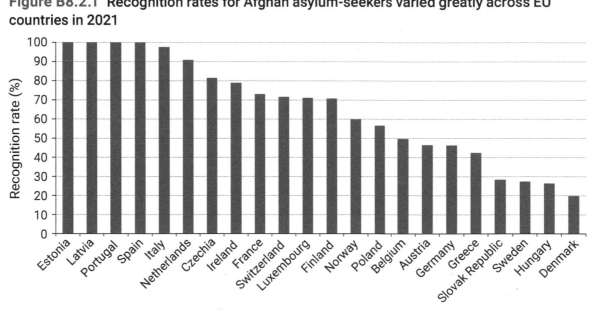

Figure B8.2.1 Recognition rates for Afghan asylum-seekers varied greatly across EU countries in 2021

Source: Refugee Data Finder (dashboard), United Nations High Commissioner for Refugees, Geneva, https://popstats.unhcr.org/refugee-statistics/download/.

Note: The figure excludes some European Union (EU) countries that received very few applications from asylum-seekers from Afghanistan.

(Box continues next page)

Box 8.2 **The evolving definition of** *refugee* *(continued)*

those who flee "because their lives, safety or freedom have been threatened by generalized violence, foreign aggression, internal conflicts, massive violation of human rights or other circumstances which have seriously disturbed public order."[e]

In a growing number of situations, host countries opt to provide complementary or subsidiary protection to those fleeing conflict and violence rather than recognize them as refugees. For example, countries hosting the largest numbers of people fleeing from recent crises—about 20 million people from Myanmar, República Bolivariana de Venezuela, South Sudan, the Syrian Arab Republic, and Ukraine—have provided them with some temporary or ad hoc protection. The reasons vary for using such protection instruments rather than a refugee status. They range from political considerations about the country of origin, to the practicality of processing large numbers of asylum claims, to concerns about setting precedents, to attempts to minimize obligations on the host country.[f]

a. United Nations (1976, 47).
b. Okoth-Obbo (2001).
c. Sharpe (2013).
d. Reed-Hurtado (2013).
e. Cartagena Declaration on Refugees, Conclusion 3 (UNHCR 1984, 36).
f. These arrangements include: (1) the Temporary Protection Directive of the European Union (EU), which enables Ukrainians to reside and work in EU countries without undergoing refugee status adjudication; (2) a regime of temporary protection for Syrians in Türkiye that was eventually codified as part of Türkiye's 2014 Law on Foreigners and International Protection; (3) a Temporary Statute of Protection for Venezuelan Migrants in Colombia, which granted 10-year residency, work permits, and other rights. On (1), see EU (2001); Ukraine Refugee Situation (dashboard), Operational Data Portal, United Nations High Commissioner for Refugees, Geneva, https://data.unhcr.org/en/situations/ukraine; UNHCR (2022). On (2), see *T.C. Resmî Gazete* (2013). On (3), see MRE (2021); Venezuela Refugee Situation (dashboard), Operational Data Portal, United Nations High Commissioner for Refugees, Geneva, https://data.unhcr.org/en/situations/vensit.

of rights, legal statuses, and scopes of application based on humanitarian principles or national interests. They take a variety of forms, such as subsidiary protection or temporary protection measures (figure 8.5). They also provide flexibility and enable international protection to be provided quickly without placing much additional pressure on asylum systems. For example, the United States provided Honduran nationals with complementary protection in 1999 in the aftermath of Hurricane Mitch[43] and Haitians with such protection in the immediate aftermath of the 2010 earthquake.[44] The global share of people receiving such complementary forms of protection has been increasing over time, particularly since 2011.

Such ad hoc systems have, however, proved insufficient to address what has become a growing human and political crisis. Complementary protection measures can be withdrawn through simple executive decisions, as occurred in the United States for Salvadorans in 2018. For some destination countries, there is simply no legal route to entry for those in need of some degree of international protection. Complementary protection regimes are also inconsistent across destination countries, with wide variations in terms of who can benefit from complementary protection and what status they receive. Although some of these differences reflect national or regional circumstances, they also lead to inconsistencies that have detrimental consequences for the affected individuals, and they diminish the potential for an effective system of responsibility-sharing.

A forward-looking approach based on coordinated, flexible international responses is needed. There is no reason to believe that the number of crises, conflicts, natural disasters, and other situations that give rise to distressed cross-border movements will significantly decline in the coming period. In fact, the acceleration of climate change suggests that extraordinary measures may be needed (box 8.3).

Figure 8.5 Complementary protection is a complex maze

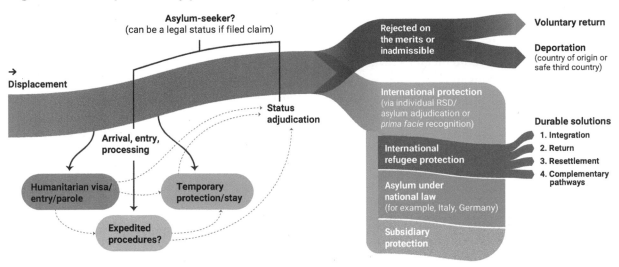

Source: WDR 2023 team.
Note: RSD = Refugee Status Determination.

Box 8.3 Climate-related mobility in Small Island Developing States

Some countries are facing high risks from climate change. For example, if and when climate change imperils the local adaptation and habitability of the Small Island Developing States and low-lying coastal settlements, the populations of these areas may need some planned relocation and a managed retreat.[a] The Global Compact for Safe, Orderly and Regular Migration includes specific commitments to better protect those involved in or affected by these movements.[b]

Many Small Island Developing States have proactively integrated climate change–related mobility into national policy frameworks. The objective is to help people to remain in place where it is viable to do so and ensure that those who choose to move have opportunities to do so. For example, Vanuatu's National Policy on Climate Change and Disaster-Induced Displacement, adopted in 2018, includes actions on return and reintegration, local integration, and planned relocation. It also incorporates mobility into development planning.[c] Fiji's Displacement Guidelines emphasize the interconnections among environmental change, human rights, and mobility.[d] In the Caribbean, two free movement agreements by the Caribbean Community (CARICOM) and the Organisation of Eastern Caribbean States (OECS) grant protection to Caribbean nationals displaced by catastrophic hurricanes, including a right of entry to other islands, a waiver of work permit requirements, and a mutual recognition of skills.[e]

Depending on the magnitude of climate impacts, migration may become unavoidable for Small Island Developing States, and planned relocation may be an option of last resort. Plans for relocation will need to empower people to make their own decisions. International assistance may be needed, including to develop a form of international protection or similar status to enable migration.[f]

a. Cissé et al. (2022).
b. Martin et al. (2018).
c. NDMO (2018).
d. Ministry of Economy, Fiji (2019).
e. Francis (2019).
f. UNHCR, Brookings Institution, and Georgetown University (2015); UNHCR, Georgetown University, and IOM (2017).

Accordingly, coordination among destination countries is needed to adopt a more coherent, predictable approach that offers some type of international protection quickly and efficiently to those who warrant it. This approach could include providing *prima facie* protection to specific groups—that is, granting protection to all persons in that group, such as citizens of a certain country of origin or members of a minority—instead of going through an individual refugee status determination process. It also could include adapting or expanding complementary protection mechanisms in particular crises and ensuring that individuals are able to secure safe legal pathways from their country of origin. Moreover, this approach would require building the institutional capacity needed for timely, transparent adjudication of protection status and for safeguarding human rights for those who need to be returned once their applications have been denied following due process.

Shifting migrants' incentives through legal pathways

Establishing legal pathways for people at all levels of skills to enter destination countries and work in the formal sector—and doing so at scale—can help reduce the incentives for distressed movements. It can also transform distressed movements into mutually beneficial migration, in which migrants bring skills and attributes in demand in the destination labor market. Such legal pathways can include temporary or even seasonal arrangements.

By providing legal pathways, destination countries shift potential migrants' incentives, including for those who otherwise would engage in high-risk movements through irregular channels.[45] For example, by offering legal entry pathways to people with certain qualifications, destination countries can encourage would-be migrants—and the communities that often help finance their movements—to acquire the skills and other attributes needed to contribute in the new country. This process can help shift the composition of migratory movements—who moves and under what circumstances—toward an outcome that more closely matches the needs and preferences of the destination society. Moreover, the availability of legal pathways reduces the incentives for migrants who are already in the country to overstay their visas and end up in a protracted irregular situation.

In designing legal pathways, destination countries need to closely reflect the needs of their labor market. In many countries, legal entry pathways are primarily available to high-skilled migrants. However, many destination countries also need lower-skilled workers. By recognizing and acknowledging unmet needs in their labor markets and providing migrants who have the corresponding skills with legal entry pathways—including for relatively lower-skilled jobs, such as in agriculture, construction, or household services—destination countries can shift potential migrants' incentives and reduce the pressure for distressed movements. This effort requires engaging with employers, labor unions, and other stakeholders to determine which skills are in demand.

In parallel, some destination countries have strengthened their cooperation with countries of origin to develop skills that are in demand and to facilitate win-win movements—for example, through Global Skills Partnerships.[46] Under this approach, destination countries finance the training of potential migrants in their origin countries and provide them with entry upon graduation. These programs can also shift incentives for would-be migrants and the communities who support them to acquire skills that are in demand. To date, such programs have largely focused on relatively high-skilled occupations, but they could be extended to include workers with lower levels of qualifications.

In addition to developing legal pathways for entry—and to ensure their sustainability—destination countries need to ensure enforcement of the existing laws and regulations aimed at discouraging irregular entries. Enforcement often requires action in several directions:

Box 8.4 Smugglers and traffickers

The people smuggling industry is complex, dynamic, and constantly evolving. According to estimates by the United Nations Office on Drugs and Crime (UNODC), at least 2.5 million migrants were smuggled in 2016 for an economic return of US$5.5–$7 billion, making it an important part of the illegal economy. This amount was roughly equivalent to the humanitarian aid budget of the United States or of the European Union that year.[a]

The organization and scale of smuggling operations vary. Smugglers may work largely on their own, within a small network in one or two countries, or as part of large, complex multinational criminal organizations. They may provide legal services such as taxi transportation or be part of sophisticated transnational criminal networks. At times, smuggling operations are based on independent actors loosely linked via social networks and communicating via digital technology, complicating efforts to combat this phenomenon. Ethnographic research suggests that portraying smugglers as criminals and migrants as their victims may oversimplify a complex and often symbiotic relationship.[b]

The line between *smuggling* (a voluntary movement of migrants by a smuggler who receives payment to take them to a destination) and *human trafficking* (movement that includes an element of extortion, exploitation, or coercion) is often blurred. Undocumented migrants make up a significant share of the victims of human trafficking: 65 percent in Western and Southern Europe, 60 percent in the Middle East, 55 percent in East Asia and the Pacific, 50 percent in Central and Southeastern Europe, and 25 percent in North America.[c] In 2014, the International Labour Organization (ILO) estimated the profits of trafficking and forced labor at about US$150 billion a year.[d] Two-thirds of this amount stems from commercial sexual exploitation and the rest from forced economic exploitation.

a. McAuliffe and Laczko (2016); UNODC (2018).
b. Achilli (2018); Campana (2018); Maher (2018); Majidi (2018); McAuliffe and Laczko (2016); UNODC (2018).
c. Koser (2010); McAuliffe and Laczko (2016); Nicot and Kopp (2018); Triandafyllidou (2018a, 2018b); UNODC (2018).
d. ILO (2014).

- *Combat smuggling.* Human smuggling operations take many forms (box 8.4), and they are increasingly assuming professionalized forms. Some smugglers behave as professional businesspersons, guaranteeing services and agreeing to receive final payment when the migrant reaches the final destination.[47] Other smuggling operations are far less benign, with migrants undergoing traumatic ordeals throughout their transit. Destination countries have launched far-reaching programs to combat smuggling through law enforcement, educational programs, and efforts to protect the rights of those who have been smuggled.[48] The programs have to rely on effective international cooperation along entire corridors.
- *Clamp down on irregular labor markets.* The attractiveness of irregular channels depends on whether there is a demand for irregular labor from employers. For distressed migrants—whose skills are not a strong match for the needs of the destination economy—such irregular labor is often exploitative. Yet the welfare gaps between origin and destination countries are often so large that they create formidable market forces that drive people to move. Efforts to restrict distressed migration cannot succeed if employers are willing and able to hire these migrants. Most countries have laws and regulations against such irregular—and often exploitative—employment,

but they are unevenly enforced, if at all. Clamping down on the irregular labor market—and reducing the costs of compliance with the law—is critical. For countries with large numbers of migrants in an irregular situation, transitioning to regular status requires policies that often include some amnesty for migrants and their employers.

- *Return migrants humanely.* Destination countries may choose to return some distressed migrants who do not face risks in their countries of origin. Deportation is always a tragedy for the individuals involved, but it may be necessary to ensure the sustainability of the migration system because it demonstrates to both citizens and would-be migrants that rules are enforced. However, enforcing returns is fraught with risks, including possible human rights violations.[49] Accordingly, the Global Compact for Safe, Orderly and Regular Migration calls for cooperation between states in facilitating safe, dignified return and readmission for migrants, as well as sustainable reintegration.[50] In practice, forced returns are exceedingly difficult if the origin countries do not cooperate. Thus to be sustainable, such agreements should reflect the interests of both the destination and origin countries[51] and possibly be framed within the broader context of bilateral migration arrangements. Some destination countries have attempted to accompany involuntary returns with support for their reintegration into their countries of origin, but with mixed results.

In some destination countries, efforts are also needed to strengthen the capacity of the institutions that process entries, including when people require asylum. For example, following the arrivals of large numbers of migrants and refugees in the summer of 2015, Germany's Federal Office for Migration and Refugees (BAMF) engaged in a modernization and digitalization effort that dramatically increased its ability to process requests for asylum.[52] Processing requests for asylum or for visas expeditiously can reduce the incentives for distressed migrants' use of irregular channels for entry.

Strengthening the match of migrants' skills and attributes through development

Over time, development can reduce the need for distressed migration. As countries develop, their citizens become better educated, and their skills better match the needs of the domestic and global labor markets. They also become more resilient to shocks, and domestic alternatives reduce the need for distressed cross-border movements.

The effects of economic development on the propensity to emigrate are complex. A review of the existing evidence suggests several patterns.[53] As middle-income countries develop, emigration steadily increases, and it is increasingly directed toward higher-income countries. By contrast, as low-income countries develop, emigration initially declines until they reach middle-income levels of development. These effects depend significantly on the size of a country's population: they are significant in smaller, less populous countries (which account for half of all countries but only 3.5 percent of the global population), and they are much more muted in larger countries. On average, emigrants from middle-income countries have more skills and easier access to attractive destinations when compared with those from low-income countries.[54]

How countries develop also matters. The gains of development are typically not distributed uniformly within a country. When development and income gains disproportionately benefit particular segments of the population, migration patterns are affected. For example, if domestic income gains accrue only to those who are relatively well-off and educated—and who are more likely to emigrate to high-income destinations—then emigration to those destinations may increase even though emigration to low-income countries remains unchanged. On the other hand, if domestic income gains from development accrue to the poorest people in low-income countries, emigration to low-income countries and neighboring countries may fall without increasing emigration to high-income countries (which is costlier).

Discussions of the effects of foreign aid on emigration[55] are taking place in a context where some donors aim to use their assistance to address the "root causes" of migration—especially distressed migration.[56] As for many development activities, the impacts vary across countries and sectors, and programs need to be tailored to each context. For example, in some countries support for better governance has dampened emigration by improving government capacity and reducing grievances.[57] Infrastructure projects can enhance market integration and increase local incomes.[58] In the long term, development assistance also helps transform the origin society, with profound consequences for migration patterns.

Development is typically associated with an improvement in institutional capacity. As countries become wealthier, they are better equipped to manage migration for their own purposes, as well as through cooperation with other countries. Development is also associated with demographic changes—a reduction in fertility rates and an increase in life expectancy. These changes affect, in turn, social dynamics, the size of the pool of potential migrants, and opportunities in the domestic labor market that can provide alternatives to cross-border movements.

Better skills matching

Economic development is almost always accompanied by improvements in human capital such as education and skills. People and countries invest more in education as they become wealthier, and, in return, their better-educated workforce becomes an engine of economic development and growth. For example, as Bangladesh's gross domestic product (GDP) per capita doubled between 1960 and 2015, the average years of schooling for the adult population increased drastically—from 1.0 years to 6.9 years—and the share of adults with some tertiary education grew from 0.33 percent to 8.6 percent.[59] This experience matches that of almost all low- or middle-income countries that have experienced economic growth.

Higher educational attainment shifts migration patterns toward better-educated and higher-skilled workers. As countries of origin develop, the skills composition of their emigrants changes. Lower-educated workers tend to be better qualified with stronger language and vocational skills, and a larger share of emigrants tends to be tertiary-educated (figure 8.6). Emigrants from more developed countries thus tend to be a stronger match for the needs of destination labor markets. This is especially true where the expectations for low-skilled workers are increasing—for example, in terms of communication, interpersonal skills, and the ability to work with autonomy—in parallel with the stepped-up demand in service occupations, such as caregiving and hospitality.[60]

Strengthened resilience

As origin countries develop, governments become increasingly able to help citizens strengthen their resilience to shocks, such as those produced by economic downturns and natural disasters.[61] Social protection systems serve as a safety net for the poor and vulnerable and for people who because of personal circumstances, such as illness or accidents, are facing temporary hardship. In Ethiopia, for example, the Productive Safety Net Programme provides assistance through public works in an adaptive manner: it expands when shocks and crises materialize.[62] Evidence of the impacts of such programs on international migration is scant, but they have reduced the need for domestic movements. An example is a place-based public works program in India.[63] Such programs essentially give people going through a difficult period more options.

Figure 8.6 Economic development changes the composition of migration flows: The education level of emigrants improves as countries develop

Education level of emigrants, by GDP per capita growth rate of origin countries

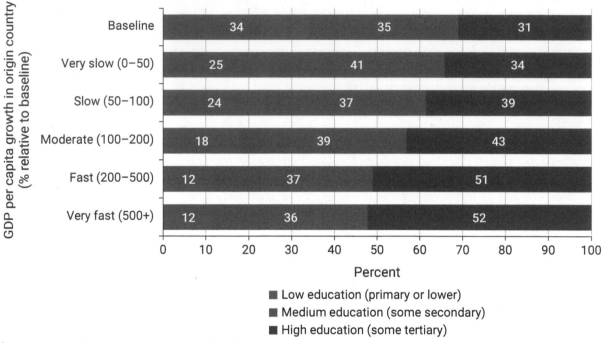

Source: Adapted from figure 9 in Shrestha (2023).

Note: The figure plots the educational composition of migrants from low- and middle-income countries to the United States as origin countries develop. The vertical axis represents the increase in gross domestic product (GDP) per capita of origin countries relative to the baseline year, defined for each origin country as the year in which GDP per capita (in constant 2017 US dollars in purchasing power parity terms, 2017 PPP$) was at its lowest level since 1960. Observations are grouped by growth, and the bars represent the average share in each group. Low- and middle-income countries were among the bottom two-thirds of all countries circa 1960 in terms of GDP per capita (2017 PPP$). Estimates exclude outliers in terms of emigration rates (Antigua and Barbuda, Bosnia and Herzegovina, Dominica, Grenada, Saint Kitts and Nevis, and West Bank and Gaza).

Development also increases the economic options at home, especially in relatively large countries. As low-income countries develop, economic activities and people shift from largely rural subsistence agriculture to manufacturing and service activities in the cities.[64] Indeed, the share of the population in urban areas in low- and middle-income countries has risen steadily, from 23 percent in 1960 to 51 percent in 2020.[65] Domestic migration offers higher incomes than in the region of origin, and it typically entails lower costs and risks than international migration. In fact, it can act as a substitute for international migration, particularly for distressed movements. Inclusive development, the availability of decent jobs at home, and their accessibility to all increase the range of options, so that migration, when it occurs, becomes the outcome of a larger rather than a smaller opportunity to choose.

Finally, development allows countries, communities, and households to adapt to the effects of climate change. Building domestic resilience to climate change means enabling people to adapt where they live when viable or to move under better circumstances, and it prepares destination areas to receive them.[66] The cities that will serve as key destinations for internal mobility in many regions will have to account for climate risks in urban planning and land use management,[67] including in the form of climate-resilient housing and infrastructure investments, connectivity networks, social services, and employment opportunities.

International migration, when it occurs, can thus take place under better circumstances. Most people putting their lives at risk while trying to enter a destination country irregularly are from low- or lower-income countries. The journeys of migrants from middle- or upper-middle-income countries tend to be less perilous. Their movement is a choice made under less stringent constraints, typically involving less suffering on their part and less excruciating policy dilemmas in their destination countries. "Leave no one behind"—the principle underpinning the 2030 Agenda for Sustainable Development—implies making migration less distressed for migrants and more fruitful for origin and destination countries.

Notes

1. Azevedo et al. (2021); Boomgaarden and Vliegenthart (2009); Heidenreich et al. (2020); Innes (2010); Madrigal and Soroka (2023); Průchová Hrůzová (2021); Slovic et al. (2017).
2. Hatton (2017); Lutz, Kaufmann, and Stünzi (2020); Pereira, Vala, and Costa-Lopes (2010); Poynting and Briskman (2020); Průchová Hrůzová (2021); Ravn et al. (2020).
3. Harris and Todaro (1970).
4. IOM (2002); Triandafyllidou, Bartolini, and Guidi (2019).
5. Irregular Migration and Return (dashboard), Directorate-General for Migration and Home Affairs, European Commission, Brussels, https://home-affairs.ec.europa.eu/irregular-migration-return_en.
6. Warren (2019).
7. Walsh (2020).
8. Bertoli, Brücker, and Fernández-Huertas Moraga (2022); McAuliffe and Laczko (2016).
9. Hatton (2009); Himmelreich (2019); Kaufmann (2021); Lutz, Kaufmann, and Stünzi (2020).
10. EUAA (2022). Eurostat data on pending cases at all instances in November 2022 were available for 28 EU+ countries, and the October value was used for the missing country. EU+ refers to the European Union, Switzerland, and Norway.
11. Bertoli, Brücker, and Fernández-Huertas Moraga (2022); McAuliffe and Laczko (2016).
12. Harris and Todaro (1970).
13. Gibney (2008); Global Detention Project (dashboard), Global Detention Project, Geneva, https://www.globaldetentionproject.org/; Könönen (2022); Majcher, Flynn, and Grange (2020).
14. See Commissioner of Law Revision, Malaysia (2006); Singapore Statutes Online (2021).
15. Burnett (2018); Rosenberg (2018).
16. Forced or compulsory labor is "all work or service which is exacted from any person under the menace of any penalty and for which the said person has not offered himself voluntarily." See Article 2, Forced Labour Convention, Convention C029 (adopted at the 14th Session of the International Labour Conference, June 28, 1930), NORMLEX, International Labour Organization, Geneva, https://www.ilo.org/dyn/normlex/en/f?p=1000:12100:0::NO::P12100_ILO_CODE:C029.
17. ILO, Walk Free, and IOM (2022).
18. Klugman and Pereira (2009); Migrant Integration Policy Index 2020 (dashboard), Migration Policy Group and Barcelona Centre for International Affairs, Barcelona, https://www.mipex.eu/; Ravn et al. (2020).
19. GMDAC (2020).
20. Black and Sigman (2022).
21. Bossard (2009); Busetta et al. (2021); Cornelius (2001); Gathmann (2008); IOM (2021); Jacobsen, Ayoub, and Johnson (2014); Koser (2000); Leyva-Flores et al. (2019); OHCHR (2016); Reques et al. (2020); Vogt (2018); WHO (2022); World Bank (2018a).
22. World Bank (2018a).
23. World Bank (2018a).
24. Albuja (2014); Infante et al. (2012).
25. Allie et al. (2021).
26. Vogt (2018).
27. Solomon (2019).
28. US Border Patrol (USBP) and Office of Field Operations (OFO) official year-end reporting for fiscal 2020 to fiscal 2022 and fiscal 2023, as of January 4, 2023. Beginning in March 2020, US Border Patrol Encounters statistics include both Title 8 Apprehensions and Title 42 Expulsions. Apprehensions refers to the physical control or temporary detainment of a person who is not lawfully in the United States, which may or may not result in an arrest. Since 2008, there has been a significant increase in unaccompanied children apprehended at the US southern border. Initially, Mexican children predominated, but as of 2012 the number of children from Central American countries was higher.
29. Düvell (2012); Nonnenmacher and Yonemura (2018); Wajsberg (2020); World Bank (2018a).
30. Frontex (2023).
31. Reuters (2016).
32. Łubiński (2022).
33. Kuschminder and Waidler (2020); Sačer et al. (2017); Wajsberg (2020).
34. Bakewell (2021); Crawley and Skleparis (2018); Erdal and Oeppen (2018).
35. Türk and Dowd (2014).
36. UNHCR Master Glossary of Terms (dashboard), United Nations High Commissioner for Refugees, Geneva, https://www.unhcr.org/glossary/.
37. UNHCR Master Glossary of Terms (dashboard), United Nations High Commissioner for Refugees, Geneva, https://www.unhcr.org/glossary/.
38. Apap (2021).
39. Betts (2013).
40. Aleinikoff and Zamore (2019).

41. Paoletti (2023); UNHCR Master Glossary of Terms (dashboard), United Nations High Commissioner for Refugees, Geneva, https://www.unhcr.org/glossary/.
42. Johns, Loschmann, and Arekapudi (2023).
43. US Immigration and Naturalization Service (1999).
44. USCIS (2010).
45. Auriol, Mesnard, and Perrault (2021); Czaika and de Haas (2013, 2017); Czaika and Hobolth (2016).
46. See chapter 5 for further details.
47. Martin (2000).
48. Martin (2000).
49. Some countries have put in place incentives and programs to soften the impact of forced returns on affected migrants. Such schemes are typically aimed at facilitating the return and reinsertion of those who are forced to return to their origin country. They may include outreach and counseling (OECD 2020) or financial incentives (Black, Collyer, and Somerville 2011). Their uptake, however, has been relatively low, and their actual impact is unclear (OECD 2020).
50. United Nations (2019).
51. Newland and Salant (2018).
52. Koch et al. (2023).
53. See spotlight 8.
54. For example, visa costs are higher for migrants traveling from low-income countries to high-income destinations. Ortega and Peri (2013) also find that migration flows to OECD destinations are very responsive to immigration policies.
55. Clemens and Postel (2018).
56. Bermeo and Leblang (2015); see also NSC (2021).
57. Dustmann and Okatenko (2014); Gamso and Yuldashev (2018).
58. Morten and Oliveira (2023).
59. Barro-Lee Estimates of Educational Attainment in the World (Barro and Lee 2013); Feenstra, Inklaar, and Timmer (2015); Penn World Table (database version 10.0), Groningen Growth and Development Centre, Faculty of Economics and Business, University of Groningen, Groningen, the Netherlands, https://www.rug.nl/ggdc/productivity/pwt/.
60. According to the US Bureau of Labor Statistics, the top three occupations that will add the highest number of jobs in the United States by 2030 are home health and personal care aides, cooks, and fast food and counter workers. Less than 20 percent of workers in these occupations have a college degree. See Occupational Outlook Handbook (portal), Office of Occupational Statistics and Employment Projections, Bureau of Labor Statistics, US Department of Labor, Washington, DC, https://www.bls.gov/ooh/.
61. For example, OECD countries spend, on average, 12 percent of their GDP on social benefits to households. World Bank data show that low- and middle-income countries spend 1.5 percent of their GDP on social assistance, with low-income countries lagging middle-income countries. See ASPIRE (Atlas of Social Protection Indicators of Resilience and Equity) (dashboard), World Bank, Washington, DC, https://www.worldbank.org/en/data/datatopics/aspire; Social Benefits to Households (dashboard), Organisation for Economic Co-operation and Development, Paris, https://data.oecd.org/socialexp/social-benefits-to-households.htm.
62. Productive Safety Net Programme in Ethiopia (dashboard), Capacity4dev, European Commission, Brussels, https://europa.eu/capacity4dev/project_psnp_ethiopia.
63. Imbert and Papp (2020); Morten (2019).
64. McMillan, Rodrik, and Sepúlveda (2017).
65. Crock and Parsons (2023).
66. Clement et al. (2021).
67. Clement et al. (2021).

References

Achilli, Luigi. 2018. "The 'Good' Smuggler: The Ethics and Morals of Human Smuggling among Syrians." *Annals of the American Academy of Political and Social Science* 676 (1): 77–96.

Albuja, Sebastián. 2014. "Criminal Violence, Displacement, and Migration in Mexico and Central America." In *Humanitarian Crises and Migration Causes, Consequences, and Responses*, edited by Susan F. Martin, Sanjula Weerasinghe, and Abbie Taylor, 113–37. Abingdon, UK: Routledge.

Aleinikoff, T. Alexander, and Leah Zamore. 2019. *The Arc of Protection: Reforming the International Refugee Regime*. Stanford Briefs Series. Stanford, CA: Stanford University Press.

Allie, Feyaad, Darin Christensen, Guy Grossman, and Jeremy Weinstein. 2021. "Using IOM Flow Monitoring Data to Describe Migration in West and Central Africa." IPL Report (September), Immigration Policy Lab, Stanford University, Stanford, CA. https://immigrationlab.org/content/uploads/2021/09/IPL-Report_African-Migration.pdf.

Andrews, Karen. 2021. "Joint Media Release with the Hon. Westly Nukundj MP: Finalisation of the Regional Resettlement Arrangement." Media release, October 6, 2021. https://minister.homeaffairs.gov.au/KarenAndrews/Pages/finalisation-of-the-regional-resettlement-arrangement.aspx.

Apap, Joanna. 2021. "The Concept of 'Climate Refugee': Towards a Possible Definition." With Capucine du Perron de Revel. EPRS Briefing (October 18), European Parliamentary Research Service, Brussels. https://www.europarl.europa.eu/RegData/etudes/BRIE/2021/698753/EPRS_BRI(2021)698753_EN.pdf.

Auriol, Emmanuelle, Alice Mesnard, and Tiffanie Perrault. 2021. "Controlling Irregular Migration: Can a Market for Temporary Foreign Work Permits Help?" CEPR Discussion Paper DP 16777, Centre for Economic Policy Research, London.

Azevedo, Ruben T., Sophie De Beukelaer, Isla L. Jones, Lou Safra, and Manos Tsakiris. 2021. "When the Lens Is Too Wide: The Political Consequences of the Visual

Dehumanization of Refugees." *Humanities and Social Sciences Communications* 8 (1): 115.

Bakewell, Oliver. 2021. "Unsettling the Boundaries between Forced and Voluntary Migration." In *Handbook on the Governance and Politics of Migration*, edited by Emma Carmel, Katharina Lenner, and Regine Paul, 124–36. Elgar Handbooks in Migration Series. Cheltenham, UK: Edward Elgar.

Barro, Robert J., and Jong-Wha Lee. 2013. "A New Data Set of Educational Attainment in the World, 1950–2010." *Journal of Development Economics* 104 (September): 184–98.

Bermeo, Sarah Blodgett, and David Leblang. 2015. "Migration and Foreign Aid." *Industrial Organization* 69 (3): 627–57.

Bertoli, Simone, Herbert Brücker, and Jesús Fernández-Huertas Moraga. 2022. "Do Applications Respond to Changes in Asylum Policies in European Countries?" *Regional Science and Urban Economics* 93 (March): 103771.

Betts, Alexander. 2013. *Survival Migration: Failed Governance and the Crisis of Displacement*. Ithaca, NY: Cornell University Press.

Black, Julia, and Zoe Sigman. 2022. "50,000 Lives Lost during Migration: Analysis of Missing Migrants Project Data 2014–2022." Global Migration Data Analysis Centre, International Organization for Migration, Berlin.

Black, Richard E., Michael Collyer, and Will Somerville. 2011. "Pay-to-Go Schemes and Other Noncoercive Return Programs: Is Scale Possible?" Migration Policy Institute, Washington, DC.

Boomgaarden, Hajo G., and Rens Vliegenthart. 2009. "How News Content Influences Anti-Immigration Attitudes: Germany, 1993–2005." *European Journal of Political Research* 48 (4): 516–42.

Bossard, Laurent. 2009. "The Future of International Migration to OECD Countries: Regional Note West Africa." Organisation for Economic Co-Operation and Development, Paris.

Burnett, John. 2018. "Transcript: White House Chief of Staff John Kelly's Interview with NPR." NPR: National, May 11, 2018. https://www.npr.org/2018/05/11/610116389/transcript-white-house-chief-of-staff-john-kellys-interview-with-npr.

Busetta, Annalisa, Daria Mendola, Ben Wilson, and Valeria Cetorelli. 2021. "Measuring Vulnerability of Asylum Seekers and Refugees in Italy." *Journal of Ethnic and Migration Studies* 47 (3): 596–615.

Campana, Paolo. 2018. "Out of Africa: The Organization of Migrant Smuggling across the Mediterranean." *European Journal of Criminology* 15 (4): 481–502.

Cissé, Guéladio, Robert McLeman, Helen Adams, Paulina Aldunce, Kathryn Bowen, Diarmid Campbell-Lendrum, Susan Clayton, et al. 2022. "Health, Wellbeing and the Changing Structure of Communities." In *Climate Change 2022: Impacts, Adaptation, and Vulnerability*, 1041–1170. Sixth Assessment Report. Geneva: Intergovernmental Panel on Climate Change; New York: Cambridge University Press.

Clemens, Michael A., and Hannah M. Postel. 2018. "Deterring Emigration with Foreign Aid: An Overview of Evidence from Low-Income Countries." *Population and Development Review* 44 (4): 667–93.

Clement, Viviane, Kanta Kumari Rigaud, Alex de Sherbinin, Bryan Jones, Susana Adamo, Jacob Schewe, Nian Sadiq, and Elham Shabahat. 2021. *Groundswell Part 2: Acting on Internal Climate Migration*. Washington, DC: World Bank.

Commissioner of Law Revision, Malaysia. 2006. "Act 155: Immigration Act 1959/63, Incorporating All Amendments Up to 1 January 2006." Reprint, 2006, Percetakan Nasional Malaysia, Kuala Lumpur, Malaysia. https://www.ilo.org/dyn/natlex/docs/ELECTRONIC/64031/99464/F1916438079/MYS64031.pdf.

Conant, Eve. 2015. "The World's Congested Human Migration Routes in 5 Maps." *National Geographic*, September 19. https://www.nationalgeographic.com/culture/article/150919-data-points-refugees-migrants-maps-human-migrations-syria-world.

Cornelius, Wayne A. 2001. "Death at the Border: Efficacy and Unintended Consequences of US Immigration Control Policy." *Population and Development Review* 27 (4): 661–85.

Crawley, Heaven, and Dimitris Skleparis. 2018. "Refugees, Migrants, Neither, Both: Categorical Fetishism and the Politics of Bounding in Europe's 'Migration Crisis.'" *Journal of Ethnic and Migration Studies* 44 (1): 48–64.

Crock, Mary, and Christopher Robert Parsons. 2023. "Australia as a Modern Migration State: Past and Present." Background paper prepared for *World Development Report 2023*, World Bank, Washington, DC.

Czaika, Mathias, and Hein de Haas. 2013. "The Effectiveness of Migration Policies." *Population and Development Review* 39 (3): 487–508.

Czaika, Mathias, and Hein de Haas. 2017. "The Effect of Visas on Migration Processes." *International Migration Review* 51 (4): 893–926.

Czaika, Mathias, and Mogens Hobolth. 2016. "Do Restrictive Asylum and Visa Policies Increase Irregular Migration into Europe?" *European Union Politics* 17 (3): 345–65.

DFAT (Department of Foreign Affairs and Trade, Australia). 2013. "Memorandum of Understanding between the Government of the Independent State of Papua New Guinea and the Government of Australia, Relating to the Transfer to, and Assessment and Settlement in, Papua New Guinea of Certain Persons, and Related Issues." DFAT, Barton, Australian Capital Territory, Australia. https://www.dfat.gov.au/sites/default/files/joint-mou-20130806.pdf.

Dustmann, Christian, and Anna Okatenko. 2014. "Out-Migration, Wealth Constraints, and the Quality of Local Amenities." *Journal of Development Economics* 110 (September): 52–63.

Düvell, Franck. 2012. "Transit Migration: A Blurred and Politicised Concept." *Population, Space and Place* 18 (4): 415–27.

EC (European Commission). 2015. "EU-Turkey Joint Action Plan." *Memo*, October 15, 2015. https://ec.europa.eu/commission/presscorner/detail/en/MEMO_15_5860.

Erdal, Marta Bivand, and Ceri Oeppen. 2018. "Forced to Leave? The Discursive and Analytical Significance of

Describing Migration as Forced and Voluntary." *Journal of Ethnic and Migration Studies* 44 (6): 981–98.

EU (European Union). 2001. "Council Directive 2001/55/EC of 20 July 2001 on Minimum Standards for Giving Temporary Protection in the Event of a Mass Influx of Displaced Persons and on Measures Promoting a Balance of Efforts between Member States in Receiving Such Persons and Bearing the Consequences Thereof." *Official Journal of the European Communities* L 212 (August 7): 12–23. https://eur-lex.europa.eu/LexUriServ/LexUriServ.do?uri=OJ:L:2001:212:0012:0023:EN:PDF.

EUAA (European Union Agency for Asylum). 2022. *Asylum Report 2022: Annual Report of the Situation of Asylum in the European Union.* Luxembourg: Publications Office of the European Union. https://euaa.europa.eu/sites/default/files/publications/2022-06/2022_Asylum_Report_EN.pdf.

European Council. 2016. "EU-Turkey Statement, 18 March 2016." Press release, March 18, 2016. https://www.consilium.europa.eu/en/press/press-releases/2016/03/18/eu-turkey-statement/.

Feenstra, Robert C., Robert Inklaar, and Marcel Peter Timmer. 2015. "The Next Generation of the Penn World Table." *American Economic Review* 105 (10): 3150–82.

FitzGerald, David Scott. 2019. *Refuge beyond Reach: How Rich Democracies Repel Asylum Seekers.* New York: Oxford University Press.

Francis, Ama Ruth. 2019. "Free Movement Agreements and Climate-Induced Migration: A Caribbean Case Study." Sabin Center for Climate Change Law White Paper (September), Columbia University, New York.

Frontex (European Border and Coast Guard Agency). 2023. "Detections in the Central Mediterranean More Than Doubled in the First Two Months of 2023." News release, March 10, 2023. https://frontex.europa.eu/media-centre/news/news-release/detections-in-the-central-mediterranean-more-than-doubled-in-the-first-two-months-of-2023-wKyDkV.

Gammeltoft-Hansen, Thomas. 2011. *Access to Asylum: International Refugee Law and the Globalisation of Migration Control.* Cambridge Studies in International and Comparative Law 77. New York: Cambridge University Press.

Gamso, Jonas, and Farhod Yuldashev. 2018. "Targeted Foreign Aid and International Migration: Is Development-Promotion an Effective Immigration Policy?" *International Studies Quarterly* 62 (4): 809–20.

Gathmann, Christina. 2008. "Effects of Enforcement on Illegal Markets: Evidence from Migrant Smuggling along the Southwestern Border." *Journal of Public Economics* 92 (10–11): 1926–41.

Gibney, Matthew J. 2008. "Asylum and the Expansion of Deportation in the United Kingdom." *Government and Opposition* 43 (2): 146–67.

GMDAC (Global Migration Data Analysis Centre). 2020. "Calculating 'Death Rates' in the Context of Migration Journeys: Focus on the Central Mediterranean." GMDAC Briefing Series: Towards Safer Migration in Africa, Migration and Data in Northern and Western Africa, GMDAC, International Organization for Migration, Berlin.

Harris, John R., and Michael P. Todaro. 1970. "Migration, Unemployment, and Development: A Two-Sector Analysis." *American Economic Review* 60 (1): 126–42.

Hatton, Timothy J. 2009. "The Rise and Fall of Asylum: What Happened and Why?" *Economic Journal* 119 (535): F183–F213.

Hatton, Timothy J. 2017. "Refugees and Asylum Seekers, the Crisis in Europe and the Future of Policy." *Economic Policy* 32 (91): 447–96.

Heidenreich, Tobias, Jakob-Moritz Eberl, Fabienne Lind, and Hajo G. Boomgaarden. 2020. "Political Migration Discourses on Social Media: A Comparative Perspective on Visibility and Sentiment across Political Facebook Accounts in Europe." *Journal of Ethnic and Migration Studies* 46 (7): 1261–80.

Himmelreich, Johannes. 2019. "Asylum for Sale: A Market between States That Is Feasible and Desirable." *Journal of Applied Philosophy* 36 (2): 217–32.

Home Office, United Kingdom. 2022. "Migration and Economic Development Partnership." *Impact Assessment,* July 4, 2022. https://www.gov.uk/government/publications/migration-and-economic-development-partnership-with-rwanda.

ILO (International Labour Organization). 2014. "ILO Says Forced Labour Generates Annual Profits of US$ 150 Billion." *News: Economics of Forced Labour,* May 20, 2014. https://www.ilo.org/global/about-the-ilo/newsroom/news/WCMS_243201/lang--en/index.htm.

ILO (International Labour Organization), Walk Free, and IOM (International Organization for Migration). 2022. *Global Estimates of Modern Slavery: Forced Labour and Forced Marriage.* Geneva: ILO; Nedlands, WA: Walk Free Foundation; Geneva: IOM.

Imbert, Clément, and John Papp. 2020. "Costs and Benefits of Rural-Urban Migration: Evidence from India." *Journal of Development Economics* 146 (September): 102473.

Infante, César, Alvaro J. Idrovo, Mario S. Sánchez-Domínguez, Stéphane Vinhas, and Tonatiuh González-Vázquez. 2012. "Violence Committed against Migrants in Transit: Experiences on the Northern Mexican Border." *Journal of Immigrant and Minority Health* 14 (3): 449–59.

Innes, Alexandria J. 2010. "When the Threatened Become the Threat: The Construction of Asylum Seekers in British Media Narratives." *International Relations* 24 (4): 456–77.

IOM (International Organization for Migration). 2002. *International Comparative Study of Migration Legislation and Practice.* Dublin: Stationery Office.

IOM (International Organization for Migration). 2021. *World Migration Report 2022.* Geneva: IOM.

Jacobsen, Karen, Maysa Ayoub, and Alice Johnson. 2014. "Sudanese Refugees in Cairo: Remittances and Livelihoods." *Journal of Refugee Studies* 27 (1): 145–59.

Johns, Melissa, Craig Loschmann, and Nisha Nicole Arekapudi. 2023. "Mexico's Policy Response as an Emerging Destination for Refugees, Asylum-Seekers, and Persons in Need of International Protection."

Background paper prepared for *World Development Report 2023*, World Bank, Washington, DC.

Kaufmann, David. 2021. "Debating Responsibility-Sharing: An Analysis of the European Parliament's Debates on the Common European Asylum System." *European Policy Analysis* 7 (1): 207–25.

Klugman, Jeni, and Isabel Maria Medalho Pereira. 2009. "Assessment of National Migration Policies: An Emerging Picture on Admissions, Treatment and Enforcement in Developing and Developed Countries." Human Development Research Paper HDRP-2009-48 (October), Human Development Report Office, United Nations Development Programme, New York.

Koch, Anne, Nadine Biehler, Nadine Knapp, and David Kipp. 2023. "Integrating Refugees: Lessons from Germany since 2015/2016." Background paper prepared for *World Development Report 2023*, World Bank, Washington, DC.

Könönen, Jukka. 2022. "Borders in the Future: Policing Unwanted Mobility through Entry Bans in the Schengen Area." *Journal of Ethnic and Migration Studies*. Published ahead of print, January 31, 2022. https://www.tandfonline.com/doi/abs/10.1080/1369183X.2022.2029375.

Koser, Khalid. 2000. "Asylum Policies, Trafficking and Vulnerability." *International Migration* 38 (3): 91–111.

Koser, Khalid. 2010. "Dimensions and Dynamics of Irregular Migration." *Population, Space and Place* 16 (3): 181–93.

Kuschminder, Katie, and Jennifer Waidler. 2020. "At Europe's Frontline: Factors Determining Migrants Decision Making for Onwards Migration from Greece and Turkey." *Migration and Development* 9 (2): 188–208.

Leyva-Flores, René, César Infante, Juan Pablo Gutierrez, Frida Quintino-Perez, Maria Jose Gómez-Saldivar, and Cristian Torres-Robles. 2019. "Migrants in Transit through Mexico to the US: Experiences with Violence and Related Factors, 2009–2015." *PLOS ONE* 14 (8): e0220775.

Longo, Matthew. 2018. *The Politics of Borders: Sovereignty, Security, and the Citizen after 9/11*. Problems of International Politics Series. New York: Cambridge University Press.

Łubiński, Piotr. 2022. "Hybrid Warfare or Hybrid Threat: The Weaponization of Migration as an Example of the Use of Lawfare; Case Study of Poland." *Polish Political Science Yearbook* 51 (1): 43–55.

Lutz, Philipp, David Kaufmann, and Anna Stünzi. 2020. "Humanitarian Protection as a European Public Good: The Strategic Role of States and Refugees." *Journal of Common Market Studies* 58 (3): 757–75.

Madrigal, Guadalupe, and Stuart Soroka. 2023. "Migrants, Caravans, and the Impact of News Photos on Immigration Attitudes." *International Journal of Press/Politics* 28 (1): 49–69.

Maher, Stephanie. 2018. "Out of West Africa: Human Smuggling as a Social Enterprise." *Annals of the American Academy of Political and Social Science* 676 (1): 36–56.

Majcher, Izabella, Michael Flynn, and Mariette Grange. 2020. *Immigration Detention in the European Union: In the Shadow of the "Crisis."* European Studies in Population Series 22. Cham, Switzerland: Springer.

Majidi, Nassim. 2018. "Community Dimensions of Smuggling: The Case of Afghanistan and Somalia." *Annals of the American Academy of Political and Social Science* 676 (1): 97–113.

Martin, Susan F. 2000. "Best Practices to Combat Smuggling and Protect the Victims of Traffickers." Paper presented at the expert group meeting, "Best Practices for Migrant Workers," University of California, Davis, Davis, CA, April 26–28, 2000. https://migration.ucdavis.edu/cf/more.php?id=100.

Martin, Susan F., Elizabeth Ferris, Kanta Kumari, and Jonas Bergmann. 2018. "The Global Compacts and Environmental Drivers of Migration." KNOMAD Policy Brief 11 (July), Global Knowledge Partnership on Migration and Development, World Bank, Washington, DC.

McAuliffe, Marie, and Frank Laczko, eds. 2016. *Migrant Smuggling Data and Research: A Global Review of the Emerging Evidence Base*. Geneva: International Organization for Migration. https://publications.iom.int/books/migrant-smuggling-data-and-research-global-review-emerging-evidence-base.

McMillan, Margaret S., Dani Rodrik, and Claudia Sepúlveda. 2017. *Structural Change, Fundamentals, and Growth: A Framework and Case Studies*. Washington, DC: International Food Policy Research Institute.

Ministry of Economy, Fiji. 2019. "Displacement Guidelines: In the Context of Climate Change and Disasters." Ministry of Economy, Suva, Fiji. https://www.adaptationcommunity.net/wp-content/uploads/2020/03/Displacement-Guidelines-Fiji-2019.pdf.

Morten, Melanie. 2019. "Temporary Migration and Endogenous Risk Sharing in Village India." *Journal of Political Economy* 127 (1): 1–46.

Morten, Melanie, and Jacqueline Oliveira. 2023. "The Effects of Roads on Trade and Migration: Evidence from a Planned Capital City." NBER Working Paper 22158, National Bureau of Economic Research, Cambridge, MA.

MPISOC (Max Planck Institute for Social Law and Social Policy). 2014. "Treaty of Friendship, Partnership, and Cooperation between the Italian Republic and the Great Socialist People's Libyan Arab Jamahiriya." Policy Document, SPLASH Database, MPISOC, Munich. https://splash-db.eu/policydocument/treaty-of-friendship-partnership-and-cooperation-between-the-italian-republic-and-the-great-social/.

MRE (Ministerio de Relaciones Exteriores, Ministry of Foreign Affairs, Colombia). 2021. "Decreto 216 del 1 de Marzo de 2021: Por medio del cual se adopta el Estatuto Temporal de Protección para Migrantes Venezolanos Bajo Régimen de Protección Temporal y se dictan otras disposiciones en materia migratoria." MRE, Bogotá, Colombia. https://dapre.presidencia.gov.co/normativa/normativa/DECRETO%20216%20DEL%201%20DE%20MARZO%20DE%202021.pdf.

NDMO (National Disaster Management Office, Vanuatu). 2018. "Vanuatu: National Climate Change and Disaster-Induced Displacement Policy." NDMO, Port Vila,

Vanuatu. https://www.iom.int/sites/default/files/press_release/file/iom-vanuatu-policy-climate-change-disaster-induced-displacement-2018.pdf.

Newland, Kathleen, and Brian Salant. 2018. "Balancing Acts: Policy Frameworks for Migrant Return and Reintegration." Policy Brief 6 (October), Migration Policy Institute, Washington, DC. https://www.migrationpolicy.org/research/policy-frameworks-migrant-return-and-reintegration.

Nicot, Morgane, and Bianca Kopp. 2018. "Policy Perspective." *Annals of the American Academy of Political and Social Science* 676 (1): 223–25.

Nonnenmacher, Sophie, and Akemi Yonemura. 2018. "Migration and Education in West Africa." Background paper, Document ED/GEMR/MRT/2018/P1/15/REV, United Nations Educational, Scientific, and Cultural Organization, Paris.

NSC (National Security Council). 2021. "U.S. Strategy for Addressing the Root Causes of Migration in Central America." White House, Washington, DC. https://www.whitehouse.gov/wp-content/uploads/2021/07/Root-Causes-Strategy.pdf.

Odysseus Network. 2017. "Memorandum of Understanding on Cooperation in the Fields of Development, the Fight against Illegal Immigration, Human Trafficking and Fuel Smuggling and on Reinforcing the Security of Borders between the State of Libya and the Italian Republic." *EU Immigration and Asylum Law and Policy* (blog), October 2, 2017. https://eumigrationlawblog.eu/wp-content/uploads/2017/10/MEMORANDUM_translation_finalversion.doc.pdf.

OECD (Organisation for Economic Co-operation and Development). 2020. *Sustainable Reintegration of Returning Migrants: A Better Homecoming.* Paris: OECD.

OHCHR (Office of the United Nations High Commissioner for Human Rights). 2016. "Situation of Migrants in Transit." Report A/HRC/31/35, OHCHR, Geneva. https://www.ohchr.org/sites/default/files/2021-12/INT_CMW_INF_7940_E.pdf.

OHCHR (Office of the United Nations High Commissioner for Human Rights). 2017. "EU 'Trying to Move Border to Libya' Using Policy That Breaches Rights–UN Experts: Moving Europe's Borders." Press Release: Special Procedures, August 17, 2017. https://www.ohchr.org/en/press-releases/2017/08/eu-trying-move-border-libya-using-policy-breaches-rights-un-experts.

Okoth-Obbo, George. 2001. "Thirty Years On: A Legal Review of the 1969 OAU Refugee Convention Governing the Specific Aspects of Refugee Problems in Africa." *Refugee Survey Quarterly* 20 (1): 79–138.

Ortega, Francesc, and Giovanni Peri. 2013. "The Effect of Income and Immigration Policies on International Migration." *Migration Studies* 1 (1): 47–74.

Paoletti, Sarah. 2023. "Temporary Protected Status in the United States: An Incomplete and Imperfect Complementary System of Protection." Background paper prepared for *World Development Report 2023*, World Bank, Washington, DC.

Pereira, Cícero, Jorge Vala, and Rui Costa-Lopes. 2010. "From Prejudice to Discrimination: The Legitimizing Role of Perceived Threat in Discrimination against Immigrants." *European Journal of Social Psychology* 40 (7): 1231–50.

Poynting, Scott, and Linda Briskman. 2020. "Asylum Seekers in the Global Context of Xenophobia: Introduction to the Special Issue." *Journal of Sociology* 56 (1): 3–8.

Průchová Hrůzová, Andrea. 2021. "What Is the Image of Refugees in Central European Media?" *European Journal of Cultural Studies* 24 (1): 240–58.

Ravn, Stiene, Rilke Mahieu, Milena Belloni, and Christiane Timmerman. 2020. "Shaping the 'Deserving Refugee': Insights from a Local Reception Programme in Belgium." In *Geographies of Asylum in Europe and the Role of European Localities*, edited by Birgit Glorius and Jeroen Doomernik, 135–53. IMISCOE Research Series. Cham, Switzerland: Springer.

Reed-Hurtado, Michael. 2013. "The Cartagena Declaration on Refugees and the Protection of People Fleeing Armed Conflict and Other Situations of Violence in Latin America." Legal and Protection Policy Research Series, PPLA/2013/03 (June), Division of International Protection, United Nations High Commissioner for Refugees, Geneva.

Reques, Laura, Ezequiel Aranda-Fernández, Camille Rolland, Adeline Grippon, Nora Fallet, Christian Reboul, Nathalie Godard, and Niklas Luhmann. 2020. "Episodes of Violence Suffered by Migrants Transiting through Libya: A Cross-Sectional Study in 'Médecins du Monde's' Reception and Healthcare Centre in Seine-Saint-Denis, France." *Conflict and Health* 14 (1): 12.

Reuters. 2016. "Norway Will Build a Fence at Its Arctic Border with Russia." *New York Times*, August 24, 2016. https://www.nytimes.com/2016/08/25/world/europe/russia-norway-border-fence-refugees.html.

Rosenberg, Eli. 2018. "Sessions Defends Separating Immigrant Parents and Children: 'We've Got to Get This Message Out.'" *Politics* (blog), https://www.washingtonpost.com/news/post-politics/wp/2018/06/05/sessions-defends-separating-immigrant-parents-and-children-weve-got-to-get-this-message-out/.

Sačer, Sabina, Mirko Palić, Marko Grünhagen, and Tihomir Kundid. 2017. "Determinants of Choice of Migration Destination: Evidence from the Western Balkan Transit Route." *International Journal of Sales, Retailing and Marketing* 6 (1): 48–60.

Sandven, Hallvard. 2022. "The Practice and Legitimacy of Border Control." *American Journal of Political Science.* Published ahead of print, August 28, 2022. https://onlinelibrary.wiley.com/doi/full/10.1111/ajps.12736.

Shachar, Ayelet. 2019. "Bordering Migration/Migrating Borders." *Berkeley Journal of International Law* 37 (1): 93–151.

Shachar, Ayelet. 2020. *The Shifting Border: Legal Cartographies of Migration and Mobility.* Critical Powers Series. Manchester, UK: Manchester University Press.

Sharpe, Marina. 2013. "The 1969 OAU Refugee Convention and the Protection of People Fleeing Armed Conflict and Other Situations of Violence in the Context of Individual Refugee Status Determination." Legal and

Protection Policy Research Series, PPLA/2013/01 (January), Division of International Protection, United Nations High Commissioner for Refugees, Geneva.

Shrestha, Maheshwor. 2023. "A Deeper Dive into the Relationship between Economic Development and Migration." Policy Research Working Paper 10295, World Bank, Washington, DC.

Singapore Statutes Online. 2021. "Immigration Act 1959: An Act Relating to Immigration into, and Departure from, Singapore." Revised Edition, Incorporates All Amendments Up to and Including 1 December 2021 and Comes into Operation on 31 December 2021. Legislation Division, Attorney-General's Chambers of Singapore, Singapore. https://sso.agc.gov.sg/Act/IA1959.

Slovic, Paul, Daniel Västfjäll, Arvid Erlandsson, and Robin Gregory. 2017. "Iconic Photographs and the Ebb and Flow of Empathic Response to Humanitarian Disasters." Proceedings of the National Academy of Sciences 114 (4): 640–44.

Solomon, Daina Beth. 2019. "U.S. Dream Pulls African Migrants in Record Numbers across Latin America." Editor's Picks, July 5, 2019. https://www.reuters.com/article/us-usa-immigration-africa-IdUSKCN1U01A4.

T.C. Resmî Gazete (Official Gazette of the Republic of Türkiye). 2013. "Law on Foreigners and International Protection." Law 6458 (adopted April 4), T.C. Resmî Gazete 53 (5): 28615 (April 11). https://www.unhcr.org/tr/wp-content/uploads/sites/14/2017/04/LoFIP_ENG_DGMM_revised-2017.pdf.

Triandafyllidou, Anna, ed. 2018a. Handbook of Migration and Globalisation. Handbooks on Globalisation Series. Cheltenham, UK: Edward Elgar.

Triandafyllidou, Anna. 2018b. "Migrant Smuggling: Novel Insights and Implications for Migration Control Policies." Annals of the American Academy of Political and Social Science 676 (1): 212–21.

Triandafyllidou, Anna, Laura Bartolini, and Caterina Francesca Guidi. 2019. "Exploring the Links between Enhancing Regular Pathways and Discouraging Irregular Migration: A Discussion Paper to Inform Future Policy Deliberations." International Organization for Migration, Geneva. https://cadmus.eui.eu/handle/1814/61251.

Türk, Volker, and Rebecca Dowd. 2014. "Protection Gaps." In The Oxford Handbook of Refugee and Forced Migration Studies, edited by Elena Fiddian-Qasmiyeh, Gil Loescher, Katy Long, and Nando Sigona, 278–89. Oxford Handbooks Series. Oxford, UK: Oxford University Press.

UNHCR (United Nations High Commissioner for Refugees). 1984. "Cartagena Declaration on Refugees Adopted by the Colloquium on the International Protection of Refugees in Central America, Mexico, and Panama, Cartagena de Indias, Colombia, 22 November 1984." Media Relations and Public Information Service, UNHCR, Geneva. https://www.unhcr.org/en-us/about-us/background/45dc19084/cartagena-declaration-refugees-adopted-colloquium-international-protection.html.

UNHCR (United Nations High Commissioner for Refugees). 2021. "UNHCR Note on the 'Externalization' of International Protection." May 28, UNHCR, Geneva. https://www.refworld.org/docid/60b115604.html.

UNHCR (United Nations High Commissioner for Refugees). 2022. "The Implementation of the Temporary Protection Directive: Six Months On." October, Regional Bureau for Europe, UNHCR, Geneva.

UNHCR (United Nations High Commissioner for Refugees), Brookings Institution, and Georgetown University. 2015. "Guidance on Protecting People from Disasters and Environmental Change through Planned Relocation." October 7, UNHCR, Geneva. https://www.unhcr.org/protection/environment/562f798d9/planned-relocation-guidance-october-2015.html.

UNHCR (United Nations High Commissioner for Refugees), Georgetown University, and IOM (International Organization for Migration). 2017. "A Toolbox: Planning Relocations to Protect People from Disasters and Environmental Change." July 28, UNHCR, Geneva. https://www.unhcr.org/protection/environment/596f1bb47/planned-relocation-toolbox.html.

United Nations. 1976. "OAU Convention Governing the Specific Aspects of Refugee Problems in Africa." Adopted by the Assembly of Heads of State and Government at its Sixth Ordinary Session, Addis Ababa, Ethiopia, September 10, 1969. Treaty Series 14691, Volume-1001-I-14691: 45–52, Treaty Section, Office of Legal Affairs, United Nations, New York.

United Nations. 2019. "Resolution Adopted by the General Assembly on 19 December 2018: Global Compact for Safe, Orderly and Regular Migration." Document A/RES/73/195 (January 11), United Nations, New York. https://www.un.org/en/development/desa/population/migration/generalassembly/docs/globalcompact/A_RES_73_195.pdf.

UNODC (United Nations Office on Drugs and Crime). 2018. Global Study on Smuggling of Migrants 2018. June. Vienna: UNODC.

USCIS (US Citizenship and Immigration Services). 2010. "Designation of Haiti for Temporary Protected Status." Federal Register 75 (13) (January 21): 3476–79, Office of the Federal Register, National Archives and Records Administration, Washington, DC.

US Immigration and Naturalization Service. 1999. "Designation of Honduras under Temporary Protected Status." Federal Register 64 (2) (January 5): 524–26, Office of the Federal Register, National Archives and Records Administration, Washington, DC.

US State Department. 2019. "U.S.-Mexico Joint Declaration." Media Note, June 7, 2019. https://2017-2021.state.gov/u-s-mexico-joint-declaration/index.html.

Vogt, Wendy A. 2018. Lives in Transit: Violence and Intimacy on the Migrant Journey. California Series in Public Anthropology 42. Oakland, CA: University of California Press.

Wajsberg, Mirjam. 2020. "'I Am Not Moving Life, But Life Moves Me': Experiences of Intra-EU (Im)Mobility among West African Migrants." In Migration at Work: Aspirations, Imaginaries and Structures of Mobility, edited by Fiona-Katharina Seiger, Christiane Timmerman, Noel B. Salazar, and Johan Wets, 91–110. CeMIS

Migration and Intercultural Studies Series 5. Leuven, Belgium: Leuven University Press.

Walsh, Peter William. 2020. "Irregular Migration in the UK." COMPAS Briefing, September 11, Migration Observatory, Centre on Migration, Policy, and Society, University of Oxford, Oxford, UK. https://migrationobservatory.ox.ac.uk/resources/briefings/irregular-migration-in-the-uk/.

Warren, Robert. 2019. "Sharp Multiyear Decline in Undocumented Immigration Suggests Progress at US-Mexico Border, Not a National Emergency." February 27, Center for Migration Studies, New York. https://cmsny.org/publications/essay-warren-022719/.

WHO (World Health Organization). 2022. *World Report on the Health of Refugees and Migrants*. Health and Migration Programme. Geneva: WHO.

World Bank. 2018a. "Asylum Seekers in the European Union: Building Evidence to Inform Policy Making." World Bank, Washington, DC.

World Bank. 2018b. "Transit Migration." Migration and Development Brief 29 (April), Global Knowledge Partnership on Migration and Development, World Bank, Washington, DC.

Spotlight 8
—
"Root causes" and development

Over the last decade, a number of high-income destination countries have developed programs aimed at tackling the "root causes" of migration, especially irregular and high-risk migration.[1] These initiatives are premised on the notion that development in the origin country would help reduce the number of emigrants. That notion has been subject to debate, however, with some observers suggesting that development would actually increase emigration.

Development and the propensity to migrate

The propensity to migrate is driven by many factors. Two are closely related to development in the country of origin: (1) the income gap with potential destination countries and (2) the availability of financial resources for would-be migrants to move to these destination countries. If the origin country grows at a sufficiently rapid pace and the income gap with potential destination countries shrinks, people will have domestic alternatives to improve their lives, making emigration less attractive. But they will also have more resources, making migration more affordable.[2] These forces pull in opposite directions. The overall impact of development on migration depends on which forces dominate.[3]

Economic development also alters the destinations of migrants. With economic development, people have more resources to finance their migration, and therefore they have a larger choice of destination countries. They also tend to have higher skills, and they are often better received in destination countries. On the other hand, development reduces the incentives to migrate to destinations where the gains will be limited—for example, if people from low-income countries move to other low-income countries.

Empirical patterns

The "migration hump"

Upper-middle-income countries have the highest ratio of emigrants to population (figure S8.1). In 2020, less than 1 percent of the population of low- and lower-middle-income countries such as Ethiopia, Madagascar, and Tanzania, as well as high-income countries such as Japan, Qatar, and the United States, lived abroad. By contrast, countries at intermediate levels of income, such as Albania and the Dominican Republic, had the highest emigration rates.

This pattern has been variously labeled the *mobility transition*,[4] the *emigration life cycle*,[5] and the *migration hump*.[6] It is consistent with the channels through which development affects the propensity to emigrate. People from middle-income countries have both the incentives to move—which are typically greater than for people from high-income countries—and the means to do so—unlike many people in low-income countries.

Figure S8.1 The propensity to emigrate is highest in middle-income countries

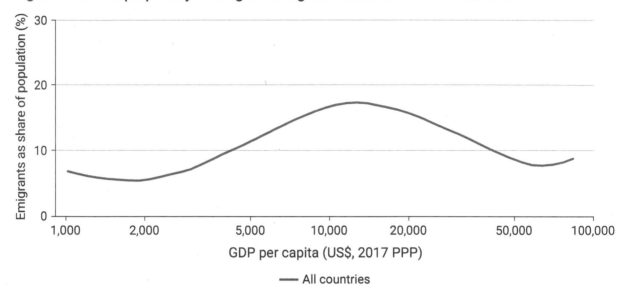

— All countries

Sources: Emigrants: International Migrant Stock (dashboard), Population Division, Department of Economic and Social Affairs, United Nations, New York, https://www.un.org/development/desa/pd/content/international-migrant-stock. Gross domestic product (GDP): Feenstra, Inklaar, and Timmer (2015), based on Penn World Table 10.0, Groningen Growth and Development Centre, Faculty of Economics and Business, University of Groningen, Groningen, the Netherlands, https://www.rug.nl/ggdc/productivity/pwt/.

Note: The figure plots the relationship between the total number of emigrants (as a percentage of the sending country population) in 2020 against GDP per capita in constant 2017 US dollars in purchasing power parity (PPP) terms in 2020. GDP for 2020 is calculated by applying the local currency real GDP growth rate for 2019–20 to 2019 GDP from Penn World Table 10.0. GDP per capita is capped at US$84,000 in the figure.

Size of the country of origin

The migration hump, however, is closely linked to the size of the country of origin (figure S8.2). It is very pronounced in countries with smaller populations (half of countries, which together account for 3.5 percent of the global population). It is, however, more muted for countries with larger populations (accounting for 96.5 percent of the global population)—until they reach upper-middle-income levels, at which point emigration rates decline. For example, the emigration rate in The Gambia, with its smaller population, is 60 percent higher than that in neighboring Guinea or Senegal, which have larger populations. Among upper-middle-income countries, the emigration rate of Uruguay, with its smaller population, is about four times higher than that of Argentina, which has a larger population.

Once again, this pattern is consistent with the channels through which development affects the propensity to emigrate. Domestic alternatives to cross-border migration reduce the incentives to migrate across borders. As larger countries develop, new opportunities emerge, including for internal migration toward, for example, a more prosperous province or a booming urban center, while such opportunities may not exist in smaller economies.

Figure S8.2 The migration hump is pronounced for smaller countries and more muted for larger countries

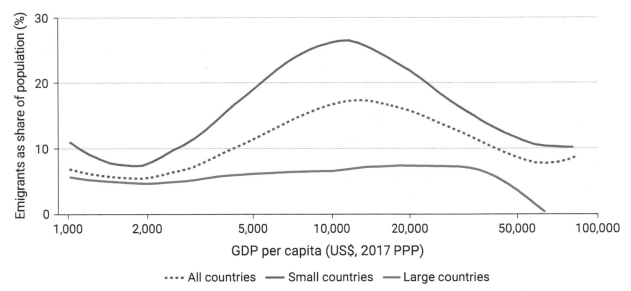

Sources: Emigrants: International Migrant Stock (dashboard), Population Division, Department of Economic and Social Affairs, United Nations, New York, https://www.un.org/development/desa/pd/content/international-migrant-stock. Gross domestic product (GDP): Feenstra, Inklaar, and Timmer (2015), based on Penn World Table 10.0, Groningen Growth and Development Centre, Faculty of Economics and Business, University of Groningen, Groningen, the Netherlands, https://www.rug.nl/ggdc/productivity/pwt/.

Note: The figure plots the relationship between the total number of emigrants (as a percentage of the sending country population) in 2020 against GDP per capita in constant 2017 US dollars in purchasing power parity (PPP) terms in 2020. GDP for 2020 is calculated by applying the local currency real GDP growth rate for 2019–20 to 2019 GDP from Penn World Table 10.0. GDP per capita is capped at US$84,000 in the figure. Small countries are those whose population is below the median (such as Israel, with a population of 9.3 million in 2020). Large countries are above the median.

Increasing propensity to migrate from middle-income countries

The migration hump provides a static perspective. It compares the propensity to migrate across countries that are at various levels of income today. However, as countries develop, say from low- to middle-income, their emigration patterns do not necessarily adjust accordingly. Therefore, to inform the debate on development and the root causes of migration, an additional perspective is needed that looks at what happens in a country when its level of income rises.[7]

From a review of emigration trends in what were middle-income countries in 1960, three key patterns emerged:

- As middle-income countries developed, emigration steadily increased. The trend continued until income reached about upper-middle-income levels—US$13,000, adjusted for purchasing power parity (figure S8.3, panel a).[8] In many of these countries, however, development was also accompanied by a decline in fertility rates, which reduced the effect of development on actual emigration flows.

Figure S8.3 As middle-income countries develop, emigration rises, mainly to high-income destinations

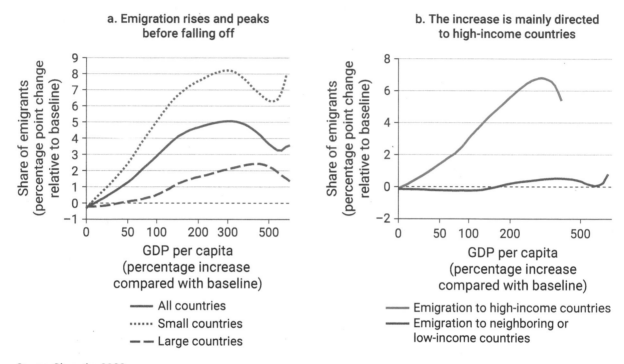

a. Emigration rises and peaks before falling off

b. The increase is mainly directed to high-income countries

Source: Shrestha 2023.

Note: In the figure, the solid lines show the smoothened relationship between increases in income and changes in emigration rate, compared with those in the baseline year for middle-income countries. Changes are relative to a baseline year, defined as the year in which the gross domestic product (GDP) per capita in constant 2017 US dollars adjusted for purchasing power parity was at its lowest level since 1960. Low-income countries are among the bottom third circa 1960 in terms of GDP per capita. Middle-income countries are among the middle third. In panel a, the dotted and dashed lines indicate the relationship for small and large countries, respectively. Small countries are below the median (3.4 million) in terms of population in 1960, and large countries are above the median. Estimates exclude outliers in terms of emigration rates (Antigua and Barbuda, Bosnia and Herzegovina, Dominica, Grenada, St. Kitts and Nevis, and West Bank and Gaza) as well as outliers in terms of high GDP growth. In panel b, the purple line indicates the smoothened relationship between increasing incomes and emigration to neighboring or low-income destinations, and the blue line shows the smoothened relationship between increasing incomes and emigration to high-income destinations.

- The differences between countries based on their size remained. Larger middle-income countries experienced a smaller rise in emigration rates, compared with smaller middle-income countries.
- Migration from middle-income countries also became increasingly directed toward higher-income destinations, which accounted for most of the increase in the propensity to emigrate (figure S8.3, panel b). By contrast, the propensity to emigrate to other destinations—to neighboring or low-income countries—remained largely unchanged. This effect is more apparent in smaller countries than in those with a larger population.

Declining propensity to migrate from low-income countries

A similar review of the experience of countries in the low range of the income distribution in 1960 highlights different patterns:

Figure S8.4 As low-income countries develop, the propensity to migrate declines, especially to low-income destinations

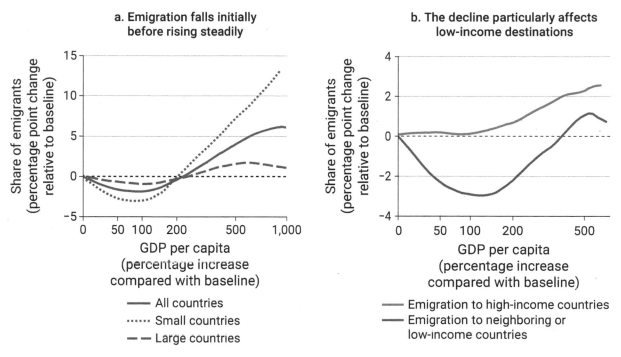

a. Emigration falls initially before rising steadily

b. The decline particularly affects low-income destinations

—— All countries
······ Small countries
– – Large countries

—— Emigration to high-income countries
—— Emigration to neighboring or low-income countries

Source: Shrestha 2023.

Note: The figure shows how emigration to high-income and neighboring or low-income countries changes as low-income countries develop. Changes are relative to a baseline year, defined for each country as the year in which GDP per capita in constant 2017 US dollars in purchasing power parity terms, was at its lowest level since 1960. In panel a, the dotted and dashed lines indicate the relationship for small and large countries, respectively. Small countries are below the median (3.4 million) in terms of population in 1960, and large countries are above the median. Estimates exclude outliers in terms of emigration rates (Antigua and Barbuda, Bosnia and Herzegovina, Dominica, Grenada, St. Kitts and Nevis, and West Bank and Gaza) as well as outliers in terms of high GDP growth. In panel b, the purple line indicates the smoothened relationship between increasing incomes and emigration to neighboring or low-income destinations, and the blue line indicates the smoothened relationship between increasing incomes and emigration to high-income destinations.

- As countries that were low-income circa 1960 developed, emigration initially declined (figure S8.4, panel a)[9] until their per capita incomes tripled, which took, on average, about 40 years. Emigration rates then followed the pattern observed in middle-income countries, increasing steadily until upper-middle-income levels. If low- and lower-middle-income countries—which account for about 27 percent of today's global population—grew at the same rate today as they did between 2000 and 2020, it would take them, on average, another 32 years to reach the average income level around which the migration rate peaks.
- Among lower-income countries as well the effects are significantly larger in countries with smaller populations and much more limited in countries with larger ones.
- The decline in emigration rates was driven largely by a reduction of emigration to other lower-income countries (figure S8.4, panel b). Emigration to high-income destinations remained stable, at a low level, until countries reached middle-income levels, at which point migration trends became similar to those of other middle-income countries. By the time the income of low-income countries had tripled, emigration to high-income countries had increased by only 0.7 percentage point.

Notes

1. Improved Migration Management (dashboard), EU Emergency Trust Fund for Africa, European Commission, Brussels, https://ec.europa.eu/trustfundforafrica/thematic/improved-migration-management.
2. For example, in low-income countries visa costs are higher for travelers to high-income destinations. According to Ortega and Peri (2013), migration flows to member countries of the Organisation for Economic Co-operation and Development (OECD) are very responsive to immigration policies.
3. Robust evidence in the literature reveals that reduction of financing constraints encourages migration. Angelucci (2016) and Gazeaud, Mvukiyehe, and Sterck (2023) find that cash transfer programs in Mexico and the Comoros increase international migration, and Bazzi (2017) and Shrestha (2017) find that higher rainfall, which raises agricultural incomes, increases international migration from Indonesia and Nepal.
4. Zelinsky (1971).
5. Clemens (2020); Hatton and Williamson (1994).
6. Clemens (2014); Dao et al. (2018); Djajić, Kirdar, and Vinogradova (2016); Martin and Taylor (1996).
7. Clemens (2020). Interpreting trends over long periods of time also raises challenges because geopolitical shifts (such as the end of the Cold War) and technological advances (which have reduced travel costs) have transformed migration dynamics across the world.
8. The baseline year for each country is the year in which GDP per capita (US$, 2017 PPP) was at its lowest level between 1960 and 2020. Countries designated as middle-income had an average initial GDP per capita of US$3,353 (2017 PPP).
9. Countries designated as low-income had an average initial GDP per capita of US$1,165 (2017 PPP).

References

Angelucci, Manuela. 2016. "Migration and Financial Constraints: Evidence from Mexico." *Review of Economics and Statistics* 97 (1): 224–28.

Bazzi, Samuel. 2017. "Wealth Heterogeneity and the Income Elasticity of Migration." *American Economic Journal: Applied Economics* 9 (2): 219–55.

Clemens, Michael A. 2014. "Does Development Reduce Migration?" In *International Handbook on Migration and Economic Development*, edited by Robert E. B. Lucas, 152–85. Cheltenham, UK: Edward Elgar.

Clemens, Michael A. 2020. "The Emigration Life Cycle: How Development Shapes Emigration from Poor Countries." IZA Discussion Paper DP 13614, Institute of Labor Economics, Bonn, Germany.

Dao, Thu Hien, Frédéric Docquier, Chris Parsons, and Giovanni Peri. 2018. "Migration and Development: Dissecting the Anatomy of the Mobility Transition." *Journal of Development Economics* 132 (May): 88–101.

Djajić, Slobodan, Murat Kirdar, and Alexandra Brausmann Vinogradova. 2016. "Source-Country Earnings and Emigration." *Journal of International Economics* 99 (March): 46–67.

Feenstra, Robert C., Robert Inklaar, and Marcel Peter Timmer. 2015. "The Next Generation of the Penn World Table." *American Economic Review* 105 (10): 3150–82.

Gazeaud, Jules, Eric Mvukiyehe, and Olivier Sterck. 2023. "Cash Transfers and Migration: Theory and Evidence from a Randomized Controlled Trial." *Review of Economics and Statistics* 105 (1): 143–57.

Hatton, Timothy J., and Jeffery G. Williamson. 1994. "International Migration and World Development: A Historical Perspective." In *Economic Aspects of International Migration*, edited by Herbert Giersch, 3–56. Publications of the Egon-Sohmen-Foundation Series. Berlin: Springer.

Martin, Philip L., and J. Edward Taylor. 1996. "The Anatomy of a Migration Hump." In *Development Strategy, Employment, and Migration: Insights from Models,* edited by J. Edward Taylor, 43–62. Paris: OECD Development Centre, Organisation for Economic Co-operation and Development.

Ortega, Francesc, and Giovanni Peri. 2013. "The Effect of Income and Immigration Policies on International Migration." *Migration Studies* 1 (1): 47–74.

Shrestha, Maheshwor. 2017. "Push and Pull: A Study of International Migration from Nepal." Policy Research Working Paper 7965, World Bank, Washington, DC.

Shrestha, Maheshwor. 2023. "A Deeper Dive into the Relationship between Economic Development and Migration." Policy Research Working Paper WPS10295, World Bank, Washington, DC.

Zelinsky, Wilbur. 1971. "The Hypothesis of the Mobility Transition." *Geographical Review* 61 (2): 219–49.

Part 4

Making migration work better requires doing things differently

A central message arising from this Report is that migration needs to be managed strategically by both countries of origin and countries of destination if it is to produce its full development gains. Global imbalances, local shocks, and societies' evolving needs will continue to generate cross-border movements. Yet the way in which migration is currently managed is failing many migrants and nationals, causing immense suffering for tens of millions, polarizing politics, and creating large inefficiencies and economic losses across both destination and origin countries.

The challenge is to manage cross-border movements in a way that benefits migrants and refugees, as well as origin and destination societies. The ultimate objective is threefold: (1) to maximize the gains for both migrants and their societies of origin and destination when migrants' skills and attributes strongly match the needs of the destination society; (2) to manage refugee situations in a sustainable manner, with a view toward medium-term development effects on both refugees and host communities and adequate responsibility-sharing within the international community; and (3) to respond to distressed migration humanely and over time to reduce the need for such movements.

Chapter 9 is an overview of policy recommendations directed at countries of origin, transit, and destination, as well as the international community. It summarizes the main findings of earlier chapters and provides examples of policies intended to enhance the management of economic migration and forced displacement. Finally, it highlights that all countries have a role to play in cross-border movements so they contribute fully to development within the broader context of the two global compacts adopted in 2018—the Global Compact for Safe, Orderly and Regular Migration and the Global Compact on Refugees.

This is a difficult time for migration reform. Political debates are polarized across countries at all income levels, and global tensions are further complicating the situation. Meanwhile, new risks, including those related to climate change, loom on the horizon. Migration reform is urgently needed. Difficult debates lie ahead, but they cannot be avoided or much delayed.

9 Recommendations

Making migration work better

Key messages

- There is significant scope for countries of origin, destination, and transit to manage cross-border movements in a strategic manner, thereby maximizing gains while mitigating costs (figure 9.1). Countries in all situations can adopt policies that enhance the development effects of migration on their societies (table 9.1).

- In most cases, the benefits of cross-border movements can be increased (and the costs mitigated) through international cooperation. Bilateral and multilateral approaches are needed.

- Although making policy on migration is often politically sensitive, lessons can be drawn from other countries to develop evidence-based approaches.

- The challenge is to determine not only what needs to be done, but also how to get it done. This will require better data and fit-for-purpose financing instruments, as well as ways to bring under-represented voices to the debate.

Figure 9.1 When strategically managed, migration maximizes gains while mitigating costs

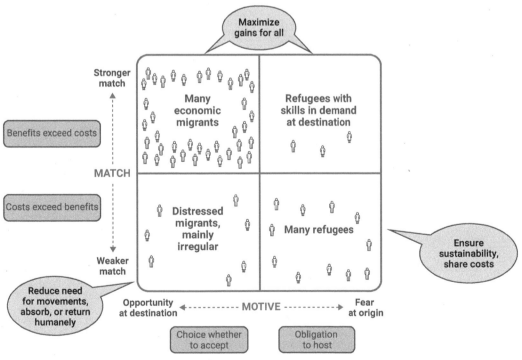

Source: WDR 2023 team.

Note: *Match* refers to the degree to which a migrant's skills and related attributes meet the demand in the destination country. *Motive* refers to the circumstances under which a person moves—whether in search of opportunity or because of a "well-founded fear" of persecution, armed conflict, or violence in their origin country.

Table 9.1 Main policy recommendations

WHEN MIGRANTS' AND REFUGEES' SKILLS ARE IN DEMAND (STRONG MATCH)		
COUNTRY OF ORIGIN Manage migration for poverty reduction	**COUNTRY OF DESTINATION** Maximize benefits, reduce costs	**BILATERAL COOPERATION** Strengthen match
Strategy. Make emigration part of development strategies. *Remittances.* Leverage remittances for poverty reduction and reduce their costs. *Knowledge.* Work with the diaspora and returnees to spur knowledge transfers and to strengthen integration in the global economy. *Skills development and brain drain mitigation.* Expand education and training in skills that are in demand in both the national and global labor markets. *Protection.* Provide citizens abroad with protection. Support vulnerable family members left behind.	*Strategy.* Acknowledge labor needs. Build a consensus on the role of migration. Ensure policy coherence. *Entry and status.* Incentivize stronger match immigration. Ensure migrants have a formal status and rights. *Economic inclusion.* Facilitate labor market inclusion. Enhance recognition of migrants' qualifications. Combat exploitation and promote decent work. *Social inclusion.* Prevent segregation and facilitate access to services. Combat discrimination. *Support to nationals.* Support citizens who are negatively affected in terms of employment outcomes and public services through social protection and public investments.	*Bilateral labor agreements.* Structure and facilitate win-win movements. Reduce recruitment costs. *Skills development.* Partner to finance the development of skills that are in demand in both the national and global labor markets.

WHEN REFUGEES' SKILLS ARE NOT IN DEMAND (WEAK MATCH, FEAR MOTIVE)	
HOST COUNTRY Manage with a medium-term perspective and enhance the match	**INTERNATIONAL COMMUNITY** Share the costs with hosting countries
Institutions and instruments. Mainstream refugee support through line ministries. Develop sustainable financing frameworks. *Internal mobility.* Facilitate and encourage refugees' movements toward opportunities. *Self-reliance.* Enable refugees to access jobs in the formal labor market. *Inclusion in national services.* Deliver education, health, and social services to refugees through national systems.	*Responsibility-sharing.* Prevent or resolve situations that cause refugees to flee. Provide adequate amounts of medium-term financing. Increase resettlement options. Broaden the base of support beyond current main contributors. Develop regional approaches. *Solutions.* Further work toward "durable solutions" (voluntary return, local integration or resettlement). Develop innovative statuses that provide state protection and access to opportunities over the medium term.

WHEN MIGRANTS' SKILLS ARE NOT IN DEMAND (WEAK MATCH, NO FEAR MOTIVE)		
COUNTRY OF ORIGIN Reduce the need for distressed movements	**COUNTRY OF TRANSIT** Coordinate with countries of destination	**COUNTRY OF DESTINATION** Respect migrants' dignity
Resilience. Enhance social protection. Create domestic alternatives to international migration. *Education.* Build skills that allow people to have more options. *Inclusion.* Promote inclusive and green development. Foster adaptation to climate change.	*Cooperation.* Work with the destination country to absorb migrants or return them humanely (for last transit country).	*Respect.* Treat all migrants humanely. *Complementary protection.* Strengthen the coherence of the current system to protect people at risk who are not refugees. *Legal pathways.* Shift migrants' incentives by establishing legal pathways for workers in demand, including lower-skilled workers. *Enforcement.* Manage necessary returns humanely. Clamp down on smugglers and exploitative employers. Strengthen institutional capacity to process entries.

MAKING MIGRATION POLICY DIFFERENTLY		
DATA AND EVIDENCE	**FINANCIAL INSTRUMENTS**	**NEW VOICES**
Harmonization. Harmonize data collection methods. *Evidence-building.* Invest in new types of surveys to inform policy making. *Open data.* Encourage research by making data widely available, while respecting migrants' and refugees' privacy.	*New or expanded instruments.* Develop medium-term instruments to support refugee-hosting countries. Provide external support to low- and middle-income countries receiving weaker match migrants. *Enhanced use of existing instruments.* Incentivize private sector engagement. Support origin countries in leveraging migration for development. Incentivize bilateral and regional cooperation.	*Affected nations.* Build coalitions among countries facing common challenges. *Domestic stakeholders.* Ensure participation of a broad range of stakeholders in decision-making processes. *Migrants' and refugees' voices.* Develop representation and accountability systems to organize migrants' and refugees' voices.

Source: WDR 2023 team.

Introduction

This chapter summarizes key policy recommendations arising from the analysis presented in this Report. This summary draws on the underlying evidence developed in earlier chapters and provides a structured outline of critical policy directions rather than an exhaustive and nuanced collection of possible approaches and experiences.

Also included are policy examples adopted by a variety of countries. Some policies have succeeded and others only partly so. Many have been controversial. Evaluating some of these policies raises methodological challenges.[1] However, regardless of their imperfections, the examples convey a wealth of experience from which policy makers can learn, bearing in mind that there is no model approach. Policy making needs to be tailored to the specifics of each situation.

This chapter is organized according to the Match and Motive Matrix, providing specific recommendations for each type of cross-border movement. There are situations in which migrants or refugees bring skills and attributes that are a strong match for the needs of the destination country; situations in which people do not bring such skills but move because of fear in their country of origin (refugees); and situations in which migrants have neither skills in demand nor international protection needs (distressed migrants). The chapter also discusses some of the essential elements that can help make reform happen.

Under each type of cross-border movement are sections that include countries of origin, countries of destination, countries of transit, and refugee-hosting countries. However, these countries are often not distinct; many could fit into all four categories. Recommendations are thus geared toward the specific "functions" of each society rather than specific groups of countries.

Strong match: Maximize gains for all

When people bring skills and attributes in demand in the destination country, there are net gains for themselves, as well as for their countries of origin and destination. These gains materialize regardless of migrants' motives, skill levels, or legal status. Countries of origin can proactively manage emigration as a force for poverty reduction in their own society. Countries of destination can also use immigration to meet their labor needs and contribute to their societies. Bilateral cooperation can help enhance the mutual gains of such movements.

Origin countries: Manage emigration for poverty reduction

Cross-border mobility can be a powerful force for reducing poverty in origin countries. The benefits for development arise from remittances, knowledge and technology flows, higher incentives and opportunities for human capital accumulation, and more efficient allocation of labor. But there are also economic, societal, and human costs when a large share of the adult population, including highly skilled professionals, emigrate, especially from smaller and poorer countries. The impacts of emigration on the country of origin—both positive and negative—are neither preset nor uniform within or across origin societies. Origin countries can shape these impacts for their own development (figure 9.2).

STRATEGY. *Make emigration part of development strategies.* In countries with relatively large numbers of current or potential labor emigrants, economic and development strategies should reflect the importance of the potential contribution of emigration to poverty reduction. These strategies should outline specific measures the government intends to take to maximize these benefits and to mitigate negative impacts. In preparing their strategies, governments would benefit from inputs from the private sector, labor unions, current and would-be migrants, and the diaspora. In some cases, dedicated institutions are needed to ensure the implementation of these strategies.

Figure 9.2 Countries of origin can manage emigration for poverty reduction

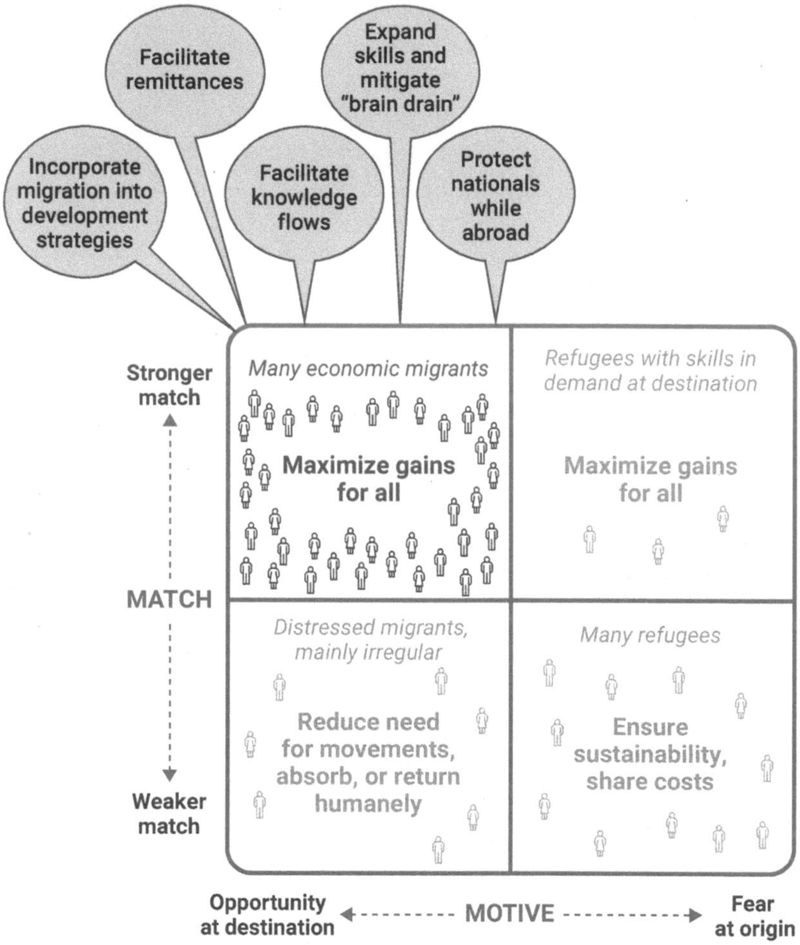

Source: WDR 2023 team.

Note: Match refers to the degree to which a migrant's skills and related attributes meet the demand in the destination country. Motive refers to the circumstances under which a person moves—whether in search of opportunity or because of a "well-founded fear" of persecution, armed conflict, or violence in their origin country.

In the Philippines, successive governments have made labor migration an integral part of the country's development strategy. The focus of such efforts has shifted with political priorities, but the determination to leverage or mitigate the complex effects of emigration has remained. Philippine Development Plan 2017–2022 aimed to mainstream migration, facilitate temporary movements, and support migrants' return.[2] Philippine Development Plan 2023–2028 is directed at supporting returning migrants' reentry into the economy and managing the social impacts of emigration, including by offering health and psychosocial services to migrants and their children. In parallel, the government set up two institutional structures to manage migration policy and regulation: the Philippine Overseas Employment Administration and the Overseas Workers Welfare Administration. They were recently consolidated into a single Department of Migrant Workers.[3]

The Bangladesh government set up a Ministry of Expatriates' Welfare and Overseas Employment in 2001. It is charged with strategic planning and programming to support regular and temporary labor migration.[4] The government also offers potential migrants services such as information and awareness campaigns (including on recruitment agencies and safety) and skills training.

Once migrants are abroad, they have access to migration attaché offices in embassies and consulates in destination countries with large numbers of migrants. However, challenges remain to ensure the full use of such services.[5]

REMITTANCES. *Leverage remittances and reduce their costs.* Remittances reduce poverty by enabling investments in health, education, and entrepreneurship; providing insurance against income shocks; and increasing recipient households' access to formal financial markets. In countries where they account for a relatively large share of income, remittances contribute to macroeconomic stability and reduce fluctuations. Reducing remittance fees and enabling remittances to flow through formal channels are critical, as articulated in the United Nations' Sustainable Development Goals. Policies that reduce remittance costs include increasing financial competition; introducing new financial products; expanding access to finance, especially in rural and poorer communities; and adopting digital payment technologies. These policies can be underpinned by cooperation with destination countries.

> To facilitate remittance flows, the Group of Twenty (G20) has created a road map (G20 Plan to Facilitate Remittance Flows) for coordination between the public and private sectors and improvements in technological infrastructure.[6] This road map includes efforts to (1) advance the provision of payment instruments and systems; (2) leverage technology to develop efficient and cheaper payment systems; and (3) increase accessibility and transparency.[7] As of 2021, the 2014 target of reducing the global average cost of transferring remittances from 10 percent to 5 percent had still not been met (the G20 average cost is 8.12 percent).

> Emigrants from Mexico enjoy relatively low remittance fees[8] because of the large size of the US–Mexico corridor and the extent of competition. As part of a broader set of financial sector reforms that can further reduce the cost of sending remittances, Mexico introduced in 2018 the Financial Technology Law, which authorizes and governs financial technology (fintech) service providers in the country and enables innovation in this sector.[9] The government also introduced a digital payments initiative, Directo a Mexico, for digital payments between Mexico and the United States. Several banks in Mexico also allow migrants to open accounts through online services[10] and to deposit remittances in US dollars to ease this flow.[11] To improve access to finance in rural areas, the Mexican government has coordinated with banks in the La Red de la Gente (People's Network) program.[12]

KNOWLEDGE. *Engage the emigrant community to encourage knowledge transfers and global integration.* In countries that have a relatively large diaspora or regular flows of returnees, knowledge transfers can invigorate the domestic economy. Migrants and diasporas can contribute to further integrating their origin countries in the global economy and facilitate trade and foreign direct investment flows. Many returning migrants, regardless of their formal education level, bring back improved skills, assets, and knowledge. Most of these contributions stem from individual or private groups' initiatives, and there may be little that governments should do. In some cases, policy interventions could even disrupt market mechanisms. Still, governments can facilitate such initiatives by maintaining a favorable business environment and easy access to a strong formal financial sector and by connecting migrants with stakeholders involved in business incubation.

> Vietnam has created mechanisms to engage its diaspora in contributing to the country's economic development plan.[13] The State Committee for Overseas Vietnamese Affairs is tasked with leveraging relations with the diaspora in fields such as economy, science and technology, education and training, and culture. In 2021, the committee launched a comprehensive survey collecting the diaspora's opinions to inform the review of a set of laws and administrative procedures.[14]

In 2010, Moldova established the Programme for Attracting Remittances into the Economy (PARE 1+1).[15] Under the program, returnees receive support to create enterprises, such as entrepreneurship and business development training, advisory and consultancy services, and matching financial resources ("one for one" up to a certain level).[16] As of 2023, over 700 returnees have benefited from the program: 1,900 financing contracts have been issued and 397 million lei (US$21.7 million) have been allocated, generating 1,153 billion lei (US$62.8 million) in investments in the economy.[17]

BRAIN DRAIN. *Expand education and training in globally transferable skills, including to mitigate the effects of brain drain.*[18] When potential migrants acquire skills in demand in destination economies, they are better matches with destination countries' needs. Better-skilled migrants often have more access to regular entry channels, enter the destination labor market in a stronger position, and are paid higher incomes. Emigration of high-skilled professionals, however, can have adverse economic and social effects, especially if they are critical to the delivery of essential services such as health care. These effects are particularly pronounced in lower-income and smaller economies. The solution partly entails expanding training and education in these areas: even if some high-skilled workers leave, others will stay, and their numbers may be sufficient for the origin country. The challenge is twofold. First, ensure that skill-building initiatives are market-driven—for example, through consultations with private employers both in the origin country and at destinations. Second, secure sufficient financing, including by facilitating private sector engagement or requiring migrants to partially repay for publicly funded education and training. Some governments have also considered mandatory public service requirements that reduce emigration soon after graduation, but enforcement is often difficult. Such requirements could complement other measures to improve the domestic conditions of high-skilled professionals over time (for example, with regard to job prospects and wages in some occupations).

In response to the growing demand for health care workers in the United States between 2000 and 2007, the Philippines expanded its nursing education programs.[19] When the United States rapidly expanded the availability of visas for foreign nurses and their families in 2000, enrollment and graduation in Philippine nursing programs experienced a significant boost.[20] Some students who were enrolled in postsecondary school switched from other fields to study nursing. Most of this response was driven by private schools, which opened or expanded nursing programs. This boost lasted until the United States returned to pre-2000 levels after 2007. For every nurse migrant, nine more nurses obtained their licenses.

PROTECTION. *Connect with and protect citizens, regardless of where they are.* Migration involves challenges and risks, including financial costs, a different language, unfamiliarity with a foreign culture and legal system, and, at times, discrimination and abuse. Migrants rely on multiple support mechanisms to overcome these challenges: friends, family, diaspora, civil society, and institutions in the destination country. Origin governments can strengthen such protection by providing migrants with accessible consular services, with properly trained staff, as well as by regulating the activities of recruitment agencies and other intermediaries.[21] Both may also help maintain bonds with citizens living abroad, which can enhance remittances and knowledge transfers, business links, and trade and investment flows that migrants facilitate while abroad.

In 2017, the Indonesian government reformed the law governing emigration with a view toward strengthening workers' protection.[22] Under the new law, regional governments—instead of private companies—oversee the provision of predeparture vocational training and the placement of workers. The changes were aimed at reining in private recruitment firms that charge migrants substantial fees, tying workers to them until they pay off their debt.[23] Although there remain many challenges to prevent the exploitation of migrant workers, the law was generally seen as an important step toward better protection.[24]

The government of Papua New Guinea is making efforts to integrate liaison officer functions as part of its Pacific Labor Mobility Scheme, which facilitates labor migration to Australia. The officer's role is to gather information on migrants' grievances and bring them to the relevant entities for redress.

Destination countries: Maximize benefits, reduce costs

When immigrants' skills and attributes match the needs of destination countries, there are net gains for both destination countries and the migrants themselves. For destination countries, the policy challenge is to maximize the benefits and reduce the costs of receiving such migrants through a multipronged agenda of economic and social integration and by supporting nationals who are negatively affected by migration (figure 9.3). This agenda applies to all migrants and to people who need international protection (refugees), as long as their skills and attributes are a strong match for the needs of destination societies.

Figure 9.3 **Countries of destination can manage immigration for their benefit**

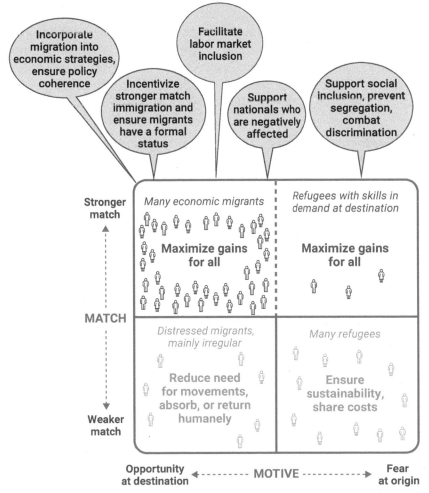

Source: WDR 2023 team.

Note: Match refers to the degree to which a migrant's skills and related attributes meet the demand in the destination country. *Motive* refers to the circumstances under which a person moves—whether in search of opportunity or because of a "well-founded fear" of persecution, armed conflict, or violence in their origin country. The dashed vertical line signifies that the five policy recommendations apply to both quadrants in the top row.

STRATEGY. *Identify and acknowledge labor needs and ensure policy coherence.* Many destination countries are facing demographic challenges and rising labor needs either because they are already aging (high-income countries) or because they are beginning to do so (middle-income countries). In most cases, automation, pro-natalist policies, and policy reforms in education, pension, and health care delivery will not be sufficient to address labor shortfalls, and some labor migration will be necessary. Each society must identify for itself the optimal combination of measures that can sustain its prosperity. Coherence of migration policies often requires coordination across multiple agencies, including with respect to migrants' entry and conditions of stay.

> Canada has adopted a proactive approach to managing immigration needs. For the current period, this approach is reflected in its 2023–2025 Immigration Levels Plan.[25] The plan is based on identification of labor needs. It embraces immigration as a strategy to attract the skills required in key sectors, such as health care, skilled trades, manufacturing, and technology. It sets a target of receiving 465,000 permanent residents in 2023; 485,000 in 2024; and 500,000 in 2025, with a greater focus on attracting newcomers to different regions of the country, including small towns and rural communities.

> To institutionalize coherence of migration policies and facilitate migrants' integration, Portugal has established a one-stop entity for migration-related issues, the National Immigrant Support Center (Centro Nacional de Apoio à Integração de Migrantes).[26] The center brings under one roof a wide range of government and support services related to immigration, independently of their legal status. It also provides other relevant support services for migrants in Portugal, such as support offices for family reunification, legal advice, and employment.[27]

ENTRY. *Create incentives for immigration by workers whose skills and attributes are a strong match with countries' specific labor needs.* Many countries have established systems to regulate the entry of migrants into their territory with a view toward favoring those who are seen as potential net contributors. Yet these systems have had varying degrees of success. For example, over half of all tertiary-educated immigrants live in only four countries: Australia, Canada, the United Kingdom, and the United States. And a number of destination countries have unmet needs for lower-skilled workers. Possible policy measures include putting in place inclusive processes to identify labor needs in consultation with employers and other stakeholders and establishing legal pathways that correspond to specific labor needs.

> The United States has as many as 185 visa categories covering both temporary and permanent visas. They include visas for permanent high-skilled workers, agricultural seasonal laborers, family reunification, and temporary stay on humanitarian grounds, among others. To meet labor market needs, there are visas for persons employed in highly specialized fields (H1B), visas for persons with extraordinary abilities in certain fields (EB1) and potential investors (EB5), and temporary visas for intracompany managers or executives (L1), but also for low-skilled workers (EW3). Although the system is cumbersome, it allows for nuanced, comprehensive responses to a wide variety of situations and needs.

> Australia's system for selecting and admitting migrants relies on consultation with employers.[28] It is adjusted regularly to respond to evolving needs and challenges.[29] Australia was one of the early adopters of a points-based system to attract skilled migrant workers via the "Skilled Independent" route.[30] In the system's early years, employment outcomes for points-tested migrants in Australia were positive, but they declined for recent cohorts because the points system did not adjust fast enough to the changing needs of the economy.[31] In response, the government expanded the number of temporary visas as a way to test and ensure that migrants' skills and attributes match labor

market needs before providing a more permanent form of stay, especially for migrants with lower skills. Temporary migrants who can find employment and integrate are granted permanent visas. Meanwhile, some policy makers have recently called for further reforms to improve the system.[32]

STATUS. *Provide migrants whose skills and attributes are a strong match with the destination country's needs with a formal status.* A regular legal status with the relevant rights and secure terms of stay are prerequisites for migrants to integrate, even temporarily, in the destination country. Granting such a status—without extended wait times—gives migrants incentives to learn the necessary skills and local language, as well as to socially integrate. Such an approach benefits not only the migrants themselves but also the destination society. Labor rights comparable to those of nationals and in line with the International Labour Organization's Fundamental Principles and Rights at Work are key to maximizing both migrants' welfare and their contribution to the destination economies.[33] A status not tied to an employer allows for movements across firms, which is more efficient for the destination economy and reduces the risk of exploitative working conditions.[34] Part of migrants' well-being and inclusion also rests on their ability to reunite with their families when they have demonstrated they can support themselves.

In 2004, the Republic of Korea established the Employment Permit System, which allows lower-skilled workers to enter and work in the country legally.[35] In 2022, more than 264,000 migrants were working in the country on such visas.[36] Since introduction of the system, the cost of hiring foreign workers has declined substantially, and migrants' households have substantially increased their spending on education and health care, as well as their savings.[37]

Experience in the United Arab Emirates highlights that migrants need not just a status, but also a set of labor rights. In 2022, the country amended its labor legislation. It now gives migrants the right to keep their legal status even if they change their employer or sponsor and allows them to stay in the country to find another job for 180 days after the termination of a work contract. Although much remains to be done to improve working conditions, this allowed workers to better negotiate renewal of their contracts and obtain higher wages.[38]

ECONOMIC INCLUSION. *Facilitate economic and labor market inclusion.* Access to decent work is critical to migrants' and destination economies' medium-term gains from migration. Labor market inclusion depends primarily on the economic conditions in the destination society and the labor market's flexibility to rapidly match supply and demand. It also depends on migrants' skills and their complementarity with those already available at the destination. High-skilled labor migrants typically need support to have their educational degrees and professional credentials recognized. Low-skilled migrants, especially those who move to low- and lower-middle-income countries, need labor rights and a range of ancillary rights, such as the ability to move freely within the country to places where there are jobs, to open a bank account, to obtain a driver's license, and to establish a company, among other things. Support programs such as matching migrants with potential employers or facilitating language acquisition also enhance migrants' productivity.

Germany has implemented foreign qualifications recognition to improve skills matching and reduce the disadvantages faced by immigrants with foreign qualifications. Under its Federal Law on Recognition of Foreign Qualifications, prospective migrants can have their foreign qualifications evaluated before their arrival in the country. Three years after recognition, immigrants who have had their credentials recognized earn 19.8 percent more and have a 24.5 percentage point greater chance of being employed than comparable immigrants.[39]

In the United States, several states are adopting policies to facilitate immigrants' economic inclusion.[40] For example, Colorado and Pennsylvania[41] passed safety standards and protections for immigrant workers, such as preventing unfair labor practices, particularly for agricultural workers in Colorado.[42]

SOCIAL INCLUSION. *Prevent segregation and facilitate access to services and inclusion.* Social inclusion can take different forms, depending on the nature of migration—permanent or temporary, with or without family—and the nature of the social contract in the destination society. Often, labor market inclusion and antidiscrimination efforts go a long way toward supporting social inclusion. Other steps include avoiding segregation of large numbers of migrants in less desirable neighborhoods and expanding opportunities for migrants and nationals to engage with one another in daily and civic life. Providing migrants with access to public services such as education or health care facilitates inclusion and reduces the risks of marginalization. Dedicated resources are often needed to expand service delivery capacity while maintaining quality. In parallel, many migrants are facing challenges arising from racism, xenophobia, or other forms of discrimination, whether overt or implicit. Political leadership to forge a constructive narrative on migration issues is key, and programs to combat discrimination need to be adjusted to each context and set of circumstances.

In Germany, the government adopted a range of measures to support social integration in the wake of the arrival of Syrian refugees and other asylum-seekers in 2015. Economic inclusion is viewed as a critical element of such broader social integration, but it has also been complemented by a range of policies and programs such as language training courses and swift integration of migrants into the health and education systems. Decentralization played a key role in this effort. Despite being under significant stress, subnational governments proved to be best placed to address emerging challenges, including local communities' concerns. Political leadership and transparent communication, integrated responses across policy areas, and the engagement of civil society were also instrumental in success.[43]

In Colombia, the government adopted an integral integrated communications strategy in 2021 to preempt and counter negative perceptions of Venezuelan migrants.[44] The strategy relied on a migration narrative for use by government and allied partners, social media campaigns, outreach through influencers and celebrities, public dialogues with diverse actors, and even cultural and gastronomical events, among other outlets.

SUPPORT FOR AFFECTED NATIONALS. *Support nationals who are negatively affected by migration.* Migration can adversely affect the jobs and wages of some citizens of the destination country. Those whose skills are similar to those of migrants, who have relatively low skill levels, or who cannot easily move are especially vulnerable, and some may lose their jobs or receive lower pay. When labor markets are flexible, people are better able to move to other jobs, occupations, sectors, or regions, and the adverse effects dissipate more rapidly. Social protection systems, such as unemployment insurance, training subsidies, and employment support programs, also help. But affected nationals also typically live in neighborhoods with high concentrations of migrants. The public services they access—such as schools and health facilities—often face pressures that can affect quality. Proactive public investment policies are needed to prevent negative impacts on nationals under such conditions.

In many member countries of the Organisation for Economic Co-operation and Development (OECD), governments use a variety of tools to help citizens cope with shocks.[45] A number of programs, including Active Labor Market Policies (ALMPs), are designed to encourage employment whenever possible.[46] Strong social protection systems can boost economic productivity by allowing individuals to invest in physical and human capital and they can be targeted to particular groups.[47] They can also increase demand and stimulate local economies by supporting economic activity.[48] Yet several lessons can be learned from trade adjustment assistance programs that provide financial and training support to workers affected by growing international competition: the adjustment is often difficult, and it may take years.[49]

To support public investments in lower-income neighborhoods, which often include a large share of migrants, France has implemented a targeted program, Politique de la Ville.[50] The program includes infrastructure investments in, for example, public housing and public transportation. It is paralleled by dedicated efforts to improve public education, including through wage premiums for teachers assigned to "priority education zones." A recent evaluation by the Court of Auditors pointed to some progress, but also highlighted areas where more needs to be done.[51]

Bilateral cooperation: Strengthen the match of migrants' skills and attributes

Because international mobility involves at least two countries, bilateral cooperation will help manage it effectively (figure 9.4). Labor migration is often disorganized and based on individual choices, noneconomic factors, and aggressive brokers driving destination choices instead of labor market needs. When countries with surpluses in certain sectors and skill sets are matched with countries with shortages,

Figure 9.4 Bilateral cooperation can improve the match of migrants' skills and attributes with destination country needs

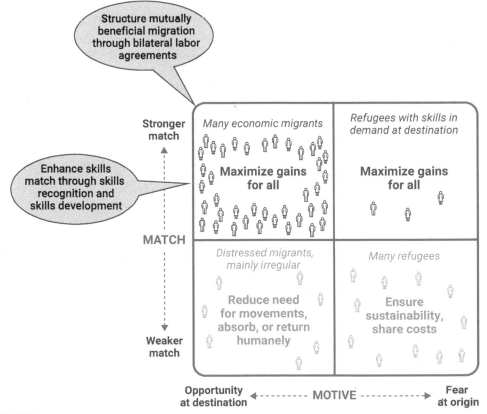

Source: WDR 2023 team.

Note: Match refers to the degree to which a migrant's skills and related attributes meet the demand in the destination country. Motive refers to the circumstances under which a person moves—whether in search of opportunity or because of a "well-founded fear" of persecution, armed conflict, or violence in their origin country.

there can be great benefits. However, migration policy has often been designed and implemented unilaterally by destination countries, despite some high-profile exceptions such as the free internal mobility scheme within the European Union. Joint policy design and implementation to structure mutually beneficial movements can yield substantive gains.

BILATERAL LABOR AGREEMENTS. *Facilitate mutually beneficial movements.* Cooperation between countries of origin and destination can be formalized through bilateral agreements. Countries typically consider bilateral labor agreements within the context of temporary migration schemes. Such agreements increase the benefits of migration for both parties—and for the migrants themselves—by specifying the terms under which migrants are admitted in order to reduce the complexity and costs of admission; by providing legal guarantees and protection against abuse and exploitation; and by regulating access to a range of services in the destination countries. Bilateral agreements should also include redress and inspection mechanisms in line with international labor standards. Where appropriate, they can also be used to reduce recruitment costs by, among other objectives, involving government in intermediation[52] or encouraging transparency and competition among intermediaries. Bilateral labor agreements can be underpinned by a range of complementary efforts by the origin country, such as posting labor attachés in embassies to provide nationals with protection and developing training programs to help prepare people for migration before they move.[53] Some destination countries have sought to link the establishment of legal channels for regular migrants with cooperation by origin countries in receiving the forced return of irregular migrants.

> Canada's Seasonal Agricultural Worker Program brings in 20,000 workers yearly to work on Canadian farms for six weeks to eight months. The program allows member countries of the Organisation of Eastern Caribbean States (OECS), as well as Anguilla, Barbados, Jamaica, Trinidad and Tobago, and Mexico, to negotiate worker contract terms annually.[54] Workers are paid at or above a minimum wage; are eligible for health insurance, pension plans, and other benefits; and pay taxes.[55] Both workers and employers can be barred from participating in the program in the future if issues are brought to the attention of government agencies or workers' organizations.[56] However, this scheme has also been criticized for its lack of provisions on recognizing migrants' particular skills and for its lack of cooperation on protecting workers' rights.[57]

> Malaysia and Bangladesh signed a memorandum of understanding in 2012 to coordinate a foreign worker program that facilitated the legal migration of Bangladeshi workers to Malaysia to work in the palm oil sector. The program began in early 2013 and was ended by Malaysia in 2018.[58] Although the program benefited fewer than 10,000 workers, program participants tripled their income and saw their per capita consumption increase by 22 percent.[59]

SKILLS PARTNERSHIPS. *Cooperate to build skills that are in demand globally.* Several pilots of Global Skills Partnership (GSP) schemes have been developed whereby the governments or the private sector in higher-income destination countries finance skill-building programs in origin countries with the understanding that the graduates of these programs will be offered an opportunity to obtain a work visa.[60] Some graduates of these programs choose to stay in their country of origin—or to return after a few years of migration—which contributes to the origin country's economy and mitigates possible brain drain concerns. These programs facilitate the movement of skilled labor across countries and their smooth inclusion in the labor market. However, the private sector must be involved to ensure that a program remains demand- and market-driven. Complementary actions can be taken at the regional level such as through regional qualification frameworks that facilitate the employment of migrants at their skill level.

> The 15-member Caribbean Community (CARICOM) has developed a scheme for mutual skills recognition under the CARICOM Single Market and Economy (CSME) initiative.[61] In the scheme, CARICOM nationals who fall within a set of approved categories[62] and seek to work in another participating CSME member state can apply for a Certificate of Recognition of Caribbean Community Skills Qualification (Skills Certificate).

> In a pilot program between Germany and Ethiopia, Bauverbände NRW, the umbrella organization of the construction firms in the federal state of North Rhine-Westphalia, is partnering with a network of local partners in Ethiopia to recruit young unemployed Ethiopians for Germany's vocational and educational training system.[63] Potential trainees are provided with German classes and a cultural introduction. Upon graduation, they receive visas, transportation, and health insurance so they can complete their professional training and seek employment in Germany.

Weak match and fear motive: Ensure the sustainability of refugee-hosting, including through responsibility-sharing

When people do not bring skills and attributes in demand at their destination, the costs to destination countries often exceed the benefits. However, under international law destination countries are obligated to host people who have a "well-founded fear" of persecution and violence in their country of origin—refugees—regardless of the costs. Thus, the challenge is to manage such costs. Because refugee situations tend to last for years or even decades, prudent policy making requires adopting approaches to providing international protection that can be sustained over time, both financially and socially. Economic outcomes for both refugees and their host communities are largely determined by host countries' policies, as well as by the international community's effectiveness in sharing responsibilities equitably.

Hosting country: Manage refugee situations with a medium-term perspective

Because they flee for safety, most refugees cross only one border. As a result, a few countries—typically low- or middle-income countries neighboring the countries of origin—host a disproportionate share of people in need of international protection. For such refugee-hosting countries, the challenge is to manage situations that can last for years—that is, provide international protection but also address refugees' specific vulnerabilities and support host communities in their own development efforts (figure 9.5). Refugee-hosting countries need to take a medium-term development perspective from the outset of a crisis, including in their institutional setups and financing arrangements. They should also aim to strengthen the match of refugees' skills and attributes with their own labor market needs. This requires permitting internal mobility, supporting access to the labor market and self-reliance, and facilitating the inclusion of refugees in national service delivery systems.

INSTITUTIONS AND INSTRUMENTS. *Ensure that institutional setups and financing instruments support a medium-term framework.* For host countries, adequate institutional arrangements are essential for managing refugee situations with a medium-term perspective. Some countries have established ad hoc agencies, often with external support, that manage refugee camps, deliver assistance, and provide education and health services. Other countries are mainstreaming these functions through relevant sectoral ministries, with a relatively small coordination structure to ensure the consistency of such distinct programs within the context of a broader strategic approach. Such models are typically more conducive

Figure 9.5 Refugee-hosting countries should from the outset adopt a medium-term perspective

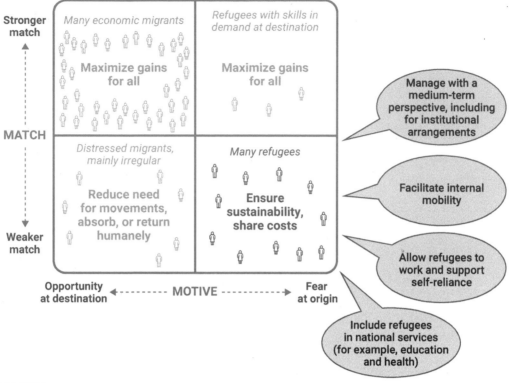

Source: WDR 2023 team.

Note: Match refers to the degree to which a migrant's skills and related attributes meet the demand in the destination country. *Motive* refers to the circumstances under which a person moves—whether in search of opportunity or because of a "well-founded fear" of persecution, armed conflict, or violence in their origin country.

to the sustainability of efforts over time. In some cases, they can include a preparedness element—for example, when refugee crises are looming or have become chronic. However, they need to be supported through medium-term financing instruments, including for external financing.

> Colombia is implementing a medium-term strategy to respond to the Venezuelan migration crisis. In 2018, the government adopted the Strategy for the Response to Migration from Venezuela (CONPES 3950), which confirmed the government's commitment to improving institutional coordination in critical areas of service provision. The government also established the Border Management Office (Gerencia de Frontera) to coordinate the response and regularize Venezuelans' migratory status and access to markets and services.[64] In March 2021, the government initiated a new phase in its strategy, focusing on the long-term integration of Venezuelans in Colombia, including by providing them with a 10-year Temporary Protected Status (Estatuto Temporal de Protección para Migrantes Venezolanos, ETPV).

> Uganda is among the first countries to integrate refugees into its national development planning under the 2016–20 and 2021–25 National Development Plans.[65] The government adopted a whole-of-government approach involving government ministries, departments, and agencies to provide integrated development solutions for refugees and host communities. The National Development Plans foresee district-level interventions to serve the entire population, both Ugandan nationals and refugees. Uganda is also pioneering an effort to strengthen the country's ability to absorb new population inflows as part of a preparedness effort.

INTERNAL MOBILITY. *Facilitate and encourage refugee movements toward economic opportunities.*
Maintaining refugees in border areas, which are often lagging economically, has often intensified pressures on host populations, increasing financing needs and social tensions. By contrast, permitting internal mobility (also referred to as "freedom of movement within the host country") could transform the management of refugee situations and their outcomes. When refugees can move freely to places where they can find a job, their skills and attributes more closely match the needs of the destination society, the pressure on communities in the areas of first arrival is dramatically lessened, and the financial costs of supporting refugees are reduced. However, permitting internal mobility can also require rethinking the ways in which international protection is provided and refugees are supported when refugees are dispersed across the country. This rethinking typically requires strengthening the focus on policies and national institutions.

> As part of its strategy, Colombia has granted Venezuelans the rights to free movement and work within the country. These rights make it possible for Venezuelans to establish themselves where their skills and attributes match the demand of the labor market and thus contribute to the economy and become self-sufficient. The International Monetary Fund (IMF) estimated that by 2030 this policy could increase Colombia's gross domestic product (GDP) by up to 4.5 percentage points.[66]

> In Türkiye, Syrian refugees mostly resided during the initial stages of the crisis in large temporary accommodation centers constructed along the Turkish-Syrian border. As the number of refugees continued to grow, the Turkish government changed its accommodation policy to an "out-of-camp" approach, allowing refugees to freely move within most parts of Türkiye. Refugees thus began to relocate based on economic incentives and location preferences, which generated a large movement from the border regions to more dynamic areas where refugees could better use their skills (mostly western regions and metropolitan areas).[67] To manage such movements, the government set a 20 percent ceiling on the share of foreign nationals allowed to live in each neighborhood. In spite of such limitations, internal mobility greatly improved the economic situation of the refugees and, as a result, lessened the financial impact on the Turkish government.

SELF-RELIANCE. *Promote refugees' access to jobs.* Refugees' self-reliance reduces the need for financial assistance. It also enables refugees to lead dignified lives and helps preparations for durable solutions. Self-reliance relies on several legal and regulatory measures such as providing refugees with predictable, secure terms of stay so they can make plans and invest in their future; granting refugees the right to work as early as possible with unhindered access to the labor market; and allowing refugees to effectively engage in the labor market, such as by allowing them to open a bank account and obtain a driver's license. These rights, however, may not be sufficient if incentives are not in place. Refugees should be encouraged to work, and humanitarian aid should focus on those who are unable to do so. Complementary incentives for the private sector can help improve the environment in which refugees can find jobs.

> Uganda has long encouraged refugees' self-reliance by offering refugee households with agricultural experience a plot of land to farm.[68] This policy has been implemented with the support of host communities and with the understanding that these communities would benefit from public investments in their areas. It has helped reduce refugees' dependency on external assistance, even though poverty rates remain high—and higher than among nationals.[69] The higher rates are linked in part to the remoteness of the areas in which refugees are hosted, the demographic composition of many households (with many working-age men having stayed behind), as well as social and language barriers.[70]

Ukrainians who moved to Poland after the Russian invasion of Ukraine in 2022 were guaranteed at least an 18-month stay in the country and were allowed to be employed in the formal sector, start businesses, and receive training services and job placement support. They also received access to selected social protection programs, including health care.[71] As of June 2022, under this policy 185,000 Ukrainian refugees were able to find jobs,[72] although additional efforts were needed to help refugees access childcare and schooling and overcome a combination of skills mismatch and language barriers.[73]

INCLUSION IN NATIONAL SERVICES. *Deliver education, health, and social services through national systems.* To ensure fairness with nationals and prevent the emergence of social tensions, refugees should be included wherever possible in national systems for the delivery of education, health, and other social services as opposed to establishing parallel service delivery systems. Such an approach can significantly lower the costs of providing such services, even though in some countries it will require strengthening national systems. In those countries with sufficient institutional capacity, even support for the most vulnerable refugees can be provided through the regular social protection system rather than through parallel humanitarian funding.

In Ethiopia, the 2019 Refugee Proclamation provides refugees with access to public education on par with that of nationals. The sixth Education Sector Development Plan (ESDP VI, 2020–25) includes refugee education for the first time. Ethiopia also pledged to issue work permits to refugee teachers, to build and improve essential services in refugee-hosting areas, and to expand the enrollment of refugee children at all levels of the education system.[74] In addition, as of June 2022 about 1,500 refugees were enrolled in 40 public universities across the country.[75]

In Poland, in addition to being granted the right to work, Ukrainians are entitled to access public services, including free health care, and to enroll their children in schools. As of September 2022, about 185,000 Ukrainian refugee children were enrolled in Polish schools.[76] Some of these schools offer separate classes for Ukrainian students or have hired assistants who speak Ukrainian and can work with children who need extra help.

Multilateral cooperation: Share responsibilities

Mutual accountability and cooperation frameworks are critical to ensuring the sustainability of refugee-hosting efforts (figure 9.6). International efforts are often needed to resolve the situations—typically conflicts—that caused refugees to flee and to restore conditions under which refugees can return to their country of origin. Parallel efforts are needed to strengthen norms—and ensure they reflect economic and development considerations—and to agree on shared goals. Such efforts can strengthen the impetus and sustainability of reforms at both the national and international levels. Two critical areas of focus are responsibility-sharing—to provide adequate support to host countries—and solutions—to help resolve refugee situations in a satisfactory manner.

RESPONSIBILITY-SHARING. *Join forces to manage large refugee flows and share costs related to hosting.* Responsibility-sharing requires providing financial and other resources to refugee-hosting countries, especially low- and middle-income, to help manage the costs of hosting refugees whose skills and attributes may not be a good match for the needs of the host economy. Countries that are not refugees' initial destinations need to increase the numbers of refugees they accept in order to help reduce

Figure 9.6 Multilateral cooperation is key to the sustainability of refugee-hosting efforts

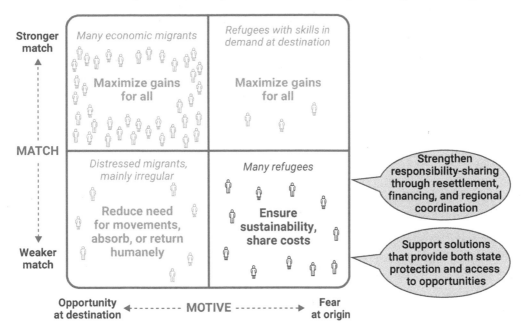

Source: WDR 2023 team.

Note: Match refers to the degree to which a migrant's skills and related attributes meet the demand in the destination country. *Motive* refers to the circumstances under which a person moves—whether in search of opportunity or because of a "well-founded fear" of persecution, armed conflict, or violence in their origin country.

costs in the main host countries. In a context of tensions within the international community, global action needs to be complemented by regional initiatives. Successful initiatives share a focus on a concrete set of issues that can be managed collectively; a constituency of countries that broadly share similar challenges and perspectives and have a history of working together; and a practical and action-oriented agenda. Additional forms of bilateral or multilateral frameworks for cooperation and mutual accountability have emerged. For example, the Global Compact on Refugees established regional support platforms to mobilize a group of like-minded stakeholders around a specific refugee situation.

> At the global level, the Global Compact on Refugees has called for enhanced responsibility-sharing using a variety of approaches.[77] Much remains to be done, however, including to broaden the base of contributing countries. Three donors (European Union institutions, Germany, and the United States) account for almost two-thirds of the total bilateral assistance,[78] and four countries (Canada, Germany, Sweden, and the United States) for almost three-quarters of all resettlements.

> Under the Quito Process, a group of Latin American countries agreed in November 2018 on a regional mobility scheme to respond to the Venezuelan migration crisis based on information exchange and regional policy coordination.[79] Eleven countries signed the Quito Declaration: Argentina, Brazil, Chile, Colombia, Costa Rica, Ecuador, Mexico, Panama, Paraguay, Peru, and Uruguay. It made it possible to achieve a degree of coherence of national approaches and to share hosting responsibilities beyond the countries of first arrival with large numbers of Venezuelan migrants moving beyond Colombia and other neighboring countries to other destinations across the region.

SOLUTIONS. *Combine state protection and access to opportunities.* Solutions are typically framed in strict terms of protection, with a focus on voluntary return and reintegration, local integration, and resettlement. However, in many cases such solutions have been elusive, and they do not always take into account refugees' economic needs and aspirations. When the situation allows, refugee-hosting societies can work with the origin country and the international community to help refugees achieve durable solutions, including voluntary returns once the situation that prompted refugees to flee has been resolved. Innovative approaches can also help improve outcomes, including approaches that disentangle citizenship and residency—political and socioeconomic rights—or that strengthen refugees' skills and attributes, for example through Global Skills Partnerships.

> Canada's Private Sponsorship of Refugees program, adopted in 1979, allows Canadians to resettle specific individuals or families who qualify as refugees under Canada's refugee and humanitarian program. These privately sponsored refugees are accepted by Canada, in addition to those resettled under government programs. Sponsoring groups are responsible for providing refugees with the settlement assistance and material and financial support needed for the duration of the sponsorship period—usually up to one year from the date they arrive in Canada.[80]

> In 1979, the Economic Community of West African States (ECOWAS) formally adopted an agreement facilitating freedom of movement and settlement across its member states.[81] This agreement and subsequent protocols grant ECOWAS citizens the right to enter any other ECOWAS state with residency rights (including the possibility of creating and managing enterprises and companies, as well as the principle of nondiscrimination). Both the United Nations High Commissioner for Refugees (UNHCR) and ECOWAS have stated that this agreement also applies to refugees.[82] While some member states have been reluctant to regularize the stay of refugees who are ECOWAS citizens,[83] many refugees from Côte d'Ivoire, Liberia, Sierra Leone, and Togo have chosen not to repatriate but to remain in ECOWAS member states.[84] Although implementation of the agreement has been lagging due to administrative capacities and other challenges, such legal frameworks can provide an alternative to a long-term refugee status in some situations.[85]

Weak match and no fear motive: Respect dignity and reduce the need for distressed movements

When people do not bring skills and attributes that are in demand at their destination, the costs to destination countries often exceed the benefits. In addition, if they are not moving because of a well-founded fear of violence and persecution in their country of origin, destination countries have no obligation under international law to accept them in their territory. Such distressed movements are often associated with suffering for those involved, and they raise difficult policy challenges for the destination country. Those who are involved in distressed migration deserve to be treated humanely. Ultimately, the challenge is to reduce the need for such movements, including by strengthening the match of migrants' skills and attributes with the needs of the destination country. This requires a combination of actions by countries of origin, countries of destination, and countries of transit.

Origin countries: Use development to reduce distressed movements

For origin countries, distressed migration brings no overall benefits, and it is prejudicial to many migrants who take high risks and can end up in exploitative situations. Over time, development can help reduce the need for distressed movements by strengthening resilience and thus the ability to absorb shocks without having to engage in high-risk international migration; by enhancing potential migrants' skills and thus their match with the needs of the destination economy; and by improving conditions in the country of origin and thus reducing the need to embark on desperate journeys (figure 9.7).

Figure 9.7 Development progress reduces the need for distressed cross-border movements

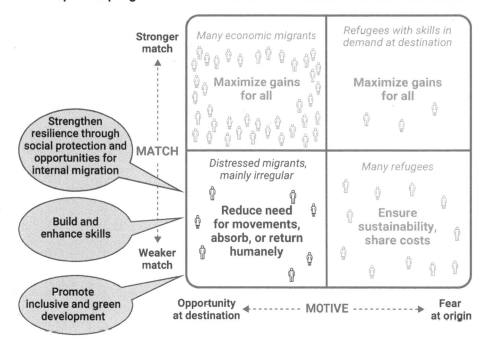

Source: WDR 2023 team.

Note: Match refers to the degree to which a migrant's skills and related attributes meet the demand in the destination country. *Motive* refers to the circumstances under which a person moves—whether in search of opportunity or because of a "well-founded fear" of persecution, armed conflict, or violence in their origin country.

RESILIENCE. *Enhance social protection and create domestic alternatives to international migration.*
Many countries across all income levels have developed social protection systems. These systems play an important role in reducing the pressure for people to engage in high-risk movements as a desperate response to a sudden shock such as a natural disaster, a bad harvesting season, a disease affecting a family member, or an accident, and they can be further strengthened. Development can create additional options for internal migration so that people do not have to engage in high-risk international migration. For example, in many lower-income countries workers and households move from rural to urban areas or from lagging to booming regions in search of better jobs and public services. Such movements, if they are successful, can reduce the need for distressed migration. Their outcome largely depends on whether destination areas are able to accommodate sizable and continuous flows of people in terms of infrastructure, housing, and service delivery, as well as local governance and institutions. Creating options for successful domestic migration is particularly important in parts of the world projected to have the largest demographic and urban growth, such as Sub-Saharan Africa.

> Ethiopia's Productive Safety Net Programme reaches about 9 million people every year. It is designed to enhance food security and stabilize asset levels through both public works employment for working-age adults, for example, to build roads, water systems, and community infrastructure, and unconditional cash transfers to households that have elderly members or are otherwise unable to work. The program has allowed beneficiaries to strengthen resilience and improve food security and nutrition, even though the effect on asset accumulation has been more modest.[86]

> Experience in Bangladesh has illustrated the potential of internal migration to enhance the resilience of rural households. In some areas, rural households face a high incidence of poverty during the lean period between the planting and harvesting seasons. Under a pilot program

implemented by an nongovernmental organization, rural villagers were offered a subsidy for round-trip transportation to a nearby urban area.[87] Twenty-two percent of households took advantage of this opportunity and sent a seasonal migrant. This resulted in a significant increase in the household's consumption. Beneficiary households who sent a seasonal migrant were more likely to send seasonal migrants to urban areas in subsequent years, even after the incentive was removed.

EDUCATION. *Enhance skills match through development.* Economic development is almost always accompanied by improvements in human capital such as education and skills. As countries become wealthier, people and governments invest more in education. In turn, the better-educated workforce becomes an engine of economic development and growth. Higher educational attainment shifts migration patterns toward better-educated and higher-skilled workers. Emigrants from more developed countries therefore tend to be a stronger match for the needs of destination labor markets. This factor can help reduce distressed movements and shift migration toward mutually beneficial outcomes.

As Bangladesh's GDP per capita more than doubled between 1960 and 2015, the average years of schooling for the adult population increased drastically—from 1.0 years to 6.9 years—and the share of adults with some tertiary education grew—from 0.33 percent to 8.6 percent.[88] This experience matches that of almost all low- or middle-income countries that have experienced economic growth. Especially important are higher-education opportunities. Youth with post-secondary education living in middle- and low-income countries have a much higher chance of finding a decent job than those with only secondary or primary education.[89]

Rwanda followed a similar progression as it developed. Primary enrollment rates climbed to over 95 percent of primary school–age children. Enrollment in tertiary education increased from about 1.3 percent in 2000 to 7.6 percent in 2021.[90] In parallel, the government created a dedicated agency—the Skills Development Fund—to upskill Rwanda's workforce for long-term economic transformation and help increase the supply of skills in high demand in the labor market by offering training programs across multiple sectors, from hospitality to construction to mining to information and communication technology, among others.[91]

INCLUSION. *Promote inclusive and green development.* Not all development trajectories have the same impact on migration. Inclusive development, which aims to provide opportunities to all, can help lift all groups within a society, reduce pressures that lead to high-risk migration among the poorest or marginalized communities, and improve options for voluntary migration. By contrast, uneven development that concentrates resources in the hands of a minority may result in further chaotic movements. Meanwhile, some countries are heavily exposed to climate risks, and they need to invest in climate adaptation to avoid the devastating impacts of flooding or sea level rises, for example, and to reduce the need for high-risk movements. Small Island Developing States at risk of being submerged may need special initiatives. Although these are extreme cases involving a relatively small number of people, managing the challenges they face will require planning.

In the face of high climate-related risks, Vanuatu proactively integrated climate change–related mobility into national policy frameworks. In 2018, Vanuatu adopted its National Policy on Climate Change and Disaster-Induced Displacement, which encompasses a comprehensive set of actions addressing return and reintegration, local integration, and planned relocation.[92]

In São Tomé and Príncipe, the government is implementing a program aimed at strengthening the resilience of people living along the shoreline in 10 coastal communities that are directly exposed to the threat of coastal erosion and flooding. The program is part of a Multi-Sector

Investment Plan, which includes policy reforms for sustainable and adaptive management of the coastal zones, a new institutional framework for disaster risk management, and strong community engagement for coastal protection.

Destination countries: Reduce distressed movements while respecting migrants' dignity

All migrants deserve fair and humane treatment, including those whose skills and attributes do not meet the needs of destination societies and who do not qualify for international protection as refugees. Most destination countries are unwilling to grant such migrants legal entry, and many distressed migrants turn to irregular channels and to the growing smuggling industry, along with the exploitative labor market it feeds. The challenge is to reduce the incentives for such movements, while preserving the dignity of all migrants (figure 9.8).

RESPECT. *Respect migrants' and refugees' dignity.* Many destination countries face difficult policy challenges to restrict the entry of migrants whose skills and attributes do not match their needs. When economic and other pressures in the countries of origin are high, people are pushed to engage in distressed migration, and difficult trade-offs can emerge to enforce entry policies while respecting migrants' dignity. Countries are addressing such situations in a variety of ways, but their responses should respect migrants' fundamental rights under applicable international laws and norms.

Figure 9.8 Human dignity should remain the yardstick of migration policies

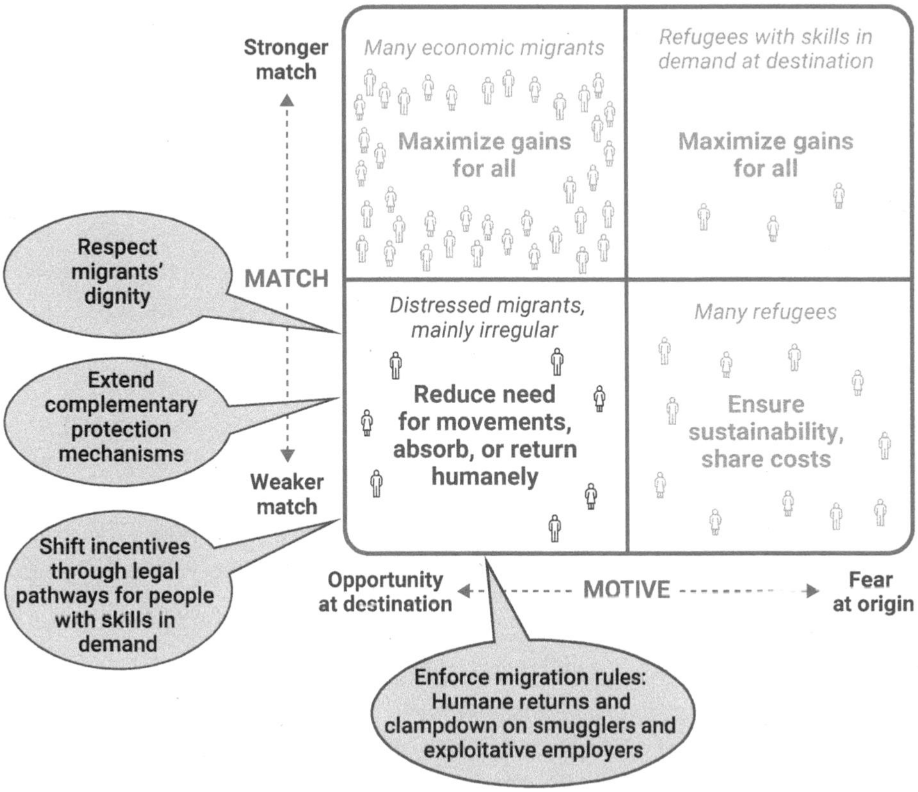

Source: WDR 2023 team.

Note: Match refers to the degree to which a migrant's skills and related attributes meet the demand in the destination country. *Motive* refers to the circumstances under which a person moves—whether in search of opportunity or because of a "well-founded fear" of persecution, armed conflict, or violence in their origin country.

> The International Labour Organization (ILO) has adopted international labor standards over the years that are important for safeguarding the dignity and rights of migrant workers. These standards include the eight fundamental rights conventions of the ILO identified in the 1998 ILO Declaration on Fundamental Principles and Rights at Work; standards of general application, such as those addressing protection of wages and occupational safety and health, as well as the governance conventions concerning labor inspection, employment policy, and tripartite consultation; and instruments containing specific provisions on migrant workers such as the Private Employment Agencies Convention, 1997 (No. 181); the Domestic Workers Convention, 2011 (No. 189); and social security instruments.

> The judiciary can play a critical role in ensuring that migrants' rights are respected. For example, in 2016 the Supreme Court of Papua New Guinea found that detention of migrants and asylum-seekers on Manus Island transferred from Australia contravened Papua New Guinea's constitution.[93] The court ruled the incarceration of asylum-seekers and refugees was in breach of their personal liberty and ordered the governments of both Papua New Guinea and Australia to immediately arrange to move people out of detention. At the time, there were about 850 men in the detention center on the island, about half of whom have been found to be refugees.[94]

COMPLEMENTARY PROTECTION. *Strengthen the coherence of the current system of ad hoc arrangements for protection.* Some distressed migrants have international protection needs, although not to a level that would qualify them as refugees. These migrants may need some form of protection for reasons that fall outside of the 1951 Refugee Convention—for example, if they are fleeing acute humanitarian crises. Amid what has become a human and political crisis, several countries have developed ad hoc legal instruments to provide temporary or subsidiary protection for distressed migrants who cannot be returned safely to their country. Such complementary protection schemes, however, remain partial, ad hoc, and often inconsistent. They should be extended in a coherent manner. Asylum-seekers should also be provided with pathways to enter their destination countries legally.

> The United States first granted Temporary Protected Status (TPS) to Honduran nationals in 1998 following Hurricane Mitch. TPS is granted to eligible foreign-born individuals who are unable to return home safely due to conditions or circumstances preventing their country from adequately handling the return. As of 2023, over 80,000 Hondurans had been granted TPS, making them eligible to receive both employment and travel authorization.[95] About 85 percent of them are in the US labor force,[96] contributing over US$1 billion in GDP annually.[97]

> The wide variation in the recognition rates for Afghan asylum-seekers observed across European Union countries in 2021—ranging from 100 percent in Estonia, Latvia, Portugal, and Spain to about 20 percent in Denmark[98]—suggests a need for improved coherence and consistency across different legal instruments and interpretations of refugee law.[99] Current disparities may contribute to increased vulnerabilities for some distressed migrants who would otherwise be granted international protection.

LEGAL ENTRY PATHWAYS. *Shift migrants' incentives through the development of legal pathways for skills that are in demand, including for lower-skilled workers.* Workers with lower levels of skills are in high demand in many destination labor markets in, for example, the agriculture, home care, food preparation, and construction sectors. Many OECD member countries have very limited legal entry pathways for such individuals, which is partly fueling irregular migration. Establishing legal pathways helps to better steer and monitor entries, to shift the incentives for people who would otherwise engage in high-risk movements, and to address the concerns of those nationals who fear loss of control of their border.

In designing such legal pathways, destination countries need to closely reflect labor market needs. Temporary migration is often part of the possible pathways, but it is appropriate mainly for temporary or seasonal jobs where job-specific human capital is not necessary.

> The experience with the US Bracero program in the 1960s highlights the pitfalls of closing legal entry pathways. Under the program, which was initiated in 1942, seasonal agricultural and railroad migrant workers from Mexico were granted a temporary work status. The program was discontinued in 1964 as part of an effort to boost employment among US nationals. However, profits among farms that had used Bracero workers fell,[100] and there is little evidence that US workers benefited.[101] Moreover, the discontinuation of this program also resulted in more migrants without legal status.[102]

> Spain and Morocco entered into an agreement on labor migration in 2001 to facilitate repeated seasonal migration for agriculture. Gradual progress in implementation of the agreement increased both the demand for seasonal migrant workers in southern Spain and the interest of low-skilled Moroccan workers (often women) in seeking an additional source of income.[103] Over 21,000 workers participated annually in 2006–08. Seasonal migration declined after the 2008 economic crisis as jobs in agriculture became desirable for a growing number of unemployed nationals and settled migrant workers. In 2013, a broader Mobility Partnership Agreement was signed between several European Union Member States (notably, Belgium, France, Germany, Italy, the Netherlands, Portugal, Spain, Sweden, and the United Kingdom) and Morocco that allowed some low-skilled migrants to access opportunities in the signatory countries, including Spain.[104]

ENFORCEMENT. *Manage involuntary returns humanely and penalize smugglers and exploitative employers.* In addition to developing legal pathways for entry—and to ensure their sustainability—destination countries need to enforce existing laws and regulations aimed at discouraging irregular entries. This effort should include combating smuggling and exploitative employment by enforcing rules and regulations that often already exist. In some cases, destination countries may choose to return some distressed migrants who do not face risks in their countries of origin as a signal to both citizens and would-be migrants that rules are enforced. Such forced returns should be managed humanely, and they may be easier if countries of destination and origin cooperate within the context of migration arrangements that are mutually beneficial. Some destination countries have also attempted to accompany involuntary returns with reintegration support, with mixed results.

> To combat human smuggling and trafficking, the United Nations Office on Drugs and Crime (UNODC) has highlighted the importance of long-term efforts that incorporate various interventions in the countries of origin, transit, and destination, with a focus on both demand and supply factors.[105] On the demand side, possible measures include expanding options for legal migration and simplifying the process of obtaining travel documents. On the supply side, countries should penalize and bring to justice migrants' smugglers and seize their unlawfully acquired assets,[106] as well as decriminalize migrants who use smugglers. Improved border management procedures and capacity and information-sharing systems are key in these efforts.

> In recent years, Germany has deported migrants from The Gambia who do not have legal status. Germany has also supported training and reintegration opportunities in The Gambia to encourage voluntary return and reduce the incentives for irregular migration, but the results have been limited.[107] Despite the risk of deportation, many Gambian migrants still feel they are better off in Germany than returning.[108] Cooperation with the country of origin has proved both important and difficult. For example, in 2021 about 2,000 Gambian returnees were denied entry by the Gambian government due to the potential economic and social impacts of their return.[109]

Transit countries: Reduce distressed movements while respecting migrants' dignity

Some distressed migrants travel through several countries before reaching their destination. In some cases, they merely pass by for a few days or a few weeks. In others, they stay longer—a few months or a few years—to earn the resources needed to pay for the next stage of their travel. In still other cases, they try to settle, and it is only when they fail to do so that they engage in further movements. These different situations call for various responses from transit countries (figure 9.9).

Figure 9.9 Cooperation between destination and "last border transit countries" is needed

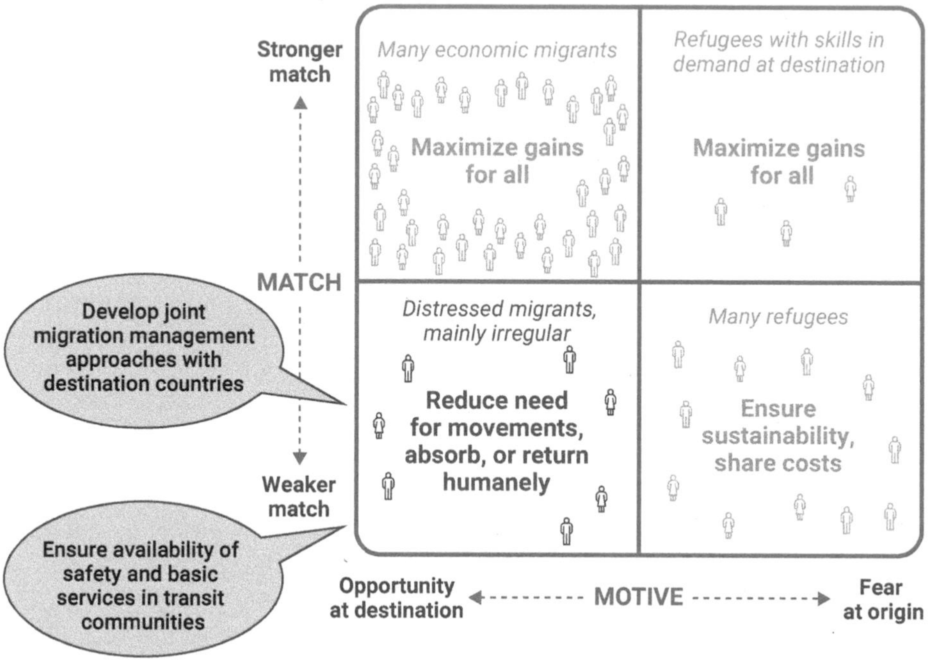

Source: WDR 2023 team.

Note: Match refers to the degree to which a migrant's skills and related attributes meet the demand in the destination country. *Motive* refers to the circumstances under which a person moves—whether in search of opportunity or because of a "well-founded fear" of persecution, armed conflict, or violence in their origin country.

BILATERAL COOPERATION. *Work with the destination countries to manage distressed movements.* Restrictive entry policies by destination countries can raise difficult challenges for the "last border transit countries" on a corridor. Many distressed migrants are stranded in these countries, sometimes for years. Last border transit countries are faced with having to accommodate an often vulnerable population, which comes at a cost. The challenges faced by last border transit countries and the intended destination countries are inextricably linked, and they cannot be resolved unilaterally. Cooperation is required to manage distressed migrants' movements in an integrated manner and to ensure that the respective entry and asylum policies of the destination and last border transit countries—and their implementation—are consistent (although not necessarily identical). There are only a few examples of such cooperation, and they have been imperfect and controversial.

Migration issues have been a consistent part of the negotiations between Mexico and the United States with a view toward developing coordinated approaches. Migration-related issues are typically discussed as part of a broader set of areas of shared interest, including economic cooperation, trade and investment, and the fight against organized crime. In the January 2023 North American Leaders' Summit, discussions focused on steps to encourage migrants to apply for legal status rather than using smugglers as they make the journey north. Such steps included the establishment of an online platform to give migrants "streamlined access to legal pathways," as well as a new legal center in southern Mexico backed by private sector funding.[110]

In 2016, Türkiye and the European Union entered into an agreement to return irregular migrants who had crossed from Türkiye into the Greek islands and whose applications for asylum had been declared inadmissible. As part of this cooperation, the European Union committed to resettling an equivalent number of Syrian refugees processed through regular channels, to provide financial support for the hosting of Syrian refugees in Türkiye, and to facilitate the issuance of Schengen visas to Turkish citizens.[111]

Essentials for reform

The international legal architecture for migration and forced displacement has been adjusted regularly over past decades to reflect changes in the patterns of movements. It is set to evolve further as part of the ongoing implementation of the Global Compact on Refugees and the Global Compact for Safe, Orderly and Regular Migration adopted by the United Nations in 2018.[112] Under the Global Compacts, forums are held to discuss states' commitments and emerging normative issues. Development considerations should be an integral part of these global conversations.[113]

At the country level, migration reform is often a complex endeavor that requires making difficult decisions. Reform can be supported by data and evidence that can help inform both public debates and policy making; financial support that can help mitigate short- or even medium-term costs as they arise; and greater engagement by all stakeholders so that a broader range of voices can be heard and contribute to policy debates in the domestic and international arenas. Such efforts are especially important when debates are highly polarized and when there are multiple competing priorities—among them, climate change, food security, and an ongoing global economic slowdown.

Improve data and evidence

Informed decision-making requires systematic, comprehensive data collection and analysis on migrants and their impacts on origin and destination societies. The first objective of the Global Compact for Safe, Orderly and Regular Migration is to improve the collection and use of data for evidence-based policy making. But several critical dimensions of data collection, processing, dissemination, and analysis need improvement in order to enhance evidence-building in priority areas (box 9.1).

HARMONIZATION. *Harmonize data collection methodologies.*[114] Censuses, specialized surveys, and administrative sources are among the building blocks of migration-related data. And yet methodologies and databases are inconsistent across countries, making aggregation, integration, and cross-country or even cross-sector comparisons impossible. In refugee situations, multiple actors, including international agencies and civil service organizations, collect at great cost a range of data with little consistency and comparability. Further technical efforts are needed to harmonize data collection systems on definitions, questions, sampling, or postenumeration surveys, and to strengthen the capacity of national statistical offices where needed. Special attention should be paid to the ethics of biometric data collection, particularly in refugee settings.

In line with the analysis developed in this Report and to support the design and implementation of a forward-looking agenda that can help enhance the development effects of cross-border movements, evidence is needed in several priority areas, including:

- Drivers of movements and their evolutions, including a better understanding of noneconomic factors; the compounding effects of climate change; and the nature of development trajectories that can reduce the need for distressed movements.
- Possible responses and adaptation strategies by countries at all income levels to manage emerging demographic imbalances.
- Skills complementarity and effects of labor migration to low- and middle-income destination countries.
- Social impacts of both labor and distressed migration on destination countries and variations across those countries at different levels of income.
- Gender dimensions and impacts of cross-border movements.
- Policy evaluations (including using longitudinal surveys of migrant, refugee, or national populations over time) in areas such as support for knowledge transfers and brain drain mitigation in countries of origin; economic inclusion, social inclusion, and support of nationals that are negatively affected in destination and refugee-hosting countries; durable solutions (including innovative approaches) for refugee situations; and, in situations of distressed migration, cross-border cooperation between transit and destination countries, establishment of legal pathways for entry, complementary protection mechanisms, and humane returns.

The Expert Group on Refugee, IDP and Statelessness Statistics (EGRISS) set up under the United Nations Statistical Commission has published a set of recommendations to harmonize definitions and methodologies in the collection of data on forcibly displaced populations.[115] This effort is underpinned by a set of initiatives aimed at strengthening the capacity of the relevant statistical offices, including through the Joint Data Center of the World Bank and the United Nations High Commissioner for Refugees.

The International Labour Organization has been collecting migration-related data. In 2018, it adopted the Guidelines Concerning Statistics of International Labour Migration, with the objective of helping countries develop their national statistical systems by collecting comparable statistics on international labor migration.[116] These efforts culminated in creation of the ILOSTAT database on International Labour Migration Statistics (ILMS), a set of indicators describing the numbers and profiles of international migrant workers, their situation in the labor market and employment patterns, their main origin and destination countries, and the magnitude of inward and outward migration flows.[117]

EVIDENCE-BUILDING. *Invest in new types of surveys.* Current data collection exercises remain incomplete. Additional types of surveys are needed to fully understand migration and to inform possible responses. For example, many of the ongoing efforts are directed at capturing a picture of the migration situation at a given moment. Such efforts are useful, but they do not help assess, among other critical policy issues, the impact of specific regulatory measures on the inclusion of migrants or the ways in which social bonds develop between migrants and their communities over time. The reason is that such effects take time to materialize. To build evidence and to determine what works, longitudinal surveys—surveys that track a given individual, household, or community over time—are critical. Similarly, most official surveys do not capture data for hard-to-reach populations, such as undocumented migrants and smaller or marginalized groups, and so new dedicated efforts are needed. Finally, because all migration-related data are currently collected in either origin or destination countries, it is not possible to follow individuals as they cross borders and to fully investigate the drivers and impacts of their mobility. This will require better coordination between origin and destination countries in their data collection efforts.

> In Chad, the Refugees and Host Communities Household Survey is fully integrated into the national household surveys as an integral part of the refugee policy dialogues among the government, the West African Economic and Monetary Union (WAEMU), and development partners.[118]

> Longitudinal studies of Mexican migrants are helping to better understand the impact of migration and integration processes.[119] For example, the Mexican Family Life Survey tracks migrants over time,[120] and the Mexican Migration Project follows migrants across borders.[121]

OPEN DATA. *Encourage research by making data available.* Collecting data is only a first step—the analysis is what really matters for building evidence for effective policy reform. Experience with other areas of development points to the significance of making databases and raw data publicly available to everyone, especially researchers and policy makers, with appropriate protections of confidentiality. And yet many migration data remain difficult to access, impeding efforts to determine what works best in managing cross-border movements. Open data have the potential to transform migration research and policies in some contexts, as long as adequate steps are taken to protect individual confidentiality and privacy. Countries should also upload existing data sets in a user-friendly manner.

> The World Bank Open Data Initiative, launched in April 2010, has shown the potential of making data available to policy makers, researchers, and civil society so they can measure results, increase knowledge, and work together to find solutions to development problems. The initiative includes a range of reforms enabling free access to more than 7,000 development indicators, as well as a wealth of information on World Bank projects and finances. It is premised on the recognition that transparency and accountability are essential to the development process.[122]

> The Development Data Partnership is a collaboration between international organizations and technology companies to facilitate the efficient and responsible use of third-party data in international development. It includes a set of rules, data license agreements, and shared secure architecture to facilitate the exchange of privately owned data.[123]

Expand financial instruments

Dedicated, medium-term development financing is required to better manage migration (figure 9.10). Such financing could be approached in the broader context of discussions around the financing of global challenges and global public goods. Additional streams of resources—over and above what is available through regular national programs—are often needed.

NEW—OR EXPANDED—FINANCIAL INSTRUMENTS. *Provide medium-term support to low- and middle-income countries who host noncitizens, either economic migrants or refugees.* To manage refugee situations with a medium-term perspective, host countries should implement a range of policies that can be sustained over time—and many need predictable, sustained external funding to make such commitments.[124] Similarly, financing is required in low- and middle-income countries that receive economic

Figure 9.10 New financing instruments and expanded use of development resources are needed to better manage migration

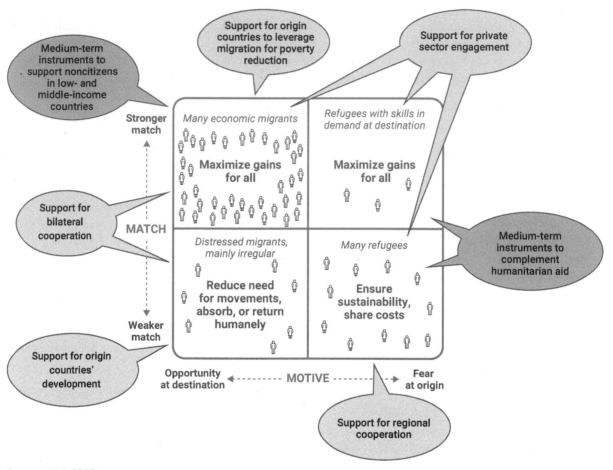

Source: WDR 2023 team.

Note: Match refers to the degree to which a migrant's skills and related attributes meet the demand in the destination country. *Motive* refers to the circumstances under which a person moves—whether in search of opportunity or because of a "well-founded fear" of persecution, armed conflict, or violence in their origin country.

migrants for a range of activities, such as service delivery or infrastructure. Over time, migrants' economic contributions will provide the necessary resources, but there may be funding gaps in the short to medium term, especially when migrants work primarily in the informal sector or when their skills and attributes are not in high demand in the labor market. For countries hosting migrants or refugees, medium-term financing instruments are needed. These instruments should be (1) grounded in the legal international protection agenda (for refugees) and respect for human dignity (for migrants); (2) underpinned by sound government policy frameworks; (3) covering both affected nationals as well as migrants and refugees; and (4) predictable over the medium term with a high degree of concessionality because such resources largely benefit nonnationals.

Within the International Development Association (IDA), the Window for Host Communities and Refugees (WHR) is an example of an instrument that finances medium-term development activities in countries that host significant refugee populations.[125] It aims to help eligible host countries create meaningful medium- to long-term development opportunities and sustainable solutions for refugees and host populations. To be eligible for support from the WHR, IDA countries must adhere to an adequate framework for the protection of refugees and have an action plan or strategy with concrete steps, including possible policy reforms for long-term solutions that benefit refugees and host communities.[126] To date, 17 countries have benefited from the WHR.[127]

Similarly, the World Bank–managed Global Concessional Financing Facility (GCFF) provides development support on concessional terms to middle-income countries affected by refugee crises. It channels donor resources to provide a grant element that improves the terms and conditions of development loans for projects benefiting host communities and refugees. Benefitting countries—which are currently Colombia, Ecuador, Jordan, Lebanon, and Moldova—must support refugees and host communities as part of their development agenda. To date, US$725 million in grant funding has been approved.[128]

ENHANCED USE OF EXISTING INSTRUMENTS. *Use development resources to maximize the development impacts of cross-border movements.* Efforts are needed in several directions. First, development resources can be used to create incentives for and facilitate private sector engagement. The necessary support may include a mix of guarantees and concessional loans for projects that would largely benefit refugees or migrants, conditional on maintaining a strong link to the protection and dignity agenda. In lower-income countries, or when migrants and refugees live in economically lagging regions, tailored support is also needed for small and medium enterprises (SMEs). Second, development resources can help origin countries better leverage migration for poverty reduction—for example, by supporting financial sector reforms to reduce the costs of sending remittances, by building skills, or by supporting SMEs to facilitate knowledge transfers. Development resources that can help reduce the pressure for high-risk migration, including in terms of social protection, urbanization, climate adaptation, and inclusive development programs, can complement these forms of assistance. Finally, development resources can incentivize regional cooperation. Financing arrangements should be tailored to specific situations and activities, according to the potential distribution of their benefits. For example, for a bilateral labor agreement or a Global Skills Partnership, the destination country that benefits from better-skilled workers may be best placed to finance the corresponding activities in the origin country, if such financing is needed. But in other cases, such as supporting regional cooperation among origin countries or acting as an incentive to formalize relationships across countries, regional financing instruments are important.

IDA has established a Private Sector Window to catalyze private sector investment in IDA-only countries, with a focus on fragile and conflict-affected states, including in refugee-hosting situations. The Window is based on the recognition that the private sector is central to achieving development impacts, but that a range of uncertainties and risks need to be mitigated for the private sector to engage at scale in such difficult environments.[129]

Bring in new voices

In an area as polarized as migration, political economy considerations often dictate the extent to which reforms can be implemented. In many countries, the current environment is difficult. Migration is an increasingly prominent topic in public debates, and the polarization of viewpoints and constituencies is growing. In the most extreme cases, the dominant political discourse has been infused with xenophobic—or even racist—vitriol. Some political forces are explicitly advocating restrictions on migration. Fewer voices are calling for a liberalization of cross-border movements. Many political leaders are seeking an intermediate position that typically balances humane considerations and calls for firm control of borders.

Figure 9.11 New voices are needed to transform migration debates

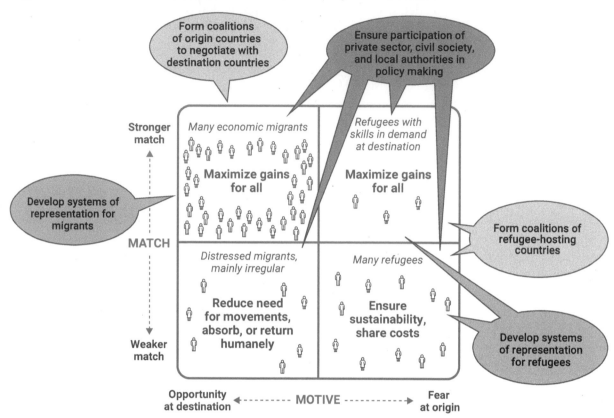

Source: WDR 2023 team.

Note: Match refers to the degree to which a migrant's skills and related attributes meet the demand in the destination country. *Motive* refers to the circumstances under which a person moves—whether in search of opportunity or because of a "well-founded fear" of persecution, armed conflict, or violence in their origin country.

To make change happen, new voices must emerge (figure 9.11). Social changes and reforms rarely occur simply through the presentation of data and evidence. When new stakeholder groups come to the forefront to make their voices heard, the terms of the debate shift. This has been true for climate change, but also for a range of controversial social issues across countries. Simply put, unless new parties join the debate, the focus and the tone of the migration debates are unlikely to change. New, and stronger, voices are needed, directed at three sets of issues, as discussed below.

AFFECTED NATIONS. *Enhance negotiating positions through coalitions.* The effective management of migration and forced displacement requires international negotiations—multilateral discussions, for example, on normative frameworks and bilateral arrangements. Developing countries, especially low-income ones, often come to the negotiating table in a relatively weak position, which undermines their ability to safeguard their interests. At times, they are constrained to remain passive witnesses in discussions that affect them, or they are pressured to help implement policies that primarily benefit destination countries. Yet low- and middle-income countries—as origin countries, destination countries, and refugee-hosting countries—have a key role to play in better managing migration. Coalition-building can help to strengthen their ability to influence the debate and make their voices better heard in international discussions, whether global, regional, or bilateral. Forming such groups, such as of the main origin countries of migrants to a particular destination, would make it easier for these countries to negotiate bilateral labor agreements that best reflect their needs and protect the interests of their citizens while they are abroad.

> Refugee-hosting countries with more than 300,000 refugees recently formed an informal group in Geneva—with a rotating chair. This "300 k + group" is aiming to coordinate the positions of large refugee-hosting countries to increase their influence in international discussions on forced displacement and to shape the dialogue with donor countries and other key stakeholders.

> The Intergovernmental Authority on Development (IGAD) has been working closely with its member states (Djibouti, Ethiopia, Kenya, Somalia, South Sudan, Sudan, and Uganda) to address the root causes and strengthen the management of forced displacement in the region, as well as advocate for more equitable international burden- and responsibility-sharing.[130] In 2019 at the first Global Refugee Forum, the IGAD Support Platform was launched as a mechanism to sustain the momentum and galvanize additional support for the implementation of IGAD's 2017 Nairobi Declaration on Durable Solutions for Somali Refugees and Reintegration of Returnees in Somalia, as well as subsequent declarations and plans of action on education (2017 Djibouti Declaration) and jobs (2019 Kampala Declaration).

DOMESTIC STAKEHOLDERS. *Ensure the participation of a broad range of domestic stakeholders in decision-making processes.* Policy making is enhanced by including multiple perspectives and achieving a degree of social consensus that can facilitate implementation. Both require engaging a wide range of stakeholders in the process. In destination countries, and to some extent in origin countries, migration should be managed by involving the entire government, not just the border control apparatus; engaging with the private sector and other social partners to assess medium-term labor needs and to identify ways to meet them; and supporting local authorities, which often are at the forefront in dealing with the response and integration challenges. The challenge for many underrepresented stakeholders is to organize themselves to make their voices heard. This is especially important when the debate is dominated by the concerns, worldviews, and proposals of constituencies that do not represent the full range of relevant stakeholders. The result may be detrimental outcomes for both underrepresented groups and society at large. Stakeholder engagement can take multiple forms that need to be adapted to each country's situation and each constituency.

> The United Kingdom established a Migration Advisory Committee (MAC) in 2007 to review labor needs in selected sectors and advise the government on the potential use of immigration as a response to those needs.[131] For example, as part of a 2023 review of MAC's Shortage Occupation List (SOL), the committee is reaching out to professional organizations to solicit inputs on migrant workers' roles and salaries and the implications of possible policy changes in order to make recommendations on (1) whether the salary requirements for occupations on the SOL should be revised; (2) which occupations on the current SOL should continue to be included and which should be removed; and (3) which occupations, if any, should be added to the SOL.[132]

> In formulating its labor force policies, Singapore continually engages stakeholders through "tripartism," which emphasizes cooperation among the government, employers, and labor unions in sustaining employment, business growth, and wage growth. Singapore created a joint task force formed by the National Trades Union Congress and the Singapore National Employers Federation, the two primary organizing bodies for unions and employers, to examine labor market policy concerns for professionals, managers, and executives. The task force consulted with more than 10,000 people and issued nine recommendations for labor market policy reform.[133]

MIGRANTS' AND REFUGEES' VOICES. *Develop systems of representation and accountability to structure migrants' and refugees' voices.* Foreign nationals typically do not have coordination mechanisms that allow their multiple voices to be represented in policy debates in the same way that elected officials represent citizens or labor unions represent workers in domestic labor markets. Migrants and refugees seldom have a forum to speak for themselves. Several countries, both origin and destination, have recognized that their decision-making process can be enhanced by listening to migrants' representatives, even if other interests and viewpoints eventually prevail. The challenge is to ensure that such "delegates" are selected in a manner that makes them genuinely representative of and accountable to the people they represent. But such mechanisms are often lacking.

> In the 1970s, several West German municipalities introduced Foreign Citizens' Advisory Councils (FCACs, Ausländerbeiräte). Residents with a foreign passport were entitled to elect a board from their own ranks that advised the municipalities on issues that especially concerned foreign nationals. Today, about 400 FCACs are in place in 12 of the 16 federal states. And yet the number of candidates standing for election to the FCACs has declined over the last few years because opportunities for political participation have increased, in particular for European Union citizens eligible to vote locally since 1992 and for the growing number of naturalized citizens. Greater social, ethnic, and national heterogeneity among migrants has also made representativity more difficult to achieve.

> In 1997, the Dominican Republic amended its constitution to allow citizens living abroad to vote in general elections from their country of residence. It also established seats for senators and deputies representing citizens abroad.[134] Under this arrangement, Dominican citizens are allowed to vote for the president, vice president, and the seven members of Parliament that represent the constituencies abroad.[135] In the 2020 general elections, there were nearly 600,000 registered Dominican voters abroad.[136]

Notes

1. See spotlight 3.
2. NEDA (2021).
3. Ang and Tiongson (2023).
4. IOM (2020).
5. IOM (2020).
6. FSB (2020).
7. DWG (2021).
8. "Sending Money from United States to Mexico," Remittance Prices Worldwide (dashboard), World Bank, Washington, DC, https://remittanceprices .worldbank.org/corridor/United-States/Mexico.
9. GPFI (2021).
10. Méndez Maddaleno (2021).
11. GPFI (2021).
12. GPFI (2021).
13. Government of Vietnam, Decree No. 74-CP on the 30th of July, 1994 of the Government on the Tasks, Authority and Organization of the Apparatus of the Committee for Overseas Vietnamese.
14. VNA (2021).
15. "The Programme for Attracting Remittances into Economy (PARE 1+1)," Organization for the Development of Entrepreneurship (Organizația pentru Dezvoltarea Antreprenoriatului), Chişinău, Moldova, https://

www.odimm.md/en/the-programme-for -attracting-remittances-into-economy.
16. ETF (2021).
17. "The Programme for Attracting Remittances into Economy (PARE 1+1)," Organization for the Development of Entrepreneurship (Organizația pentru Dezvoltarea Antreprenoriatului), Chişinău, Moldova, https://www.odimm.md/en/the-programme-for -attracting-remittances-into-economy.
18. Abarcar and Theoharides (2021); Chand and Clemens (2008); Shrestha (2011).
19. Abarcar and Theoharides (2021).
20. Cortés and Pan (2015).
21. Fernando and Lodermeier (2021).
22. Indonesia replaced its Law No. 39/2004 on the Placement and Protection of Indonesian Workers Overseas with Law No. 18/2017 on the Protection of Indonesian Migrant Workers.
23. Missbach and Palmer (2018).
24. UN Women (2019).
25. IRCC (2022).
26. See Centro Nacional de Apoio à Integração de Migrantes, National Immigrant Support Center (website), CNAI, Lisbon, https://www.acm.gov.pt/-/cnai-lisboa.

Details about the Lisbon support center can be found at Centros Nacionais de Apoio à Integração de Migrantes, National Immigrant Support Centers (website), CNAIM, Lisbon, https://lisboaacolhe.pt/apoio-ao-a-imigrante/centros-nacionais-de-apoio-a-integracao-de-migrantes-cnaim/.

27. "One-Stop-Shop / National Immigrant Support Centres (CNAI)," European Website on Integration, European Commission, Brussels, https://ec.europa.eu/migrant-integration/integration-practice/one-stop-shop-national-immigrant-support-centres-cnai_en.
28. Crock and Parsons (2023).
29. Crock and Parsons (2023).
30. Department of Home Affairs (2023).
31. Crock and Parsons (2023).
32. Haydar (2023).
33. ILO (2022).
34. This has been discussed extensively in the context of the Gulf Cooperation Council (GCC) countries. For example, the United Arab Emirates (2011), Qatar (2020), and Saudi Arabia (2021) have relaxed the *kafala* sponsorship system and are now allowing migrants to seek other employers once their initial contract has expired.
35. Employment Permit System (dashboard), Global Skill Partnerships, Center for Global Development, Washington, DC, https://gsp.cgdev.org/legalpathway/employment-permit-system-eps/; Park (2017).
36. Employment Permit System (dashboard), Global Skill Partnerships, Center for Global Development, Washington, DC, https://gsp.cgdev.org/legalpathway/employment-permit-system-eps/; MOEL (2022).
37. Clemens and Tiongson (2017).
38. HRW (2014).
39. Brücker et al. (2021).
40. Figueroa and Hinh (2022).
41. An Act amending the act of June 1, 1937 (P.L. 1168, No. 294), known as the Pennsylvania Labor Relations Act.
42. Colorado General Assembly, SB21-087, Agricultural Workers' Rights: Concerning agricultural workers' rights, and, in connection therewith, making an appropriation.
43. Koch et al. (2023).
44. Rossiasco et al. (2023).
45. OECD (2018).
46. Tesliuc (2006).
47. OECD (2019).
48. DFAT (2014).
49. Park (2012); Schochet et al. (2012).
50. Politique de la Ville (dashboard), Agence nationale de la cohésion des territoires, Paris, https://agence-cohesion-territoires.gouv.fr/politique-de-la-ville-97.
51. Cour des Comptes (2020).
52. For example, when the government of Bangladesh experimented in 2013 with direct recruitment of migrant workers to work in Malaysia, it was able to bring down migration costs to a sixth of the market costs (Mobarak, Sharif, and Shrestha 2023).
53. Sáez (2013).

54. See Canada.ca (2023).
55. Canada.ca (2023); IOM (2008).
56. *Rural Migration News* (2019).
57. Hennebry and Preibisch (2012).
58. Malaysia-Bangladesh G2G Program (dashboard), Global Skill Partnerships, Center for Global Development, Washington, DC, https://gsp.cgdev.org/legalpathway/malaysia-bangladesh-g2g-program/.
59. Shrestha (2019).
60. Clemens (2015).
61. CARICOM (2017).
62. According to Article 46 of the Revised Treaty of Chaguaramas, the following categories of CARICOM nationals have the right to seek employment in any of the participating CSME Member States: university graduates, artists, musicians, media workers, sportspersons, nurses, teachers, artisans, holders of associate degrees, domestic workers, agricultural workers, and private security officers. See CARICOM (2001).
63. There is an oversupply of workers in the Ethiopian labor market, but few permanent positions are available. Thus many unemployed civil engineers are interested in undergoing technical training in the German construction sector and working there as specialists.
64. Rossiasco et al. (2023).
65. Government of Uganda (2020).
66. Alvarez et al. (2022).
67. Tumen (2023).
68. Momodu (2019).
69. Betts et al. (2019).
70. UNHCR (2021b).
71. Government of Poland, Amendment to the law on assistance to Ukrainian citizens in connection with the armed conflict on the territory of the country, March 26, 2022.
72. EC (2022).
73. Jacoby (2022).
74. Bengtsson (2018).
75. UNHCR (2022).
76. Maza (2023).
77. United Nations (2018).
78. OECD (2021).
79. MREMH (2018).
80. UNHCR (2021a).
81. Under its 1979 Protocol A/P.1/5/79 relating to Free Movement of Persons, Residence and Establishment. In terms of the free movement of people, Article 27 (1) of the founding treaty clearly spells out the objective of establishing a free movement zone. It states: "Citizens of Member States shall be regarded as Community citizens and accordingly Member States undertake to abolish all obstacles to their freedom of movement and residence within the Community."
82. See, for example, the final report of the meeting of the ECOWAS Trade, Customs and Free Movement of Persons Committee in Accra, Ghana, September 25–27, 2007. It endorses the views that refugee status and ECOWAS residence are not incompatible and urges ECOWAS member states to issue travel documents to

their nationals who are refugees; that host states formally confer the right of residence on ECOWAS citizens who are refugees; and that the validity of such residence be for three years and renewable (paras. 21–23). See ECOWAS (2007a, 2007b).

83. Adepoju, Boulton, and Levin (2010).
84. ECOWAS (2007b).
85. Jegen and Zanker (2020).
86. Abay et al. (2023); Berhane et al. (2014); Sabates-Wheeler et al. (2021).
87. Bryan, Chowdhury, and Mobarak (2014).
88. Barro-Lee estimates of educational attainment in the world (Barro and Lee 2013); Feenstra, Inklaar, and Timmer (2015); Penn World Table (database version 10.0), Groningen Growth and Development Centre, Faculty of Economics and Business, University of Groningen, Groningen, the Netherlands, https://www.rug.nl/ggdc/productivity/pwt/.
89. Sparreboom and Staneva (2014).
90. School Enrollment, Primary (% Gross): Rwanda (dashboard), World Bank, Washington, DC, https://data.worldbank.org/indicator/SE.PRM.ENRR?locations=RW.
91. "Who We Are" (website), Rwanda Skills Development Fund, Kigali, Rwanda, https://sdfrwanda.rw/newsite/who-we-are.
92. NDMO (2018).
93. Namah v. Pato, SCA 84 (Supreme Court of Justice of Papua New Guinea, 2013).
94. Tlozek and Anderson (2016).
95. National Immigration Forum (2023).
96. Warren and Kerwin (2017).
97. Baran and Magaña-Salgado (2017).
98. Refugee Data Finder (dashboard), United Nations High Commissioner for Refugees, Geneva, https://popstats.unhcr.org/refugee-statistics/download/.
99. Some of the differences stem from the way these rates are computed.
100. San (2023).
101. Clemens, Lewis, and Postel (2018).
102. Meissner (2004).
103. Triandafyllidou, Bartolini, and Guidi (2019).
104. Triandafyllidou, Bartolini, and Guidi (2019).
105. UNODC (2018).
106. IOM (2017).
107. Dreyer and Scheibach (2020); Hunt (2020).
108. Hunt (2020).
109. African Courier (2021); Mefo Takambou (2021).
110. Shear, Sullivan, and Jordan (2023).
111. EC (2015); European Council (2016).
112. United Nations (2018, 2019).
113. Under the Global Compact for Safe, Orderly and Regular Migration, the first International Migration Review Forum was held in 2022 with the participation of a broad range of stakeholders. It will meet every four years. Under the Global Compact on Refugees, the first Global Refugee Forum was held in 2019 and will also meet every four years.
114. Molnar (2020).
115. See "About," Expert Group on Refugee, IDP and Statelessness Statistics, EGRISS, UN City, Copenhagen, http://egrisstats.org/about/.
116. ILO (2018).
117. International Labour Migration Statistics (database), ILOSTAT, International Labour Organization, Geneva, https://ilostat.ilo.org/resources/concepts-and-definitions/description-international-labour-migration-statistics/.
118. Nguyen, Savadogo, and Tanaka (2021).
119. UNECE (2020).
120. Rubalcava et al. (2008).
121. Durand and Massey (2006).
122. World Bank (2012).
123. Verhulst and Young (2017). Also see Development Data Partnership (dashboard), World Bank, Washington, DC, https://datapartnership.org/.
124. This problem was flagged during the 2015 World Humanitarian Summit and in the discussions leading to the 2019 Grand Bargain between some of the largest donors and humanitarian organizations to improve the effectiveness and efficiency of the humanitarian action.
125. For more on the Window for Host Communities and Refugees, see IDA (2022). See also Window for Host Communities and Refugees, International Development Association, World Bank, Washington, DC, https://ida.worldbank.org/en/replenishments/ida19-replenishment/windows-host-communities-refugees.
126. Window for Host Communities and Refugees, International Development Association, World Bank, Washington, DC, https://ida.worldbank.org/en/replenishments/ida19-replenishment/windows-host-communities-refugees.
127. The 17 countries are Bangladesh, Burkina Faso, Burundi, Cameroon, Chad, the Democratic Republic of Congo, Djibouti, Ethiopia, Kenya, Liberia, Mauritania, Niger, Pakistan, the Republic of Congo, Rwanda, South Sudan, and Uganda.
128. Global Concessional Financing Facility (dashboard), World Bank, Washington, DC, https://globalcff.org/.
129. IEG (2021).
130. This work resulted in the 2017 Nairobi Declaration on Durable Solutions for Somali Refugees and Reintegration of Returnees in Somalia (IGAD 2017); the 2017 Djibouti Declaration on Education (von Freeden 2021); and the 2019 Kampala Declaration on Jobs, Livelihoods, and Self-Reliance (IGAD 2019)—all referred to as the "IGAD Process."
131. Migration Advisory Committee (dashboard), MAC, London, https://www.gov.uk/government/organisations/migration-advisory-committee.
132. MAC (2023).
133. Pan and Theseira (2023).
134. OECD (2009).
135. IFES (2016).
136. IFES (2020).

References

Abarcar, Paolo, and Caroline B. Theoharides. 2021. "Medical Worker Migration and Origin-Country Human Capital: Evidence from U.S. Visa Policy." *Review of Economics and Statistics*. Published ahead of print, October 15, 2021. https://doi.org/10.1162/rest_a_01131.

Abay, Kibrom A., Guush Berhane, John F. Hoddinott, and Kibrom Tafere. 2023. "COVID-19 and Food Security in Ethiopia: Do Social Protection Programs Protect?" *Economic Development and Cultural Change* 71 (2): 373–402. https://doi.org/10.1086/715831.

Adepoju, Aderanti, Alistair Boulton, and Mariah Levin. 2010. "Promoting Integration through Mobility: Free Movement under ECOWAS." *Refugee Survey Quarterly* 29 (3): 120–44.

African Courier. 2021. "Gambia Rejects Deportation Flights from Europe." *News: Migration*, September 6, 2021. https://www.theafricancourier.de/news/migration /gambia-rejects-deportation-flights-from-europe/.

Alvarez, Jorge A., Marco Arena, Alain Brousseau, Hamid Faruqee, Emilio William Fernandez-Corugedo, Jaime Guajardo, Gerardo Peraza, and Juan Yépez Albornoz. 2022. "Regional Spillovers from the Venezuelan Crisis: Migration Flows and Their Impact on Latin America and the Caribbean." IMF Departmental Paper DP/2022/019 (December), International Monetary Fund, Washington, DC.

Ang, Alvin, and Erwin R. Tiongson. 2023. "Philippine Migration Journey: Processes and Programs in the Migration Life Cycle." Background paper prepared for *World Development Report 2023*, World Bank, Washington, DC.

Baran, Amanda, and Jose Magaña-Salgado. 2017. "Economic Contributions by Salvadoran, Honduran, and Haitian TPS Holders: The Cost to Taxpayers, GDP, and Businesses of Ending TPS." With Tom K. Wong. Policy Report (April), Immigrant Legal Resource Center, San Francisco.

Barro, Robert J., and Jong-Wha Lee. 2013. "A New Data Set of Educational Attainment in the World, 1950–2010." *Journal of Development Economics* 104 (September): 184–98.

Bengtsson, Stephanie. 2018. "Who Teaches Refugees? Policy Study Launches in Ethiopia." December 18, International Institute for Educational Planning, United Nations Educational, Scientific, and Cultural Organization, Paris.

Berhane, Guush, Daniel O. Gilligan, John F. Hoddinott, Neha Kumar, and Alemayehu Seyoum Taffesse. 2014. "Can Social Protection Work in Africa? The Impact of Ethiopia's Productive Safety Net Programme." *Economic Development and Cultural Change* 63 (1): 1–26. https://doi.org/10.1086/677753.

Betts, Alexander, Imane Chaara, Naohiko Omata, and Olivier Sterck. 2019. "Refugee Economies in Uganda: What Difference Does the Self-Reliance Model Make?" January, Refugee Studies Centre, Oxford Department of International Development, University of Oxford, Oxford, UK.

Brücker, Herbert, Albrecht Glitz, Adrian Lerche, and Agnese Romiti. 2021. "Occupational Recognition and Immigrant Labor Market Outcomes." *Journal of Labor Economics* 39 (2): 497–525.

Bryan, Gharad T., Shyamal K. Chowdhury, and Ahmed Mushfiq Mobarak. 2014. "Underinvestment in a Profitable Technology: The Case of Seasonal Migration in Bangladesh." *Econometrica* 82 (5): 1671–1748. https://doi.org/10.3982/ECTA10489.

Canada.ca. 2023. "Hire a Temporary Worker through the Seasonal Agricultural Worker Program: Overview." February 8, Digital Transformation Office, Treasury Board of Canada, Ottawa, Canada. https://www .canada.ca/en/employment-social-development /services/foreign-workers/agricultural/seasonal -agricultural.html.

CARICOM (Caribbean Community). 2001. *Revised Treaty of Chaguaramas Establishing the Caribbean Community Including the Caricom Single Market and Economy.* Signed by Heads of Government of the Caribbean Community on July 5, 2001, at their Twenty-Second Meeting of the Conference of Heads of Government in Nassau, Bahamas, Georgetown, Guyana, July 7, 2001. https://treaty.caricom.org/.

CARICOM (Caribbean Community). 2017. "Single Market and Economy: Free Movement, Travel and Work." CSME Unit, Caribbean Community Secretariat, St. Michael, Barbados. https://csme.caricom.org/documents /booklets/65-free-movement-travel-and-work-3rd -edition/file.

Chand, Satish, and Michael A. Clemens. 2008. "Skilled Emigration and Skill Creation: A Quasi-Experiment." CGD Working Paper 152 (September), Center for Global Development, Washington, DC.

Clemens, Michael A. 2015. "Global Skill Partnerships: A Proposal for Technical Training in a Mobile World." *IZA Journal of Labor Policy* 4 (2): 1–18.

Clemens, Michael A., Ethan G. Lewis, and Hannah M. Postel. 2018. "Immigration Restrictions as Active Labor Market Policy: Evidence from the Mexican Bracero Exclusion." *American Economic Review* 108 (6): 1468–87.

Clemens, Michael A., and Erwin R. Tiongson. 2017. "Split Decisions: Household Finance When a Policy Discontinuity Allocates Overseas Work." *Review of Economics and Statistics* 99 (3): 531–43.

Cortés, Patricia, and Jessica Pan. 2015. "The Relative Quality of Foreign-Educated Nurses in the United States." *Journal of Human Resources* 50 (4): 1009–50.

Cour des Comptes. 2020. "L'évaluation de l'attractivité des quartiers prioritaires: Une dimension majeure de la politique de la ville." Communiqué de Presse, December 2, 2020. https://www.ccomptes.fr/system /files/2020-12/20201202-communique-quartiers -prioritaires.pdf.

Crock, Mary, and Christopher Robert Parsons. 2023. "Australia as a Modern Migration State: Past and Present."

Background paper prepared for *World Development Report 2023*, World Bank, Washington, DC.

Department of Home Affairs, Australia. 2023. "Points Calculator." Version of March 20, 2023, Department of Home Affairs, Canberra, Australia. https://immi.homeaffairs.gov.au/help-support/tools/points-calculator.

DFAT (Department of Foreign Affairs and Trade, Australia). 2014. "Briefing: Social Protection and Growth." DFAT, Canberra, Australia. https://www.dfat.gov.au/sites/default/files/social-protection-and-growth-briefing.pdf.

Dreyer, Lena, and Andrea Scheibach. 2020. "Pilot Measure in The Gambia: Skills for Reintegration." March, Deutsche Gesellschaft für Internationale Zusammenarbeit, Bonn, Germany.

Durand, Jorge, and Douglas S. Massey, eds. 2006. *Crossing the Border: Research from the Mexican Migration Project*. New York: Russell Sage Foundation.

DWG (Group of Twenty Development Working Group). 2021. "Financial Inclusion and Remittances: G20 Plan to Facilitate Remittance Flows." September, G20 Secretariat (rotating), Rome. https://dwgg20.org/app/uploads/2021/09/g20-plan-to-facilitate-remittance-flows.pdf.

EC (European Commission). 2015. "EU-Turkey Joint Action Plan." *Memo*, October 15, 2015. https://ec.europa.eu/commission/presscorner/detail/en/MEMO_15_5860.

EC (European Commission). 2022. "Poland: 185 000 Refugees from Ukraine Start Work under Simplified Procedure." European Website on Integration, June 8, European Commission, Brussels. https://ec.europa.eu/migrant-integration/news/poland-185-000-refugees-ukraine-start-work-under-simplified-procedure_en#:~:text=Since%20the%20introduction%20of%20a,personal%20identifier%20issued%20to%20residents.

ECOWAS (Economic Community of West African States). 2007a. "Final Report: Meeting of the Trade, Customs, and Free Movement of Persons Committee, Accra, Ghana, September 25–27, 2007." ECOWAS Commission, Abuja, Nigeria.

ECOWAS (Economic Community of West African States). 2007b. "Memorandum: Meeting of the Committee on Trade, Customs, Immigration, Accra, 25–27 September 2007." ECOWAS Commission, Abuja, Nigeria. https://www.unhcr.org/49e47c8f0.pdf.

ETF (European Training Foundation). 2021. "Skills and Migration: Country Fiche, Moldova." September, ETF, Turin, Italy.

European Council. 2016. "EU-Turkey Statement, 18 March 2016." Press Release, March 18, 2016. https://www.consilium.europa.eu/en/press/press-releases/2016/03/18/eu-turkey-statement/.

Feenstra, Robert C., Robert Inklaar, and Marcel Peter Timmer. 2015. "The Next Generation of the Penn World Table." *American Economic Review* 105 (10): 3150–82.

Fernando, Asanga Nilesh, and Alison Lodermeier. 2021. "Understanding Adverse Outcomes in Gulf Migration: Evidence from Administrative Data from Sri Lanka." *International Migration Review* 56 (1): 155–75.

Figueroa, Eric, and Iris Hinh. 2022. "More States Adopting Inclusive Policies for Immigrants." *Off the Charts* (blog), April 12, 2022. https://www.cbpp.org/blog/more-states-adopting-inclusive-policies-for-immigrants.

FSB (Financial Stability Board). 2020. "Enhancing Cross-Border Payments: Stage 3 Roadmap." FSB, October 13, Basel, Switzerland. https://www.fsb.org/2020/10/enhancing-cross-border-payments-stage-3-roadmap/.

Government of Uganda. 2020. "Third National Development Plan (NDPIII) 2020/21–2024/25." National Planning Authority, Kampala, Uganda. http://www.npa.go.ug/wp-content/uploads/2020/08/NDPIII-Finale_Compressed.pdf.

GPFI (Global Partnership for Financial Inclusion). 2021. "G20 National Remittance Plan, Mexico 2021: Biennial Update." GPFI, World Bank, Washington, DC. https://www.gpfi.org/sites/gpfi/files/sites/default/files/Mexico.pdf.

Haydar, Nour. 2023. "Clare O'Neil Pledges an Overhaul of Australia's 'Broken' and 'Backwards' Migration System." *abc.net.au: News*, February 21, 2023. https://www.abc.net.au/news/2023-02-22/clare-oneil-migration-economic-impact-work-to-do/102007886.

Hennebry, Jenna L., and Kerry Preibisch. 2012. "A Model for Managed Migration? Re-examining Best Practices in Canada's Seasonal Agricultural Worker Program." *International Migration* 50 (s1): e19–e40.

HRW (Human Rights Watch). 2014. "'I Already Bought You': Abuse and Exploitation of Female Migrant Domestic Workers in the United Arab Emirates." News Release, October 22, 2014. https://www.hrw.org/report/2014/10/22/i-already-bought-you/abuse-and-exploitation-female-migrant-domestic-workers.

Hunt, Louise. 2020. "Warnings over Gambian Migrant Returns as Democratic Transition Wobbles." *Migration News Feature*, January 28, 2020. https://www.thenewhumanitarian.org/news-feature/2020/1/28/migration-deportation-asylum-refugees-Gambia-Germany.

IDA (International Development Association). 2022. *Building Back Better from the Crisis: Toward a Green, Resilient and Inclusive Future; Additions to IDA Resources: Twentieth Replenishment*. Report from the Executive Directors of the International Development Association to the Board of Governors, February 17. Washington, DC: IDA, World Bank.

IEG (Independent Evaluation Group). 2021. "The World Bank Group's Experience with the IDA Private Sector Window: An Early-Stage Assessment." What Works Series, July 8, World Bank, Washington, DC.

IFES (International Foundation for Electoral Systems). 2016. "Elections in the Dominican Republic: 2016 General Elections; Frequently Asked Questions." May 13, IFES, Arlington, VA.

IFES (International Foundation for Electoral Systems). 2020. "Elections in the Dominican Republic: 2020 General Elections; Frequently Asked Questions." June 30, IFES, Arlington, VA.

IGAD (Intergovernmental Authority on Development). 2017. "Nairobi Declaration on Durable Solutions for Somali Refugees and Reintegration of Returnees in Somalia." March 25, IGAD Secretariat, Djibouti, Republic of Djibouti. https://igad.int/communique-special-summit-of-the-igad-assembly-of-heads-of-state-and-government-on-durable-solutions-for-somali-refugees/.

IGAD (Intergovernmental Authority on Development). 2019. "Kampala Declaration on Jobs, Livelihoods, and Self-Reliance." March 28, IGAD Secretariat, Djibouti, Republic of Djibouti. https://igad.int/kampala-declaration-on-jobs-livelihoods-and-self-reliance/.

ILO (International Labour Organization). 2018. "Guidelines Concerning Statistics of International Labour Migration." Report ICLS/20/2018/Guidelines, 20th International Conference of Labour Statisticians (Geneva, 10–19 October 2018). Department of Statistics, ILO, Geneva. https://www.ilo.org/wcmsp5/groups/public/---dgreports/---stat/documents/meeting document/wcms_648922.pdf%0Ahttp://files/376/wcms_648922.pdf.

ILO (International Labour Organization). 2022. "ILO Declaration on Fundamental Principles and Rights at Work and Its Follow-Up: Adopted at the 86th Session of the International Labour Conference (1998) and Amended at the 110th Session (2022)." ILO, Geneva.

IOM (International Organization for Migration). 2008. "Seasonal Agricultural Workers Program: Guatemala-Canada." December, Guatemala Mission, IOM, Guatemala City.

IOM (International Organization for Migration). 2017. "Countering Migrant Smuggling." Global Compact Thematic Paper, IOM, Geneva.

IOM (International Organization for Migration). 2020. *Bangladesh Migration Governance Framework*. Dhaka, Bangladesh: IOM.

IRCC (Immigration, Refugees and Citizenship Canada). 2022. "An Immigration Plan to Grow the Economy." Press release, November 1, 2022. https://www.canada.ca/en/immigration-refugees-citizenship/news/2022/11/an-immigration-plan-to-grow-the-economy.html.

Jacoby, Tamar. 2022. "Living in Limbo: Displaced Ukrainians in Poland." *MPI Feature*, November 2, 2022. https://www.migrationpolicy.org/article/living-limbo-displaced-ukrainians-poland?jr=on.

Jegen, Leonie, and Franzisca Zanker. 2020. "The Economic Community of West African States." With research assistance by Nanzala Gonda, Abdur Rehman Zafar, and Rebecca Schmid. *Migration Control Info* (Wiki), December 2020. https://migration-control.info/en/wiki/the-economic-community-of-west-african-states/.

Koch, Anne, Nadine Biehler, Nadine Knapp, and David Kipp. 2023. "Integrating Refugees: Lessons from Germany since 2015/2016." Background paper prepared for *World Development Report 2023*, World Bank, Washington, DC.

MAC (Migration Advisory Committee). 2023. "A Guide to the Shortage Occupation List (SOL) and Companion to the SOL Call for Evidence 2023." MAC, London. https://assets.publishing.service.gov.uk/government/uploads/system/uploads/attachment_data/file/1139466/CfE_Guidance.pdf.

Maza, Christine. 2023. "In Poland, Refugees Confront Tough Choices as the School Year Starts." Heinrich Böll Stiftung, Washington, DC. https://us.boell.org/en/2023/01/24/poland-refugees-confront-tough-choices-school-year-starts.

Mefo Takambou, Mimi. 2021. "EU, Gambia Tussle over Expelled Migrants." *Politics: Africa*, May 9, 2021. https://www.dw.com/en/eu-escalates-row-with-gambia-over-expelled-migrants/a-59072367.

Meissner, Doris. 2004. "U.S. Temporary Worker Programs: Lessons Learned." *MPI Feature*, March 1, 2004. https://www.migrationpolicy.org/article/us-temporary-worker-programs-lessons-learned.

Méndez Maddaleno, Rodrigo. 2021. "Remittances in Central America: The Role of CABEI." Office of the Chief Economist, Central American Bank for Economic Integration, Tegucigalpa, Honduras. https://www.bcie.org/fileadmin/user_upload/Remittances_in_Central_America_the_Role_of_CABEI.pdf.

Missbach, Antje, and Wayne Palmer. 2018. "Indonesia: A Country Grappling with Migrant Protection at Home and Abroad." *MPI Profile*, September 19, 2018. https://www.migrationpolicy.org/article/indonesia-country-grappling-migrant-protection-home-and-abroad.

Mobarak, Ahmed Mushfiq, Iffath Sharif, and Maheshwor Shrestha. 2023. "Returns to International Migration: Evidence from a Bangladesh-Malaysia Visa Lottery." *American Economic Journal: Applied Economics*. Published ahead of print, March 15, 2023. https://www.aeaweb.org/articles?id=10.1257/app.20220258&from=f.

MOEL (Ministry of Employment and Labor, Republic of Korea). 2022. "Over 84,000 Foreign Workers on E-9 Visas Have Entered Korea." *MOEL News*, December 21, 2022. https://www.moel.go.kr/english/news/moelNewsDetail.do?idx=3138.

Molnar, Petra. 2020. "Technological Testing Grounds: Migration Management Experiments and Reflections from the Ground Up." European Digital Rights, Brussels; Refugee Law Lab, York University, Toronto. https://edri.org/wp-content/uploads/2020/11/Technological-Testing-Grounds.pdf.

Momodu, Sulaiman. 2019. "Uganda Stands Out in Refugees Hospitality." *Africa Renewal* 32 (3). https://www.un.org/africarenewal/magazine/december-2018-march-2019/uganda-stands-out-refugees-hospitality.

MREMH (Ministerio de Relaciones Exteriores y Movilidad Humana, Ministry of Foreign Affairs and Human Mobility, Ecuador). 2018. "Declaración de Quito sobre Movilidad Humana de Ciudadanos Venezolanos en la Región." September 4, MREMH, Quito. https://www.cancilleria.gob.ec/2018/09/04/declaracion-de-quito-sobre-movilidad-humana-de-ciudadanos-venezolanos-en-la-region/.

National Immigration Forum. 2023. "Fact Sheet: Temporary Protected Status (TPS)." Updated, February 1, 2023,

National Immigration Forum, Washington, DC. https://immigrationforum.org/article/fact-sheet-temporary-protected-status/.

NDMO (National Disaster Management Office, Vanuatu). 2018. "Vanuatu: National Climate Change and Disaster-Induced Displacement Policy." NDMO, Port Vila, Vanuatu. https://www.iom.int/sites/default/files/press_release/file/iom-vanuatu-policy-climate-change-disaster-induced-displacement-2018.pdf.

NEDA (National Economic and Development Authority, the Philippines). 2021. *Updated Philippine Development Plan 2017–2022*. Pasig City, the Philippines: NEDA. https://pdp.neda.gov.ph/updated-pdp-2017-2022/.

Nguyen, Nga Thi Viet, Aboudrahyme Savadogo, and Tommomi Tanaka. 2021. *Refugees in Chad: The Road Forward*. Washington, DC: World Bank.

OECD (Organisation for Economic Co-operation and Development). 2009. "Dominican Republic." In *Latin American Economic Outlook 2010*, 233–36. Paris: OECD.

OECD (Organisation for Economic Co-operation and Development). 2018. "Social Protection System Review: A Toolkit." OECD Development Policy Tools, OECD, Paris.

OECD (Organisation for Economic Co-operation and Development). 2019. "Can Social Protection Be an Engine for Inclusive Growth?" Development Centre Studies, OECD, Paris.

OECD (Organisation for Economic Co-operation and Development). 2021. "Financing for Refugee Situations 2018–19." Forced Displacement Series, OECD, Paris.

Pan, Jessica, and Walter Edgar Theseira. 2023. "Immigration in Singapore." Background paper prepared for *World Development Report 2023*, World Bank, Washington, DC.

Park, Jooyoun. 2012. "Does Occupational Training by the Trade Adjustment Assistance Program Really Help Reemployment? Success Measured as Occupation Matching." *Review of International Economics* 20 (5): 999–1016.

Park, Young-bum. 2017. "South Korea Carefully Tests the Waters on Immigration, with a Focus on Temporary Workers." *MPI Profile*, March 1, 2017. https://www.migrationpolicy.org/article/south-korea-carefully-tests-waters-immigration-focus-temporary-workers.

Rossiasco, Paula Andrea, Patricia de Narvaez, Ana Aguilera, Greta Granados, Paola Guerra, and Taimur Samad. 2023. "Adapting Public Policies in Response to an Unprecedented Influx of Refugees and Migrants: Colombia Case Study of Migration from Venezuela." Background paper prepared for *World Development Report 2023*, World Bank, Washington, DC.

Rubalcava, Luis N., Graciela M. Teruel, Duncan Thomas, and Noreen Goldman. 2008. "The Healthy Migrant Effect: New Findings from the Mexican Family Life Survey." *American Journal of Public Health* 98 (1): 78–84.

Rural Migration News. 2019. "Canada's Seasonal Workers Program." *Rural Migration News* (blog), December 20, 2019. https://migration.ucdavis.edu/rmn/blog/post/?id=2372.

Sabates-Wheeler, Rachel, Jeremy Lind, John F. Hoddinott, and Mulugeta Tefera Taye. 2021. "Graduation after 10 Years of Ethiopia's Productive Safety Net Programme: Surviving but Still Not Thriving." *Development Policy Review* 39 (4): 511–31.

Sáez, Sebastián, ed. 2013. *Let Workers Move: Using Bilateral Labor Agreements to Increase Trade in Services*. Directions in Development: Trade Series. Washington, DC: World Bank.

San, Shmuel. 2023. "Labor Supply and Directed Technical Change: Evidence from the Termination of the Bracero Program in 1964." *American Economic Journal: Applied Economics* 15 (1): 136–63.

Schochet, Peter Z., Ronald D'Amico, Jillian Berk, Sarah Dolfin, and Nathan Wozny. 2012. *Estimated Impacts for Participants in the Trade Adjustment Assistance (TAA) Program Under the 2002 Amendments*. Mathematica Policy Research Report (August 30). Princeton, NJ: Mathematica.

Shear, Michael D., Eileen Sullivan, and Miriam Jordan. 2023. "Biden Announces Major Crackdown on Illegal Border Crossings." *Politics*, January 10, 2023. https://www.nytimes.com/2023/01/05/us/politics/biden-border-crossings.html.

Shrestha, Maheshwor. 2019. "Impact Evaluation of a G2G Migration Program." Jobs, Labor, and Migration Course, World Bank, Washington, DC. https://thedocs.worldbank.org/en/doc/966591574377914275-0160022019/original/SPJCC19JLMD8S3BLAGroupExMaheshShrestha.pdf.

Shrestha, Slesh Anand. 2011. "Effect of Educational Returns Abroad on Domestic Schooling: A British Gurkha Army Experiment." Unpublished working paper, Department of Economics, University of Michigan, Ann Arbor.

Sparreboom, Theo, and Anita Staneva. 2014. "Is Education the Solution to Decent Work for Youth in Developing Economies? Identifying Qualifications Mismatch from 28 School-to-Work Transition Surveys." W4Y Work4Youth Series 23 (December), Youth Employment Programme, Employment Policy Department, International Labour Office, Geneva.

Tesliuc, Emil D. 2006. "Social Safety Nets in OECD Countries." Social Safety Nets Primer Note 25, World Bank, Washington, DC.

Tlozek, Eric, and Stephanie Anderson. 2016. "PNG's Supreme Court Rules Detention of Asylum Seekers on Manus Island Is Illegal." *abc.net.au: News*, April 26, 2016. https://www.abc.net.au/news/2016-04-26/png-court-rules-asylum-seeker-detention-manus-island-illegal/7360078.

Triandafyllidou, Anna, Laura Bartolini, and Caterina Francesca Guidi. 2019. "Exploring the Links between Enhancing Regular Pathways and Discouraging Irregular Migration: A Discussion Paper to Inform Future Policy Deliberations." International Organization for Migration, Geneva. https://cadmus.eui.eu/handle/1814/61251.

Tumen, Semih. 2023. "The Case of Syrian Refugees in Türkiye: Successes, Challenges, and Lessons Learned." Background paper prepared for *World Development Report 2023*, World Bank, Washington, DC.

UNECE (United Nations Economic Commission for Europe). 2020. Guidance on the Use of Longitudinal Data for Migration Statistics. Document ECE/CES /STAT/2020/6. Geneva: United Nations. https://unece .org/sites/default/files/2021-03/ECECESSTAT20206 .pdf.

UNHCR (United Nations High Commissioner for Refugees). 2021a. "Global Compact on Refugees: Indicator Report 2021." UNHCR, Geneva.

UNHCR (United Nations High Commissioner for Refugees). 2021b. "Using Socioeconomic Evidence to Promote Solutions for Refugees in Uganda." Uganda Employment Policy Brief (July), UNHCR, Geneva.

UNHCR (United Nations High Commissioner for Refugees). 2022. "Ethiopia: Education Factsheet 2022." UNHCR, Geneva. https://data.unhcr.org/en/documents /details/94021.

United Nations. 2018. "Global Compact on Refugees." United Nations, New York. https://www.unhcr.org /5c658aed4.

United Nations. 2019. "Resolution Adopted by the General Assembly on 19 December 2018: Global Compact for Safe, Orderly and Regular Migration." Document A/RES/73/195 (January 11, 2019), United Nations, New York. https://www.un.org/en/development/desa /population/migration/generalassembly/docs/global compact/A_RES_73_195.pdf.

UNODC (United Nations Office on Drugs and Crime). 2018. Global Study on Smuggling of Migrants 2018. June. Vienna: UNODC.

UN Women (United Nations Entity for Gender Equality and the Empowerment of Women). 2019. "Gaining Protection for Indonesia's Migrant Workers and Their Families." July 12, UN Women, New York. https:// www.unwomen.org/en/news/stories/2019/6/feature -story-of-change-protection-for-indonesias-migrant -workers.

Verhulst, Stefaan G., and Andrew Young. 2017. "Open Data in Developing Economies: Toward Building an Evidence Base on What Works and How." July, Governance Lab, New York University, New York. https://odimpact.org /files/odimpact-developing-economies.pdf.

VNA (Vietnam News Agency). 2021. "State Commission for Overseas Vietnamese Affairs Launches Portal." VietNamNet Global News, October 25, 2021. https:// vietnamnet.vn/en/state-commission-for-overseas -vietnamese-affairs-launches-portal-786607.html.

von Freeden, Julia Annette. 2021. "Increasing the Accessibiltiy of the Djibouti Declaration on Refugee Education in IGAD Member States." December 8, Deutsche Gesellschaft für Internationale Zusammenarbeit, Bonn, Germany. https://igad.int /communique-special-summit-of-the-igad-assembly -of-heads-of-state-and-government-on-durable -solutions-for-somali-refugees/.

Warren, Robert, and Donald Kerwin. 2017. "A Statistical and Demographic Profile of the US Temporary Protected Status Populations from El Salvador, Honduras, and Haiti." Journal on Migration and Human Security 5 (3): 577–92.

World Bank. 2012. "Learning About the Open Data Initiative." Feature Story, March 22, 2012. https://www .worldbank.org/en/news/feature/2012/03/22 /learning-about-the-open-data-initiative.